COMRADES ESTRANGED

COMRADES ESTRANGED

Labor and Citizenship in the Twentieth-Century Persian Gulf

Alex Boodrookas

Stanford University Press
Stanford, California

Stanford University Press
Stanford, California

Library of Congress Cataloging-in-Publication Data
Names: Boodrookas, Alex author
Title: Comrades estranged : labor and citizenship in the twentieth-century Persian Gulf / Alex Boodrookas.
Description: Stanford, California : Stanford University Press, [2026] | Includes bibliographical references and index.
Identifiers: LCCN 2025041136 (print) | LCCN 2025041137 (ebook) | ISBN 9781503645653 cloth | ISBN 9781503646476 paperback | ISBN 9781503646483 ebook
Subjects: LCSH: Labor unions—Political activity—Persian Gulf States—History—20th century | Foreign workers—Civil rights—Persian Gulf States—History—20th century | Noncitizens—Civil rights—Persian Gulf States—History—20th century | Citizenship—Persian Gulf States—History—20th century
Classification: LCC HD6799.5.Z65 B66 2026 (print) | LCC HD6799.5.Z65 (ebook) | DDC 331.880953—dc23/eng/20250911
LC record available at https://lccn.loc.gov/2025041136
LC ebook record available at https://lccn.loc.gov/2025041137

Cover design: Lindy Kasler
Cover art: Houshang Pezeshknia, *Khark*, 1958. Alamy.
Typeset by Newgen in Minion Pro 10.2/14.4

The authorized representative in the EU for product safety and compliance is: Mare Nostrum Group B.V. | Doelen 72 | 4831 GR Breda | The Netherlands | Email address: gpsr@mare-nostrum.co.uk | KVK chamber of commerce number: 96249943

Printed and bound by CPI Group (UK) Ltd, Croydon, CR0 4YY

I once asked Mubarak [Ruler of Kuwait, 1896–1915]
why he didn't build a wall around his capital.
His answer was characteristic and a statement of fact.
"I am the wall," was all he said.

—*Stanley Mylrea,* Kuwait Before Oil[1]

Contents

	Note on Transliteration and Translation	ix
	Acknowledgments	xi
	Introduction	1
One	**Deportation States | 1900–1950**	24
Two	**The Wages of Oil | 1940–1955**	49
Three	**Arab Labor, Arab Oil | 1945–1959**	75
Four	**The Fear Complex | 1952–1961**	100
Five	**Are We Really Independent? | 1960–1965**	125
Six	**The Radical Sixties | 1965–1970**	155
Seven	**Exporting Oil, Importing Labor | 1971–1976**	182
	Conclusion	216
	Notes	225
	Bibliography	317
	Index	345

Note on Transliteration and Translation

This book utilizes a simplified version of the transliteration system used by the *International Journal of Middle East Studies* (IJMES), omitting all diacritics. Places and proper names are transliterated according to their common spelling when available. All translations are my own unless otherwise noted.

Acknowledgments

This book could not have been written without the benefit of many years of scholarly generosity. At NYU, I was fortunate to have been surrounded by a remarkably sharp and supportive intellectual community. Arang Keshavarzian pushed me to expand my horizons and provided invaluable advice, feedback, and encouragement. Zachary Lockman has been thoughtful, grounded, and reassuring. I am inexpressibly grateful to them both. Manu Goswami profoundly shaped my ideas about scholarly inquiry and its value, while Frederick Cooper helped me navigate a complicated project and provided insightful suggestions. Leslie Pierce has long been a source of knowledge and advice, while Guy Burak and Nelida Fuccaro provided invaluable help at critical moments. I would also like to thank Benoit Challand, Ahmed Ferhadi, Ali Adeeb Alnaemi, Maya Mikdashi, Eman Morsi, Suneela Mubayi, Jane Burbank, Lauren Benton, Linda Gordon, Mehdi Khorrami, Sheida Dayani, and Amir Moosavi. Over the years I have been repeatedly bailed out by Greta Scharnweber, Chelsea Rhodes, Jim Ryan, Kieran Lettrich, and Chrystyna Banks, who grappled with university bureaucracies on my behalf. Finally, at GW, I learned critical thinking from the American Studies Department, where James A. Miller, Melani McAlister, and Ramzi Fawaz built a supportive scholarly community.

This project would have been impossible without the assistance of dozens of scholars, archivists, and activists in Kuwait. I was hosted by the Gulf University of Science and Technology, where Fahed Al-Sumait kindly served as an advisor and source of support. I would also like to thank Farah Al-Nakib, Mohammad Al Awadi, and Reem Al Ali at the American University of Kuwait. Khalid al-Diyyan at the Kuwait National Library, and the staff of the Center for Gulf and Arabian Peninsula Studies at Kuwait University and the Center for Research and Study of Kuwait, allowed me to collect and organize the many newspaper articles on which this project relied. At the Kuwait Trade Union Federation, Mohammad Abdullah al-ʿAradih and Mohammad Juma'an al-Hudainih welcomed me with open arms, while Hussein al-Mashmoum kindly provided advice and assistance. Ali Hussein al-Awadhi, Ahmad al-Diyyan, and Ghanim al-Najjar were guides to the intricacies of Kuwaiti politics. The organizing work of Bibi al-Sabah and Mary Ann Abunda shaped the trajectory of this project. My deepest thanks are reserved for my interviewees, particularly Hassan Falah, Hussein al-Youha, Hussein Saqr, Dr. Ahmad al-Khatib, Qabalan ʿAjnan al-ʿAzimi, and Daifullah Falah Sultan. I hope that this work will help to preserve their story.

The research for this project took me to seven countries, in each of which I benefited from invaluable assistance. In Oman, Professor Mohammad al-Muqaddam warmly welcomed me back, while Professor Sultan al-Hashimi provided invaluable research advice and an illuminating interview. I cannot thank Professor Ali al-Riyami enough for his help locating interviewees. Khawla Abdelhamid and Hazem Kayali provided information on their relative Ashraf Lutfi. In India, Radhika Singha and Vijaya Ramaswami hosted me at the remarkable institution that is Jawaharlal Nehru University, while Pavitra Soram at the Fulbright office in New Delhi patiently navigated bureaucratic hurdles. I am also deeply indebted to the dozens of archivists whose work make this historical research possible.

Over the years, a number of scholars have assisted me with advice, information, and useful sources. Some may not remember, but I do: Toby Jones, Laleh Khalili, Touraj Atabaki, Paula Chakravartty, Adam Hanieh, Ayşe Baltacıoğlu-Brammer, Pete Moore, Faisal Hamadah, Fahad Bishara, Reem Alissa, Ervand Abrahamian, Begüm Adalet, Omar AlShehabi, Jill Crystal, and Mandana Limbert. I would also like to thank the Association of Gulf and Arabian Peninsula Studies, particularly Gwenn Okruhlik and Fahed Al-Sumait, for defending the field from the corrupting influence of money and censorship. Essential funding for this project came from a MacCracken Fellowship at NYU, Foreign Language and Area Studies and Fulbright-Hays Fellowships from the U.S. Department of Education, and a Dissertation Prospectus Development Fellowship from the Social Sciences Research Council.

At the Crown Center for Middle East Studies at Brandeis University, Gary Samore and Naghmeh Sohrabi were patient and flexible, allowing me to enrich this manuscript while working remotely. I also enjoyed the company, and humor, of Hayal Akarsu, Mohammad Ataie, Youssef El Chazli, Huma Gupta, Ekin Kurtiç, Pascal Menoret, and David Patel. Kate Wahl at Stanford University Press has been the ideal editor in every way. I am also grateful to two anonymous reviewers whose suggestions helped me refine several key arguments.

I am fortunate to have landed in a remarkably collegial history department at Metropolitan State University of Denver. My chairs, Matt Makley and Kim Klimek, have been inexpressibly supportive even though I have taken a disproportionate amount of their time. Meg Frisbee, Derek Everett, and Todd Laugen provided invaluable comments on my book proposal, while every member of the department has provided advice and support. I feel lucky to have landed where I am.

This book was made possible by two unions. GSOC (UAW Local 2110) is the reason why I was able to live in New York on a graduate worker stipend, while the MSU Denver Faculty Federation (AFT Local 6321) is why tenure still exists at my current institution. I would like to thank both, and especially my fellow MSFF Steering Committee members, for fighting to ensure that the university lives up to its ideals. The germ of this project emerged from the fight against the exploitative labor policies of NYU at its campuses in both New York and Abu Dhabi. I learned much about organizing and solidarity from my fellow members of the NYU Coalition for Fair Labor. I completed this manuscript while facing criminal charges after armed riot police arrested dozens of antiwar demonstrators on my campus. I would like to thank Leslie Boyd, Andrea Maestrejuan, Kyle Montanio, and my fellow defendants. I would especially like to thank my attorney, Azra Taslimi, and the firm of Rathod Mohamedbhai for taking my case pro bono and fighting for me in court, as well as those members of the university administration who opposed institutional sanctions against students and faculty engaging in peaceful protest.

Many friends and colleagues have been a source of both personal and professional support. Laura Goffman has provided invaluable comments on nearly everything I have written for the past decade. She has also helped me navigate writer's block, academia, and a myriad of personal challenges.

I am inexpressibly grateful for her insights and her friendship. At NYU, Isaac Hand, Jennifer Pineo-Dunn, Hannah Scott Deuchar, and Ian VanderMeulen were a wonderful community of colleagues and friends. I am also deeply appreciative of Amanda Perry, Nick Wirtz, Gayatri Kumar, Lâle Can, Matt MacLean, Noora al-Meer, Laura Phillips, Daniel Tavana, Cyrus Roedel, Shimrit Lee, Mohammad al-Subhi, Yassine Ben Yaacoub, and Abdullah al-Ziadi. In Denver, Rob Prince, Carole Woodall, Andrea Stanton, and Karim Mattar have welcomed me into yet another new community.

My parents have been supportive despite long absences, long distances, the incomprehensible expectations of the academy, and an education that must have seemed suspiciously prolonged. My sister Diane made sure I never got too full of myself and has become a close friend as we have navigated adulthood. Allison Korinek has been my closest partner in every way. She also provided invaluable feedback as I transformed an absurdly long first draft of this manuscript into a more readable book. Her endless well of kindness and humor have been an inexpressible comfort. Words cannot fully express my gratitude.

Introduction

IN MAY 1975, THE Kuwaiti newspaper *al-Taliʿa*, or *The Vanguard*, published a series of articles defending the rights of noncitizen workers. Two years earlier, a sudden rise in oil prices had triggered both an economic boom and a surge of immigration, which in turn sharpened a long-running debate over the exploitative conditions facing the noncitizen residents who made up the majority of Kuwait's population. The articles showcased a series of interviews with Hussein al-Youha, the vice president of the Kuwait Trade Union Federation (KTUF) and one of the most prominent leaders of the Kuwaiti labor movement. He explained that workers in Kuwait were subject to three separate labor laws, one each for the oil, public, and private sectors. The result was systemic discrimination on the basis of nationality. Workers in the private sector, who were overwhelmingly noncitizen, possessed fewer rights than workers in the government sector, which was dominated by Kuwaitis. Moreover, even when covered by the same law, noncitizen workers routinely received lower pay, inferior benefits, and fewer protections than their citizen colleagues.

Al-Youha articulated an unambiguous message: "We demand equality between Kuwaiti and non-Kuwaiti workers." The solution was simple: pass a single, unified labor law to provide all workers with equal rights and benefits. It was self-evidently unjust, he argued, that non-Kuwaitis faced systemic discrimination and "terrible" conditions in the workplace. Noncitizens even received less vacation time than Kuwaitis even though most had to travel abroad to spend time with their families. In addition to these ethical considerations, he argued that the rights of Kuwaiti workers were inextricably intertwined with the rights of their noncitizen colleagues. The effective ban on noncitizen membership in trade unions weakened the labor movement and therefore undermined efforts to improve wages and working conditions for all workers, regardless of their nationality. Because noncitizen workers could be paid less, received fewer benefits, and were easier to fire, employers preferred hiring noncitizens to citizens, which exacerbated the problem of citizen unemployment. The labor market included all workers, regardless of nationality, so lifting the wages for the lowest-paid noncitizens would benefit the entire working class. For al-Youha, solidarity was both a practical necessity and a moral imperative.[1]

Al-Youha's call for noncitizen rights was no aberration.[2] Like many Kuwaiti labor activists, he was steeped in an ethos of internationalism and working-class solidarity forged during the middle of the twentieth century. While in many ways his life story is remarkable, it also reflects the struggles over decolonization, labor, citizenship, and democracy that dominated regional politics. Al-Youha was born in Dubai in 1933. After the death of his parents, he moved to Kuwait, where he was raised by a relative and received an elementary school education. Like many families in the region, his was immersed in the ties of trade that connected the Persian Gulf and wider Indian Ocean world, working as sailors, traders, and ship captains. But by the late 1940s, this centuries-old maritime economy was collapsing under the combined weight of war, depression, and global competition. So, at the age of fourteen, he began working as a messenger at the Kuwait Oil Company (KOC), the oil firm jointly owned by British Petroleum and U.S.-based Gulf Oil, which had become one of the region's largest employers.[3]

Al-Youha's experience mirrored that of many other workers in the early years of the Gulf oil industry. He lived in a shack in a dilapidated settlement that the company called the "Arab village," earning a meager five rupees per day. The company classified him as a "coolie," a term that was both derogatory and commonplace, and provided no opportunities for advancement. Al-Youha, like many others, was most offended by the racial discrimination that permeated every aspect of the oil industry. Compared to their Kuwaiti colleagues, Indian and Pakistani workers, as well as Arab "skilled" workers hired abroad, received higher wages and better benefits while monopolizing mid-ranking jobs. Exclusively white "senior staff" lived in what was virtually another world, cloistered in segregated suburbs and lavished with benefits, including servants, cinemas, swimming pools, and tennis courts. Al-Youha soon left the oil firm, leveraging his experience to find work as a taxi driver and, eventually, a municipal firefighter.

It was while working as a taxi driver that al-Youha was introduced to trade unionism. In 1954, he met with members of the Kuwaiti branch of the Arab Nationalist Movement, including its leaders Ahmad al-Khatib and Sami al-Munais, who viewed workers as a pillar of their anticolonial alliance. Their unionization effort never got off the ground, as it was stifled by British imperial repression and the fact that mass politics and anticolonial nationalism were only beginning to gain a foothold in the Gulf. But after Kuwait won its independence in 1961 and introduced a constitution that protected essential freedoms of speech and association, al-Youha became an active labor organizer. In 1964, he founded the Municipal Workers Union—the first legal trade union in Kuwait—and in 1967, he became the second president of the Government Sector Union Federation, a post he held while taking night classes in order to earn his high school diploma. The following year, he helped found the Kuwait Trade Union Federation (KTUF), eventually becoming its president in 1979.

Like many other labor leaders, al-Youha came to believe that unions could only flourish in a democratic state. His labor advocacy drew him inexorably into politics. He spoke out against the rigging of Kuwaiti elections in 1967, thus earning the enmity of the regime. In the aftermath of Egypt's shattering defeat in the 1967 war with Israel, al-Youha, like many other Arab nationalists, took a more radical turn. He helped found the People's Revolutionary Movement (al-Haraka al-Shaʿbiyya al-Thawriyya), which supported armed struggle against British colonialism and orchestrated a series of bombings against both the autocratic Shah of Iran and the Kuwaiti officials responsible for undermining the 1967 elections. While the bombs were not intended to cause bloodshed and the extent of his own involvement was unclear, al-Youha was arrested and sentenced to a year in prison. In 1972, he helped organize a series of popular committees connecting women's rights, trade unionism, and democracy in an effort to broaden participation in the labor movement.[4] Four years later, he was arrested again, this time for protesting the suspension of constitutional rule. The arrests did not stifle his activism. He continued to speak out on behalf of workers, including noncitizens, for decades to come.[5] Al-Youha's advocacy brought him into contact with some of the best-known anticolonial figures of the twentieth century. He met Gamal Abdel Nasser in Egypt and Houari Boumédiène in Algeria; at one conference in Cuba, he found himself trying to make small talk with Fidel Castro. He lectured in Marxist South Yemen and visited Moscow on multiple occasions. But despite his ties to the communist world, he identified as a trade unionist first and foremost and always stressed his belief in democracy.

Al-Youha's life connects the sweeping transformations of the midcentury Persian Gulf. He witnessed the consolidation of British imperial power, the emergence of autocratic states, the rise of mass politics, the explosion of oil wealth, and the transformative, if incomplete, process of decolonization. This book traces how social movements, and especially the labor movement, shaped all of these transformations. Specifically, it follows the debate over the meaning of citizenship and the rights of noncitizens, centering three interrelated questions at the heart of regional politics: Who should be granted citizenship? What rights should citizens have? And what rights should be granted to noncitizens? These struggles not only forged the Persian Gulf, but they also shed light on some of the fundamental questions of twentieth-century historiography: citizenship and exclusion, race and capitalism, decolonization and the nation-state.

The narrative begins in the early twentieth century, as the British empire tightened its grip on the Persian Gulf. By establishing a sprawling network of nationality laws, passport regulations, and movement restrictions, imperial authorities and their increasingly autocratic local allies deployed control over borders to reshape politics within them, seizing unprecedented power over their populations. British officials worked hand in glove with local elites, oil companies, and technical experts to etch corporate strategies of labor control—arbitrary deportation, racial hierarchy, divide and rule, and contract labor—into the legislative foundations of the Gulf states. Thus even as formal imperial power receded, the apparatus of empire remained largely intact. But the deportation state was not just an imperial initiative. Regional regimes and business elites viewed ready access to labor as an essential economic interest. They lobbied to transform labor into an even more readily available and disposable commodity by facilitating the hiring, firing, and deportation of noncitizen workers. Their efforts to expand their hiring pool and restrict access to nationality preserved imperial forms of governance well into the twenty-first century, demonstrating the inextricability of empire, migration, and authoritarianism.

But the struggle over citizenship also generated solidarities. In the 1950s, workers launched a campaign of protests and strikes that won a series of sweeping reforms, including worker protections, social welfare, and a more equitable distribution of oil wealth. Formulating and popularizing critiques of the racially segregated oil firms that dominated the industry, workers positioned themselves as the vanguard of anticolonial nationalism and played a central role in the movement for decolonization. In the aftermath of Kuwaiti independence in 1961, they became powerful opponents of absolutist rule and exclusionary citizenship, winning the desegregation of the oil industry and the nationalization of oil. In so doing, the Kuwaiti labor movement played a key but overlooked role in forging a global consensus—that control over natural resources is a fundamental right of sovereignty. But while organized labor achieved its anticolonial nationalist objectives, its effort to unite workers across the boundaries of nationality foundered in the face of powerful opposition. The failure to win rights for noncitizens set the stage for the suspension of constitutional rule in 1976. The story of citizenship in the Gulf thus demonstrates how the rights of citizens are inextricably bound to those of noncitizens.

Today, the Persian Gulf hosts one of the largest noncitizen populations on earth. When Kuwait gained independence in 1961, noncitizen residents already outnumbered citizens, a demographic balance—or, as it is often and tellingly described, "imbalance"—that shows no sign of abating.[6] As of 2020, more than thirty million noncitizen residents lived in the Gulf Cooperation Council (GCC) states of Bahrain, Kuwait, Oman, Qatar, Saudi Arabia, and the United Arab Emirates (UAE), representing an estimated 52 percent of their combined population. Kuwait was estimated to be 70 percent noncitizen, while in the UAE and Qatar the number reached over 85 percent.[7] Despite their small populations, three GCC states—Saudi Arabia, the UAE, and Kuwait—have long been among the world's twenty countries with the largest absolute number of noncitizen residents.[8]

Perhaps as remarkable as the scale of migration to the Gulf is the extent to which legislation across the region treats noncitizens as transitory. In all GCC states, noncitizen residents have little or no chance of naturalization, or even of gaining the right to long-term residency. Virtually all rely on short-term labor visas subject to arbitrary revocation. The path to citizenship is so narrow that the region is home to hundreds of thousands of stateless people—colloquially termed the "bidun," meaning "without"—who struggle to obtain the necessities of life. Though noncitizens are diverse and experience varying levels of privilege and vulnerability, all are permanently temporary.[9] Citizenship in the Persian Gulf can also be tiered. Only Kuwaitis who can trace their descent to ancestors resident in Kuwait in 1920 are classified as "original" or "founding" citizens. They are distinguished from "naturalized" citizens, who have access to fewer state benefits and are denied political rights until thirty years after their naturalization. Naturalized citizens can also be stripped of their nationality on a variety of grounds—a threat that has been carried out with increasing frequency.[10] Thus for most residents of the Gulf, citizenship is the exception, rather than the norm. It is also of little use when making claims or exercising rights. Rather, it is first and foremost a mechanism of exclusion.

The Persian Gulf is often stereotyped as exceptional or even irrational, whether as an oil-fueled parody of conspicuous consumption or a netherworld of exploitation and authoritarianism. Building on scholarly critiques of Gulf exceptionalism, this book argues that, when studied like any other place, the region is no exception; rather, it is a valuable site for reconfiguring popular and academic understandings of citizenship.[11] When freed from the blinders of methodological nationalism and addressed as a global phenomenon, citizenship can be understood as a mechanism of exclusion as much as a guarantor of rights. Few wealthy nation-states have not, at one time or another in the past century, turned to temporary noncitizen labor to simultaneously placate the exclusionary demands of xenophobic nationalism and the voracious labor requirements of capital.[12] The Gulf also vividly demonstrates the importance of denizenship—or the rights of noncitizens—on which the success of movements for democracy and social justice across the region would ultimately hinge.[13] Around the globe, movements for the rights of immigrants and workers, and for democracy and freedom of speech, grapple with states that can deport their critics at will. As borders are increasingly hardened, immigration regimes militarized, and citizenship weaponized, the Gulf must be seen not as an exception, but as the rule.

* * *

Recovering the contingencies that shaped the citizenship regime requires a rethinking of some of the central tropes of Gulf studies. The field has long been overshadowed by two discourses of economic inevitability that have minimized the role of popular movements in regional history. The first is rentier theory, which for decades has been the dominant theoretical lens through which social science has conceptualized the Persian Gulf. In brief, rentier theory argues that oil rents enable resource-rich states to buy off political opponents through the provision of government jobs and social services. It presumes a perverse social contract phrased in the language of exchange: material affluence for political quiescence.[14] While a number of works informed by rentier theory have added nuance or qualifications to this basic equation, its framework posits oil as an overpowering structural variable that steamrolls historical contingency and non-elite agency.[15] At its worst, rentier theory frames Gulf citizens as the lucky recipients of unearned wealth, lacking in work ethic and entrepreneurial spirit and determined to exclude noncitizen residents from their undeserved bounty.

Discourses of economic inevitability are also deployed to explain the rise of mass migration. With the oil rush and its concurrent construction boom, so the story goes, the region faced a "manpower shortage"—especially of "skilled workers"—and so naturally turned to recruitment abroad. Other accounts stress the "push" and "pull" factors, generated by oil wealth and the inequities of the global economy, that made mass migration inevitable. John Chalcraft critiques this as the framework of "hydraulics," in which labor becomes a natural resource that some regions intrinsically lack, like water or oil, and that has to be obtained elsewhere.[16] These are the terms of neoclassical economics, which understands labor, like all other commodities, in terms of supply and demand.[17] Narratives that frame migration as the inevitable result of global economic forces can be traced back to the earliest years of the oil boom, saturating imperial reports, newspaper articles, and academic analysis.[18] These accounts were often accompanied by predictions of a future equilibrium. Most observers believed that after an initial "construction period," demand for labor would subside, and noncitizen workers would return home. This belief is well illustrated by a conversation in Kuwait recorded by the anthropologist Peter Lienhardt during the 1950s, in which a "well-educated and liberal-minded young Kuwaiti" explained: "When their work is finished, we shall simply take the immigrants to the Iraqi border and say, 'Thank you very much. Goodbye.'"[19]

These entrenched discourses of economic inevitability go a long way toward explaining why scholarship on the Persian Gulf often sidelines contingency and popular protest. When the rise of mass migration and the growth of authoritarian states are framed as the unavoidable corollaries of oil wealth, there is little reason to study their history. They are narratives of path dependency in which oil and the state are all-powerful actors. They have consequently led to the scholarly neglect of popular politics, and even of social history writ large.

In recent years, a new wave of scholarship has subjected these discourses to sustained critique, opening the door for more balanced narratives of Persian Gulf history. A number of social scientists influenced by rentier theory have abandoned the idea that "rentierism alleviates class conflict," instead stressing the importance of historical contestation and contingency.[20] Scholars more critical of the rentier framework have noted that oil wealth did little to diffuse dissent; if anything, it raised the material stakes of politics.[21] A growing body of scholarship on the powerful, even revolutionary social movements that have swept the Gulf over the past century has made a theory premised on social peace look increasingly absurd.[22] As Adam Hanieh has noted, rentier theory cannot explain a region characterized by "near-constant capital versus labor struggle."[23] *Comrades Estranged* builds on these critiques by offering a novel reconceptualization of state formation that reverses the chain of causality proposed by rentier theory. By tracing the history of popular movements for social and economic justice across the mid-twentieth century, it argues that the benefits of the welfare state, including universal healthcare, education, social security, and accessible housing, were not the free gifts of benevolent autocrats. Nor were they the inevitable result of oil wealth, or the fruit of a cynical ploy to "buy off" the opposition. These benefits had to be won. They are the hard-fought victories of a prolonged struggle, during which workers and activists fought for what T. H. Marshall called "social citizenship," or the idea that citizens have a right to a certain minimum quality of life.[24] For all of the inequities of the Gulf economy and the authoritarianism of Gulf regimes, citizens won access to an enviable social safety net, enabled by an enormous, if imperfect, redistribution of resources.[25]

Neoclassical models of migration have also come under scholarly attack, both in the Gulf and elsewhere.[26] Their explanatory shortcomings have become increasingly self-evident over the decades. Is Kuwait really in desperate need of workers when 85 percent of its workforce is noncitizen? Or is Qatar, where the percentage is 95 percent?[27] Numbers are even more stark in the private sector, where in 2010, noncitizens comprised an estimated 95 percent of the workforce in Kuwait and a stunning 99 percent in Qatar.[28] The idea of economic "dependence" on noncitizen labor also ignores a longstanding unemployment crisis facing young Gulf citizens, who are often passed over by employers in favor of cheaper and more vulnerable noncitizen workers.[29] Migration to the Gulf simply cannot be explained in the language of supply and demand when both have proven to be insatiable.[30] *Comrades Estranged* builds on these efforts to challenge the discourses of economic inevitability that have erased residents of the Persian Gulf from their own history.

But an alternative history is still needed, in part because of the structure of the field. Scholarship addressing migration and citizenship is disproportionately written by social scientists whose work addresses the present day. Most histories of migration, though invaluable, focus on the lived experience of specific diasporas, and so only occasionally interface with the historiography of political struggle. Citizens and noncitizens are therefore addressed in separate and self-contained analytical spheres, resembling what, in another context, Zachary Lockman has critiqued as a "dual society" model.[31] Perhaps most limiting is a widespread reliance on English-language sources, which overemphasize the role of imperial officials and oil executives. The result is an elision of local agency and a proliferation of smoothly teleological narratives that miss the contestation and contingencies of history.

This book puts forward a counternarrative by mobilizing previously unused sources and drawing on heterodox scholarship on the racialized and gendered devaluation of labor. Building on generations of scholarship in the fields of critical geography and migration studies, its starting point is the belief that migration was not the inevitable result of global economic forces.[32] Rather, so-called "migrant workers" were and are perpetually in demand precisely because they are migrant workers: They are easier to underpay, intimidate, fire, and deport. In the words of Saskia Sassen, demand exists because "immigrant labor is not just any labor"—it is cheap, deportable, and therefore desirable.[33] To understand the history of migration, then, we must trace how a protracted and contingent political struggle created a vast "labor reserve" of alienated noncitizens. As Doreen Massey has noted, labor reserves "are the product of social relations; they don't just happen."[34] In the Persian Gulf, imperial, business, and state elites battled to exclude noncitizens from the protections of labor law and union organizing, and to deal with "labor shortages" by searching for more workers abroad rather than by improving wages and working conditions at home. With remarkable consistency across the decades, they sought to forge, and profit from, a migrant working class. Their efforts faced a challenge from workers and their allies, who fought the apparatus of exclusion. The story of this struggle—the history of exclusion—is the central thread of this book.

Comrades Estranged further departs from previous scholarship by tracing the history of economic debates within the Gulf itself. Critiques of neoclassical migration models are neither new nor limited to academic scholarship. Rather, rival frameworks for understanding the economics of oil and labor migration circulated freely in the midcentury press. Employers and the business press championed the idea that a "manpower shortage," especially of "skilled" or "experienced" workers, threatened economic prosperity, and called for an increase of migration in response.[35] They kept wages low by arguing that raises would trigger a spiral of inflation, which was a widespread concern in the midcentury Gulf. But workers and their supporters presaged later academic discourse by tearing apart the narrative of absolute shortage, framing a corporate failure to attract workers as the predictable result of an unwillingness to pay decent wages, provide adequate housing and other amenities, and train their workforce. In 1976, a headline summarized this view with a concise turn of phrase: "There is no shortage of labor in Kuwait, only a maldistribution."[36] These debates pivoted on conceptual terms—such as monopoly, inflation, manpower shortage, and reverse migration—that became political flashpoints. Representations of the economy thus played a key role in shaping reality. A central goal of *Comrades Estranged* is to write the intellectual contributions of employers, workers, technocrats, and radicals back into the history of the Persian Gulf.

To avoid reifying the category of the "migrant worker" by treating noncitizens as a predetermined object of study, *Comrades Estranged* interrogates how noncitizens were produced as such—as temporary, deportable, and excised from the body politic. In so doing, it draws on the work of Nicholas De

Genova and Mae Ngai, who frame exclusion, rather than immigrants themselves, as their object of study.[37] It therefore is distinct from a rich literature on the experiences of particular diasporic or noncitizen communities in the Gulf: Iranians, South Asians, the enslaved, the stateless.[38] It also consciously eschews the most common term for noncitizens in the Gulf context: the "migrant worker." While the term permeates academic and popular discourse, it is itself a form of exclusion, as Attiya Ahmad has argued.[39] Far from transient interlopers or undifferentiated packets of labor, noncitizens are dynamic actors whose lived experience has been shot through with both belonging and alienation.[40] Indeed, the assumption that noncitizens are merely transitory migrants is not only inaccurate but implicitly justifies their exclusion.[41] Finally, the figure of the "oppressed migrant worker," exemplified by images of South Asian men laboring on construction sites, has been a central trope in othering, exceptionalizing, and Orientalizing the Persian Gulf—despite the fact that, as Ahmed Kanna has noted, "the racialized exploitation of foreign workers is perhaps the aspect of Gulf societies that is *most* similar to the neoliberal societies of the North."[42] By historicizing the figure of the migrant worker, this book highlights the contingencies of its production and challenges its connotations of temporariness.[43]

Citizenship is the thread that ties these interventions together. As scholars of citizenship have argued, its form can vary widely. It can be "thin," involving only a minimum of protections, or "thick," granting its holders a bundle of social and economic rights.[44] This diversity generates contestation, making citizenship a "framework for debate" within every polity.[45] The outlines of citizenship are also diverse. It can be relatively accessible to noncitizens or closely guarded as an exclusive privilege. Scholars have traced how citizenship regimes are shaped by an array of actors in a variety of historical contexts.[46] In the Persian Gulf, where most people were not citizens, the question of the rights of noncitizens was perhaps just as pivotal as the question of the rights of citizens. A key intervention of *Comrades Estranged* is thus its discussion of not only citizenship, but the rights of noncitizens—what Linda Bosniak terms "alienage," or what other scholars have referred to as "denizenship." Bosniak notes that citizenship and denizenship are usually discussed separately, a division that reflects a split between academic works on citizenship and those on nationality.[47] While the two terms are often used as synonyms, their difference in meaning is significant: Citizenship stresses the participation and rights of individuals within a given polity, while nationality emphasizes access to citizenship itself.[48] This book not only addresses both, but argues that they are fundamentally interdependent.

In a context where most people lack the protections of citizenship, the question of denizenship takes on central importance. Noncitizens are often understood as lacking, in Hannah Arendt's well-known phrase, the very "right to have rights."[49] But this is misleading. Noncitizens are rarely, if ever, bereft of rights. At a minimum they are usually protected from murder or theft, while many are granted further protections from workplace discrimination or arbitrary deportation.[50] But these rights vary widely, and the variability in forms of denizenship, like the variability in forms of citizenship, is a key node of contestation. This book argues that in the midcentury Persian Gulf, the meanings of both citizenship and denizenship were forged in tandem as workers, activists, and radical organizations battled for a more equitable distribution of wealth and power. Noncitizens always have the right to some rights. The question is what those are.

* * *

The history of citizenship in the Persian Gulf begins with empire. Abdel Razzaq Takriti has described the region as "a part of the world where imperial political engineering was exceedingly successful."[51] Without exception, the authoritarian monarchies consolidated under the dominion of the British empire remain in place today. During the first half of the twentieth century, British imperial authorities transformed "the monopolization of the legitimate means of movement" into the foundational mechanism of their autocratic control.[52] Deportation was the go-to imperial solution to a wide range of social and political problems, from unemployment and crime to disease and dissent. British authorities and their local client rulers first introduced nationality laws as an appendage to the deportation state to legitimize their arbitrary power over movement by creating the category of the deportable alien. The Gulf thus illustrates Yael Berda's argument that citizenship in the British imperial context must be seen, first and foremost, as a "mobility regime."[53] *Comrades Estranged* argues that Gulf monarchies began as deportation states, forged from the surveillance and regulation of migration in the imperial era.

Perhaps the most striking characteristic of the imperial deportation state is its longevity. It became the core of authoritarian regimes after independence, regimes that preserved legislation and personnel inherited from the British. A coalition of elites found that the creation of a class of deportable noncitizens suited their interests. Ruling families silenced dissent by arbitrarily seizing passports or even revoking citizenship. Some granted nationality to handpicked allies in order to gerrymander elections and build dependent constituencies. Business elites transformed nationality into a generator of wealth. As Étienne Balibar has noted, borders do not halt migration; rather, they are designed "actively to *differentiate* between individuals in terms of social class."[54] Employers, landlords, and monopolistic importers found that they could profit from the structural exclusion of noncitizens, who became their customers, tenants, and workers, injecting value into what Karl Polanyi calls "fictitious commodities"—land, labor, and money.[55] In defense of their material interests, business elites tried to limit noncitizen landholding, naturalization, and business ownership even as they encouraged mass migration, consciously forging a permanently impermanent and dispossessed working class. The perpetuation of the imperial deportation regime thus illustrates the incompleteness of decolonization.[56] If the postcolonial, in the words of Stuart Hall, "is characterised by the persistence of many of the effects of colonisation, but at the same time their displacement from the coloniser/colonised axis to their internalisation within the decolonised society itself," then the Gulf is a model postcolonial society. Indeed, the very first examples cited by Hall are the states of the Persian Gulf.[57]

Some of the most enthusiastic proponents of the deportation state were British and U.S.-owned companies—especially oil companies—whose role raises the thorny question of the relationship between race and nationality. As numerous scholars have noted, from their earliest days in the Gulf, oil multinationals replicated the racial segregation familiar across global resource frontiers.[58] *Comrades Estranged* builds on this work by tracing how, precisely, white supremacy functioned as a mechanism of power. To maintain control of their workforce and the oilfields in which they labored, oil companies relied on a strategy of divide-and-rule. Their standard procedure during strikes, executed repeatedly in the midcentury Gulf, was to deploy their exclusively white "senior staff" as strikebreakers, trusting—accurately—that racism would supersede solidarity. But with the rise of anticolonial nationalism and organized labor in the 1950s and 1960s, oil companies faced insurmountable pressure to hire more local nationals, numbers of white senior staff dwindled, and racist strikebreaking grew increasingly untenable. To try and salvage their position, they turned to another tested strategy of the oil industry: noncitizen workers.[59] By making much of their workforce deportable, they deliberately deployed a powerful form of vulnerability to counter the threat of labor organizing.

This strategy relied on the consent of Gulf regimes—consent which was forthcoming. Indeed, it was Gulf states, rather than oil companies, that spearheaded efforts to fragment workers along the lines of nationality. Even national oil companies, established with the explicit aim of breaking the stranglehold of the oil majors, replicated the strategies of divide-and-rule favored by the U.S.- and British-owned firms that they sought to supplant. They found willing allies in a new class of technocrats schooled in the fields of law, economics, or industrial relations whose expertise provided new and sophisticated justifications for a range of longstanding corporate and imperial policies. Business elites and their monarchical allies thus replaced a strategy of divide-and-rule based on race with one based on nationality, etching their preferences into the legal apparatus of Gulf states. The nationality regime that emerged thus reflected the "racialized global inequality" embodied by the labor relations strategies of the global oil industry.[60]

The framework of racial capitalism can help to elucidate the relationship between citizenship and race. Though developed in the context of the Atlantic world, this body of scholarship has, to cite Cedric Robinson, provided an invaluable template for understanding the tendency of capitalism "not to homogenize, but to differentiate—to exaggerate regional, subcultural, and dialectical differences."[61] This differentiation produces "edge populations," which are systematically disempowered, devalued, excluded, and, more often than not, racialized.[62] As Eve Troutt Powell has noted, race has long been central to Middle Eastern history, even as the outlines of these "racisms" differ from those in other contexts.[63] In recent years, a small but invaluable scholarship on race in the Middle East has inestimably enriched our understanding of these racisms.[64] But in the Gulf, race remains understudied, while the role of racism as a mechanism of control is only beginning to be unearthed.[65] Moreover, the twentieth-century Gulf remains a particularly challenging context in which to discuss race, in part because it hosted a variety of interlaced racisms: the white supremacy that saturated Anglo-American oil firms; enslavement and debt bondage across the Indian Ocean; and a longstanding East African slave trade that grew increasingly racialized during the export boom of the nineteenth century. These conceptions of race were crosshatched by other hierarchies and forms of difference with their own genealogies that cannot simply be collapsed into the same analytical category.[66]

The history of citizenship in the Gulf illuminates the interconnectedness of empire, race, gender, and nationality—an interconnectedness with a global resonance.[67] While, to quote Gargi Bhattacharyya, "racial capitalism does not emerge as a result of a plan," labor practices in the Gulf oil industry are about as close to a plan as it is possible to imagine.[68] This observation is no flash of scholarly insight: Midcentury newspapers, petitions, and memoirs written by workers and anticolonial nationalists are replete with condemnations of corporate and imperial racism in the Persian Gulf, as well as comparisons with Jim Crow segregation and South African apartheid. The comparison was, and is, apt. Apartheid itself, out of which the term racial capitalism first emerged, was a strategy "to translate the facts of racial domination and segregation (already well established in South Africa) into the terms of *national* difference" with a network of Bantustans and labor camps.[69]

This work thus challenges Benedict Anderson's conceptual division between nationality, an imagined community resting on the belief in a shared historical destiny, and racism, built on "eternal contaminations" outside of history.[70] It builds on histories of exclusion and segregation in the Gulf, some of the best-documented of which are studies of urban space.[71] It also illustrates Maya Mikdashi's argument that "there is no practice of sectarianism, sovereignty, or citizenship that is not marked by sexual difference," as gender repeatedly intersects with race and nationality in the Gulf citizenship regime.[72] The relationship between migration and exclusion has always been central to theories of racial capitalism; indeed, Cedric Robinson begins his own analysis with the othering of migratory workers in medieval Europe. Immigration historiography in the United States is especially rich with examples of how immigration controls and nationality legislation, and especially "guestworker" programs, generated new racialized subjects.[73] As Radhika Mongia has argued, "A blurring of the vocabularies of nationality and race is a founding strategy of the modern nation-state," and thus nationality "enabled a covert racism."[74] In the Persian Gulf, the racism was not particularly covert.

* * *

The creation of an exclusionary citizenship regime is only part of the story. *Comrades Estranged* centers the many residents of the Gulf who fought for the rights of both citizens and noncitizens in the name of social and economic justice. Anticolonial and antiauthoritarian activists condemned the use of nationality as a form of patronage and fought against the deployment of movement restrictions as a weapon against dissent. Arab nationalists defended the rights of all Arabs, regardless of citizenship, and called for easier access to naturalization in order to provide longtime residents with a sense of stability and belonging. Feminists condemned patriarchal legislation that passed nationality from father to son, leaving the children of many Gulf women as either noncitizens or stateless people. Growing to a crescendo in the mid-1970s, the calls of these dissidents focused on more inclusive and egalitarian conceptions of citizenship, nationality, and denizenship.

The figure of the worker most forcefully collided with the figure of the citizen. As labor organizing accelerated in the 1940s and 1950s, workers allied with Arab and anticolonial nationalists to argue that citizens deserved to share in the nation's natural wealth. They were particularly prominent in Kuwait, becoming key advocates for the creation of an independent state apparatus that could defend them from the rapacity of the multinational oil companies. In the aftermath of Kuwaiti independence in 1961, the labor movement deployed strikes, sabotage, and the discourses of citizenship and anticolonial nationalism to become a powerful force in Kuwaiti politics. Workers played a central role in building systems of welfare, universal healthcare, and social security, and they became prominent antagonists of empire.

What workers and their allies recognized better than anyone else was that their power, and their rights, were directly proportionate to the rights of noncitizens. For reasons both practical and ideological, labor leaders determined that they needed to organize noncitizen workers. Like Hussein al-Youha, many were inspired by Arab nationalism or socialism or both, and they believed in the necessity of unifying the working class. All recognized that a class of deportable and systematically underpaid noncitizen workers would undercut wages, harm the employment prospects of citizens, and make labor organizing difficult—if not impossible. Many simply thought that it was the right thing to do. Thus, through the mid-1970s, the labor movement fought for noncitizen rights both in the workplace and outside of it, including for the right to join unions, earn a minimum wage, and enjoy the protections of labor law and social security. In so doing, Kuwaiti unions emerged as perhaps the most powerful champions of noncitizen rights in the midcentury Gulf.

This was not an inevitable choice. The question of who to include under the banner of labor has haunted labor movements, and labor scholars, from the time of Marx and Engels.[75] In many times and places, unions enforced exclusion. In the Persian Gulf, access to cheap and deportable noncitizen labor is often seen as one of the many forms of rent that accrues to citizens.[76] But if it is a form of rent, it is both unequal and unsustainable. For employers, cheap labor boosts profits. For the wealthy, it provides easy access to domestic work. But for citizen workers whose income comes primarily from their labor, the presence of a vulnerable noncitizen class lowers their wages, disincentivizes their employment, and undercuts their ability to organize.[77] Thus, the category of citizenship was always crosshatched by the category of class. For citizen workers, the dwindling rights of noncitizens represented a threat to their own position.

What gave workers in the Persian Gulf their remarkable power was their control over oil. As Kaveh Ehsani has noted, scholarship on oil often erases the role of workers.[78] One of the most influential and useful recent works on the politics of hydrocarbons—Timothy Mitchell's *Carbon Democracy*—reflects this elision. Mitchell argues that industrialization allowed coal miners to seize unprecedented disruptive power, which in turn led to an expansion of democratic rights in nineteenth-century Europe. But he argues that the oil industry, with its global markets, geographic isolation, smaller workforce, and technically sophisticated production process, was more difficult to disrupt, leading to "the weakening of democratic forces" around the globe.[79] These conclusions have come under fire from social historians of oil who have demonstrated that oil networks could be, and were, subject to disruption.[80] *Comrades Estranged* enlarges this critique by narrating a new history of oil labor that utilizes Mitchell's argument about the power of hydrocarbon disruption to different ends. By disrupting the flow of oil with strikes and sabotage, workers in the Persian Gulf wielded enormous structural power out of all proportion to their numbers. Carbon-based fuels—including oil—could empower labor movements, and in the midcentury Persian Gulf, they did.

Perhaps the most world-historic victory championed by the labor movement was the nationalization of oil. It was a staggering transformation, underlining Arang Keshavarzian's argument that the Gulf was "a site for purposive participation in the making of global capitalism."[81] The one-sided oil concessions negotiated between Gulf monarchies and Anglo-American oil firms in the early years of the twentieth century granted multinational corporations control of production and profits. In the 1950s, anticolonial nationalists and oil workers combined to rein in corporate power and, eventually, win sovereign control over natural resources. The concessionary system was finally extinguished across the Gulf in the 1970s, following decades of popular criticism and protest. Oil nationalization reconfigured the distribution of value in the global economy and represented what has been convincingly described as "the most concentrated nonviolent transfer of global wealth in human history."[82]

Until recent years, the dominant English-language historiography of oil demeaned nationalization, personalizing or even pathologizing it as the product of supposedly self-serving politicians like Mosadegh, Qasim, or Nasser.[83] Emblematic of this literature is *The Prize*, Daniel Yergin's best-selling book, which was turned into a PBS miniseries and remains the first point of reference for nonspecialists looking for a comprehensive history of the oil industry. It is a corporate history of "pioneering" entrepreneurs and innovators, almost exclusively men, building globe-spanning empires. In over eight hundred pages on one of the most segregated industries of the twentieth century, racism barely merits a mention, while oil concessions are framed as a reasonable price for corporate expertise. Though resource nationalism dominates the second half of his volume, Yergin does little to try to understand its causes, framing it as irrational fanaticism. The result is that the nationalization of oil is narrated as a violation of the sanctity of contract, or even a stupendous act of ingratitude.[84] Such histories reflect the biases of their corporate sources, which are steeped in midcentury racism and dismissive of local politics.

A new and invaluable set of global oil histories has demolished this paradigm by unearthing the unscrupulous means by which multinational oil firms acquired their concessions, the pervasiveness of corporate racism, and the linkages between resource nationalism and decolonization.[85] These works have opened the door for a new narrative of oil nationalization. Understanding how oil was nationalized—how the "oil revolution" was won—requires fine-grained social histories of individual nationalizations. Each is, by definition, simultaneously circumscribed within the borders of the nation-state and shaped by regional and global forces.[86] *Comrades Estranged* contributes to this effort.[87] It argues that in the Persian Gulf, it was oil workers and their allies who built the arguments behind nationalization, became its most influential advocates, and took control of the production process, literally bringing oil nationalization about. The "oil revolution," then, was a bottom-up social movement that emerged from the experience of racial discrimination in the oilfields. Well into the 1970s, regional monarchies were reluctant to alienate oil multinationals and the powerful governments—notably Britain and the United States—that defended them. Regimes understood that their survival rested more on security agreements and arms sales than on the consent of their own populations. Nationalization represented a step into the abyss that many were reluctant to take. It was the force of popular opinion and economic disruption, both orchestrated by oil workers, that forced them to take that fateful step.

Workers in the Gulf thus represent the connecting tissue between revolutionary movements and mainstream politics, and incorporate the region into the history of the global left.[88] As a popular, left-wing mass movement, labor was a vehicle for—and advocate of—an array of ideas that would reshape the politics of the Persian Gulf.[89] Its story challenges narratives of economic inevitability and reveals how ordinary people in the Gulf fought for a more just and equitable future. But while workers succeeded as anticolonial nationalists, they faced far stronger opposition when fighting for their rights as workers. As happened to so many of the labor movements at the forefront of decolonization, the very state that workers fought to build in opposition to empire turned against them once independence was won.[90] Alarmed by the prospect of an alliance transcending the boundaries of nationality, state authorities, oil companies, and major employers combined to split the ranks of organized labor, granting special privileges for Kuwaiti workers and shutting noncitizens out of the movement. In the aftermath of the 1973 oil boom, employers successfully lobbied the Kuwaiti state to further facilitate the recruitment of labor abroad, making noncitizen workers increasingly available, and therefore increasingly expendable. The ruling family shut down movements for both citizen and noncitizen rights by suspending constitutional rule in 1976 and unleashing the coercive apparatus on the trade union movement, bringing an end to Kuwait's first democratic experiment. Workers lost the battle to unite a multinational working class, and with it, the interrelated struggles for more capacious conceptions of both citizenship and denizenship. Their story thus illustrates the limits of nationalism as an emancipatory framework. It also sheds light on the paradox haunting the formerly colonized world: that independence did not mean decolonization.

* * *

To tell a history that is, by necessity, theoretically and geographically sprawling, this book draws on a wide array of sources and spans a series of geographic scales. It focuses on Kuwait, which is particularly significant and well-documented. Ever since the 1950s, and especially in the years following the promulgation of its constitution in 1962, Kuwait has enjoyed a more open political sphere than any other Gulf state, which has made it host to the region's freest trade union movement. Thanks to a flourishing press, debates that took place across the Persian Gulf are best documented in Kuwait. Moreover, Kuwait was something of a political nexus. Its newspapers and periodicals were read, and its politics followed, across the region, and it served as a hub for activists and opposition movements around the Arabic-speaking world. And because Kuwait's first oil boom took place in the early 1950s, before all smaller Gulf states except for Bahrain, it became a model for the region in the hydrocarbon age.

Finally, Kuwait played a prominent role in the global story of oil nationalization and resource nationalism. Many oil histories trace a smooth progression of nationalizations across the mid-twentieth century, beginning with the Soviet Union, followed by Mexico in 1938, succeeded by the "OPEC radicals"—Algeria, Libya, and Iraq—in the late 1960s and early 1970s, and ending with the "moderates" that nationalized oil following the 1973 war with Israel. This narrative obscures the fact that the spread of nationalization across the globe was anything but inevitable. Teleological narratives of the triumph of resource nationalism bear a distinct resemblance to domino theory—one nationalization inexorably following another. But the Gulf states, led by the conservative Saudi oil minister Ahmed Zaki Yamani, showed considerable reluctance to alienate their longtime imperial patrons by nationalizing oil. As the first Gulf state to take that momentous step, Kuwait occupies a key position. Kuwaiti oil workers organized strikes that brought production to a halt, allying with journalists and opposition politicians and overcoming corporate strategies of divide-and-rule. Together, they pressured the Kuwaiti parliament to reject several proposed compromises, such as "participation" agreements, which would have stopped short of complete nationalization. Kuwait thus occupied the pivotal if unglamorous position as the most radical of the moderates, delivering the final blow to the empire of oil.

But while Kuwait is an invaluable case study, it cannot be understood in a vacuum. It has long been enmeshed in the wider Persian Gulf, which is itself embedded in the Indian Ocean, Arabic-speaking, and formerly colonized worlds. Until independence, the Persian Gulf was governed by the Foreign Department of the India Office, effectively as an appendage to a colony. British authorities redeployed technologies of rule from British India, East Africa, or even farther afield. Anglo-American oil firms transplanted corporate practices and racist stereotypes across a variety of resource frontiers, especially the United States. Political activists defined themselves as Arabs or Kuwaitis, Marxists or workers, identifiers that made their own claims to the universal and the particular. This work therefore follows what Keshavarzian calls a "multiscalar approach to regionalization."[91] If a geographical trend to the narrative can be discerned, it is a gradual narrowing. *Comrades Estranged* begins by examining the Gulf as a whole but becomes more grounded in Kuwait as nation-states consolidate their power and people increasingly think, and act, in national terms. A nimble strategy is required to draw out the myriad connections that tied Kuwait and the Gulf to the rest of the world.

Much of what is written here will be new even to those familiar with the historiography of the Persian Gulf. This is principally because *Comrades Estranged* relies on a range of underutilized sources. The neglect of social history in the Persian Gulf is exacerbated by an overreliance on British records. While these documents provide rich depictions of official thinking, they are clouded by overblown fears of communism, an elite-centered understanding of politics, and a heavy dose of racism. Imperial officials generally viewed left-wing social movements as either temporary deviations from the "natural xenophobia" of Kuwaitis or as the work of outside agitators. The idea that an inclusive movement for social justice could be organized and led by Kuwaitis simply did not register in the imperial mind and is therefore silenced by the British sources. Even a prominent figure like Hussein al-Youha is rarely mentioned by name in the imperial files.[92] Moreover, the Gulf suffers from a dearth of accessible post-independence state archives, ensuring that histories often elide the role of local officials.[93] Internal documents from non-state organizations, such as the influential clubs that shaped midcentury Kuwaiti politics, are also nearly impossible to find. Historical scholarship thus tapers off with its imperial source base and only picks up again when studies based on contemporary fieldwork begin, skipping over the critical decades that witnessed nationalization and decolonization.

This erasure is particularly apparent in the case of the Kuwaiti labor movement. Its early records were lost in a government raid on union headquarters in 1965.[94] Then in 1991, the entire union archive was seized by Saddam Hussein's forces and deposited somewhere in Iraq, where it subsequently disappeared.[95] This may be part of the reason why there is no comprehensive history of the movement in any language. Its significance has been most obviously ignored in the English-language scholarship. Only the foundational work of Falah al-Mdairis has taken Kuwaiti workers seriously as historical actors.[96] The shadow of imperial logic preserved in the archival record has thus amplified the dismissiveness of rentier theory.

But to quote Sara Pursley's comment on Iraq, "Hand-wringing about missing sources might better be left to a time when more of the existing ones have been utilized."[97] The rich archive of the Arabic-language press demolishes the claim that the Gulf suffers from a dearth of historical sources. Kuwaiti newspapers represent an incredibly rich—and often the only—source for detailed information on Gulf politics and popular movements, particularly during the years 1955 through 1976. Remarkably, though most historic Kuwaiti newspapers are publicly available, few scholars have used them. They provide perhaps the most critical source base for this book.[98] Also sidelined are memoirs and Arabic-language historiography, especially from the first half of the century. As Fahad Bishara has noted, this neglect can in part be explained by limited conceptions of "what constitutes a legitimate source of historical truth," as many of these works are based on oral history or popular memory.[99] The result of this elision of Arabic-language source material has been a historiographic tendency to attribute change to abstract forces like the resource curse or the rentier state, or to corporate and imperial policy. Voices from the Gulf itself are either distorted through an unsympathetic filter or elided altogether.

In order to deconstruct the logics of power, this book draws on corporate and imperial records, including several archives that have hitherto been neglected. But it most depends upon records produced locally and written in Arabic, especially newspapers, memoirs, local histories, and oral history interviews. These sources have not only provided valuable information, but they have shaped my interventions and arguments. The periodization of this work is influenced by the memoirs of the legendary Kuwaiti opposition leader Dr. Ahmad al-Khatib; its arguments about the role of corporate racism and the labor movement in oil nationalization emerged from interviews with labor leaders; its focus on empire and decolonization was inspired by the coverage of anticolonial and pro-democracy publications like *al-Shaʿb* (The People) and *al-Taliʿa* (The Vanguard). This archive, preserved in opposition to the state, represents a form of resistance to the creeping power of authoritarian rule and the silences of official records. If I have to any degree succeeded in piecing together a narrative that escapes the tropes of economic determinism and teleological nation-building, it is thanks to those who have fought to preserve the social history of the Persian Gulf.

1 Deportation States | 1900–1950

ON JANUARY 27, 1957, three men disembarked from a British ship to begin their terms of exile. Leaders of a mass movement for political reform and self-determination, Abdul Aziz Shamlan, Abdu Ali Alewat, and Abdul Rahman al-Bakir were three of the most prominent anticolonial activists in Bahrain.[1] But their demands challenged the autocratic power of British authorities and the Bahraini ruling family, who waited for an opportunity to strike back. The moment came in late October 1956, after British, French, and Israeli forces attacked the Suez Canal. With the eyes of the world drawn by events in Egypt, British troops occupied Bahrain, arrested the leaders of the reform movement, and put them on trial in an ad hoc tribunal.[2] The men refused to defend themselves, arguing that the court itself was illegitimate. The verdict was never in doubt. Shamlan and al-Bakir were sentenced to fourteen years imprisonment, and Alewat to ten.[3]

But their forced removal from political life did not satisfy the British authorities. Concerned that the continued presence of the men in Bahrain could encourage further protest, British and Bahraini authorities arranged for their terms of imprisonment to be served far from the Persian Gulf.[4] So it was that they were deported to St. Helena, the notorious island prison in the south Atlantic where Napoleon Bonaparte had died in exile after his defeat at Waterloo. In his memoirs, al-Bakir writes with amazement—and a hint of bitter pride—that he was deemed such a threat by imperial authorities that he received the dubious honor of a cell on St. Helena. But these feelings were tempered by indignation at both the injustice of the trial and the severity of the sentence.[5] Shamlan, al-Bakir, and Alewat would be released only after an international campaign forced a British Parliamentary inquiry into their detention.[6] Meanwhile, back in Bahrain, the heavy hand of imperial repression crushed what had been a powerful reform movement.

If their place of incarceration was exceptional, their expulsion was not. By 1950, British imperial authorities and their local clients had come to rely on deportation as their go-to mechanism of social and political control across the Persian Gulf. This chapter traces the interconnected rise of deportation, nationality, and autocratic rule in Bahrain and Kuwait during the first half of the twentieth century. Regional rulers had long deployed banishment to neutralize their enemies. As imperial interests deepened, the British built deportation into the legal foundations of their hegemony.[7] By the 1930s, imperial officials, oil companies, local rulers, and elite families had transformed deportation into an everyday tool of governance across the region. Cheap, efficient, and unencumbered by the inconveniences of legal due process, deportation allowed a stripped-down imperial apparatus to displace, rather than address, issues of poverty, disease, and dissent. In the Gulf as elsewhere, the regulation of movement across borders transformed politics within them, granting nascent states a new and unchecked power over their populations.[8]

Deportation was a central if overlooked aspect of the consolidation of national sovereignty along territorial lines.[9] Perhaps its greatest legacy was nationality legislation. At the turn of the twentieth century, the Persian Gulf was a largely "anational society."[10] But over the course of the next five decades, nationality would become perhaps the most important legal category in everyday life. This transformation has become a central object of historical study in the Gulf—indeed, Nelida Fuccaro argues that it was the shifting position of noncitizens that "measured the pace of state and nation building" in Bahrain.[11] There is, however, no history of the deportation state and its wide-ranging social and political effects.[12] British officials in Bahrain drafted the region's first nationality legislation in the 1920s and '30s in large part to facilitate, and legitimate, their frequent recourse to deportation by clarifying overlapping claims to legal jurisdiction. They also made nationality a privilege to be granted by the state, rather than a right. In so doing, imperial authorities and their local allies seized the formidable power to grant or deny nationality at will. Thus the tools of the deportation state—denial of entry, expulsion, the withholding of passports, and citizenship stripping—have all been deployed not just against noncitizens, but also citizens, as weapons against dissent.

Most studies of migration controls in the Persian Gulf foreground what is usually called the *kafala* system. In brief, this immigration regime ties noncitizens to citizen-guarantors—"*kafils*," from the word "to guarantee"—for their residency visas. The sponsorship system has led to the systematic exploitation of noncitizens, as private employers are effectively granted the power of deportation over their workers.[13] Short-term contract migration is, of course, not unique to the Gulf. It was quite common in the twentieth century, from Germany to California, and remains prevalent in many places to this day.[14] Nor is it a novel practice in the wider Middle East—the Ottoman Empire, for instance, deployed sponsorship as it sought to quash political dissent and track seasonal labor migration during the Hamidian era.[15] As a number of scholars have noted, sponsorship reflects the hierarchies of British imperialism and global capitalism rather than the supposed cultural peculiarities of the Persian Gulf.[16] For that reason, I will refer to this legal apparatus as sponsorship, rather than *kafala*, as the Arabic term unnecessarily exceptionalizes a common practice.[17]

But short-term labor sponsorship in the Persian Gulf is remarkable in at least one respect—its longevity and scale. This chapter therefore traces a history that, to paraphrase Foucault, eschews the search for origins.[18] It focuses on how and why a wide range of actors in the Persian Gulf lent their support to the deportation state and the sponsorship system, ensuring its remarkable durability and scope. Understanding the "origins" of sponsorship, in other words, is far less illuminating than tracing how and why elites across the Persian Gulf have buttressed it across time. The deportation regime was not a purely imperial creation. Once introduced into the regional political lexicon, nationality became a node of political debate, while a remarkable array of elites took upon themselves the task of defining and enforcing the line between citizen and noncitizen. A regional lens, and a reading of Arabic-language sources, reveals how the deportation state won the backing not just of imperial officials but of business elites and ruling families. If Bahrain foregrounds the role of Anglo-American officials and oil companies, Kuwait witnessed a remarkable convergence of elite and imperial interests. Adopting a narrow and exclusionary view of Kuwaiti nationality based on patrilineal descent and determined to forge a modern and efficient state and security apparatus, Kuwaiti elites played a central role in building the deportation state even as they sought to rein in the unchecked power of the monarchy. Even some anticolonial nationalists supported the deportation of their perceived enemies. In so doing, they inadvertently undermined their own campaigns for democracy and independence . It was these interests that would maintain the system after independence.

The deportation state is thus central to the wider processes of autocratic state formation and imperial resource extraction and to legitimating their continuation after the end of formal empire. This history of the nationality and deportation regime enriches a growing literature that has overturned the conventional association of citizenship with political participation—a literature that has, not coincidentally, emerged from imperial or settler-colonial contexts.[19] In the Gulf, nationality was conceived not to delineate the category of the rights-bearing citizen, but to create the figure of the deportable alien. Gulf states were forged as deportation states, their power over movement across borders buttressing autocratic rule within them.

EMPIRE & EXILE | 1900–1929

The nineteenth-century imperial presence in the Persian Gulf was an ad hoc and minimalistic affair. For the British, the region was significant less for its own sake than because it lay on the route to their far more profitable possessions in India. It thus was governed not directly from London, but by the Foreign Department of the India Office, making the Gulf administration a bureaucratic appendage of a subject colony. While the British justified their hegemony by arguing that they were suppressing piracy and slavery, they pursued neither with much vigor.[20] Instead, they focused on excluding their rivals from the region's constellation of port cities, eschewing the imposition of direct rule. The official British presence was limited to a handful of Political Agents, who served as the proverbial men on the spot, under the supervision of a Political Resident. Accompanied by a smattering of coaling depots, naval bases, and quarantine stations at strategic locations along the coast, they were the only imperial representatives in the region until the twentieth century.[21] But even this light imperial footprint irrevocably altered the balance of power in the Gulf. To maintain their empire on the cheap, the British adopted the classic imperial tactic of outsourcing governance to elites on the ground. They preferred to empower a single individual in each port city, endowing them with absolute sovereignty and the title of "Ruler." By protecting their handpicked allies with the classic strategies of divide-and-rule and gunboat diplomacy, they gradually transformed the port cities of the Gulf from mercantile oligarchies into centralized monarchies, laying the foundations of autocratic governance.[22]

The legal scaffolding of British hegemony in the Gulf was comprised by a series of nineteenth-century secret treaties, known as "Exclusive Agreements," which forced local sovereigns to conduct foreign relations exclusively through British representatives and to pledge "that I will on no account cede, sell, mortgage or otherwise give for occupation any part of my territory save to the British Government."[23] Regional empires, from the Ottomans to the British, had long deployed bans on foreign landholding to exclude their rivals, reflecting what Lâle Can describes as a widespread understanding of the "connection between ownership of land and sovereignty."[24] The British employed the land clauses to repel their rivals, such as when they vetoed a German effort to extend the Berlin to Baghdad railway into Kuwait.[25] As they tightened control over the Gulf, they invoked the Exclusive Agreements with greater frequency, ensuring that even the most mundane land deals involving foreigners would require their approval. If, as David Graeber has argued, property is fundamentally a negative right held "against all the world"—the right to prevent others from using one's property—then the ban on foreign landholding can be interpreted as a British claim to possession of the Gulf.[26]

The dilemma facing imperial officials was that there was no agreed-upon definition of a foreigner.[27] As late as 1930, the Political Agent in Bahrain could report that "no difference of nationality is recognised between the subjects of the various Shaikhs of the Gulf area. A man transferring his domicile from Dubai to Abu Dhabi for instance would have no further claim on the Shaikh of Dubai."[28] At first, this ambiguity did not perturb the British. On the contrary, the fuzziness of nationality gave their men on the spot the power to arbitrarily alter its inclusions and exclusions based on political expediency, determining subjecthood, and thus jurisdiction, on a case-by-case basis.[29] This flexibility was useful. In exchange for the sweeping privileges granted in the Exclusive Agreements, the British had pledged to protect subjects of Gulf rulers who lived abroad, usually in Saudi, Iranian, or Ottoman territory. Imperial officials generally viewed this responsibility as an unwelcome burden that threatened their diplomatic relationships across the region. A fluid definition of foreigner allowed them to dodge difficult cases.[30] Fluidity also helped fend off the encroachments of rival powers, such as an Ottoman effort to pressure Mubarak Al Sabah, the Ruler of Kuwait at the turn of the twentieth century, to adopt Ottoman nationality in an effort to bring Kuwait back into their imperial orbit.[31]

If control over land provided the legal justification of informal empire, control over movement was its means of enforcement. Exile, expulsion, and banishment have a long history in the Persian Gulf, as they do elsewhere.[32] By the turn of the twentieth century, British authorities regularly employed ad hoc movement restrictions and expulsions against an array of individuals deemed inimical to their interests.[33] Everyone from an Iranian bookseller to the headstrong nephew of the Ruler of Bahrain could find themselves labeled a threat and expelled.[34] Deportation was particularly useful for dealing with notables who were considered to be more useful alive than dead, whether because a future reconciliation was possible or because their execution could trigger a political earthquake.[35] It could also serve as an exemplary form of punishment.[36] Local rulers also utilized banishment, whether as a form of social control, penalty for misbehavior, or just to rid themselves of troublesome people. Around the turn of the century, Shaikh Mubarak of Kuwait deported one man "for shooting and killing his slave while in a drunken state" and expelled any Muslim who was reported to be "addicted to drinking."[37]

Indeed, deportation was not just the prerogative of authorities. Communities reserved the right to banish individuals whom they did not want living in their midst, which was a longstanding practice in the Ottoman empire.[38] In 1911, a movement led by the chief *Qadi* (judge) of Bahrain reportedly demanded the deportation of "Foreign Bad Characters" who opened "houses of ill-fame."[39] Nearly three decades later, several hundred Kuwaitis petitioned their Ruler to expel a British missionary on the grounds that his "bitter and domineering manner" had made him universally unpopular.[40] The power to exile could even be delegated to private persons. Abdul-Azeez Al-Shaya remembers that his father, who helped found the district of Mirqab just outside the city walls of old Kuwait, was given "responsibility" over "all the foreign residents" of the new district.[41] This included the power of expulsion, which he reputedly used on at least one occasion.[42] Because most deportations were conducted entirely within British imperial jurisdiction, they required little paperwork, and imperial officials could continue surveillance of deported persons even when they were in exile.

Changing circumstances at the turn of the twentieth century led the British to deepen, and formalize, their role in the Persian Gulf. As they did, they etched deportation into the legal apparatus of empire. The impetus for this shift came from rising global demand for pearls and dates, two of the Gulf's most important exports, which triggered a regional economic boom. This in turn generated increased competition for Gulf products and markets from rival imperial powers. Lord Curzon, the British Foreign Secretary, adopted what he called a "forward policy" to aggressively defend the borders of British India. The discovery of oil in Iran in 1908, and the prospect of oil discoveries elsewhere in the region, added to this pressure. The result was the imposition of a formal legal apparatus that brought the British into everyday affairs with the goal, according to the Political Resident, of putting imperial power on "a more precise footing."[43]

The entrenchment of British power began in Bahrain, where their presence was unusually heavy. From 1900 to 1905, a series of legal disputes involving a German mercantile firm generated concerns that European merchants would claim extraterritorial protection from their own governments if they were tried in "native courts," thus challenging British hegemony.[44] As Omar AlShehabi has noted, the incident sparked off a long-running skirmish between the British and the Bahraini ruling family over legal jurisdiction that centered around the definition of "foreigner."[45] The British eventually seized jurisdiction over all foreigners in Bahrain in 1909.[46] They formalized their position in 1913 with a pivotal Order in Council, their most explicit claim to sovereignty in the Gulf to date, which granted the Political Agent the power to deport any British subject who had committed, or was deemed "likely to commit," a criminal offense.[47] In practice, British powers were even more sweeping. While Bahraini subjects were technically exempted from British jurisdiction, many were "informally deported" by local authorities on the "recommendation" of the British.[48] Further articles specified that British subjects who failed to pay a monetary fee to "guarantee" their behavior were also subject to expulsion, a clause that built the concept of sponsorship into the earliest legal codification of British rule in the Gulf.[49]

The outbreak of World War I led authorities around the world to organize the international system of borders and passports that remains familiar today.[50] The Gulf was no different. In the nineteenth century, the only British-enforced movement restrictions in the Gulf were customs duties and quarantine regulations. As Laura Goffman has noted, "Gulf quarantines emerged as a justification for British empire and a mechanism of monarchical power."[51] They also divided residents of the Gulf along the lines of race, class, and gender—setting a precedent for future movement restrictions.[52] World War I entrenched this system of surveillance, as imperial authorities imposed strict controls over imports and exports and embraced paranoid fears of pan-Islamic anticolonialism.[53] Empowered by the Defense of the Realm and Defense of India Acts, imperial authorities implemented movement controls across the Gulf.[54] Two durable practices emerged from the war: the use of passports and mass deportations. In 1915, as a "war measure," the British announced that any person traveling to or from the Gulf would be required to carry a British-issued Certificate of Identity.[55] These were supplemented by "Letters of Recommendation," issued by local Rulers and endorsed by British authorities, which authorized individual trips and thus functioned as a kind of visa.[56] New requirements were paired with an unprecedented wave of mass deportations. Across the region, from Kuwait to Oman, imperial authorities partnered with local authorities to expel dozens of "foreign malefactors" as the war exacerbated fears of political subversion.[57] The dragnet was wide; in one instance, a man was deported from Kerman despite the fact he "seemed too stupid to be dangerous."[58] These wartime measures transformed residency into an increasingly restricted privilege that could be granted or withdrawn by the state.

INVENTING NATIONALITY | 1920–1940

In the Gulf as in much of the world, the exigencies of war became the routines of peace. During the 1920s, as they accelerated deportations and tightened movement restrictions, British officials institutionalized their hitherto ad hoc regime in response to pressure from Anglo-American oil firms, challenges from rival imperial powers, and pushback from deportees themselves. To legitimize these actions and clarify questions of legal jurisdiction, they turned to nationality. As in other parts of their Middle Eastern empire, the British deployed citizenship legislation to underpin a new "mobility regime" that would become the central prop of their power.[59]

As British interests and involvement deepened after the end of the First World War, deportation became an even more integral pillar of their power. In 1920, imperial authorities turned Henjam Island, formerly a naval base and quarantine station, into an "internment camp" for political prisoners from Iran and Iraq.[60] By 1922, the Political Resident, concerned about a popular backlash, was reporting that he was "anxious not to have to be continually deporting people."[61] But deportations only became more common. In fact, the following year witnessed a series of particularly high-profile expulsions following the enforced deposition—and deportation—of Shaikh Isa of Bahrain (whom the British themselves had placed on the throne decades earlier) along with a number of prominent reformers.[62] But even as deportations accelerated, they faced their first legal test. Three political deportees who had been leaders of the Bahraini reform movement—Mulla Hafiz, Jassim bin Muhammad al-Shirawi, and Abdul Wahab Zayani—challenged their deportations in the High Court at Bombay on the grounds that they were Bahraini subjects and therefore exempted from British jurisdiction.[63] Remarkably, all three won. The court ruled that the Ruler of Bahrain could not arbitrarily cede jurisdiction over his own subjects.[64] The rulings threatened the emerging deportation regime by undermining the ad hoc attribution of jurisdiction routinely practiced by British authorities in the Gulf. The frustrated Political Agent suggested interning Zayani in the Hanjam concentration camp, but it was clear that a more systematic solution was needed.[65]

The expansionism of rival powers exacerbated British concerns. The 1920s witnessed the consolidation of nation-states in Iran, Iraq, and Saudi Arabia, in addition to expanding commercial competition from Japan, Germany, and the United States. The ballooning Saudi state actively projected power across the region and harassed Bahrainis in Saudi Arabia, particularly Shia, by imposing arbitrary taxes or confiscating land.[66] As Lindsey Stephenson has argued, Iran would play a key role in pushing the British to formalize their position in the Gulf.[67] The centralizing regime of Reza Shah not only managed to impose its will across its southern Gulf provinces and enforce its own system of movement restrictions, but claimed sovereignty over Bahrain, which had once been an Iranian possession and hosted a large number of Persian-speaking residents. Though many Bahrainis of Iranian descent had lived on the islands for generations and considered themselves Bahraini, some Iranian nationalists vocally expressed their loyalty to the Pahlavi regime.[68] A turning point came in 1929, when the Iranian government passed a nationality law and restricted the rights of foreign subjects to own property, putting severe pressure on British-protected subjects in their domain.[69]

In the face of these escalating issues of sovereignty and jurisdiction, the British turned to nationality legislation.[70] In 1929, the Government of Bahrain—under its imperious British "Advisor," Charles Belgrave—and the Political Agency released simultaneous proclamations that read, "It is hereby notified that persons born in Bahrain of foreign parents unless registered in the Agency, will be considered for all purposes as subjects of the Bahrain State. Women adopt the nationality of their husbands."[71] The proclamation, the first of its kind on the western shore of the Persian Gulf, was one of several nationality laws imposed across British territories in the Middle East at roughly the same time. While each responded to varied local conditions, all—from Palestine to Egypt—can be seen as reinforcing, and legitimating, a nascent deportation state.[72] They also drew on global precedent. The Bahraini proclamation greatly resembled the Iraqi Nationality Law, imposed by British Mandatory authorities in 1924, which was based on the Ottoman Nationality Law 1869, passed as part of the Tanzimat-era reforms and itself inspired by the Napoleonic Code.[73] Across the region, the British would take the lead in establishing a regional regime of nationality in order to advance their interests.

The British also created a new system of documentation. After the 1929 proclamation, Belgrave's government of Bahrain began issuing its own Nationality Certificates.[74] It also required the use of passports, for the cost of seven rupees, in addition to a special travel document for use within the Gulf.[75] By 1931, "many hundreds" of Bahrainis abroad were visiting Bahrain to apply for passports and nationality certificates.[76] This bureaucratic infrastructure was distinctly imperial—the office was even organized by an India Office employee, Jelaluddin Ahmed, while the Immigration Branch of the Bahrain State Police would be led by a British advisor.[77] For decades, Bahraini passport officials would be trained by the British.[78]

Imperial officials were not alone in valuing nationality and deportation as mechanisms of exclusion. As early as 1922, the Anglo-Persian Oil Company had first proposed the idea of using nationality regulations to "exclude foreigners" from potentially oil-rich Bahrain.[79] Imperial authorities would take their advice. When oil concessions were signed in Bahrain in 1930 and in Kuwait in 1934, the British convinced their client rulers to include "nationality clauses," which required oil companies to give priority in employment to local nationals first, and to British subjects second. They were designed to prevent an influx of foreign oil workers who could be used by rival powers to gauge oil resources, justify an increased diplomatic presence, or even claim extraterritorial jurisdiction. The India Office inserted nationality clauses into every oil concession in the Persian Gulf, even in jurisdictions without nationality legislation.[80] Imperial authorities energetically enforced these clauses, and citizens of rival powers, particularly the United States, remained systematically excluded from the region's oil industry for years to come.[81] Nationality was thus not just an imperial intervention, but the product of an alliance between state and corporate power.

British officials soon came to view the 1929 declaration as too ambiguous and began discussing the draft of a formal Bahraini nationality law in late 1935.[82] This legislation, eventually passed as the Bahrain Nationality Law of 1937, would serve as a template for laws across the region. A key addition was Article Five, which granted the Ruler of Bahrain the power to personally grant or retract nationality—a staggering accretion of state power. The India Office warned that "there might be serious objections" to "allowing the Sheikh of Bahrein the unfettered right to make and unmake Bahrein nationals."[83] But the article remained.[84] A second key clause specified that women would be tied to the nationality of their fathers, and then husbands in marriage.[85] This was inserted with little or no discussion; when they took notice of it at all, British officials characteristically attributed the gendering of nationality law to the supposedly patriarchal nature of Gulf society. In fact, the clause mirrored British legislation, in addition to many other contemporary nationality laws.[86] Imperial officials in the Gulf, on their own initiative, thus chiseled their own patriarchal conceptions of nationality into the region's legislation. The article proved critically important, and not just for women. It both impeded gender equality—especially marriage rights—and framed Gulf citizenship not as civic, but as genealogical: as *jus sanguinis*—by blood—rather than *jus soli*—by birth.[87] This conception presumed that noncitizens, especially immigrants, were indelibly different and foreign, laying the foundations for the narrow and exclusive conception of nationality that would dominate the region.

The clause with the most immediate impact concerned land.[88] By the 1930s, imperial officials had come to understand land ownership as a litmus test for both respectability and nationality. In their view, to own land in a particular place was tantamount to a declaration of nationality and a literal investment in belonging.[89] In fact, well into the fifties, voting rights in Bahraini municipal elections were not determined by nationality, but by landholding.[90] In this view, presumably responsible landholders were the converse of a migratory "floating population," referred to by Belgrave as the "dregs of the Gulf," who were blamed for everything from criminality to disease.[91] As a means of countering Iranian claims to Bahrain, British officials decided to ban Iranian landownership.[92] Iranian landholders would then have "to choose between continuing their Persian nationality and parting with their property," just as Bahrainis in Iran had been forced to do.[93] On May 8, 1937, the new nationality law was published alongside a separate decree, targeting Iranians, which forbade nationals whose home countries banned noncitizen landownership from owning land in Bahrain.[94] At the same time, to force the "floating population" of "indigents" to either leave Bahrain or accept Bahraini nationality, the British imposed an annual registration fee and documentation requirement on noncitizen residents.[95] In the following years, further restrictions were put on noncitizen landownership, until it was finally banned altogether.[96] Thus, through the medium of land, imperial officials inscribed divisions of class into nationality law, creating a *de jure* divide between noncitizen renters and citizen rentiers.

Belgrave and his imperial allies used the 1937 National Law to manufacture a citizenry dominated by Arab men of property, while subjecting undesirable subjects—particularly landless or unemployed Iranians—to the unchecked power of the deportation state. Even if they abandoned their property, Iranians and the landless faced deliberate hurdles to the acquisition of nationality.[97] The burden of proof rested entirely on the applicant, even though the Bahraini government acknowledged that, in an era before documentation, hard evidence "cannot easily be produced."[98] As the nationality regime designed in Bahrain was replicated across the Gulf, its exclusions were always the greatest part of its appeal.

DEPORTATION STATES | 1935–1955

Reading India Office files in the decades following the passage of the 1937 Nationality Law, one is struck by the ever-present ubiquity of deportation. It was in the 1930s and '40s—as Charles Belgrave tightened his grip on the archipelago—that deportation reached its full potential as a mechanism of autocratic governance. Enhancing his already sweeping powers with emergency legislation passed during World War II, Belgrave could exile virtually anyone in Bahrain without recourse to judicial review. He exercised this power energetically.[99] Two-year banishment sentences were routinely given to anyone deemed to be "likely to conduct himself in a manner so as to be dangerous to good order."[100] Local and imperial authorities sometimes turned to expulsion precisely because they were unable to gather sufficient evidence for a criminal trial.[101] Even the most mundane interactions could lead to deportation. In 1939, three people seen "walking in a suspicious manner" were questioned, detained, and deported for landing without passes.[102] In a revealing case, Belgrave requested the Political Agent to deport a Somali man who he himself had hired but who "has now developed consumption" and "cannot recover." Belgrave requested that he be deported immediately, as he would soon be too ill to travel and "the Bahrain Government will be liable for considerable expense to provide for him during the time that he lives." No further trace of him can be found in the files, but penciled at the bottom of the letter is a terse note: "We should repatriate this man."[103]

Movement restrictions did not affect all residents of the Gulf equally. Political dissidents were perhaps the most susceptible. In 1932, for instance, one "Iraqi agitator" was, in the euphemistic words of the Political Agent, "provided with a free ticket to another port."[104] Expulsion could also stifle the press. For years, negative coverage across the Gulf was suppressed by the simple expedient of preventing journalists from acquiring visas.[105] The movement regime also advanced imperial economic interests. In 1929, imperial officials persuaded the rulers of Kuwait and Bahrain to exclude all "Russian steamers" in order to stifle Soviet economic competition.[106] Measures taken to deny entry to "indigents" and "paupers," usually pilgrims passing through the Gulf on the way to Iraq or Saudi Arabia, reduced imperial expenditure on social services.[107] In the early 1940s, the Bahraini Government empowered the police to deport "destitute immigrants" without judicial review, leading to what Belgrave called a regular "round up of beggars."[108] Belgrave even used passport fees to generate revenue for his administration.[109] For a time, the Passport Department became the third largest income stream for the Bahraini government, transforming the deportation state into a profitable enterprise.[110]

While anyone could be subject to deportation, authorities targeted certain groups more than others. Iranians faced a disproportionate amount of scrutiny. British and Bahraini authorities devised a number of stratagems to identify people of Iranian origin, and justifications to expel them.[111] As late as 1959, Bahraini authorities denied entry to people suspected of being of "Persian" origin, believing that "a simple conversation with a gutteral or 'heavy' Arabic pronunciation is usually sufficient to establish this."[112] The ill were also targeted. In 1938 and 1942, British authorities reported that "lepers" and "diseased persons" were "rounded up and repatriated."[113] Conceptions of health often intersected with those of gender. Women in the sex industry were subjected to arbitrary restrictions and deportations in the name of protecting public health, even though Belgrave himself reported that in Bahrain, "male prostitutes were almost as numerous as women."[114] Imperial authorities also instituted a policy requiring "women of European race" to receive authorization from imperial officials before their arrival in the Gulf, a measure that was, according to the Political Agent in Kuwait, essential to protecting British "prestige."[115] The deportation state thus allowed the British and their allies to cement the social hierarchies of empire.

It was the struggle against labor, once again led by Belgrave, that led to the systemization of the sponsorship regime. Hearkening back to Ottoman practice, Bahraini authorities had long used guarantors, or *kafils*, in a variety of circumstances, often as a form of bail.[116] The term was used for an Ottoman surety system imposed on seasonal workers in Istanbul in 1903.[117] In the Gulf, an early sponsorship requirement linked to employment targeted Iranian pearl divers. Beginning in the late 1920s, any Iranian nonresident wanting to visit Bahrain needed not only special permission from the Bahraini Government, but "the written and stamped guarantee of a respectable local merchant, who assumes responsibility for the person returning and for his good conduct in Bahrain."[118] In 1928, the Bahraini government allowed pearl divers to visit Bahrain without passports as long as they held "Diving Books," documents that recorded their indebtedness to Bahraini ship captains, on the condition that their captain be "responsible" for the eventual departure of his crew.[119] As Omar AlShehabi has noted, this system would become a forerunner of the labor sponsorship system across Bahrain.[120] Thus debt served as a passport in itself.

Belgrave formalized this process in 1936 by requiring that employers seeking to hire Indian workers obtain "permission" from the government in the form of a "No Objection Certificate."[121] A longstanding bureaucratic mechanism in British India, NOCs authorized travel to and from the Gulf, and they allowed local authorities to confirm that they had "no objection" to a particular traveler.[122] They also had wider uses; a NOC was required to import firearms, for instance.[123] They were little more than the formalization of the ad hoc practice of clearing an action with another part of the imperial bureaucracy. One of the most remarkable admissions about NOCs came in 1959, when the Foreign Office acknowledged that despite decades of use, "there is no basis in law for the No Objection Certificate system."[124] This did not prevent its widespread proliferation. Belgrave ordered that to receive permission to hire Indian workers, the Bahrain Petroleum Company (Bapco) was required to "investigate their credentials" and obtain a NOC; in effect, the system allowed for screening.[125] Critically, they also prevented workers from changing employers without the permission of the Bahraini state. No Objection Certificates eventually became a pillar of the sponsorship system—in some Gulf states, they endured well into the twenty-first century.[126] The ban on changing jobs gave unprecedented power to employers, as any worker in Bahrain on an NOC would be automatically deported when leaving their job.

Sponsorship requirements grew increasingly strict as the years progressed. Belgrave tightened the screws in 1949, when he banned noncitizens from changing jobs without their employer's permission and required that every employer "guarantee" that they would pay the repatriation expenses of their noncitizen employees by leaving a monetary deposit with the Political Agency.[127] This, he argued, forced employers to "take responsibility" for their noncitizen employees.[128] The decision highlights the significance of corporate practice in the formation of the deportation regime. Bapco had for years automatically deported employees who left its service; Belgrave was effectively ordering that all employers in Bahrain follow their example.[129] He argued that it would be unfair to allow companies to poach employees from rivals who had gone through the trouble and expense of finding, testing, hiring, and transporting them, and that the repatriation deposits ensured that Bahrain would never be flooded by unemployed foreigners.[130] But the regulations also left employees tied to a particular sponsor, and thus vulnerable to exploitation. The impact of these measures was felt immediately. Employers began reporting "runaway" former employees—meaning those who changed jobs without permission—to state and imperial authorities so they could be deported.[131] Sometimes, such employees had not even run away; deportation was simply a convenient way to dispose of them. One man, for instance, asked the Agency to "repatriate" a "servant" on the grounds that he was "lazy and insolent."[132] Thus, to remain in Bahrain, employees needed to remain on good terms with their former employers, which created a new and powerful form of employer leverage.[133]

International oil firms came to value deportation, and sponsorship, as tools to discipline their labor force. The use of deportation in labor conflicts was nearly as old as the Gulf oil industry itself. In 1922, when Arab, Indian, and Iranian workers organized a strike at the Anglo-Persian Oil Company refinery at Abadan, the company deported all two thousand Indian strikers in what the Political Resident described as a "show of force."[134] Another refinery strike in Abadan was crushed by mass deportations in 1929.[135] In Saudi Arabia, Aramco officials and local authorities repeatedly deported labor organizers who called for an end to racial discrimination in the segregated oil firm.[136] Sometimes, as in the case of a strike of 125 Pakistani workers in Qatar, workers were blacklisted—the company sent their names to oil firms across the region, described them as "ring-leaders and sub-ring-leaders in openly opposing authority," and suggested that they not be granted further employment.[137] In the early 1930s, the Bahrain Petroleum Company even tried to negotiate a special clause in its concession giving it the power to deport its employees itself, though the Political Agency vetoed the idea on the grounds that a private corporation "cannot be given judicial powers of deportation."[138] But nothing in the archives indicates that local or imperial authorities ever refused a corporate request to deport a worker.

DEPORTATION & CLASS | 1920–1950

Corporate and imperial officials were not the sole architects of the deportation state. Though nationality was first deployed as a tool of imperial control, once introduced into the legal lexicon of the Persian Gulf it would become a subject of popular contestation. As Nelida Fuccaro has noted, popular anti-Iranian feeling led many Bahrainis—ranging from Arab nationalists to supporters of the Al Khalifa—to lend their support to the exclusionary nationality regime.[139] The role of local agency would become particularly apparent in the case of Kuwait, where local elites who viewed themselves as modernizing statebuilders spearheaded the creation of the deportation state. In the early twentieth century, a group of reformers launched a campaign to place Kuwait on the map of the wider Arab *Nahda*, or renaissance. Centered around Qasim bin Muhammad al-Ibrahim, Nasir bin Mubarak Al Sabah, , Abdul Aziz al-Rushaid, and Yusuf bin ʿIsa al-Qinaʾi, and inspired by the work of Rashid Rida, this circle worked to forge a national identity, modern education system, and literary culture.[140] Their ideas would shape Kuwait's pivotal six months of parliamentary rule in 1938 and 1939, part of the Majlis Movement that swept Kuwait, Bahrain, and Dubai. Though usually remembered as an experiment in democracy, it was also an early effort to police the boundaries of the Kuwaiti polity.

Early representations of the Kuwaiti nation abound in the work of Abdul Aziz al-Rushaid, whose *History of Kuwait* (Tarikh al-Kuwait), published in 1926, and *Kuwait Magazine* (Majallat al-Kuwait), which ran from 1928 to 1930, are germinal works of Kuwaiti letters. Based largely on oral sources, his historical work falls within the "safhat" genre, presenting a scattered assortment of events, stories, customs, and descriptions that knit together a national narrative.[141] Born in Kuwait at the end of the nineteenth century, al-Rushaid was educated at venerable institutions in Hasa, Zubair, and Baghdad, became the head of Kuwait's famous Mubarakiyya school in 1917, helped found the Ahmadiyya school in 1921, and organized an influential Literary Club in 1923, before dying in Java in 1938.[142]

An inclusive conception of "being Kuwaiti" emerges when al-Rushaid traces folk culture. These descriptions complement Farah Al-Nakib's argument that the proximity of residents in the pre-oil town led to "shared experiences and everyday relations," and built a sense of community.[143] Kuwaiti traditions, including holidays, food, customs, and other aspects of popular culture, while often segmented by class, convey the impression of a population simultaneously celebrating, praying, eating, or conducting business.[144] Instead of attacking colloquial Kuwaiti Arabic as the language of the uneducated, *Majallat al-Kuwait* dedicated a section in nearly every issue to defining unique words from Kuwaiti dialect and explaining their etymology and origins.[145] But more importantly, to be Kuwaiti meant sharing a narrative of historical time, based on the knowledge of important events.

Each had its own nickname: there is "al-Rajaiba," a terrible downpour that destroyed many mud-brick houses in the month of Rajab, 1289 (1872); "the famine," so terrible that Kuwaitis were forced to drink "the blood of beasts"; "the drowning," when a series of storms devastated the Kuwaiti merchant fleet; and "the plague," which killed much of the town's population.[146] The collective memory of these events proved enduring: over twenty years later, a Kuwaiti paper could reference the "year of destruction" with the expectation that its audience would know exactly what it referred to.[147] Particularly important were the events of 1920: the construction of the last fortified wall around Kuwait town[148] and the subsequent battle of Jahra, when Ikhwan raiders, under the expansionist Saudi regime, were defeated by British and Kuwaiti forces, thus preserving Kuwaiti independence.[149] These events and customs are also recorded in other works in the *safhat* genre, thus serving as the foundational shared experiences of the Kuwaiti imagined community.[150]

However, al-Rushaid's work also reflects the elitism characteristic of the Kuwaiti mercantile class.[151] He highlights tribal lineage, the role of merchants as the entrepreneurial and philanthropic core of the city-state, and the politics of the ruling Al Sabah family.[152] Al-Rushaid begins his story by speculating that the ruling Al Sabah may have left their homelands because of the kind of insult that "pure/true Arabs (*al-ʿarabi al-samim*)" cannot stand or ignore, or due to their deep-seated desire for "independent government."[153] If the heart of Kuwait was Arab, its lifeblood was commerce. According to al-Rushaid, "Trade is the greatest pillar for advancing the country and the strongest reason for its progress," an activity with "the supreme place in the civilized world."[154] The most notable Kuwaitis, besides the ruling family, were merchants who had invested in Kuwait, literally and figuratively, alongside a handful of religious scholars.[155] *Majallat al-Kuwait* includes regular biographies of Kuwaiti personalities that reflect a "great man" understanding of Kuwaiti history and reinforce fissures of class, tribe, and education.[156] These early works thus divide the Kuwaiti population into hierarchical, even primordial categories: urban or rural, Sunni or Shi'a, Arab or Iranian.

Perhaps most revealing is al-Rushaid's history of Kuwaiti state formation. He writes that when the first settlers arrived in Kuwait, "governance was not of the first importance." They were like "one family," sharing together in the joys and sorrows of their city. Leadership was based on the venerable principle of consultation (*shura*), which allowed for transparency and participation in governance. Kuwaitis shunned formal institutions because they feared the emergence of a tyrant. But, says al-Rushaid, everything changed with the arrival of "foreigners." Not only were these "migrants" strangers to the Kuwaitis, but they often had different customs and ways of living. When they began to "mix" with the Kuwaitis, a set of defined rules was needed to regulate the interactions between these two communities. Thus, for the first time, a state became an imperative necessity.[157] His work thus privileges the role of Sunni, upper-class, urban Arab men and both introduces—and enforces—a sharp divide between "Kuwaiti" and "foreign." These dueling narratives would eventually become what Mary Ann Tétreault has described as a "tabiʿiyya" conception of citizenship, based "on actual or fictive blood relationships arranged in a hierarchy," and "jinsiyya," based on conceptions of equality before the law.[158] Their outlines, and their contradictions, would be central to Kuwaiti politics for decades to come.

These reformists would become some of the most prominent opponents of absolute monarchy. The Al Sabah family had ruled Kuwait as a kind of mercantile oligopoly from the eighteenth century, their authority kept in check by a wealthy and powerful class of merchants and pearling captains. That began to change during the reign of Mubarak Al Sabah, who ruled from 1896 to 1915. After seizing power by murdering his own brothers, Mubarak took Kuwait out of the Ottoman orbit, signing a secret agreement with Britain in 1899. He then began building the kind of centralized monarchy that would become familiar across the Gulf. This was, as elsewhere, accompanied by the creation of a regime for regulating migration, established during World War I with British assistance.[159] The Kuwaiti merchant elite pushed back against this attack on their prerogatives. In 1921, after the death of Emir Salim Al Sabah, members of Kuwait's most important merchant families, including al-Rushaid, formed a council to demand an official role in the succession process. While the effort failed, the council remained a touchstone for influential Kuwaitis who continued to press for more say in government.[160]

These tensions came to a head during the Majlis Movement, a six-month period of parliamentary rule from 1938 to 1939 that is still seen as a pivotal moment in Gulf political history. The movement took power after the Ruler's decision to grant a series of monopolies to favored allies and sign the first Kuwaiti oil concession in 1938, which threatened to provide the regime with spectacular wealth and unprecedented power.[161] In response, a group of mercantile elites seized legislative authority and began to enact a series of sweeping reforms. They drafted a Basic Law that effectively functioned as a written constitution, reestablished a quasi-independent judiciary, canceled or reshuffled the monopoly agreements, separated the public treasury from the privy purse, and generally tried to instill a spirit of more "democratic government" in Kuwait. To build mass support, they founded a popular Arab nationalist movement, the National Youth Block, which expanded the circle of political participation.[162] They also specified that Kuwaiti nationality should be clearly defined and only granted or withdrawn according to law, rather than at the whim of the Ruler.[163]

But the Council paired these reforms with a hierarchical and narrow conception of the Kuwaiti nation. This reflected its membership—it was dominated by Sunni merchants from elite families elected on a very limited franchise.[164] Moreover, it spent much of its time and energy "stopping the torrent (*sil*) of foreign migration."[165] In his memoirs, the Secretary of the Legislative Council, Suleiman al-ʿAdsani, explains that after World War I, a wave of foreigners came to Kuwait to escape political instability and famine in other parts of the Gulf, especially southern Iran. While expressing sympathy for their plight, he writes that their numbers soon exceeded ten thousand people, and they began to beg in the streets or practice their crafts in competition with established Kuwaitis. Worse, with their different "language, customs, and spirit of nationalism," this "flood," now implied to be made up of Iranians, threatened to "overwhelm" the Arab countries of the Gulf. The Council responded with vigor, ordering ship captains and guards to "stop this torrent of migration."[166] To strengthen enforcement, it established a new police force of sixty trained men from "pure (*ʿariiqa*) families," founded a border patrol equipped with a fleet of cars, and hired a passport officer under the supervision of "patriotic youth."[167] It deemed these measures necessary to stop the immigration of "thieves" and "infiltrators," terms that would become ingrained in the Kuwaiti political lexicon.[168] It was thus the quasi-democratic Assembly that took the lead in hardening Kuwait's borders.[169]

The Legislature also conducted the first systematic attempt to police the outlines of nationality. ʿAdsani explains that one of the chief difficulties in fighting immigration was the inability to distinguish between "the national and the foreigner." In response, the Legislature launched a comprehensive census. Teams fanned out across the city, traveling door to door to count inhabitants, record their names in a central registry, and systematically divide Kuwaitis from non-Kuwaitis for the first time.[170] The census was accompanied by a wave of deportations targeting two groups that would remain at the center of public ire: Iranians and the impoverished. In his memoirs, Dr. Ahmad al-Khatib, later a leader of the Kuwaiti pro-democracy opposition, writes that he would never forget the sight of poor Iranian families in his neighborhood being rounded up "like cattle" and deported because of racism and religious intolerance.[171] This was not the first mass expulsion of impoverished Iranians from Kuwait. In 1931, the Ruler deported hundreds of Iranians without a "visible means of support" to the banks of the Shatt al-Arab.[172] But it was the Council that established the institutions that would become the core of the deportation state.

The Council itself did not last. After just six months, the Ruler of Kuwait, with the tacit support of the British, mobilized his allies—notably nomadic Bedouin—to crush the parliamentary movement, imprison its supporters, and even publicly crucify one of its leaders.[173] Its collapse launched a decade of deeply autocratic rule.[174] Many commentators, both then and now, blamed the Council's collapse on its inability to attract a following outside the Sunni urban mercantile elite.[175] The use of Bedouin forces to suppress the movement proved particularly significant. Excluded from elite and urban conceptions of the Kuwaiti nation, people of nomadic descent would be stereotyped as undemocratic and politically backward for decades to come.[176] Many elite Kuwaitis retained the narrow vision of the Kuwaiti nation that found its expression in 1938 to 1939. The Kuwaiti press of the late 1950s could still condemn a "special class" of Kuwaitis, "Arabs whose grandparents protected their Arab blood and did not mix with others," who refused to marry those deemed beneath their station.[177] Elite families claimed a special status as Asili, or "original" residents of Kuwait. Tracing their lineage back to noble tribes and maintaining their exclusivity through intermarriage, they tried to maintain an elite position within the wider category of Kuwaiti.[178] These exclusionary and elitist ideas would exert an enduring influence on the outlines of Kuwaiti nationality.

With the collapse of the Assembly, the British and their local allies once again took the lead in constructing the deportation state. As Kuwaiti oil production resumed in 1946, the British seized control over movement with an order modeled on the 1937 Bahrain Passport Regulation, imposing a passport and visa requirement for travel.[179] In 1949, the Kuwaiti Department of Security began issuing its own bright green passports from a new passport office.[180] The first Kuwait Passport Regulation was passed in 1952.[181] Sponsorship was already common practice in Kuwait by that time—in fact, to work as a driver for the Kuwaiti government, noncitizens needed to find a guarantor to cover expenses in case they were found liable for an accident.[182] The British Political Agency reported its pleasure that Kuwaiti authorities, despite their "rather primitive" administration, were "exercising some form of control" over migration.[183] Throughout the fifties, the British continued to pressure the Ruler of Kuwait to impose stricter restrictions on movement and for more deportations of political dissidents, arguing that "strong-arm methods" were required in order to prevent "considerable public security anxieties."[184] Internal Kuwait Oil Company documents also reveal strong support of mass deportations, driven by fears of an "ever-present danger" of radical or communist subversion "under the guise of Arab nationalism."[185] As in Bahrain, the British also provided expertise. The first director of the Residence and Passports Department in Kuwait was a Palestinian from Jaffa, Hani al-Qaddumi, who had formerly worked for the Department of Travel and Immigration in Mandate Palestine.[186]

Kuwait adopted sponsorship on local initiative with imperial backing. In 1949, the Public Security Department, under ruling family member Abdullah Mubarak, ordered that all "foreigners" planning to stay in Kuwait for longer than sixteen days needed to request a "Residential Book" from his department, which required an "undertaking" from "a responsible person i.e. Sheikh, Mayor, Government Officer, Land Lord, Prominent Merchant, Bank Manager, President or Manager of a local firm or Company etc."—in short, a guarantor.[187] By the mid-1950s, Kuwait had a two-pronged system of No Objection Certificates, one managed by the Kuwaiti government for Kuwaiti sponsors, and the other by the Political Agency for British subjects or protected persons, most of whom were employed by the oil company.[188] The imposition of a regime of movement controls corresponded with a wave of mass deportations, as the ruling family, imperial authorities, and the Kuwait Oil Company worked together to deport waves of newly designated noncitizens.[189]

As in Bahrain, the consolidation of the Kuwaiti deportation state was accompanied by nationality legislation. But the first Kuwaiti nationality law, passed in 1948, was drafted by an Egyptian legal advisor without imperial input. Remarkably, the Political Agent only learned of the law in 1950, nearly two years after its passage—a testament to the fact that it was never enforced.[190] It defined Kuwaiti nationals as anyone who had either resided in Kuwait continuously since 1899; been born in Kuwait of a Kuwaiti father, or to a Kuwaiti mother without an established legal connection to a father; or born of a foreign father in Kuwait "provided such a foreigner is of a country the majority of whose nationals is of the Arabic speaking language or whose religion is Islamic"—making it much more open than nationality laws elsewhere in the Gulf.[191] As in Bahrain, women followed the nationality of their closest male relative.[192] The law is most notable because, in light of later legislation, it provided a remarkably easy path to nationality. In fact, imperial authorities were concerned that it would allow "Persians and others" to become Kuwaiti citizens, and these authorities waited for an opportunity to amend the law and make nationality more difficult to obtain.[193]

In the event, however, the law was ignored. Instead, Kuwaiti authorities arbitrarily handed out nationality certificates, transforming them into a powerful form of patronage.[194] The Kuwait Oil Company was the first institution in Kuwait to confront the nationality question because of the "nationality clause" in its oil concession, which required that it give priority in employment to Kuwaitis without defining who, precisely, Kuwaitis were.[195] When it resumed operations after World War II, KOC almost exclusively hired workers with official nationality certificates.[196] The practical effect of the policy was to empower Abdullah Mulla Saleh, the Ruler's Chief Secretary and the official representative of the Kuwaiti Government to KOC.[197] Mulla handed out nationality certificates personally, liberally, and arbitrarily, even to people who he knew were not Kuwaiti, building a network of dependents in the process.[198] KOC encouraged this practice as it broadened their pool of potential workers.[199] The Kuwait Development Board, established to oversee infrastructural development in 1952, took similar measures. As it reviewed immensely profitable tenders and contracts, which were required to go to Kuwaitis, it asked contractors to submit passports or sworn statements.[200] But even passports were mistrusted, as individuals could easily acquire them under false pretenses, or simply because Abdullah Mubarak, the mercurial head of Public Security, took a liking to them.[201] Eventually, in order to dodge public criticism, they followed the example of KOC and turned to Abdullah

Mulla, who would make the determination himself.[202] Decisions regarding nationality were just as arbitrary, but the Board no longer had to take the criticism.[203]

After establishing the deportation regime in Bahrain and Kuwait, local and imperial authorities replicated the system across the Gulf. Immigration legislation tended to cascade across the region. As one Gulf administration restricted movement, people seeking employment or fleeing hardship traveled to another jurisdiction, which would in turn impose its own restrictions on movement. The first passport regulations in the Trucial States—the contemporary United Arab Emirates—were implemented in 1952 to check Saudi expansionism and prevent the area from becoming a haven for people banished from Kuwait and Bahrain.[204] The Trucial States Passport Regulation, which gave the power for the Political Agent to deport anyone who lacked proper travel documents, was the model for later legislation in Bahrain, Kuwait, and Qatar.[205] Sponsorship was implemented in Qatar in 1955 at request of the Ruler, who asked imperial authorities to draft legislation giving him "power to restrict a person's Residence Permit to the duration of his work for a particular employer."[206] As before, the bureaucratic technologies of the deportation state ricocheted around imperial space. Abdul Ghafar Mohammad, from the Bahraini immigration department, established a passport and sponsorship system in Abu Dhabi, which eventually became the basis of the immigration regime in the United Arab Emirates.[207] Thus by 1960, an interlocking network of nationality, deportation, and sponsorship was in place across the entire region.

CONCLUSION

For many residents of the Gulf, the rise of the deportation state led to disempowerment, vulnerability, and frustration. It also met criticism from regional papers, many of which supported the reform movements undermined by the threat of expulsion.[208] One of the most powerful first-hand accounts comes from Abdul Rahman al-Bakir, the activist and St. Helena deportee. When he returned home to Bahrain in mid-1948 after a period working abroad, "the first thing I did immediately upon my return was ask to be given a Bahraini passport." As he was born in Bahrain to a well-known family, his application should have been straightforward. But Belgrave opposed granting him nationality, presumably because of his political activism. Al-Bakir had to visit the Ruler to petition for support, pleading that "I am Bahraini, that my family has long been known in Bahrain, and that all of the officials of the government and the police testified that I am Bahraini and born in Bahrain." Only when his appeal to the Ruler succeeded, and he received his passport, did he feel that he could continue participating in politics.[209] The incident illustrates the new and terrible fear of statelessness sweeping across the Gulf. It also reveals al-Bakir's sense of indignation that the state was claiming the power to ascribe or retract a fundamental part of his own sense of self. In a way, he believed that he had a right to nationality. Al-Bakir's fears proved to be well-founded: to end his persistent activism, Bahraini authorities stripped him of both his passport and his nationality when he was deported to St. Helena.[210] He would die in exile.

2 The Wages of Oil | 1940–1955

IF MIDCENTURY KUWAIT CAN be said to have had a central forum, it was undoubtedly Safat Square. Located in the heart of the old city, it had its origins as a market space where Bedouin from the outlands sold their wares.[1] Kuwaiti historiography represents Safat as a node of civic practice.[2] It was overlooked by Naif Palace, home of the ruling family, and later by the first government buildings that served as the physical embodiment of the Kuwaiti state. Safat Square was where citizens gathered to protest, political leaders delivered speeches, one of the leaders of the 1938 Majlis Movement was publicly executed, and Abdullah al-Salem Al Sabah was crowned Ruler in 1950.[3] Safat was also a cultural center. Its cafés brought the radio to a popular audience, and it housed the country's first cinema. When oil wealth began to transform the built environment, it became a symbol of modernity, where some of the first multistory concrete buildings in the Persian Gulf rose above a town of wood and mud brick.[4]

But between demonstrations of popular protest and sovereign spectacle, Safat served a more quotidian but no less significant purpose. As oil fueled an economic boom in the early 1950s, the square was transformed into a vast, informal labor market. In 1953, one Kuwaiti paper reported that "if you go to the New Road or Safat square before sunset, and especially on Fridays, you will find yourself a stranger in your own land."[5] Immigrants in search of jobs congregated in the square, braving the relentless sun. The operations of this market became a popular topic of discussion in the Kuwaiti press, which reported on how a network of brokers connected workers with employers.[6] While definitive evidence is hard to come by, it appears that in the midcentury period, many domestic workers were undocumented men or boys from the southern Gulf.[7] By the 1970s, domestic work had become so ubiquitous that one newspaper reported that it was becoming commonplace to "consider a servant as part of the 'furniture (*athath*)' of a modern Kuwaiti household."[8] As domestic workers were exempted from labor laws and rarely experienced government scrutiny, many could often find work without valid residence permits, funneling the undocumented into private homes.[9]

In the middle of the century, a new kind of domestic worker began to emerge—the contracted noncitizen. Many Gulf oil companies, including Aramco and the Kuwait Oil Company (KOC), recruited men from India to work in the bungalows supplied to their white senior staff.[10] Bureaucratization did not rein in coercion. On the contrary, employers enjoyed the power to reject—and therefore deport—domestic workers who did not meet their expectations, with the oil company dealing with all logistical arrangements.[11] Nor did this new form of labor replace the old. Long after the creation of a regime of residency permits and labor laws, Safat remained a bustling labor market.[12] Everyday life in the square thus revolved less around the practices of citizenship than its exclusions. It embodied a new labor market for a new kind of subject: the so-called "migrant worker."

The Gulf's first oil boom began in Iran; swept through Bahrain, Saudi Arabia, and Kuwait in the 1940s and 1950s; and reached the southern Gulf states of Qatar, Oman, and the UAE in the 1960s and 1970s. Contemporaries generally remember the coming of oil as an epochal shift. For a region reeling from the effects of economic depression, oil wealth reconfigured everyday life with stunning rapidity. Its impact proved especially abrupt in Kuwait, where British Petroleum quickly transferred much of its production after Iranian oil nationalization in 1951. Ambitious infrastructure projects transformed the built environment; the provision of healthcare, education, and housing created a massive public sector and welfare state; new subjectivities—the wage worker, the consumer, and the contractor—emerged, proliferated, and became the norm. It also triggered an influx of immigration, as inhabitants of neighboring countries followed the opportunities that accompanied oil wealth. But if oil was a catalyst, its effects were volatile.[13] The question of how to distribute this unprecedented wealth became the central concern of politics, transforming labor, citizenship, and the economy into highly contested topics. In the early years of the oil boom, nationality became increasingly significant, in Will Hanley's words, "case by case"—when crossing a border, getting a job, winning a contract, or receiving a loan.[14] It also became the subject of debate in the flourishing press, which discussed questions that would remain at the center of Kuwaiti politics: Who is a Kuwaiti? How should that determination be made? And who deserves to share in the benefits of the nation's natural wealth? This chapter traces the debates that began during the first oil boom and shaped the region for decades to come.

During the 1950s, a class of employers and business owners learned that they could profit from the line between citizen and noncitizen. Many were scions of the same merchant families who had orchestrated the 1938 Majlis Movement and dominated the heights of the Kuwaiti economy for generations. Organizing themselves in Chambers of Commerce, these elites transformed nationality into a generator of profit by manipulating the value of what Karl Polanyi describes as "fictional commodities": land, labor, and money.[15] By restricting the ownership of land to citizens, they transformed noncitizens into a class of perpetual renters. In arranging special monopoly agreements with foreign manufacturers, they cornered markets and squeezed out competition. And by employing ever-growing numbers of noncitizen workers, they gained access to a reserve army of labor at rock-bottom prices. Mobilizing their formidable resources, business elites sought to open the door to immigration while closing it to naturalization in the hope of building a class of permanently dispossessed noncitizens. The creation of a citizen business class was thus the corollary, and the inverse, of the production of a noncitizen working class.[16]

Anglo-American-owned oil companies and technical experts became key political actors as they strove to build the largest and cheapest possible pool of labor. In so doing, they deployed strategies familiar across the world's resource frontiers—classifying locally hired workers as "unskilled" or inexperienced, segregating workers by race and nationality in purpose-built labor camps, taking advantage of preexisting social divisions to fragment their workforce, and hiring noncitizens on short-term contracts.[17] All of these workers—with the notable exception of their exclusively white "senior staff"—were paid bare subsistence wages. They justified their actions with arguments of political economy that would remain influential for decades. They claimed that international recruitment was necessary in order to overcome a regional shortage of labor—especially skilled labor. Low wages, meanwhile, were justified as a means of fighting inflation.

Scholars of labor and migration, including in the Persian Gulf, have critiqued supply and demand conceptions of labor migration, as well as how the concept of skill was deployed to justify hierarchies of race, class, and nationality.[18] But there is no comprehensive account of how representations of the economy in the midcentury Gulf emerged as a node of contestation in regional politics, shaping the outlines of the nascent nationality, labor, and migration regimes. Such arguments were both spurious and self-serving. Employers grappled not with an absolute lack of laboring bodies, but from a lack of the right kind of bodies—cheap, available, and subject to arbitrary deportation. Their struggle to recruit a sufficient workforce was the predictable result of their unwillingness to institute training programs, pay a living wage, provide opportunities of advancement, or imagine women as paid workers. Discourses of political economy were not just misunderstandings of economic principles. Rather, they did analytical work for employers and imperial officials, justifying low wages, systemic discrimination, and the turn to exploited contract labor. The discourses of economics depoliticized and naturalized these choices, framing them as the inevitable outcome of market forces rather than as what they were: a deliberate choice.

These representations of the economy did not go unchallenged. The 1950s witnessed the emergence of a cohort of reformers who contested the policies and arguments that kept wages low and prices high. Some adopted exclusionary conceptions of nationality that legitimized the deportation state. But these were accompanied by sweeping and increasingly influential critiques of the exclusions of nationality and the inequities of the oil economy. Kuwaitis launched a discursive battle over the questions of immigration, inflation, and labor policy that put forward alternate explanations for economic phenomena, presaging academic arguments made decades later. They did not act like the prototypical *homo economicus*, seeking to maximize their individual share of the "rent" generated by oil wealth. Rather, their demands for more equitable access to citizenship and distribution of wealth laid the groundwork for a wider movement for democratic governance, economic justice, and political independence in the years to come.

THE ARMY OF OIL | 1930–1955

Oil was only one of a series of epochal shifts transforming the midcentury Gulf. Its impact was crosshatched by a series of other factors, from the remaking of the regional economy to the reconfiguration of centuries-old networks of migration and trade. Nevertheless, Anglo-American oil firms and technical advisors brought a series of new and transformative technologies of labor control to the Gulf—the contract, the labor camp, and racial segregation. Along with local and imperial authorities, they also developed a series of arguments to justify their practices. Couched in the language of economics, these arguments, and these technologies, would prove remarkably durable.

The Persian Gulf has been a nexus of migration for centuries, crisscrossed by enslaved people, pearl divers, sailors, and merchants.[19] Individuals, families, or entire tribal groups would circulate in an annual migration from the desert to the coast and back again, linking the pastoral, agricultural, and pearling economies in a regional ecosystem of labor.[20] Migration did not entail freedom. All labor operated on a continuum in which coercion remained essential. The *sukhra*, or forced labor, was used by ruling families across the Gulf until it was abolished by sustained popular pressure in the 1920s and 1930s.[21] Another common form of bondage was enslavement, which expanded in the late nineteenth century alongside surging global demand for pearls and dates.[22] Enslavement survived into the second half of the twentieth century in part due to British reluctance to alienate an influential class of slaveholders by enforcing abolition.[23] The most common form of bondage operated through debt. Pearling captains kept their divers in perpetual servitude by rolling over debts year after year, and generation after generation.[24] Framing coerced labor as "debt bondage" was a useful means of dodging the opprobrium of imperial officials, who rhetorically condemned slavery but were more than willing to track down indebted workers who fled across the Gulf.[25]

In the decades following World War I, a devastating regional depression reconfigured this longstanding web of migration. The invention of the cultured pearl in Japan, the rise of the California date industry, and the general collapse of demand during the Great Depression devastated the largest industries in the Gulf. As Matthew Hopper has argued, it was regional depression, rather than British intervention, that brought enslavement to an end, as slaveholders found that the cost of maintaining enslaved people exceeded the value of their labor.[26] Abolition was aided by changing popular feeling, as reformers criticized enslavement as both a moral abomination and a hinderance to modern development.[27] In his memoirs, Abdul Rahman al-Bakir wrote that his press campaign for the abolition of slavery in Qatar was one of his proudest accomplishments.[28] Debt bondage declined alongside the pearling industry that had sustained it.[29] The 1920s and 1930s also witnessed the collapse of the pastoral economy. Nomadic Bedouin saw demand for their products undermined by competition from the global market, their military power shattered by the rise of mechanized warfare, and their grazing lands fragmented by national borders and devastated by drought. By World War II, regular reports on nomads compiled by British imperial officials had shifted from analyses of tribal politics to wrenching accounts of poverty.[30] Many abandoned their nomadic lifestyle and moved into the rapidly expanding shanty settlements on the outskirts of Gulf cities. By the 1950s, camps outside of Kuwait housed an estimated 28 percent of the total population and were growing at a rapid clip.[31]

It was at this moment of economic collapse that U.S.- and British-owned oil firms began to transform life in the Gulf. Most of the region's oil concessions were signed in the 1920s and 1930s, while production ramped up after World War II. The rise of oil did not lead to a smooth transition to a wage economy. On the contrary, the oil companies inserted themselves into preexisting networks, etching older hierarchies into supposedly "modern" forms of labor discipline. As late as 1951, at least one oil company in the southern Gulf employed dozens, if not hundreds, of enslaved people, paying a part of their wages to their enslavers.[32] This appears to have been common knowledge in the industry. In his 1959 book, longtime oil man Henry Longhurst complained that in the Gulf, "the most difficult employees were former slaves, who, after years of pampering by their masters, were inclined to be intolerant of the Company's hours and conditions of work"—a comment that may have said more about the prevalent working conditions in Anglo-American oil firms than Longhurst intended.[33] At times, however, oil companies attacked non-wage systems if they believed they could grow the potential pool of wage labor. In both Bahrain and Kuwait, they instituted programs by which divers could pay off their debts by working for the oil company, allowing them access to an even broader pool of labor.[34] In general, they benefited from, and so encouraged, a surfeit of dispossessed wage labor.

Most of the first locally hired oil workers were former nomads and pearl divers. What initially brought KOC into contact with the Bedouin was not oil, but water. In the 1930s, the company began drilling water wells around the Kuwaiti desert as a public relations measure.[35] These reconfigured the geography of nomadic life during the drought of the early 1940s.[36] When oil operations resumed after the war, the Bedouin were already at hand. H. R. P. Dickson, a former British Political Agent hired by the oil company who fancied himself an expert on Bedouin life, proved the most forceful advocate for the hiring of former nomads. According to imperial reports, Dickson persuaded the company "to put up with the waywardness and irresponsibility of Bedouin employees" because of their other supposed qualities.[37] He and other KOC officials believed that Bedouin were "more religious" and "less susceptible to Communist influence" than workers from urban areas.[38] They also believed that Bedouin were naturally subservient to tribal authority—a subservience they consciously tried to cultivate. The company even hired an anthropologist to study "the adaptation of bedouins to KOC labor conditions."[39] Her report encouraged the company to promote men deemed to have social "standing" in an effort to transfer their obedience to the oil firm.[40] Similar policies became standard practice around the Gulf.[41]

The oil boom also attracted a wave of immigration. Immigrants from the southern Persian Gulf, where oil exploitation would not begin until the 1960s and 1970s, left to escape grinding poverty, or to access social services like healthcare and education.[42] It was easy for them to acquire forged documents, or, because passports were often issued to families, rather than individuals, to slip through border controls by pretending to be a relative of someone with a valid passport.[43] The oil company also prioritized their employment on the theory that "the most docile and manageable workers are the immigrants from the southern part of the Arabian Peninsula."[44] Palestinians, expelled from their homes during or after 1948, became an influential diaspora, especially in Kuwait. Many were from the intelligentsia and played a key role in staffing the growing educational system and state bureaucracy.[45] They were also exempted from many restrictions on movement and residency because of pan-Arab sentiment. Shafeeq Ghabra has traced the ties of family and kinship that knit the diaspora together, reinforced by a flurry of clubs, organizations, and federations.[46] Iranians comprised another large and variegated immigrant population.[47] The diversity of the Iranian diaspora can be in part explained by the fact that they arrived in a series of distinct migrations—during the economic instability of the late Qajar period and the First World War, the consolidation of the Pahlavi regime in the 1920s, the crash following oil nationalization in 1951, and a period of prolonged drought and rural dislocation in the 1960s. Most Iranians, however, were hired in menial jobs; indeed, in 1970, an estimated 70.1 percent of Iranians in Kuwait were illiterate.[48] Moreover, while many Arab immigrants were granted exceptions to passport regulations, Iranians were subject to the full force of the deportation state.[49] The result was that, by 1963, the British embassy reported that of the estimated 32,961 Iranian immigrants in Kuwait, 93 percent had entered Kuwait without authorization, compared to only 7 percent of "Gulf Arabs."[50] What united all of these migrations was their domination by men. By the late fifties, the population of men in Kuwait was 50 percent higher than the population of women, an imbalance that would last for decades.[51]

But while oil companies found immigrants, nomads, and pearl divers to be an ideal source of manual labor, to staff their intermediate ranks, they turned to British India, which already had a vast contract recruitment infrastructure in place.[52] The British government had turned to contract workers in World War I to support their Mesopotamia campaign and maintain essential oil operations at Abadan.[53] Oil firms would play a leading role in bringing contract labor into the broader Persian Gulf. Contract workers were essential to the Gulf oil industry from its inception, beginning with the Anglo-Persian Oil Company (APOC) in Iran.[54] In 1928, APOC opened its own recruiting office in India, which would become a model for oil firms across the Gulf.[55] The turn to contract workers was not always their first choice. The Bahrain Petroleum Company (Bapco) at first hired Indian workers in Bahrain itself, without providing them with any contracts at all. Only after the Government of India effectively banned the company from hiring in India did they relent, opening a Bombay office in 1936.[56] By the fifties, nearly all oil companies in the region were recruiting from India, forming the connecting tissue between Indian indenture and the system of sponsorship and contract labor familiar in the contemporary Gulf.[57]

The genealogy between indenture and contracting can be most easily traced in Kuwait. The Kuwait Oil Company (KOC), which was half-owned by British Petroleum and thus a sister company to APOC, recruited Indian workers through the APOC office in Bombay before hiring its own recruitment staff after the oil boom.[58] KOC appreciated that British authorities in India agreed to screen job applicants "from the security aspect," thus weeding out political radicals and labor organizers.[59] A police check on new recruits would become standard practice across the region and another "benefit" of contract labor.[60] In 1950, when the cash-flush Kuwaiti government decided to hire workers abroad to complete its ambitious construction project, it turned to KOC for advice.[61] The government adopted exactly the same contracts, in some cases using the same forms, literally crossing out the words "Kuwait Oil Company" and replacing them with "Kuwait Government."[62] For well over a decade, the Kuwaiti government recruited contract labor through the British Petroleum office in Bombay, effectively transforming the oil company into a state labor recruiter.[63] These workers lived in a system of segregated labor camps built to house workers who were then hired out to construction companies, laying the foundations of the contracting system.[64]

Perhaps the primary benefit of noncitizen labor—at least from the perspective of employers—was its deportability. Here the exception proves the rule, and the exception, as was so often the case, was Palestinian. Because they could not return to their homes, Palestinian refugees faced systematic discrimination in hiring. The problem, as one Kuwaiti contractor explained, was "the possible difficulty of exporting such labor at the termination of the contract."[65] This is clearly evidenced by correspondence between UNRWA and William Hasted, a British "technical expert" hired to lead the Kuwait Development Board, an agency tasked with overseeing a vast infrastructure construction program. In 1952, the UNRWA reached out to ask local employers to help facilitate the hiring of Palestinian refugees.[66] Hasted refused, explaining that "state policy is not to encourage the use of Palestinian Arab refugee labor until the future is clearer . . . owing to the difficulty of resettling them on completion of their contract."[67] Only when they could be deported would Palestinians be hired.

Just as significant as these new methods of recruitment were the arguments used to justify them. At first, the Political Agent in Kuwait was concerned by the political repercussions of contract labor. He counseled that workers from the Gulf states should be given priority over any foreigners and warned that workers from abroad could bring dangerous political ideas to the Gulf.[68] But in the end, he acquiesced. He was persuaded by the company's claim that it was facing a labor shortage, which in turn had generated rising wages and inflation. Inflation had long been a central focus of imperial policy in the Gulf. World War II had witnessed the imposition of sweeping rationing measures and price controls designed to minimize the impact of wartime economic dislocation.[69] Imperial authorities generally agreed that higher prices "would automatically have caused another general demand for higher wages," generating higher prices and necessitating still higher wages in a dangerous and disruptive spiral.[70] Writing to his superiors in 1945, the Kuwait Political Agent described wages as "fantastically high," and warned that local hiring by the oil company would likely increase them. He therefore reported that he was "in favour of the company importing labour if local labour is not forthcoming at a competitive rate."[71] Approval was quickly granted.

As the Political Agent's language makes clear, the problem was not a lack of labor, but a lack of labor at wages deemed "competitive." These wages were low. KOC took its cue from Bapco in Bahrain, which set its wage rates for locals based "largely on the cost of a diet containing the requisite number of calories to keep a man and his family properly nourished."[72] Also like Bapco, these wages failed to keep pace with the cost of living. A survey conducted in 1951 found that KOC workers simply could not survive on basic rates of pay.[73] In 1956, another survey found that the expenses of workers with more than five dependents would outweigh their earnings, and some had to depend on cattle herding to supplement their wages. But even then, the company held off a wage increase, in case "our employees concluded that wage increments might be expected every six months or so."[74] The result was that many employees of Gulf oil firms received wages that were insufficient even to pay for adequate food.[75]

The company justified their subsistence wages by arguing that higher pay would, in the words of British advisor to the Bahrain Government Charles Belgrave, "start a dangerous whirl of inflation."[76] This was a ubiquitous shibboleth of oil firms, imperial officials, and their hired technical experts.[77] In Saudi Arabia, Aramco officials went even further, arguing that such inflation would threaten "a further drift from agriculture and date cultivation" and a concomitant increase in political instability.[78] To combat inflation, imperial and corporate officials coordinated a series of wage suppression efforts. In Bahrain, the effort was led by Charles Belgrave, who, beginning in 1950, organized and enforced a set wage rate on all major employers and penalized those who stepped beyond it.[79] This strategy was enforced by what officials described as a "black list" of workers who had asked for what was deemed to be more than their due, which was circulated around all major Anglo-American firms in the region.[80] In Kuwait, wage suppression was spearheaded by the Kuwait Development Board's Labour Committee, headed by yet another British technical expert, which set a maximum wage, determined wage levels across the Kuwaiti state based on conceptions of experience and skill, and oversaw overseas recruitment efforts, in close coordination with KOC and major British construction firms.[81]

The other essential corporate innovation was the labor camp. Nearly all oil companies in the region operated from segregated enclaves, usually built from scratch in isolated areas near the oilfields: Abadan in Iran, Awali in Bahrain, Dhahran in Saudi Arabia, and Ahmadi in Kuwait. These company towns, like their counterparts in the United States, enabled complete corporate control over all aspects of life and deployed a racialized hierarchy of divide-and-rule to govern their workforce.[82] The first camps outside of the oil industry were built by Hasted's Kuwait Development Board, which viewed the Aramco camps as a model.[83] Replicating corporate practices of segregation, Hasted decided to build not one camp, but two—Jewan Camp, built for Indian and Pakistani contract workers, and the Shuwaikh Camp, otherwise known as the "Supervisory Camp," which housed "skilled" workers who were exclusively white.[84] Shuwaikh Camp—but not Jewan—was designed to provide amenities including air conditioning and tennis courts, giving it the feel of a suburb more than a camp.[85] Segregation was common sense to most of these administrators, who, like Hasted, often referred to two distinct groups: "Europeans and labour."[86] The latter were often classified as "bachelors" because they were housed separately and not allowed to bring their families, from whom they were separated for months or years at a time.[87]

The construction of Jewan Camp provides a rare window into corporate and imperial thinking on labor camps. The Development Board discussed several benefits of spatial segregation. First, corporate control would help avoid the "infiltration of Communists" or other potential subversives. The threat of communism—used as a synonym for virtually all forms of labor organizing—was often couched in the language of contagion. In this model, the camp was another form of quarantine.[88] Workers could be easily policed by a force coordinated by contracting companies and the Kuwaiti state.[89] Second, Jewan was designed to be insulated from the rest of the Kuwaiti economy—a "self-contained" economic unit, with its own food supply and shopping facilities. This would prevent its residents from contributing to rising inflation.[90] It would even have its own financial system, including a "sub-branch" of British Bank of the Middle East.[91] Furthermore, by adding to Kuwait's housing stock and "thus freeing houses in the town," it would open space for new workers and reduce housing costs for employers.[92]

Emblematic of this logic was the provision of food. As Hasted explained, "The most important factor in keeping labour contented was a supply of good and cheap food, and if food prices rose, labour would demand a higher wage, and if this were granted, food prices would again rise in their turn, and the result would be inflation which it would be impossible to control."[93] The Board therefore decided to distribute the "catering" contracts and shop permits to private contractors, creating a new system of patronage without the burden of an enlarged state bureaucracy.[94] The camp, like the country itself, would become an economic terrarium that placed citizen business elites in the profitable position of gatekeepers and transformed even the most low-income workers into dependent, revenue-generating subjects. Workers were expected to arrive, eat their assigned rations, spend their surplus funds on predetermined commodities from handpicked intermediaries, and leave. Arguments of inflation, communism, and segregation thus intersected in the logic of the labor camp.

Perhaps the most clearly contradictory corporate argument was the so-called "skilled labor shortage." As Natasha Iskander has noted, "skill" has often been deployed in the Persian Gulf to justify hierarchy rather than describe ability.[95] This critique could be expanded to terms such as "experience," "qualifications," or "seniority," which oil firms systematically defined to the advantage of their white "senior staff." Especially in the early years of the oil boom, some workers did in fact require significant amounts of training to suit them for particular jobs. Many former nomads and pearl divers were illiterate and so could not immediately gain clerical employment, while advancement in the technically complex oil industry required a long apprenticeship process. Across the Gulf, and indeed across the global oil industry, oil workers, and oil-producing countries, demanded training schemes that would provide opportunities for advancement to local employees.[96] But companies almost always resisted such calls, even as they bemoaned a lack of skilled workers. Training was expensive and time-consuming, especially when easily deportable and experienced workers could be hired abroad. Moreover, as will be seen in the next chapter, oil companies tried to keep operations in the hands of their white workers, who they accurately presumed would remain loyal in case of a strike. Thus, Arab workers were systematically denied access to training and promotion.

Perhaps the most glaring evidence of the constructed nature of the "manpower shortage" was the discursive erasure of women's labor.[97] Early imperial calculations of the working population excluded women altogether—the most comprehensive study of the era, the 1955 Bahrain employment census, surveyed only the "total male labour force."[98] The gendered term "manpower" would remain a staple of the discourse for decades, in both English and Arabic. Corporate and imperial authorities across the Persian Gulf generally assumed that women would never work outside the home and made no effort to encourage them to do so, an assumption that rested on stereotypes of Gulf culture as static and patriarchal.[99] In fact, British sexism proved just as, if not more, significant. The first girls schools in Bahrain to be organized by the British were opened only after girls began showing up to boys schools on their own initiative.[100] Even those girls who were able to secure a precious spot in school were subjected to a separate curriculum that emphasized needlework.[101] Belgrave reasoned that "in a country where very few of the girls are allowed to earn their living or are likely to be allowed to work for some time except in the schools, it seems to be a valuable subject."[102] The school year culminated in a crafts exhibition organized by Mrs. Belgrave.[103] The practice was only phased out in 1956, when the girls of the Secondary School went on strike in sympathy with Egyptian forces during the Suez Crisis.[104] Thus even when white-collar jobs began to open up to Arab workers in the 1960s and 1970s, proportionately few women had received the education necessary to fill them.

The final and greatest hurdle to professional advancement was racism. According to one analyst with extensive experience in the midcentury oil industry, "the firm but only privately expressed conviction on the part of many Western oil men, including some who know the Middle East well, that training is a 'myth,' in the sense that it is impossible to raise a backward people to a level of industrial competence in less than two or three generations."[105] A typical KOC report presumed that Kuwaitis possessed "little sense of responsibility" and were unlikely to ever be truly fitted for important jobs.[106] Thus, training schemes across the region were implemented only under duress and were often deliberately undermined by the companies that created them.[107] When KOC launched a training program in 1950, even company officials acknowledged that it was designed to promote the "preservation of industrial peace" and deflect political criticism as much as it was supposed to provide actual training.[108] Moreover, KOC wages were so low that nearly all of the workers who completed the training program left the company to take better-paying jobs in Kuwait City.[109]

KOC recruitment efforts in the 1950s illustrated both the significance and disingenuousness of many of the economic arguments put forward by oil firms and their imperial allies. In response to popular demands for the hiring of more Arab and Kuwaiti workers, KOC sent recruiters around the Arabic-speaking world in 1957.[110] Concerned about the "political unreliability of 'northern area' Arabs," imperial officials suggested that KOC limit their hiring "as far as possible."[111] They need not have worried. KOC officials reassured the authorities they were making trips not so much in the hope of actually hiring anyone, "so much as of appearing to leave no possible source of Arab labour untouched."[112] In any event, this superficial effort was, as the company acknowledged, a "complete failure."[113] The simple fact was that "our present pay scales are unlikely to attract the right type of men."[114] Out of over a thousand applicants in Iraq, they had "not found one willing to go to Kuwait on the terms offered by the Company."[115] An effort the following year failed for the same reasons.[116] In 1958, when KOC opened an office in Beirut to coordinate recruitment in Lebanon, Jordan, Syria, and Egypt, it was framed as a public relations measure rather than a good-faith recruiting effort.[117] The newspapers chosen for advertisements were "those most generally favoured in Kuwait," rather than in the countries where KOC was supposedly recruiting, so that job advertisements would succeed "in gaining goodwill for the Company."[118] As the Political Agency summarized, KOC recruitment of Arab workers was more "a face saving gesture than anything else."[119]

Corporate arguments of political economy had one flaw—they lacked evidentiary backing. A strike wave in 1945 to 1946, discussed in the next chapter, led the Foreign Office to send labor specialists to the Gulf in the hope of preventing unrest by studying its causes, including the cost of living. At first, these specialists supported the oil companies. During a visit to Bahrain in

1949, Labor Attaché M. T. Audsley determined that while over 80 percent of the lowest-paid Bapco workers were making less than four rupees per day, the amount was perfectly sufficient.[120] When he visited again two years later, however, he found that prices had risen, wages had stagnated, none of his suggestions had been taken, and workers on the lowest pay scale barely reached "the lowest subsistence level."[121] Audsley's visit triggered a series of investigations that chipped away at longstanding arguments about inflation within the imperial bureaucracy itself. After his departure, Bapco ordered a cost of living study that found that 80 percent of the Arab staff were "receiving wages below the minimum subsistence level" and raised its pay rates twice in quick succession.[122] Notably, when Audsley visited Bahrain in 1953, he found that higher wages had "not resulted in an inflationary spiral of food retail prices."[123] In fact, one official advocated a further wage increase, noting that "based on a sufficient diet of 2,900 calories per day," some of his own workers were still living on less than a subsistence diet.[124] Even Belgrave acknowledged that the material and living conditions of workers had "noticeably improved," a transformation that the Attaché attributed to rising wages and that did not generate the much-feared specter of inflation.[125]

But regardless of this lack of evidence, these arguments survived even after formal British withdrawal, sustained by employers who found them just as useful as Anglo-American oil firms did. The result was that recruitment abroad became a favored stratagem of wage suppression, while workers hired locally were confined to manual labor at wages barely enough to keep them alive. But as mass political movements emerged alongside a popular press, workers, reformers, and anticolonial nationalists would challenge both Anglo-American firms and the arguments they deployed.

THE WAGES OF NATIONALITY | 1948–1959

In July of 1953, a group of workers presented a petition to the Kuwait Development Board claiming that their employer had violated state regulations by firing hundreds of people without regard to their nationality. Just a few months earlier, the Ruler of Kuwait, Abdullah al-Salem Al Sabah, had ordered all government contractors to give priority in employment first to Kuwaitis, and second to the "sons of Arab countries," employing non-Arabs only if absolutely necessary.[126] The petition raised a dilemma: namely, the "difficulty of distinguishing between Kuwaiti and non-Kuwaiti labourers."[127] The first oil concession, signed in 1934, mandated the oil company to "employ subjects of the Shaikh as far as possible for all work for which they are suited."[128] But this requirement was written over a decade before the first legal definition of Kuwaiti nationality. Moreover, most residents of Kuwait possessed no documentation whatsoever. Unable to determine whether or not the petitioners were citizens, the Development Board requested the help of some "elder policemen" who could "assist in the identification of Kuwaitis."[129] Eventually, six policemen deemed to have "a good knowledge of Kuwait" were dispatched to the worksite.[130] It was clearly their age and experience, more than their official position, that qualified them to make this determination. When the officers had finished their task, the workers were reinstated, and the company sternly reminded to give "priority in engagement" to Kuwaitis.[131] But the larger question of nationality remained unanswered.

This story exemplifies the pressing material questions generated by the oil boom of the 1950s. The opening sentence of a 1952 article summarized the popular consensus: "The issue facing Kuwait right now is the issue of petrol income."[132] The intense and multi-sided debate over the distribution of this income came to revolve around the concepts of political economy and citizenship. In Kuwait, nationality was imbued with important material benefits even before it was clearly defined. As Jill Crystal has noted in the case of Qatar, material questions, notably employment, would shape the outlines of nationality in the early oil years.[133] Nationality became a battleground for two opposing camps. On the one side was an increasingly wealthy business class, dominated by Kuwait's longstanding merchant families, which sought to transform the line between citizen and noncitizen into a generator of profit. They fought to frame what Manu Goswami calls a "bounded national space and economy" that granted special privileges to citizens.[134] By the end of the 1950s, the exclusions of nationality had generated their own well-heeled constituency. But other Kuwaitis understood the interrelated questions of oil income and nationality in terms of economic justice. While the 1950s witnessed a surge of popular xenophobia, political reformers also condemned the practices of oil multinationals and the business elite and called for a more inclusive definition of Kuwaiti citizenship and a more equitable distribution of wealth.

Land, along with housing, again proved to be a critical material wedge dividing citizens from noncitizens. In 1952, Kuwait followed the Bahraini example by forbidding noncitizens from owning land, yet another law that would become the standard across the Persian Gulf.[135] At the same time, the Kuwaiti state launched a housing program for low-income citizens that by 1960 was annually building four thousand homes.[136] As it did across the Gulf, land and housing transformed nationality into a much-sought-after status, imbuing it with enormous material significance even as it created new forms of spatial segregation.[137] Perhaps the most significant policy was the Kuwaiti Land Acquisition Program, launched in 1951, which, as Ghanim al-Najjar has argued, became a key means of "redistributing wealth among a few property owners."[138] Justified as a means of acquiring necessary land for state development projects by purchasing it from its legal owners, the program consumed approximately 11 percent of Kuwaiti public expenditure from 1951 to 1979, peaking at a staggering 42.8 percent in 1959, most of which went to only two dozen well-connected families.[139] Redistributive policies also created patronage networks. Abdulrahman Alebrahim has traced how Kuwaitis petitioned ruling family members for access to land and housing, reinforcing monarchical power.[140] Finally, land underlined state strategies of divide-and-rule. Because new neighborhoods separated formerly nomadic and formerly urban residents, citizens and noncitizens, and even people who had lived in different neighborhoods within the walls of old Kuwait, public housing entrenched, in the words of Farah Al-Nakib, "clear socioeconomic distinctions between members of the urban community."[141]

Citizen business elites also monopolized trade. To do so, they turned to a venerable legal instrument: the agency agreement. Agency agreements were contracts that granted a particular individual or firm the exclusive right to sell the goods of a particular exporter or manufacturer within a particular territory.[142] In the nineteenth century, they were usually given to large firms with British managers, which covered broad swaths of territory, usually the entire Persian Gulf or Indian Ocean.[143] But by the 1930s, a handful of traders from the Gulf, usually those connected to imperial officials and ruling families, began accumulating agency agreements on their own.[144] Their significance was staggering. The anthropologist Peter Lienhardt complained that agencies "offered too many possibilities for arbitrary privilege."[145] Many a mercantile empire began with a fortuitous agency agreement acquired in the critical early decades of the oil boom.[146] By the 1980s, just thirteen people imported 48 percent of goods into Kuwait, in no small part due to their monopolization of agency agreements.[147] Citizen-capitalists also successfully lobbied for legislation requiring that agency agreements be restricted to particular national territories and individuals, culminating in a 1960 Kuwaiti law that required that all "agents" be citizens.[148] Also important were oil company contracts and purchasing agreements, which oil firms used to build local support, reward local clients, and reinforce hierarchies within the boundaries of nationality. In 1950, for instance, Dickson warned that he could tell that the owners of several shops on KOC property "from their very names, are not Kuwaiti Arabs at all, but are either foreigners (Persian or Iraqi) or Domiciled Persians," and argued that preference "should always be in favour of Kuwaiti Arabs proper," rather than "domiciled Persians."[149]

Chambers of Commerce emerged as the most important institutional advocates for what increasingly came to be called the "national economy" (*al-iqtisad al-watani*) and for the citizen-capitalists who came to dominate it.[150] Chambers coordinated business interests, resolved disputes, and served as brokers between local importers and global manufacturers.[151] Perhaps most significantly, they played a crucial role in policing the outlines of nationality by excluding noncitizen merchants.[152] Their newsletters connected foreign exporters to citizen importers, while their lobbying shaped legislation that protected "the interests of merchants and the national economy."[153] The Kuwaiti Chamber would continue to play a key role in the drafting of legislation in the interests of its wealthy members.[154] In so doing, like Chambers of Commerce across the region, it systematically excluded and marginalized noncitizens.[155]

The final pillar of citizen-businessperson wealth was labor. Noncitizens served not just as tenants and customers, but also as workers. Citizen-capitalists also profited directly as middlemen in a growing labor recruitment industry. Starting in the fifties, a group of firms began to emerge as specialist "labor contractors."[156] When it resumed operations in 1946, the Kuwait Oil Company relied on three "bulk labor" contractors to rapidly build up a reserve army of workers.[157] Alghanim, for instance, employed 790 people, almost all of whom were recruited from Iraq with the personal permission of the Ruler, highlighting the connection between patronage and profit.[158] They were supplemented by nine "Agents," working on 10 percent commission, who provided what was called "Bulk Labour" or "daily labour," hired daily within Kuwait itself. In total, KOC paid £152,731 to labor contractors in 1948 alone, of which £22,764 was paid as commission—a significant sum.[159] While even the British embassy acknowledged that "there were frequent complaints by the men that they had not received the wages due to them," the system continued for years.[160] Through the 1960s, international oil, transportation, and construction firms relied heavily on bulk labor contractors.[161] These labor contractors were the nucleus of the "manpower" industry, which would become a powerful political and economic force across the Gulf.[162]

By the mid-1950s, citizen merchants had effectively lobbied for special privileges over land, labor, and trade that transformed nationality into a generator of profit. But their efforts also faced forceful pushback. In Kuwait, the accession of the moderately reformist Ruler Abdullah al-Salem in 1950 began a fifteen-year period that witnessed the rise of mass politics and perhaps the most open period of political debate in Kuwaiti history. The first influential press outlets in the Gulf were imported from elsewhere, particularly Egypt. By 1951, imperial authorities in Kuwait were reporting that "no less than seven Egyptian newspapers cram-full of politics were in circulation in the town," bringing with them "the seeds of organized labour."[163] Perhaps even more significant was the *Voice of the Arabs*, broadcast in Cairo and disseminated by an ever-increasing number of radios, which helped transform Arab nationalism into the dominant ideological current in the region. In 1957, it began a regular program that exclusively focused on news from the Gulf.[164] With remarkable rapidity, Kuwaitis were incorporated into an Arabic-language media sphere that oriented their politics toward the Arab world.

The Gulf also became host to a collection of independent newspapers that often blended their anticolonialism with a broadly pro-reform and pro-labor editorial line. In Bahrain, such publishing revolved around the personage of the aforementioned Abdul Rahman al-Bakir. Born to a family of Bahraini merchants, he spent many years sailing the well-worn trade routes of the Persian Gulf and Indian Ocean.[165] After a few years in Muscat, he returned to Bahrain in 1936 to work for the oil company and organize the 1938 protests.[166] At about the same time, his brother was killed in a "painful accident" while working for the Qatar Petroleum Company, which al-Bakir blamed on lax safety standards and an absence of effective medical care.[167] On his return to Bahrain in mid-1948, he resumed his political activities, working to unify the various political and literary clubs across Bahrain and publishing a variety of secret pamphlets and newspapers, including *al-Qafila* (The Caravan).[168]

Perhaps the most successful was the *Sawt al-Bahrain* (The Voice of Bahrain), which would inspire new publications across the Gulf.

Kuwait came to host the freest and most active media sphere in the Persian Gulf, emerging as something of a forum for the entire region. In the early 1950s, paper after paper emerged, many of which were affiliated with one of the clubs that sprang up around the country and became important forums of debate. The most prominent figure in these circles was Ahmad al-Khatib. Unlike many Kuwaiti politicians, al-Khatib was not from a wealthy family. His father and grandfather worked for the ruling family as guards. In his memoirs, he remembers watching them ride out of the fortified gates of Kuwait to protect caravans as they crossed the desert, and spending anxious days gazing out to the horizon, awaiting their return. One day those fears were realized—his father was wounded in battle and rendered unable to work. He received no disability benefits whatsoever, and the family was forced into poverty.[169] They suffered another blow when a member of the ruling family arbitrarily confiscated a significant portion of their property.[170] But with the support of both his mother and Yusuf bin ʿIsa al-Qinaʾi, the educational reformer, he was able to win a coveted scholarship to study at the American University of Beirut, eventually earning his M.D.[171] There, he met Kuwaitis active in the 1938 Majlis Movement, as well as Palestinian activists like George Habash, and under the tutelage of AUB professor Constantine Zureiq he became a dedicated Arab nationalist.[172] Viewed as Black by the university administration, he also faced the ugly reality of American racism, an experience that informed his Third Worldist perspective. On his return to Kuwait in 1952, Dr. al-Khatib (as he was universally known) founded Kuwait's first official branch of the Arab Nationalist Movement (ANM). He soon established himself as one of the de facto leaders of the pro-democracy political opposition, a position he would retain for nearly half a century.[173]

The explosion of press activity in the early 1950s created a new and powerful public sphere. Citizenship would become one of its most prominent topics of debate. At first glance, one of the most striking elements of the Kuwaiti press in the 1950s was its xenophobia. In May 1952, *al-Raʾid*, the publication of the Kuwaiti Teachers Club, called on the government to "take the necessary steps to stop this rushing torrent" of migration that is "nearly drowning us."[174] The problem of "migrant beggars" as a threat to the "image" of Kuwait emerged as a recurring theme in *al-Raʾid*, which repeatedly called for the state to deport offenders.[175] This stance reflected the paper's politics: the Teachers Society restricted voting and executive committee membership to Kuwaitis even though many teachers were from Egypt and Palestine.[176] Noncitizens became scapegoats for a remarkable range of social ills, from poverty to unemployment.[177] Iranians were subject to the most vitriol, including from Arab nationalist publications that advocated for the rights of Arab noncitizens.[178] In 1953, *al-Iman*, published by the influential Arab nationalist National Culture Club, reported that "Kuwait is enduring a terrifying exodus of foreigners" who hang pictures of "their leaders" in their shops and coffeehouses while "massing" and "occupying" the streets.[179] The paper contrasted "unmixed/unadulterated (*al-iqhah*) Arabs" with the dangers of the "infiltration" of "al-ʿAjam"—a derogatory term for Iranians.[180] It even described "the wandering poor" as "colonizers."[181] Another article complained of the public use of "repugnant jibberish"—presumably Persian.[182] The only solution, the paper argued, is for the state to "shut the door" on migration.[183] Cairo's *Voice of the Arabs* took the lead in warning of the dangers of "such illegitimate immigration into this sensitive part of our Arab homeland" by Iranians.[184] At times, papers even called for mass deportations in order to "solve" the problems of unemployment and begging and, in the case of Arab nationalists, to reinforce Arab demographic predominance.[185] This position would come back to haunt the reformist movement.

Beneath the xenophobia, however, were fissures and nuances, and even efforts to push back against the interlocking regimes of nationality and deportation. A crucial divide began to form between Arab and Kuwaiti nationalists. The Arab nationalist *al-Iman* framed Kuwaitis as, first and foremost, part of the wider Arab nation, going so far as to rebrand the Persian Gulf as the "Arab Gulf."[186] While this discourse could be viciously anti-Iranian, it also opened the door of integration to Arab immigrants, blurring the line between citizen and noncitizen. The Arab nationalist press also condemned the deportation of political activists, especially anticolonial nationalists like Abdul Rahman al-Bakir.[187] Kuwaiti nationalists embraced Arabist rhetoric to a point, but supported a more exceptionalist, and therefore restrictive, form of Kuwaiti nationalism.[188] *Al-Raʾid* called for Kuwaiti students to be trained by Kuwaiti teachers, and continued the effort to forge a unique, and often exclusionary, conception of the Kuwaiti nation redolent of the perspective advanced by the *Nahda* reformers decades earlier.[189] But the overwhelming popularity of Arab nationalism, combined with the fact that many immigrants were Arab, left the door open for solidarities across the boundaries of nationality.

Perhaps the most sweeping and powerful critiques in the Kuwaiti press targeted the narratives of political economy deployed by economic and political elites. Given its destructive impact, especially during the World Wars, inflation was one of the most popular topics of discussion. In May of 1952, *al-Ra'id* even published a poem entitled "Inflation (*al-ghla'a*)," written in a formal meter, which decried the devastating effects of rising prices and described how traditional bonds between the rich and the poor, or parents and their children, were disintegrating as the wealthy abandoned their responsibility to society.[190] While some authors framed rising prices as the product of moral decay or sudden wealth, more blamed them on the greed and avarice of elite families.[191] Even *al-Ma'had al-Dini*, a conservative religious periodical, included *fatawa* addressing the ethics of price gouging.[192] Reformist and Arab nationalist papers went beyond moral condemnation, coupling accusations of greed with specific policy recommendations. They called for an end to state land purchasing programs and exclusive Agency agreements that did little more than create monopolies that funded the conspicuous consumption of well-connected businesspeople.[193] Newspapers also attacked the use of land as a mechanism to recycle oil wealth into the hands of the wealthy, exemplified by exploding rents and greedy landlords who, in the words of one commentator, "only understand the principle of acquiring as much money as they can."[194]

The Arab nationalist press was particularly vociferous. In its very first issue in January 1953, *al-Iman* condemned inflation as the "hand tightening its grip on the laboring class."[195] It blamed traders for "price fixing," selling goods at whatever price they liked to "gain a profit that they determine for themselves." It argued that the question was not one of "supply and demand," but rather of agency agreements that created an "unofficial monopoly."[196] Critiques of inflation would grow even sharper as the decades progressed, while "monopoly"—also a flashpoint in 1938—became a ubiquitous term of abuse. Future issues of the paper provided a platform for advocates of rent freezes, price controls, and redistributive taxation.[197] The paper placed the blame for the "storm of inflation" squarely on the shoulders of importers and landlords who made "fantastic profits" by taking advantage of the weakness of consumers.[198]

Reversing the arguments of imperial officials and oil company representatives, the Kuwaiti press largely agreed that the cost of living was rising to unsustainable levels because wages failed to keep up with prices.[199] The solution, they argued, was for the state to actively intervene in the labor market in the name of economic redistribution.[200] High wages were seen as a means not just to provide for workers, but to transfer national wealth away from the foreign corporations and well-connected business owners reaping the lion's share of the profit from Kuwaiti oil.[201] Papers also provided a megaphone for worker efforts to raise wages. When Kuwaiti teachers petitioned the government for higher wages to offset the cost of housing, for instance, *al-Iman* provided regular and supportive coverage.[202] Kuwaiti publications also reframed the concept of the skilled manpower shortage, arguing that it resulted from a lack of industrial education programs and the discriminatory practices of the oil company. *Al-Ra'id* threw its support behind the idea of a "College of Industry" in order to train "an army of skilled workers" so that Kuwaitis could build a modern economy.[203] Newspapers also criticized the deliberately discriminatory classification systems employed by the oil companies, which allowed, for instance, "experience in the Indian Army" to take the place of a secondary school degree for British employees but showed no similar flexibility to their Arab workers.[204] One short story published by *al-Ra'id* narrates the travails of a respected, self-taught Kuwaiti employee fired from his job because of his lack of formal credentials.[205] Some papers also adopted a self-consciously reformist position with regards to women's education, which they described as essential to economic development and reform.[206] Thus, directly contradicting imperial and corporate discourse, higher wages were framed as the solution to the disruption of inflation, rather than its cause.

The intersection of discourses of citizenship, social justice, and political economy were exemplified by a series of articles written by Fahad al-Dueiri, an influential member of the Teachers' Club and editor of *al-Ra'id*, in the paper's first issues. The piece helped launch a long-running debate over social insurance, inclusion, and economic justice.[207] Al-Dueiri argued that unlike most states, which relied on a "base" of taxpayers, Kuwait's enormous oil revenues represented a "new phenomenon" that transformed "the solidarity (*tadamun*) between the people and the government" and threatened a decline in civic virtue.[208] His solution was a social insurance regime based on the principle that Kuwaitis are all "one family."[209] His revealing and detailed breakdown of the ideal bureaucratic structure of a social security administration modeled his conception of an idealized Kuwaiti society, tied together with metaphors of kinship.[210] A Kuwaiti nationalist, he argued that the Kuwaiti system should be administered by a group of expert-managers with an in-depth understanding of what he considered the unique conditions prevailing in Kuwait, which he viewed as inherently "Bedouin."[211] While "outsiders" could be brought in as experts or advisors, he was adamant that only "pure (*samim*)" Kuwaitis—a term he never defines—should serve in leadership positions.[212] The administration would be broken down into sections, each of which corresponded to what al-Dueiri saw as a distinct segment of Kuwaiti society, divided along the lines of class.[213]

Most revealing were two unusual suggestions. The first was for a "loan department," which would provide loans to "pure (*'ariiqa*) Kuwaiti families" with generous terms and conditions.[214] The second was the "settlement office," which would transform unruly nomads into "simple laborers." Al-Dueiri believed that two distinct problems, a labor shortage and a "Bedouin problem," could be solved with one grand plan. In exchange for the debt the Bedouin would owe to the Ruler for the granting of nationality, they "can supply a labor force in Kuwait." The state could thus "supervise the cultivation of health and soul, and the appropriate level of material development" until the Bedouin reach an appropriate level of development, "become Kuwaitis," and finally share in the "rights and responsibilities" of citizenship.[215] As will be seen, the position of Bedouin would become a major point of debate, especially after independence.[216] Simultaneously inclusive and discriminatory, al-Dueiri's conceptualization exemplifies how elite Kuwaitis, including in the press, understood the link between labor and citizenship and etched the hierarchies of class into discourses of nationality.

The press also echoed with calls to reform the nationality regime. Some of this discourse was driven by xenophobia. Arab nationalist papers were most upset that some Iranians "have, with little effort, received Kuwaiti passports, while Arabs, whether Syrian or Iraqi, Hijazi or Bahraini, have not."[217] But anti-immigrant rhetoric also generated pushback. One letter to the editor published in *al-Iman* attacked the paper's anti-immigrant coverage with remarkable forcefulness, accusing it of deploying contradictory arguments, muddled reasoning, and flimsy logic that relied on a mix of "nationalism (*qawmiyya*) and racism (*'ansuriyya*)" reminiscent of Nazi Germany.[218] Indeed, calls for nationality legislation were not simply driven by the desire to exclude. Many authors were concerned not so much with preventing naturalization as with regularizing it in order to halt the use of nationality as an arbitrary form of patronage.[219] It was a matter of fairness, an effort to make sure that people who considered themselves Kuwaitis actually received nationality, while well-connected foreigners were not able to take advantage of special favors.[220] In general, *al-Iman* argued that nationality should be granted to anyone who truly felt Kuwaiti, rather than only by descent—a significant departure from both British and monarchical practice.[221] Finally, pro-democracy activists also noted that an accurate census and straightforward nationality law would help to verify and expand the electoral lists, thus defending democratic procedures and bringing more Kuwaitis into the political process.[222] The question came to the fore during the first contested municipal elections of 1954, when a group of Kuwaiti clubs organized a petition calling for the Ruler to establish special committees of "knowledgeable dignitaries" to draft electoral lists of Kuwaitis, and again during local elections in 1958.[223] A clear definition of Kuwaiti nationality would thus advance both social justice and democracy.

As the decade progressed, demands to reform the nationality regime grew louder and more radical. *Al-Sha'b* (The People), a left-wing Arab nationalist paper published from 1958 to 1959, launched a campaign to reform nationality law in the name of fairness. The paper highlighted the experience of self-described Kuwaitis who were unable to prove their nationality: "His work permit affirms that he is Kuwaiti. His driver's license recognizes that he is Kuwaiti. And those who know him testify that he is Kuwaiti! But the land registration department refused to register the house which he purchased in his name, because he does not carry a Kuwaiti passport!"[224] This was particularly galling at a time when state officials handed out nationality to people lacking "any connection to the society."[225] Another piece noted that the many inequities resulted from the fact that the primary definition of a Kuwaiti was "those who own land or a house in Kuwait."[226] But many poorer residents never owned houses or land, while "many non-Kuwaitis were able to acquire houses and land thanks to their contacts and connections" and then use their land deeds to obtain a passport. The solution, it suggested, would be to assemble a committee of twenty people from all "factions, classes, neighborhoods, and districts" of Kuwait to guarantee that applicants for passports and nationality were, in fact, Kuwaiti.[227] This was in fact precisely the solution that the state would adopt. *Al-Shaʿb* thus introduced a fundamental challenge to the nationality regime: that any Arab living in, and loyal to, Kuwait should have access to nationality, regardless of class or gender.[228]

CONCLUSION

The 1950s introduced arguments, institutions, and forms of labor discipline that would dominate the region for decades to come. They also witnessed sharpening divisions of nationality and class and the rise of popular movements for democracy, anticolonialism, and social justice. But the most powerful challenge to the exclusions of citizenship and class would come from organized labor. Allying with journalists, anticolonial activists, and Arab nationalists, workers challenged not just the idea that good economics dictated their survival on subsistence wages, but also the racial segregation that dominated the oil industry. The alliance between workers and anticolonial nationalists, and the arguments of resource nationalism that they championed, would transform Kuwait into a global node of politics.

3 Arab Labor, Arab Oil | 1945–1959

ASHRAF LUTFI WAS BORN in Jaffa, Palestine, in 1919. The son of a translator employed by the Mandate government, he enjoyed a comfortable middle-class upbringing, eventually working as a language teacher and principal in the state school system. But in his twenties, his life was upended by the political violence and mass expulsions sweeping across Palestine. In January of 1948, he was wounded in a bombing orchestrated by the Stern Gang, which left him with a permanent scar under his eye. As Zionist forces enveloped Jaffa later that year, Lutfi and his family fled their home with nothing but some clothes and a small bundle of valuables. They would never return.[1] Lutfi eventually found his way to Kuwait, where he was hired by Abdullah Mulla Saleh, the powerful "Secretary" of the Ruler and the official point of contact between the ruling family and the Kuwait Oil Company (KOC). Lutfi quickly made himself indispensable, playing a central role in oil concession negotiations in 1955 and 1958 and eventually running the Office of the Emir himself.[2] The U.S. Consulate described him as the "real brains of the State Secretariat," where he "prepares his case as carefully as a lawyer, buttressing it with statistics."[3] Lutfi repeatedly outmaneuvered the oil companies by outmatching their research. By 1957, the U.S. Consulate had concluded that "Lutfi seems well on his way to becoming a kind of 'Tariki of Kuwait,' although more moderate"—a reference to Abdullah Tariki, the first oil minister of Saudi Arabia and one of the architects of the global oil cartel known as the Organization of Petroleum Exporting Countries, or OPEC.[4]

This prediction proved prescient. Within a decade, Lufti would emerge as a prominent member of a new generation of Arab oil reformers who championed the idea of "permanent sovereignty"—that sovereign control over natural resources is fundamental to the principle of self-determination.[5] Ashraf Lutfi is a particularly illuminating figure because he connects the high-level international conferences that are usually the subject of oil history to the popular struggles that played a pivotal if underappreciated role in what has come to be called the "oil revolution." In his 1959 book entitled *Arab Oil: A Plan for the Future*, Lutfi presented an accessible step-by-step plan for seizing control over oil. Articulating what Nelida Fuccaro calls "Petroleum Arabism," he argued that Arab states needed to build integrated national oil firms that could manage every aspect of the industry, from exploration and production to refining and shipping, in order to break the stranglehold of the oil multinationals.[6] The first step would be to train a cadre of skilled Arab workers capable of running the industry without foreign technical assistance. As a caution, he cited World War II, when British oil experts refused to supply the Iraqi government with its own oil because of its pro-Axis policies.[7] Control of oil needed to start from the production process itself.

His priorities reflected his on-the-ground experience. In negotiations with the Kuwait Oil Company, Lutfi was particularly adamant about two points: that the corporation had to hire a larger proportion of Kuwaiti and Arab workers, and that it had to end its policies of racial discrimination.[8] These corporate policies were perhaps the two biggest targets of criticism in the Kuwaiti press. Segregation was endemic at KOC, as it was in every oil firm in the Persian Gulf. But as Lutfi clearly recognized, segregation was not just demeaning—it was a mechanism of control. In order to prevent Arab and Kuwaiti workers from shutting down production during a strike, oil companies deliberately kept them away from key positions in the production process, instead hiring a surfeit of white "senior staff" who could serve as reliable strikebreakers. Eventually, Lutfi's pointed observations—that British butchers and foremen were listed as "senior staff" while more skilled Arab workers were not, for instance—helped force the company to begin reconfiguring its hiring policies.[9] He viewed these efforts as the first step in a longer process that would culminate in the consolidation of state sovereignty over national resources. Perhaps as remarkable as the ambition of Lutfi's arguments was their significance. *Arab Oil*, in addition to his role in successive oil conferences, transformed Lutfi into an internationally prominent figure. He represented Kuwait at the pivotal Arab Petroleum Congress of 1959, and eventually, in 1965, he was appointed the third Secretary General of OPEC.[10]

Arab Oil encapsulated a series of arguments popularized by workers, anticolonial activists, and journalists that reconfigured the politics of the Persian Gulf in the 1950s. This chapter traces the emergence of the labor and Arab nationalist movements and the forging of an alliance that would shape Kuwaiti politics for two decades.[11] Workers responded to abysmal wages, dangerous working conditions, and the daily indignities of racial segregation by immigrating across the Gulf in search of better job opportunities or by going on strike in unprecedented numbers. As workers and newspapers crisscrossed the region, they brought new expectations and ideas with them. The result was a series of strike waves that became increasingly regional in their repercussions, accompanied by the growth of class consciousness. Links between anticolonial nationalism and organized labor were not unique to the Gulf; indeed, they have a long tradition across the Arabic-speaking world and beyond.[12] What distinguished the Persian Gulf was the size of the region's oil reserves and the consequent stakes of the struggle, as well as the dominance of a handful of major oil firms. In Kuwait, the most important firm was the Kuwait Oil Company, a joint U.S. and British venture. Workers and their allies honed and popularized arguments of resource nationalism—that the citizenry, in the words of Fernando Coronil, should possess the "collective ownership of the nation's natural body," defined as ownership and control of oil.[13] In making this argument, they linked their daily struggles against corporate segregation with Arab nationalist, and even global, movements for racial justice and decolonization. Workers and local papers therefore played a key role in forging what Laleh Khalili calls a "political petroscape" that framed oil as "a general public good for all Arabs across borders," setting the stage for nationalization in the decades to come.[14]

Central to these arguments was the question of race. Scholars have begun to excavate the corporate racism that permeated the Gulf oil industry.[15] This chapter builds on their work by demonstrating that racism was not just a lingering vestige of the past ingrained in corporate culture. It was, first and foremost, a calculated strategy of control. Ensconced in segregated compounds and spacious bungalows, pampered by servants in exclusive clubs, and socializing only among themselves, white "senior staff" saw their interests as more aligned with their employers than with their non-white colleagues. Whiteness underpinned a strategy of divide-and-rule that represented the last line of defense for the oil majors and became a form of privilege that has proved remarkably enduring.[16] Gulf oil firms can thus be best understood as yet another example of the centrality of race in global capitalism.[17] Ashraf Lutfi had discerned a critical point: in the battle for permanent sovereignty over natural resources, decolonization needed to begin with desegregation.

SEGREGATION & ITS DISCONTENTS

The alliance between labor and anticolonial nationalism that burst forth in the 1950s can be seen as the product of inequities dating back to the beginning of the oil industry. These began with the notoriously one-sided oil concessions, signed in the early decades of the century, that provided the legal underpinnings of petroleum extraction. Nearly all concessions were held by one or more of the world's seven largest multinational oil companies headquartered in Europe or the United States. They were all signed by regional autocrats dependent on British imperial power, without public input or consent—in fact, most were negotiated in secret. They were all supposed to last for decades, sometimes as long as seventy or eighty years. And they all granted the oil companies control over production decisions, exemption from taxation, and special legal privileges. These privileges were secured by an initial cash payment and a royalty that amounted to a fraction of annual income.[18] The oil companies used these concessions to extract spectacular profit margins from the region's oil, which, in addition to being untaxed, enjoyed the lowest production costs in the world.[19]

What entrenched the alliance between labor and Arab nationalism was the racial segregation that saturated Anglo-American oil firms. The global oil industry was notorious for its racism, and the Gulf was no exception.[20] Oil companies were run as a tiered hierarchy, with white "senior staff" on top, and locally hired workers, usually classified as "unskilled" or "bulk labor," at the bottom. Sandwiched in between were "skilled" or "artisan" employees, usually Arab noncitizens or Indian and Pakistani workers hired on contract from Bombay or Karachi. The firms operated out of segregated oil cities, usually built from scratch in remote areas adjacent to the oilfields—Ahmadi in Kuwait, Awali in Bahrain, American Camp in Saudi Arabia, and Abadan in Iran.[21] In Kuwait, the oil town of Ahmadi confined its Arab inhabitants to a ramshackle quarter officially called the "Arab Village" and its Indian and Pakistani workers to the "Indian Village."[22] In the first postwar years, KOC tried to avoid building housing for their locally hired workers, which they feared "could lead to the attraction of families and the creation of comprehensive social obligations."[23] Instead, the company encouraged what it called a "slum settlement" to spring up on the fringes of its operations.[24] Non-white KOC workers lived in insect-infested shacks that lacked electricity and running water.[25] Such divides meant that, as the Kuwaiti paper *al-Sha'b* reported in 1958, any visitor to KOC housing could instantly determine "which house belongs to an Englishman and which to an Arab."[26]

What rankled the most was the gratuitously racist and dehumanizing treatment meted out to non-white employees. In 1952, the British labor attaché bluntly acknowledged that "a good deal of racial prejudice exists" in KOC, while plans to develop a "system of payment and grading according to merit and not to race" never fully materialized.[27] Instead, white workers received superior retirement benefits, vacation time, and wages.[28] The company club excluded Kuwaitis from membership, while Indian and Pakistani workers had a club of their own with inferior facilities.[29] In the company hospital, "Asiatic" workers were assigned fewer beds per worker than white "expatriate staff."[30] Even water was segregated.[31] This was standard practice—in Bahrain, the U.S.-owned oil firm built separate drinking water taps for "Europeans" and "Asiatics."[32] Racist epithets were so common that they became official corporate classifications. KOC management in London repeatedly requested that their colleagues in Kuwait refrain from using the word "coolie," explaining that it "is an extremely unpopular term with our Arab friends."[33] The campaign was unsuccessful, and the term continued to be used throughout the 1950s.[34] In 1956, it fell to Shaikh Jabir al-Ahmad to suggest that the company stop describing its cafeteria for non-white workers as a "Feeding Centre," explaining that the term "gave one the impression of feeding sheep as it were."[35] Bill Mulligan of Aramco blamed the British for importing imperial racism, claiming that American oil company employees visiting Bahrain "would come back and have the natives calling them Sahib—'You call me Sahib boy.'"[36] But in fact, Aramco had established segregated labor camps on its own initiative, a point that British observers often liked to emphasize.[37] In the Persian Gulf, as around the world, racial segregation was a way of life in the oil industry.

Racism was so open and prevalent that U.S. and British officials worried that it could generate a political backlash that would threaten their position in the Gulf.[38] In 1952, the British labor attaché M. T. Audsley reported that even the new housing for Arab workers "is much too primitive and will sooner or later be a subject of much criticism."[39] After describing the company's "extremely inadequate" sanitary provisions, he concluded that, "I could not help having the utmost sympathy with everyone who had to work yet alone eat and sleep under these conditions."[40] U.S. officials agreed, describing the "shanty towns" as "sprawling eyesores" of miserable "hovels."[41] In 1949, the Political Resident began losing his patience with Bapco, reporting that "their chief concern is to make as much money as possible for their shareholders," and that only Belgrave's iron fist and liberal use of deportation was preventing an explosion.[42] However, government officials generally sympathized with their fellow countrymen. In a representative comment, Rupert Hay, a former Political Resident, acknowledged that "there is a certain amount of racial segregation," but, in the same sentence, claimed that "there is nothing in the nature of a color bar." The problem, he explained, was that "closer contact might well lead to incidents and the embitterment of racial relations."[43] Such sentiments ensured that state officials did little to pressure the companies to change their ways.

The racism saturating Anglo-American oil firms has been documented by a new generation of oil historians who have thoroughly demolished earlier, uncritical accounts informed by the impressive public relations apparatus of the oil industry.[44] But what still needs to be centered in analyses of corporate racism, and what underlines its significance, is the fact that racial segregation was a deliberate—and critical—mechanism that allowed oil firms to control the production process. Early labor organizers in the oil industry repeatedly expressed frustration that their strikes were incapable of halting the production process.[45] This was by design.[46] State and corporate documents confirm that KOC, like every other oil company in the Persian Gulf, utilized a strategy that it referred to as its "strike plan." The company systematically hired enough white employees to ensure that if all of its non-white workers walked off the job, "basic operations can continue."[47] The strategic deployment of segregation was, alongside arbitrary deportation, standard corporate practice across the Persian Gulf, dating back as early as 1922.[48] White workers took the place of their non-white counterparts during strikes in Dhahran in 1953, in both Bahrain and Basra in 1954, and in Qatar in 1959.[49] When Indian and Pakistani workers struck at KOC in 1948, the company was able to shrug off the action because "much of the work ordinarily handled by Indian artizans was done by Senior Staff"—the standard euphemism for white personnel.[50] The threat of the "strike plan" hung over every labor action in the oilfields until the 1970s, by which time, as will be seen, popular and worker pressure had forced the employment of more locally hired workers.[51]

Imperial authorities not only knew of the strike plans, but encouraged and helped coordinate them.[52] While some British officials worried that the negative publicity generated by segregation outweighed its usefulness, many acknowledged that the plans could serve imperial interests "in the event of various possible contingencies affecting the supply of oil from or through Middle Eastern countries."[53] In 1960, when KOC considered abandoning the strategy in the face of popular criticism, they asked imperial authorities for their input.[54] The Political Resident and Political Agent eventually agreed that while the company should "give way a little" to avoid negative press, they thought the plan should continue.[55] U.S. Consular officials also knew of, and supported, the strike plans.[56] Indeed, in the business press, the strategic deployment of segregation was an open secret.[57]

White supremacy was also a pillar of corporate policing. In 1940, Bapco hired a group of British ex-servicemen, whom the Political Agent then appointed as "special Police officers."[58] In a moment of candor, officials described the men as "White guards," while the Political Agent specified that "the Sergeant selected should be of pure European parentage."[59] In 1953, the head of the KOC security department reported that "if we ever had a situation of unrest and damage to our vital installations was an immediate threat," he would "not hesitate" to replace his usual guards with "Europeans."[60] This in fact happened in 1956, during the Suez Crisis, when "Europeans" and "Westerners" were strategically deployed to replace "Arab and Eastern employees," "Moslems," and "Indians" across KOC facilities. The company even distributed fifty rifles and two machine guns to "Western employees" in case state security forces would "at any time prove unreliable," thus creating an exclusively white, private militia to defend its prerogatives.[61]

The strike plan shaped all corporate policies, but perhaps the most significant was hiring. The corporate determination to maintain a large white workforce stalled the employment, training, and promotion of Arab and Kuwaiti workers well into the 1960s.[62] Even after completing months-long training courses, they could only ever become "assistant" electricians or carpenters under white supervision.[63] This disincentivized locally hired workers from entering the oil industry. This was not merely a KOC policy; in Bahrain, Belgrave acknowledged that training programs were hampered by the oil company's discriminatory practices, as "there is nothing to suggest that a youth who starts his career in a workshop will ever rise to a position of importance."[64] Aware that their careers would inevitably plateau in low-level positions, young people logically chose to work elsewhere. Compounding official policies of segregation was the racism of individual managers. Corporate officials who believed that Kuwaitis "have little sense of responsibility" were reluctant to promote them to management positions.[65] In 1958, KOC found that Kuwaiti workers were promoted less often than non-Kuwaitis in all but one department.[66] As one imperial official noted, on the rare occasions that Kuwaitis did reach higher-level posts, they were kept away from essential aspects of oil production—where they could prove dangerous in case of a strike—and instead "seem to find their way ineluctably into the Public Relations Department and the Display Centre," where they were literally put on display as the token Kuwaiti face of a segregated company.[67]

THE RADICAL FIFTIES

Unsurprisingly, systemic racism was not conducive to harmonious labor relations. Rather, it would contribute to a rising tide of labor activism that swept the oilfields of the Persian Gulf. While the region has a long history of labor organizing, it was in the 1950s that the rise of mass politics, anticolonial nationalism, and the press transformed worker activism from localized and sporadic actions into events with broader political resonance.

In the Persian Gulf, labor activism was neither a foreign import nor a strategy restricted to the modern industrial workforce. Denial of work had long been a means by which those who earned a living from their labor could defend their rights and privileges, while organization along the lines of a craft, guild, or industry was a time-honored custom.[68] While imperial authorities denigrated the workforce, especially migratory pearl divers, as "ruffians and semi savages," the British also understood their potential power.[69] With the arrival of Anglo-American employers in the Persian Gulf, differing expectations—and blatant racism—generated new disputes with local workers. In 1902, workers building a missionary hospital in Bahrain shut down construction.[70] The first recorded oil-related work stoppage in Kuwait occurred as early as the 1920s, when workers drilling exploratory wells for a British engineer walked off the job.[71]

However, it is remarkable how rarely these early actions, localized and spontaneous as they were, are cited as significant events in the historiography of Gulf labor movements. Most participants and chroniclers date the movement's origins from the moment when workers began connecting their workplace struggles to broader political questions in the 1930s, 1940s, or 1950s.[72] In both Kuwait and Bahrain, the connection between nationalist and labor movements dates back to the aforementioned Majlis Movement of 1938 to 1939.[73] In 1937, Kuwaiti taxi drivers struck in response to unilateral government decision that significantly cut into their wages.[74] Armed men ended the action by arresting and beating its leaders. But the strike also demonstrated the role of non-elites in the political moment of 1938: One of the arrested drivers was Mohammad al-Barrack, a prominent anticolonial activist.[75] In Bahrain, Bapco workers went on strike in 1939 after state authorities arrested Ahmad al-Shirawi, a Bapco employee, and Saʿad Shamlan, a prominent Arab nationalist lawyer with close ties to the workers.[76] The future St. Helena deportee Abdul Rahman al-Bakir, then working for Bapco, helped to organize the strike, with assistance from the political and literary clubs of Manama.[77] Critically, the strike drew on nationalist ideas to make workplace demands, criticizing the predominance of Indian workers in skilled jobs and the relatively low wages paid to Arab workers.[78] But as in Kuwait, the strike was crushed by the combined force of imperial, corporate, and Bahraini authorities, who deported its most prominent leaders.[79] Rejecting the demand for collective representation for the redress of grievances, the company utilized Shaikh Ali Al Khalifa to serve as a go-between with its labor force, thus reinforcing monarchical authority through corporate practice.[80]

Rampant inflation during World War II generated another regional wave of labor activism. In December 1943, about six hundred Arab Bapco workers went on strike, demanding equality with Indian "artisan" workers, protection from arbitrary discipline, improved housing, and higher wages.[81] Even the British Political Resident acknowledged that "Bahrain Petroleum Company and Bahrain Government have only got themselves to thank for this trouble as they have both of them been underpaying Arab employees for some time past"—though when push came to shove, he backed the company and deported the leaders of the strike.[82] The following year, anonymous posters and letters began cropping up across Bahrain, calling for higher pay, workman's compensation, and benefits equal to those of Indian "artisan" workers, while in 1945, both butchers and municipal workers walked off the job to demand wage increases.[83] In Saudi Arabia, Indian workers alarmed corporate authorities not only by going on strike, but by attempting to convince their Arab colleagues to join them.[84] The British quickly deported the instigators, and the strike collapsed.[85] Even in Muscat, under the unsparing eye of a repressive Sultan, employees of the customs department struck for higher pay in 1944.[86]

A new strike wave at the end of the war far surpassed the scale of earlier actions. In 1945, Aramco workers conducted a major labor stoppage, winning the support of Saudi authorities and forcing the company to make a series of concessions.[87] In July of 1946, workers of the Iraq Petroleum Company in Kirkuk went on strike and, with the support of the Iraqi Communist Party, forced their employer to dramatically improve worker housing in an action that reconfigured the politics of the Iraqi oilfields.[88] Just days later, Tudeh, the Iranian Communist party, helped organize a stunningly successful strike in the Iranian oil industry, winning the eight-hour day, overtime pay, higher wages, and the first comprehensive labor law in the region.[89] Less spectacular but still significant actions took place in the smaller states of the Gulf. Qatari workers struck over inedible food and low wages, forcing the company to dramatically improve working conditions, while Kuwaiti workers launched the first attempt to form a union in the Kuwait Oil Company.[90] Particularly unsettling to corporate and imperial authorities was the regional nature of these labor actions. News of one successful strike inspired workers elsewhere, and ideas and expectations ricocheted across the Gulf along with newspapers and workers, knitting together an integrated labor market and leading to a general rise in wages.[91]

The rise of mass politics, the press, and Arab nationalism in the 1950s transformed labor activism, and particularly oil labor activism, into a potent political force. The year 1952 proved especially pivotal. The Free Officers coup in Egypt elevated Gamal Abdel Nasser into an international symbol and transformed Arab nationalism into the most widely popular political ideology in the Gulf. Dr. Ahmad al-Khatib graduated from medical school in Beirut and opened the first cell of the Arab Nationalist Movement (ANM) in Kuwait.[92] After his expulsion from Qatar, Abdul Rahman al-Bakir returned to Bahrain and helped form the Higher Executive Committee, which challenged imperial and autocratic rule from 1954 to 1956.[93] While most of the first oil workers, hired straight from pearling ships or the desert, had not yet been exposed to Arab nationalism, by the mid-1950s, many began to see themselves as members of a broader working class or Arab nation, imbuing their actions with greater significance and generating new solidarities.[94] Interviewed years later, the prominent oil worker and trade unionist Daifullah Falah Sultan described the early Arab nationalists as the intellectuals (*muthaqafiin*) of the movement.[95] The rising tide of Arab nationalism was further buoyed by the new mass education system. As Talal al-Rashoud has noted, many teachers were Egyptian or Palestinian and saw schools as a means of forming a modern and politically "conscious (*wa'i*)" generation.[96] Kuwaiti students established their own newspapers, inculcating nationalist and pan-Arab ideas.[97] The popularity of Arab nationalism became apparent in 1956, when Britain, France, and Israel attacked Egypt in retaliation for the nationalization of the Suez Canal. The Gulf exploded in protest, much of it directed against the oil companies.[98]

Domestic pressure gained added force from its potential to connect with new pan-Arabist labor movements. Until the mid-1950s, oil companies had largely managed to fend off pressure from non-communist international labor organizations either by persuading imperial officials to deny them visas, or by framing themselves as exemplary modern corporations. Shepherded through company operations on stage-managed tours, even the few U.S. labor leaders who visited the Gulf ignored systematic segregation and affirmed corporate claims that their exemplary practices rendered labor unions unnecessary.[99] But the International Confederation of Arab Trade Unions (ICATU), founded in 1956, emerged as a counterweight to the rabidly anticommunist International Confederation of Free Trade Unions (ICFTU). Immediately after its founding, the ICATU began building a presence in the Gulf. Oil companies were particularly concerned that the union explicitly called for the hiring of more Arab workers in the petroleum industry, which directly threatened their strike plans.[100] Imperial authorities viewed the ICATU primarily as a tool of Gamal Abdel Nasser, and therefore worked with the oil companies to thwart its organizing efforts.[101]

In 1956, for instance, KOC worked with British officials to deny a visa to Anwar Salama, an oil worker and one of the most prominent trade unionists in Egypt, on the grounds that he could undermine "British and Western oil interests in the Middle East."[102] Instead, they invited the ICFTU for an official visit on the theory that, if unionization were inevitable, it could at least take place under the auspices of an anticommunist federation. The invitation was remarkably brazen, given that when an ICFTU official had planned to visit the Gulf only one year earlier, there had been "difficulties" with his visa that had forced him to cancel his trip.[103] The Foreign Office reported that the ICFTU were "touchy about being 'used,'" now that "the I.C.F.T.U. is regarded as the lesser of two evils and could perhaps be useful to British diplomacy."[104] In the end, the ICFTU consented to be "used" and the trip went ahead—but their belated efforts proved utterly incapable of stemming the tide of Arab nationalism.

It was also in the 1950s that labor organizing in the Gulf began to intersect with the broader oil revolution. After World War II, resource nationalism gained momentum alongside decolonization, drawing inspiration from the successful nationalization of Mexican oil in 1938.[105] Rising criticism of the concession regime, coupled with corporate fears of nationalization, led to the global adoption of a new "fifty-fifty" principle first negotiated by OPEC cofounder Juan Pablo Pérez Alfonzo in Venezuela in 1948, which evenly divided profits between oil companies and producing countries.[106] Resource nationalism began the 1950s with a setback in Iran. In 1951, the anticolonial prime minister Mohammad Mosaddegh nationalized the oil industry. In response, the oil majors set aside their differences to blackball Iranian oil, making it impossible to ship or sell. Their efforts devastated the Iranian economy and undermined Mosaddegh, who was subsequently toppled in a coup orchestrated by the CIA and MI6.[107] In the years to come, the story of Mosaddegh, in the words of former OPEC head Francisco Parra, "threatened anyone who got too far out of line."[108]

But despite this setback for resource nationalism, avoiding "another Abadan"—the specter of nationalization—became an ever-present concern for the oil companies.[109] While they justified the concessionary system by arguing that they alone possessed the expertise required to produce oil, those claims were spurious and Iranian nationalization proved it. Iranian oil workers, who benefited from the most comprehensive training program in the region thanks to nationalist pressure on the oil company, proved perfectly capable of running the industry without British assistance.[110] After Iranian nationalization, imperial officials began to pressure the oil companies to institute reforms in order to placate popular opinion, and oil companies in both Kuwait and Qatar raised the wages of their local workers.[111] The Kuwait Oil Company (KOC) was half-owned by British Petroleum and regularly shuffled personnel between Kuwait and Abadan, and so was particularly rattled.[112] What made Iranian nationalization an existential crisis for Britain was not just oil, but currency. Anglo-Iranian had been Britain's single largest source of foreign exchange because its oil was sold in Pounds Sterling. After nationalization, British Petroleum (BP), which was half-owned by the British government, ramped up oil production at KOC, which also priced its oil in Sterling. Henceforth, Kuwait played a central role in propping up not just British Petroleum, but the tottering British Pound, the British economy, and even the centuries-long position of London as a financial entrepôt.[113]

Out of this context emerged a new wave of worker activism, centered in the oilfields of the Gulf, that was unprecedented in both its scale and radicalism. The protests that rocked Aramco in 1953 invigorated supporters of reform. The strike lasted for ten days, with workers condemning corporate segregation and calling for the recognition of a trade union. While the strike was crushed by the combined power of the company and the state—Aramco implemented its strike plan while the Saudi government sent in troops—workers also won some concessions, along with the sympathy of the Arab world.[114] Aramco was a common point of comparison for officials and workers, so the strikes took on a regional significance.[115] Kuwaiti newspapers covered Aramco labor struggles throughout the decade.[116] *Sada al-Iman*, for instance, condemned the company for its "ugly racism" in privileging "foreigners" over "citizen-workers," a practice, the paper pointedly noted, that was shared by "all of the monopolistic companies."[117] In Bahrain, newspapers allied with anticolonial nationalists reprinted the demands of Aramco workers and covered the strikes and negotiations in detail.[118]

Bahrain would become the center of one of the decade's first and most notable anticolonial labor struggles. Bahraini nationalists, including Abdul Rahman al-Bakir, had long viewed organized labor as a potentially powerful political base.[119] When taxi drivers in Bahrain struck in response to a new government regulation in September 1954, anticolonial activists quickly transformed the struggle into a nationwide campaign.[120] What emerged was *al-Ha'ya*, a mass movement organized by a body that came to be called the Higher Executive Committee (HEC).[121] Self-consciously cross-sectarian, it called for institutions of representative government, the legalization of trade unions, and the passage of a reformed criminal code and comprehensive labor law.[122] To force the issue, the HEC organized a general strike. From December 4 through 10, 1954, Bahrain came to a virtual standstill.[123] Imperial authorities were worried, and some even concluded that the increasingly imperious Advisor Charles Belgrave was losing control.[124] What concerned the authorities most was the HEC's call for a single, unified union including all of the workers of Bahrain.[125] While the British would eventually put down the HEC with armed force, it had an enduring impact, demonstrating the potential power of mass politics across the Persian Gulf.[126]

While less publicized than the struggles in Bahrain, other Gulf states experienced radical worker protests in the 1950s. In 1950, oil workers in Abu Dhabi struck for higher wages, reportedly because an Abu Dhabi man who had worked for the Kuwait Oil Company had returned home and reported on the better pay rates in Kuwait.[127] In the same year, a "mutiny"—really a labor dispute over "low pay and poor conditions of service"—led to the firing of ninety members of the Muscat Infantry.[128] In 1956, workers on the Royal Air Force base in Sharjah halted work to demand higher wages.[129] In Qatar, workers struck on a near-annual basis, calling for the hiring and promotion of Qataris and an end to racial discrimination.[130] As Jill Crystal has argued, these strikes forced the nascent Qatari state, along with imperial authorities and the oil company, to establish a system of labor relations and define Qatari nationality.[131] Many of the strikes of the 1950s were launched to bring wages in Qatar up to regional standards.[132] In 1958, for instance, Qatari workers went on strike when they learned from an Iraqi driller that the parent company of the Qatar Petroleum Company, the Iraq Petroleum Company, paid higher wages in Kirkuk than in Qatar.[133] The strike only ended when the company promised to bring the Qatari wage scales into line with those in Iraq.[134] Thus oil workers traveling across the Gulf brought rising expectations with them, connecting both a regional labor market and a rising tide of protest.

The most common, if least dramatic, worker strategy of resistance was migration itself. Workers voted with their feet by traveling in search of better-paid work. Throughout the 1950s, oil companies were forced to raise wages in response to their counterparts in other parts of the Gulf, underlining the regional nature of the labor market and the power of workers to seek better conditions by traveling somewhere else.[135] In 1953, imperial authorities were speaking of a "Persian Gulf labour market" experiencing an "upward movement" of wages.[136] Interviews with Kuwaiti labor organizers suggest that while there were not necessarily direct lines of communication with counterparts elsewhere, workers constantly compared their conditions with those prevalent in other parts of the region.[137] Indeed, by 1960, KOC had resigned itself to matching whatever pay raises or benefit schemes were implemented by Aramco.[138] Thus by playing companies off each other, voting with their feet, and repeatedly going on strike, workers slowly won an ever-greater share of the region's wealth. They also forged new and powerful arguments that combined labor solidarity and anticolonial nationalism. These would prove profoundly influential in Kuwait, where workers and their allies built a transformative coalition.

LABOR & NATIONALISM IN KUWAIT

The first efforts to institutionalize trade unions in Kuwait emerged at this pivotal moment. According to Mohammad Massud al-ʿAjmi, author of the only extant history of the Kuwaiti labor movement, the first unionization attempt in Kuwait took place at the tail end of the 1946 strike wave, though it failed due to fears of harsh reprisals.[139] Indeed, imperial and corporate authorities were closely monitoring any potential organizing efforts at KOC.[140] Nevertheless, on November 15, 1949, KOC witnessed its first major strike of Arab workers. The stoppage was impromptu and unorganized, triggered by a delay in the payment of wages. But after getting the company's attention, the workers, nearly all of whom were Arab or Kuwaiti, took the opportunity to air a range of other grievances—notably the unequal treatment meted out to Arab, South Asian, and white workers. They were helped by the fact that "sympathisers from the Labour Camp" rallied to join the strikers.[141] This challenge, however, faced significant obstacles. In the years before the rise of Arab nationalism, unions were anathema to most workers.[142] According to Hussein Saqr, not only did most Kuwaitis know little about trade unions, but many saw labor organizing as politically subversive, disloyal, or dangerous.[143]

By framing the strike as an attack not just on themselves, but against the Kuwaiti state, the oil company quickly divided the workers and won the support of the authorities. Abdullah Mulla Saleh, the Ruler's secretary and official representative, was "invited to come in and deal with" the situation.[144] He and a number of high-ranking ruling family members obligingly visited the worksite and berated the workers, while Shaikh Abdullah Mubarak, the notorious chief of the Public Security Department, asked for the names of all of the men on strike "so that he could deal with them himself."[145] Faced with the combined power of the state and the corporation, the strike collapsed without achieving any of its objectives.[146]

But the transformations of the 1950s turned the political associations of trade unionism from a liability into an asset and provided examples of successful organizing campaigns. A renewed attempt to unionize took place in 1951, when a group of workers created a "workers' association"—notably, not a union—with the goal of encouraging "worker cooperation" and founding a cooperative store.[147] Though the idea of forming a union was abandoned, the effort demonstrated the usefulness of collective action.[148] Most historians of, and figures in, the Kuwaiti labor movement cite the KOC transportation workers strike of February 20 to 22, 1952, as a turning point.[149] The action seems to have been better prepared than its predecessors. Before resorting to a strike, the workers elected a committee of five representatives to negotiate with both government and company representatives for a month. The delegation even met personally with the Ruler, Abdullah al-Salem. KOC was intransigent. A company representative told the workers not to worry because their housing demands were scheduled to be resolved by the company's development plan in about eight years—a response that did nothing to allay worker frustration. The strike was total, as port workers and other Kuwaiti employees of the oil company joined the striking drivers.[150] Many of those involved were former pearl divers, sailors, or Bedouin. Notably, its participants were all self-described Kuwaitis. Khalid al-Rumi later recollected that in the 1940s and early 1950s, "Every strike action was only of Kuwaitis on their own, as the other workers were segregated from them to a significant extent."[151] Two of its most prominent leaders, ʿAshur ʿAisi and Fahad ʿAtia al-Khashti, grew up together in the neighborhood of Dahla, inside the walls of the old city.[152] The strike was organized by KOC drivers frustrated by the "abuse and oppression" experienced by Kuwaitis, and the privileges enjoyed by "foreign workers," meaning white "senior staff" and Indian and Pakistani "artisan" workers.[153] As these demands demonstrate, the strikers utilized an argument that would become their most effective weapon: deploying nationalist discourse to attack corporate racism.

As in 1949, Kuwaiti authorities swiftly crushed the strike. Shaikh Jabir al-Ahmad framed it as an attack on national security and warned that his Public Security Department would bring the "trouble-makers" to "trial and retribution." A loyal worker should resolve "not to listen to sedition-mongers, but to stick to his job and come forward and inform us of those who stir up sedition or are suspected of doing so."[154] He was as good as his word. When the workers ignored the warning and struck anyway, their leaders were fired, arrested, and imprisoned.[155] A group of workers tried to reconstitute their organization under the Islamic Guidance Society, a social and welfare organization that, as the last remaining authorized club in Kuwait, served as an umbrella organization for Kuwaiti activists. But security forces quashed an attempt by ʿAshur ʿAisi to establish a more permanent organization, and ʿAisi himself was arrested.[156]

Despite this setback, most workers remember the strike as a moral victory that transformed public perceptions of organized labor. Many Kuwaitis saw the strikers' demands as more than reasonable and began connecting their plight with the increasingly popular nationalist cause. The workers also won important concessions, earning two weeks of annual leave and one day off a week.[157] In fact, the strike had more of an impact than was understood at the time. Under the combined pressure of the Iranian oil nationalization crisis and the KOC strike—which overlapped—the oil company undertook a reappraisal of its approach to its Arab and Kuwaiti workers.[158]

The KOC strike proved to be the start of an unprecedented period of labor unrest. In April of 1952, a group of Pakistani workers in the employ of the state threatened to go on strike.[159] While the walkout failed to materialize, it led state officials to begin formalizing labor policy, as discussed in the following chapter.[160] In the summer of 1953, a series of strikes rippled through government departments. Workers, Kuwaiti and non-Kuwaiti, complained that wages and hours were set arbitrarily and demanded a more just compensation scheme.[161] In June, Kuwaiti clerks at the National Bank of Kuwait threatened to go on strike over a policy of hiring workers abroad rather than training Kuwaitis.[162] By 1955, the Kuwaiti Department of Social and Labor Affairs was reporting that it had been involved in thirteen labor disputes, ten of which concerned government departments.[163] News of the strikes even reached U.S. Secretary of State John Foster Dulles, who worried that "disruptive political movements . . . are beginning to operate in Kuwait."[164] The strike wave coincided with a renewed drive for unionization. In 1954, a group of drivers affiliated with the National Committee of Clubs and the Arab Nationalist Movement met to consider the formation of a union. Among them was Hussein al-Youha, an early and active member of the Arab Nationalist Movement who would found the Municipal Workers Union in 1964. While they received the encouragement of Dr. Ahmad al-Khatib, they decided to suspend their unionization drive after a majority of drivers voted against it.[165] Government employees also tried to unionize in the mid-fifties.[166] Though these efforts failed to create durable institutions, unionization was clearly gaining in popularity.

Political and labor activism exploded during the Suez Crisis of 1956. Kuwait witnessed mass demonstrations, marches, and one of the largest labor actions in Kuwaiti history. During the crisis, oil company officials obtained a copy of a pamphlet calling for "a general and full strike" against "the Imperialists and traitors," and preemptively shut down all nonessential operations.[167] Unlike in other parts of the Gulf, the strike was nonviolent, and workers returned to their posts the following day. But combined with mass marches and student demonstrations, it underlined the new power of Arab nationalism and labor. Moreover, pressure continued by other means. On the night of December 10, ten explosions rocked KOC facilities, igniting Well No. 5.[168] An estimated 9,500 barrels of oil gushed into the sea, while smoke and flames could be seen from miles away.[169] While the Kuwaiti government tried to keep the news quiet, the explosions were covered around the world.[170] The U.S. Consulate worried that the attackers had inside help.[171] The oil company immediately reevaluated its security procedures, doubling the budget of the Security Department and installing state-of-the-art "Autocall" motion sensors to detect possible saboteurs.[172] It also issued new passes incorporating not just photographs, but the thumbprints of "local employees."[173] However, given that oil facilities across the wider Middle East were damaged by sabotage operations encouraged by the ICATU, it appeared that security would never solve the problem.[174] The specter of sabotage would hang over oil company operations for decades.[175]

Perhaps the most significant tailwind for the labor movement was the support it received in the press.[176] Once again, Bahrain served as a model, as nascent political clubs and an increasingly active press took up the cause of workers' rights. Starting in the late 1940s, the *Voice of Bahrain* launched what its editor Abdul Rahman al-Bakir later described as a "war" against the "monopolistic" Anglo-American oil firms in the Gulf, particularly Aramco and Bapco.[177] In addition to supporting workers' rights and Arab nationalism, the *Voice of Bahrain* took a broadly reformist and pro-democratic line that transformed it into the mouthpiece of a popular movement.[178] The Kuwaiti press followed its example. The Arab nationalist *al-Iman* introduced trade unionism to a broader public, publishing, for instance, glowing articles on the Tunisian labor movement and its role in the nationalist and anticolonial struggle.[179] Closer to home, it called on the oil company to release more detailed statistics about production and wages.[180] Following its closure, the cause of labor was taken up by *Sada al-Iman*, which began publication in the mid-1950s under the editorship of Dr. al-Khatib. *Sada al-Iman* self-consciously sought to play a "pioneering" role in "promoting the consciousness of our workers," calling on workers to consider the publication as "their official newspaper" in their campaign for "freedom, dignity, independence, and social justice."[181] It actualized this intention by publishing a regular "Workers' Column" to serve as "a voice for our workers."[182] In issue after issue, the paper demanded the legalization of trade unions and the formation of a general labor federation.[183] It argued that unions were important not just for workers, but for all of society. Free and fair union elections could provide a basis for democratic rule.[184] By participating in the rational and cooperative formation of industrial policy, unions could assist in the forging of a modern state and the maintenance of "security and order."[185] They could also help in the fight against inequality. Describing poverty as a political choice, rather than an economic inevitability, the paper argued unionization would help build a social safety net to look after the basic needs of all Kuwaitis.[186] Finally, it framed workers and unions as the vanguard of struggles for Arab unity and freedom, as nationalist consciousness was linked with worker consciousness.[187] These arguments would remain influential in Kuwaiti political discourse for decades.

In addition to serving as the most vocal supporter of unionization, the paper provided regular coverage of working-class issues. It published demands from workers across Kuwait to bring their concerns to the attention of both state authorities and the wider public.[188] In 1955, a series spanning several weeks reprinted worker reports of exploitive conditions in the construction industry and called on the authorities to improve conditions.[189] It also covered pan-Arab labor conferences and regional labor issues.[190] All of these articles unapologetically articulated a message of class consciousness. The oppression of "capitalists" could only be successfully overcome, the paper argued, with collective action led by workers.[191] *Sada al-Iman* was soon followed later in the decade by a wave of publications that openly championed workers' rights, notably *al-Fajr* (The Dawn), published by the Kuwait Graduates' Club, and *al-Sha'b* (The People).[192] *Al-Sha'b* relayed so many worker complaints that the head of the KOC Employee Affairs Department asked for, and received, space to publish a rebuttal of its accusations.[193] Thus, through the Arab nationalist press, the language of class began to permeate the Kuwaiti political discourse.

Just as significantly, in their critiques of the oil companies, Kuwaiti papers began building the arguments for resource nationalism and desegregation that would dominate Kuwaiti politics for two decades.[194] The most important were Arabization and Kuwaitization—the hiring of more Arab and Kuwaiti workers.[195] In a representative piece, *al-Sha'b* reported that "from time to time, the company declares that it gives priority in employment to Kuwaitis and Arabs, but when a Kuwaiti or Arab applies for a job, his application is invariably refused."[196] *Al-Fajr* added to the chorus, noting that virtually no "senior staff" were Kuwaiti: "Aren't there competent persons among the Arabs to fill these posts?"[197] The most strident criticism of all was directed at racial segregation. *Al-Sha'b* republished letters from workers who recounted instances of racist treatment and condemned policies designed to reinforce hierarchies based on race.[198] One piece argued that with its racial segregation, intrusive surveillance, and disregard for labor law, the company was "living with a nineteenth-century mentality in an age of satellites and ballistic missiles."[199]

As the decade progressed, calls for desegregation were increasingly paired with demands for sovereign control of oil exploitation. Even the moderate *al-Ra'id* argued that Kuwait should seize "its rights" by taking greater control over the exploitation of oil.[200] *Sada al-Iman* emerged as the most forceful advocate of resource nationalism, coupling descriptions of anti-Arab and anti-Kuwaiti discrimination in the company with calls for Kuwaiti control over the production and sale of oil.[201] Its very first issue criticized the ability of a foreign corporation to control, and profit from, natural resources that rightfully belonged to the people of Kuwait.[202] Another piece, revealingly entitled "The Oil Company Ignores Government Decisions," criticized the company for acting like a state within a state—an increasingly popular critique that connected segregation to sovereignty.[203] The paper explicitly linked the "oppression and injustice" faced by Kuwaiti oil company workers to the imperialistic nature of the oil company.[204] By the end of the decade, the press reached a broad consensus that oil companies needed to hire, train, and promote more citizens, or at least more Arabs, and that this would be the first step toward Kuwait gaining control over its natural resources.

The argument that multinational oil firms inherently infringed on Kuwait's sovereign rights logically morphed into calls for sovereign control over oil. Gamal Abdel Nasser's seizure of the Suez Canal introduced the concept of nationalization to the broader public.[205] In January of 1958, *al-Sha'b* turned a news report on a Japanese bid for an oil concession into a call for the nationalization of Kuwaiti oil.[206] Noting that the pledged capital of the company, £3.5 million, was less than the assets held by the Kuwaiti government, and that Kuwait was already training a new generation of technical specialists, the paper argued that there was no reason why Kuwait should continue to grant concessions. Oil concessions, it argued, were simply a modern form of "economic colonialism." It argued that a Department of Industry should be established and tasked with overseeing local oil production, including the construction of a new refinery that could serve as the basis of a new petrochemical industry.[207] The timing and content of the article make clear that popular feeling surrounding oil nationalization was running ahead of elite thinking. A month after the article was published, Abdullah Tariki, the future OPEC architect, visited Kuwait to persuade the Ruler to grant an offshore concession to the Japanese firm.[208] The paper, in other words, was taking a harder line than one of the architects of OPEC.

Perhaps most remarkably, the Kuwaiti press framed Kuwait as a colonized nation fighting for its independence, part of a rising tide of self-determination. Anticolonial movements, and particularly the war in Algeria, became popular topics of coverage. *Al-Sha'b* explicitly connected imperialism and racial justice, for instance, linking U.S. oil firms to the backlash against the desegregation of Little Rock High School.[209] In June of 1958, *al-Sha'b* interviewed Kwame Nkrumah, first prime minister of independent Ghana, about his accomplishments in the first year of independence. Nkrumah specifically discusses his wish to liberate the country from dependence on a single export commodity, in this case, cocoa, drawing an implied parallel between Ghana and the oil-exporting countries.[210] The idea of "sovereign rights" over natural resources, the concept enshrined in the final communiqué of the Bandung Conference, would have been familiar to readers of the Kuwaiti press well before the groundbreaking Arab Petroleum Congress of 1959.[211]

Sustained press attacks and strikes slowly began to reshape the policies of the Kuwaiti state. In the immediate aftermath of articles in *al-Fajr* and *al-Sha'b*, Shaikh Jabir al-Ahmad sent a letter to the manager of KOC accusing the company "Intelligence Office" of spying on employees and creating "a spirit of distrust and hatred." He also called on the company to appoint Kuwaitis "or Arabs if Kuwaitis cannot be found," to raise employee standards of living, and to "find a solution to the housing crisis."[212] KOC responded not by changing its policies, but by trying to plug the leaks.[213] It initiated a series of security measures, even cutting down on the amount of written material that "could be turned against them if it got into the wrong hands."[214] KOC concerns were amplified by the accuracy of the press reports.[215] State authorities also began to adopt the position that the company needed to take more active measures to Arabize and Kuwaitize the workforce.[216] The longstanding relationship between the state and the oil company was coming under unprecedented strain.

KOC struggled to respond to press attacks. Its first strategy to deflect criticism was therefore to suppress the press itself. Throughout the late 1950s, KOC representatives pressured Kuwaiti officials to impose strict censorship, and on at least one occasion even threatened to sue a paper for libel.[217] Imperial authorities also supported the shuttering of critical papers.[218] After a series of temporary suspensions, *Sada al-Iman*, *al-Sha'b*, and *al-Fajr* had all been forcibly closed by the end of 1959. At the same time, KOC tried to improve its image. It founded its own publication to generate good publicity, though the effort somewhat backfired when its first editor, Khalid Khalaf, quit to edit *al-Sha'b*.[219] To expand its influence beyond its desert compound at Ahmadi, it opened a "town office" to serve as a conduit between the city of Kuwait and the oil company.[220] Like Aramco, KOC also paid substantial sums of money to various newspapers across the Arabic-speaking world in order to generate positive coverage.[221] Perhaps the most remarkable KOC public relations effort also seems to have been inspired by Aramco, which in 1955 had hired the prominent American writer Wallace Stegner to write a book about its operations in the hope of generating positive publicity.[222] KOC, half-owned by BP, took a more British approach. In 1960, it hired Ian Fleming—the creator of James Bond—to write a positive review of its operations. Fleming visited Kuwait for two weeks at the company's expense and drafted a manuscript entitled "Kuwait: State of Excitement." However, Fleming reported that "The Sheikhs" objected to "the passages referring to the adventurous past of the country which now wishes to be 'civilised' in every respect."[223] It was never published. Its existence, however, testifies to the lengths to which the Kuwait Oil Company was willing to go to avoid desegregating its operations.

EXCLUSIONS

While the growing alliance between labor and anticolonial nationalism reshaped regional politics in the 1950s, it could also be a double-edged sword. As Nelida Fuccaro has noted, "the nationalist and anti-imperialist lore which surrounds the turbulent popular politics of 1954–6 has tended to underplay the shortcomings of Arabism and Pan-Arabism as ideologies of popular mobilization" capable of appealing to a "cosmopolitan and communitarian tradition."[224] The result was that, for the time being, non-Arab workers, especially from Iran, India, and Pakistan, found themselves excluded not just from organizing efforts, but from the imagined history of the labor movement. This was most evident during two of the largest early strikes in Kuwait led by Indian and Pakistani workers, who faced the same racial segregation, and many of the same daily humiliations, as their Arab colleagues.[225] In 1948, an effort to form an "Artisan Welfare Society" led to the summary deportation of its leaders and triggered a strike that in turn led to yet another mass deportation.[226] Though Indian and Pakistani workers would increasingly turn to their newly independent states for help, these states would prove incapable of protecting the rights of their citizens.[227] Five years later, on the morning of December 17, 1953, the strike of an estimated nine hundred Indian and Pakistani workers housed at Jewan Camp only underlined this point.[228] Once again, the strike ended with deportation, this time of thirty-nine workers.

But it also rattled both state and imperial authorities, and the workers won some of their most pressing demands, including the provision of accessible medical care. Indeed, the strike had a greater impact than the workers realized at the time. It successfully pressured the Kuwaiti government to raise the wages of its noncitizen employees, though the decision was delayed "because the Government did not wish it to appear that the rise had been extorted by the strike."[229] It also led to the regulations, discussed in the next chapter, that would become the basis for Kuwaiti labor law.

But despite their size and significance, neither strike is featured in any of the memoirs or retrospective histories of the Kuwaiti labor movement, which frame labor protest as part of the story of Arab nationalism or Kuwaiti statebuilding and thus excise non-Arab workers from its core narrative. South Asian workers, with only a handful of exceptions, received limited outside support, or even attention, when they went out on strike in the 1940s and 1950s.[230] Only *al-Iman* covered the second strike, and its report consisted of a single sentence noting an action of "Indian and Pakistani workers"—an attitude strikingly different from its blanket coverage of Arab labor issues.[231] Of course, company officials, with the assistance of both imperial and Kuwaiti authorities, had tried to drive such a wedge between workers of various nationalities, segregating them in different camps and job classifications.[232] Just as important was the threat of deportation.[233] Qabalan ʿAjnan al-ʿAzimi, for instance, remembered that because they faced the "fate of expulsion" if they spoke out, noncitizen workers had "no role" in labor organizing with Kuwaitis.[234] Efforts to organize noncitizen workers placed them at disproportionate risk. Corporate strategies of divide-and-rule thus proved effective through the 1950s. But as will be seen, their success would not last.

CONCLUSION

By the end of the 1950s, labor and Arab nationalism had cemented a powerful alliance. With their attacks on segregated Anglo-American oil firms and their championing of anticolonial causes around the globe, they had built an enormous popular following and challenged the underpinnings of the concessionary system. But their reach had clear limits. While most Arab nationalists understood their fellow Arabs to be their comrades, other immigrants did not fit into their schema, while Iranians faced outright hostility. One expatriate frustrated by the turn toward exclusivity was Ashraf Lutfi, who expressed bitterness that the Kuwaiti elite had turned their backs on "a chance to give the expatriates a permanent stake in Kuwait and thus to win their loyalty."[235] As more and more of the working population was comprised of noncitizens, questions of inclusivity would become increasingly existential.

4 The Fear Complex | 1952–1961

IN 1949, NEWLY INDEPENDENT India sent a delegation to Bahrain to investigate a series of complaints from Indian employees of the Bahrain Petroleum Company (Bapco). The workers explained that although they faced repeated contract violations, low wages, abysmal working conditions, and rampant racial discrimination, they were afraid to bring even their most minor grievances to the notice of management. Whenever they raised concerns, they were summarily fired and deported. In his report to New Delhi, the chief investigator expressed both concern and exasperation. The system, he believed, led to inefficiency as it penalized employees for taking the initiative in "bringing genuine grievances to the notice of the management." More fundamentally, arbitrary deportation ensured that the protections of labor law, corporate grievance procedure, and even legal contract were rendered meaningless. The result, he explained, was that noncitizen workers were "living under a fear complex" from which there was no escape.[1]

By 1960, the fear complex blanketed the whole of the Persian Gulf. At its core was an interlocking network of labor, immigration, and nationality laws imposed across the region during the 1950s. This chapter traces how and why an array of often unexpected actors cemented the legal underpinnings of this complex on the eve of independence in the two pivotal cases of Bahrain and Kuwait. While nationality laws had metastasized for decades, labor legislation represented a dramatic reversal of imperial policy. British officials, transnational oil firms, and local rulers had long rejected basic legal protections for workers. Oil companies had successfully convinced many observers that they embodied the cutting edge of industrial relations and thus required no state regulation, while political authorities were reluctant to jeopardize their relationships with local elites by inquiring too closely into their labor practices. But the rising tide of labor activism described in the previous chapter altered their political calculus. Oil companies and their imperial patrons came to believe that labor legislation was not only inevitable but even useful, as a means of transferring both the responsibility—and the blame—for controlling their workforce onto the state. This meshed with postwar imperial strategy, which determined that "British influence would be sustained indirectly rather than through the formal trappings of the old imperial system."[2] The efforts of corporate and imperial officials were paradoxically facilitated by the labor and anticolonial nationalist movements, which viewed the regulation of Anglo-American oil firms as a step toward building sovereign and independent states. Thus, for their own conflicting reasons, a remarkably broad coalition of workers, anticolonial activists, labor relations experts, imperial officials, and corporate managers all turned to the state to regulate labor.

In a sense, this chapter builds on the work of a generation of scholars who have shown how labor and anticolonial movements in the Persian Gulf forced multinational corporations to desegregate their operations and accept at least some responsibility for the wellbeing of their workers.[3] But it also demonstrates how popular protest shaped the growth of what Michael Mann calls the "infrastructural power" of the state.[4] It was through regulation of labor and migration that state power percolated into the lives of all of the residents of the Persian Gulf as it never had before, with labor permits, manpower surveys, and work visas. While this power put limits on the arbitrary actions of private firms, it also internalized the most exclusionary and discriminatory aspects of corporate and imperial practice. State formation in the Persian Gulf, so often framed as the inevitable and elite-led product of oil wealth, was driven not just from the top down, but from the bottom up. In their struggle against corporate segregation, anticolonial activists and labor organizers played a central role in constructing the state apparatus by reining in the near-sovereign powers of U.S.- and British-owned oil firms.

The legislation drafted in the waning days of empire reflected a curious mixture of corporate and imperial expertise. On the one hand, it grew out of a belief in both the inevitability and the desirability of modern development that was virtually hegemonic across the political spectrum. With their technologically sophisticated production process and slick public relations departments, oil firms were widely seen as the embodiment of modernity and progress. In recent years, scholars have thoroughly dismantled this corporate myth.[5] However, this idealized vision of the model oil corporation proved alluring to an array of experts—British and Egyptian—whose training in the discipline of industrial relations imbued them with remarkable influence and whose fingerprints can be found on virtually every major policy implemented during the 1950s. These technical advisors believed that oil firms embodied modern "best practices" of industrial relations and viewed them as models to be emulated. The result was labor legislation inspired by, or even directly copied from, corporate practice.[6]

At the same time, this cohort of experts pathologized residents of the Gulf as backward and unmodern, replicating stereotypes of the "Arab worker" or the "African worker" prevalent across midcentury empires.[7] The result was a turn to precedent in other parts of the Arabic-speaking world—especially that of Egypt. Industrial relations specialists replicated a British imperial labor policy prevalent across the postwar Middle East designed to channel labor activism toward bread-and-butter issues and away from broader political objectives, especially anticolonial nationalism.[8] The significance of regional precedent and its intersection with stereotypes of the Persian Gulf and its residents are most vividly demonstrated in Kuwait, where labor regulations were drafted not by British authorities but by Egyptian industrial relations experts.[9] While deriving their authority from their supposedly universal expertise, they drafted laws that were more profoundly shaped by their prejudice. They found ready allies in local business interests, whose support, as will be seen in future chapters, proved essential in shaping labor law after independence. Corporate and imperial officials thus allied with industrial relations experts and local business interests to transplant restrictive labor legislation across the Persian Gulf, dividing citizens and noncitizens, public and private sectors, and white- and blue-collar workers. Though, as will be seen, Kuwaiti labor law would be revisited immediately after independence—the 1959 legislation would be in place for only five years—the alliances and discourses forged in the imperial era would endure.

Labor and citizenship legislation intersected with the nascent deportation state to preserve the hierarchies of empire in the era of decolonization.

Even as imperial and corporate officials resigned themselves to the inevitability of independence, they sought to build the "right kind" of state, one that would enforce labor discipline and police dissent even after the end of formal empire. Their efforts were ironically, and unintentionally, facilitated by labor and anticolonial activists who viewed labor legislation as an important step on the road to sovereignty. Discrimination thus emerged in a new form, with a reconfigured set of justifications and a powerful cast of local supporters.[10] Rather than reining in the discriminatory practices of the oil industry, Gulf states internalized them. In so doing, they incorporated an array of corporate and imperial strategies—including segregation, divide-and-rule, and mass deportation—into their legal systems on the eve of independence.

THE BAHRAIN LABOR LAW | 1954–1957

Like much imperial legislation, labor laws across the Gulf influenced each other. They freely borrowed ideas and language, drawing on the same models in pursuit of the same objectives, and were often written by the same people. Indeed, labor laws were one of the last sweeping legislative efforts of the British empire in the Persian Gulf. The specific circumstances of their passage varied across the region, but they shared striking similarities. All were imposed only after extensive press criticism and labor organizing forced imperial officials and oil companies to abandon their opposition to any form of state regulation. All were profoundly shaped by a new generation of labor experts, either British or Egyptian, whose views were in turn shaped by the conservativism that characterized the midcentury field of labor relations and by stereotypes about the supposed backwardness of the Persian Gulf. And all were imposed during periods of heightened repression following popular protests. Merging expertise and blunt force, the laws set the stage for intense battles following independence.

A cursory glance at the state of legal worker protections in the Gulf before 1950 is enough to explain why workers across the region prioritized the passage of labor laws. In Kuwait, the only labor legislation was the archaic and draconian 1940 Pearling Law, passed in the aftermath of the 1938 Majlis Movement, which allowed pearling captains to confiscate the possessions of indebted divers who were killed on the job in order to posthumously recover their debts.[11] The Government of Bahrain banned forced labor, but had imposed no broader protections for workers. The oil industry was virtually unregulated. Across the region, workers had no regularized means for the redress of grievances.[12] As late as 1952, the Kuwait Oil Company (KOC) had no system of industrial relations whatsoever.[13] The Employee Handbook listed twenty loosely defined violations that could be grounds for dismissal, including laziness, malingering, and "agitation of Company employees."[14] As the decade progressed, KOC instituted a system of labor and welfare officers to whom workers could address complaints. However, cases were decided at the whim of white officers—or, as the Personnel Manual euphemistically called them, "American or European" foremen—according to vague policies.[15] Even KOC officials acknowledged that many of these managers "do not have a sufficiently sympathetic attitude towards labour."[16] In Bahrain, compensation for workplace injuries was decided by an ad hoc committee consisting of a Bapco representative, the Political Agent, and the British Advisor, Charles Belgrave. Payments were entirely voluntary, and many employers repudiated any responsibility for compensation whatsoever.[17]

Without institutionalized rights or formal outlets for dissent, workers often sought the redress of grievances by petitioning ruling family members who were seen as potentially sympathetic. In Kuwait, Shaikh Jabir al-Ahmad was known for raising worker complaints with the company.[18] In Bahrain, Shaikh Ali bin Ahmad informally oversaw labor issues.[19] Such elite mediation had been common before the 1940s in Egypt, where dissident princes sought popular influence by positioning themselves, however dubiously, as friends of the working class.[20] Oil companies seem to have tacitly accepted this practice because it redirected criticism of their policies back onto regional monarchies, while ruling families appreciated that they could claim to be protecting the interests of their people.[21] But monarchical intermediaries had little patience for collective action organized by workers themselves.[22] KOC officials expressed satisfaction that "there is no doubt" that "the sheikhs," who often accepted corporate narratives of subversion and outside agitation, "are determined to stamp out any tendency to strike"—a determination that would be borne out many times.[23]

The first labor law in the British-protected states of the Gulf emerged as a direct result of popular pressure in Bahrain, which was an early hub of both political activity and imperial interest. The Higher Executive Committee (HEC), which by 1954 had forged a mass anticolonial movement, made the passage of a modern labor law one of its priorities. While the British and their allies implacably opposed the HEC plan to create a union encompassing all workers in Bahrain, they compromised on the demand for labor legislation on the logic that it could help redirect worker organizing away from anticolonialism and towards bread-and-butter issues like wages and working conditions.[24] To do so, they turned to a cadre of imperial labor advisors schooled in the field of industrial relations and seconded to the Foreign Office.[25] Perhaps the most important was Labor Attaché M. T. Audsley, described by Joel Beinin and Zachary Lockman as "the chief architect of postwar British labor policy in Egypt."[26] Audsley had already been dispatched to Bahrain in the late 1940s, in response to the postwar strike wave, when he had dismissed calls for higher wages as the result of "unrestrained nationalism" that would warp the natural laws of the labor market.[27]

In early March 1955, Audsley visited the archipelago once again, this time to negotiate the outlines of Bahraini labor law. On arrival, he met with HEC leaders to try and dissuade them from organizing a state-wide labor union. As an alternative, Audsley proposed forming Joint Consultative Committees in major industries and organizing an industrial census and a cost-of-living inquiry, which would facilitate vocational training and set a minimum wage. Then a tripartite Labour Law Advisory Committee, comprised of employer, government, and worker representatives on the model of the International Labor Organization, would draft a comprehensive labor law.[28] Al-Bakir and his HEC colleagues agreed, and hotly contested elections were held on April 18 and 19, 1955, to select the labor representatives for the labor law committee.[29] Candidates affiliated with the HEC won a clear victory, a result that was generally seen as indicative of widespread grassroots support for the movement.[30] In mid-1955, the committee began discussing the outlines of the first labor law to be imposed in the Gulf.

But even before discussions began, British labor experts had worked to set their terms in favor of employers. Audsley's first draft of the proposed labor law, which would be the basis of discussion, embodied imperial and technocratic efforts to channel and diffuse dissent. It drew on British colonial legislation from Sudan and Libya that had already been cleared by the Legal Department of the Foreign Office, adding provisions from Egyptian law.[31] It also drew on corporate practice. After leaving Bahrain, Audsley visited Kuwait, where he took detailed notes on Kuwait Oil Company labor policies. He then forwarded his notes on to his successor in Bahrain,

Cyril Marshall, who heavily reworked the draft to incorporate KOC practice into the legislation on the argument that it was best suited for the particular circumstances of the Persian Gulf.[32] In order to further "prepare the public mind," the draft was published in the weekly government gazette, and when the Labour Law Advisory Committee met for the first time it was used as the basis for discussions.[33] Thus the segregation characteristic of British colonial law and U.S. corporate practice, buttressed by the imprimatur of technical expertise, became the basis of the law.

Audsley's efforts replicated his earlier work in Egypt, where he had sought to "promote a nonpolitical trade union movement."[34] While Audsley believed in the inevitability of labor unions, he sought to restrict their scope of action to basic workplace issues of wages and working conditions and thus separate organized labor from wider political questions—especially anticolonial nationalism. This policy continued under Audsley's successor, Cyril Marshall, who led the labor law negotiations.[35] Marshall even visited British Aden in order to learn how imperial authorities there had contained a powerful labor and anticolonial alliance.[36] Marshall was encouraged to find that the National Front in Aden had scaled back its labor activism with the establishment of the Trade Union Congress, which took over responsibility for resolving bread-and-butter workplace issues and thus cleaved organized labor from the anticolonial cause. Marshall concluded that the creation of a trade union apparatus in Bahrain could serve as a means of separating "political" disputes from "industrial" ones.[37] The experts found allies in the oil company. In London, representatives of Caltex (the California Texas Oil Company)—the joint venture between the Texas Company and Standard Oil of California that owned Bapco—lobbied British authorities to defang the labor law by banning union federations, sympathy strikes, and even "peaceful picketing."[38] Like Audsley, they drew on examples from labor legislation across the Middle East to buttress their position, thus transforming the decisions of regional autocracies or imperial administrations into legal precedent.[39] While British officials could not promise to implement the company's requests, they suggested advising the Bahraini Government to unilaterally amend the law after its passage, regardless of Committee negotiations.[40] The suggestion proved prescient.

From mid-1955 until mid-1956, the Labour Law Advisory Committee met over fifty times to hash out the details of the Bahraini labor law. Its main dynamic was the tension between the employers' representatives, particularly those from Bapco, and the representatives of the workers, allied with al-Bakir's Higher Executive Committee.[41] Marshall unsurprisingly sympathized with the employers and even convinced the Higher Executive Committee to ban strikes during the course of negotiations.[42] The worker spokesman, Muhammad Qasim al-Shirawi, proved an able negotiator who won the grudging respect even of the employer representatives. Al-Shirawi and his colleagues emphasized three concerns. First of all, they noted that the law as written did not in fact improve wages or working conditions.[43] Marshall argued that minimum wage legislation would eventually rectify this absence, though the Political Resident privately acknowledged that a "publicity" campaign would be needed to counter widespread disappointment at this exclusion.[44] For its part, Bapco opposed all concessions, particularly the idea of promoting all Arab workers to monthly status after a fixed period of employment. Such a policy would undermine the power of arbitrary dismissal as well as their strategy of racial segregation by uniting their Arab workers, usually paid by the day, with their Indian and Pakistani "artisan" workers.[45] Keeping their Arab workers on short-term contracts would remain a priority.

Second, workers argued for the legalization of a federation to unite all unions in Bahrain, which they viewed as not just essential for workers, but for the anticolonial nationalist movement as a whole. Al-Shirawi exasperated the employer representatives by pointing out that such a federation was permitted under British law.[46] Eventually, recognizing that workers were likely to form a de facto alliance whatever the language of the law, separate negotiations between Bapco and the nascent Bahrain Labor Federation reached a tentative agreement to allow a single "federation" broken into multiple "branches."[47] Finally, the worker representatives tried to improve the position of Bahraini workers by setting a limit on the number of noncitizens who could be hired by particular firms and by equalizing wages and benefits between Arab "daily" workers and South Asian "artisans."[48] The problem, they explained, was that noncitizens "obtain work at the expense of the Bahrainis because they are prepared to accept lower wages and to live on a very low standard."[49] Bapco, however, successfully opposed the proposal by arguing that it would constitute an abridgement of the rights of management.[50] They therefore not only retained their concessionary power to hire workers from abroad, but saw it further enshrined in Bahraini law.

Finally, after a year of negotiations, on July 25, 1956, the Political Resident reported that the committee "has reached practical agreement on the draft."[51] For Bahraini workers, it left much to be desired. On the advice of Marshall, and unlike Egyptian labor law, it excluded agricultural workers.[52] In a cover letter accompanying the draft, the committee explained that these workers could later be covered by separate legislation, though that was never written.[53] It also did not set a minimum wage or a quota for Bahraini workers on the argument that the committee was awaiting a comprehensive employment census to ensure that such a provision would not trigger inflation.[54] Again, the specter of inflation silenced demands for higher wages. Two unresolved points of tension remained to be sorted out by the Bahraini government: The draft allowed for both solidarity strikes and the immunity of labor unions from tort action, concessions that the employer representatives had refused to make. The Political Resident, however, argued that any attempt to amend the draft would lead anticolonial nationalists to oppose the law and thus "seriously reduce the chance of keeping labour outside politics in the future."[55] The Resident therefore supported its passage. On October 10, it was forwarded on to the Government of Bahrain for final revision and approval.[56]

For a brief moment it appeared that Bahraini activists had won a major victory. But less than three weeks later, while the draft was still awaiting the Ruler's signature, British, French, and Israeli forces launched a surprise attack on the Suez Canal. Bahrainis responded with massive protests, which were in turn crushed by two thousand British troops—one of the largest direct deployments of imperial forces in the history of the Gulf. Abdul Rahman al-Bakir and other prominent leaders of the HEC were quickly arrested and put on trial. Some were imprisoned, some deported, and the leaders exiled to St. Helena.[57] When the Labour Law Advisory Committee met again in 1957 to finalize the law after a long hiatus, even imperial officials acknowledged that because of the crackdown, "the Labour Law Advisory Committee has no-one who can represent the workers' point of view adequately," so "the Government's representatives and the employers' representatives are having a field day with no opposition."[58] The law was amended to significantly reduce the rights of trade unions, restrict the power of the strike, and, critically, exclude noncitizens "at the option of the Bahrain Government."[59] Interestingly, imperial authorities had initially supported the inclusion of noncitizens in trade union legislation, believing that a militant union comprised only of citizens could become a potent nationalist force. Diluting unions with non-citizens, they believed, would restrain their militancy.[60] This interpretation, however, was rejected by corporate officials, who wanted to keep their workforce divided. A Bapco representative also reinserted a provision excluding all domestic workers from the law, a decision that would have long-term consequences for the gendering and devaluing of labor.[61]

The modifications came under sustained attack from the remnants of the political opposition. The *Voice of the Arabs*, broadcasting from Cairo, argued that the modifications were "laid down to protect the interests of the foreign monopolist companies with no regard to the workers' rights."[62] Even imperial authorities were uneasy about the extent to which the law deviated from legislation in the United Kingdom.[63] But while acknowledging that the law would do little to affect the lives of workers, the Political Resident nevertheless defended it as a "thoroughly progressive measure" that would demonstrate that "Bahrain retains its capacity to give a lead in standards of administration in this part of the world by taking expert advice and applying it to local conditions"—illustrating the intersection of the universal and the particular in imperial discourse.[64]

In practice, even the limited provisions of the draft were never enforced.[65] Many accidents went unreported, and employees regularly worked well beyond allowable hours in dangerous conditions.[66] Moreover, the promised minimum wage legislation was never passed.[67] Bapco and the Residency made the familiar argument that any wage increase could trigger inflation.[68] When the Bahraini government finally drafted a regulation on the employment of foreign workers in 1960, it lacked teeth, as it was "almost entirely" drafted by Hal McCullouch, Labour Relations Manager at Bapco, and "designed purely and simply to bring the provisions of the Labour Ordinance into line with the internal regulations or arrangements of BAPCO."[69] The legislation thus enshrined corporate and imperial precedent into local legislation.

EGYPTIAN ORIENTALISM IN KUWAIT | 1952–1959

While they emerged out of a political context very different from that of Bahrain, labor regulations in Kuwait were also the product of popular pressure. In the immediate aftermath of the strikes of 1952 discussed in the previous chapter, KOC representatives approached imperial authorities with a surprising request: They asked for the passage of a workers' compensation law. The problem, as KOC saw it, was that "they found themselves having to set out conditions of labour and compensation for industrial injuries," which led to payments that "fall much below what is paid in neighboring countries."[70] These arbitrary decisions generated resentment.[71] As one imperial official explained, "They would much prefer to have to conform to a law rather than be put in the position of making a law themselves."[72] In the face of rising political pressure, the company believed that labor legislation would place both the responsibility and the blame for compensation decisions in the hands of the state. In calling for legislation, KOC received the support of its most strident critics. During the 1950s, anticolonial nationalists repeatedly condemned the oil companies as neocolonial "states within a state" that needed to be restrained by legislation.[73] In their view, labor law was an essential step on the road to independence. The legal regulation of labor became one of the few things that all parties could agree on.

The Kuwaiti state therefore began building an embryonic system of industrial relations in the early 1950s. Following a wave of strikes in 1953, the British-led Development Board drafted new "terms of reference" for its contractors specifying, among other things, that "preference [in hiring] will be given to Kuwaiti workers, and then the sons of Arab countries."[74] It also began to monitor and regulate rates of pay across the government.[75] Later in 1953, in response to the aforementioned strike of Indian and Pakistani workers at Jewan Camp, the Board established a permanent Labor Committee, run by a "labor expert" and including British and Kuwaiti representatives from across government departments, to coordinate labor issues.[76] The Committee would play a central role in forcing the imposition of labor legislation in Kuwait.

A major shift in state action came with the escalation of tensions in 1954. Events in Bahrain reverberated across Kuwait, underlining the regional nature of labor protest and legislation. KOC officials reported that statements from the Higher Executive Committee "are freely circulated and discussed" around Kuwait city.[77] The Kuwaiti paper *Sada al-Iman* covered events surrounding the HEC and Bahraini labor law, praising the creation of the tripartite labor law committee as a "victory for the Arab people of Bahrain."[78] The National Culture Club and the Teachers' Club both sent letters of support to the HEC, with the former lauding it as a "great contribution to the struggle against colonialism" in the Arab world.[79] Another impetus to action was a minor recession triggered when the Emir of Kuwait halted the work of the five largest British construction firms in the country, which he accused, with justification, of making excessive profits from cost-plus contracts. When the firms simultaneously laid off an estimated ten thousand employees, wages dropped for the first time in years, and state authorities ordered mass deportations of non-Kuwaitis.[80] The downturn also triggered the first efforts to distinguish between Kuwaiti and non-Kuwaiti workers.[81] After the layoffs, unemployed Kuwaitis picketed state departments, arguing that the state should help them find jobs and that noncitizens should bear the brunt of the firings.[82] But as the state kept no records of births or deaths, distinctions based on nationality were virtually impossible to enforce. The regulation of labor would thus force the state to clearly define the border between citizen and noncitizen for the first time.[83]

In 1954, these tensions led Kuwaiti officials to commission a British expert to comprehensively study what they called the issue of "foreign labor."[84] The British did not want to draft a comprehensive labor law, hoping to delay legislation until the negotiations in Bahrain had been settled.[85] But they wanted to appoint a specialist to oversee a system of unemployment registration and noncitizen labor permits.[86] The resulting recommendations—nicknamed the Strover Report, after its author—would transform the nascent Kuwaiti state.[87] Strover recommended that every worker in Kuwait, citizen or noncitizen, be registered by the Social Affairs Department and issued a labor card. Employers would be forbidden from employing workers without cards, which were only to be given to noncitizens who entered the country legally, possessed a valid passport and residency permit, and were deemed to be "of good conduct."[88] Permits for noncitizens were valid for a maximum of six months and could be withdrawn by the Department if they competed with "national labor" in the "labor market," or, crucially, if the worker remained unemployed for over a month.[89] Thus the report tied residency to employment, reinforcing the sponsorship system. This program would be supplemented by a state-funded technical training school, opened in 1956, to provide skilled Kuwaiti workers for the labor market.[90]

Beginning in 1955, Egyptian labor experts in the Department of Social Affairs used its comprehensive registry to regulate the labor market according to Strover's suggestions, connecting employers with workers in a vast, centralized recruiting system.[91] They were further spurred on by a survey that found that only 22 percent of the workforce was Kuwaiti, and that of the non-Kuwaitis who registered with the state over 60 percent were undocumented. Within two years, the Social Affairs Department had issued 40,638 cards, representing a significant proportion of the working population.[92] By 1958, it was registering nine thousand arrivals annually, with about 75 percent coming from the southern Persian Gulf.[93] The system proceeded in tandem with a wider expansion of state infrastructural power. An official census, completed in 1957, launched a flurry of statistical studies and planning surveys.[94] Strover's report and the labor bureaucracy it generated thus built on the efforts of the 1938 Majlis Movement, making the population of Kuwait further visible to the state.

The Strover Report also led to the passage of the Government Workers' Cadre of 1955, which set baseline standards for wages, hours, and working conditions across state departments. Standardization was a central demand of many labor leaders, who condemned the special favors granted to well-connected workers.[95] While the authorities framed the Cadre as an effort to end arbitrary wage inequities, it was also designed to break the power of labor. Workers were denied the right to form unions or even to discuss the reasons for dismissal if they were fired.[96] Instead, the Cadre created a Labor Committee within the Social Affairs Department, which would act as the ultimate arbiter of disputes between employers and employees.[97] In 1955 alone, it resolved thirteen incidents.[98] A turning point came when the staff of six bakeries went on strike in 1956. When the leaders of the strike—all non-Kuwaitis, and likely Iranians—were fired, the Department of Social Affairs forced their reinstatement and negotiated a compromise. As the U.S. Consulate reported, "a precedent in Kuwait labor relations was thereby set," as the state took up the role of arbiter in labor disputes.[99]

The Kuwaiti press supported comprehensive labor legislation in part because of its firmly held belief in the importance of embracing modern methods of labor management and reining in favoritism and arbitrariness. The generally pro-regime *al-Ra'id* complained that the Cadre underpaid low-ranking employees in comparison with the inflated salaries of their managers, but supported many of its provisions, notably the special privileges meted out to citizen workers.[100] Arab nationalist papers proved more critical. *Al-Iman*, for instance, qualified their support of the Cadre by arguing that it was not a complete solution "as long as prices are in a race with the rise in wages."[101] But even they proved susceptible to the discourse of expertise deployed by British labor specialists.[102] *Sada al-Iman* took a similar line.[103] *Al-Shaʿb* even praised the systematic deportation of noncitizens, and especially non-Arabs, as a means of combating unemployment, once again highlighting the exclusionary elements of Arab nationalism.[104]

The mid-1950s left one more institutional legacy that would later prove significant to the nascent Kuwaiti trade union movement. In 1956, as political clubs proliferated across Kuwait, a group of students at the government technical school began discussing the idea of establishing a club for workers. The student group, which included Hussein Saqr, the future founding president of the Kuwait Trade Union Federation, created a committee to pursue the project, and asked for the support of the new Department of Social Affairs.[105] The Department agreed, apparently because it believed that the club could fight illiteracy and channel, or at least aggregate, labor dissent.[106] The Center for Workers' Culture, as it came to be known, thus received state funding, but its board was elected, giving it a certain amount of independence.[107] It even organized lectures about trade unions, some of which were given by labor specialists from Social Affairs.[108] As a centralized gathering place for workers, it became a hub for pro-union organizers, including most of the founding members of the Kuwaiti trade union movement of the 1960s.[109]

The policing of labor accelerated alongside the growth of the security services and the deportation state. Imperial officials reported that the new Social Affairs Department acted "in close touch and friendly liaison with the Police," who "tour the town in search of beggars" and "expel all who are not Kuwaitis."[110] A revealing microcosm of the transition from corporate to state control of labor is the story of the KOC "Investigation Force." Created by KOC in 1948, it was composed of six "special security officers," all of whom were non-Kuwaitis, who were given the power of special police officers by the Political Agent.[111] Starting in the late 1940s, Shaikh Abdullah Mubarak, the head of the Kuwait Police, argued that "all police and security functions should be in the hands of the State, rather than the Company," seemingly because this would increase his own power.[112] Corporate and imperial officials eventually concluded that state control would relieve KOC of the onus of policing labor protests.[113] Thus, in late 1953, the force was absorbed into the Kuwait security forces under Abdullah Mubarak, its remaining members literally putting on the uniform of the State Security Force.[114] KOC also handed over its "card index of political suspects" to the Political Agency and helped the Kuwaiti security forces organize a Fingerprint Bureau and Photographic Section.[115] The security apparatus designed by the oil company would become not just the nucleus of the deportation state, but also the germ of the Kuwaiti police.[116]

Pressure on the oil company and its imperial patrons only increased in the late 1950s, reinforcing their determination to pass comprehensive labor legislation. In July 1957, KOC dockworkers won a large raise after a short strike.[117] New opposition papers like *al-Sha'b* (The People) and *al-Fajr* (The Dawn) launched an even more determined attack on the discriminatory practices of the oil company than had their predecessors. The failure of its campaign to recruit Arab workers from Iraq, Jordan, and other northern countries, discussed in the previous chapters, forced KOC to acknowledge that its Arabization and Kuwaitization efforts were ineffectual.[118] British plans to grant Kuwaiti independence, part of a broader imperial strategy of divesting power to handpicked client regimes, further encouraged the drafting of legislation. Imperial officials believed that a labor law would both help rein in labor activism and shield an independent Kuwait from the accusation that it remained colonized in all but name, especially if it wanted to join the International Labor Organization (ILO)—a key symbol of membership in the community of nations.[119] Even members of the ruling family began to push for the legislation. Those on the Labor Committee grew frustrated that they bore responsibility for resolving labor disputes but had no clear framework for how to do so.[120] For its part, the Foreign Office reported that "because of fierce attacks on the Company in the Kuwait Press they want the [labor] law introduced as quickly as possible"—an acknowledgment that labor legislation was designed to protect employers, rather than workers, and that it was popular protest that forced the issue.[121]

Opposition newspapers, imperial and Kuwaiti officials, and corporate managers thus all came to view the regulations imposed following the Strover Report as insufficient and called for more detailed legislation. Concerns about immigration and labor often intersected. In 1954, as much of the Kuwaiti press railed against immigration, the Foreign Office increasingly conflated immigration and communist infiltration.[122] The Political Agent pressured the Ruler to impose a tighter system of visas and residency permits on Arabs, heretofore exempted from movement restrictions.[123] Imperial officials tried to persuade their Kuwaiti counterparts of "the communist danger," citing intelligence reports finding "continuing communist activity."[124] Oil company officials agreed. L. T. Jordan, the manager of KOC, warned London of political agitation "under the guise of labour unrest" and advised installing further security measures.[125] Something, he believed, had to be done. Thus, by the late fifties, workers, employers, imperial officials, and anticolonial nationalists had all improbably decided that the time had come for comprehensive legislation to regulate migration and labor in Kuwait.

THE KUWAITI LEGISLATION OF 1959

Like their Bahraini counterparts, Kuwait's foundational labor and nationality laws were drafted in a period of repression. While the Ruler, Abdullah al-Salem, may have permitted greater freedoms of speech and the press than any other Gulf monarch, his tolerance had its limits. In 1959, Arab nationalists organized a rally at Shuwaikh School to celebrate the first anniversary of the union between Syria and Egypt. During the rally, the Kuwaiti Arab nationalist Jassim al-Qatami gave a speech during which he called for sweeping political reform and the reining in of monarchical power. In response, the regime shuttered virtually every independent newspaper in the country, suspended political clubs and organizations, and banned public protests, a crackdown on dissent that would last until after independence in 1961.[126] It was at precisely this moment that the state and its allies would impose pivotal labor and nationality legislation without fear of a popular backlash.

Curiously, one of the last holdouts opposing new labor legislation was the man tasked with writing it. The Egyptian labor advisor to the Kuwaiti government, Amin ʿIzz al-Din, deemed a law unnecessary. ʿIzz al-Din was a prominent "labor expert" with a British degree in industrial relations. While he is best known to scholars for his encyclopedic history of the Egyptian labor movement, in the mid-1950s he was sent to Kuwait by the Egyptian government as a "labor expert" tasked with designing a basic institutional and legal framework of industrial relations.[127] But despite his fame as a labor historian, ʿIzz al-Din proved far more ideologically aligned with management. He reasoned that the state and the oil company, the two largest employers in Kuwait, already used "comprehensive" employment guidelines that guaranteed "minimum standards of employment and conditions of work." If anything, he believed, the existing regulations simply needed to be enforced.[128] As it happened, ʿIzz al-Din was a longtime friend of both M. T. Audsley and Cyril Marshall, the British labor attachés, whom he had met in Egypt, and he had largely come to see the Kuwaiti situation as they did. On a visit to Cairo in the spring of 1955, Audsley persuaded ʿIzz al-Din to extend his "full cooperation" with the British "in order to avoid too serious a divergence between our proposals for Bahrain and his for Kuwait."[129] In Kuwait, Audsley put ʿIzz al-Din into touch directly with the Political Agency.[130] At the request of the British, ʿIzz al-Din put the draft of the Kuwaiti labor law "into cold storage until the results of the Bahrain deliberation were well advanced."[131] Instead, he prioritized the creation of the Social Affairs Department and the employment exchange. He also rebuffed a request from a member of the Bahraini High Executive Committee to advise them in their labor law negotiations, telling them to have "every confidence and trust" in the British labor experts.[132]

Amin ʿIzz al-Din, like other Egyptian advisors, seems to have imbibed developmentalist narratives that framed Kuwait as a backward society and Anglo-American institutions, particularly the oil companies, as the embodiment of modern industrial relations. This can be clearly seen in ʿIzz al-Din's 1958 booklet entitled *Workers of Kuwait from Pearls to Oil*, published by the Kuwaiti Government Press. Its preface, written by Hamad al-Rujaib of the Kuwaiti Social Affairs Department, frames Kuwait as a "simple society" at "the beginning of the path" toward modernity and development.[133] ʿIzz al-Din agrees. His booklet describes Kuwait as a place where "remnants of ancient social and economic relations" still survive, redolent of the guild system "as known by Europe and the countries of the Arab East during the Middle Ages."[134] Captains were analogous to master craftsmen, sailors to journeymen, and the young boys who did various odd jobs to apprentices.[135] But these former sailors, captains, and divers found that their "ancient skills and expertise" had lost their value in the new labor market.[136] Moreover, they faced unprecedented competition from foreign workers, who could easily "infiltrate (*tasallil*)" Kuwait across its long and undefended borders.[137] Today, "there is no doubt that the manpower problem in Kuwait can be summarized as the failure of national manpower (*al-qawa al-ʿamila al-wataniyya*)—in terms of its abundance and technical capacity—causing a reliance on foreign manpower."[138] This skilled manpower shortage, which understandably led to "feelings of enmity" against foreigners, was exacerbated by a lack of planning.[139] Now, explained ʿIzz al-Din, the Department of Social Affairs was preparing legislation to rationalize labor relations and protect the Kuwaiti workers left behind by modernity. This paternalistic and developmentalist paradigm underpinned his thinking about Kuwait and the legislation he drafted.[140]

When in late 1957, ʿIzz al-Din finally did draft a labor law, even imperial officials were disappointed by its conservatism. In the years leading up to the drafting process, ʿIzz al-Din had asked British authorities for films, booklets, or other information on workplace safety, workers' compensation, and labor law, which was obligingly forwarded by the Ministry of Labour and National Service.[141] He then proceeded to ignore them. His first draft retained the archaic system of pearling compensation payments and said nothing about trade unions, which ʿIzz al-Din believed could, perhaps, be covered by regulations "in ten years' time."[142] The draft was so conservative that it was discarded.[143]

Like its Bahraini predecessor, the draft of what would become the Kuwait Labor Law of 1959 was modeled on corporate and imperial precedent.[144] ʿIzz al-Din openly advertised this fact in his introduction, which lists the "sources of the law," including surveys conducted by the Kuwaiti Department of Social Affairs, a comparative study of Arab labor legislation, recommendations of the Arab League, international labor agreements, and ILO reports. Remarkably, ʿIzz al-Din acknowledged that an important "origin" of Kuwaiti labor law was the KOC Employee Handbook, which had been consulted on a wide variety of substantive matters including "classification of workers, employment, covenanted workers, organization, end of service, compensation, working hours, wages, allowances, trade training, leave, social welfare, medical services, precautions against accidents, accommodation and other detailed matters."[145] In conversations with imperial officials, ʿIzz al-Din affirmed that he used KOC labor regulations as a guide.[146] This decision seems to have been made at the suggestion of Audsley, broached after conversations with "senior executives" of the oil companies.[147] ʿIzz al-Din thus gave the imprimatur of the Kuwaiti state to the corporate and imperial policies he so admired.[148]

The resulting law deepened the fissures that divided the Kuwaiti workforce, setting several crucial precedents that would be replicated across the

Persian Gulf. First, it reified the division the public and private sectors by excluding workers covered by the Government Workers Cadre.[149] This bifurcation was significant in a context where the private sector workforce was overwhelmingly noncitizen and the public sector workforce increasingly Kuwaiti. Citizens and noncitizens found themselves under different laws, with the latter receiving distinctly inferior protections. It also reified divisions of class, gender, and nationality. Workers in temporary positions of under six months in length were entirely exempted from protection, thus incentivizing employers to hire short-term contract workers. Workers classified as "private domestics and the like" were also left unprotected.[150] The latter exemption channeled undocumented workers into domestic labor, where they would be vulnerable to exploitation—a problem that was foreseen, but not addressed.[151] It also forbade women from working at night or in "dangerous professions," framing the state as the "protector" of women. Finally, the law systematized the work permit system and reaffirmed that "priority in employment" was to be given to Kuwaitis, Arabs, and foreigners, in that order. The Social Affairs Department, already reconfigured after the Strover Report, received sweeping powers of inspection and enforcement, transforming it into the core of the new bureaucratic state.[152]

Perhaps most notable were restrictions on labor organizing. While the law legalized trade unions, it did so only in accordance with "decisions issued by the Social Affairs Department," which never materialized. It also banned strikes, limiting unions to selecting worker delegates to "Arbitration Committees," run by Social Affairs, which were given the final power to settle all labor disputes. This arrangement reflected contemporary Egyptian labor legislation, which also compelled arbitration.[153] Committees would be comprised of representatives of the Court of Appeals, the office of the Prosecutor General, and the Department of Social Affairs and Labour, plus up to three representatives of both the employer and the workers.[154] In fact, the law was so heavily weighted toward the interests of employers that worker representation on the committees was only guaranteed by a 1960 amendment.[155]

Upon reading the draft legislation, corporate and imperial authorities generally recognized that it would prove a boon to their interests. The Political Residency was pleased to find that it was "in some ways less generous than the Bahrain Law."[156] In fact, they noted, "the Kuwait Oil Company would have little difficulty in applying the Law in its present form," given that "Amin ['Izz al-Din] used the Company's Labour Regulations as a guide to much of what he did."[157] KOC agreed, acknowledging that the law would actually "strengthen the Company's hand" by making it easier to fire workers.[158] The head of the KOC labor department reported that "we were repeatedly told by representatives of the Department of Social Affairs in discussing various Clauses that 'of course you offer your employees more generous terms than those required by the Law.'"[159]

The Department of Social Affairs then allowed employers to suggest modifications to the law in a series of private meetings.[160] The discussion is illuminating. KOC worried that the legislation could unify its workforce by blurring the color line between white "senior staff" and non-white workers.[161] The company preferred that their relations with noncitizens—and especially white "senior staff"—be governed exclusively by employment contracts, rather than labor law, and feared that if subjected to the law, managers would "be virtually required to join local Trade Unions, or pilloried if they refused."[162] To counter this possibility, KOC lobbied to exempt managers from legislation.[163] Here as elsewhere, they cited the example of Egypt, where many unions were divided in two, with one representing "workers" and another representing white-collar "employees."[164] The U.S.-owned American Arabian Oil Company, or Aminoil, argued that the conflation of workers and staff differed from standard practices "elsewhere in the world," citing the example of General Motors.[165] Employers need not have worried. Saleh Ayoub, the Egyptian labor expert, affirmed that because "K.O.C. practice is generally more favourable to Labour than the terms of the proposed law," the legislation would not affect the oil company.[166] In effect, the main argument in favor of the legislation was that it would do little.

Kuwaiti employers, also invited to comment on the draft, backed the oil companies in their drive to separate white- and blue-collar employees. Their support not only proved politically crucial but presaged an alignment of state and business interests after Kuwaiti independence. Perhaps the most revealing were the comments of Jassim al-Qatami, invited in his capacity as the manager of the Kuwait Cinema Company, who argued that "the manual worker should be distinguished from the brain worker (the Staff Worker), because their work was different and prevailing custom had established a distinction between them."[167] This division was "current custom in every organization in the world," recognized not just in KOC but also by "small concerns" in Kuwait. He was seconded by Khalid al-Kharafi, who owned the al-Kharafi Steel Construction Company.[168] Al-Qatami also criticized the proposed labor permit system for noncitizen workers, not on the grounds of noncitizen rights, but because he believed that the requirement to have permits would hamper the free recruitment of workers.[169] The vocal intervention of al-Qatami in particular was notable because, in addition to being the scion of a prominent family, he was one of the leaders of the Kuwaiti branch of the Arab Nationalist Movement, ostensibly an ally to labor. During the Suez Crisis protests in 1956, he famously resigned his position as Chief of Police when ordered to put down an anticolonial nationalist demonstration, penning a resignation letter in which he stated that he would not suppress ideas that he himself believed in.[170] Al-Qatami represented the conservative wing of the movement and, in this instance, the sometimes contradictory position of Arab nationalists on issues of labor rights in the 1950s, when many of its members were drawn from elite circles and therefore had a personal interest in siding with employers over their workers.[171] His positionality highlighted the potential for tension between anticolonial nationalism and labor.[172]

The law was passed in 1959 and immediately began to reshape working life in Kuwait. Kuwait Radio even started a weekly program discussing the law "with the aim of making its provisions known to the public."[173] In the days following its passage, hundreds of noncitizen workers lined up outside the Kuwaiti Department of Social Affairs to apply for work permits. However, few possessed identity papers or could provide written evidence of their legal entry into Kuwait. Undocumented applicants were given only a temporary pass that allowed them to continue working in their present jobs "but would be of no use to them when they resigned or were laid off and wanted to find new work."[174] British officials reported that "this is an absurd situation," leaving "well over half the labour force" in a new bureaucratic position: as undocumented immigrants.[175] The absurd, however, would become the new normal. A crucial test of the law came soon after its passage. In 1960, a lull in land expenditures and construction led many contractors to make ends meet by underpaying their workers. In response, the Social Affairs Department began mediating a wave of disputes and encouraging the firing of non-Kuwaiti workers before Kuwaitis.[176] The U.S. consulate reported that the legislation was unlikely to "change labor practices in Kuwait" and "will certainly hamper if not hamstring union activity."[177] For its part, KOC hoped and expected "that special treatment given the Kuwaitis will assure a lack of solidarity with other workers"—an expectation that proved inaccurate.[178] Rather than collective bargaining, KOC instituted official grievance committees to formalize the "teaparties," organized by Shaikh 'Ali, where workers conveyed their requests to the company.[179] The law did exactly what KOC hoped it would: Its labor policies were kept intact, but responsibility for their enforcement, and blame for their inadequacies, would now rest with the state.

The second pivotal piece of legislation passed during the 1959 crackdown on dissent was the nationality law. Paired with legislation targeting the rights of noncitizens, it initiated a sweeping re-evaluation of who was or was not Kuwaiti and consolidated the regime of exclusion on the eve of independence.[180] While before its passage authorities deemed that a passport or other official document was sufficient evidence of Kuwaiti nationality, the law significantly raised evidentiary requirements and narrowed the bounds of who could become a naturalized citizen. "Founding (*asasi*)" Kuwaitis were deemed to be those who inhabited Kuwait from 1920 and their patrilineal descendants. The date was significant: It was the year of the Battle of Jahra and the building of the wall around Kuwait City. The building of the wall was not just a significant historical marker but a memorable date, making it easier to remember who lived in Kuwait at that time. The Public Security Department was also empowered to naturalize "Arabs" who legally immigrated after eight years, and non-Arabs after fifteen, provided that the latter learned Arabic. These naturalized citizens, however, were denied the full rights of citizenship, including the right to vote, for a set period of time. This created a "second-tier" form of citizenship without political rights that would become a key point of contestation in the ensuing decades. A 1960 amendment then limited the number of people who could be naturalized in any given year. As in British imperial legislation, women were to follow the nationality of their closest male relative. Finally, the state reserved the right to strip the nationality of naturalized citizens who made false statements in their application, served an enemy power, or committed a crime "involving a breach of honor."[181]

The question of who fulfilled requirements for naturalization would prove another contentious issue. In order to determine who was a bona fide resident of Kuwait, the law empowered the Police and Public Security Department to form special "Nationality Committees," comprised of several preparatory committees of five members, and a "high committee" of seven, which were to operate from 1959 to 1965. These committees, made up of elderly men from each of the districts of the old town of Kuwait, would testify to whether or not an individual fulfilled the requirements of Kuwaiti citizenship.[182] Bedouin, meanwhile, were to be naturalized by tribe, with their appointed "sheikhs" serving in the place of the urban nationality committees.[183] To reach into outlying areas, the state posted public notices asking those who wanted to apply for Kuwaiti nationality to record their names at the nearest police station, setting a deadline for applications.[184] Those who failed to apply before the Nationality Committees disbanded in 1965, or who lacked sufficient witnesses, would be denied Kuwaiti citizenship. The result of the law was that, in the words of Claire Beaugrand, nationality became "a matter of personal networks."[185] Given the tremendous repercussions of statelessness, the process was nerve-wracking, especially as the burden of proof rested on the applicant, not the state.

At the same time as the nationality law came into effect, a barrage of legislation restricted the rights of noncitizen residents. Now only Kuwaitis could receive a state pension, practice law, or open a pharmacy.[186] In July 1959, the Department of Social and Labor Affairs announced that "any attempt by a laborer to attain his goals in any manner other than by one of the three approved methods"—meaning a strike—would result in the loss of their work permit and their expulsion from Kuwait.[187] Some of the most significant new laws were passport regulations, notably the Aliens Residence Law 17 of 1959, which permitted administrative deportation without appeal or due process. It remains in place to this day.[188] The law also reinforced the gendered nature of movement restrictions, ordering that "a wife may not hold a separate passport except with the agreement of her husband"—the same restriction applied to "feeble-minded people." Finally, it granted police and public security authorities the power to withdraw passports at will.[189] This last power was employed immediately. After the Shuwaikh incident of 1959, Shaikh Abdullah Mubarak, the head of Public Security, personally confiscated the passports of several reformist leaders, a tactic that would be routinely employed after independence.[190]

As so often happened, crackdowns on citizens and noncitizens proceeded in tandem. On edge following a nationalist coup that toppled the British-allied monarchy in neighboring Iraq the previous year, the Kuwaiti state undertook what imperial authorities described as a "purge" of "undesirable foreigners." While "the official reason for all this business is of course anti-Communist," in truth "the net is wider than the Communists" and many deportees "may well be victims of jealous rivals."[191] The Acting Ruler privately admitted that "he was working on the principle that 30% proof qualified for expulsion" on the argument that "when dealing with Communists it was better to be sure than sorry."[192] Notably, this was an issue on which they agreed with Arab nationalists. Yaʿqub al-Humaidi reports that the movement "prepared lists of the communists' names and numbers and informed the authorities who took the procedures to deport many of them," describing this as a national duty "to protect the Arabism of Kuwait from this tide dominating Iraq."[193] While Arab nationalists would, in time, emerge as some of the most trenchant critics of the nationality regime, their efforts would be undermined by their earlier support of the deportation state.

CONCLUSION

By the time Kuwait won its independence in 1961, a remarkable amount of corporate and imperial policy had become Kuwaiti law, thanks not just to the British, but to local officials, business elites, and Arab experts. Legislation had further entrenched the schism between citizen and noncitizen and created a new legal distinction between "original" Kuwaitis and the naturalized. Arab descent, urban upbringing, merchant family connections, and landownership could be transmuted into a Kuwaiti passport. Those deemed less desirable received nationality last, or not at all. If the regime of passports and visas helped give the state control over its borders, the regime of labor permits and nationality law brought state power into daily life. For noncitizens, deportability meant perpetual precarity.

However, the debates over what rights workers should have, and who should or should not be granted nationality, only grew more heated as the implications of the nationality regime became clear. Despite years of British lobbying for a narrower nationality law, even some imperial observers worried that the law threatened to create a generation of stateless people "who will clearly resent being an under-privileged existence in what is and always has been their home."[194] This was precisely what happened. As Claire Beaugrand has documented, the loss fell heaviest on the landless Bedouin.[195] Lacking any evidence of their residency in Kuwait, they found it impossible to win recognition from the resolutely urban citizenship committees. The result was mass statelessness. In 1974, Abdulrasoul al-Moosa carried out a study of "shanty settlements" on the outskirts of Kuwait, which were populated largely by former nomads. He found that while 78.3 percent of residents described themselves as Kuwaiti, only 14.4 percent possessed documentation of their nationality.[196] Moreover, the creation of the category of "noncitizen" generated a new debate that would only intensify after independence: What rights should be accorded to citizens, and to noncitizen residents? While the ruling family and its allies continued to defend their interests, an alliance of reformers, anticolonial nationalists, and workers united to "thicken" conceptions of both citizenship and denizenship in the name of social justice.[197]

5 Are We Really Independent? | 1960–1965

IN THE SUMMER OF 1964, the newly minted National Assembly of Kuwait gathered to discuss the draft of a new labor law. Nearly all of its elected members had come to the conclusion that revised legislation was necessary. Over the course of the previous year, an unprecedented succession of strikes had swept the country, bringing renewed attention to long-simmering worker grievances and leading Kuwaitis across the political spectrum to conclude that without a reformed legal apparatus to govern industrial relations, workers had few means of redress. A revitalized press, deploying the massively popular rhetoric of Arab Socialism, kept the labor question on the front page of Kuwait's many newspapers. The National Assembly brought to power a cohort of Arab nationalist MPs who, though a minority in the chamber, had long been advocates of workers' rights and were able to turn parliamentary attention to labor affairs. Reflecting the mood of the moment, even the most conservative members of the Assembly had grudgingly come to believe that something needed to be done, if only to fend off calls for more radical change.

Consensus collapsed, however, around several key issues—most notably, the position of noncitizen workers within organized labor. Saʿud al-ʿAbd al-Razzaq, the Vice President of the National Assembly, argued that it would be dangerous to allow noncitizens to join trade unions, especially given their numerical predominance in the private sector. Presuming that noncitizens would continue to sympathize with their home countries, he argued that their incorporation into the labor movement would create powerful domestic organizations under foreign control, thus undermining Kuwaiti sovereignty. Khalid al-Ghanim, one of the many MPs from elite merchant families, agreed, expressing a vague but widely held concern that allowing noncitizens to join unions could generate instability and strife (*fitna*). These elites, many of whom personally employed noncitizen workers on short-term contracts, were already uncomfortable with the legalization of trade unions, and viewed noncitizen membership as a profound threat to both their political and economic interests.[1]

Mohammad al-Rashid, the only former oil worker in the legislature, most clearly articulated the position of the pro-labor Arab nationalists. He argued that denying rights to noncitizen workers would rebound on their Kuwaiti counterparts. How, he asked, could a strike succeed if it were limited to the minority of Kuwaiti workers, who could not shut down production on their own? Dr. Ahmad al-Khatib, now the Vice President of the Assembly and universally recognized leader of the opposition, agreed. Dressed in one of his trademark suits, he noted that many non-Kuwaitis had refused to participate in the recent strike at the Kuwait Oil Company because they feared retribution, undermining the power of the stoppage and, therefore, the rights of their Kuwaiti colleagues. Jassim al-Qatami made a complementary, if more cerebral, case, tracing the historical importance of worker solidarity across world history. Debate was somewhat derailed when he mentioned Karl Marx, which caused a stir amongst the assembled legislators. But he stuck to his position, reiterating that workers could only secure their rights within an inclusive movement.[2] A number of early labor organizers—many of whom were themselves naturalized—attended Assembly sessions to lobby for the bill and against nationality-based restrictions on union membership.[3] The Arab nationalists tied their case together with a central thread: the inextricability of the rights of citizen and noncitizen workers.

For anticolonial nationalists and their allies, the winning of Kuwaiti independence in 1961 was an enormous victory. It also represented a moment of promise. Under a relatively reformist Emir and a new constitution, the press flourished as never before, turning Kuwait into something of a political nexus of the Arabic-speaking world. The exclusionary citizenship regime enacted in 1959 faced its first challenge both in the press and in Parliament as it began to create a class of stateless people. A young generation of labor organizers took advantage of their newfound rights by forming the first legal trade unions in Kuwaiti history. By becoming the most trenchant critics of the racial segregation that permeated the foreign-owned oil companies, organized labor emerged as a cornerstone of the pro-democracy and Arab nationalist movements and constructed the case that would eventually lead to a Kuwaiti takeover of the oil industry.[4]

A debate over the rights of two interrelated groups—noncitizens and workers—soon dominated the politics of the new nation-state. This struggle was pivotal in a country where most of the population, and the overwhelming majority of the private sector workforce, was not Kuwaiti. Feminists proved powerful critics of a nationality regime that often rendered the children of Kuwaiti women and noncitizen men stateless.[5] Other social movements—from pro-democracy advocates to people of nomadic background—found themselves similarly excluded or marginalized by a deliberately hierarchical nationality regime. Activists believed that the battle over the outlines of citizenship would shape not just the rights of noncitizens, but the fate of the social movements on which Kuwaiti democracy relied. Despite occasional defections, the Kuwaiti trade union leadership fought to include Arab noncitizens—and, eventually, all noncitizens—in their movement. They viewed the issue as existential. Exclusion would create an underclass of poorly paid contractors, driving down wages for all workers, citizen and noncitizen, and disincentivizing the employment of better-paid citizens. It would also render strikes ineffective, thus dooming organized labor to irrelevance. Practical considerations meshed with ideological ones. The close relationship between the labor and Arab nationalist movements meant that both considered all Arabs, regardless of nationality, as their countrymen. The hardening of national divides thus generated an increasingly powerful movement to overcome them.

But despite the new freedoms of political independence, Kuwaiti reformers in the early constitutional period could not overturn the structural inequities that persisted from the imperial era. The same elites remained atop the same state apparatus. Legislation drafted and imposed under imperial rule was still in effect, often enforced by the same bureaucrats. The old merchant families dominated the new National Assembly and viewed movements for worker and noncitizen rights as an attack on their supply of cheap and pliable labor, while the monarchy, its insecurity only heightened by British withdrawal, framed mass political movements as threats to their power. The regime and its elite allies adopted many of the same stereotypes favored by their former overlords—Bedouin backwardness, nativism, patriarchy, and anticommunism. Even British influence persisted, as Political Agents-turned-ambassadors defended the interests of oil multinationals with the connivance of an increasingly invested United States. British-orchestrated coups in Sharjah in 1965, Abu Dhabi in 1966, and Oman in 1970 vividly illustrated what would happen if a Gulf state drifted too far from Anglo-American hegemony.[6] In law and personnel, discourse and infrastructure, the long arm of empire remained largely intact. For Kuwaitis who had led the victorious fight for independence, what stood out was continuity, rather than change. Indeed, more than a decade later, in the midst of yet another battle in the seemingly endless war with the oil companies, a Kuwaiti paper could still publish the banner headline: "Are we really independent?"[7]

For nascent trade unions, the contradictions of building an internationalist movement within the framework of the nation-state proved just as challenging as imperial continuities. Their ubiquitous call for "Arabization" and "Kuwaitization"—primarily a demand to desegregate the oil industry by replacing white managers with Arab and Kuwaiti workers—at times rebounded on other noncitizens, who lost opportunities for employment and advancement. In their critiques of contractors who hired undocumented workers, workers and their allies indirectly aligned with supporters of stricter immigration enforcement, reinforcing the very deportation state that disempowered their noncitizen colleagues. Perhaps the most glaring exclusion of organized labor was an inheritance from Arab nationalism—a profound distrust, even hatred, of Iranians, who often received more hostility than solidarity in the first years of independence. In the newly independent nation-state, labor seemed to win only when it pursued nationalist objectives or defended the rights of citizens. The often valiant efforts of labor organizers on behalf of their noncitizen colleagues met, in virtually every case, powerful opposition and eventual defeat. The result was that the structural fissure between citizens and noncitizens only grew wider, even as the labor movement became an increasingly prominent critic of the citizenship regime.

Kuwaiti independence was, in many ways, revolutionary. But the early constitutional era also underlined its limits. To paraphrase Frederick Cooper,

Kuwaitis had won their sovereignty—but nothing else.[8] The end of British suzerainty did little to stem the inequities of an international oil regime that benefited Anglo-American oil firms as much as, if not more than, oil-producing states. Their operations remained segregated, and their upper ranks dominated by managers in Britain and the United States. Nor was independence accompanied by a dramatic change in the domestic power structure. If anything, the new Kuwaiti constitution preserved the late imperial balance of power, epitomizing what Julian Go calls the "historical institutionalization" of a colonial instrument.[9] While reformers hoped that the constitution would provide the foundation of a new, democratic order, its passage proved to be a high-water mark for Kuwaiti democracy. Kuwaitis also increasingly found themselves sundered from their fellow Arabs, as national interests trumped anticolonial solidarities. Thus, like their counterparts around the world, anticolonial nationalists in Kuwait would find that independence did not mean decolonization.

CONTINUITIES OF INDEPENDENCE | 1960–1963

In Kuwait, independence was something of a paradox. A rising tide of anticolonial activism had convinced imperial authorities that they could not indefinitely maintain formal hegemony. British prerogatives—an independent court system, advisors embedded in the state apparatus, special rights of military deployment—appeared increasingly anachronistic as more and more colonized states won their independence. However, independence was also carefully stage-managed in order to preserve British interests and the status quo, including many of the institutions that had appeared so anachronistic. Imperial officials were convinced that their most vital concerns, notably oil and sterling, would be protected by a monarchy that, whatever its official status, would remain dependent on British arms and influence. As independence loomed, British legal advisors began crafting regulations regarding courts, passports, and administration to prepare for formal withdrawal.[10] Finally, on June 19, 1961, with a rather mundane "exchange of notes," Emir Abdullah al-Salem terminated the Anglo-Kuwaiti Treaty of 1899 and Kuwait became an independent state.

The move immediately triggered a crisis. The following week, the regime of Abdul Karim Qassim claimed Kuwait as Iraqi territory and threatened military intervention. In response, the Kuwaiti government requested and received seven thousand British troops to forestall a potential invasion, highlighting the uncomfortable reality that the monarchy, whatever its legal status, still relied on British arms. To counter the public relations backlash triggered by this turn to its former imperial overlord, the fledgling Kuwaiti government launched a diplomatic blitz to win wider international support, especially within the Arabic-speaking world. The effort succeeded, and the Arab League sent its own forces to protect the country—though this may have been due less to the effectiveness of Kuwaiti diplomacy than to the growing rivalry between Qassim and Nasser. While the crisis dissipated, it highlighted Kuwait's uncertain international position and its continued dependence on the British.[11]

These foreign policy developments unfolded alongside a domestic transformation. Heartened by spontaneous demonstrations in support of his rule that erupted during the Qassim crisis, and by the eventual support of the Arab League, Abdullah al-Salem felt less threatened by both Nasserism and democracy. In late 1961, he began lifting the political restrictions imposed two years earlier. In need of an effective policy apparatus, he staffed the new Foreign Ministry with well-known Arab nationalists from the political opposition. Most significantly, he agreed to a constitution.[12] The document, largely written by Egyptian legal expert Othman Khalil Othman, guaranteed an array of new liberties to Kuwaiti citizens. These included a qualified right to free speech, a free press, legal due process, and assembly—including the right to form trade unions.[13] After holding elections in which all adult, non-naturalized men were eligible to vote, the National Assembly opened for its first session on January 29, 1963.[14] In spite of its shortcomings, the early constitutional period enabled an unprecedented level of popular and labor organizing. The flourishing press, led by Arab nationalist papers like *al-Tali'a* (The Vanguard), not only covered the local political scene but brought the radical movements of the global sixties into the homes of ordinary Kuwaitis. However, the exclusion of stalwart pro-democracy advocates like Dr. al-Khatib from the constitutional drafting committee, the presence of the autocratic prince and Interior Minister Sa'ad al-Abdullah, and a heavy reliance on Egyptian legal advisors who viewed Kuwait as a backward and tribal society not yet ready for popular political participation led to the creation of a constitutional monarchy rather than a republic.[15] It remained unclear just how democratic the constitution would prove to be.

Hopes for sweeping reform and Arab unity were quickly dashed as panic over unemployment and immigration came to dominate Kuwaiti politics. These interrelated debates unfolded in the context of a decline in oil prices that began in 1957 and continued into the 1970s, putting the brakes on the country's explosive economic boom. While few observers had expected, or even wanted, the feverish growth to last forever, the slowdown generated a spike in citizen unemployment, which in turn triggered alarm in the press. Newspapers demanded state action, describing joblessness as a "crisis," a "dangerous social problem," or even a "source of evil and crime."[16] Citizen unemployment became a central question of early parliamentary politics; indeed, one of the first reports issued by the new National Assembly studied the rise of joblessness, particularly amongst formerly nomadic people.[17]

Whatever the causes of unemployment, many Kuwaitis blamed noncitizens, especially undocumented ones. The second, related panic thus concerned "infiltration" (*tasallil*), which had become the standard if charged shorthand for undocumented immigration. Newspapers across the political spectrum called for a crackdown, including stronger border enforcement and mass deportations. Opinion pieces argued that "infiltrators" should be not just expelled, but punished with fines or imprisonment in order to "teach them a lesson" and discourage further undocumented migration.[18] Others called not just for stricter border controls to stop undocumented migration, but even for an end to the "open door" policy for legal Arab immigrants, who were excepted from many residency restrictions.[19] Statistics provided by the Ministry of Social Affairs and Labor became a staple of newspaper headlines, such as "7 thousand infiltrators in four months."[20] Photographs of captured "infiltrators" became a ubiquitous trope of press coverage, often accompanied by articles calling for stricter enforcement.[21]

As in the 1950s, the management of migration justified the creation of a new state apparatus of planning and surveillance under the auspices of the Ministry of the Interior and the newly renamed Ministry of Social Affairs and Labor.[22] Many officials took the view that the rise of both mass immigration and modern industrial production necessitated a centralized state bureaucracy tasked with the regulation of manpower—the gendered term that would remain a staple of the discourse.[23] Such ideas, of course, predated independence. In a typical 1960 article, a state labor expert argued that the "violent stream" of immigrants with diverse "customs and traditions" needed to be forged into a "united family" through state intervention and rational planning.[24] State action accelerated during the panics of mid-1963, when the Ministry launched a highly publicized "manpower survey" that dramatically expanded the apparatus of surveillance.[25] The press closely followed the results, with conservative newspapers in particular keeping close tabs on the number of noncitizen residents. In the wake of the survey, the Ministry opened a network of new offices across Kuwait to oversee the registration of noncitizen workers and the distribution of work cards, to be managed by employees trained, ironically, in the United Arab Republic.[26] It also ramped up inspections and threatened to fine employers who hired workers without documentation.[27] At the same time, the Interior Ministry launched an energetic and well-publicized campaign to halt "infiltration" along Kuwait's borders.[28] It doubled the number of border posts, increased its deployments of guards, and even installed a radar system to intercept speedboats.[29] It coupled increased surveillance with the mass deportation of thousands of people, most of whom were Iranian.[30] Thus, in the early years of independence, the deportation state grew even more pervasive, fueled in part by popular support.

This newly empowered bureaucracy responded to the migration and unemployment panics with an organized campaign to displace the effects of the recession onto the shoulders of noncitizens. On March 31, 1962, thousands of non-Kuwaiti government employees suddenly learned that their contracts would not be renewed, seemingly in response to fears about the ballooning public sector.[31] The following year, the Interior Ministry announced that it would only grant residency permits (*iqamat*) with permission from the Ministry of Social Affairs and Labor so as not to generate "unemployment in the [presumably citizen] working class."[32] The Ministry of Social Affairs and Labor temporarily halted the issuance of all work cards until they had taken "comprehensive steps to organize labor."[33] The Kuwaiti state then began winnowing its own ranks of noncitizen workers. By early 1964, an estimated 3,500 to 4,000 non-Kuwaiti government employees had been laid off.[34] As noncitizens came to be blamed for the problem of unemployment, they were increasingly subject to firing and deportation.

Few individuals embodied the continuities in the immigration regime more than Suleiman al-Masha'n. The head of the passport office in the Ministry of Social Affairs and Labor, al-Masha'n became something of a celebrity bureaucrat. Like much of the legislation he enforced, he was a holdover from the imperial era, having worked on immigration issues since the 1940s.[35] In interviews, he justified the crackdown on "infiltration" as a means of combating citizen unemployment. There were too many "idle hands" in the country, he argued, and "human pressure" was increasing daily. In response, his department undertook measures to "lighten the migration" and make sure that everyone entering the country first received a residency permit. He also began defending the system of individual visa sponsorship in paternalistic terms. Every person who "guarantees" (*yakfil*) or "employs" a foreigner, he explained, took "direct responsibility" for them. They cannot simply expel them into the street without work.[36] His paternalism only increased with time. In 1973, al-Mashaʿn argued, in the face of voluminous evidence, that most of the problems of the sponsorship system stemmed from the kindness and sympathy of Kuwaitis, who were too easy on their workers.[37] In public statements across the decades, he consistently defended the deportation state.

The questions of labor and citizenship generated two of the most contentious debates in the young National Assembly that together drove yet another wedge between citizen and noncitizen workers. Shortly after the first parliamentary session of January 1963, the National Assembly took up the case of "ungraded" Kuwaiti workers in the government sector. Paid by the day and exempted from the benefits accorded to salaried workers, they faced low pay and little opportunity for promotion.[38] The National Assembly agreed to promote Kuwaiti workers to monthly status—but it left out noncitizens.[39] The decision was controversial. Arab nationalist deputies forcefully argued that all daily workers should be promoted, regardless of their nationality. Dr. Ahmad al-Khatib argued that to be a truly advanced (*mutaqadama*) country and to defend its international reputation, Kuwait needed to treat all workers equally.[40] But despite his impassioned appeal, he lacked the votes to block the measure.

The incident highlighted the potentially transformative impact of a region-wide decision by the Arab Nationalist Movement (ANM) to adopt a socialist line in 1961 to 1962. In the Gulf, and particularly in Kuwait, this debate led to a prolonged struggle between socialist and conservative elements within the movement. While conservatives, usually middle- or upper-class activists, were the ascendant faction in the Kuwaiti branch until 1967, many

Arab nationalists nevertheless vocally supported the rights of Arab noncitizens.[41] In a remarkable article splashed across pages one to six, *al-Tali'a* responded to the growing tensions between citizens and noncitizens by arguing that "justice for Kuwaiti workers does not conflict with justice for their brother Arab workers." It bemoaned that recent debates over noncitizen workers had created a "hostile spirit" between Kuwaitis and Arabs, which could only advance an "imperialist plan" to weaken the Arab cause. Rather than viewing the rights of Kuwaiti and Arab workers as mutually exclusive, the Arab nationalist press argued that all workers were interdependent, and that the rights of one group rebounded on the rights of all.[42] *Al-Tali'a* also rejected the framing of immigrants as the source of unemployment, instead blaming employers for hiring cheap and deportable labor from abroad. Rather than excluding noncitizens, the Assembly needed to raise the floor of wages for everyone.[43]

Labor contractors came under special scrutiny. A series of reports attacked firms that recruited workers abroad, managed their residency paperwork, and then hired them out to larger employers, including the oil companies, for a fee.[44] Newspapers described the practice as both illegal and unethical, a means of profiting off of underpaid workers.[45] They also singled out contractors for employing a disproportionate number of Iranians.[46] Conservative papers joined in the criticism, but only because contracting firms reputedly employed many undocumented workers. A representative article accused labor contractors of conducting a "trade in infiltrators."[47] While labor brokers certainly embodied the worst inequities of the labor regime, they could also be a scapegoat, deflecting attention away from structural problems.

Arguments for solidarity across the lines of nationality were buttressed by a growing number of articles detailing the harsh conditions faced by noncitizen workers, especially in the Arab nationalist or left-wing press.[48] These described systematic exploitation, with workers facing grueling hours, low pay, and dangerous conditions. Complaints to the Ministry of Social Affairs faced long delays or went entirely unanswered, leaving workers under the perpetual threat of deportation, and therefore "at the mercy of employers."[49] While the oil companies attracted the bulk of the criticism, a number of local employers, particularly the brick factory, also became symbols of abuse.[50] In response, Arab nationalists called for not only stronger labor legislation, but for the unionization of noncitizens, which was framed as the primary means by which they could claim their rights. Furthermore, Arab nationalist papers argued that while "the fracturing of the working class" threatened to create a "false sense of competition" between workers of different nationalities, unionization was the solution.[51]

The second major National Assembly debate of 1963 to 1964, however, highlighted the limits of Arab nationalist solidarity. It centered around the question of whether noncitizens should be allowed to serve as government aides. Many political figures, including Arab nationalists, pushed for a citizenship restriction on the grounds that many officials had been appointed by the British because of their willingness to collaborate with imperial interests. But to others, placing such restrictions on noncitizens was a betrayal of the Arab cause. When the measure passed, Kuwait faced criticism across the Arabic-speaking world.[52] The increasingly powerful binary of citizen/noncitizen clashed with the Arab nationalist vision of a world divided between Arabs and non-Arabs.

The movement's most glaring exception again involved non-Arab immigrants, and especially Iranians.[53] In the "infiltration" debates, Arab nationalists took a hard line. They continued to propagate the theory that Iranian immigrants were pawns of an Iranian regime allied with imperialist powers and determined to expand its influence across the Gulf.[54] Their language could be shocking. Articles with titles like "Iranians are everywhere!" compared Iranian immigration to Zionism, and even warned of "another Nakba" if Iranians were allowed to overwhelm the Gulf—a deliberately provocative reference to the expulsion of Palestinians.[55] Opposition to Iranian immigration was even framed as part of the anti-imperial struggle of "Asian and African peoples," on the grounds that Iranian immigrants were the agents or puppets of the Shah.[56] Cartoons in *al-Taliʿa* popularized a startlingly bigoted image of Iranians, an ape-like caricature with dangling arms and a vapid expression, which greatly resembled representations of Irish immigrants in the nineteenth-century U.S. press.[57] Moreover, dislike of "Persians" even extended to those with Kuwaiti citizenship. The paper popularized the slur "Kuvaiti" to refer to Kuwaitis of Iranian descent who spoke with an accent, implying that they were countrymen in name only.[58] These stereotypes would haunt the formal Arab Nationalist Movement until its eventual dissolution in the late 1960s.

KUWAITIS WITHOUT NATIONALITY

Alongside a surge of xenophobia, the early parliamentary years also witnessed the first challenge to the restrictive nationality regime imposed in 1959. By 1963, it was clear that the system of citizenship committees, which put the onus on applicants to "prove" their nationality to a panel of elderly Kuwaitis, was both imprecise and arbitrary, and left many people entirely stateless. The plight of two groups disproportionately denied nationality became the focus of discussion: Bedouin, and Kuwaiti women married to noncitizens. The debate over Bedouin revealed the extent to which, despite rising calls for reform, many urban and elite Kuwaitis shared stereotypes favored by corporate and imperial officials. Virtually all believed that Bedouin needed to be educated and civilized before receiving the political rights of citizenship, and few questioned the patriarchal nature of nationality law. Indeed, the question of the political role of formerly nomadic people would become a staple of political and academic debate for decades.[59] Kuwaiti feminists leveled a more fundamental challenge to the exclusionary regime of citizenship as they grappled with the fact that the child of a Kuwaiti women and her non-Kuwaiti husband would not receive Kuwaiti nationality. But the elitism of even this critique meant that the most forceful critics of the nationality regime—feminists, Bedouin, and workers—rarely worked in tandem, or even viewed their struggles as interconnected. These fissures would undermine reformist efforts for decades to come.

The post-independence debate over nationality began with discussions of the draft of the Kuwaiti constitution. Dominated as it was by representatives of elite families and the monarchy, the drafting committee did not challenge the paradigm introduced in 1959, and in fact further reinforced state power over the granting, and stripping, of nationality. One of the ruling family's picks for the committee, Interior Minister Saʿad al-Abdullah, insisted on removing the phrase "Kuwaitis by birth" from the draft, apparently to emphasize his unwillingness to grant citizenship on any basis but descent. Another monarchical appointee, the minister of justice, argued for the imposition of even tighter restrictions on nationality as there was "no other country" on earth so "full of foreigners." As a result, Othman modified his draft text by adding a clause to legalize citizenship stripping "within the bounds of the law," while leaving more specific requirements undefined.[60]

The constitution thus ensured that nationality would remain a privilege granted or retracted by the state and determined at birth.

The nationality regime faced a challenge in the early constitutional era as journalists and members of parliament critiqued the inequities of the citizenship committees. One article recounted the story of a man who spent three years waiting for various ministries and committees to examine his nationality application, only to have it rejected on the grounds that the deadline for applications had passed.[61] Cases of mixed-status families, in which some members were granted nationality and others denied it, underlined the arbitrariness of the process, as such decisions should have been impossible given the genealogical basis of Kuwaiti nationality.[62] Arab nationalists warned that the poor often struggled to obtain nationality, and that many were effectively becoming stateless.[63] Many Kuwaitis agreed that the "right people" were not reliably receiving nationality, while the "wrong people" often were. There was some agreement on who the "right people"—fellow Arabs who had long lived in Kuwait—and the wrong people—Iranians—were, but such terms were of course the crux of the debate.[64] There was also widespread agreement that Palestinians should be prevented from obtaining Kuwaiti nationality on the grounds that mass naturalization could legitimate the Israeli occupation of Palestine and undermine the right of return.[65]

The most vexing question remained that of other Arab noncitizens and formerly nomadic people—would they have access to naturalization? A 1963 series of articles published by *al-Hadaf* on what it called the "Bedouin problem" illustrates the major points of debate. The paper argued that it was clearly in the "political and economic interest" of Kuwait to increase its population, which could be achieved by naturalizing the Bedouin. But "settlement" and "stability," which would bring an end to their nomadic lifestyle, would not necessarily lead to "civilization." Before becoming citizens, they would need to transform their "customs and traditions," which, the paper argued, were antithetical to the modern idea of citizenship and to participation in industrial society. Bedouin needed not just "outward change," but "fundamental change" to behavior, customs, and beliefs. In order to preserve "national unity," the Bedouin would need to abandon their tribal loyalties and develop nationalist sentiment. They would also need to overcome their traditional aversion to manual labor in order to be integrated into industrial society, especially as their lack of job skills would relegate the first generation of former nomads to low-ranking jobs. After interviewing several "experts" on the "Bedouin question," *al-Hadaf* argued that rather than plunging nomads directly into Kuwaiti society, the government should establish agricultural settlements in border areas with sufficient water resources. Once the Bedouin were settled, the rootedness of agricultural life would gradually erode their nomadic mindset, and, over the course of one or two generations, transform them into suitable candidates for citizenship.[66]

This mélange of popular stereotypes and modernization theory underpinned many assumptions made by journalists and policymakers alike.[67] In 1967, Mohammad AlHashimy of the Kuwait Planning Board compiled a comprehensive report on "Bedouins and Bedouin Life in Kuwait," which set out to answer the question of whether former nomads could become productive citizens. From his position as a technical expert, he asserted that Bedouin were fundamentally flawed citizens in two ways: They "are not loyal to any political entity but only to their tribe," and they have "an aversion to manual work," which they saw as "an affront to their pride." Like *al-Hadaf*, he viewed these characteristics as an "obstacle to national unity." He also viewed them as fundamentally spatial. The issue, he argued, was that most former nomads were living together in ramshackle dwellings on the outskirts of Kuwait City, recreating their preexisting tribal practices in the process. "Passive urbanization," he believed, would be "insufficient" if Bedouin continued to live in tribal groupings. Instead, planned "agricultural settlement," based on building a conception of private property through the ownership of individual plots of land, would "allow him [the Bedouin] to move gradually into the industrial society without shattering his personality" and help change their "concepts of work, social status, leadership and power."[68]

The National Assembly debate over granting nationality to formerly nomadic people encapsulated the contradictory pressures of the nationality debate. In 1963, there was significant parliamentary support for naturalizing more Bedouin on the grounds that many were longstanding and loyal residents of Kuwait, or, more practically, that they were needed to boost the country's population.[69] Many MPs framed the issue as one of special importance because of the prominence of Bedouin in the police and armed forces.[70] In 1964, the Defense Committee of the National Assembly recommended the formation of a special committee to investigate the question of Bedouin naturalization.[71] But many Kuwaitis, especially those from elite families with roots inside the walls of old Kuwait, remained firmly against Bedouin naturalization, and their opposition only hardened with time. In 1964, a number of MPs argued that nearly all "known Bedouin" had already received nationality, and that those Bedouin now registering their names in police stations—which was required to receive nationality—were largely interested in getting access to state benefits, particularly low-income housing.[72] Conservative publications began linking the question of granting nationality to Bedouin with the danger of infiltration, an association that would grow increasingly popular and that effectively denied that people of nomadic descent were truly Kuwaiti.[73] The press also relentlessly associated the Bedouin with poverty. A series of "how the other half lives" articles in the mid- to late 1960s linked the problems of informal dwellings, Bedouin, and nationality. While they could be sympathetic, their tone, which framed the former nomads as tragically romantic figures left behind by the modern world, also played into the stereotype that Bedouin were simply not prepared for modern life.[74] Indeed, as Farah Al-Nakib has shown, Kuwaitis of Bedouin descent were spatially segregated by state housing projects, preserving a divide within Kuwaiti society for decades to come.[75]

Fears that the "wrong people" were obtaining nationality proved inextricable from the panic over "infiltration." At a stormy National Assembly session in late 1963, members reaffirmed that they would not grant nationality to "infiltrators" who entered the country illegally, citing the article granting nationality to property holders as a loophole that was enabling mass Iranian naturalization. Many MPs persistently questioned the loyalty of anyone of Iranian descent. Arab nationalists proved particularly vocal not just in their condemnations of Iranian "infiltrators" but of their efforts to gain nationality. Even more common was the accusation that many nationality seekers simply hoped to benefit from the material rewards of being Kuwaiti. Embedded in all of these arguments was the assumption that nationality was not a right. Calls for sweeping reform would emerge only in the 1970s.[76]

THE FEMINIST CHALLENGE | 1964–1975

Along with left-wing Arab nationalists, perhaps the most forceful critics of the Kuwaiti nationality regime were feminists. Starting in the early 1960s, a panic over the phenomenon of "foreigner (*ajanib*) marriage" swept across Kuwait. The press generally discussed the marriage of Kuwaiti women to noncitizen men, and of Kuwaiti men to noncitizen women, as two separate questions, an implicit recognition of the fact that Kuwaiti men and women faced different challenges when marrying noncitizens. Writing in the mainstream press in response to the growing number of young Kuwaiti men marring noncitizen women, Kuwaiti feminists reframed the debate to highlight the inequities of Kuwaiti nationality law and the hierarchies within the category of citizen. They also challenged the framing of marriage to noncitizens as, to cite Sara Rahnama's work on Algeria, a form of national betrayal.[77] The debate is particularly notable because it reveals the relationship between nationality and citizenship. By arguing that the patriarchal Kuwaiti nationality law restricted the right of Kuwaiti women to freely choose their partners, Kuwaiti feminists deployed the language of citizenship to challenge the exclusions of nationality.

The "foreigner marriage crisis" emerged out of intersecting anxieties about the mobility and sexuality of young Kuwaiti men in the aftermath of the oil boom.[78] The first articles to use the term, which were published by the mainstream press in the early 1960s, generally focused on Kuwaiti scholarship students who married European or American women. Most presumed that foreigner marriage represented a crisis. But they were less sure as to why. Some argued that marriage needed to be based on a shared sense of being Arab, and that cross-cultural matches were likely to fail or produce children who would be fundamentally conflicted about their true identity.[79] In this narrative, the word "foreigner" effectively meant "non-Arab"; legal nationality seemed less important as women married to Kuwaiti men automatically received Kuwaiti nationality.[80] Thus, most articles understood cultural incompatibility to be the main "problem" of foreigner marriage.[81] Beyond the supposed threat to individual marriages, some commentators feared broader social implications. A number of articles argued that too many foreigner marriages could threaten the survival of a unique Kuwaiti culture in future generations. Others expressed concern that they would produce a class of Kuwaiti "spinsters" unable to find husbands. Virtually all agreed, however, that the phenomenon was real and concerning.[82]

Commentators also disagreed on why such marriages were taking place. A few viewed foreigner marriage as the natural result of youthful male mobility. Impressionable Kuwaiti men spent years abroad at a time when their thoughts, it was assumed, naturally turned toward women. But the actions of the men themselves received disproportionately little scrutiny from many early articles; most simply presumed that "boys would be boys." Instead, these authors—almost exclusively men—focused on the sexuality of American and European women. Seductive women with blond hair, high heels, and short skirts became a popular trope for cartoonists. Some articles blended misogyny and modernity, arguing that it was natural that cosmopolitan Kuwaiti men returning home from an education abroad would not wish to marry "ignorant, illiterate, narrow-minded" Kuwaiti women stifled by outmoded norms and traditions.[83] A few authors used the debate to critique Kuwaiti social norms. According to one MP, gender segregation limited opportunities for courtship between Kuwaitis. A solution to the crisis, he argued, would be to gender-integrate Kuwait University, thus enabling relationships to blossom.[84] Nearly all commentators agreed that the skyrocketing cost of dowries played a key role in discouraging Kuwaiti men from pursuing Kuwaiti women, and some suggested reforming the system.[85] As a rule, however, the focus was on men—their behavior, regulation, and agency.

But as the 1960s progressed, the standard tropes of the "foreigner marriage" debate faced a forceful challenge from Kuwaiti feminists, many of whom wrote for publications aimed at women readers. Two central figures were Ghnaima al-Marzouq, the first woman to serve as editor-in-chief of a Kuwaiti publication, and Laila al-Othman, a prominent Kuwaiti journalist, poet, and novelist who was married to a Palestinian doctor.[86] They redirected the debate onto the plight of Kuwaiti women marrying foreign men, whose children were deprived of Kuwaiti nationality.[87] In so doing, they raised new and profound questions about law, class, and gender inequality, and became central actors in debates surrounding citizenship and nationality. By refocusing the foreigner marriage debate on the injustices of nationality law, Kuwaiti feminists created an aperture through which they could critique both the exclusions of citizenship and the hierarchies preserved within it.

The central forum for feminist critique was *Usrati* (My Family), a women's publication edited by Ghnaima al-Marzouq. The most intense debate was launched in 1966 by Laila al-Othman, who critiqued the restrictions of both law and custom that discouraged Kuwaiti women from marrying foreigners and even challenged the idea that foreigner marriage represented a crisis at all. Discussing her happy marriage to the Palestinian doctor Hosni Mansur, she told an interviewer that she hoped that her story would serve as inspiration for other Kuwaiti women who wanted to marry non-Kuwaiti men—though her husband's position as an educated Arab Muslim meant that hers was one of the less controversial foreigner marriages.[88] Her critique generated a flurry of impassioned responses. Unlike the male-dominated discussions in other publications, Kuwaiti women focused on their experience of legal discrimination and its repercussions, especially the looming threat of statelessness for the children of Kuwaiti women and non-Kuwaiti men.[89]

Kuwaiti women redeployed the debate around the foreigner marriage crisis to attack not just patriarchal marriage practices but the gendered inequities that remained within the category of citizenship. Many noted that Kuwaiti women often married foreigners to escape either their own families or the prospect of an arranged marriage to a man they did not love. One *Usrati* article, for instance, framed the right of Kuwaiti women to marry non-Kuwaiti men as the next step in a long struggle for the rights of Muslim women, going so far as to describe unhappy forced marriages as a kind of living death.[90] Other women redeployed the foreigner marriage debate to condemn the exclusivist marriage practices of the *ʿAsli* Kuwaitis—a term used to refer to the elite families who dominated the heights of politics and the economy and habitually intermarried. "Why not consider marrying from the *biasir*," asked one interviewee, identified only by a pseudonym, using the derogatory term for non-elite Kuwaitis. The foreigner marriage debate, she argued, was simply a distraction from the fundamental class tensions within Kuwaiti society. Another woman even compared the reluctance of elite families to "marry down" to racial discrimination in the United States.[91] Other observers also noted, and critiqued, the relationship between foreigner marriage and class discrimination.[92] Some Kuwaiti feminists challenged the very premise of the marriage crisis. Interviewed in *al-Nahda* in 1971, Laila al-Othman argued that the most dangerous marriage crisis in Kuwait was not foreigner marriage, but the rising percentage of Kuwaiti "spinsters." This crisis, she believed, could be resolved by making it easier for Kuwaiti women to marry the man of their choosing, whatever his nationality.[93] Another woman explained the turn to noncitizen marriage by accusing Kuwaiti men of failing to treat their wives as intellectual partners, or of going "from one wife to another."[94]

Feminist critiques thus opened up wider political horizons. Ghnaima al-Marzouq, for instance, defended the rights of noncitizens and condemned what she called collective punishment against them.[95] Under her editorship,

Usrati also came to the defense of stateless women and called for the revision of nationality law.[96] But at other times, feminists reinforced hierarchies both within and without the boundaries of citizenship, reflecting what Haya al-Mughni sees as a vein of elitism running through the Kuwaiti feminist movement.[97] Activists from privileged families made little effort to reach out to other critics of the nationality regime, notably labor and Bedouin activists, who came from less exalted circles. In so doing, they eschewed the potentially sweeping implications of their critiques of nationality. Even many defenders of foreigner marriage qualified their support by condemning women who married their servants or drivers, which was often psychologized as the result of social isolation.[98] The accusation that noncitizens only wanted to marry Kuwaiti women for their money was a common refrain, and would be used as a justification for the tightening of nationality law. Indeed, Laila al-Othman's father was so concerned about even the suggestion that his daughter had been married for money that he refused to accept a dowry.[99] Many commentators also distinguished between different kinds of foreigners, especially between Arabs and non-Arabs and Muslims and non-Muslims. By explicitly privileging marriage to the former, they defended foreigner marriage by reinforcing a hierarchy of non-Kuwaitis.[100] Again, the experience of Laila al-Othman is indicative. She explained that at first, her father hesitated to give his consent to the marriage, but on reflection, decided that after all, "my daughter hasn't married a Jew!" Mansur was a doctor, and a respectable Arab Muslim, not a "stranger" or a "foreigner."[101] In short, even if women should have the right to marry noncitizens, some foreigners were less foreign than others.

THE INDUSTRIAL BEDOUIN

The issue that would most closely link the rights of citizens and noncitizens was labor. The early constitutional period presaged a significant shift in the legal position of trade unions. While the 1959 Labor Law officially legalized unionization, even P. C. D. Archer, the British Labour Advisor, acknowledged that it "did not confer a genuine freedom to form trade unions," as it required the Department of Social Affairs and Labor to issue appropriate regulations that were never in fact drafted.[102] Moreover, Emiri Decree 43 of 1960 amended the law by requiring binding arbitration in every labor dispute, which effectively rendered strikes illegal.[103] But Article 43 of the new constitution, proposed by the Egyptian constitutional law expert Othman Khalil Othman, protected "the liberty of forming societies and unions on a national basis and by peaceful means."[104] Interior Minister Saʿad al-Abdullah was able to add the clause "in conformity with the conditions and stipulations specified by Law," thus weakening the protection.[105] Nevertheless, it gave hope to workers that their efforts to organize would be constitutionally protected.

The general atmosphere of reform that followed independence also invigorated organizing. Workers launched a flurry of petitions to newspapers, ministers, and the National Assembly.[106] With the lifting of censorship, newspapers from across the political spectrum once again took up the cause of labor. Even conservative papers were willing to broadcast the concerns of employees of the segregated oil companies.[107] Arab nationalist papers championed the call for unionization.[108] They were led by *al-Taliʿa*, which would become the most powerful mouthpiece of the pro-democracy and Arab nationalist movements in ensuing decades. It argued that unions were essential not just for workers, but also in the wider struggle for democracy, social justice, and anti-imperialism.[109] Aspiring trade unionists also benefited from the geopolitics of decolonization in which recognition by international organizations was a prized asset. The nascent Kuwaiti state viewed membership in the International Labor Organization (ILO) as a badge of sovereignty. But when the Kuwaiti delegation arrived in Geneva in the immediate aftermath of independence, Egypt and the Communist bloc challenged the credentials of its "workers' representative," who was a KOC Personnel Officer. Kuwait was only allowed to take its seat after the Arab League mediated a compromise, in which the delegation agreed to formally allow trade unions in the near future.[110] Kuwaiti membership in the ILO would remain insecure if it failed to legalize any actual trade unions, and pro-labor publications in Kuwait raised the specter of international condemnation if the National Assembly failed to act.[111] Even the British embassy believed that unions were "the obvious next step in the development of the state," reflecting a widespread midcentury faith in teleological modernization.[112]

The germ of what would become the first legal Kuwaiti trade unions emerged from a small group that first met at the Center for Workers' Culture, which, by the early 1960s, had become a node where workers from across the country could discuss issues, meet with allies, and learn about unions.[113] It was while representing the Center at the 1959 Asian Youth Conference in Cairo that the future Kuwaiti labor leader Hussein Saqr met with Fathi Kamil, the Egyptian labor leader, beginning a long relationship between labor organizers in Kuwait and Egypt.[114] Before the constitutional era, labor organizers viewed their work as sufficiently subversive that they would meet in secret, often in private homes.[115] A key moment came in 1961, when a group of workers affiliated with the Center for Workers' Culture reached out to prominent leaders of the Arab Nationalist Movement, including Dr. Ahmad al-Khatib and Sami al-Munais, to request their support in organizing a labor movement.[116] After independence, in 1963, the Kuwaiti branch of the ANM founded a special labor committee to expand its working-class base and "deepen the existing differences between the workers and the regime in general."[117] Al-Munais and al-Khatib would play a longstanding role in supporting the movement from the Assembly as elected MPs, while Arab nationalists like Hussein al-Youha would become key labor leaders.[118] The alliance between labor and the ANM would play a critical role in shaping the positions of the young labor movement, and in maintaining its independence from the regime.

As repression lifted during the early constitutional period, Kuwait witnessed a wave of labor activism by both citizens and noncitizens. On April 2, 1963, hundreds of workers at Shuwaikh Port went on strike to demand overtime pay, more vacation days, and an end to "ungraded" work, which meant that some workers had spent years being paid on an ad hoc, daily basis. Their demands received widespread coverage in the press and got the attention of the authorities.[119] Shortly afterwards, Arab workers at Aminoil (the American Arabian Oil Company) went on strike to demand the same number of vacation days as their "Artisan" colleagues.[120] In June, municipal watchmen struck for the five-day week.[121] In July, nurses at al-ʿAdtham Hospital—most of whom were noncitizen women—went on strike over hours, wages, and the quality of food.[122] In March of 1964, predominantly non-Kuwaiti workers at the Ministry of Public Works struck after the department unilaterally extended the length of the work week.[123] The Ministry reacted swiftly and sternly, condemning the action as "harmful to the security and stability of Kuwait."[124] Then in April, strikes took place at the Ministry of Electricity and in a private contracting firm.[125] Workers also sent a flurry of petitions to government departments and newspapers calling for labor rights and a better quality of life.[126]

The labor action with the most political resonance took place at the Kuwait Oil Company. In the early 1960s, workers continued to face systemic racial discrimination and a reluctance to hire and promote Arab and Kuwaiti workers. Many workers and their families were still living in ramshackle huts on the outskirts of oil operations.[127] KOC maintained its policy of "going slow" with Kuwaitization, largely to, as one official reported, "retain a nucleus of European personnel who could maintain production in an emergency for a limited period after Arab and Indian staff had withdrawn their labour"—in other words, to break strikes.[128] In fact, KOC even went so far as to estimate the precise number of white staff—about six hundred—that would be required to implement its strike plan.[129] The company also made little effort to hire more Arabic-speaking workers, instead hiring "only as suitable Arabs became available in Kuwait."[130] In 1960, the number of Arab KOC employees actually decreased, while in a 1966 report to the ILO, KOC acknowledged that they "expect to continue to rely on recruitment of skilled employees from neighboring countries" for five more years and that only 24 of their 737 salaried employees were Kuwaitis.[131]

The sustainability of their strike plan, however, was being thrown into question. The hiring and promotion of Arab and Kuwaiti workers, particularly in the oil industry, became one of the central points of discussion in the press and National Assembly.[132] Newspapers excoriated foreign oil companies for their failure to promote Kuwaiti workers.[133] Furthermore, the sixties brought growing popular recognition and condemnation of the strike plan. Newspapers reported—accurately—that oil companies hesitated to train Kuwaiti workers "to distance the Kuwaiti from the actual fields of oil operations."[134] Even the ruling family voiced open criticism. At a November 1962 press conference, Shaikh Jabir al-Ahmad accused KOC of "some not altogether straight dealings" with regards to Arabization. The comments were picked up by the company, which denied their validity but acknowledged that they represented popular sentiment.[135] Even British authorities began to worry about political backlash undermining their oil interests in Kuwait.[136] One report argued that the isolated enclave of Ahmadi was becoming "an increasingly unacceptable anachronism," as "a completely foreign city, inhabited and run by foreigners, detached mentally and physically from its hinterland cannot survive long in the days of the Voice of the Arabs, the National Assembly and the national press."[137]

Tensions boiled over in a strike on April 16, 1963, just two weeks after the Shuwaikh Port strike and two months after the first National Assembly elections. The company reported that over the course of the day, 1,625 of 3,981 workers were absent, representing the majority of the company's Arab and Kuwaiti workforce, though some noncitizens seem to have stayed on the job due to fear of dismissal and deportation. The action was well organized, a point that alarmed the oil company.[138] Rather than heading to work, workers brought pre-prepared banners and signs to protest the company's practices. The workers were careful to demonstrate their loyalty to the state, hoisting and applauding a photograph of the Emir, and to frame their struggle in nationalist terms. This previewed a strategy that would become central to the movement: an effort to drive a wedge between the oil companies and the state.

The protest was sympathetically covered in the press, particularly the Arab nationalist papers, nearly all of which republished worker demands.[139] The workers declared victory and returned to work the following day after receiving assurances that the company would arrange a meeting to discuss their grievances. The company had been taken by surprise. In a report written in the aftermath of the strike, company officials stated that their primary concerns were to keep production going and to protect the families of their white staff—though the latter were never threatened. The company was able to maintain continuous operations thanks to its strike plan, carried out by its British and American employees. Interestingly, many of its Indian and Pakistani workers asked not to come to work because of reported intimidation. From the extant records, it is impossible to tell if these workers stayed away because they actually feared retaliation—a claim that may have been an excuse—or because they wanted to support their Arab colleagues. Either way, the effect was the same.[140]

The first promised meeting between workers and management, which took place a week after the strike, was derailed because no workers were invited. Their interests were supposed to be represented by the Assistant Undersecretary for Oil from the Ministry of Finance and Industry, but as he was not in direct contact with the strikers, he had no clear idea of what they wanted. The attendees had to rely on lists of demands published by Kuwaiti newspapers. Eventually, on April 29 and May 1, the Ministry of Social Affairs and Labor hosted a meeting between the company and a group of elected worker representatives, including the soon-to-be prominent labor leader

Hassan Falah. The worker representatives put forward fourteen demands that would remain at the heart of their struggle with the oil companies for the next twelve years. The first and most important was that "a workers' union should be formed to include all our fellow workers in the Company." Their second key demand was "complete equality between Arab and non-Arab workers in rights and duties." Challenging the exclusions of nationality, workers pressed not just for Kuwaitizaiton, but Arabization, and for Arab workers to be given equal access to training facilities in addition to better pay and more opportunities for promotion. Other demands struck at the heart of the corporate system of divide-and-rule. The workers condemned the "contracting out" of work, arguing that the practice allowed the oil company to hire short-term workers with lower pay and fewer rights. They attacked the special privileges granted to white workers, and the preferential treatment accorded to Indian and Pakistani mid-level employees. And finally, they called for a comprehensive pension scheme, rejecting the company's assertion that it was waiting for the state to launch a social security system first.[141]

The workers did not win at the bargaining table. The oil company refused to recognize the legitimacy of the elected worker delegation and agreed only to review their demands and submit them "to the competent authorities."[142] The Ministry of Social Affairs and Labor, which mediated the dispute, agreed with the company that unionization was a matter for the Kuwaiti government to decide, rather than KOC, and informed workers that their demand should thus be redirected.[143] KOC officials also tried to split Kuwaiti from non-Kuwaiti workers, pushing back against pan-Arab solidarities, but to little effect.[144] The strike proved to be a major step forward for labor. All attendees of the meeting had acknowledged the right of workers to collectively organize, which even conservative newspapers considered a significant victory.[145] Moreover, reporting on the strike, as well as conditions in the oil company more generally, linked organized labor to the increasingly popular cause of resource nationalism.[146] *Al-Taliʿa* provided sustained and positive coverage, praising Arab workers for battling for "the right for a dignified life" and for moving the Arab world toward a "socialist society."[147]

Remarkably, publications from across the political spectrum supported the legalization of trade unions and an end to discrimination against Arab and Kuwaiti workers.[148] The strike received attention in papers as far away as Beirut.[149] Criticism of the oil company in *Akhbar al-Kuwait* was so vociferous that the minister of social affairs tried to pressure its editor to tone down its coverage.[150] As the interminable negotiations dragged on, a sustained drumbeat of coverage called for an end to the discriminatory and degrading conditions faced by oil workers.[151] The low percentage of Kuwaiti workers in the oil industry was also a regular topic of debate in the National Assembly.[152] On January 12, 1964, KOC representatives were summoned to a testy hearing of the Health and Social Affairs and Grievances and Petitions committees of the National Assembly, where they were grilled by Arab nationalist MPs.[153]

Unwilling to acknowledge the injustice, or even the reality, of racial discrimination, corporate and imperial authorities were at a loss to understand the strike. Rather than viewing the action as the outgrowth of legitimate grievances, they justified the dominance of white managers by arguing that they possessed superior temperament, skill, experience, and qualifications. One British labor attaché even blamed the tensions with workers on the few Arab managers in the company, complaining that "there is no quick method of making the Arab supervisors as considerate of the subordinates as their British predecessors generally were."[154] Most corporate and imperial officials attributed the failures of Kuwaitization to the supposed laziness and backwardness of non-white workers.[155]

Most perplexingly for the British, the strike demonstrated the mutual exclusivity of three of their most firmly held beliefs: that the strike was "political" in nature (and was therefore illegitimate), that it was organized by the many KOC workers of nomadic descent along tribal lines (and was therefore irrational), and that Bedouin were "backward" and "traditional" and therefore disinclined to participate in politics, which, as chapter 2 explained, was precisely why KOC had hired them in the first place. To solve this conundrum, British observers came up with a curious logic that would recur throughout the decade. As a disproportionate number of KOC workers were from the ʿAzmi tribe, authorities argued that the strike was instigated by outside agitators—usually described as non-Kuwaiti Arab or Palestinian workers—who took advantage of the Awazim's supposed proclivity to oppositional politics.[156] A 1965 report improbably described the Awazim as a tribe with "Nasserist inclinations" that was "noted for its hostility to the Sabah family."[157] Three years later, imperial officials described the oil union as "an institution for the industrial bedouin," who organized along tribal lines within the framework of modern labor relations.[158] These primordial proclivities were supposedly reinvigorated by the arrival of politicized Arabs, particularly "clever, lazy and politically conscious Palestinians."[159] KOC inaccurately concluded that "the originators of the move were non-Kuwaiti Arabs and that Kuwaitis were being coerced into joining them."[160] Fears of an alliance between Bedouin intransigence and Palestinian cunning, and thus implicitly of citizens and noncitizens, would underpin much of British policy for the next decade.

The strike rattled KOC.[161] A series of further strikes across the region during the summer of 1963 only amplified their concerns. Oil workers struck in Abu Dhabi from May 21 to 24; on Das Island, off the coast of Abu Dhabi, on June 1; and again in Qatar from April 21 to May 7.[162] The latter strike in Qatar represented such a large action that it was described as an "abortive revolution" that only failed to interrupt production due to what the company described as "heroic efforts" on the part of their white employees.[163] To add to KOC worries, these strikes were extensively covered in the Kuwaiti press, which connected struggles in Abu Dhabi and Aden with a broader campaign against what was often described as the neo-imperialism and discrimination practiced by Anglo-American oil firms in the Gulf.[164]

The 1963 strike launched a prolonged struggle at KOC that helped shift public opinion on the question of unionization. Workers threatened to strike again during the summer, as their demands had been discussed but not addressed.[165] In mid-September, Kuwaiti security forces reportedly thwarted a second attempted strike the day before it was scheduled by arresting thirty-four organizers.[166] After another unsuccessful round of negotiations, workers walked out of a December meeting in protest, accusing the company of stonewalling.[167] Negotiations continued, over the same demands, all the way into 1965.[168] By repeatedly refusing to compromise, KOC became a lightning rod for criticism and the perfect foil for labor organizers, who built popular support for trade unionism by linking it to anticolonial nationalism.[169] The popular mood finally forced a shift in policy, as the Kuwaiti state granted workers institutional recognition. On April 28, 1963, the Ministry of Social Affairs and Labor announced the creation of a Higher Advisory Committee for Labor Affairs comprised of sixteen members, including four workers and four employer representatives, to study potential reforms to labor legislation and mediate disputes.[170] The effort was only advisory, but it nevertheless built a framework for debate.

By the end of 1963, popular opinion in Kuwait had coalesced around the idea that a new labor law was needed to resolve industrial disputes. This consensus included the largely Egyptian industrial relations specialists working within the Ministry of Social Affairs and Labor.[171] Some even issued public statements of support that framed unions as useful for promoting democratic governance, protecting workers' rights, and building a modern economy.[172] The minister of social affairs himself expressed his support for a bill legalizing labor unions, saying that they would help confront the problems of low wages, long hours, and insufficient housing. He even echoed the call for an end to "the discrimination between workers, foreigner and Kuwaiti."[173] On the questions of worker training and Arabization in particular, officials were inclined to support the workers, noting company statistics that revealed a systematic failure to hire and promote Arab workers.[174] The seductive discourses of modernity and development thus blended with those of anti-discrimination, anticolonialism, and social justice.

UNIONIZATION | 1964–1965

By late May 1964, a new labor law—one that would guarantee the right to unionize—had become the nexus of parliamentary discussion. Of all the aforementioned arguments in its favor, supporters homed in on the fight against neocolonialism, positioning workers as the front line of resistance against foreign oil companies. Sami al-Munais stressed that "unions are the answer" to the "dictatorship of the company," which *al-Tali'a* had come to call the "Ahmadi empire."[175] The framing of the labor law as a nationalist measure proved effective.[176] On August 9, 1964, after a protracted debate, Law 38 of 1964 was officially published.

The legislation would shape Kuwaiti labor law for decades to come. Pro-labor and Arab nationalist deputies managed to secure several of their key demands. Most importantly, unionization and collective bargaining were finally legalized. The law also limited working hours and required employers to supply their workers with adequate drinking water, transportation, and healthcare. And it addressed some of the most exploitative practices of labor recruiters. Finally, it reiterated the requirement that "priority" in employment be given first to Kuwaiti nationals, then to Arabs, and finally to "foreigners."[177]

But the legislation also created new restrictions. Article 72 required that Kuwaitis could only join unions if they received "Good Conduct" certificates from the reactionary Interior Ministry, handing the Kuwaiti state enormous leverage. Article 73 banned unions from "indulging in political, religious, or sectarian matters," or accepting donations without the consent of the Ministry of Social Affairs and Labour, while Articles 74 to 76 empowered the Affairs Ministry to inspect union accounts, membership lists, and even meeting minutes. Strikes could only be launched after arbitration, and violations of law could lead to the suspension, or even dissolution, of a union. Just as significant were its limitations on membership. As a private sector labor law, it excluded government workers, "temporary workers engaged for a period not exceeding six months," workers in firms that employed no mechanical machinery and fewer than five workers, and all domestic workers. The law thus exacerbated the divide between labor law governing the public sector, with its largely Kuwaiti workforce, and the private sector, which was dominated by noncitizens. Its provisions limiting the length of the work week did not apply to the workers with the longest hours in "hotels, restaurants, watchmen and hospitals." It also specified no minimum wage.[178]

The sharpest controversy arose over the role of noncitizens. The first draft of the bill, written by Egyptian experts at the Ministry of Social Affairs and Labor, had proposed that Kuwaitis should be guaranteed a majority of executive committee seats in trade unions, but that union membership and elected office should be open to all.[179] The pro-labor Arab nationalists vocally demanded that all workers should have equal rights in unions.[180] *Al-Taliʿa* put equivalence between Arab and Kuwaiti workers at the center of its coverage, attacking exclusions on the basis of nationality as a form of "discrimination (*al-tafriq*)" that would shatter Arab unity and weaken the anti-imperialist cause.[181] Condemnation of nationality restrictions had also been a hallmark of Arab nationalist articles on the labor struggles of 1963 and 1964.[182] After the Shuwaikh Port strike, for instance, *Sawt al-Khalij* reported that "some opportunists tried to discriminate between Kuwaiti workers and their brother non-Kuwaiti Arabs," but that workers rejected such "racism (*al-ʿansuriyya*)."[183]

But despite the mass appeal of Arab nationalism, conservatives held a majority of seats in the Assembly. Even many of those who had come around to the idea of unionization demanded that union membership be restricted to Kuwaiti citizens.[184] Some even tried to further restrict union rights in the law by limiting membership not just to Kuwaitis, but to "first-tier" Kuwaitis, thus excluding naturalized citizens.[185] Their perspective eventually triumphed. The Assembly placed strict limits on noncitizens, allowing them to join unions only after five years of residency, and only five years from the passage of the law. Even then they were prohibited from voting in union elections or holding office, and without protection from dismissal and deportation, they would still face insurmountable obstacles to union activity.[186] In effect, noncitizens were excised from the movement by the National Assembly. A relieved KOC reported that "the point of view of Arab Unity, whilst being accepted by the Assembly in principle, were not supported when it came to adopting measures which would harm interests of pure Kuwaitis."[187]

The final text of the bill disappointed supporters of labor. They described the exclusion of noncitizens from many of the law's protections as discriminatory and a violation of international norms, and they accused "capitalists" in the National Assembly for "stirring up factional chauvinism" in order to pursue their class interest.[188] Their effort to force contractors to take "responsibility" for their workers, a clause that would have effectively outlawed the exploitative subcontracts proliferating in major industries like oil, had failed, a defeat that *al-Tali'a* blamed on lobbying by the influential Chamber of Commerce.[189] Arab nationalists, reflecting the increasingly class-based analysis of the movement, explained that the law's shortcomings partly resulted from the fact that most deputies and ministers were employers, rather than workers. Further, the paper asserted, many deputies passed a labor law less to protect the rights of workers than to please the international community, and particularly the ILO.[190] In the years following the law's passage, Kuwaiti labor leaders and their allies continue to attack its shortcomings in articles and public meetings.[191] The debate was anything but over.

Despite the law's many weaknesses, it nevertheless provided an opening for labor organizers. Just days after its passage, and with the encouragement of the Arab nationalist press, workers affiliated with the Workers' Culture Center and the Arab Nationalist Movement began collecting the signatures required to form unions.[192] In September 1964, they petitioned the Ministry of Social Affairs and Labor for permission to form unions in the Health, Municipality, and Education Ministries, in addition to KOC.[193] The process was not smooth. At first, the Ministry hesitated, yielding only when Dr. Ahmad al-Khatib personally intervened.[194] Then the minister of the interior held up their applications for Certificates of Good Conduct. The unions were only recognized when a group of workers went straight to the Emir and, notably, received his personal support.[195] Finally, after a meeting at the venerable Independence Club on October 21, 1964, the first unions in Kuwait were officially incorporated.[196] By the end of 1964, four trade unions had been registered, in the Municipality, Ministries of Health and Education, and the Kuwait Oil Company, soon followed by two more in Aminoil and the Japanese-owned Arabian Oil Company.[197] The division between unions in the government sector, where most citizens worked, and the private sector, mainly oil, would be a bureaucratic fixture of the movement. While the unions remained small, with about one thousand to two thousand members each, their early months witnessed slow but sustained growth.[198] With an elected leadership, allies in the press and the Arab Nationalist Movement, and a presence in the most significant industries in the country, the Kuwaiti labor movement had an institutional base.

CONCLUSION

As the unions mediated their first disputes, they began to negotiate their relationship with the Kuwaiti state. Their role was anything but predetermined. The Egyptian labor movement, which many Kuwaiti trade unionists viewed as a model, had, by the Nasserist era, taken a corporatist turn, surrendering its independence in exchange for material concessions on wages and benefits.[199] Many early union organizers were anticolonial nationalists who hoped that, after independence, their new government would become an ally. Like many other voluntary organizations at the time, the unions applied for, and received, a 3,000-dinar annual government subsidy. It was seemingly designed to control the unions as much as to help them, but it provided an important financial boost nonetheless.[200] The unions also began bringing labor actions under their purview, reining in independent strikes that had now become wildcats.[201] But the Kuwaiti labor movement would firmly reject corporatism. As the fledgling constitutional regime came under attack, Kuwaiti unions would emerge as powerful proponents of democratic rule, resource nationalism, and noncitizen rights.

6 The Radical Sixties | 1965–1970

IN 1965, THE KUWAITI government launched a campaign to fracture the nascent labor movement along the lines of nationality. It began with a transparently calculated decision to grant retroactive overtime payments to state employees. This answered a longstanding demand of government workers—but came with a caveat. While citizens were granted retroactive payments for overtime worked since 1955, noncitizens were offered significantly less.[1] Union leadership faced a stark choice: Would they support a policy that materially benefited their membership—which was, by law, exclusively Kuwaiti—or reject it as a matter of principle? In the aftermath of the announcement, government-sector unions, led by Hussein Saqr and Nasser al-ʿArfi, the head of the Ministry of Finance and Industry union, organized a public meeting to discuss the proposal. Both men condemned the decision in forceful terms, describing it as discriminatory, unjust, and directly opposed to the union's position on noncitizen rights. But at the end of the meeting, al-ʿArfi broke with Saqr by announcing that he would support the measure on the grounds that it was in the best interest of his membership. *Al-Taliʿa* (The Vanguard) expressed shock and alarm at this decision, but it also reported that some rank-and-file members voiced similar feelings.[2] Would the trade union movement, only one year old, be nipped in the bud by the nationality question?

British expectations that xenophobia would override solidarity proved inaccurate. Despite coordinated pressure from the state, the oil companies, and British officials, union leaders launched a sustained and aggressive campaign for the equal treatment of citizen and noncitizen workers. In the aftermath of the controversy, the trade union leadership scrambled to prevent their young movement from splintering, traveling the country to convince workers to oppose any measure that discriminated against their noncitizen colleagues. Speaking to Aminoil workers in Fahahil, Hussein Saqr attacked the government's position as an attempt to divide the working class, comparing it to the ban on noncitizen union membership. The Aminoil workers agreed, opposing any such overtime plan on the grounds that it was blatantly discriminatory.[3] After a series of public meetings held to discuss the overtime proposal, Kuwaiti public sector unions formed a three-person joint committee consisting of Hussein al-Youha, Ahmad Said al-Asbahi, and Hussein Saqr to convey their opposition to the Ministry of Social Affairs and Labor.[4] Though the government refused to change its decision, workers and their allies continued to fight for its reversal. For years afterwards, trade union leaders pointed to their statements on nondiscrimination during this period as some of the foundational texts of their movement.[5]

This chapter traces the years 1965 to 1970, when the new trade union movement weathered a withering crackdown on dissent to emerge as one of the most powerful forces in Kuwaiti politics. The period was a time of transformation and revolution on the Arabian Peninsula. Nasser's staggering defeat in the 1967 war against Israel splintered the Arab Nationalist Movement and radicalized its left wing. South Yemen won its independence from Britain as a socialist state in 1967 after years of struggle, injecting new energy into Marxist movements across the region. The following year, the Dhofar Liberation Front, which launched a revolution against the repressive British-backed Sultan of Oman in 1965, changed its name to the Popular Front for the Liberation of the Occupied Arab Gulf (PFLOAG), embraced Maoism, and transformed itself into an international movement for the overthrow of British-backed autocrats across the Gulf.[6] In Bahrain, the "Constitutive Committee," a mass movement of Bahraini reformists, radicals, and workers, demanded a constitution, rule of law, and the democratization of governance, culminating in a major uprising in 1972.[7] Even Saudi Arabia witnessed the emergence of Marxist-Leninist factions out of the remnants of underground Ba'athist or Arab nationalist parties, despite a vicious state crackdown.[8] Radicalism gathered strength as empire retreated. In January 1968, the cash-strapped British suddenly announced that they would withdraw from the Persian Gulf, triggering alarm in the Nixon administration and jubilation in the ranks of anticolonial activists. Reflecting the British belief that regional autocracies were now capable of quelling calls for revolutionary change, Bahrain, Qatar, and the United Arab Emirates all gained their independence in 1971.[9]

In Kuwait, as elsewhere, the foreclosure of legal avenues of political participation fueled political radicalism. In 1965, Abdullah al-Salem Al Sabah, who had ruled for fifteen years, died, leaving the throne to his more autocratic brother, Sabah al-Salem. What followed was an assault on the vibrant political culture of the early constitutional period. The next six years witnessed a crackdown on dissent that strained the new constitution past its breaking point. By rigging elections, muzzling the press, and shuttering political clubs, the state sharpened tensions with the political opposition until the situation became explosive. It also allied with business interests and elite families to narrow access to nationality.[10] Revealingly, the state directed its attack, first and foremost, against campaigns for noncitizen rights—especially in the workplace. It framed the specter of noncitizen participation in trade unionism as an especially pernicious threat to Kuwaiti sovereignty. The crackdown corresponded with and encouraged a new and unprecedented radicalism in the left wing of the Kuwaiti opposition. In 1968, the Arab Nationalist Movement expelled its Kuwaiti branch on the grounds that the Kuwaitis had neither hewed to the new socialist line nor challenged the authority of the monarchy. In response, the Kuwaiti movement split, with a radical faction including Ahmad al-Ruba'i—who fought in the Dhofar Revolution—forming al-Haraka al-Thawriyya al-Shaʿbiyya fi al-Kuwait, or The Popular Revolutionary Movement (PRM). It broke from the founding generation of Arab nationalists and called for direct struggle against the Al Sabah.[11] By 1970, it appeared to some observers that Kuwait was tottering on the brink of a revolution.

The nascent Kuwaiti labor movement found itself at the intersection of suppression and radicalization. It also faced the same question as other labor movements in the postcolonial era. What would be its relationship to the state? And how would it respond to efforts to divide citizen and noncitizen workers? In the era of decolonization, many labor movements in the Arabic-speaking world embraced corporatism, surrendering their independence in exchange for either material benefits or official position.[12] Kuwaiti trade unionists broke with that precedent. In the face of a violent crackdown, organized labor emerged as a pillar of the pro-democracy opposition, attained the power to shut down oil production, and positioned itself as the vanguard of resistance to the oil firms that embodied neocolonialism in Kuwait. The result was a remarkable flourishing in an atmosphere of repression. Despite the forced exclusion of noncitizens from the movement, workers, especially petroleum workers, wielded power out of all proportion to their numbers by positioning themselves as defenders of Kuwaiti sovereignty and leveraging their newfound capacity to shut down oil production. By launching a series of strikes and adopting the rhetoric of anticolonial nationalism, oil workers demonstrated that they could overpower the combined force of the state and the oil companies. Moreover, their embrace of radical politics and abandonment of many exclusionary elements of nationalism led trade union leaders to campaign on behalf of all workers, citizen and noncitizen.[13] The founding of the Kuwait Trade Union Federation (KTUF) embodied a conscious effort to unite labor struggles across the public and private sectors, and therefore across the boundaries of nationality. Their actions in this period thus laid the groundwork for a sweeping challenge to the Kuwaiti nationality regime in the early 1970s.

In a broader sense, the radical moment of the late 1960s illuminates how the category of nationality perpetuated the hierarchies of the imperial era.[14] Julian Go has noted that, despite its value, scholarship on racial capitalism has not forged an agreed-upon conceptualization of race, and is still just beginning to trace its intersection with other identifiers in specific historical contexts.[15] This chapter seeks to provide one such case study. In the Gulf, nationality perpetuated racialized strategies of labor control after decolonization. It thus proved analogous to Jaakko Heiskanen's critique of the concept of ethnicity, "filling in the gaps created in our conceptual organisation of the world as nineteenth-century categories were repurposed for twentieth-century ends"—a process "inseparable from the consolidation of a global international system populated by formally equal and sovereign nation-states."[16] The wages of nationality—more benefits, better pay, and priority in hiring and promotion—were ingrained in law and legitimated by the principles of the international order.[17] They were also calculated, the product of an alliance between business elites, oil firms, and authoritarian monarchies who all feared the rise of organized labor.

Despite their internationalism, Kuwaiti labor leaders struggled to counter the exclusions of nationality and at times even found themselves abetting them against their will. Indeed, the greatest source of their power—the ability to shut down oil production—depended on the Arabization and Kuwaitization of the oil sector, policies that often came at the expense of noncitizens.

Even as labor leaders repeatedly condemned nationality as a new form of racism, and compared Gulf oil companies to apartheid and Jim Crow, they struggled to effectively oppose a category ingrained in the global system of nation-states. Emblematic of this conundrum was the decision to draft a new labor law in the oil sector and frame its enforcement as a matter of national sovereignty. While enormously popular, the campaign sidelined the rest of a private sector dominated by noncitizen workers. The result was that even their victories threatened to further cleave them from their non-Kuwaiti comrades. This fissure, accurately predicted and consciously opposed, threatened to undermine the unity on which labor depended for its strength.

CRACKDOWN

In his memoirs, Dr. Ahmad al-Khatib frames the crackdown of 1965 as a turning point, when the state began to claw back the democratic gains won over a generation of struggle.[18] The death of Abdul Karim Qassim, combined with rising tensions between Egypt and Saudi Arabia, seem to have convinced the Al Sabah that their geopolitical position had stabilized and that they could therefore risk the international opprobrium likely to result from the suppression of dissent.[19] The resulting shutdown of legal avenues for political participation would, once again, be paired with efforts to even further restrict access to Kuwaiti nationality and undermine the rights of noncitizens. But in forcing politics underground, it would also radicalize the opposition and turn organized labor firmly against the regime.

The crackdown began in the National Assembly. The government introduced a measure to give the Council of Ministers the right to fire state employees, prevent their future employment, and even strip them of political rights. Arab nationalist deputies concluded that the Assembly was no longer an effective political platform and resigned their positions.[20] With their departure, the National Assembly became, as a British official said, "little more than a rubber stamp."[21] Then student organizations and clubs, which had been centers of political activity, were shuttered. In 1966, *al-Tali'a* was suspended for a year, sending a chill through the Kuwaiti press.[22] The regime also conducted mass deportations of politically active noncitizens, including the deliberate targeting of journalists.[23] While the surviving Arab nationalist press condemned the deportations as a distraction from the failures of the government, many conservative papers came out in open support of the regime's actions.[24] So did the British. Even before the death of Abdullah al-Salem, they had called for the suppression of *al-Tali'a*.[25] The paper only survived because Abdullah al-Salem had flatly refused, even when the British hinted at the prospect of abandoning their "military commitments" to Kuwait.[26] British authorities seconded another liaison officer to the Kuwaiti Security Forces to help counter "subversive activities by non-Kuwaitis."[27] They also hoped that a resurgence of what they called "little Kuwaiti" nationalism could become a means of bludgeoning the opposition, especially given that "only Kuwaitis vote."[28] To that end, they expressed satisfaction that the deportations had persuaded noncitizens "to isolate themselves yet more completely from politics" and brought the National Assembly "nicely to heel," even if, as one official put it, "there does not seem to be any opportunity for a review of, or appeal against, the decision and it is not a procedure that would stand up to investigation by Amnesty International."[29]

As with the crackdown on dissent in 1959, the regime and its allies took the opportunity to narrow access to nationality. In 1965, the Assembly made naturalization even more difficult by upping its requirements.[30] Then in 1966, the ten-year waiting period during which second-tier citizens were denied political rights, scheduled to expire in 1969, was extended until 1986, reinforcing a profound fissure within the citizenry itself.[31] And in the same year, the Interior Ministry decided to grant nationality to the noncitizen wives of Kuwaiti men only after a five-year waiting period.[32] Suleiman al-Masha'n defended the decision with the rhetoric of the marriage crisis, claiming that many noncitizen women only wanted to marry Kuwaiti men for the purpose of obtaining the material benefits of nationality.[33] These legislative changes corresponded with a discursive shift in the press, as conservative papers increasingly argued that many people who saw nationality as "just a business deal" had been naturalized.[34] But perhaps the regime's most significant decision was to illegally grant first-tier nationality—with full voting rights—to tens of thousands of Bedouin in the hope of creating a loyalist voting bloc.[35] The move exacerbated tensions between Kuwaitis of nomadic and urban descent, and further undermined the legitimacy of the nationality regime in the eyes of the Kuwaiti population.[36] It also previewed a strategy of electoral gerrymandering that would become a favored tactic in future decades.

A striking element of the crackdown was its focus on trade unions, specifically their relationship to noncitizens. Like the oil companies, the ruling family and its allies seemed most alarmed by the potential of an alliance between citizen and noncitizen workers. The most open explication of the crackdown, delivered by the prime minister on May 3, 1966, made this clear:

> Not all of them [noncitizens] respect the sanctities of this country, or appreciate its hospitality. There are some who do not respect our traditions and laws. Some work for foreign interests and in the service of principles which are alien to us. They try to attract citizens to their principles to use them in their harmful activities. Thus an activity which aims at shattering the ties of our national unity appeared in our country. They sow the seeds of rancour, hatred and jealousy among brothers, fathers and sons and families. They also try to spread a rash spirit of disregard for the values which are sacred to us and for the traditions in which we were brought up. They cast doubt on our social, political and economic systems. The advocates of these activities, which are harmful to the interests of the homeland, come from among the newcomers and from a few of our weak and deceived citizens who yielded to these activities without realising the great danger to themselves and to their country. Everyone knows the exposed methods which this group uses to implement its plan. They strenuously try to win the trade unions and federations over to their activities. We encourage these trade unions and federations. We work for their establishment. We supply them with funds in the interest of their members if they care for their rights and if they remind themselves of their own and their homeland's interests. This is so that they may stress their existence in the real national attitudes required of them. However, we will never permit them to be exploited by certain tendentious individuals for their subversive purposes or to be deflected from the ideas for which they were established.[37]

The British also remained fixated on the prospect of an alliance between citizen workers and noncitizens, especially "the Palestinian element in Kuwait." Meeting in 1966, imperial authorities and KOC officials concluded that if Palestinians were to be "drawn into Kuwaiti politics," they could mobilize "real industrial strength."[38] This concern only deepened as a new generation of Palestinian refugees moved to Kuwait in the wake of the 1967 war, and as 1969 approached—the fifth anniversary of the Kuwaiti labor law, meaning that non-Kuwaitis would be eligible to join trade unions.[39] While British authorities hoped that the Kuwaiti government would take action to preemptively amend the law, their concern that "outside agitators" would take over the movement did not abate.[40]

The weight of the crackdown therefore fell heavily onto the shoulders of the nascent trade union movement. Government departments repeatedly threw up barriers to labor organizing. When workers of the Ministry of Public Works attempted to unionize, the Interior Ministry refused to grant them Good Conduct Certificates on the grounds that the group included "managers," rather than workers.[41] Interior also prevented Aminoil workers from unionizing on the argument that they needed at least one hundred founding members, despite the fact that the company only employed sixty-three Kuwaitis.[42] By 1965, Good Conduct Certificates had become a significant problem, while *al-Tali'a* was accusing the Interior Ministry of actively impeding unionization.[43] When workers attempted to publish a newsletter, "The Voice of the Worker," state officials not only shut it down but arrested several workers on the charge of "publishing a magazine without a license."[44] Permission to publish a union organ would be repeatedly denied.[45] In September 1965, security forces even raided the headquarters of the government sector union federation, seizing documents and detaining a janitor who refused to cooperate with the search.[46]

To prevent the much-feared alliance of citizen and noncitizen workers, the Kuwaiti state partnered with British officials and the oil companies to update their policies of divide-and-rule. One widespread strategy was the selective payment of allowances. Allowances had long been utilized by oil companies to provide extra compensation to employees posted to remote locations or engaged in hazardous work. But beginning in the 1960s, oil companies and government departments began paying special "cost of living" or "social" allowances exclusively to Kuwaitis, often scaling them based on the size of a worker's family.[47] This was a popular imperial strategy around the world—French colonial officials in West Africa had used family allowances to discriminate between French and African workers.[48] Labor activists and their allies blamed—and strongly condemned—the oil companies for using allowances to divide their workforce by giving citizen workers additional privileges to defend. However, their strategic deployment seems to have originated with the state.[49] In 1968, it was the state of Kuwait that pressured KOC into paying special social allowances only to their Kuwaiti employees, with the minister of finance and oil reportedly telling the company "to take no notice of the unions, the Assembly, or the press."[50]

Another essential tactic was hiring noncitizens on labor contracts.[51] A revealing moment came after the wave of strikes that swept the oilfields of the Gulf in 1963, when representatives of nearly every major oil firm in the region—Aramco, Qatar Petroleum Company, Shell Qatar, Abu Dhabi Petroleum Company, Bapco, ADMA Das Island, and the Kuwait Oil Company—traveled to Bahrain to coordinate their response.[52] Their remarkably frank discussion revealed that virtually all of the Gulf oil firms were gradually phasing out their divide-and-rule strategy based on race and replacing it with one based on nationality, turning to recruitment of contract workers abroad. As labor nationalization campaigns made it increasingly difficult to hire white middle managers—on whom oil firms had relied as strikebreakers—the employment of deportable noncitizens allowed corporate authorities to retain control. Subcontracting had long been standard practice across the world's oil frontiers.[53] Now it would become a way of life across the Persian Gulf, embraced not just by oil firms but by the well-connected local employers and ruling families who became its new champions.

Oil firms also tried to create systems of worker representation that could perpetuate divide-and-rule. At the 1963 meeting, the attendees unsurprisingly agreed that labor organizing was an existential threat. When the KOC representative reported that the Kuwaiti government was on the verge of legalizing trade unions, the news "aroused sharp reaction from all other representatives."[54] Most tried to stave off unionization with a policy of "joint consultation," which opened lines of communication between workers and management without the threat of collective action. This also allowed the oil companies to "provide separate channels of communication for the different national groups in their employment," thus dividing the workforce even further.[55] Bapco restricted their consultative committees to Bahrainis, while Qatar Petroleum organized five separate negotiating groups. Similar meetings held by the region's oil firms throughout the mid-sixties made clear that noncitizens, rather than white workers, were becoming the pivotal players in corporate strike plans, and that oil companies were giving special privileges, such as allowances, benefits, and higher wages, to their citizen employees to cleave them from their noncitizen colleagues.[56]

The granting of special prerogatives to citizen workers and systematic hiring of noncitizen contractors threatened to split the young trade union movement. Fissures within labor are difficult to trace. The limitations of the written source material, and an understandable reluctance to air dirty laundry, can erase internal conflict from the historical record. Nevertheless, it seems clear that potentially serious divisions emerged in 1965. A glimpse of these tensions emerges in an *al-Tali'a* article published that April. The paper reported that major employers and government departments were using special regulations to divide Kuwaitis and Arabs, as well as blue- and white-collar employees. This was generating a dangerous "social and material" divide between different workers and different sectors, notably the noncitizen-dominated private sector and citizen-run public sector workforces. The paper criticized unions for not sufficiently fighting against these divisions, and particularly the efforts to grant special privileges to Kuwaiti workers.[57] A few weeks later, an opinion piece condemned workers who focused on who "is of Kuwaiti origins" or who is not, or that "so and so is Shammari and so and so is 'Azmi and so and so is Rashidi." In collapsing "tribal" identifiers and nationality, the paper framed both as "outmoded" and backward—not a basis on which a modern and effective trade union movement could be built.[58]

Two incidents in 1965 demonstrated the divisive power of nationality. The first was the overtime decision discussed at the beginning of this chapter. The second took place in December, when some eight hundred contracted port workers walked off the job in Shuwaikh. The strike was organized by noncitizens who, in addition to demanding unpaid wages, were protesting the detention and deportation of several workers. But unlike nearly every other strike during the decade, it received stunningly negative coverage in the Arab nationalist press, including *al-Tali'a*. The workers were Iranian. The paper accused the strike of defending "infiltrators" and chauvinistically opposing efforts to Arabize the port workforce. It also condemned the strike as political, and thus unrelated to wages or working conditions—despite the fact that it actively encouraged the Kuwaiti labor movement to take political positions.[59] This was not an isolated incident. In 1966, the paper blamed the difficulties of labor organizing in Bahrain and Qatar on British imperial power, the oil companies, and Iranian "infiltrators," who they reported were used to break strikes and undermine worker power.[60] Anti-Iranian bigotry undermined efforts to unite workers of all nationalities and left the Arab nationalists vulnerable to accusations of a double standard.

But despite this notable blindspot, workers and their allies did not compromise in their fight for noncitizen rights. On the floor of the National Assembly, the Arab nationalist MP and former oil worker Rashid Saif condemned the selective distribution of social allowances as a racist and discriminatory stratagem to divide the working class.[61] In correspondence with the ILO, Kuwaiti trade unions repeatedly expressed their frustration with the exclusion of noncitizens from their movement and recounted their efforts to amend Kuwaiti labor law to enable noncitizen participation.[62] In July of 1968, the KOC union released a petition, reprinted in *al-Taliʿa*, demanding that the company implement compensation policies "without discrimination between Kuwaiti and Arab."[63] Workers repeatedly compared discrimination on the basis of nationality with discrimination on the basis of race, attacking both in the strongest possible terms.[64] So did their allies in the press. In the late 1960s, *al-Taliʿa* published a succession of articles hammering home the argument that unequal allowances and overtime payments were just another form of racism.[65] Indeed, after a visit to Kuwait in 1969, the U.S. labor attaché reported that he "had been impressed by the determination of the labour leaders to work for equality of treatment between Kuwaitis and non-Kuwaiti arabs," and noted that worker representatives "had likened the policies of the Kuwait government to those of apartheid in South Africa."[66]

Union leadership paired condemnations of discrimination with more strategic arguments. Many noted that their strength was directly proportional to the size of their membership and would therefore increase with the participation of noncitizens.[67] Hussein al-Youha, a particularly forceful advocate of noncitizen worker rights, made this relationship clear in a 1967 speech.[68] He framed the exclusion of noncitizens from the labor movement as its greatest weakness. The strength of any labor movement, he explained, was determined by the percentage of the workforce that it includes. Kuwaiti legislators had deliberately weakened the movement. This, he argued, had made it difficult for the oil unions to bring a majority of the workforce into their membership, undermining their struggle against the foreign-owned oil companies. And it had left workers in the overwhelmingly noncitizen private sector unprotected.[69]

As the crackdown continued, the labor movement cemented its alliance with the pro-democracy opposition by entering electoral politics. In the second elections to the National Assembly, scheduled for January 1967, several labor representatives, including Hassan Falah and Rashid Saif, ran for office as part of a reformist alliance that included youthful members of old merchant families and longtime Arab Nationalist Movement (ANM) members like Dr. Ahmad al-Khatib.[70] During the campaign, union candidates supported new labor legislation that would grant equal rights to noncitizens, challenging the government's stance head-on. Coming just three years after the first unions were authorized, the participation of worker representatives in the elections illustrated both the independence and the rapid ascent of the labor movement. But this new alliance was thwarted by the state. The election campaign, and its aftermath, were characterized by vicious attacks on unions from both state officials and the conservative press.[71] ILO officials visiting Kuwait at the time described union activities as effectively "banned" and organizing efforts at "a virtual standstill."[72] Indeed, attacks on labor were so forceful that the ILO representative in Kuwait requested an extension to his mission because the authorities had made it virtually impossible for him to meet with union representatives or even sympathetic Kuwaiti officials.[73] British officials reported that Hassan Falah, key founder of the KOC union and now a candidate for the National Assembly, was summoned by Shaikh Abdullah al-Jabir, the governor of Ahmadi, for a "dressing down," and reportedly warned that if the union did not stay out of politics, he would be stripped of his nationality.[74] The government also launched a failed effort to dislodge the leadership of the KOC union.[75] The regime ended the challenge by rigging the elections, ensuring the defeat of nearly all members of the opposition. Of the trade union candidates, only Rashid Saif won a seat.[76]

In the aftermath of the 1967 elections, relations between state and the unions reached a nadir. Minister of Labor Abdul Aziz Sarawi, who had usually been responsive to worker demands, resigned in protest.[77] He was replaced by the far less sympathetic Khalid al-Madaf, whom *al-Tali'a* accused of abetting anti-union forces within his Ministry.[78] The switch exemplified a broader trend of noncitizen Arab technical experts, hired in the early oil years to staff high-level government positions, being replaced by regime loyalists who turned the state bureaucracy against organized labor. The new leadership quickly heightened restrictions on unions.[79] When employees of the Ministry of Post and Electricity applied to form a union, their application was rejected by the Ministry of Social Affairs and Labor, despite the fact that they had assembled the necessary paperwork.[80] The Interior

Ministry further restricted access to Certificates of Good Conduct, slowing the growth of union membership.[81] Legal avenues for political participation seemed increasingly foreclosed.

THE RADICAL SIXTIES

Though their electoral strategy faltered, Kuwaiti labor organizers built their organizational capacity and public profile in a sustained battle against the oil companies. They discursively mobilized longstanding nationalist critiques, arguing that the oil companies ignored or willfully misinterpreted Kuwaiti law, operated like a state within a state, discriminated against their non-white employees, and, in short, represented the institutional embodiment of neocolonialism. In so doing, they successfully framed their labor struggle in terms of sovereignty and citizenship and positioned themselves as representatives of both Arab nationalism and anti-imperialism. The arguments and institutions that emerged from this period, particularly the Kuwait Trade Union Federation (KTUF), would transform Kuwaiti politics.

Despite the founding of OPEC in 1960, the 1960s were not an auspicious moment for resource nationalism. Surplus production capacity led to low oil prices and pitted oil-producing countries against each other in a bid to convince the oil multinationals, who still controlled the oil spigot, to maintain the production levels on which their economies depended. Moreover, between 1962 and 1965, OPEC began to split into two camps: the "moderates," usually U.S.-allied monarchies in favor of perpetuating the concession system, and the "radicals," led by Venezuela, Algeria, and Iraq, who called for more fundamental change, including the possibility of nationalization. The fissure, which opened due to disagreements on taxation, undermined OPEC for over a decade. During the 1960s, in country after country, the moderates beat out the radicals, usually because autocratic regimes proved unwilling to break with their imperial allies. In a representative move, Abdullah Tariki, the prominent Saudi oil minister and OPEC founder, was removed from his post and exiled in 1962. Though he remained an influential voice in oil affairs, he would never hold public office again.[82]

But despite these setbacks, Christopher Dietrich has argued that resource nationalism became "even more mainstream" as decolonization swept the globe.[83] Kuwait would be pivotal to this paradigm shift. The divide within OPEC reflected the divide within Kuwaiti politics. While the regime and its allies sided with the conservatives, Arab nationalists and oil workers backed the radicals.[84] Tensions exploded when a new oil agreement was proposed in 1965. While it would have increased royalties through direct taxation, it would also have perpetuated the concessionary system and the independent power of the oil multinationals.[85] Arab nationalist deputies invited Tariki to personally address the National Assembly during the debate, and the body subsequently exercised its considerable power to say no by vetoing the deal.[86] Kuwaiti newspapers and oil unions championed Tariki's internationalist project for the rest of the decade, in effect serving as a juncture between nascent "petro-periodicals" and the mainstream discourse.[87] Tariki had become a fixture in *al-Tali'a* beginning in 1963.[88] By 1964 he was publishing a semi-regular column, entitled "Bitruliyyat," on global oil affairs, and openly calling for nationalization. He viewed Arab control over oil and its revenues as the solution to a slew of political and economic problems, from Palestine and Bedouin settlement to agricultural and industrial development, and like Ashraf Lutfi called for the creation of new national oil companies, staffed by Arab citizens, that could supplant the multinational oil corporations.[89] Tariki felt comfortable in Kuwaiti politics. Indeed, while he was a Saudi national, he had attended primary school in Kuwait, and his first job was as a clerk working for a Kuwaiti businessman. His personal biography bridged the centuries-old ties of trade that knitted together the Indian Ocean and the new bonds of solidarity that bound the Third World. It was therefore no surprise that when Tariki proposed the establishment of an "oil university" to train the new generation of Arab technical experts, he suggested that it be located in Kuwait.[90]

An especially popular issue was the hiring and promotion of Arab and Kuwaiti workers. Distancing oil workers from production remained an effective corporate strategy, keeping oil-producing states dependent on imported managers and expertise.[91] In March 1967, the KOC head of government relations met with the minister of finance and oil and found himself facing blistering criticism of the failures of Kuwaitization. The minister said that "not only had the Company failed to develop an adequate number of Kuwaitis to occupy 'leading positions' in its organisation, but it had failed to retain those who joined it with some qualifications." In fact, the minister reported that his own brother Mohammad, like many other qualified Kuwaitis, "was put in the Display Centre doing nothing until he was made to feel he was not wanted."[92] Critics linked the longstanding failure to implement Kuwaitization with rising citizen unemployment numbers.[93] The opposition blamed the Kuwaiti government for failing to force the oil companies to hire more Kuwaitis. In a particularly heated exchange in 1968, Rashid Saif reportedly attacked the oil minister over the low percentage of Kuwaitis in Aminoil by calling him "an oil company hireling" and "a donkey," though the terms were stricken from the official record.[94]

Perhaps the most universally popular measure for combating the strike plan was the creation of worker training programs to prepare Kuwaitis for higher-level positions in the oil industry. Virtually all parties believed that effectual control of production could only be carried out by a critical mass of trained Kuwaiti workers.[95] Worker training thus became a central objective of the trade union movement, and the oil unions in particular, especially given that the oil companies justified their systematic privileging of white managers by arguing that they possessed necessary technical and managerial skills and experience.[96] The oil workers framed training as essential for securing Kuwait's economic sovereignty.[97] In 1968, a flurry of calls for new training programs followed a KOC report that showed that its workforce was only 18 percent Kuwaiti.[98] Technical training in the oil industry was also seen as a means of reducing citizen unemployment.[99] The Kuwaiti state had launched several technical training schemes in the 1950s. They accelerated in the 1960s, when Kuwait, like other Gulf states, approached the ILO for advice.[100] The trade unions were key participants in, and advocates for, worker training efforts.[101] On January 20, 1968, with the prodding of the government sector union federation, the Ministry of Social Affairs and Labor opened a new Vocational Training Center.[102]

But training schemes proved ineffectual. Students at the technical college complained that they received insufficient stipends, faced confusing bureaucratic hurdles, and often did not even receive textbooks.[103] One ILO official visiting in 1961 disdainfully dismissed the "so-called Technical Training College."[104] More fundamentally, labor training did not address the real reasons behind the domination of white managers in the oil industry: racism and the strike plan. The latter led the oil companies to continue promoting presumably loyal white workers and to deliberately distance Kuwaitis, or even sympathetic Arab noncitizens, from the production process. As the years progressed, it became increasingly clear that worker training could not, on its own, incentivize the hiring of more citizen workers.[105] Sami al-Munais pointed out that whatever worker training measures were put in place, private sector employers were simply not paying wages high enough to attract Kuwaitis.[106] While the growing number of Kuwaitis with formal qualifications made it harder for the oil companies to justify their anemic Kuwaitization, training programs did nothing to change structural incentives.[107]

It was the strike that proved the pivotal tactic of the era. Kuwaiti unions consolidated their position during a series of work stoppages in the oil industry from 1965 to 1967. The first flashpoint was the Japanese Arabian Oil Company at Khafji, in the Neutral Zone between Kuwait and Saudi Arabia. The Japanese-owned firm, which had a special concession from the two governments, was notorious for its poor working conditions.[108] In early 1965, an explosion killed four contracted workers and injured several more.[109] Then on July 18, its workers went on strike, accusing the company of ignoring Kuwaiti law and taking advantage of its position in the Neutral Zone to use Saudi security forces to put down worker protests. While most of the strikers were Kuwaiti, a number of Saudi workers joined in solidarity, despite the fact that they had no right to strike or join a union under Saudi law. In response, the company cut off telephone communications, electricity, and water to workers living in remote housing that left them dependent on company infrastructure. It then asked the Saudi authorities to put down the strike. While workers tried to protect Kuwaitis and any "Arab carrying a Kuwaiti Iqama [residency permit]" from retaliation, Saudi forces detained an Arab resident of Kuwait—a move that generated stinging press criticism.[110] *Al-Tali'a* framed the strike as evidence that the Kuwaiti state was failing to protect the rights of workers, and it called for the formation of a trade union federation so that workers could better assist each other across sectors.[111]

Conditions did not improve. Two years later, in 1967, Khafji workers struck again, and the scenario repeated itself—the company cut off essential utilities to workers stranded in isolated oilfields. Though the strike again failed to achieve its demands, it left behind an important institutional legacy. After learning of the situation, Hassan Falah of the KOC union and Hussein Saqr of the government workers federation traveled to the Interior Ministry to try and convince Interior Minister Sa'ad al-Abdullah to intervene on the workers' behalf. But when the government sector unions released a statement of solidarity with the Khafji workers, the Ministry of Social Affairs and

Labor threatened to sanction them, arguing that they were not authorized to work in the private sector. Meeting to respond to the Ministry's threat, union leaders decided to create a national labor federation, with Hussein Saqr as President and Hussein al-Youha as Vice President.[112] The Kuwait Trade Union Federation (KTUF) united the public and private sector federations and became the overarching structure of the labor movement.

The strike that would demonstrate the strength of the oil unions—and heighten tensions with the regime—took place on June 11, 1967, in the wake of the war between Israel and the surrounding states. From its inception, the labor movement had taken an active role in foreign policy issues, especially pan-Arabism and anticolonialism. Its forceful positions further distinguished it from the regime while reinforcing ties to other social movements both within Kuwait and around the world.[113] When the war began, the International Confederation of Arab Trade Unions called on all Arab oil workers to shut down production, deploying sabotage if necessary, and strikes swept across much of the Middle East.[114] In Kuwait, *al-Tali'a* and its allies called for an oil embargo in support of Palestine.[115] Oil workers informed the government that they would conduct a solidarity strike and received authorization to stop work for twenty-four hours. But in a demonstration of independence and opposition, they stayed off the job for an extra day, with the British reporting that "it was only on firm intervention by the Government that normal production was resumed."[116] The extended strike reflected anger at the government's position. While all Arab oil exporters threatened Israel with retaliation, the OPEC moderates, including Kuwait, did not back their threats with action, fearing a break with the United States.[117] The oil workers thus positioned themselves as the most effective foes not just of the oil companies, but of Israel and its allies.

While the strike failed to force an effective embargo, it demonstrated the power and popularity of the trade union movement. KOC reported that the newly formed Federation of Petroleum Workers was "becoming swiftly more efficient and sophisticated in its dealings," while the British embassy grudgingly extended this evaluation to the labor movement as a whole.[118] The worried British labor attaché found that the unions had managed to become "important in the internal politics of the sheikhdom, and as a potential base for directing agitation elsewhere."[119] The strike also underlined the pivotal position of noncitizen workers. British and Kuwaiti government officials were concerned at the enthusiasm for the strike shown by noncitizen Arab workers, particularly Palestinians, who had only backed down when threatened by forceful government action.[120] The strike thus demonstrated the continued potentialities for solidarity across the boundaries of nationality.

By 1967, labor leaders were losing patience with the limitations of Kuwaiti labor law, especially in the oil sector. Facing the intransigence of both the companies and their own government, they took matters into their own hands. Hassan Falah traveled personally to Cairo to meet with Egyptian oil union officials and sympathetic labor lawyers. One was the Egyptian attorney Ahmad al-Khoajih, who, at Falah's request, drafted a new labor law for the oil sector. Rashid Saif, the oil worker turned MP, then introduced the draft law in the National Assembly.[121] Union officials built popular support for the legislation by organizing a press campaign and holding a series of open seminars near KOC headquarters in Ahmadi, during which they discussed the law and its components with workers and journalists. According to Ahmad al-Asbahi, the seminars built a sense of collective leadership among workers and pressured the government to pass the legislation.[122] The strategy succeeded, and the law was passed, with remarkable rapidity, as Law 43 of 1968.

Its passage proved significant in several respects. First, in the long term, it had the seemingly unintended effect of further dividing citizen and noncitizen workers. When asked why he supported a law specifically for the oil sector, Hassan Falah explained that oil workers had different responsibilities and skills from other workers and therefore required special legislation.[123] This was a widespread opinion at the time. In a 1968 interview, the minister of social affairs and labor agreed that there was "no doubt" that oil workers had a "special character" that required unique legislation with provisions that "exceed the advantages that are provided in labor legislation in the private sector."[124] The decision also made political sense. It was far easier to demand regulation of a segregated industry that was popularly regarded as a paragon of neocolonialism. Moreover, the power to shut down the most profitable sector of the Kuwaiti economy did, in fact, place oil workers in a unique position. But by focusing only on the oil sector, the law contributed to the deterioration of conditions in the rest of the private sector, which disproportionately employed noncitizens. Thus, even as the oil unions battled for the rights of their noncitizen colleagues, the vast majority of noncitizen workers were left behind.

Just as significantly, the law initiated a battle over enforcement that pitted the oil unions directly against the Kuwaiti state. It did not overturn the provisions of the 1964 law that had most hindered unionization, such as the barriers to noncitizen union membership or the power of arbitrary dismissal, which would likely have provoked insurmountable opposition. But the law provided a slew of new benefits to oil workers. It required that all labor contracts must be put into writing, set the work week at forty hours, provided twelve days of annual vacation for official holidays and six weeks paid sick leave, and set requirements for housing, healthcare, and allowances.[125] Its most crucial clauses extended the protection of labor law to short-term employees and required that contracted workers be given the benefits of full employees, thus negating the corporate strategy of labor contracting.[126] This would become the flashpoint. British authorities believed that pro-regime MPs had passed the legislation without understanding its full implications and worried that it would "increase the prestige of the labour movement" and "rally the non-Kuwaiti workers behind it."[127] In response, the Kuwait Oil Company stonewalled, asking the government to clarify—or even modify—the law before implementation.[128] They argued that because many of their contracted workers were not directly involved in the actual extraction and refining of oil, but instead were engaged in "ancillary operations" such as construction and transport, they were not covered by the law's provisions.[129]

The unions and their allies were infuriated by both the company's response to the law and the government's refusal to enforce it.[130] The KOC request to amend the legislation was especially galling because it was first sent to the ruling-family-controlled ministries and only handed to the National Assembly after a delay.[131] Union officials, with the support of the Arab nationalist press, framed the issue as a matter of sovereignty. They argued that the oil companies were violating Kuwaiti independence and undermining Kuwaiti democracy, and that the regime was neglecting its duty to implement its own legislation.[132] The oil companies were acting like states within the state, all in the name of perpetuating discrimination against Arab and Kuwaiti workers.[133] In an interview, Hassan Falah noted that after twenty-five years and much trumpeting of its programs of worker training and education, the company had still not trained a new generation of skilled

Kuwaiti workers.[134] The unions thus positioned themselves as the guardians of Kuwaiti independence.[135]

After issuing a series of ineffectual statements, in September of 1968, the Petroleum Workers Federation announced that they would order a forty-eight-hour strike in all foreign-owned oil companies if the law was not implemented—notably excluding the new, state-run National Petroleum Company.[136] The declaration led to another showdown with the state. The Ministry of Social Affairs claimed that the unions had ignored the procedures laid out by the labor law, and that therefore the strike was illegal.[137] The union leadership called off the strike, but only after the Council of Ministers and Interior Ministry agreed to meet with representatives of the Petroleum Workers Federation to discuss their grievances. *Al-Taliʿa* claimed victory, reporting that the workers had achieved their objective without needing to strike.[138] But discussing grievances did not mean resolving them, and soon *al-Taliʿa* renewed its attack.[139] Discussions broke down in January 1969 when the government announced that, after consultation with the oil companies, it would seek to amend the legislation. In a combative parliamentary session, Rashid Saif walked out of the National Assembly in protest.[140] The Petroleum Workers Federation, accusing the government of being "untruthful" in negotiations and abandoning the "hopes and aspirations" of oil workers, announced a strike to begin on the morning of January 21.[141] After a failed meeting with the minister of social affairs and labor, the workers walked out.[142]

The 1969 strike proved to be a turning point. The workers predictably framed the shutdown in terms of national sovereignty.[143] Notably, they directed much of their ire toward government departments, including Social Affairs and Labor, for failing to come to their defense.[144] British Petroleum, the half-owner of KOC, determined that the strike could best be interpreted as a "direct challenge" to the authority of the Kuwaiti state.[145] Reflecting the increasingly militant rhetoric of the labor movement, particularly in the oil sector, the union strike announcement ended with a defiant "long live the working class."[146] The press provided blanket coverage, given that the strike shut down the heart of the Kuwaiti economy. A representative article in *al-Taliʿa* accused the "lightweight" government of yielding to pressure by "cutting a deal" with the oil companies and failing to defend the basic rights of oil workers.[147]

The strike proved even more complete than its 1963 predecessor. KOC estimated that a remarkable 95 percent of its non-staff workers were absent.[148]

It was also broader, hitting not just KOC, but Aminoil and the Japanese Arabian Oil Company.[149] The companies activated their strike plans and were able to maintain production with their "western staff," assisted by a handful of noncitizen contract workers.[150] The use of noncitizens as strikebreakers was an ominous sign for labor, even if most noncitizens participated in the walkout.[151] But by strategically pressuring workers in the Export Operations Group, the KOC union was able to bring exports to a halt—a critical shift that demonstrated that workers could now circumvent corporate countermeasures and seize control of the oil spigot.[152] For the labor movement, the moment was a watershed.

The walkout triggered an immediate and powerful backlash. Confident that Kuwaiti officials would view the strike as a challenge to their authority, the oil company called on state security forces to respond.[153] Public Security obliged, breaking up a mass meeting and bringing union leaders into custody for questioning.[154] In fact, in the aftermath of the strike, the director of KOC went so far as the send a thank-you note to Shaikh Abdullah al-Jabir, the governor of Ahmadi, for his "cooperation" during "this difficult period."[155] The strike thus underlined the close relationship between the oil firms and the state. But the workers had made their point. Union officials called off the strike after two days not due to state pressure, but to avoid a loss of public support if a prolonged shutdown of oil exports triggered an economic crisis.[156] Government officials and the conservative press amplified these concerns by stressing the impact on oil production.[157] The strike demonstrated that despite the failure of Kuwaitization, the labor movement could shut down oil production and effectively wield the language of sovereignty.

While the regime feigned unconcern, Kuwaiti officials were rattled. In a meeting with the company, the Ruler privately acknowledged that his government "was in fact very much concerned," and "fully appreciated the effects of such action on the stability of the country."[158] He assured the company that "next time, if there is a next time, there will be immediate intervention coupled with dismissals and deportations if necessary."[159] Once again, an alliance between citizen and noncitizen workers was his greatest fear. The Council of Ministers circulated a warning to noncitizen oil employees warning that "anyone who went on strike would be deported."[160] Shaikh Jabir al-Ahmed confidentially informed the oil company that "while the Government were prepared to allow Kuwaiti workers to strike, they would act to prevent strike action by non-Kuwaitis."[161] In fact, KOC informed British officials that the Kuwaiti government had even dropped "a confidential hint to go slow on 'Kuwaitisation'" in order to make it easier to break strikes.[162] This was a startling revelation—in effect, the Kuwaiti state had endorsed the strike plan.

Even as the 1969 strike reinforced the alliance between the oil company and the state, it also secured the political position of organized labor. Years later, Hussein Saqr would credit the struggle against the oil companies with improving the popular image of the trade union movement and drawing public attention to labor issues.[163] It also placed the labor movement even more firmly in the political opposition. Indeed, at the time, KOC concluded that "relationships between Government and Trade Unions (and perhaps the family and the Bedu) are never going to be quite the same again."[164] The prediction would prove prescient.

EXPLOSION | 1969–1970

The growth in union power faced a check in 1969. In the late 1960s, with the National Assembly discredited by electoral fraud and the Arab nationalists out of power, the far left seized the headlines. They first struck when the Shah of Iran, the *bête noire* of Marxists and Arab nationalists alike, made a diplomatic visit to Kuwait. On November 14, 1968, the PRM detonated a series of bombs outside the Iranian Embassy, along the airport road, and near al-Salam Palace—where the Shah was being hosted by the ruling family. They then planned another attack on the second anniversary of the rigged 1967 elections. Three more bombs exploded outside the National Assembly building, the Ministry of the Interior, and even the home of the Interior Minister, sending shockwaves through the Kuwaiti political scene. Though the attacks were not—and were not designed to be—fatal, they would have a profound effect on organized labor. The PRM had openly supported the 1969 oil strike and included workers, including trade unionists, in its ranks.[165] And the anniversary of the elections, and thus the bombings, fell on January 25—during the middle of the walkout.[166]

The simultaneous bombings and strike triggered a powerful backlash. Nearly the entire PRM leadership was arrested and put on trial, and the organization collapsed. The attacks received little public support. Even the PRM's central committee condemned its Kuwaiti branch. The trial, however, complicated matters. Facing a special national security court of dubious constitutionality, Ahmad al-Rubaʿi put forward a spirited defense. He condemned "capitalist monopolies" that controlled the nation's oil wealth and operated as a "state within a state," and described the Al Sabah as an autocracy determined to hold on to power through the use of sham elections and violence. The court convicted al-Rubaʿi and many of his colleagues, including the trade unionist Hussein al-Youha, and sentenced them to prison terms. The crackdown initiated a period of leftist fragmentation that lasted through the mid-1970s, as younger activists broke with the founding generation of the Arab Nationalist Movement. With legal routes of politics foreclosed, many young and leftist Kuwaitis were turning to other means. The regime used the 1969 bombings as a pretext for an especially violent crackdown on the opposition in general, and the labor movement in particular. By highlighting the involvement of a handful of labor organizers in PRM activities, and its distribution of political leaflets to workers during the 1969 strike, the regime tried to brand the entire trade union movement as a criminal enterprise.[167] *Al-Taliʿa* was once again suspended, and press censorship tightened.[168] Of the accused PRM members put on trial, six were trade unionists, and several were convicted of involvement in the bombings.[169] In this crackdown, according to British authorities, the regime resorted to physical abuse. Labor organizers, including Hassan Falah, were reportedly detained, hung up by their feet, and beaten, even those not involved in the plot.[170]

The government also used the crackdown to amend the 1968 oil sector labor law.[171] By reclassifying a wide variety of workers in the oil industry as not essential to oil operations, it exempted many contractors from its protections, thus gutting its key provisions.[172] It also excluded all noncitizen workers at the government-owned National Oil Company.[173] In fact, one conservative MP had even proposed going further by excluding naturalized Kuwaiti citizens. The final legislation was rammed through the rigged National Assembly with a vote of 37–3 over the opposition of the KTUF and even the usually pro-regime minister of social affairs and labor. *Al-Taliʿa* accused the Ministry of Finance and Oil of effectively acting as a "lawyer" for the oil companies, undermining both workers' rights and Kuwaiti sovereignty.[174] Even the British acknowledged that the new law contravened "the spirit of the I.L.O. conventions" and lacked legitimacy given the rigged nature of the Assembly.[175] But it won the support of the pro-government press—now the only outlets allowed to publish freely—such as *al-Ra'i al-'Am*, which argued that Kuwaitis deserved special privileges in the workplace.[176]

Predictably, the oil companies responded by ramping up their use of noncitizen workers. By hiring them for less than a year, they could classify them as "temporary," skirting requirements to provide termination payments, benefits, and renewal clauses. Their continued employment would remain contingent on a new contract, giving companies yet another mechanism of control.[177] Additionally, the special benefits given to salaried Kuwaiti employees further incentivized the oil companies to hire non-Kuwaiti contracted workers.[178] The unions and their allies continued to attack KOC for skirting its Kuwaitization obligations and condemned the exploitation of contracted workers and the systematic discrimination against noncitizens.[179] The press once again accused the oil companies of violating Kuwaiti sovereignty and working "to distance the Kuwaiti from the actual fields of oil operations."[180] In a published interview, Hassan Falah commented that because of government inaction, "the workers alone are in the battle" against the companies.[181] Suspicions were confirmed in 1970, when *al-Tali'a* received another batch of KOC documents suggesting that the company was deliberately firing permanent employees and replacing them with workers on short-term contracts.[182]

The crackdown of 1969 also proved to be a turning point for Arab noncitizens. That year, the Kuwaiti state reversed its longstanding policy of granting them special residency exceptions. In March, the government declared that it would begin to officially treat non-Palestinian Arabs like other foreigners, subjected to all visa and other restrictions, despite the repudiation of the Arab League.[183] The decision triggered a flurry of condemnation in the press both within Kuwait and across the Arab world.[184] Even business interests protested, reporting that the sudden restrictions dampened consumer demand.[185] The decision made it much more difficult for noncitizen Arab residents to live with other members of their family, and led to an entrenchment of the demographic predominance of noncitizen men and a flurry of reportage on the problem of "bachelors."[186] But despite its unpopularity, this policy shift proved durable. Opposition parliamentarians tried to overturn it in 1971, but they were defeated by pro-regime MPs.[187] The line between citizen and noncitizen, long shot through with gray due to the power of pan-Arabism, was becoming increasingly black and white.

Palestinians faced a particularly wrenching situation. A wave of Palestinian refugees—many of whom were children—arrived in Kuwait after the 1967 war with Israel. The state responded by withdrawing Palestinian access to social services, most notably public education.[188] While the Department of Education still provided children classified as "Gulf Arabs" with free admission to government schools, it capped the number of Palestinian students with a quota system. In response, the Palestinians of Kuwait organized two parallel education systems: one private, the other public, under the auspices of the PLO. The latter faced a perpetual financial crisis, as it was funded by sporadic grants from PLO headquarters and by a 5 percent tax levied on Palestinians working for the Kuwaiti state. Without a state apparatus to enforce taxation, the PLO could only impose revenue increases with Kuwaiti consent, which was not always forthcoming. By the 1970–71 school year, only 3,854 Palestinian students were in government schools, while the PLO was educating 13,817 largely low-income students.[189] The rise of labor nationalization policies further exacerbated the economic challenges facing Palestinians in Kuwait by systematically promoting and hiring citizens above their Palestinian counterparts. Only a few select Palestinians were able to gain Kuwaiti nationality.[190] For Palestinians in Kuwait, perhaps more than for anyone else, battles for noncitizen rights proved existential.

CONCLUSION

By 1970, the succession of rigged elections, strikes, and bombings had generated a remarkably tense political situation. The British embassy even predicted that "there is probably going to be a revolution in Kuwait in the not too distant future."[191] The ambassador wrote that "a system of tribal oligarchy," combined with a "fantastic difference" between the rich and the poor, "cannot resist the pressures of the modern world for very long."[192] But just as tensions reached a new height, the government backed down. Shaikh Jabir al-Ahmad issued a self-critical statement in which he promised not to repeat the mistakes of 1967, and to hold a fair election in 1971. His statement opened a new period of dialogue and political debate. The years 1971 through 1976 became a moment of remarkably fluid politics, where leftists, workers, and radicals questioned the very basis of the state and economic apparatus. Dr. Ahmad al-Khatib reentered electoral politics by disbanding the Kuwaiti Arab Nationalist Movement, which he had himself founded two decades earlier, and forming a more broadly reformist Kuwaiti Progressive Democratic Movement. He was joined by well-known oppositionists Sami al-Munais, Ahmad al-Nafisi, and Abdullah al-Nibari.[193] This new electoral bloc supported democratic reforms and embraced scientific socialism and Marxism-Leninism as its "guide" rather than its "overriding ideology," thus breaking from both the right and the left.[194]

The early 1970s also opened the door for a new and radical era of labor activism. A striking feature of the 1971 election campaign was the centrality of worker candidates and worker issues in mainstream politics. The bloc led by Dr. al-Khatib centered labor demands, especially the push for the Arabization and Kuwaitization of the workforce.[195] It also included three labor candidates who ran explicitly as workers. Hussein Saqr, who was concurrently KTUF president; Mohammad Abdul Mohsin al-ʿAsimi, president of the Government Sector Federation and Municipality union; and Ajnaan ʿAjnan al-ʿAzimi, a respected member of the Petroleum Workers Federation, sought election in three different districts. They received the vocal support of *al-Taliʿa*, which argued that, given their numbers, workers should receive appropriate representation in the Assembly.[196] Their campaign centered worker issues and connected questions of oil, labor, and national sovereignty. Al-ʿAzimi attacked labor contracting and the strike plan and made Kuwaitization and worker training pillars of his campaign. Hussein Saqr drew the clearest line between labor issues and anti-imperialism, demanding "the liberation of the oil wealth from the control of the foreign companies" to make "Arab petroleum for the Arabs." Labor training programs, and sovereign control over oil, would be the first steps in a national program to build a diversified and sustainable industrial economy and free Kuwait from the control of foreign monopolies.[197] While Saqr lost his election, the coalition elected enough MPs in 1971 that labor could once again count on friends in high places.

Perhaps the most striking legacy of the 1960s was the reconfiguration of power in the oil industry. This transformation is clearly illustrated by Ashraf Lutfi, whose story opened chapter 3. In 1968, Lutfi, now an internationally recognized political figure, published his second work, entitled *OPEC Oil*. From its first pages, the work highlights the remarkable progress made in just nine years. Lutfi marvels at the accomplishments of the raft of new national oil companies and of efforts to train a new generation of local oil specialists—just as he had advised.[198] Most significantly, Lutfi credits these transformations not to OPEC, but to a rising tide of popular pressure. In fact, he frames himself not as a leader of the movement for resource sovereignty, but as a technocratic voice of moderation in opposition to the "political agitators and self-interested oil 'experts'" who describe foreign oil corporations as an "imperialist monster."[199] It was they, he argues, who eschewed compromise. "Outside the immediate confines of government and oil circles," he wrote, "the general public—and this applies at all levels from the man in the street to the intelligentsia—are firmly convinced that the foreign oil companies operating in their territories are earning excessively high returns unparalleled elsewhere in the world. The nation, it is maintained, is not getting the maximum benefit from its natural resources and the government is criticized for not doing enough to improve the conditions of exploitation."[200] Oil-producing countries—and citizen oil workers—were slowly consolidating control over their oil exports—with potentially far-reaching consequences.[201]

In Kuwait, this reconfiguration in oil politics built on foundations laid by workers from 1964 to 1971. The Kuwaiti trade union movement had evolved from a small, clandestine group into one of the most powerful forces in Kuwaiti politics. This power derived from their capacity to shut down oil production, their alliances with the press and members of parliament, their impeccable anticolonial nationalist credentials, and the popular goodwill built over decades of organizing. Their influence now reached far outside the realm of labor and had transformed trade union leaders into national figures. But even as they emerged as the vanguard of anticolonial nationalism, the unions were increasingly at odds with the Kuwaiti state. And while the unions had vocally supported their Arab noncitizen colleagues, they faced the ever-present threat of division along the lines of nationality. In the 1970s, workers and their allies would launch their most radical campaign for noncitizen rights and reshape the global oil industry.

7 Exporting Oil, Importing Labor | 1971–1976

IN 1974, MOHAMMAD YASIN, a specialist from the International Labor Organization (ILO), arrived in Kuwait to oversee a "manpower assessment and planning project." A staggering rise in oil prices over the previous year had dramatically increased the income of the Gulf states, making a seemingly unquenchable demand for labor even more voracious. Employers warned that they were suffering from a severe "manpower shortage," and the Kuwaiti state turned to the ILO for advice. Yasin set out to conduct a wide-ranging survey of the factors shaping the Kuwaiti labor market, including everything from demographics, wages, and collective bargaining to gender norms, housing, and income distribution. His approach was representative of that taken by the ILO, which framed labor migration as embedded in broader social, political, and economic trends.[1]

But Yasin soon found himself facing unexpected resistance. It quickly became apparent that business interests, with the support of the Kuwaiti state, wanted the ILO to help facilitate international labor recruitment rather than to study the questions of wages, working conditions, housing, and quality of life that could explain why Kuwaiti employers struggled to attract workers in the first place. These political and economic elites therefore tried to limit his study to "a rather restricted exercise on supply and demand." The reason for this opposition, he believed, was that for "business and trading interests the relatively cheap foreign labor is an asset," helping them drive down wages in the private sector. They therefore were "sensitive even to a hypothetical possibility of a reduction in the availability of foreign labor" that could be triggered by a wider examination of the conditions facing noncitizen workers.[2]

When he tried to broaden the scope of his report, state officials brusquely denied Yasin relevant information, logistical support, and the opportunity to meet with officials, especially at the tight-lipped Ministry of the Interior. They even refused to provide him with adequate office space.[3] Spurned by the bureaucracy he was supposedly advising, he told his superiors in Geneva that he was himself being treated like an "expatriate employee"—in other words, as just another migrant worker.[4]

Yasin found that when he noted that labor recruitment was hindered by low wages, high living costs, or inadequate housing, his arguments fell on deaf ears. He told his superiors that his problems stemmed from the fundamental structure of Kuwaiti politics. "In the National Assembly and the top executive positions," he explained, "the country's few businessmen and traders and their relatives monopolize power. They are interested to continue to have a saturated labor market comprising of expatriates not able to ask for higher wages."[5] When Yasin published a critical final report, the Kuwaiti government objected, especially with regards to his descriptions of chaotic interdepartmental relations and the uncooperative attitude of the Interior Ministry.[6] At the request of the Kuwaiti government, the ILO—which received significant amounts of funding from Gulf states—labeled the report "classified and confidential." It was buried.[7]

Mohammad Yasin's experience encapsulated the debates over immigration, citizenship, and political economy that swept Kuwait in the early 1970s. The lifting of political censorship in Kuwait in 1971 launched a remarkable period during which Kuwaitis challenged the fundamental assumptions of the deportation state, the nationality regime, and the global oil industry. The struggle was centered around a series of interrelated dilemmas. First, rising oil prices generated unprecedented demand for labor and led employers to warn of a "manpower shortage." Second, at the same time, many longtime noncitizen residents were leaving Kuwait, frustrated by stagnating wages, abysmal working conditions, and the impossibility of attaining the stability of nationality, or even permanent residency, a phenomenon that came to be referred to as the "reverse migration." Third, citizen unemployment remained high, especially for young people who struggled to compete with cheaper and more vulnerable noncitizen workers in the private sector. And finally, the repercussions of the restrictive Kuwaiti citizenship regime were becoming impossible to ignore. By the 1970s,

Kuwait had come to host an underclass of stateless people denied access to employment, education, and other necessities. For many Kuwaitis, these issues highlighted the unsustainability, and the injustice, of the nationality and migration regimes.

The response to these challenges revealed a widespread recognition of the inextricability—and interdependence—of the rights of citizens and noncitizens. A broad coalition of reformers argued that the dilemmas of the 1970s were the predictable result of an exclusionary nationality regime and exploitative labor and residency legislation. The solution, they argued, was to improve the lives of noncitizen residents, create a gateway to permanent residency, and open access to Kuwaiti nationality. Reformers paired ethical arguments with practical ones, explicitly challenging the narrative of "manpower shortage" by arguing that easing access to residency and nationality would help attract and retain much-needed workers. Kuwaiti unions proved to be a pillar of the reform movement. Though they faced insurmountable obstacles to organizing noncitizens, they nevertheless battled for noncitizen rights and for a more open nationality regime, proposing an alternative future designed to solve problems of manpower, nationality, and inequality by improving the conditions of all workers across Kuwait. Their efforts transformed the Kuwaiti labor movement into perhaps the most powerful citizen-led movement for noncitizen rights in the history of the Persian Gulf.

But reformers faced united and powerful opposition. Wealthy employers, who allied with—and often controlled—the conservative press, fought any effort to improve wages or working conditions in a private sector that benefited enormously from its access to cheap noncitizen workers. Instead, they successfully called on the state to facilitate the recruitment of workers abroad, making labor even more readily available. Ironically, they found willing partners across the global south. As rising oil prices forced low-income countries to spend an unprecedented share of their precious U.S. dollars on fuel, many decided to redress the currency imbalance with remittances, encouraging their citizens to work abroad and send their savings back home. These governments actively encouraged their citizens to move to the Gulf just as the Gulf states began scouring the world for labor. The oil boom thus triggered a double movement: As oil flowed out, people flowed in, in a cycle underpinned by the inequities of the global currency regime.[8]

The sweeping victories and defeats of the Petroleum Workers Federation, which reached the peak of its power in the early 1970s, exemplified the paradoxes of the period. Oil workers played a central role in pressuring the Kuwaiti National Assembly to reject the "participation" system, a last-ditch effort by the oil companies to avoid outright nationalization.[9] Deploying their newfound power to shut down oil production and pushing decades-old arguments for permanent sovereignty to their logical conclusion, they forced the Kuwaiti regime to turn on its longtime imperial patrons and become the first Gulf state to nationalize oil. In shattering the coalition of regional regimes that had been the final holdouts against nationalization, Kuwaiti workers reshaped the outlines of the postwar petroleum order. Kuwaiti oil nationalization emerged not as a top-down diplomatic initiative, but out of the long-running struggles over labor, sovereignty, and discrimination in the oilfields. But, under enormous pressure, oil workers reluctantly compromised on the principle of equality between citizen and noncitizen workers, agreeing to contracts that granted special privileges to the former. In the long term, this decision would do exactly what labor organizers had long feared—fracture the Kuwaiti labor movement and fatally undermine its power.

The events of 1971 to 1975 are thus a particularly vivid illustration of both the power and the limits of the discourses of citizenship and the nation-state. They also demonstrate the interdependence of the rights of citizens and noncitizens. Kuwaiti oil workers deployed the language of national sovereignty to remarkable effect, reshaping the economic history of the twentieth century. But the question of noncitizen rights proved to be an insuperable barrier. The nationalization of oil did not conflict with the interests of either capital or the state; in fact, it enriched both, despite the geopolitical risks it initially posed to the regime. But when workers and their allies challenged efforts to forge a migrant working class, deportable and underpaid, they faced an overpowering backlash and eventual defeat. That defeat would have sweeping implications for all residents of Kuwait, undermining democratic rule by shattering the social movements that sustained it.

CHALLENGING THE NATIONALITY REGIME | 1970–1975

The reopening of Kuwaiti politics coincided with a rapidly changing economic and political context. Beginning in 1971, oil prices crept up for the first time in a decade as global demand caught up with surplus capacity.

The actions of OPEC and the Organization of Arab Petroleum Exporting Countries, or OAPEC, led to skyrocketing oil revenues, especially following the 1973 war with Israel. The result was a surge of wealth, and demand for labor, across the Gulf states. These economic transformations occurred just as the wave of radicalism suppressed during the late 1960s reentered mainstream politics. In 1973, the remnants of the PFLOAG determined that democratic activism could be effective in Kuwait and so restricted their armed struggle to Dhofar. In response, Ahmad al-Diyyan and Ahmad al-Rubaʿi, who had gained prominence during the 1969 bombing trials, formed "The Movement for Democratic Work in Kuwait" (*al-Harakat al-ʿAmal al-Dimuqrati fi al-Kuwait*), which sought to build a socialist movement by peaceful means and focused on organizing workers.[10] Finally, the decline of Arab nationalism corresponded with a new spirit of leftist internationalism. New links between left-wing movements in Iran and the Arabic-speaking Gulf vividly illustrate the breadth of new solidarities.[11] *Al-Taliʿa* revised its anti-Iranian line and adopted a more internationalist orientation, calling on a united working class to champion reforms.[12] The Kuwaiti political field had never been more radical, or more capacious.

Noncitizens forced the issue of migration into prominence by once again voting with their feet. They had many reasons to leave Kuwait in the early 1970s: new residency restrictions, declining real wages, and Kuwaitization, which led many noncitizens to lose opportunities for employment and promotion.[13] The oil boom only exacerbated their precarity, leading to a dramatic rise in the cost of living without a commensurate rise in wages. Noncitizen workers also benefited from new opportunities elsewhere. Oil production expanded rapidly in southern Gulf states like Abu Dhabi and Qatar and generated unprecedented regional competition for labor, while improved economic conditions in Jordan, Egypt, and Iraq gave many Arab expatriates an incentive to return home.[14] The result was what came to be popularly called the "reverse migration (*al-hijra al-ʿaksiyya*)." For the first time in decades, departures of Arab residents began to outnumber arrivals.[15] The phenomenon expanded alongside renewed warnings of a "manpower shortage."[16] By 1974, the Kuwaiti press had come the conclusion that the situation was a full-fledged crisis for both ideological and economic reasons: because Arab workers were being replaced by "Asian" ones, and because the country faced a shortage of labor just as demand was rising.[17]

The reverse migration triggered a flurry of statistical reports, economic studies, and press coverage.[18] State efforts once again centered around statistical studies and bureaucratic reshuffling.[19] On April 14, 1974, the Council of Ministers transferred responsibility for the distribution of work permits to the Ministry of Social Affairs and Labor, a symbolic recognition of the ascent of "manpower" as the defining paradigm of immigration policy.[20] Then in October, Mohammad Yasin of the ILO published a study that concluded that more accurate census data would be required to organize manpower needs.[21] His recommendations led to a remarkably detailed effort to estimate Kuwait's labor needs for the next five years, organized by profession, down to individual economists, barbers, and even "men of religion."[22] The early 1970s also witnessed a state effort to encourage more Kuwaiti women to enter the workforce, though it included few resources or actionable suggestions.[23]

What distinguished the migration debate of the early 1970s was its radical challenge not just to residency regulations, but to the entire nationality regime. The devastating human impact of exclusionary Kuwaiti nationality legislation had by now become incontestable. In 1970, Ahmad Mohammad Ahmad, a stateless father of six, attempted to take his own life after spending years struggling to find stable employment.[24] A similar attempted suicide the following year generated further coverage.[25] Critics highlighted the arbitrariness and injustice of nationality determinations.[26] One man told a newspaper that his application for nationality was rejected because he failed to identify the position of the old Shamlan well. Another reported that his denial resulted from his inability to pinpoint the location of the donkey stables in pre-oil Kuwait, explaining, in exasperation, that he had never owned a donkey.[27] Several MPs proposed amendments to the nationality law designed to unify the citizenship status of "split families," whose members ended up with different nationalities.[28] The early 1970s also witnessed rising criticism of tiered nationality and growing support for its abolition, as many citizens had spent over a decade without the right to vote.[29] Even government officials were beginning to acknowledge the flaws of nationality law.[30] Suleiman al-Mashaʿn, the very bureaucrat charged with its implementation, reported that the rigid requirements of the law meant that nationality committees often had to turn down people whom they believed to be deserving.[31]

By 1972, one newspaper was describing the reformist wave as the "naturalization movement (*harakat al-tajnis*)."[32] An array of actors called on the state to "open the door" of naturalization, which had closed with the Nationality Committees in 1965. Their arguments often intersected with those over the reverse migration and "manpower shortage." Advocates of reform argued that a more humane system of migration, residency, and naturalization would not only redress a string of injustices, but it would also allow Kuwait to retain much-needed workers. The idea that large-scale naturalization could provide economic benefits gained new legitimacy in late 1971 when it received the backing of Ahmad al-Daʿij, a specialist on the government's influential Planning Committee. Al-Daʿij wanted to grant nationality to Arabs born and raised in Kuwait and to Arab technicians who possessed "valuable skills." He argued that these new citizens would both contribute to economic development and diversification and correct Kuwait's demographic balance of citizens to noncitizens, which al-Daʿij believed was a "problem." Granting nationality would solve the skilled labor shortage, discourage the emigration of qualified workers, and provide the stability required for economic growth and long-term planning.[33] His ideas received widespread coverage in the press and were officially presented to the government for consideration, lending technocratic legitimacy to the reform movement.[34]

But the core arguments of the naturalization movement were ethical. Reformers centered their critique around four sympathetic and prototypical figures whose exclusion from the national community was deemed particularly unjust. In part, these figures were tropes, but they reflected the experiences of real individuals whose lack of nationality profoundly disrupted their lives. Two popular figures were long-resident Arab experts, Kuwaiti in all but name, and, in the women's press, the children of Kuwaiti women and non-Kuwaiti men, an issue raised during the aforementioned "marriage crisis" debates of the 1960s. Perhaps the most widely sympathetic was the stateless high school graduate. By the early 1970s, more and more stateless young people were graduating from high school and finding that they lacked the paperwork required to go on to higher education, get a job, marry, access public benefits, travel outside the country, or even legally reside in Kuwait.[35] Their impossible position led even some pro-regime publications to support their naturalization.[36] The final figure was the Bedouin soldier or police officer, stateless despite many years of service, which proved particularly compelling for government officials or conservatives who were otherwise skeptical of reform.[37] A law providing for the naturalization of Bedouin working for the army or police thus received widespread support when it was proposed in 1973.[38]

Some of the most compelling testimony came from stateless people themselves. In the early 1970s, Kuwaiti newspapers published a slew of testimonials on the personal impact of what one author called the "harsh and merciless" nationality law.[39] "I am not a foreigner," wrote one stateless woman whose father died in the early 1950s, before he could register as a Kuwaiti national.[40] Many felt that an essential part of their sense of self was being denied and feared expulsion from the country where they had spent most of their lives and considered their home.[41] A typical, if unusually detailed story, is that of Abdullah Suleiman Mohammad. A former sailor, as a youth he worked for a well-known captain, or *nakhuda*. When KOC began operations, he was hired as a contractor in the oilfields. In later years, he bounced around jobs, working for some of the most prominent people and institutions in Kuwait: for Shaikh Salem, as a driver for the Ministry of Water and Electricity, for the Planning Council, Kuwait University, the businessman Abdul Mohsin al-Kharafi, and for the newspaper *al-Raʾi al-ʿAm*. None ever asked for proof of nationality, simply treating him as a Kuwaiti. But he never held an official passport, only a travel pass from the pre-independence era. While this level of documentation proved sufficient to get basic medical care and receive employment as a daily or "unskilled" worker, it became an increasingly greater burden. He could not travel abroad, feared losing his right to residency, and struggled to marry. His application to the Nationality Committee was never answered, though it was backed by several prominent Kuwaiti witnesses. By the time it became clear that he would need official documentation, it was already too late.[42]

Many supporters of a more open nationality regime believed that it should be accompanied by a system of permanent residency, without a sponsorship requirement, and by the abolition of citizenship "tiers" that denied naturalized citizens the right to vote. Some argued that permanent residency could serve as a stepping stone to nationality, especially for long-resident Arab professionals.[43] This would provide them with a much-needed sense of stability that would benefit the Kuwaiti economy by increasing consumption, ending the "skilled manpower shortage," and countering the effects of the reverse migration.[44] The proposal received the backing of al-Daʿij and the Planning Council.[45] Indeed, the questions were bureaucratically inextricable—the same office within the Ministry of Social Affairs managed both nationality and residency. Critics of tiered nationality—which denied voting rights to naturalized citizens—also gained increasing prominence as the decade progressed.[46] Al-Daʿij even went so far as to compare tiered citizenship with South African apartheid.[47]

This insistence on linking the rights of noncitizens, stateless people, and second-tier citizens reflected a growing understanding that their struggles were inextricable. This point was driven home by the prominent oppositionist Sami al-Munais. He noted that if permanent residents were given access to all the rights of citizenship minus the vote—such as healthcare, education, and property ownership—then they would have exactly the same rights as second-tier citizens. He could have noted that they would also have the same rights as women with first-tier citizenship, who would only win the right to vote in 2005. The proposal to grant rights to one of these groups would have repercussions for all the others. If some noncitizens gained access to permanent residency, would that provide ammunition to advocates for women's suffrage, or to opponents of tiered citizenship? And relatedly, would that undermine the relative voting power of first-tier citizens, or the supply of cheap and deportable labor on which major employers depended? For al-Munais, as for many activists in this period, the answer was solidarity. In addition to calling for broader access to naturalization, he condemned the division of citizenship into two tiers as both unsustainable and unethical, and even attacked the Planning Council's proposal for the naturalization of "skilled" workers on the argument that it would simply give employers another incentive to avoid training their workforce while bypassing the people who needed nationality the most. Instead, he called for the naturalization of people of all backgrounds, based on fair and just criteria.[48]

Some of the most vocal advocates for nationality reform came from organized labor. This reflected a wider belief, held by the unions and their allies, that the working class should take an active role in politics. In a 1975 interview, Hussein Saqr explained that "it is a mistake to divide social and economic issues from political issues," as "they are all connected to each other." To make his case, he referenced the condition of the labor movement before Kuwaiti independence. How could a union win equal pay or workplace rights in a country under colonial occupation? Political struggle, he argued, is necessary for any labor movement, and therefore the KTUF would continue to press for constitutional rule, women's rights, freedom of speech, and freedom of the press.[49] Throughout the decade, Kuwaiti unions would become prominent supporters of the Palestinian cause, of anticolonial movements across the Gulf and the wider Third World, and of extending the right to vote to women in Kuwait.[50]

The unions, especially oil unions, viewed the reform of nationality law as a cause closely linked to their own. Because the oil companies preferred to hire workers of nomadic descent, and because former Bedouin were the population most often left behind by nationality laws, a significant percentage of workers in the oil industry were stateless.[51] KOC employed so many stateless workers that "Kuwaiti unproven" remained one of their official categories into the 1970s.[52] The unions attacked the oil company practice of denying benefits to "Kuwaitis without nationality," as union leaders defiantly called them.[53] Some trade unionists proposed ending the payment of special allowances to citizens by simply naturalizing stateless workers.[54] In 1968, *al-Taliʿa* published a remarkable petition from 133 stateless KOC workers to the Crown Prince. Describing themselves as "people of the desert," they explained that despite the fact that many of them had worked for the oil company for decades, they were denied many of the benefits of their long service because they were not Kuwaiti citizens.[55] By the early 1970s, the paper was effectively framing stateless oil workers as another "figure" of the stateless person.[56]

Two incidents in 1971 reiterated the connection between the labor movement and nationality reform. In November, it became apparent that the Japanese-owned Arabian Oil Company, which operated in the Neutral Zone between Kuwait and Saudi Arabia, was deliberately hiring stateless workers because they were banned from joining unions until they had been continuously employed for five years—a provision that was easy to dodge with the use of short-term labor contracts. In response, Hussein Saqr, president of the Kuwait Trade Union Federation, issued a statement condemning the company for treating its workers like "foreigners in their own land," despite the fact that they were "100 percent" Kuwaiti.[57] Because their children were denied full access to the state education system, one of the key demands of the stateless oil workers was the provision of an educational allowance, a dilemma that vividly illustrated the connection between nationality and workers' rights.[58] Later that year, in an effort to cut back on labor costs, the Kuwait Oil Company fired 250 noncitizen workers, most of whom were stateless people who considered themselves Kuwaiti and so lacked protection from dismissal.[59] Throughout the 1970s, Saqr called on the state to amend the nationality law "to allow all those who deserve nationality to obtain it," to halt the practice of citizenship stripping, and to end the "disgraceful discrimination" between first and second-tier citizens.[60]

The unions thus backed efforts to reform the nationality regime, with their leadership condemning discrimination based on nationality as a form of racism.[61] The systematic exploitation and abysmal conditions facing private sector workers became a recurring theme, particularly in *al-'Amil* (The Worker), the official magazine of the KTUF, which began publication in 1975.[62] This reflected a belief that noncitizen unionization remained existential for the labor movement. As early as 1970, the KTUF drafted a new labor law for the government sector that specified that all workers, regardless of nationality, should enjoy equal benefits under the law, including allowances and the right to join unions.[63] The leftist Ahmad al-Diyyan condemned the "deluded" Kuwaiti worker who thinks "that his class interests conflict with those of the foreign worker and not with the oil companies that he works for." He cited the example of the 1969 oil strikes, when some noncitizens had remained on the job even though a successful action would have improved the conditions of citizen and noncitizen workers alike.[64] The labor movement and its allies also challenged the idea that citizen unemployment and the "manpower shortage" were simple questions of supply and demand. Instead, they argued that employers struggled to recruit noncitizen workers because they were underpaid, denied access to social security and education, and subject to the insecurity that came with the ever-present fear of deportation.[65] The unions received support from allies in the National Assembly who encapsulated this argument in their "Program of National Work." It argued that the "manpower crisis" could be solved only by a comprehensive strategy that empowered workers and their unions and attracted workers with competitive wages and benefits.[66]

A key locus of the struggle would once again be labor law. By 1970, it was clear that the division of labor legislation into private, public, and oil sectors left most noncitizens, disproportionately concentrated in the private sector, with distinctly inferior workplace protections.[67] The KTUF condemned this as "discrimination" against non-Kuwaitis, and out of sync with "modern legislation" in "civilized countries."[68] They further pointed out that as long as private sector employers were incentivized to hire disproportionately underpaid and deportable noncitizens, citizen unemployment would persist.[69] Thus, in 1974, the labor movement launched a campaign to "unify" labor law in order to provide all workers in Kuwait with equal and more powerful protections.[70] The KTUF spearheaded the effort, with its president, Nasser al-Faraj, condemning the "discrimination between Kuwaitis and non-Kuwaitis" built into the structure of labor legislation.[71] Hussein al-Youha, now KTUF vice president, framed the issue as a fundamental question of equity.[72] They found allies in both the General Federation of Arab Workers and the ILO, with the latter questioning whether Kuwait was in compliance with the essential Forced Labor Convention of 1957.[73] In response, the Kuwaiti government acknowledged the flaws of separate legislation and claimed that it was attempting to "fuse them in one standardized labour law."[74] In reality, the regime was undermining a union drive to do exactly that.

Finally, the unions launched a concerted effort to broaden their base. The KTUF "Program for Trade Union Work," compiled by the Center for Workers' Culture under the leadership of Hussein al-Youha in November of 1974, focused on two groups that it had long struggled to organize: noncitizens and women.[75] The private sector, the program acknowledged, remained largely outside KTUF jurisdiction, and while women only comprised an estimated 3 percent of the workforce, they were beginning to enter wage work in unprecedented numbers.[76] Sexism proved especially rampant in the oil industry. Sarah Akbar, the first Kuwaiti woman to work in the field as a petroleum engineer, recollected that even the most qualified women were given only desk work at KOC until she successfully fought for a position on an oil rig in 1981.[77] Moreover, as Laura Goffman notes, sexist and paternalistic discourses saturated press discussions of women in the workforce, especially in the case of care work.[78] But nevertheless, in March of 1974, KTUF officials formed a special "women's committee" and organized meetings with Kuwaiti women's organizations.[79] The committee would become a permanent part of the trade union movement, playing a prominent role in the struggle for gender equality.[80] By the end of the year, the task of organizing "without discrimination" had become the movement's rallying cry.[81]

By early 1975, a radical revision of Kuwaiti legislation appeared to be possible, or even imminent. Throughout the first half of the year, nationality was the subject of a string of parliamentary debates and blanket press coverage.[82]

When a new draft law was presented to the National Assembly, it not only "opened the door" for new naturalizations, but provided a step-by-step process from arrival to citizenship that totally reconfigured the nationality regime.[83] Labor law was also being fundamentally reconsidered. In 1974, the social affairs minister acknowledged "holes" in private sector labor law and announced that he planned to revise it.[84] Then in May 1975, the Ministry of Social Affairs and Labor announced that it would form a "high committee" comprised of representatives from the government, "leading businessmen" from the Chamber of Commerce, union officials, and "experts" to discuss new legislation.[85] The deportation state, nationality regime, and labor apparatus, constructed in the imperial era and reinforced after independence, looked like they could be on the verge of transformation.

DOUBLE EXCLUSION | 1973–1976

The relationship between labor, nationality, and immigration reinforced solidarities in the 1970s. But this interdependence also incentivized an array of elites to unite in defense of their vested interests. Even as they bemoaned a manpower shortage, employers fought efforts to attract workers by improving wages and working conditions in the private sector. Instead, they blamed government regulations for restricting their access to labor and called on the Kuwaiti state to engage in aggressive recruitment efforts abroad. Despite widespread recognition of the inequities and contradictions of the citizenship and labor regimes, reform efforts faltered in the face of implacable opposition.

Unions and their allies faced new and powerful opponents in the 1970s. One was the Federation of Kuwaiti Contractors, founded in 1965. These contractors were explicitly Kuwaiti—its membership was restricted to firms with at least 51 percent Kuwaiti capital.[86] It soon became a key lobbying group that pushed for the accelerated hiring of noncitizens.[87] Along with conservative papers such as *al-Raʾi al-ʿAm*, they blamed the supposed manpower shortage, particularly in the construction industry, on overly restrictive state regulations, accusing government ministries of being too "rigid" in their visa procedures and calling on the Ministry of Social Affairs and Labor to ease its restrictions on hiring.[88] In a complete reversal of the logic of the unions, they argued that the main crisis was, in fact, rising wages, which reduced their profits.[89] They blamed citizen unemployment on the disinclination of citizens to engage in hard work, echoing stereotypes of laziness popular among imperial officials of the early twentieth century.[90] Rather than attracting and retaining workers with higher wages or better working conditions, the contractors argued that the state should actively seek out new sources of "manpower" outside the Arab world.[91] They received support from the conservative press, which had close ties to major contractors.[92] Well-connected and well-resourced, the contractors were effective antagonists of organized labor.[93]

For the first time, unions also faced opposition from a popular movement: Islamic activists. After a decade of marginalization during the heyday of Arab nationalism, the Kuwaiti branch of the Muslim Brotherhood, the Kuwaiti Social Reform Society, reorganized in 1968 and began to play an increasingly prominent role in politics.[94] These activists adopted the same idealized vision of a classless Islamic society as their counterparts in Egypt.[95] While they expressed respect for the dignity of work and general support for workers' rights, they viewed strikes, unions, or any form of class-based organizing as unnecessarily disruptive to social peace. Their newspaper, *al-Mujtamaʿ*, illustrates how Islamic activists tended to support workers in theory but turned on organized labor when it took action to advance working-class interests. Like many contemporary publications, the paper included a regular "workers' column" in its early issues, with labor news from across Kuwait and the Arabic-speaking world. It also publicized efforts by the Social Reform Society to lend support to workers. That support, however, proved to be of limited practicality. The Society would, for instance, donate volumes on Islam to a trade union library to promote the spiritual development of the membership.[96] Moreover, the paper often published pieces openly opposed to trade unionism. One representative article, written by the prominent thinker Yusuf al-Qaradawi, argued that Islam respects the dignity of workers, as well as their right to a dignified life. Islam, al-Qaradawi argued, governs social, economic, and political life according to principles of justice. While positive, his message was not particularly specific, yet alone actionable. Beyond individual piety, he, and the paper, provided no roadmap toward this ideal of justice.[97] Instead, *al-Mujtamaʿ* centered individual initiative, self-reliance, and hard work in an editorial line that reflected Muslim Brotherhood thought elsewhere.[98] Moreover, news about workers and unions was interspersed with far more frequent—and virulent—attacks on communism, Marxism, and socialism, written in a conspiratorial tone and replete with bigoted stereotypes of "Judeo-Bolshevism."[99] The workers' column eventually disappeared altogether. The paper never reconciled collective action, yet alone class struggle, with its ideal of Islamic tranquility.

As the decade progressed and the unions adopted an increasingly militant posture, *al-Mujtama*ʿ positioned itself as a critic of the labor movement. In a representative 1974 piece, it accused the unions of engaging in "political exploitation (*istaghlal al-siyyasi*)." The paper argued that while unions could help address the inevitable grievances of workers in industrial society, in some parts of the world, "communist parties" and "leftist movements" used unions "for the sake of political gains with no relation to the conditions of the workers," echoing arguments of "bread-and-butter unionism." The solution, the paper argued, was to more aggressively police trade union participation in politics and ensure that unions were only allowed to bargain over wages, working conditions, and other workplace issues.[100] Allied with a regime that viewed them as less dangerous than secular nationalists and drawing on lucrative charitable contributions and government subsidies, religious conservatives would only grow in strength during the 1970s.[101]

Reformers also faced a National Assembly dominated by opponents of radical change. In 1972, Jassim al-Qatami, the prominent merchant, Arab nationalist, and former police chief, broke from his old allies and founded the "National Bloc" to serve as a "middle current" between nationalism and Marxism. His movement attracted many wealthy former members of the Arab Nationalist Movement and further split the political opposition.[102] In late 1973, tensions between organized labor and al-Qatami's bloc erupted when the latter proposed privatizing Kuwaiti port operations, a move that threatened to turn most port workers into contractors.[103] By 1975, even Dr. Ahmad al-Khatib's nationalist bloc discussed noncitizens largely in terms of "economic and social development" and the need for "stability."[104] The simple fact was that noncitizen residents were not voters.[105] The waning of pan-Arab sentiment also dampened sympathy for Arab noncitizens. A revealing legislative defeat took place in 1971, when the National Assembly proposed a raise to citizen workers in the government sector that would bypass noncitizens. *Al-Tali*ʿ*a* and its allies attacked the proposal as discriminatory, racist, and ultimately detrimental to the Kuwaiti economy, which relied on noncitizens as both workers and customers. But while they won a raise for non-Kuwaiti workers, the final compromise fell well short of equality.[106] Differential wages for citizens and noncitizens in the public sector thus grew even more entrenched.

But perhaps the greatest hindrance for advocates of noncitizen rights, especially in the workplace, was the virtual exclusion of noncitizens from the labor movement. The unions had long struggled to organize noncitizen workers. Because employers possessed nearly unchecked powers of deportation, very few noncitizens joined unions even when they were legally able to do so. Labor organizers were often reluctant to reach out to noncitizens, which itself could put the latter at risk.[107] Even noncitizens willing to take the risk of joining unions often had their applications for Certificates of Good Conduct rejected by the Interior Ministry.[108] In 1973, nearly five years after noncitizens could officially join unions, the KTUF was still over 95 percent Kuwaiti.[109] While the KTUF repeatedly expressed its frustration with the exclusion of noncitizens, it remained hamstrung by the law.[110] Thus, in their everyday work, union officials rarely represented, or even interacted with, noncitizens, who consequently faded from view.[111]

Thus, while the early 1970s witnessed a series of strikes led by noncitizens in the private sector, the major trade unions were only peripherally involved.[112] In May of 1973, about six hundred mostly noncitizen workers at Shuwaikh Port went on strike. But they were quickly crushed by Kuwaiti security forces. Press coverage makes clear that unions felt incapable of providing effective support, while the intensity of the state response vividly demonstrated its continued willingness to resort to physical force against noncitizen workers.[113] At roughly the same time, over a thousand workers at Kuwait's chemical fertilizer plant, only forty-six of whom were Kuwaiti, threatened to strike over low wages, insufficient healthcare, dangerous working conditions, and, notably, "discrimination between nationalities."[114] The strike was especially revealing because it was a private sector labor battle in which workers explicitly opposed granting special privileges to Kuwaitis.[115] But while workers were able to win retroactive wages by threatening to strike, these were once again divided by nationality, with far fewer benefits going to non-Kuwaitis.[116] Another indicator came the same year when about 350 workers from the Ministry of Public Works, many of whom were Palestinian, were fired and replaced by contractors despite press and union criticism.[117]

The only success story of private-sector organizing during the early 1970s was in banking, which itself is the exception that proves the rule—outside of oil, it was the industry with the highest percentage of citizen workers.[118] In June 1974, the banking union launched a successful and highly publicized eight-day strike, demanding that their wages keep pace with those in the government sector.[119] Women, more prominent in banking than in most other sectors, played an important role in all of these efforts, raising their profile within the labor movement.[120] So did noncitizens, thus making banking one of the few industries in which labor organizing successfully breached the boundaries of nationality.[121] But its success was something of an anomaly, and it generated powerful pushback from employers and their allies in the press.[122] While labor leaders fought to keep the plight of noncitizen workers in the public eye, they found it difficult to provide more than rhetorical support.[123]

Indeed, even many proposals for nationality reform came with qualifications that reinforced hierarchies of class, gender, or place of origin. Critics of the arbitrariness of naturalization complained that it seemed to be easier for "foreigners" to obtain nationality than Arabs.[124] The stereotype of Bedouin backwardness often blighted calls for a more open nationality regime.[125] Warnings about the dangers of Bedouin nationality only heightened after the regime's illegal naturalizations, with articles cautioning that the "sons of the desert" could not "understand the true meaning of democracy," and that their acquisition of voting rights would mean that "the tribe will become the axis on which the political and social apparatus will pivot."[126] Perhaps the most common barrier to nationality reform was classism. One representative article condemned the fact that a naturalized Arab university professor was ineligible for elected office, while a lowly janitor with first-tier nationality was.[127] One paper aptly summarized the rallying cry as "nationality to those who deserve it," a description that encapsulated contradictory currents of hierarchy and inclusivity.[128]

The exclusion of noncitizens from the Kuwaiti social security system exemplified the politics of the period. Social security legislation was first introduced to incentivize Kuwaiti citizens to work in the private sector, where benefits were usually inferior to those offered to government employees. This was seen as a means of diversifying the economy and reducing state expenditures.[129] The KTUF, which had long fought for comprehensive state-run social insurance, managed to win a seat at the table in discussions of the new system.[130] The unions put forward a series of demands, the first of which was the inclusion of non-Kuwaitis. They argued that noncitizen exclusion from social security law would undermine the goal of incentivizing private sector employment for citizens and be a form of "racial discrimination."[131] The ILO specialists who wrote the first draft pushed for the broadest possible access to social security benefits, in part for reasons of equity, but also because it would encourage fluidity in the labor market, as workers would be assured that their pensions would remain intact even if they changed jobs.[132] But against the advice of both the ILO and the Planning Board, the social security plan finally delivered to the National Assembly excluded noncitizens altogether. During the debate over the bill, the KTUF launched a sustained campaign to try and amend the legislation to include noncitizens.[133] But their efforts failed.[134] When new legislation was introduced a few years later, the unions reprised their role, once again battling for noncitizen inclusion.[135] But while they won significant benefits for Kuwaitis—a victory seen as an important legacy—they lost their battle to include noncitizens.[136]

The plight of stateless people, and the campaign for their rights, eventually led the state to undertake a few selective reforms. In 1972, the National Assembly began selectively naturalizing stateless people who were born in Kuwait, completed their high school education, and possessed no other nationality, a move designed to address the plight of the "stateless high school graduate."[137] In 1974, a nationality committee was formed to study applications from longtime residents, usually trained specialists, who had demonstrated "tangible services" to Kuwait.[138] And in 1976, the Interior Ministry formed another committee to review nationality applications from long-serving police officers.[139] Thus by 1974, several new nationality committees, each designed to address a different sympathetic figure of "Kuwaitis without nationality," were reviewing applications.[140] But these amendments were largely superficial. The government, and particularly the Interior Ministry, enforced stringent restrictions.[141] When the naturalization of "highly-Qualified Arabs" began in 1974, the committee granted nationality to only fifteen people despite receiving over two thousand applications.[142] Naturalizations approved by the committees remained a trickle, making a mockery of the problem.[143] Indeed, even as the regime granted nationality to a handful of carefully selected applicants, it was stripping the nationality of others. In 1973, the regime denaturalized three men who supposedly obtained nationality through false testimony in the early 1960s.[144] Similar investigations over the following years led to yet more cases of citizenship stripping.[145] Allies of the ruling family positioned themselves as defenders of the integrity of the nationality regime, with Interior Minister Saʿad al-Abdullah calling on Kuwaiti citizens to adopt the slogan "every citizen a watchman."[146] While the stripping of citizenship was seen by many as a dangerous phenomenon, it remained a powerful mechanism of repression.[147]

In the event, the forceful opposition of the monarchy doomed efforts to reform nationality. In April of 1975, just as that "naturalization movement" appeared to be on the brink of success, Saʿad al-Abdullah, minister of defense and the interior, quashed any hopes for reform. He announced that the regime opposed any major changes to nationality law, denied systemic flaws in the nationality regime, and called on the National Assembly to move on to other issues.[148] The president of the Assembly, a regime loyalist, sided with the government.[149] Just days later, the Planning Committee, with the support of the Crown Prince, called for second-tier citizens to be denied political rights for a further five to ten years, restricted permanent residency to a select few, and allowed only limited naturalizations for noncitizens with special skills or longstanding service records who would "benefit" Kuwait.[150] The announcements triggered a furious response from opposition MPs and their supporters, who argued that the abrupt decision was both undemocratic and unrepresentative of the popular will.[151] Meeting at the venerable Independence Club, they condemned the government's position in the strongest terms.[152] But while reformers refused to give up the fight, the constitutional power of the monarchy rendered significant change impossible.[153]

The regime also sided with employers on the question of noncitizen rights. At first, the Kuwaiti state, led by the Ministry of Social Affairs and Labor, defended itself against the accusations of bureaucratic sluggishness made by the contractors. The Ministry argued that the manpower crisis "is not a government issue" but, echoing the unions, was the predictable result of private sector employers failing to pay sufficient wages or to train their workforce.[154] In 1973, it hired a new cohort of labor inspectors to address violations of labor law.[155] The following year, Social Affairs sponsored a survey that found that private sector workers were routinely denied access to sufficient housing, food, water, and safety equipment, in violation of the law.[156] When it formed a High Committee for Solving the Manpower Issue in 1975, its members condemned private sector employers for "failing to provide suitable wages or housing" and instead relying on an endless supply of noncitizen labor.[157] It even considered restricting the number of noncitizen work permits it distributed in order to encourage employers to hire more citizens.[158] But it was not clear that Social Affairs was willing to act on their own reports. Indeed, Kuwaiti labor inspectors were so underpaid and overworked that, in September of 1975, some went on strike themselves.[159]

Even as it conceded the legitimacy of union demands in the private sector, the regime rejected their proposed solutions. At roughly the same time that the government announced its position on nationality, it reconfigured immigration regulations along the lines proposed by the employers. On March 5, 1975, Suleiman al-Masha'n of the Department of Social Affairs and Labor announced that new arrivals to Kuwait would no longer require Good Conduct or No Objection Certificates, but would only need approval from the Manpower Department. He explained that the heightened demand for labor in the wider Gulf region had led them to ease their "strict" requirements, explicitly acknowledging that he was acting on suggestions made by "businessmen, including contractors and others." He also announced that a system of permanent residency would not be on the table.[160] The decision eased documentary requirements and concentrated decision-making in the Ministry of Social Affairs, rather than Interior.[161] But the new policy also required that noncitizen workers apply for permission to change jobs from a new "Department of Renewing and Transferring Iqamas," thus entrenching the system of sponsorship.[162] Noncitizens leaving Kuwait were also banned from returning with a new job for a year, disincentivizing resignation.[163] Finally, the department's work was divided into two sections: one for "breadwinners" and another for "house servants," effectively dividing visa operations along the lines of increasingly gendered domestic labor.[164] The new regulations gave the contractors nearly all of what they wanted.

The regime also began acting as a labor broker itself. In the early 1970s, the minister of social affairs began actively visiting labor-exporting countries and signing state recruitment agreements.[165] The process accelerated after the Arab manpower conference in 1975, when the Kuwaiti Department of Manpower Organization announced its intention to systematically pursue bilateral labor deals.[166] Kuwaiti embassies around the world began actively cooperating with employers to find new workers abroad.[167] In 1975, Shaikh Salim Sabah al-Salim, the minister of social affairs, explained that he saw the "importation" of manpower and the protection of the rights of employers as two of the most important priorities of his department.[168] These efforts received the support of the pro-business press, which framed migration as a means of providing people from low-income countries with an opportunity to improve their circumstances.[169] Their efforts were aided by the rapid rise in oil prices after 1973, which had triggered a fiscal crisis in much of the developing world as countries were forced to purchase expensive oil with precious dollars. Thus oil nationalization—perhaps the most significant victory of the labor movement—led to the hiring of even more noncitizen workers.[170]

The situation of domestic workers—as is so often the case—exemplified the increasing marginalization of noncitizens. With the proliferation of bilateral labor agreements, increasing numbers of domestic workers were women contracted in South Asia.[171] As domestic work was increasingly feminized, their labor was increasingly gendered, generating yet another media panic. Newspapers framed domestic workers as potential victims of rapacious employers in need of special protections—thus justifying their exclusion from the protections of ordinary labor law—while also framing them as potential threats—whether as undocumented "infiltrators" or as "bad characters" tempting the men of Kuwaiti families.[172] When the government released statistics revealing a high suicide rate among domestic workers, a police official blamed not just low salaries and prolonged separation from family, but unrealistic expectations generated by "contact with the people of her own country," implying that further isolation could be a solution.[173] The concurrent anxiety around the phenomenon of "fleeing maids" (*huruub al-khidim*) reveals the agency of domestic workers—their costly but significant power to vote with their feet.

In 1975, the state responded to the oil boom and the "maid panic" with an array of paternalistic regulations focused on domestic workers. These were designed to reinforce the integrity of the patriarchal Kuwaiti household, led by the presumably male "head of house (*rub al-usra*)."[174] The Ministry of Social Affairs and Labor created a special regime for domestic workers in 1975 on the argument that "the nature of the work of a servant differs from the nature of the work of a worker." The Ministry would oversee the international recruitment process of domestic workers by signing bilateral agreements with labor exporting countries.[175] At the same time, the Department of Manpower Protection attempted to crack down on unscrupulous labor brokers by opening a series of offices to regulate the employment of noncitizen domestic workers.[176] But at exactly the same time, the Ministry of Social Affairs forbade noncitizen workers from changing employers without its permission, tying them even more closely to their employers.[177] Two years later, in 1977, it ordered that the residency permits of all domestic workers who left their employer without permission would be suspended indefinitely, making them unemployable in Kuwait. The decision was explicitly designed to halt the prominent "problem" of "fleeing maids."[178] In effect, it created a state-run blacklist of domestic workers.

While the movement for nationality reform had been checked, it nevertheless altered Kuwaiti politics and demonstrated that a fundamental transformation of the nationality and residency regime was not just possible, but popular. The potentially revolutionary transformations of the period were most apparent in the struggle over the control of oil. The story of oil workers would demonstrate just how powerful Kuwaiti unions had become. But at the same time, it underlines the continued power of the exclusions of nationality, which proved even more enduring than the foreign-owned oil firms that for so long seemed unassailable.

NATIONALIZATION & FRAGMENTATION | 1970–1975

The reopening of the political sphere in Kuwait corresponded with a global revolution in oil politics. Because of rapidly accelerating demand, there was no more surplus capacity in the system. This new environment of scarcity meant that the longtime corporate strategy of playing one oil producing country off of another was no longer viable, and that producers could feasibly wield the threat to reduce, or even temporarily halt, oil exports—the so-called "oil weapon."[179] Moreover, a new generation of trained technical experts from oil-producing countries ensured that white workers no longer dominated the production process, undermining the power of corporate strike plans. And with the triumph of decolonization, gunboat diplomacy could no longer serve as the option of last resort for multinational oil firms. The stage was set for Kuwaiti oil workers, who would bring the "oil revolution" to its conclusion.

The chain of events that would culminate in the final wave of oil nationalizations began with a coup in Libya that brought Muammar Gaddafi to power and transformed an OPEC moderate into a resource radical. In September of 1970, the Libyan regime pressured the independent Occidental Petroleum, which was almost totally dependent on Libyan crude, into paying higher taxes and royalties per barrel, breaking the longstanding principle of corporate control over pricing. Just a few months later, in February 1971, President Houari Boumédiène nationalized the Algerian oil industry. Iraq, with its long history of petro-nationalism, nationalized the Iraq Petroleum Company in June 1972, followed by Libya in 1972 to 1973. Only a coalition of conservative Gulf monarchies eschewed nationalization: notably Saudi Arabia, Kuwait, Qatar, and the United Arab Emirates. Led by Ahmed Zaki Yamani, a regime loyalist appointed to replace Abdullah Tariki as Saudi oil minister, the OPEC "moderates" sought to hold back the tide. In 1968, Yamani founded the Organization of Arab Petroleum Exporting Countries (OAPEC), first comprised of Saudi Arabia, Kuwait, and Libya, in the hope of forming a bloc to counter the radicals. In a rearguard action against outright nationalization, he supported "participation," which would give oil-producing countries a greater stake in the oil industry, but without complete control.[180] It was at this moment that the Kuwaiti labor movement forced the Kuwaiti state into a binary choice: to side with them or with the oil companies. While the OPEC radicals understandably receive the lion's share of attention in histories of the "oil revolution," as Christopher Dietrich has noted, nationalization "would have been impossible without the support of gradualist oil elites."[181] As thoughtful historians of oil have noted, this shift was the product of power pressure.[182] Kuwaiti workers would be central to this project.

The transformative strikes of the 1970s began at the American Arabian Oil Company (Aminoil). By 1970, it had a workforce of about 800, including about 160 Kuwaitis and 580 workers classified as "Other Arabs."[183] Labor relations had been tense for years.[184] Pensions, housing, and wages were perennial issues, as was pervasive racial discrimination.[185] Despite nearly a decade of organizing, Aminoil workers lived under conditions that were widely seen as some of the worst in the industry.[186] The situation exploded when, even after the Affairs Ministry's Arbitration Committee ruled in favor of the workers in a housing dispute, the company dragged its feet in implementing the decision, leaving its workers in dilapidated buildings. In March of 1972, the Aminoil union, with the support of the Petroleum Workers Federation, threatened to strike unless the company improved its housing and raised wages.[187]

Subsequent events exacerbated tensions not only between workers and the company, but also between workers and the state, foreshadowing a widening rift. On the night before the planned strike, six members of the union, including its president, Daifullah Falah Sultan, were arrested by security forces, triggering a "wave of resentment" amongst the workers. While *al-Tali'a* blamed the oil company for the arrests, it also accused the government of failing to stand with labor.[188] The unions countered state pressure with a powerful organization of their own. The small group of Aminoil workers could count on support from both the wider Petroleum Workers Federation and its umbrella organization, the Kuwait Trade Union Federation (KTUF), both of which quickly came to their aid. The KTUF threatened to launch a solidarity strike on March 12, ratcheting up the pressure.[189] Friendly MPs also supported the workers, generating more popular attention.[190] The combined strategy convinced state authorities to side with the workers. The Ministry of Social Affairs and Labor ordered Aminoil to compromise, and the company caved.[191] Workers won a cost-of-living allowance, a clause banning retaliation against strikers, a pledge to investigate the issue of housing, and a one-time payment of 250 dinars to workers to compensate for the failure to implement Law 28 of 1969.[192]

A second important action took place a few weeks later, when the Petroleum Workers Federation threatened to organize a strike of KOC workers starting on April 1, 1972. The union argued that the company was failing to implement provisions of the oil sector law on issues including wages, hours of work, housing, and allowances.[193] A key point of contention was the position of noncitizens. As in the Aminoil strike, the union demanded retroactive raises on the grounds that they would compensate for the delays in implementing the labor law. But the company offered these only to Kuwaiti workers. The union rejected the plan, arguing that the rapidly rising cost of living "affects everyone without exception or distinction."[194] The union won the support of the state and achieved its main demands. The Kuwait Oil Company, once seen as virtually untouchable, had caved under the mere threat of a strike.

These two victories, won in quick succession, demonstrated both the power of the oil unions and their commitment to their noncitizen colleagues. British officials were unnerved. The ambassador reported that the unions "have recently made a remarkable advance towards a position of power and have demonstrated their ability to take on oil companies and win."[195] Moreover, they "have fought skillfully and have outmaneuvred both Government and oil companies," forcing the state to decide between "confronting the strikers or the companies."[196] Once again, the British were particularly concerned that noncitizens were overcoming their fear of deportation and actively participating in union actions.[197] British authorities noted that in KOC, "contingency planning has always assumed that non-Kuwaiti non union staff would continue working for fear of losing their jobs and work permits"—an assumption they could no longer make.[198] The oil firms were most alarmed that workers had managed to circumvent their strike plans. During the Aminoil strike, "determined and effective" picketing led the company to conclude that they "were by no means sure that they could or would wish to pass their expatriate staff through hostile picket lines even for the maintenance of the essential services."[199] Their "expatriate"—overwhelmingly white—managers were thus pinned down. At KOC, meanwhile, "the union has complete control over the marine terminal and has thus a stranglehold on the company," enabling it to shut down oil exports at will.[200] By targeting a few key chokepoints, workers managed to immobilize the most critical points of the oil complex.

The strikes of April 1972 initiated a sustained period of labor struggle. In a series of coordinated actions across multiple oil firms, the Petroleum Workers Federation launched a campaign to match the wages and benefits of the government sector, ban the hiring of noncitizen subcontractors, and end discrimination on the basis of nationality.[201] The demand that oil sector salaries match those in the citizen-dominated public sector was itself an indirect challenge to the nationality regime, complementing efforts to unify labor law by creating a floor for wages and benefits that would extend to all workers in Kuwait. On June 9, 1972, KOC workers threatened another strike, accusing the company of failing to live up to its promises to raise wages and hire Arab and Kuwaiti workers.[202] The unions continued to frame the question in terms of sovereignty and patriotism and sought to avoid antagonizing the ruling family, going so far as to petition the Crown Prince for aid.[203] As with the

Aminoil strike, the key point of tension was their demand that all workers, regardless of nationality, receive equal allowances, and that the company end the use of noncitizen contractors.[204] Heightening the pressure still further, on November 30, 1972, KOC storage and shipping workers went on strike, returning a few days later when the government agreed to restart negotiations.[205] By arguing that they were simply pressuring the Kuwaiti government to implement its own legislation, the labor movement forced the state to come to its defense and won a series of concessions.

But union efforts on behalf of noncitizen workers also exacerbated tensions with the state, and particularly the Ministry of Social Affairs. The Petroleum Workers Federation continued accusing the oil companies of violating the spirit of the 1969 oil labor law by relying on, and deliberately misidentifying, contracted workers.[206] Arco, one of the contractors, did not employ a single Kuwaiti, while many firms engaged undocumented workers who were especially vulnerable to deportation.[207] The Petroleum Workers Federation warned that the differential treatment accorded to Kuwaiti and non-Kuwaiti workers threatened to "fracture the unity of the workers."[208] While the Ministry of Social Affairs and Labor acknowledged the accuracy of union arguments, it took no direct action.[209] The minister of social affairs also disputed the union's characterization of the struggle as a question of national sovereignty, instead describing it as a wage dispute.[210]

Perhaps nowhere was the rising tension between the oil unions and the government more apparent than in the state-owned Kuwait National Petroleum Company (KNPC). As a Kuwaiti company, it at first proved immune to union attacks on imperialist corporations; in fact, when the company was founded, *al-Tali'a* framed it as a means of breaking the grip of foreign oil companies on the model long proposed by Ashraf Lutfi and Abdullah Tariki.[211] Wary of a popular backlash, the unions had at first avoided taking direct action against it, and KNPC had in turn been given a series of special exemptions from labor law.[212] A KNPC union had been founded in 1968 only after being repeatedly denied authorization by the Ministry of Social Affairs.[213] But KNPC proceeded to adopt virtually the same labor practices as the other oil companies.[214] Tensions escalated in 1972 when the company blamed high fuel prices on rising worker salaries, triggering a furious response from the unions.[215] *Al-Tali'a* began accusing it of acting just like the foreign oil companies, ignoring labor law and implementing racist policies that discriminated against noncitizens, especially in the provision of allowances.[216] The company refused a union request for mediation from the Ministry of Social Affairs and Labor, and the union rejected two proposed wage increases that were only offered to Kuwaiti workers. Instead, workers threatened a strike, explaining that while they had "been tolerant from the start" because KNPC was a "national company," its "exploitative behavior" forced their hand.[217] They consistently argued that the company was attempting to "exacerbate factionalism" between its workers and called instead for "solidarity and unity of the working class."[218] It was a remarkable moment: a Kuwaiti union was challenging a national oil company on the issue of noncitizen rights.

The strike would be the first in a series of qualified victories in which the unions won across-the-board raises for their members but at the cost of conceding special privileges to citizens. On November 18, 1972, KNPC agreed to raise the salaries for both Kuwaiti and non-Kuwaiti workers. But while the union declared victory, won a raise, and reiterated its support of "all demands of all workers, without exception or discrimination," it also consented to what was effectively a special bonus for citizens. Given the union's rhetoric, this was a significant concession. Even the union press release, which included the now-standard call for the unity of the working class, acknowledged that the company's divide-and-rule tactics were threatening to open a gap between Kuwaitis and non-Kuwaitis.[219] The precedent of a special allowance for Kuwaitis in the oil industry had been endorsed, if reluctantly, by the unions themselves.[220]

Over the following months, this precedent would be extended across the Kuwaiti oil industry, even as oil unions continued to oppose it in principle. In May of 1973, KOC workers threatened to strike over the issue of social allowances.[221] At the end of July, KOC agreed to better social and housing allowances, housing, vacation, and pay, but like KNPC, it gave special benefits to Kuwaitis.[222] The last and most rancorous struggle took place at Aminoil.[223] Like the other oil companies, in early 1973 Aminoil proposed a series of raises that included special allowances for citizens. However, workers voted it down because it discriminated against non-Kuwaitis.[224] Through the summer, the union released a barrage of press statements and strike authorization votes that framed discrimination on the basis of nationality as a form of racism.[225] In late August, the union rejected a proposal, backed by the Ministry of Social Affairs, that would have given a special raise to citizen workers.[226] On September 9, workers finally went on strike, issuing a statement excoriating corporate discrimination against noncitizens.[227] In a provocative response, the oil company called on the government to "provide necessary security."[228] It also led to a violent incident that shocked the Kuwaiti political scene. As workers gathered for negotiations on the afternoon of September 10, an Employee Training manager pulled out a handgun and shot one of the striking workers. While the shooting seems to have resulted from panic, rather than premeditation, Aminoil had made such violence possible by providing its high-ranking managers with weapons—a long-standing corporate practice.[229] Exasperated by the company's unwillingness to compromise, the union circumvented it by winning the support of the Council of Ministers, which, under massive popular pressure and in the context of the strain on the international oil companies, forced a settlement.[230]

The final agreement, concluded in mid-November, addressed all key worker demands. It reclassified daily workers as monthly workers, created a new wage classification system, introduced new social allowances, and provided retroactive increases for Kuwaitis and non-Kuwaitis. The press, even the conservative publications, was enthusiastic, framing it as a victory for both Kuwaiti sovereignty and the working class.[231] Indeed, the long struggle with the foreign corporation won the unions broad popular support. In his memoirs, Ahmad al-Asbahi remembers the strike as a moment of triumph.[232] But like their compatriots at KOC and KNPC, the Aminoil union conceded special social allowances for Kuwaitis.[233] Even at the zenith of their power, the oil unions conceded their demand for equality between citizens and noncitizens.

It is impossible to know exactly why the oil unions abandoned a principle for which they had fought for so long. There is no written record of their internal deliberations, and former union officials did not discuss the thorny issue in detail during interviews. Labor leaders had long condemned discrimination on the basis of nationality as racist, divisive, and cynical. Many viewed the question as existential. Indeed, oil workers repeatedly went on strike in 1972 and 1973 in no small part to defend the rights of noncitizens, and they repeatedly expressed regret when compromising on the point. There are also hints of internal dissention, especially with left-wing labor leaders such as Hussein al-Youha. What is clear, however, is that on no other issue did they face so much resistance, especially from the Kuwaiti state.

During the Aminoil strike, which centered the question of noncitizen rights to a remarkable degree, Kuwaiti security forces detained union leaders at the company's request.[234] Then the day after the strike ended, Minister of Social Affairs and Labor Hamad Mubarak al-ʿAyyar blamed the workers not just for the labor dispute, but even for the shooting, arguing that the gunman had tried to "defend himself" and that if the workers had shown more "responsibility," the incident would never have happened.[235] Workers found that the language of sovereignty could be powerful, whether framed in terms of anticolonialism, resource nationalism, or the rule of law. Equality, however, was a tougher sell.

The failure of the oil unions to secure equality for noncitizens reflected a wider trend—unions tended to win when pursuing nationalist objectives but lost when they challenged the exclusions of nationality. This was vividly demonstrated by the fact that, even as the labor movement was losing the battle for noncitizen rights, it was demonstrating its effectiveness as a champion of Kuwaiti sovereignty in the campaign for oil nationalization. While the Kuwaiti state may have been an OPEC moderate, Kuwaitis largely sided with the radicals. *Al-Taliʿa* openly championed the oil revolution. It reported on events in Libya and the nationalizations in Algeria and Iraq, continued providing a platform to Abdullah Tariki, and reiterated its calls for oil nationalization.[236] It also emphasized the importance of labor in resource sovereignty.[237] Articles about control over natural resources continued to center discrimination in the oilfields, worker training, and Kuwaitization, with the paper arguing that Kuwaiti workers possessed sufficient expertise to run production themselves.[238]

Kuwait became a key player on the diplomatic front of the oil revolution in late 1972. Negotiating on behalf of the moderate OPEC members, Ahmed Zaki Yamani signed a participation agreement with the oil majors that granted the Gulf states a 25 percent share in their oil concessions, which would gradually rise to 51 percent by 1982.[239] But in Kuwait, the agreement required ratification in the National Assembly, many of whose members viewed participation as a means of avoiding full nationalization. The parliamentary debate triggered a political firestorm. *Al-Taliʿa* hammered the proposal.[240] The paper argued that while gradualists viewed participation as a step on the road to sovereign rights, there was nothing inevitable about nationalization. Indeed, participation threatened to supplant, rather than lead to, sovereign control over Kuwait's natural resources.[241] In the National Assembly, opposition MPs pointed out that the agreement only perpetuated oil company control over production.[242] The KTUF emerged as a major player in the debate, organizing rallies in opposition to participation and calling for full nationalization.[243] Union leadership also continued to attack the corporate policy of distancing Kuwaitis from production, though now they also expressed confidence that they no longer relied on the expertise of the multinational oil companies.[244] In an embarrassing blow to Yamani, the monarchy, and the principle of participation, the National Assembly voted the agreement down in mid-1973.[245]

Almost immediately, the question of Palestine radicalized the oil debate once again. The war that began on October 6, 1973, led OAPEC to orchestrate an oil boycott of countries allied to Israel and unilaterally raise the "posted price" used to calculate royalties. This transformation in oil pricing would eventually lead to the "oil crisis" of the 1970s.[246] In Kuwait, the trade unions led the call for the use of what they themselves called the "oil weapon" in the battle for Palestine.[247] Given the labor movement's longstanding advocacy of pan-Arab and anticolonial causes, their vocal support for Arab forces in the 1973 war was unsurprising.[248] But what made their advocacy especially significant was their ability to physically shut down production themselves. Barely a week after the end of hostilities, the KTUF held a meeting that concluded with a call for the immediate nationalization of U.S. oil interests in Kuwait.[249] As days turned into weeks, oil workers decided to take more direct action. In late October, the Oil and Petrochemical Workers Federation called for a targeted strike in the oil industry to serve as a warning to the United States. They argued that the Kuwaiti government's proposed response—a 10 percent reduction of shipments to the United States—did not go nearly far enough. Pointing out that Kuwaiti oil represented only 2 to 3 percent of U.S. consumption, the union argued that the only way to truly pressure the United States would be to drive up global oil prices, and that only direct action could effect sufficient pressure.[250] The strike began on October 23, 1973, bringing production to a halt for three days. The workers demanded not only a pause in production but the nationalization of at least 51 percent of the Kuwait Oil Company, and they threatened successive strike actions until "our patriotic people" were given control over the nation's natural wealth.[251] Linking the colonization of

Palestine to the neocolonialism of the oil companies, the unions demanded nationalization to combat both.

The strike proved both effective and popular. Union statements were remarkably militant—oil workers even threatened to sabotage oil facilities if their demands were not met, a threat that, given Kuwait's previous experience, had to be taken seriously.[252] It also attracted glowing press coverage.[253] Drawing on arguments made over the preceding two decades, newspapers again linked the exploitation of workers with oil sovereignty.[254] Given the widespread popularity of the Palestinian cause, the strike provoked no retaliation from the state, even though it included noncitizen workers.[255] Indeed, as oil workers could now shut down production at will, there was little that the state could do short of a massive—and enormously unpopular—display of force.

Fearing a break from its U.S. and British allies, the Kuwaiti state remained reluctant to take the final step and nationalize oil. It was clear that Britain and the United States at least considered retaliating. "I know what would have happened in the nineteenth century," grumbled Henry Kissinger at a staff meeting in late October. "But we can't do it. The idea that a bedouin kingdom could hold up Western Europe and the United States would have been absolutely inconceivable. They would have landed, they would have divided up the oilfields, and they would have solved the problem."[256] But it was no longer the nineteenth century—or even the 1950s. After two decades of organizing, Kuwaiti workers had rendered corporate strike plans obsolete and seized physical control over Kuwaiti oil.[257] Only military force could have dislodged them, and force was no longer politically feasible. The Kuwaiti debate over nationalization reached its climax in the spring of 1974.[258] The press, led by *al-Tali'a*, kept up a steady stream of demands for nationalization, supported by the unions and their allies.[259] The ruling family and Council of Ministers found themselves under constant attack as defenders of the oil companies.[260] Eventually, the pressure became impossible to resist. On May 14, 1974, the Assembly nationalized Kuwaiti oil.[261]

Nationalization momentarily thrust Kuwait into the center of global politics. Francisco Parra, the fifth OPEC secretary general, described the move as a "turning point" in the history of the oil industry. As the first Gulf state to make this momentous decision, it shattered Yamani's coalition of conservative monarchies. The result was a dramatic transfer of ownership of a significant proportion of the world's oil.[262] While officials such as Parra tend to frame their fellow oil elites as the midwives of nationalization, more recent histories of oil, not to mention contemporary Kuwaiti political observers, had no doubt that oil workers deserved much of the credit.[263] In his memoirs, Dr. Ahmad al-Khatib singles out the unions for their "pioneering role" in oil nationalization.[264] In later years, union officials would remember their championing of resource sovereignty as one of the most significant legacies of their movement.[265] Curious but revealing evidence of Kuwait's key role in oil politics came in 1975, when Ilich Ramírez Sánchez, better known as Carlos the Jackal, attacked OPEC headquarters in Vienna in an attempt to pressure the organization to take more radical action in support of the Palestinian cause. After seizing control of the meeting hall, he divided the delegates into groups of "friends" and "enemies," depending on the political stance of their country of origin, with the plan of taking his enemies as hostages. He moved quickly through the room until he reached the Kuwaiti delegation—when he paused, evidently unsure of what to do. After some deliberation, he decided that the presumably relieved Kuwaiti delegates qualified as friends.[266]

But even as it reached the apex of its power, the Kuwaiti labor movement came up against its limits. This became apparent in a series of strikes in 1974 and 1975. Tensions between the unions and the state—centered on the question of sovereignty—came to a head, fittingly enough, at the Kuwait National Petroleum Company. In March 1974, KNPC workers threatened to strike, arguing that workers had a right to share in the company's windfall profits and that the company was employing foreign oil servicing firms that took advantage of contracted workers.[267] At KNPC, workers had extra leverage because the company dominated the domestic Kuwaiti market. A strike could therefore disrupt local supply, triggering long lines at gas stations across Kuwait. But this also underlined the fact that the strike was directed against a company that was itself seen as an embodiment of Kuwaiti resource sovereignty.[268] On July 27, 1974, representatives of the four major oil company unions met in the headquarters of the Petroleum Workers Federation in Ahmadi to try and drive home their point that salaries were lagging far behind the cost of living, and that workers were not sharing in the profits of the oil boom.[269] Negotiations at KNPC reached a dead end in August, when workers demanded salary parity with workers in the government sector.[270] On August 23, the strike began.[271]

The unions won a number of concessions, including surprise inspections of the conditions of contracted workers in the oil industry.[272] But they also faced some of the most forceful pushback they had ever encountered. In their rhetorical battle with the government over who truly represented the national interest, the unions were no longer winning the public debate.[273] Government ministers condemned the threatened strike as unauthorized and unjustified, and warned that it would affect public services across the country, including water and electricity.[274] Yacoub al-Jauaʿn, manager of the Bank of the Gulf and an increasingly prominent spokesman for Kuwaiti business elites, took the opportunity to call for "alternatives" to unions, like "internal federations" or "shared committees," which could resolve disputes without having to resort to the strike.[275] In private conversations with visiting ILO officials, representatives from the Ministry of Social Affairs and Labor and the Chamber of Commerce argued that unions were overreaching by demanding parity between oil and government salaries.[276] Even previously sympathetic papers expressed skepticism, and published attacks from business leaders and other critics of the union movement.[277] As the *Voice of the Gulf* argued, even as the Kuwaiti labor movement reached the heights of power, it found itself sandwiched between the state, the National Assembly, and major employers.[278] Ironically, its very success had eliminated its strongest argument—after independence and nationalization, organized labor could no longer position itself as the standard-bearer of anticolonialism. Perhaps the most ominous strike took place at Conoco in the summer of 1975. Frustrated by the standard grievances of oil workers—stagnating wages, limited benefits, and the hiring of deliberately vulnerable noncitizen contract workers—workers walked off the job. Even though the company was facing nationalization, it broke the strike by firing the key organizers. They were noncitizens.[279]

CONCLUSION

A detailed recounting of Kuwait's oil revolution makes clear the significance, as well as the inextricability, of the linkages between nationality and labor, migration and democracy, and the rights of both citizens and noncitizens. By seizing physical control over the oilfields and deploying the language of sovereignty, Kuwaiti workers played a key role in reshaping the global economy. But when they centered ideals of equality, they faced powerful pushback and eventual defeat. Elite efforts to frame labor and migration as economic and apolitical masked a project that labor leaders and their allies recognized as an existential threat not just to their movement, but to democracy in Kuwait. Their fight for noncitizen rights was not just a demonstration of solidarity, but an act of self-defense. It also cannot be read simply as a failure. It highlights the contingencies of a process too often framed as the inevitable result of oil or empire. In their drive to challenge the nationality regime, Kuwaiti workers and their allies put forward alternative analytical frameworks that pointed toward a more equitable future. Their efforts reveal that underneath the fissures of nationality, the possibility of solidarity and transformative change has always existed.

Conclusion

IN 1976, THE REGIME dissolved the National Assembly and suspended several key political rights, including freedoms of speech and assembly. The decision brought an end to the first constitutional period and ushered in an era of authoritarian rule that lasted, with one interregnum, until 1992. It also marked a dangerous precedent, setting the stage for future suspensions of the constitution. The crackdown strangled the reformist campaigns that had gained so much popular support in the early 1970s. Longtime advocates of democracy, like Dr. Ahmad al-Khatib, felt that their hard-earned victories were slipping away.[1] The ensuing half-century would be a prolonged rearguard action for supporters of labor and democracy in Kuwait.

The most impacted were once again the most vulnerable—especially noncitizens and stateless people. The shutdown of formal politics silenced calls for the reform of nationality law, while official justifications for tiered citizenship grew more forceful.[2] A slew of newspaper reports in the late seventies accused noncitizens of marrying Kuwaiti women for the purpose of obtaining nationality as the censored press jumped to the defense of the regime.[3] The plight of the stateless *bidun* grew even worse as the years progressed, especially following the imposition of austerity measures after a fall in oil prices in the early 1980s. Along with other Gulf states, Kuwaiti authorities began restricting access to essential services, including jobs, education, and healthcare.[4] In the early twenty-first century, the United Arab Emirates signed a remarkable deal with the Comoro Islands in which, in exchange for Emirati direct investment, the Comoros agreed to provide over 100,000 stateless people with passports—on the condition that their holders never be allowed to visit the Comoro Islands. The deal created a class of permanent exiles, a form of nationality stripped of the rights of citizenship. Kuwait considered, but declined, a similar offer.[5] The scheme, which effectively represents the commodification and export of citizenship itself, highlights the connection between two groups usually discussed separately—the stateless *bidun* and noncitizen residents—by effectively transforming the former into the latter.[6]

In recent years, movements for *bidun* rights have revived thanks to the efforts of stateless people themselves. In 2012, the publication of Saud Alsanousi's award-winning novel *The Bamboo Stalk*, which follows the struggles of a man with a Filipina mother and a Kuwaiti father, triggered a national conversation about the exclusions of Kuwaiti nationality, so much so that regimes across the Gulf censored a miniseries based on the book.[7] As Claire Beaugrand has documented, a wave of *bidun* activism that began that same year has forced the question of naturalization back into the center of Kuwaiti politics. While the naturalization of *bidun* has once again won significant support, conservative elites have blocked all such efforts, demonstrating their continued interest in, and power to impose, narrow conceptions of nationality.[8] Control over nationality also remains a powerful weapon against dissent. When regimes across the region faced protests in 2011, many, including Kuwait, responded by stripping dissidents of their citizenship.[9]

The weakening of Kuwaiti democracy exacerbated the vulnerabilities of noncitizens. Low oil prices led to a new era of austerity and another outflow of migration.[10] The regime also began taking a harder line against efforts to improve conditions in the private sector. In 1985, the Kuwaiti delegate to an ILO meeting in Jakarta placed the blame for abuses of noncitizen workers on "Asian" governments and "Asian" recruitment agencies, claiming that they were responsible for unrealistic expectations and "false promises."[11] Years of censorship ensured that labor could no longer count on allies in the press. When, in 1989, 1,200 noncitizen workers went on a hunger strike after working for months without pay, coverage of labor issues was so threadbare that Kuwaiti newspapers published a translated report from the Associated Press.[12] The Iraqi occupation and its aftermath proved particularly traumatic. International attention to the plight of noncitizen workers helped generate a series of reforms targeting recruitment agencies, which once again became the scapegoat for systemic abuses.[13] At the same time, however, a vocal bloc accused noncitizens of "collaborating" with the occupiers, and called for a purge of both legal and "illegal" residents.[14] The heaviest weight of the backlash fell on Palestinians, in part because of the Palestinian Liberation Organization's decision to side with Iraq. Hundreds of thousands of Palestinian residents of Kuwait were deported, devastating a community that had been central to the building of Kuwait and the maintenance of Palestinian nationhood in diaspora.[15]

While the return of electoral politics in 1992 opened avenues for protest, it also provided an opportunity for a new generation of politicians to deploy xenophobia for political gain. Perhaps the most notorious recent example is the former MP Safa al-Hashem, who has referred to noncitizens as "opportunistic bacteria," tried to restrict their access to essential services, and supported mass deportations.[16] The COVID-19 pandemic had a devastating impact on noncitizen residents, especially the undocumented. Concentrated in crowded quarters, employed in dangerous service professions, and denied access to free healthcare, they died in disproportionate numbers and faced new economic hardships.[17] They also encountered another wave of xenophobia that reflects a growing racialization of South Asian workers.[18] As Neha Vora and Amélie Le Renard have noted, the rise of terms like "Indian," popularly used to refer to all South Asians in the Persian Gulf, reflect the intersection of race and nationality.[19] But as in the past, racism and xenophobia have generated their own backlash. Many Kuwaitis reacted with glee when al-Hashem lost her reelection bid in 2020. Moreover, like the deportation state she defends, al-Hashem cannot be seen as a solely Kuwaiti phenomenon—she holds academic credentials from Penn State and Harvard Business School.[20]

The rights of noncitizen workers have increasingly become the subject of international diplomacy. Beginning in the early 2010s, Kuwait and the Philippines clashed over the rights of the latter's citizen residents in Kuwait, who represent a significant percentage of the domestic worker population.[21] In 2018, a diplomatic crisis erupted when the body of Joanna Demafelis, a twenty-nine-year-old Filipina domestic worker, was discovered in a freezer in an abandoned apartment. The Philippines suspended all official migration for several months, but relented when it became clear that the ban only encouraged undocumented immigration and rebounded on their own citizens.[22] Later that year, the government of Kuwait then expelled the Filipino ambassador after embassy officials posted a video of an effort to remove a domestic worker from an abusive household.[23] While the Philippines has consistently pressured the Kuwaiti state to improve the position of domestic workers, the ineffectiveness of these efforts testifies to the difficulties of protecting noncitizen rights in a world of nation-states.

In recent decades, particularly dystopian attacks on noncitizen rights in the Persian Gulf have generated international attention.[24] In 2019, for instance, the Indian press covered the arrest of a ring of medical personnel who surgically altered fingerprints so that noncitizens blacklisted from Kuwait could evade biometric surveillance.[25] The 2022 World Cup in Qatar brought a veritable explosion of coverage. International attention is often seen as a means of pressuring Gulf states to carry out reforms. Unfortunately, such coverage can also be sensationalist, stereotyped, or bigoted, framing the Gulf as exceptionally repressive or unjust.[26] Such representations miss the underlying structural causes of disempowerment that are fundamentally global. Moreover, as Faisal Hamadah has noted, discussions of domestic workers have increasingly been conducted in the depoliticizing framework of human rights.[27] The NGO-ification of noncitizen labor threatens to shatter the solidarities—and obscure the shared political interests—that have long connected citizens and noncitizens in Kuwait and the wider Gulf.

Regardless of the international situation, noncitizens remain their own most effective advocates. In Kuwait, a key figure is the remarkable Mary Ann Abunda, who arrived in Kuwait from the Philippines in 2000 at the age of twenty-two and began organizing her fellow workers nine years later.[28] Working with Sandigan, the Filipino trade union, she has helped create a mutual aid organization that provides valuable legal information, material assistance, and other services to noncitizen workers in Kuwait. Sandigan organized Kuwait's first Domestic Workers Conference and even opened an office in KTUF headquarters to help respond to the complaints of workers themselves.[29] Their efforts have been complemented by the work of advocacy and awareness groups based in the Gulf itself. Together, these citizen and noncitizen activists have kept the question of noncitizen rights, and the reform of the nationality regime, on the political agenda.

* * *

Repression has fallen with particular force on organized labor. In late September of 1976, Kuwaiti security forces arrested eight prominent members of the trade union movement, including both the president and vice president of the KTUF, Nasser al-Faraj and Hussein al-Youha. Charged with "anti-state activities," they were accused of distributing anonymous leaflets that condemned the suspension of constitutional rule.[30] Their imprisonment launched a period of unprecedented repression of organized labor and political freedom writ large.[31] By the late 1970s, the only organizations beyond the grasp of government control were the Graduates Society and the Kuwait Trade Union Federation.[32] Islamic activists began to win elections within the trade union movement itself, in no small part because they faced less repression than the secular reformers whom the regime viewed as their most dangerous enemies.[33] Government officials continued their tactics of red-baiting, aided by a subservient press.[34] The institution of autocratic rule swept away the protections under which labor organizing had flourished, along with key allies in parliament and the media. While the trade union movement would survive, it would never again dominate Kuwaiti politics. It was undermined by the independent state that it had fought so hard to build.

The Kuwaiti trade union movement nevertheless remained a steadfast supporter of constitutional rule.[35] In the wake of the first suspension of parliament, the KTUF joined other political organizations in calling for the restitution of democracy. But state authorities responded with ferocity, threatening to suspend the unions altogether on the argument that they were constitutionally required to abstain from politics. In a move that demonstrated the new balance of power between the unions and the state, the workers backed down.[36] By the 1980s, the ILO and ICATU accused the Kuwaiti government of restricting their access to KTUF headquarters.[37] When the constitution was suspended again in 1986, the KTUF objected forcefully, but to no avail.[38] Organized labor has also continued to fight to broaden and deepen the rights of citizenship, demanding nationality for *bidun* and that naturalized citizens receive full voting rights and protection from citizenship stripping.[39] Left-wing factions continue to battle for social justice, women's rights, and working-class solidarity, regardless of nationality. A number of the most prominent pro-democracy politicians in Kuwait got their start in the trade union movement.[40] For many Kuwaiti labor leaders, the uncompromising defense of democratic rule remains a central tenet of their movement.

As trade unionists began to narrate Kuwaiti labor history—and their own role in it—they tended to describe themselves as one branch of a wider reformist movement that transformed Kuwait, in Dr. al-Khatib's words, "from an emirate into a state." In the past several decades, the pro-democracy opposition has adopted this teleological narrative of statebuilding as the central thread of Kuwaiti history. It serves the double purpose of both legitimizing its long struggle with the ruling family and framing democracy as not only desirable, but inevitable. Labor leaders have generally adopted this rhetoric. In an interview, Hussein al-Youha volunteered the "emirate to state" expression verbatim, and described the labor movement as a key player "in building this state, developing it, and making it better."[41] Hussein Saqr even lists select articles of the Kuwaiti constitution in the preface to his memoirs.[42] This narrative of the trade union movement as modern statebuilder has become hegemonic, recounted in interviews, newspaper articles, and popular histories.

Within this metanarrative, trade unionists often frame oil nationalization as their most significant legacy.[43] Kuwaiti oil unions have continued the fight to keep both the production process, and oil itself, in Kuwaiti hands, and remain the best-organized and most powerful segment of the movement for resource sovereignty.[44] In 1995, a wave of strikes prevented a round of wage cuts in the oil industry.[45] Then in 2016, a government proposal to cut wages and sell off portions of Kuwaiti oil production to private firms triggered a general oil workers strike.[46] The issue of privatization provoked impassioned responses. In a remarkable gesture, Hassan Falah came out of retirement to address the striking workers. By then in his eighties, he nevertheless gave the impression of a man who knows how to make a speech. He excoriated privatization as a betrayal of the labor movement and the long struggle it waged against imperial powers and multinational oil companies. Oil wealth, he argued, can only be the property of the nation and of the people, and privatization would be not only unjust, but unconstitutional.[47] The strike slashed production by 50 percent, and after a standoff, the government backed down.[48] It affirmed that even in their weakened state, oil unions and their allies remained capable of winning a significant political battle. But nationalization was no panacea. As Laleh Khalili argues, national oil companies "reproduced a kind of knowledge that ratified the exploitation of labor and nature just as they had been exploited in the colonial period."[49] Continued struggles to diversify the economy, equitably redistribute wealth, and—especially—combat climate change have ensured that Kuwaiti oil remains a flashpoint.

The dominant statebuilding narrative of the labor movement also contains a glaring omission—the battle for noncitizen rights. The memoirs and histories written by trade unionists rarely discuss the persistent efforts of the labor movement to improve the lives of noncitizens. This silencing seems to reflect a hegemonic political discourse that is dominated by what Fahad Bishara calls "the celebratory narratives of nation-building."[50] For trade unionists, even the most internationalist, stressing their support for noncitizen rights does little to legitimate their work in a political climate in which contributing to the construction of an independent state is deemed to be the most significant metric. But in eliding their defense of noncitizens, labor leaders minimize both their historical significance and their temerity. The threat of a multinational working class was, in no small part, what enabled them to play such a significant role in building the Kuwaiti welfare state and defending parliamentary rule. It forced corporate and state authorities to compromise at the bargaining table and challenged their narratives of economic inevitability. It also demonstrated that Kuwaitis did not relentlessly pursue their perceived self-interest as privileged citizens or act as individual rent-seekers looking to maximize their share of oil wealth. Instead, Kuwaitis thought of themselves in a variety of ways—as workers, Arabs, trade unionists, or democrats—and constructed their conceptions of economic interest alongside diverse visions of social justice. These conceptions could be radically inclusive and egalitarian.

The mid-1970s proved to be the high-water mark of union interest in noncitizens. In the following years, some members of the labor movement turned their attention from improving the working conditions of noncitizen workers to restricting immigration.[51] By the late eighties, a candidate for a KTUF position could describe "Asian workers" as "the most important issue" facing his union.[52] In 1993, Kuwaiti KOC workers threatened to strike when the oil company posted recruitment advertisements in Indian newspapers.[53] Unions struggled to build noncitizen membership, especially among domestic workers.[54] While the KTUF leadership has at times allied with advocates for noncitizen rights, members of its leadership have sometimes dismissed or even demeaned such work.[55] But the labor movement never abandoned its struggle for noncitizen rights. Unions have continued to fight for wages and benefits in the private sector, including for noncitizens.[56] They have also kept up their criticism of the labor sponsorship system.[57] In 1993, the KTUF opened a "Migrant Workers Office."[58] Along with the Bahraini trade union federation, it also launched an official partnership with GEFONT Support Group-Kuwait, an organization for Nepali workers affiliated with the General Federation of Nepali Trade Unions, which works with Nepali workers around the Gulf.[59] The KTUF also partners with the ILO and various NGOs to push for an end to the labor sponsorship system. In a 2014 interview, the president of the KTUF went so far as to describe sponsorship as a modern-day "system of slavery."[60] Such efforts underline a faith in solidarity that, while always fragile, has never been extinguished.

* * *

In May of 2024, the new emir of Kuwait suspended parliament for the first time in over thirty years. In justifying his imposition of monarchical rule, he again turned to nationality, emphasizing his determination to "protect" Kuwaiti citizenship and "Kuwaiti identity."[61] The months preceding the suspension of parliament had been marked by another immigration and citizenship panic. The regime even created an anonymous hotline that allowed Kuwaitis to report cases of "citizenship fraud."[62] The suspension of constitutional rule was immediately followed by an unprecedented wave of citizenship stripping. Within months, tens of thousands of people lost their nationality in the largest denaturalization effort in Kuwaiti history—indeed, one of the largest anywhere on earth. Many face the prospect of statelessness. The regime then passed a series of measures restricting access to nationality, once again targeting noncitizens married to Kuwaiti men.[63] The denaturalizations proved devastating for those impacted—upending lives, dividing families, and shattering hopes for the future. They also cast a further chill over every aspect of politics. Asked if the inquiry would include cabinet ministers or members of parliament, the Minister of the Interior responded with a terse statement: "All of Kuwait is under review."[64]

But despite the resurgence of authoritarianism, there is still value to narrating the twists and turns of the making of the migrant working class. The actions of immigrants and workers, of radicals and activists, reveal a remarkable array of alternate possibilities and roads not taken—and which have never been foreclosed. Rather than a narrative of defeat, it is a story in which the working class was present at its own making and fundamentally shaped the history of the Persian Gulf. The contingencies of this history serve as a powerful antidote to narratives of economic inevitability, or to pessimists who believe that the region is doomed to economic stratification and political repression. They provide encouragement to those who hope that the autocratic present may be but a passing phase in the history of a diverse and cosmopolitan region. That hope has been preserved in a fragmentary archive of oral histories, anonymous petitions, shuttered newspapers, and banned books, passed from one generation to the next. This counter-archive remains what it was designed to be: a source of solace for those who struggle for a more just and equitable future for all residents of the Persian Gulf.

Notes

Acknowledgments

1. C. Stanley G. Mylrea, *Kuwait Before Oil: Memoirs of Dr. C. Stanley G. Mylrea, Pioneer Medical Missionary of The Arabian Mission Reformed Church of America* (Unpublished: Library of the Center for Research and Studies on Kuwait), 39.

Introduction

1. "Hussein al-Youha: Nutalib bi-Musawat al-ʿUmmal al-Kuwaitiyyin bi-ghayr al-Kuwaitiyyin," *al-Taliʿa*, May 6, 1975; "Tawhid Qawanin al-ʿAmal fi al-Kuwait," *al-Taliʿa*, May 13, 1975.

2. "Nashʾat al-Haraka al-ʿUmmaliyya fi al-Kuwait," *al-Risala*, December 1968. KU Newspaper Archive (hereafter KU) 10/H/220.

3. Unless otherwise cited, personal details from al-Youha's life come from Hussein al-Youha, Personal interview, November 27, 2017; "Hussain Al-Youha," AUK Oral History, accessed May 24, 2024, https://oralhistory.auk.edu.kw/items/show/4; and "al-Sunduq al-Aswad: Hussein al-Youha," https://www.youtube.com/playlist?list=PLL95OS4M68S9K_NL31JK-qHDCSJDftoSA, accessed May 26, 2024.

4. "Kul Shayʾ ʿan al-Ijtimaʿ al-Awwal lil-Hayʾat al-Shaʿbiyya," *Mirʾat al-Umma*, December 20, 1972, KU 10/z/310.

5. "Bidayat al-Haraka al-ʿUmmaliyya wa al-Naqabiyya ʿala Lisan Ruwwadha," *al-ʿamil*, October 15, 1984, KU 10/z/100.

6. FO 371/156928, Letter from J. C. B. Richmond to A. R. Walmsley, June 17, 1961; State of Kuwait Department of Planning and Statistics, *Statistics Abstract in 25 Years* (Kuwait: Central Statistics Office, 1990), 21.

7. Gulf Labour Markets and Migration [Hereafter GLMM], "GCC: Total Population and Percentage of Nationals and Non-nationals in GCC Countries," https://gulfmigration.grc.net/gcc-total-population-and-percentage-of-nationals-and-non-nationals-in-gcc-countries-national-statistics-mid-2020-2/.

8. United Nations, Department of Economic and Social Affairs, Population Division (2016); *International Migration Report 2015: Highlights* (ST/ESA/SER.A/375).

9. This formulation is from Noora Lori, *Offshore Citizens: Permanent Temporary Status in the Gulf* (Cambridge University Press, 2019). See also Anh Nga Longva, *Walls Built on Sand: Migration, Exclusion, and Society in Kuwait* (Westview Press, 1997), 181.

10. Zahra Babar, "The 'Enemy Within'—Citizenship-Stripping in the Post–Arab Spring GCC," *Middle East Journal* 71, no. 4 (2017): 525–43; "Darajat al-Jinsiyya al-Kuwaitiyya 2025," *Kuwait Services*, accessed May 31 2025, https://kuwaitservices.org/2961/%D8%AF%D8%B1%D8%AC%D8%A7%D8%AA-%D8%A7%D9%84%D8%AC%D9%86%D8%B3%D9%8A%D8%A9-%D8%A7%D9%84%D9%83%D9%88%D9%8A%D8%AA%D9%8A%D8%A9/; "'Stateless Overnight': Authoritarian Crackdown Strips 42,000 Kuwaitis of Nationality," *France24*, March 15, 2025, https://www.ft.com/content/03f51141-ddde-439e-ba57-e82f5ffb2696. On tiered citizenship in the UAE, see Lori, *Offshore Citizens*, 7.

11. Ahmed Kanna, Amélie Le Renard, and Neha Vora, *Beyond Exception: New Interpretations of the Arabian Peninsula* (Cornell University Press, 2020); Harvey Molotch and Davide Ponzini, eds., *The New Arab Urban: Gulf Cities of Wealth, Ambition, and Distress* (NYU Press, 2019). Historical critiques of Gulf exceptionalism include Nelida Fuccaro, *Histories of City and State in the Persian Gulf: Manama since 1800* (Cambridge University Press, 2009); Farah Al-Nakib, *Kuwait Transformed: A History of Oil and Urban Life* (Stanford University Press, 2016); and Laura Frances Goffman, *Disorder and Diagnosis: Health and the Politics of Everyday Life in Modern Arabia* (Stanford University Press, 2024).

12. Cindy Hahamovitch, "Creating Perfect Immigrants: Guestworkers of the World in Historical Perspective," *Labor History* 44, no. 1 (February 2003): 69–94, 85–86.

13. Nicholas De Genova, "Denizenship," in *Precarity and Belonging: Labor, Migration, and Noncitizenship*, ed. Catherine S. Ramírez, Sylvanna M. Falcón, Juan Poblete, Steven C. McKay, and Felicity Amaya Schaeffer (Rutgers University Press, 2021): 227–42; Tomas Hammar, *Democracy and the Nation-State: Aliens, Denizens, and Citizens in a World of International Migration* (Gower Pub. Co., 1990); Aristide R. Zolberg, "The Dawn of Cosmopolitan Denizenship," *Indiana Journal of Global Legal Studies* 7, no. 2 (Spring 2000): 511–18.

14. Hazim Beblawi, "The Rentier State in the Arab World," in *The Rentier State*, ed. Hazem Beblawi and Giacomo Luciani (Croom Helm, 1987), 49–71; Michael L. Ross, *The Oil Curse: How Petroleum Wealth Shapes the Development of Nations* (Princeton University Press, 2012).

15. Makio Yamada and Steffen Hertog, "Introduction: Revisiting Rentierism—with a Short Note by Giacomo Luciani," *British Journal of Middle Eastern Studies* 47, no. 1 (2020): 1–5; and Project on Middle East Political Science, "The Politics of Rentier States in the Gulf," *POMES* 33 (January 2019), https://pomeps.org/wp-content/uploads/2019/02/POMEPS_Studies_33.pdf.

16. John Chalcraft, *The Invisible Cage: Syrian Migrant Workers in Lebanon* (Stanford University Press, 2008), 2, 9.

17. Douglass S. Massey et al., "Theories of International Migration: A Review and Appraisal," *Population and Development Review* 19, no. 3 (September 1993): 431–66;

Douglass S. Massey, "Towards a Theory of International Migration," *Eastern Journal of European Studies* 3, no. 2 (December 2012): 9–35; Michael Burawoy, "The Functions and Reproduction of Migrant Labor: Comparative Material from Southern Africa and the United States," *American Journal of Sociology* 81, no. 5 (1976): 1050–87.

18. I. J. Seccombe and R. I. Lawless, "Foreign Worker Dependence in the Gulf, and the International Oil Companies: 1910–50," *International Migration Review* 20, no. 3 (Autumn, 1986): 548–74; Amin ʿIzz al-Din, *ʿUmmal al-Kuwait min al-Luʾluʾ ila al-Batrul* (*Workers of Kuwait from Pearls to Oil*) (Kuwait Government Press, 1958), 16.

19. Peter Lienhardt, *Disorientations, A Society in Flux: Kuwait in the 1950s*, ed. Ahmed Al-Shahi (Ithica Press, 1993), 50.

20. Michael Herb, *The Wages of Oil: Parliaments and Economic Development in Kuwait and the UAE* (Cornell University Press, 2014), 16; Jill Crystal, *Oil and Politics in the Gulf: Rulers and Merchants in Kuwait and Qatar* (Cambridge University Press, 1990).

21. An early and trenchant critique of rentier theory is Gwenn Okruhlik, "Rentier Wealth, Unruly Law, and the Rise of Opposition: The Political Economy of Oil States," *Comparative Politics* 31, no. 3 (1999): 295–315. More recent works in this vein include Fuccaro, *Histories of City and State*, 6; Kaveh Ehsani, "Social Engineering and the Contradictions of Modernization in Khuzestan's Company Towns: A Look at Abadan and Masjed-Soleyman," *International Review of Social History* 48, no. 3 (2003): 361–99; Matthew MacLean, "Spatial Transformations and the Emergence of the 'National': Infrastructures and the Formation of the United Arab Emirates, 1950–1980" (PhD diss., New York University, 2017), 13–14, 339–40; Kevan Harris, *A Social Revolution: Politics and the Welfare State in Iran* (University of California Press, 2007), 30; Michael Watts, "Resource Curse? Governmentality, Oil and Power in the Niger Delta, Nigeria," *Geopolitics* 9, no. 1 (2004): 50–80; Timothy Mitchell, "Ten Propositions on Oil," in *A Critical Political Economy of the Middle East and North Africa*, ed. Joel Beinin, Bassam Haddad, and Sherene Seikaly (Stanford University Press, 2021), 68–84, 77.

22. These can be traced back to the 1970s in books such as Fred Halliday, *Arabia without Sultans* (Penguin, 1974); Helen Lackner, *A House Built on Sand: A Political Economy of Saudi Arabia* (Ithaca Press, 1978); Fawwaz Traboulsi, *Dhufar: Shahada min Zaman al-Thawra* (Riyad al-Rays lil-Kutub wa al-Nashr, 2004). Some of the best are unpublished dissertations: Falah al-Mdairis, "The Arab Nationalist Movement of Kuwait from its Origins to 1970" (PhD diss., University of Oxford, 1987); Ghanim Hamad al-Najjar, "Decision-Making Process in Kuwait: The Land Acquisition Policy as a Case Study" (PhD diss., University of Exeter, 1984). Recent examples include Abdel Razzaq Takriti, *Monsoon Revolution: Republicans, Sultans, and Empires in Oman 1965–1976* (Oxford University Press, 2013); Robert Vitalis, *America's Kingdom: Mythmaking on the Saudi Oil Frontier* (Stanford University Press, 2009); Omar AlShehabi, *Contested Modernity: Sectarianism, Nationalism, and Colonialism in Bahrain* (Oneworld Academic, 2019); Talal al-Rashoud, "Modern Education and Arab Nationalism in Kuwait, 1911–1961" (PhD diss., School of Oriental and African Studies, 2016); Rosie Bsheer, "A Counter-Revolutionary State: Popular

Movements and the Making of Saudi Arabia," *Past and Present* 238, no. 1 (February 2018): 233–77.

23. Adam Hanieh, "Rethinking Class and State in the Gulf Cooperation Council," in *A Critical Political Economy of the Middle East and North Africa*, ed. Joel Beinin, Bassam Haddad, and Sherene Seikaly (Stanford University Press, 2021), 105–22, 107; Ahmed Kanna, "Class Struggle and De-exceptionalizing the Gulf," in *Beyond Exception: New Interpretations of the Arabian Peninsula,* Ahmed Kanna, Amélie Le Renard, and Neha Vora (Cornell University Press, 2020), 100–22.

24. T. H. Marshall and Tom Bottomore, *Citizenship and Social Class and Other Essays* (Pluto Press, 1992).

25. For a complementary account of the role of popular agency in Gulf healthcare, see Goffman, *Disorder and Diagnosis.*

26. Andrea Wright, *Between Dreams and Ghosts: Indian Migration and Middle Eastern Oil* (Stanford University Press, 2021), Introduction; Andrew M. Gardner, "Why Do They Keep Coming? Labor Migrants in the Persian Gulf States," in *Migrant Labor in the Persian Gulf*, ed. Mehran Kamrava and Zahra Babar (Columbia University Press, 2012), 41–58, 58; Adam Hanieh, "Overcoming Methodological Nationalism: Spatial Perspectives on Migration to the Gulf Arab States," in *Transit States: Labour, Migration & Citizenship in the Gulf*, ed. Abdulhadi Khalaf, Omar AlShehabi, and Adam Hanieh (Pluto Press, 2015), 65.

27. GLMM, "Percentage of Nationals and Non-nationals in GCC Countries' Employed Populations (2020)," May 7, 2022, https://gulfmigration.grc.net/media/graphs/Graph%20Employment%202020%20by%20country%20-%202022-07-05.pdf.

28. GLMM, "Percentage of Non-nationals Employed by Sector of Activity (Public/private and Other Sectors) in GCC Countries (around 2010)," November 8, 2013, https://gulfmigration.grc.net/media/graphs/GLMM%20-%20Website%20-%20GCC%20Graph%208%20-%2008%20Nov%202013.pdf.

29. This is extensively discussed in Herb, *The Wages of Oil*; and Crystal A. Ennis, *Millennial Dreams in Oil Economies: Job Seeking and the Global Political Economy of Labour in Oman* (Cambridge University Press, 2024).

30. Hanieh, "Overcoming Methodological Nationalism"; Andrea Wright, "Imperial Labour: Labour, Security and the Depoliticization of Oil Production in the Arabian Peninsula," in *South Asian Migrations in Global History: Labor, Law, and Wayward Lives*, ed. Neilesh Bose (Bloomsbury, 2021), 63–84; Crystal Ennis and Nicolas Blarel, "Mapping and Theorizing Migration Governance: Insights from the South-to-West Asian Migration Corridor," in *The South Asia to Gulf Migration Governance Process*, ed. Crystal Ennis and Nicolas Blarel (Bristol University Press, 2022).

31. The only exceptions are article-length, for instance John Chalcraft, "Migration and Popular Protest in the Arabian Peninsula and the Gulf in the 1950s and 1960s," *International Labor and Working-Class History*, no. 79 (2011): 28–47; and Toby Matthiesen, "Migration, Minorities, and Radical Networks: Labour Movements and Opposition Groups in Saudi Arabia, 1950–1975," *International Review of Social History* 59, no. 3 (2014): 473–504. My argument is influenced by Zachary Lockman, *Comrades and*

Enemies: Arab and Jewish Workers in Palestine, 1906–1948 (University of California Press, 1996), 4.

32. Giovanni Arrighi and Fortunata Piselli, "Capitalist Development in Hostile Environments: Feuds, Class Struggles, and Migrations in a Peripheral Region of Southern Italy," *Review (Fernand Braudel Center)* 10, no. 4 (Spring 1987): 649–751; Jamie Peck, *Work-place: The Social Regulation of Labor Markets* (The Guilford Press, 1996); Tithi Bhattacharya, *Social Reproduction Theory: Remapping Class, Recentering Oppression* (Pluto Press, 2017); Doreen Massey, *Spatial Divisions of Labour: Social Structures and the Geography of Production* (Macmillan, 1995); Saskia Sassen, *The Mobility of Labor and Capital: A Study in International Investment and Labor Flow* (Cambridge University Press, 1988).

33. Sassen, *The Mobility of Labor and Capital*, 37; Nicholas P. De Genova, "Migrant 'Illegality' and Deportability in Everyday Life," *Annual Review of Anthropology* 31 (2002): 419–47, 439; Charanpal Singh Bal, "Dealing with Deportability: Deportation Laws and the Political Personhood of Temporary Migrant Workers in Singapore," *Asian Journal of Law and Society*, no. 2 (2015): 267–84.

34. Massey, *Spatial Divisions of Labour*, 54.

35. These narratives have been critiqued in the Gulf context by Natasha Iskander, *Does Skill Make Us Human? Migrant Workers in 21st-Century Qatar and Beyond* (Princeton University Press, 2021), and Wright, *Between Dreams and Ghosts*, Introduction.

36. "La Yujad ʾazmat fi al-ʿaydi al-ʿamila fi al-Kuwait bal Suwʾ Tawziʿ laha," *Ajiyal*, March 21, 1976, KU 10/Ha/200.

37. De Genova, "Migrant 'Illegality,'" 423; Mae Ngai, *Impossible Subjects: Illegal Aliens and the Making of Modern America* (Princeton University Press, 2004).

38. Notable accounts of migration and exclusion in the Gulf include Nelida Fuccaro, "Pearl Towns and Early Oil Cities: Migration and Integration in the Arab Coast of the Persian Gulf," in *The City in the Ottoman Empire: Migration and the Making of Urban Modernity*, ed. Ulrike Freitag (Routledge, 2011), 99–116; Shafeeq Ghabra, *Palestinians in Kuwait: The Family and the Politics of Survival* (Westview Press, 1987); Matthew S. Hopper, *Slaves of One Master: Globalization and Slavery in Arabia in the Age of Empire* (Yale University Press, 2015); Claire Beaugrand, *Stateless in the Gulf: Migration, Nationality and Society in Kuwait* (I. B. Tauris, 2017); Andrea Wright, "Migratory Pipelines: Labor and Oil in the Arabian Sea" (PhD diss., University of Michigan, 2015); Mohammad Taghi Razavian, "Iranian Communities in the Persian Gulf: A Geographical Analysis" (PhD diss., University of London, 1975); Lindsey R. Stephenson, "Rerouting the Persian Gulf: The Transnationalization of Iranian Migrant Networks, c. 1900–1940" (PhD diss., Princeton University, 2018).

39. Attiya Ahmad, "Beyond Labor: Foreign Residents in the Persian Gulf States," in *Migrant Labor in the Persian Gulf*, ed. Mehran Kamrava and Zahra Babar (Columbia University Press, 2012), 21–40.

40. Vora, *Impossible Citizens*, 9. See also Abdulhadi Khalaf, Omar AlShehabi, and Adam Hanieh, eds., *Transit States: Labour, Migration and Citizenship in the*

Gulf (Pluto Press, 2015); Andrew Gardner, *City of Strangers: Gulf Migration and the Indian Community in Bahrain* (Cornell University Press, 2010); Attiya Ahmad, *Everyday Conversions: Islam, Domestic Work, and South Asian Migrant Women in Kuwait* (Duke University Press, 2017); Pardis Mahdavi, *Crossing the Gulf: Love and Family in Migrant Lives* (Stanford University Press, 2016); Lori, *Offshore Citizens*; Longva, *Walls Built on Sand.*

41. Elizabeth F. Cohen, "The Political Economy of Immigrant Time: Rights, Citizenship, and Temporariness in the Post-1965 Era," *Polity* 47 (2015): 337–51; David Cook-Martín, "Temp Nations? A Research Agenda on Migration, Temporariness, and Membership," *American Behavioral Scientist* 63, no. 9 (2019): 1389–403.

42. Kanna, "Class Struggle and De-exceptionalizing the Gulf," 101, 111.

43. See Nicolas P. De Genova, "The Legal Production of Mexican/Migrant 'Illegality,'" *Latino Studies* 2 (2004): 160–85.

44. Marshall and Bottomore, *Citizenship and Social Class*; "Thick" and "thin" conceptions come from Charles Tilly, *Citizenship, Identity, and Social History* (Cambridge University Press, 1996), 8; Gershon Shafir, ed., *The Citizenship Debates: A Reader* (University of Minnesota Press, 1998), 1–28.

45. Frederick Cooper, *Citizenship, Inequality, and Difference* (Princeton University Press, 2018), 6, 90, 144.

46. Examples include Laurent Dubois, *A Colony of Citizens: Revolution and Slave Emancipation in the French Caribbean, 1787–1804* (University of North Carolina Press, 2004); Martha S. Jones, *Birthright Citizens: A History of Race and Rights in Antebellum America* (Cambridge University Press, 2018); James Holston, *Insurgent Citizenship: Disjunctions of Democracy and Modernity in Brazil* (Princeton University Press, 2008); Annette K. Joseph-Gabriel, *Reimagining Liberation: How Black Women Transformed Citizenship in the French Empire* (Illinois University Press, 2019); Frederick Cooper, *Citizenship between Empire and Nation: Remaking France and French Africa, 1945–1960* (Princeton University Press, 2014).

47. Linda Bosniak, *The Citizen and the Alien: Dilemmas of Contemporary Membership* (Princeton University Press, 2006), 2, 11. On the rights of denizenship, see Hiroshi Motomura, *Americans in Waiting: The Lost Story of Immigration and Citizenship in the United States* (Oxford University Press, 2006).

48. Will Hanley, *Identifying with Nationality: Europeans, Ottomans, and Egyptians in Alexandria* (Columbia University Press, 2017), 5.

49. Margaret Somers, *Genealogies of Citizenship: Markets, Statelessness, and the Right to Have Rights* (Cambridge University Press, 2008); Hannah Arendt, *The Origins of Totalitarianism* (Penguin, 2017, originally published 1951).

50. Yasemin Nuhoğlu Soysal, *Limits of Citizenship: Migrants and Postnational Membership in Europe* (University of Chicago Press, 1994).

51. Abdel Razzaq Takriti, "Colonial Coups and the War on Popular Sovereignty," *American Historical Review* 124, no. 3 (June 2019): 878–909.

52. John C. Torpey, "Coming and Going: On the State Monopolization of the Legitimate Means of Movement," *Sociological Theory* 16, no. 3 (November 1998): 239–59;

and *The Invention of the Passport: Surveillance, Citizenship and the State* (Cambridge University Press, 2000), 3.

53. Yael Berda, *Colonial Bureaucracy and Contemporary Citizenship: Legacies of Race and Emergency in the Former British Empire* (Cambridge University Press, 2023), 27, chapter 5; Nadim Bawalsa, *Transnational Palestine: Migration and the Right of Return Before 1948* (Stanford University Press, 2022), Introduction; Lana Tatour, "Citizenship as Domination: Settler Colonialism and the Making of Palestinian Citizenship in Israel," *Arab Studies Journal* 27, no. 2 (Fall 2019): 8–39.

54. Étienne Balibar, "What Is a Border?" in *Politics and the Other Scene* (Verso, 2002), 75–86, 81.

55. Karl Polanyi, *The Great Transformation: The Political and Economic Origins of Our Time* (Beacon Press, 2007, 1st ed. 1944), Chapter 6.

56. For comparative examples see Sunil Amrith, *Crossing the Bay of Bengal: The Furies of Nature and the Fortunes of Migrants* (Harvard University Press, 2013); Kalyani Ramnath, *Boats in a Storm: Law, Migration, and Decolonization in South and Southeast Asia, 1942–1962* (Stanford University Press, 2023); Ronald Aminzade, *Race, Nation, and Citizenship in Postcolonial Africa: The Case of Tanzania* (Cambridge University Press, 2013).

57. Stuart Hall, "When was 'the Postcolonial'? Thinking at the Limit," in *The Post-Colonial Question: Common Skies, Divided Horizons*, ed. Iain Chambers and Lidia Curti (Routledge, 1996): 242–60, 248.

58. Ian J. Seccombe, "'A Disgrace to American Enterprise': Italian Labour and the Arabian American Oil Company in Saudi Arabia, 1944–54," *Immigrants & Minorities: Historical Studies in Ethnicity, Migration and Diaspora* 5, no. 3 (1986): 233–57; Vitalis, *America's Kingdom*; Kaveh Ehsani, "The Social History of Labor in the Iranian Oil Industry" (PhD diss., Leiden University, 2014); Laleh Khalili, *Sinews of War and Trade: Shipping and Capitalism in the Arabian Peninsula* (Verso, 2021); Wright, *Unruly Labor*; Katayoun Shafiee, *Machineries of Oil: An Infrastructural History of BP in Iran* (MIT Press, 2018), chapter 4; Reem Alissa, "The Oil Town of Ahmadi since 1946: From Colonial Town to Nostalgic City," *Comparative Studies of South Asia, Africa and the Middle East* 33, no. 1 (2013).

59. For accounts of contracting in the oil industry see Touraj Atabaki, Elisabetta Bini, and Kaveh Ehsani, eds., *Working for Oil: Comparative Social Histories of Labor in the Global Oil Industry* (Palgrave Macmillan, 2018); Hannah Appel, *The Licit Life of Capitalism: US Oil in Equatorial Guinea* (Duke University Press, 2019); and Wright, *Unruly Labor*, Chapter 7.

60. Appel, *The Licit Life of Capitalism*, 2, 27; Myrna I. Santiago, *The Ecology of Oil: Environment, Labor, and the Mexican Revolution, 1900–1938* (Cambridge University Press, 2006).

61. Cedric J. Robinson, *Black Marxism: The Making of the Black Radical Tradition* (University of North Carolina Press, 2000), 26; Nancy Fraser, "Roepke Lecture in Economic Geography—From Exploitation to Expropriation: Historic Geographies of Racial Capitalism," *Economic Geography* 94, no. 1 (2018): 1–17; Jodi Melamed,

"Racial Capitalism." *Critical Ethnic Studies* 1, no. 1 (2015): 76–85; Yousuf Al-Bulushi, "Thinking Racial Capitalism and Black Radicalism from Africa: An Intellectual Geography of Cedric Robinson's World-system," *Geoforum* 132 (June 2022): 252.–62, 258.

62. Gargi Bhattacharyya, *Rethinking Racial Capitalism: Questions of Reproduction and Survival* (Rowman & Littlefield International, 2018), 5, 27.

63. Eve M. Troutt Powell, *Tell This in My Memory: Stories of Enslavement in Egypt, Sudan and the Late Ottoman Empire* (Stanford University Press, 2012), 17.

64. See Sumayya Kassamali, "Understanding Race and Migrant Domestic Labor in Lebanon," *Middle East Report Online*, July 13, 2021; Muriam Haleh Davis, *Markets of Civilization: Islam and Racial Capitalism in Algeria* (Duke University Press, 2022); Beeta Baghoolizadeh, *The Color Black: Enslavement and Erasure in Iran* (Duke University Press, 2024); Kyle J. Anderson, *The Egyptian Labor Corps: Race, Space, and Place in the First World War* (University of Texas Press, 2021).

65. See Mandana E. Limbert, "Caste, Ethnicity, and the Politics of Arabness in Southern Arabia," *Comparative Studies of South Asia, Africa, & the Middle East* 34, no. 3 (2014): 590–98; Goffman, *Disorder and Diagnosis*; Hopper, *Slaves of One Master*; Khalili, *Sinews of War and Trade.*

66. Hisham Aidi, "Exporting Race: Norms, Categories, & 'The All-American Skin Game,'" *Daedalus* 154, no. 2 (2025): 204–28.

67. This thus historicizes, and builds on, arguments made in Amélie Le Renard and Neha Vora, "Interrogating Race in Gulf Studies," in Hisham Aidi, Marc Lynch, and Zachariah Mampilly, eds., "Racial Formations in Africa and the Middle East: A Transregional Approach," *POMES Studies*, no. 44 (September 2021): 96–101; Neha Vora and Amélie Le Renard, "Who Is 'Indian' in the Gulf? Race, Labor and Citizenship," *Middle East Report Online*, June 16, 2021; Hessa Alnuaimi, "The Role of Colonial Knowledge in Building the Arab Gulf's Migration Regime," *Asian Journal of Middle Eastern and Islamic Studies* 16, no. 4 (2022): 382–401.

68. Bhattacharyya, *Rethinking Racial Capitalism*, ix.

69. James Ferguson, *Global Shadows: Africa in the Neoliberal World Order* (Duke University Press, 2006), 56.

70. Benedict Anderson, *Imagined Communities: Reflections on the Origin and Spread of Nationalism* (Verso, 1983), 149, and chapter 8.

71. Al-Nakib, *Kuwait Transformed*, and "Revisiting Hadar and Badu in Kuwait: Citizenship, Housing, and the Construction of a Dichotomy," *International Journal of Middle Eastern Studies* 46, no. 1 (2014): 5–30; Arbella Bet-Shlimon, *City of Black Gold: Oil, Ethnicity, and the Making of Modern Kirkuk* (Stanford University Press, 2019); MacLean, "Spatial Transformations and the Emergence of the 'National'"; Fuccaro, *Histories of City and State.* For more detail see Alex Boodrookas and Arang Keshavarzian, "The Forever Frontier of Urbanism: Historicizing Gulf Cities," *International Journal of Urban and Regional Research* 43, no. 1 (2019): 14–29.

72. Maya Mikdashi, *Sextarianism: Sovereignty, Secularism, and the State in Lebanon* (Stanford University Press, 2022), 47.

73. Ngai, *Impossible Subjects*; Maria L. Quintana, *Contracting Freedom: Race, Empire, and U.S. Guestworker Programs* (University of Pennsylvania Press, 2022); Julie Greene, "Rethinking the Boundaries of Class: Labor History and Theories of Class and Capitalism," *Labor* 18, no. 2 (2021): 92–112.

74. Radhika Mongia, *Indian Migration and Empire: A Colonial Genealogy* (Duke University Press, 2018), 113, 136.

75. This is influenced by W. E. B. Du Bois, *Black Reconstruction in America: An Essay toward a History of the Part Which Black Folk Played in the Attempt to Reconstruct Democracy in America, 1860–1880* (Oxford University Press, 2007), Chapter 2, "The White Worker"; and Joan Scott, *Gender and the Politics of History* (Columbia University Press, 1988). See also Hanan Hammad, *Industrial Sexuality: Gender, Urbanization, and Social Transformation in Egypt* (University of Texas Press, 2016); and Lockman, *Comrades and Enemies*.

76. Longva, *Walls Built on Sand*, 68–69, 107–109; Hélène Thiollet, "Immigration Rentier States," *Journal of Ethnic and Migration Studies* 50, no. 3 (2024): 657–79.

77. This builds on Herb, *The Wages of Oil*, 34.

78. Kaveh Ehsani, "Disappearing the Workers: How Labor in Oil Has Been Made Invisible," in *Working for Oil*, ed. Atabaki, Bini, and Ehsani, 11–34; Nelida Fuccaro and Mandana E. Limbert, "Scouting for Oil in the Middle East," in *Life Worlds of Middle Eastern Oil: Histories and Ethnographies of Black Gold*, ed. Nelida Fuccaro and Mandana E. Limbert (Edinburgh University Press, 2023), 3–27, 3.

79. Timothy Mitchell, *Carbon Democracy: Political Power in the Age of Oil* (Verso, 2011), 5, 9, 145.

80. Ehsani, "Disappearing the Workers," 16; Tyler Priest, "Crude History," *Reviews in American History* 43, no. 2 (2015): 333–39; Peyman Jafari, "Linkages of Oil and Politics: Oil Strikes and Dual Power in the Iranian Revolution," *Labor History* 60, no. 1 (2019): 24–43, 25; Zachary Davis Cuyler, "Tapline, Welfare Capitalism, and Mass Mobilization in Lebanon, 1950–1964," in *Working for Oil*, ed. Atabaki, Bini, and Ehsani, 337–68, 339; On Barak, "Outsourcing: Energy and Empire in the Age of Coal, 1820–1911," *International Journal of Middle East Studies* 47, no. 3 (2015): 425–45.

81. Arang Keshavarzian, *Making Space for the Gulf: Histories of Regionalism and the Middle East* (Stanford University Press, 2024), 6.

82. Christopher R. W. Dietrich, *Oil Revolution: Anticolonial Elites, Sovereign Rights, and the Economic Culture of Decolonization* (Cambridge University Press, 2017), 4.

83. J. H. Bamberg, *The History of The British Petroleum Company, Vol. 2: The Anglo-Iranian Years, 1928–1954* (Cambridge University Press, 1994), 143, 166.

84. Daniel Yergin, *The Prize: The Epic Quest for Oil, Money, and Power* (Touchstone, 1992); Bamberg, *The History of The British Petroleum Company, Vol. 2*, 474.

85. Examples include *Giuliano Garavini, The Rise and Fall of OPEC in the Twentieth Century* (Oxford University Press, 2019); Dietrich, *Oil Revolution*; Nathan J. Citino, *From Arab Nationalism to OPEC: Eisenhower, King Sa'ud, and the Making of U.S.-Saudi Relations* (Indiana University Press, 2002), 12, 57–60, and 100–101;

Brandon Wolfe-Hunnicutt, *The Paranoid Style in American Diplomacy: Oil and Arab Nationalism in Iraq* (Stanford University Press, 2021).

86. Christopher Dietrich has called for more localized histories of nationalization in "H-Diplo Roundtable Review of Oil Revolution," *Roundtable Review* XX, no. 10 (October 29, 2018).

87. I significantly expand on al-Mdairis, *al-Mujtamaʿ al-Madani wa-al-Haraka al-Wataniyya fi al-Kuwait*, 154–55, the only other study that touches on the role of oil workers and nationalization in Kuwait. See also Mattin Biglari, "Making Oil Men: Expertise, Discipline and Subjectivity in the Anglo-Iranian Oil Company's Training Schemes," in *Life Worlds of Middle Eastern Oil: Histories and Ethnographies of Black Gold*, ed. Nelida Fuccaro and Mandana E. Limbert (Edinburgh University Press, 2023), 221–50; Stefano Tijerina, "The Zero-Sum Game of Early Oil Extraction Relations in Colombia: Workers, Tropical Oil, and the Police State, 1918–1938," in *Working for Oil*, ed. Atabaki, Bini, and Ehsani, 37–68; Santiago, *The Ecology of Oil*; and Elisabetta Bini, "Oil Workers, Trade Unions and the Emergence of Oil Nationalism in Libya, 1956–1969," *EUI MWP* no. 27 (2012).

88. The few works that address midcentury Gulf labor movements include Vitalis, *America's Kingdom*; Khalili, *Sinews of War and Trade*; Chalcraft, "Migration and Popular Protest in the Arabian Peninsula and the Gulf in the 1950s and 1960s"; Matthiesen, "Migration, Minorities, and Radical Networks"; and Wright, *Unruly Labor.*

89. Takriti, *Monsoon Revolution.*

90. Frederick Cooper, "The Dialectics of Decolonization: Nationalism and Labor Movements in Postwar French Africa," in *Tensions of Empire: Colonial Cultures in a Bourgeois World*, ed. Frederick Cooper and Ann Laura Stoler (University of California Press, 1997), 406–35; Frederick Cooper, *Decolonization and African Society: The Labor Question in French and British Africa* (Cambridge University Press, 1996).

91. Keshavarzian, *Making Space for the Gulf*, 11.

92. LAB 13/2141, Letter J. C. Radcliffe to A. Ibbott, December 3, 1968.

93. Omnia el Shakry, "'History without Documents': The Vexed Archives of Decolonization in the Middle East," *American Historical Review* 120, no. 3 (2015): 920–34.

94. Muhammad Masʿud al-ʿAjmi, *al-Haraka al-ʿUmmaliyya wa al-Naqabiyya fi al-Kuwait: al-Nashʾa wa Bidayat al-Takwayn* (The Labor and Trade Union Movement in Kuwait: Its Establishment and Early Formation) (Kuwait: Sharikat al-Rabiʿan li-l-Nashr, 1982), 6.

95. Hussein Saqr, *Rihla Dakhil al-Dhakira maʿ al-Haraka al-ʿUmaliyya al-Kuwaitiyya* (A Trip Down Memory Lane with the Kuwaiti Workers' Movement) (Kuwait: The Kuwait Trade Union Federation Press, n.d.), 17.

96. The few extant works on the Kuwaiti labor movement, while invaluable, are short in length and therefore lacking in detail. See al-ʿAjmi, *al-Haraka al-ʿUmmaliyya wa al-Naqabiyya fi al-Kuwait*; Falah Abdullah al-Mdairis, "al-Dawr al-Siyāsī li-l-Ḥaraka al-Niqābiyya al-ʿummāliyya fī al-Kuwait" (The Political Role of the Trade Union Movement in Kuwait, 1964–1994), *Shuʾūn al-Ijtimāʿiyya* no. 44

(Winter 1994); al-Mdairis, *al-Mujtama' al-Madani wa-al-Haraka al-Wataniyya fi al-Kuwait.*

97. Sara Pursley, *Familiar Futures: Time, Selfhood, and Sovereignty in Iraq* (Stanford University Press, 2019), 28.

98. Some of the only exceptions are al-Mdairis, "The Arab Nationalist Movement"; Fuccaro, *Histories of City and State*; al-Rashoud, "Modern Education and Arab Nationalism in Kuwait"; Wafa Alsayed, "Beyond Instrumentalism: Arab Nationalism and the Foreign Policy of Kuwait in the 1960s and 1970s," *The Middle East Journal* 76, no. 2 (Summer 2022): 199–221; and Goffman, *Disorder and Diagnosis.*

99. Fahad Ahmad Bishara, "Narrative and the Historian's Craft in the Arab Historiography of the Persian Gulf," in *The Persian Gulf in Modern Times: People, Ports, and History*, ed. Lawrence G. Potter (Palgrave Macmillan, 2014), 47–72.

Chapter 1

1. For an excellent history see AlShehabi, *Contested Modernity*, Chapter 4.

2. Abd al-Rahman al-Bakir, *Min al-Bahrain ila al-Manfa Saint Helena* (From Bahrain to Exile in St. Helena) (Beirut: Dar Maktabat al-Haya, 1965), 288.

3. "Annual Report for Year 1956," in *The Bahrain Government Annual Reports, Vol. V: 1952–1956* (Cambridge Archive Editions, 1986), 347.

4. Miriam Joyce, "The Bahraini Three on St. Helena, 1956–1961," *Middle East Journal* 54, no. 4 (Autumn, 2000): 613–23.

5. Joyce, "The Bahraini Three on St. Helena."

6. Al-Bakir, *Min al-Bahrain ila al-Manfa Saint Helena*, 282.

7. One of the only histories of deportation in the Arabic-speaking world is Rim Naguib, "The Ideological Deportation of Foreigners and 'Local Subjects of Foreign Extraction' in Interwar Egypt," *Arab Studies Journal* 28, no. 2 (Fall 2020).

8. For more on the role of borders and passports in global processes of state formation, see Jane Caplan and John Torpey, eds., *Documenting Individual Identity: The Development of State Practices in the Modern World* (Princeton University Press, 2001); Radhika Mongia, "Race, Nationality, Mobility: A History of the Passport," *Public Culture* 11, no. 3 (Fall 1999): 527–56; Bridget Anderson, Matthew J. Gibney, and Emanuela Paoletti, eds., *The Social, Political and Historical Contours of Deportation* (Springer, 2013), Introduction.

9. For more accounts of this process see Keshavarzian, *Making Space for the Gulf*, Chapter 3; MacLean, "Spatial Transformations and the Emergence of the 'National'"; and Stephenson, "Rerouting the Persian Gulf."

10. Frederick F. Anscombe, "An Anational Society: Eastern Arabia in the Ottoman Period," in *Transnational Connections in the Arab Gulf*, ed. Madawi al-Rasheed (Routledge, 2005), 21–38.

11. Fuccaro, *Histories of City and State*, 221, and Chapters 3 and 6. See also al-Mdairis, "The Arab Nationalist Movement of Kuwait from its Origins to 1970"; Abdullah F. al-Nafisi, *al-Kuwait: al-Ra'i al-Akhar* (Kuwait: Another Opinion) (Dar Taha,

1978); Crystal, *Oil and Politics in the Gulf*; Fuccaro, "Pearl Towns and Early Oil Cities"; Al-Nakib, *Kuwait Transformed*; Beaugrand, *Stateless in the Gulf*; Lori, *Offshore Citizens*; Stephenson, "Rerouting the Persian Gulf"; AlShehabi, *Contested Modernity*; Wright, *Unruly Labor*; Goffman, *Disorder and Diagnosis*.

12. The continued significance of deportation is discussed in Longva, *Walls Built on Sand*, 97–100.

13. Human Rights Watch, "Building Towers, Cheating Workers: Exploitation of Migrant Construction Workers in the United Arab Emirates," November 11, 2006.

14. Hahamovitch, "Creating Perfect Immigrants."

15. İlkay Yılmaz, *Ottoman Passports: Security and Geographic Mobility, 1876–1908* (Syracuse University Press, 2023), 7–8, 147, and chapter 5.

16. Ian J. Seccombe, "Labour Migration to the Arabian Gulf: Evolution and Characteristics 1920–1950," *British Society for Middle Eastern Studies Bulletin* 10, no. 1 (1983): 3–20; Omar Hesham AlShehabi, "Policing Labour in Empire: the Modern Origins of the Kafala Sponsorship System in the Gulf Arab States," *British Journal of Middle Eastern Studies* (2019): 1–20; Neha Vora and Natalie Koch, "Everyday Inclusions: Rethinking Ethnocracy, *Kafala*, and Belonging in the Arabian Peninsula," *Studies in Ethnicity and Nationalism* 15, no. 3 (December 2015): 540–52; Wright, *Between Dreams and Ghosts*, 137–42.

17. Kanna, "Class Struggle and De-exceptionalizing the Gulf."

18. Michel Foucault, "Nietzche, Geneology, History," in *Language, Counter-Memory, Practice: Selected Essays and Interviews*, ed. D. F. Bouchard (Cornell University Press, 1977).

19. Berda, *Colonial Bureaucracy and Contemporary Citizenship*; Bawalsa, *Transnational Palestine*; Shira N. Robinson, *Citizen Strangers: Palestinians and the Birth of Israel's Liberal Settler State* (Stanford University Press, 2013); Lauren Banko, *The Invention of Palestinian Citizenship, 1918–1947* (Edinburgh University Press, 2016); Tatour, "Citizenship as Domination."

20. Hopper, *Slaves of One Master*.

21. James Onley, *The Arabian Frontier of the British Raj: Rulers, Merchants, and the British in the Nineteenth-Century Gulf* (Oxford University Press, 2007); Keshavarzian, *Making Space for the Gulf*, Chapter 1.

22. Fuccaro, *Histories of City and State*, Chapter 1; Takriti, *Monsoon Revolution*, Chapter 1; Keshavarzian, *Making Space for the Gulf*, Chapter 2.

23. Lorimer, *Gazetteer* Volume I, 946; IOR/R/15/5/314, "Agreement of 23rd January 1899 with Ruler of Kuwait, signed M. J. Meade, Resident Gulf, and Mubarak al Subah, and ratified by Viceroy and Governor-General of India," February 16, 1899.

24. Lâle Can, *Spiritual Subjects: Central Asian Pilgrims and the Ottoman Hajj at the End of Empire* (Stanford University Press, 2020), 112. See also Camille Cole, "Empire on Edge: Land, Law, and Capital in Gilded Age Basra" (PhD diss., Yale University, 2020), 300; Fahad Ahmad Bishara, *A Sea of Debt: Law and Economic Life in the Western Indian Ocean, 1780–1950* (Cambridge University Press, 2017), Chapter 8; IOR/L/PS/12/3795, Letter C. Belgrave to Agent Bahrain, July 17, 1939; IOR/V/27/820/18,

K. P. S. Menon, "Report on the effect on Indian interests of certain decrees passed by the Government of Zanzibar. 1935."

25. IOR/L/PS/12/3795, India Office Memorandum B.422/P.1632/30, "Exercise of Jurisdiction in Cases affecting Foreign Subjects in Bahrein by the British Political Authorities," signed J. G. Laithwaite, March 3, 1930; CLC/B/123/MS27733A; INA, F, E-A, 55–58. Note H. S. Barnes, July 1, 1901; INA, F, Secret E, 156–58, Letter A. Godley to the Under Secretary of State, India Office, August 1, 1901.

26. David Graeber, *Debt: The First 5,000 Years* (Melville House Publishing, 2011), 198–99.

27. For more see Fuccaro, "Port Towns and Early Oil Cities."

28. NAI 464-N, Letter H. V. Biscoe to the Secretary of State for the Colonies, Colonial Office, March 24, 1930.

29. See examples in IOR/R/15/1/299, and IOR/R/15/2/150, Letter Gordon Loch Agent Bahrain to Resident Gulf, June 20, 1934.

30. IOR/R/15/2/486, Letter Agent Bahrain to Charles Belgrave, May 16, 1934.

31. Cole, "Empire on Edge," Chapters 4 and 5.

32. J. M. Beattie, *Policing and Punishment in London, 1660–1750* (Oxford University Press, 2001), 290; Matthew P. Fitzpatrick, *Purging the Empire. Mass Expulsions in Germany, 1871–1914* (Oxford University Press 2015); Julia Rose Kraut, *Threat of Dissent: A History of Ideological Exclusion and Deportation in the United States* (Harvard University Press, 2020).

33. NAI, F, General-B, July 1910. Letter J. B. Wood, Deputy Secretary to the Government of India in the Foreign Department to P. Z. Cox, Resident Gulf, March 9, 1910.

34. Many deportations are recorded in annual Administration Reports.

35. An especially prominent example can be found in "Persian Gulf Administration Report (1904–5)," in *Persian Gulf Administration Reports, Vol. V* (Cambridge Archive Editions, 1989), 544–45.

36. "Administration Report of the Muscat Political Agency (1913)," in *Persian Gulf Administration Reports, Vol. VII* (Cambridge Archive Editions, 1989), 234.

37. "Administration Report of the Kuwait Political Agency (1913)," in *Persian Gulf Administration Reports, Vol. VII* (Cambridge Archive Editions, 1989), 256; Lorimer, *Gazetteer*, Volume II, Part B, 1075.

38. Leslie Peirce, *Morality Tales: Law and Gender in the Ottoman Court of Aintab* (University of California Press, 2003), 263; "Administration Report of the Bahrain Political Agency (1911)," in *Persian Gulf Administration Reports, Vol. VI* (Cambridge Archive Editions, 1989), 688.

39. "Administration Report of the Bahrain Political Agency (1911)," in *Persian Gulf Administration Reports, Vol. VI* (Cambridge Archive Editions, 1989), 688.

40. IOR/R/15/5/314, "Office Note of 6th September, 1938."

41. Abdul-Azeez Mohammad Al-Shaya, *Echoes of Memory* (Kuwait: The National Council for Culture, Arts & Letters, 2015), 39.

42. Al-Shaya, *Echoes of Memory*, 39.

43. IOR/L/PS/12/3795, Letter P. Z. Cox to Secretary to the Government of India in the Foreign Department, February 25, 1906. For more see AlShehabi, *Contested Modernity*, 141–46; Fuccaro, *Histories of City and State*.

44. IOR/L/PS/12/3795, Letter Major P. Z. Cox to Secretary to the Government of India in the Foreign Department, February 25, 1906; IOR/L/PS/12/3795, Morley of Blackburn, Secret Letter No. 11, India Office, May 21, 1909.

45. AlShehabi, *Contested Modernity*, 143–46. See also Fuccaro, *Histories of City and State*, 81.

46. NAI, F, Secret E, No. 464–66, February 1908, Letter H. Minto et al. to John Morley, November 14, 1907; IOR/L/PS/12/3795, "Exercise of Jurisdiction in Cases affecting Foreign Subjects in Bahrein by the British Political Authorities," signed J. G. L., March 3, 1930.

47. IOR/L/PS/12/3329, "The Bahrain Order in Council, 1913," August 12, 1913.

48. IOR/R/15/2/104, Letter Resident Gulf to Agent Bahrain, June 5, 1922; NAI, FP/E, 1922, No. 358, Letter Resident Gulf to E. B. Howell, Deputy Secretary to the Government of India in the Foreign and Political Department, June 21, 1922.

49. IOR/L/PS/12/3329, "The Bahrain Order in Council, 1913," August 12, 1913.

50. John Torpey, "The Great War and the Birth of the Modern Passport System," in *Documenting Individual Identity: The Development of State Practices in the Modern World*, ed. Jane Caplan and John Torpey (Princeton University Press, 2001): 256–70; Naguib, "The Ideological Deportation of Foreigners"; Jordi Tejel and Ramazan Hakkı Öztan, eds., *Regimes of Mobility: Borders and State Formation in the Middle East, 1918–1946* (Edinburgh University Press, 2022); Yael Berda, "Managing Dangerous Populations: Colonial Legacies of Security and Surveillance," *Sociological Forum* 28, no. 3 (Sept. 2013): 627–30.

51. Goffman, *Disorder and Diagnosis*, 22. See also Michael Christopher Low, *Imperial Mecca: Ottoman Arabia and the Indian Ocean Hajj* (Columbia University Press, 2020), Chapter 3.

52. Low, *Imperial Mecca*, Chapter 3.

53. NAI, FP, Secret-War, September 1915, Nos. 93–106, Letter General Officer Commanding Bombay Brigade to Chief of the General Staff Army Headquarters, June 22, 1915.

54. IOR/R/15/2/84, Letter Agent Bahrain to Resident Gulf, December 10, 1931.

55. IOR/R/15/2/84, Memorandum Agent Bahrain to Resident Gulf, April 19, 1922; IOR/R/15/2/84, Letter F. B. Prideaux Resident Gulf to P. L. Loraine Minister to the Court of Persia, May 20, 1926. For examples see IOR/R/15/5/202.

56. For examples see IOR/R/15/5/202.

57. These are documented in wartime Administration Reports. Quote is from "Administration Report of the Bahrain Political Agency (1914)," in *Persian Gulf Administration Reports, Vol. VII* (Cambridge Archive Editions, 1989), 325.

58. "Administration Report of the Kerman Political Agency (1916)," in *Persian Gulf Administration Reports, Vol. VII* (Cambridge Archive Editions, 1989), 440.

59. Berda, *Colonial Bureaucracy and Contemporary Citizenship*, chapter 5.

60. "Administration Report of the Political Residency (1920)" and "Administration Report of the Bandar Abbas and Lingah Political Agency (1920)," in *Persian Gulf Administration Reports, Vol. VII* (Cambridge Archive Editions, 1989), 731, 740; "Administration Report of the Bandar Abbas and Lingah Political Agency (1924)," in *Persian Gulf Administration Reports, Vol. VIII* (Cambridge Archive Editions, 1989), 99.

61. IOR/R/15/2/106, Memorandum Agent Bahrain to Resident Bushire, January 22, 1922.

62. IOR/R/15/2/108, Memorandum Agent Bahrain to Resident Gulf, January 26, 1925; "Administration Report of the Bahrain Political Agency (1923)," in *Persian Gulf Administration Reports, Vol. VIII* (Cambridge Archive Editions, 1989), 216; IOR/R/15/1/346, Letter F. B. Prideaux to Foreign Secretary to the Government of India in the Foreign and Political Department, Delhi, December 4, 1926.

63. AlShehabi, *Contested Modernity*, 176–210.

64. These cases are comprehensively covered in IOR/R/15/2/104; IOR/R/15/2/106; IOR/R/15/2/107; NAI, FP, E, 1923, No. 798; NAI, FP, E, 1922, No. 358, and NAI, FP, 1923, No. 976-X.

65. IOR/R/15/2/107, Memorandum Political Agent Bahrain to Political Resident Persian Gulf, March 23, 1924.

66. See IOR/R/15/2/101, including Letter Political Resident Bushire to Foreign Department of the Government of India, April 27, 1923; and NAI 464-N, Letter C. G. Prior to H. V. Biscoe, January 26, 1930.

67. Stephenson, "Rerouting the Persian Gulf."

68. Stephenson, "Rerouting the Persian Gulf," 22; Lindsey R. Stephenson, "Between Modern and National Education: The 'Ajam Schools of Bahrain and Kuwait," *Arabian Humanities* (2020); Shahnaz R. Nadjmabadi, "Cross-Border Networks: Labour Migration from Iran to the Arab Countries of the Persian Gulf," *Anthropology of the Middle East* 5, no. 1 (Spring 2010): 18–33; Chelsi Mueller, *The Origins of the Arab-Iranian Conflict: Nationalism and Sovereignty in the Gulf between the World* Wars (Cambridge University Press, 2020).

69. IOR/R/15/2/1460, Translation of Circular Memorandum, Persian Minister for Foreign Affairs to British Legation, July 10, 1929; IOR/R/15/2/486, Letter E. Watkinson to Reginald H. Hoare, February 6, 1934; Stephenson, "Rerouting the Persian Gulf."

70. IOR/R/15/2/150, Letter S. G. Loch to Laithwaite September 30, 1933; CLC/B/207/MS39073, "Extract from Bahrain Exchange Circular Dated 7th July, 1937."

71. IOR/R/15/2/150, Letter C. Belgrave to Agent Bahrain, May 17, 1933. Attached is a copy of Alan No. 1101/17/1347, dated February 27, 1929.

72. Bawalsa, *Transnational Palestine*, 7; Banko, *The Invention of Palestinian Citizenship*, 8, 51; Lauren Banko, "Claiming Identities in Palestine: Migration and Nationality under the Mandate," *Journal of Palestine Studies* 46 (2017): 26–43; and Lauren Banko, "Keeping Out the 'Undesirable Elements': The Treatment of Communists, Transients, Criminals, and the Ill in Mandate Palestine," *The Journal of Imperial and Commonwealth History* 47, no. 6 (2019): 1153–80; Berda, "Managing Dangerous Populations."

73. Zainab Saleh, "On Iraqi Nationality: Law, Citizenship, and Exclusion," *The Arab Studies Journal* 21, no. 1 (2013): 48–78.

74. These are repeatedly cited in IOR/R/15/2/486, including Letter C. D. Belgrave to Agent Bahrain, March 14, 1934.

75. Administrative Condensed Report, 1926–1937," in *The Bahrain Government Annual Reports, Vol. II: 1937–1942* (Cambridge Archive Editions, 1986), 58.

76. "1930–31 Annual Report for the Year 1349," in *The Bahrain Government Annual Reports, Vol. I: 1924–1956* (Cambridge Archive Editions, 1986), 238–39.

77. "1942–43 Annual Report for Year 1361," in *The Bahrain Government Annual Reports, Vol. III: 1942–1947* (Cambridge Archive Editions, 1986), 47.

78. "1952–53 Annual Report for Year 1372," in *The Bahrain Government Annual Reports, Vol. V: 1952–1956* (Cambridge Archive Editions, 1986), 51; 1956 Annual Report for Year 1956," in *The Bahrain Government Annual Reports, Vol. V: 1952–1956* (Cambridge Archive Editions, 1986), 411.

79. The relevant correspondence can be found in IOR/R/15/1/618, including Letter H. E. Nichols, Managing Director Anglo Persian Oil Company Ltd., to the Under Secretary of State Colonial Office, May 31, 1922.

80. IOR/R/15/1/638, especially Letter Resident Gulf to Secretary of State for the Colonies, November 9, 1930, and letter H. R. P. Dickson to Resident Gulf, September 22, 1930; and IOR/R/15/1/639, Letter A. L. Greenway to T. C. W. Fowle, July 2, 1931.

81. A summary of this strategy can be found in Seccombe and Lawless, "Foreign Worker Dependence in the Gulf," 550–57; and Gennaro Errichiello, "Foreign Workforce in the Arab Gulf States (1930–1950): Migration Patterns and Nationality Clause," *International Migration Review* 46, no. 2 (Summer 2012): 389–413.

82. Retaliatory measures are discussed throughout IOR/R/15/2/486, and the law is proposed in IOR/R/15/2/150, Letter G. W. Rendel to Under Secretary of State, India Office, November 16, 1934.

83. IOR/R/15/2/150, Letter M. Clauson to T. C. Fowle, October 11, 1935.

84. "1946–7 Annual Report for Year 1366," in *The Bahrain Government Annual Reports, Vol. III: 1942–1947* (Cambridge Archive Editions, 1986), 444; "1947–8 Annual Report for Year 1367," in *The Bahrain Government Annual Reports, Vol. IV: 1947–1952* (Cambridge Archive Editions, 1986), 48.

85. See IOR/R/15/2/150.

86. M. Page Baldwin, "Subject to Empire: Married Women and the British Nationality and Status of Aliens Act," *Journal of British Studies* 40, no. 4 (2001): 522–56; 537; Candice Lewis Bredbenner, *A Nationality of Her Own: Women, Marriage, and the Law of Citizenship* (University of California Press, 1998).

87. For more on gender and nationality law see Suad Joseph, ed., *Gender and Citizenship in the Middle East* (Syracuse University Press, 2000), and Maya Mikdashi, "Sex and Sectarianism: The Legal Architecture of Lebanese Citizenship," *Comparative Studies of South Asia, Africa, & the Middle East* 34, no. 2 (2014): 279–93.

88. For more on land and nationality see Fuccaro, *Histories of City and State*, Chapter 4, 133-36, and Stephenson, "Rerouting the Persian Gulf," Chapter 3. Outside

the Gulf, see Katherine Verdery, "Transnationalism, Nationalism, Citizenship, and Property: Eastern Europe Since 1989," *American Ethnologist* 25, no. 2 (May 1998): 291–306; and Cooper, *Citizenship, Inequality, and Difference*, 64–65.

89. Examples abound in IOR/R/15/2/486 and IOR/R/15/2/1460.

90. Fuccaro, *Histories of City and State*, 207.

91. IOR/R/15/2/150, Letter J. G. to P. G. Loch, July 15, 1933; IOR/R/15/2/1405, Letter Charles Belgrave to Agent Bahrain, July 30, 1929.

92. IOR/R/15/2/486, Letter T. C. Fowle to H. A. F. Metcalfe, November 17, 1934.

93. Stephenson, "Rerouting the Persian Gulf," 137–39; IOR/R/15/2/150, Express Letter T. C. Fowle to Government of India, March 2, 1935; Express Letter Agent Bahrain to Resident Bushire, November 24, 1935; IOR/R/15/2/151, Note signed Political Agent entitled "Law Regarding Ownership of Landed Property by Foreign Subjects."

94. IOR/L/PS/12/3795, Letter Resident Gulf to Aubrey Metcalfe, February 15, 1938.

95. IOR/R/15/2/150, Express Letter T. C. Fowle to Government of India, March 2, 1935; IOR/L/PS/12/3795, "Extract from the Annual Report on Iran for the year 1938."

96. CLC/B/207/MS39073, Letter Grant Manager Bahrain to G. M. Eastern Bank London, May 14, 1949; "1948–9 Annual Report for Year 1368," in *The Bahrain Government Annual Reports, Vol. IV: 1947–1952* (Cambridge Archive Editions, 1986), 102; "1952–53 Annual Report for Year 1372," in *The Bahrain Government Annual Reports, Vol. V: 1952–1956* (Cambridge Archive Editions, 1986), 48.

97. This is evident in Bahrain Government Annual Reports from 1937–52.

98. "1952–53 Annual Report for Year 1372," in *The Bahrain Government Annual Reports, Vol. V: 1952–1956* (Cambridge Archive Editions, 1986), 51.

99. NAI, EA, NE, 1937, Nos. 565, Judgment in Criminal Case No. 224 of 1937, September 24, 1937.

100. NAI, EA, G, 1937, Nos. 1–45, Order by the District Court, Bahrain, February 19, 1937.

101. FO 371/114730, Letter I. T. M. Lucas to J. C. Thomas, November 29, 1955.

102. IOR/L/PS/12/3327, Criminal Case No. 153 of 1939.

103. IOR/R/15/2/1394, Letter Charles Belgrave to Agent Bahrain, June 25, 1927.

104. "1932–33 Annual Report for the Year 1351," in *The Bahrain Government Annual Reports, Vol. I: 1924–1956* (Cambridge Archive Editions, 1986), 418.

105. "1930–31 Annual Report for the Year 1349," in *The Bahrain Government Annual Reports, Vol. I: 1924–1956* (Cambridge Archive Editions, 1986), 237–38; "Annual Report for the Year 1352 (1933–34)," in *The Bahrain Government Annual Reports, Vol. I: 1924–1956* (Cambridge Archive Editions, 1986), 489.

106. "Administration Report of the Bahrain Political Agency (1929)," in *Persian Gulf Administration Reports, Vol. VIII* (Cambridge Archive Editions, 1989), 601; "Administration Report of the Kuwait Political Agency (1929)," in *Persian Gulf Administration Reports, Vol. VIII* (Cambridge Archive Editions, 1989), 605.

107. IOR/R/15/2/1405, Letter Director of Customs to Agent Bahrain, September 30, 1929.

108. "1943 Annual Report for Year 1362," in *The Bahrain Government Annual Reports, Vol. III: 1942–1947* (Cambridge Archive Editions, 1986), 111.

109. NAI, FP, NE, 1931, No. 73, Letter Agent Bahrain to Resident Gulf, June 28, 1931.

110. "Administrative Condensed Report, 1926–1937," in *The Bahrain Government Annual Reports, Vol. II: 1937–1942* (Cambridge Archive Editions, 1986), 58.

111. "1943–4 Annual Report for Year 1363," in *The Bahrain Government Annual Reports, Vol. III: 1942–1947* (Cambridge Archive Editions, 1986), 177; IOR/R/15/2/490, Letter C. J. Pelly to Charles Belgrave, April 4, 1948; FO 371/140234, Letter Agency Bahrain to Residency Bahrain, August 1, 1959.

112. FO 371/140234, Letter Agency Bahrain to Residency Bahrain, August 1, 1959.

113. "1938–39 Annual Report for Year 1357," in *The Bahrain Government Annual Reports, Vol. II: 1937–1942* (Cambridge Archive Editions, 1986), 194; IOR/R/15/2/1297, Memorandum Agent Bahrain to Adviser Bahrain, June 17, 1942; IOR/R/15/2/1394, Letter Charles Belgrave to Agent Bahrain, June 25, 1927.

114. IOR/R/15/2/1216, Letter Agent Bahrain to Residency Gulf, August 31, 1927; Charles Dalrymple Belgrave, *Personal Column* (London: Hutchinson & Co. Ltd., 1960), 103; IOR/R/15/2/594.

115. NAI, FP, NE, 1935, No. 187. Note, May 11, 1935; Agent Kuwait to Resident Gulf, November 29, 1933.

116. IOR/R/15/1/334, Memorandum, Political Agent Bahrain to Resident Gulf, April 22, 1923; IOR/R/15/2/101, Letter Agent Bahrain to Resident Gulf, April 22, 1923; Peirce, *Morality Tales*, 73.

117. Yılmaz, *Ottoman Passports*, 146–50, 168–69.

118. "Administrative Condensed Report, 1926–1937," in *The Bahrain Government Annual Reports, Vol. II: 1937–1942* (Cambridge Archive Editions, 1986), 58.

119. IOR/R/15/2/1405, Notice, Government of Bahrain, December 25, 1928, and Passport Regulations, January 9, 1929.

120. Alshehabi, "Policing Labour in Empire."

121. IOR/L/PS/12/3866, Letter Petroleum Concessions Limited to M. J. Clauson, December 3, 1936.

122. Alshehabi, "Policing labour," 8; Berda, *Colonial Bureaucracy and Contemporary Citizenship*, 108.

123. FO 371/104353, Aide Memoire, British Embassy, Washington, D.C., June 5, 1953.

124. FO 371/140234, Letter A. R. Walmsley to E. F. Given, June 29, 1959.

125. IOR/R/15/2/1717, Letter G. W. R. Smith, Chief Local Representative Bapco to Agent Bahrain, May 21, 1936.

126. Seccombe and Lawless, "Foreign Worker Dependence in the Gulf," 560; Errichiello, "Foreign Workforce in the Arab Gulf States," 399.

127. IOR/R/15/2/1723, Letter C. D. Belgrave to Agent Bahrain, November 23, 1949.

128. There are many examples in IOR/R/15/2/1589, including letter Agent Bahrain to John Birch & Co., Bahrain, June 23, 1949, and Letter Gray, Mackenzie & Co. Ltd. to Agent Bahrain, November 29, 1949.

129. IOR/R/15/2/1723, Letter Charles Belgrave to Agent Bahrain, November 23, 1949.

130. IOR/R/15/2/1723, Letter Agency Bahrain to M. B. Jacob, November 27, 1950.

131. IOR/R/15/2/1396, Letter to Agent Bahrain, May 5, 1946; IOR/R/15/2/1589, Letter S. M. Afimiwalla to Agent Bahrain, June 10, 1949, and Letter, The Hashmi Engineering Works to Agent Bahrain, April 15, 1950.

132. IOR/R/15/2/1589, Letter O. J. Fonseca to Agent Bahrain, September 13, 1950.

133. See for instance IOR/R/15/2/1589, Letter British Overseas Airways Corporation to Agent Bahrain, May 18, 1950.

134. NAI, FP, Mid-Asia, 1932, No. 349, Press communiqué, T. G. B. Wauch, March 28, 1922; Telegram 515, Resident Gulf to the Foreign Secretary to the Government of India in the Foreign and Political Department, March 17 1922; and Letter A. P. Trevor to the Foreign Secretary to the Government of India in the Foreign and Political Department, Delhi, March 28, 1922. For an account of this strike see Touraj Atabaki, "Far from Home, But at Home: Indian Migrant Workers in the Iranian Oil Industry," *Studies in History* 31, no. 1 (2015): 85–114.

135. ARC 59010, Telegram 82, Abadan to Tehran, May 12, 1929; Stephanie Cronin, "Popular Politics, the New State and the Birth of the Iranian Working Class: The 1929 Abadan Oil Refinery Strike," *Middle Eastern Studies* 46, no. 5 (2010): 699–732.

136. NAI, EA, Near East, 1943, Nos. 8(5), Letter California Arabian Standard Oil Co. Bahrain Island Persian Gulf to Agent CASOC, Bombay, March 2, 1943, and Letter CASOC Ltd. Bahrain to CASOC San Francisco, March 9, 1943; IOR/L/PS/12/1386, Memorandum by Ghayur Khairat Hussain, Pakistani Employees Aramco to J. Mac Pherson, Dhahran, February 27, 1949.

137. FO 371/82130, Copy of letter from Fields Manager, Qatar, January 24, 1950.

138. IOR/R/15/1/674, Letter no. 6412/36 to Longrigg, Petroleum Concessions Ltd., September 24, 1936.

139. Fuccaro, *Histories of City and State*, 176–86.

140. Suliman Al-Atiqi, "The Origins of Kuwaiti Nationalism: Rashid Rida's Influence on Kuwaiti National Identity," *The Arab Studies Journal* 23, no. 1 (2015): 78–122.

141. Bishara, "Narrative and the Historian's Craft," 54.

142. Al-Atiqi, "The Origins of Kuwaiti Nationalism," 94.

143. Al-Nakib, *Kuwait Transformed*, 43, 77, and chapter 3.

144.Abd al-ʿAziz al-Rushaid, *Tarikh al-Kuwait* (History of Kuwait) (Beirut: Dar Maktabat al-Haya, 1978; 1st ed. 1924), 95–96.

145. *Majallat al-Kuwait* (Reprinted Kuwait: Qurtas Publishing, 1999), 26, 87, 226.

146. *Tarikh al-Kuwait*, 95–96.

147. "al-Kuwait fi Shahr," *al-Raʾid* Issue 10, Year 1, March 1953 (Republished by the Center for the Research and Study of Kuwait [Hereafter CRSK], Kuwait, 1999), 1033.

148. *Tarikh al-Kuwait*, 250.

149. *Tarikh al-Kuwait*, 254–62.

150. For instance Yusuf bin ʿIsa al-Qinaʿi, *Safhat min Tarikh al-Kuwait* (Pages from the History of Kuwait) (Kuwait: Dhat al-Salasil, 1988; original 1946).

151. Abdulrahman Alebrahim, "The Balancing Powers in Kuwait and the 1938 Majlis Movement," *AlMuntaqa* 4, no. 2 (December 2021/January 2022): 8–26, 11.

152. Al-Rushaid, *Tarikh al-Kuwait*, 19.

153. Al-Rushaid, *Tarikh al-Kuwait*, 34.

154. Al-Rushaid, *Tarikh al-Kuwait*, 61.

155. "Abd Allah Al Faraj," *Majallat al-Kuwait*, no. 1 (February/March 1928); and "al-Shaykh Muhammad bin Faris," *Majallat al-Kuwait*, nos. 2–3 (March/April 1928) (Reprinted Kuwait: Dar Qurtas li-l-Nashr, 1999), 24, 83.

156. "Sections of the Magazine," *Majallat al-Kuwait*, Year 1, Issue 1, February/March 1928 (Reprinted Kuwait: Qurtas Publishing, 1999), 4–5.

157. al-Rushaid, *Tarikh al-Kuwait*, 90–92.

158. Tétreault, *Stories of Democracy*, 48.

159. "Administration Report of the Kuwait Political Agency (1918)," in *Persian Gulf Administration Reports, Vol. VII* (Cambridge Archive Editions, 1989), 624; IOR/R/15/5/94, Letter Agent Kuwait to Political Secretary to the High Commissioner, Baghdad, May 12, 1921.

160. Crystal, *Oil and Politics in the Gulf*, 18–26; Rosemarie Said Zahlan, *The Making of the Modern Gulf States: Kuwait, Bahrain, Qatar, the United Arab Emirates, and Oman* (Ithaca Press, 1989; updated ed. 1998), 33–40.

161. For a summary of the period, see Abdulrahman Alebrahim, *Kuwait's Politics Before Independence: The Role of the Balancing Powers* (Gerlach Press, 2019), chapter 4.

162. Alebrahim, "The Balancing Powers in Kuwait and the 1938 Majlis Movement," 19.

163. The text can be found at the end of Khalid Sulayman al-ʿAdasani, *Nisf ʿam li-l-Hukm al-Niyabi fi al-Kuwait* (Half a Year of Parliamentary Rule in Kuwait) (Beirut, 1947). I am grateful to Ghanim al-Najjar for providing me with a copy.

164. Alebrahim, "The Balancing Powers in Kuwait and the 1938 Majlis Movement."

165. Alebrahim, "The Balancing Powers in Kuwait and the 1938 Majlis Movement," 32.

166. Alebrahim, "The Balancing Powers in Kuwait and the 1938 Majlis Movement," 32.

167. al-ʿAdasani, *Nisf ʿam li-l-Hukm al-Niyabi fi al-Kuwait*, 15, 20–21, 32–33.

168. al-ʿAdasani, *Nisf ʿam li-l-Hukm al-Niyabi fi al-Kuwait*, 33.

169. For more on the Council and policing, see Jill Crystal, "Public Order and Authority: Policing Kuwait," in *Monarchies and Nations: Globalisation and Identity in the Arab States of the Gulf*, ed. Paul Dresch and James Piscatori (I. B. Taurus, 2005).

170. Al-ʿAdasani, *Nisf ʿam li-l-Hukm al-Niyabi fi al-Kuwait*, 33.

171. Ahmad al-Khatib and Ghanim al-Najjar, *al-Kuwait, min al-Imara ila al-Dawla: Dhikrayyat al-ʿamal al-Watani wa al-Qawmi* (Kuwait, from Emirate to State: Memoirs of National and Patriotic Work) (Beirut: al-Markaz al-Thaqafi al-ʿArabi, 2007), 34.

172. "Administration Report of the Kuwait Political Agency (1932)," in *Persian Gulf Administration Reports, Vol. IX* (Cambridge Archive Editions, 1989), 149.

173. Al-Khatib and al-Najjar, *al-Kuwait, min al-Imara ila al-Dawla*, 35.

174. Al-Khatib and al-Najjar, *al-Kuwait, min al-Imara ila al-Dawla*, 36.

175. Crystal, *Oil and Politics in the Gulf*, 50–54; Al-Nakib, *Kuwait Transformed*, 77.

176. For more see Khaldoun al-Naqeeb, *Siraʿ al-Qabila wa al-Dimuqratiyya: Halat al-Kuwait* (The Struggle of Tribalism and Democracy: The Situation of Kuwait) (Saqi,

1996); Beaugrand, *Stateless in the Gulf*, 60; Al-Nakib, *Kuwait Transformed* and "Revisiting Hadar and Badu in Kuwait."

177. "Ana wa al-Tabaqat," *al-Sha'b*, Issue 48, October 9, 1958.

178. Alebrahim, *Kuwait's Politics Before Independence*, 31–38.

179. FO 371/61431, Letter A. C. Galloway to Secretary of State for India, London, July 2, 1947; IOR/R/15/5/319, Letter Agent Kuwait to Resident Bahrain, April 4, 1949; FO 371/82137, Letter Residency Bahrain to Eastern Department, Foreign Office, March 30, 1950.

180. "Administration Report of the Kuwait Political Agency (1949)," in *Persian Gulf Administration Reports, Vol. XI* (Cambridge Archive Editions, 1989), 88.

181. FO 371/120658, Letter B. A. B. Burrows to Selwyn Lloyd, March 26, 1956.

182. HSTD 1/1/1, Minutes of the 50th Meeting of the Kuwait Development Board, January 13, 1953.

183. FO 371/82137, Letter Residency Bahrain to Eastern Department Foreign Office, March 30, 1950.

184. FO 371/114588, Letter B. A. B. Burrows to C. J. Pelly, May 31, 1955; FO 371/109811, Telegram C. J. Pelly to Foreign Office, April 25, 1954; FO 371/120550, "Brief for official talks with the Americans," January 12, 1956.

185. ARC 106835, Letter E. A. V. de Candole to C. A. P. Southwell, May 16, 1956.

186. Ghabra, *Palestinians in Kuwait*, 37.

187. IOR/R/15/5/319, "Application for permission to stay (or extension of stay) in KUWAIT," Government of Kuwait, Directorate of Public Security, Immigration and Travel Section; Letter from Abdulla Mulla Salah, February 7, 1949, enclosing the "Announcement to the foreigners"; and Letter Agent Kuwait to Kuwait Oil Company, August 31, 1949.

188. FO 371/140274, Letter D. J. McCarthy to C. G. Man, August 26, 1959; ARC 106835, "News for August," to E. A. V. de Candole, August 31, 1954.

189. FO 371/82137, Letter Residency Bahrain to Eastern Department, Foreign Office, March 30, 1950.

190. FO 1016/126, Letter J. Gethin to C. J. Pelly, September 27, 1950.

191. FO 1016/126, Law No. 2 of 1948, "Kuwait nationality [*jinsiyya*]."

192. Mary Ann Tétreault and Haya al-Mughni, "Gender, Citizenship and Nationalism in Kuwait," *British Journal of Middle Eastern Studies* 22, no. 1/2 (1995): 64–80; Al-Nakib, *Kuwait Transformed*, 94–95.

193. FO 1016/126, Letter Resident Bahrain to Judge C. H. Haines, October 28, 1950.

194. For a more detailed account see Boodrookas, "The Making of a Migrant Working Class."

195. ARC 106985, Memorandum entitled "Kuwait Oil Company, Labour Personnel Management," Labour Superintendent Kuwait to Assistant General Manager Kuwait, March 9, 1949.

196. IOR/R/15/5/251, Letter Resident Gulf to M. P. O'C Tandy, July 7, 1946.

197. HQ BBME 0054, "Reports on Progress: Kuwait" 1949–52.

198. ARC 106992, Letter Abdullah Mulla Saleh to L. T. Jordan August 23, 1948. As Jill Crystal has noted, a similar process took place in Qatar. Crystal, *Oil and Politics in the Gulf*, chapter 5.

199. ARC 106992, Letter L. T. Jordan to C. A. P. Southwell, November 7, 1949; ARC 106890, Letter A. H. Knowles to General Manager, June 23, 1957.

200. HSTD 1/1/1, Minutes of the 60th Meeting of the Kuwait Development Board, March 30, 1953; HSTD 1/1/2, Minutes of the 64th Meeting of the Kuwait Development Board.

201. HSTD 1/1/2, Minutes of 78th Meeting of the Kuwait Development Board, August 3, 1953.

202. HSTD 1/1/2, Minutes of 66th Meeting of the Kuwait Development Board, May 11, 1953.

203. HSTD 1/1/2, Report of the 70th Meeting of the Kuwait Development Board, June 9, 1953; HSTD 2/2 Part I, "APPRECIATION OF CONTRACT SITUATION IN KUWAIT," July 9, 1953.

204. FO 371/82137, Letter Residency Bahrain to Eastern Department Foreign Office, March 30, 1950; FO 371/114730, Note, D. M. H. Riches, December 19, 1955.

205. FO 371/120658, Note F. A. Vallat to Lord Reading, July 18, 1956; and Letter Residency Bahrain to Eastern Department, Foreign Office, October 2, 1956.

206. FO 371/149104, Letter J. C. Moberly, Agency Doha to J. A. Ford, Bahrain, November 28, 1960.

207. Khaled M. Kanoo, *The House of Kanoo: A Century of an Arabian Family Business* (The London Centre of Arabian Studies, 1997), 191; FCO 8/70, R. L. Morris, British Embassy, Beirut, "Report on Labour, Social and Industrial Developments in Abu Dhabi," December 5, 1967.

208. IOR/R/15/2/106, Memorandum Agent Bahrain to Resident Gulf, April 22, 1923; IOR/R/15/5/202, "Translation of an article, which appeared in AL NAS newspaper of Basra on the 10th September 1937" entitled "The withdrawal of Visas from Kuwait Subjects," signed by "Pained."

209. al-Bakir, *Min al-Bahrain ila al-Manfa Saint Helena*, 22.

210. "al-Sha'b Taqaddam: 'Abd al-Rahman al-Bakir," *al-Sha'b*, February 20, 1958.

Chapter 2

1. Reem Alissa, "Building for Oil: Corporate Colonialism, Nationalism and Urban Modernity in Ahmadi, 1946–1992" (PhD diss., U.C. Berkeley, 2012), 22.

2. Asseel al-Ragam, "Towards a Critique of an Architectural Nahda: A Kuwaiti Example" (PhD diss., University of Pennsylvania, 2008), 35–39, 275–81; Farah Al-Nakib, "Public Space and Public Protest in Kuwait, 1938–2012," *City* 18, no. 6 (2014): 723–34; Muhammad 'Abd al-Hadi Jamal, *Aswaq al-Kuwait al-Qadima* (The Old Markets of Kuwait) (Kuwait: Center for Research and Study of Kuwait, 2001).

3. Al-Nakib, "Public Space and Public Protest in Kuwait."

4. Alissa, "Building for Oil," 22.

5. "Min Mata'ib al-Muwatinin," *Al-Iman*, Issue 9, November 1953 (Republished CRSK: Kuwait, 2011), 586.

6. See for instance "al-Bahithun 'an al-'Amal fi Saha," *Majallaat al-Kuwait*, June 1, 1974.

7. Personal interview, Dr. Sultan Mohammad al-Hashmi, October 26, 2017.

8. "al-Wik'ind al-Hindi fi Shari' al-Jahra'!" *al-Yaqutha*, March 17, 1975, KU 10/zay/540.

9. FO 371/140274, Note, C. H. Haines, June 25, 1959; FO 1016/714, Letter D. F. Hawley to E. T. Davies, June 28, 1961; FO 371/127015, Minutes of the Sixty-Second Meeting of the Labour Law Advisory Committee, April 21, 1957.

10. ARC 37023, "The Anglo-Persian Oil Company Limited (APOC) Persian Compendium: Labour Department"; ARC 106789, Letter J. G. Considine to General Manager, April 3, 1951; ARC 106985, Memorandum Labour Superintendent Kuwait to Assistant General Manager Kuwait, March 9, 1949; Rentz Papers, Box 1, Folder 4, Letter George S. Rentz to F. W. Ohliger, October 5, 1949.

11. ARC 106889, Letter Mrs. A. R. Smith, Johnie Patrick Club Kuwait, to D. A. Campbell, KOC, April 25, 1951.

12. "Rackets within rackets?" *Kuwait Times*, January 25, 1978, KU 10/ha/321.

13. Arbella Bet-Shlimon, *City of Black Gold*, 7; Fuccaro, *Histories of City and State*, 120.

14. Hanley, *Identifying with Nationality*, 2; Jill Crystal, *Oil and Politics in the Gulf*, 78–80.

15. Karl Polanyi, *The Great Transformation: The Political and Economic Origins of Our Time* (Beacon Press, 2007), 71.

16. A longer account of mercantile efforts can be found in Boodrookas, "The Making of a Migrant Working Class," chapter 2.

17. For more on racism in the Gulf oil industry, see Vitalis, *America's Kingdom*; Ehsani, "The Social History of Labor in the Iranian Oil Industry"; and Wright, *Unruly Labor.*

18. In the Gulf, the concept of skill is critiqued in Iskander, *Does Skill Make Us Human*, while the concept of the labor shortage is critiqued by Andrea Wright in *Between Dreams and Ghosts*, page 6 and Introduction. Outside the Gulf context, see Introduction, footnote 33 on critiques of supply and demand conceptualizations of labor migration. The concept of skill has long been critiqued by labor historians. See for instance Kathleen Canning, *Languages of Labor and Gender: Female Factory Work in Germany, 1850–1914* (Cornell University Press, 1996).

19. Yacoub Yusuf al-Hijji, *Kuwait and the Sea: A Brief Social and Economic History*, trans. Fahad Ahmad 'Isa Bishara (Arabian Publishing, 2010), 27.

20. Lorimer, *Gazetteer of the Persian Gulf*, Volume II, Part A, 266, 1010–11.

21. Lorimer, *Gazetteer of the Persian Gulf*, Volume II, Part B, 1535 and Part A, 248; "Report of the Persian Gulf Administration (1904–5)," in *Persian Gulf Administration Reports, Vol. V* (Cambridge Archive Editions, 1989), 545; "Administration Report of the Bahrain Political Agency (1922)," in *Persian Gulf Administration Reports, Vol. VIII* (Cambridge Archive Editions, 1989), 138; al-'Adasani, *Nisf 'am li-l-Hukm al-Niyabi fi al-Kuwait.*

22. Hopper, *Slaves of One Master*, 8, 10.

23. See Suzanne Miers, "Slavery and the Slave Trade in Saudi Arabia and the Arab States on the Persian Gulf, 1921–63," in *Abolition and its Aftermath in Indian Ocean Africa and Asia*, ed. Gwen Campbell (Routledge, 2005).

24. "Administration Report of the Bahrain Political Agency (1923)," in *Persian Gulf Administration Reports, Vol. VIII* (Cambridge Archive Editions, 1989), 219; Al-Hijji, *Kuwait and the Sea*, 33.

25. Johan Mathew, *Margins of the Market: Trafficking and Capitalism Across the Arabian Sea* (University of California Press, 2016), 56; IOR/R/15/2/1959, Letter Agent Bahrain to Residency Agent Sharjah, June 19, 1934, and Letter Charles Belgrave to Agent Bahrain, December 18, 1935.

26. Hopper, *Slaves of One Master*, chapter 6.

27. "Hukm Bayʿ al-Raqiq wa Sharaʾih," *Majallat al-Kuwait*, Issue 6, July/August 1928 (Reprinted Kuwait: Dar Qurtas, 1999), 231; Al-Bakir, *Min al-Bahrain ila al-Manfa*, 26.

28. Al-Bakir, *Min al-Bahrain ila al-Manfa St. Helena*, 26.

29. See Bahrain Government Annual Reports and Hijji, *Kuwait and the Sea*.

30. This can be traced in Kuwait Weekly Newsletters in ARC 30707 and in Administration Reports from the Kuwait Political Agency. See also "Taashih al-Aghlat fi Hawadith al-Jazira," *Majallat al-Kuwait*, Issue 4–5, May–July 1928 (Reprinted Kuwait: Dar Qurtas, 1999), 188; Anthony B. Toth, "Tribes and Tribulations: Bedouin Losses in the Saudi and Iraqi Struggles over Kuwait's Frontiers, 1921–1943," *British Journal of Middle Eastern Studies* 32, no. 2 (2005): 145–67.

31. Abdulrasoul A. al-Moosa, "Bedouin and Shanty Settlements in Kuwait" (PhD diss., University of London, 1976), 91.

32. "Administration Report of the Sharjah Political Agency (1951)," in *Persian Gulf Administration Reports, Vol. XI* (Cambridge Archive Editions, 1989), 240; Seccombe, "Labour Migration to the Arabian Gulf," 5–6.

33. Henry Longhurst, *Adventures in Oil: The Story of British Petroleum* (Sidgwick and Jackson, 1959), 210–11.

34. "Administration Report of the Bahrain Political Agency (1936)," in *Persian Gulf Administration Reports, Vol. IX* (Cambridge Archive Editions, 1989), 452; ARC 30707 Kuwait Weekly Newsletters for the week ending June 12, 1942.

35. ARC 30707, Kuwait Weekly Newsletters for the week ending February 13, 1942.

36. ARC 30707, Kuwait Weekly Newsletters for the weeks ending February 20, 1942, March 20, 1942, and May 29, 1942.

37. "Administration Report of the Kuwait Political Agency (1945)," in *Persian Gulf Administration Reports, Vol. X* (Cambridge Archive Editions, 1989), 484.

38. ARC 106831, Letter L. T. Jordan to C. W. Hamilton, Gulf Oil Corporation, November 25, 1953; Letter L. T. Jordan to C. A. P. Southwell, November 14, 1953.

39. NARA, RG 469, ID 2990419, Entry P140, Box 1, Despatch 179, US Consulate Kuwait to Department of State, January 3, 1959.

40. ARC 106428, Inter-departmental Memorandum on "Recruitment of Arab Staff," E. A. V. de Candole to General Manager, January 16, 1958.

41. Dawn Chatty, "The Bedouin of Central Oman," *The Journal of Oman Studies* 6, no. 1 (1983): 149–62; "Administration Report of the Muscat Political Agency (1948)," in *Persian Gulf Administration Reports, Vol. XI* (Cambridge Archive Editions, 1989), 54; GU, Mulligan Papers, Box 2, Folder 15, Letter George S. Rentz to T. C. Barger, July 25, 1950.

42. Personal interviews, September 21 and 22, 2017, Muhammad ʿAmir Saʿid ʿUmri, *al-Hijrat al-Sukkaniyya wa Atharuha fi al-Tarikh al-ʿOmani, 1913–1970* (The Population Migrations and their Influence in Omani History) (Oman: 2011), 157, 166; Department of Planning and Statistics, State of Kuwait, *Statistics Abstract in 25 Years* (Kuwait: Central Statistics Office, 1990), 274.

43. Nasser al-Othman, *With their Bare Hands: The Story of the Oil Industry in Qatar*, trans. Ken Whittingham (Longman, 1984), 87–89; personal interviews, September 21 and 22, 2017.

44. NARA, RG 469, ID 2990419, Entry P140, Box 1, Despatch 179, U.S. Consulate Kuwait to Department of State, January 3, 1959.

45. Ghabra, *Palestinians in Kuwait*, chapter 3.

46. Numerous articles on Palestinian organizations can be found in KU 18/z/520.

47. Razavian, "Iranian Communities in the Persian Gulf"; Stephenson, "Rerouting the Persian Gulf," chapter 2.

48. Razavian, "Iranian Communities in the Persian Gulf," 156–57, 164, 206, 302.

49. Razavi, "Iranian Communities in the Persian Gulf," 156, 256, 293–94, 300.

50. FO 371/168782, Letter M. C. S. Weston to S. M. Black, October 30, 1963.

51. FO 371/168782, Letter M. C. S. Weston to T. A. H. Tyler, April 21, 1963; Abbas Masoudi, *Idari az Shaikh Nishinha-yi Khalij-i Fars* (Observations of the Shaikh on the Persian Gulf) (Tehran: Iran-i-Chap, 1345/1966), 21.

52. Andrea Wright, "From Slaves to Contract Workers: Genealogies of Consent and Security in Indian Labor Migration," *Journal of World History* 32, no. 1 (March 2021): 29–43; and *Unruly Labor*, 21–24; Hugh Tinker, *A New System of Slavery: The Export of Indian Labour Overseas 1830–1920* (Hansib Publishing Limited, 1993).

53. Radhika Singha, "Finding Labor from India for the War in Iraq: The Jail Porter and Labor Corps, 1916–1920," *Comparative Studies in Society and History* 49, no. 2 (April 2007): 412–45; Atabaki, "Far from Home."

54. Atabaki, "Far from Home, But at Home"; Wright, *Unruly Labor*, chapter 1; IOR/L/PS/11/167.

55. ARC 68877, "REPORT AND RECOMMENDATIONS regarding the future organisation of Recruitment of Labour, Stores Purchasing & Steamer Agency work in Bombay & Karachi after 30th. June, 1928."

56. See IOR/R/15/2/1717 and NAI, EA, Near East, 1939, No. 50, Letter T. C. Fowle to Aubrey Metcalfe, January 13, 1939; IOR/R/15/2/419, Letter C. Harvey Cole to Agent Bahrain, October 28, 1945; Letter George S. Smith, Electrician to Agent Bahrain, October 28, 1945; IOR/R/15/2/419, Letter W. P. Anderson to Agent Bahrain, October 31, 1945.

57. Wright, "From Slaves to Contract Workers" and *Unruly Labor.*

58. ARC 106784, "Agenda and Notes for Meeting on 15th November, 1948."

59. ARC 106841, Letter C. A. P. Southwell to L. T. Jordan, January 31, 1951.

60. FO 371/109945, Letter C. Coatley-White to C. T. Ewart Biggs, January 11, 1954.

61. ARC 106889, Letter L. T. Jordan to Abdulla Mulla Saleh, June 3, 1951.

62. ARC 106889, Letter L. W. Sinclair to J. G. Considine, KOC, May 23, 1951.

63. "al-Nuhud bi-al-Quwa al-ʿUmmaliyya fi al-Kuwait," *al-Muwazzaf*, Issue 7, June 1963, 48.

64. FO 371/104450, Memorandum, "Permanent Labour Committee," August 1953; HSTD 1/1/1, Minutes of the 14th Meeting of the Kuwait Development Board, June 30, 1952.

65. HSTD 2/2 Part III, Letter Sahra Developments Company (Kuwait), July 29, 1952 and Letter Hasted to A. C. Brighton, Sahra Developments Company (Kuwait), August 12, 1952.

66. HSTD 2/2 Part III, Letter C. L. Hyka, Placement Officer UNRWA, to R. D. McLeod, Sahra Development Co, July 21, 1952.

67. HSTD 2/2 Part III, Letter Hasted to A. C. Brighton, Sahra Developments Company (Kuwait), August 12, 1952.

68. IOR/R/15/5/251, Letter M. P. O'C. Tandy to W. R. Hay, July 24, 1946.

69. For more see Boodrookas, "The Making of a Migrant Working Class," chapter 2.

70. "1945 Annual Report for Year 1364," in *The Bahrain Government Annual Reports, Vol. III: 1942–1947* (Cambridge Archive Editions, 1986), 209.

71. IOR/R/15/1/648, Note M. P. O.'C Tandy to A. C. Galloway, June 15, 1945.

72. Rupert Hay, "Impact of the Oil Industry on the Persian Gulf Shaikhdoms," *Middle East Journal* 9, no. 4 (1955): 361–72, 364; LAB 13/1128, "Report on visit to Bahrain, 2nd to 7th March, 1951," M. T. Audsley, British Middle East Office, Cairo, April 23, 1951; FO 371/98466, Note, C. M. Rose, February 4, 1952; ARC 67329, Telegram Kuwait to London, June 6, 1945.

73. FO 371/98467, Note C. M. Rose, "Kuwait Oil Company Labour Relations," February 12, 1952.

74. ARC 106906, J. G. Considine, "Notes on a Conversation with H.E. Shaikh Jabir al Ahmad held on 4th November 1956."

75. Personal interview, Daifullah Falah Sultan, December 4, 2017; personal interview, Hussein al-Youha, November 27, 2017; al-Othman, *With Their Bare Hands*, 54.

76. "1950–51 Annual Report for Year 1370," in *The Bahrain Government Annual Reports, Vol. IV: 1947–1952* (Cambridge Archive Editions, 1986), 292.

77. See for instance FO 371/74942, Letter W. R. Hay to Ernest Bevin, June 15, 1949; FO 371/98398, Letter W. P. Cranston to Rupert Hay, May 23, 1952. These ideas are also found in many Gulf and Bahrain Government Administration Reports.

78. FO 371/110132, Letter Embassy Jedda to Anthony Eden, February 3, 1954.

79. FO 371/98398, Letter Ministry of Labour and National Service to E. M. Errock, March 4, 1952; FO 371/120690, Letter C. Marshall to K. J. Hird October 2, 1956.

80. IOR/R/15/2/1717, Letter G. W. R. Smith to Agent Bahrain, September 17, 1936. IOR/R/15/2/981 is comprised of files on the Bahrain blacklist.

81. HSTD 1/1/1, Minutes of the 30th Meeting of the Kuwait Development Board, September 3, 1952, and Minutes of the 45th Meeting of the Kuwait Development Board, December 8, 1952.

82. See Vitalis, *America's Kingdom*, chapters 3–4; Alissa, "The Oil Town of Ahmadi since 1946"; Ehsani, "Social Engineering and the Contradictions of Modernization in Khuzestan's Company Towns"; Boodrookas and Keshavarzian, "The Forever Frontier of Urbanism"; Bet-Shlimon, *City of Black Gold*; Wright, *Unruly Labor.*

83. HSTD 1/1/1, Minutes of the 14th Meeting of the Kuwait Development Board, June 30, 1952.

84. HSTD 1/1/1, Minutes of the 15th Meeting of the Kuwait Development Board, July 6, 1952.

85. HSTD 1/2/2, Notes Technical Sub-Committee Meeting, January 26, 1954; HSTD 1/1/1, Minutes of the 24th Meeting of the Kuwait Development Board, August 10, 1952; HSTD 2/2 Part I, Handwritten note, undated.

86. HSTD 2/2/2, Letter Hasted to Holland & Hannen and Cubitts, Ltd.

87. The term is used repeatedly in the HSTD files.

88. FO 371/98432, Letter C. M. Rose to Rupert Hay, November 10, 1952.

89. FO 1016/367, Despatch C. J. Pelly, Agency Kuwait to Secretary of State for Foreign Affairs, Foreign Office, May 10, 1954.

90. HSTD 1/2/2, T. N. Smith, "First Report of the Transport Sub-Committee," January 28, 1954; ARC 106812, Review of Construction Programme for Kuwait.

91. HQ BBME 0221, Confidential Letter No. 64/18, H. E. A. Platt, October 3, 1952.

92. HSTD 1/1/1, Minutes of the 16th Meeting of the Kuwait Development Board, July 9, 1952.

93. HSTD 1/1/1, Minutes of the 56th Meeting of the Kuwait Development Board, February 23, 1953.

94. HSTD 1/1/1, Minutes of the 43rd Meeting of the Kuwait Development Board, November 24, 1952; and Minutes of Sub-Committee meeting at Baladiyya, December 10, 1952.

95. Iskander, *Does Skill Make Us Human?*

96. Shafiee, *Machineries of Oil*; Michael Edward Dobe, "A Long Slow Tutelage in Western Ways of Work: Industrial Education and the Containment of Nationalism in Anglo-Iranian and ARAMCO, 1923–1963" (PhD diss., Rutgers University, 2008.).

97. Maria Mies, *Patriarchy and Accumulation on a World Scale: Women in the International Division of Labor* (Zed Books, 1986), 16.

98. "1949–50 Annual Report for Year 1369," in *The Bahrain Government Annual Reports, Vol. IV: 1947–1952* (Cambridge Archive Editions, 1986), 199; FO 371/114772, A. Porter, Development Division Beirut, "A Census of Employment in Bahrain," November 16, 1955.

99. FCO 51/36, "Joint Research Memorandum LR 6/12," October 20, 1967.

100. IOR/R/15/2/208, Adrian Vallance, "Report on Progress in Education, December 1939 to May 1940," May 9, 1940.

101. This was not unique to Bahrain. As Sara Pursley has argued, education "experts" from the United States played a central role in gendering the educational system of Iraq in the mid-twentieth century. Sara Pursley, "The Stage of Adolescence: Anticolonial Time, Youth Insurgency, and the Marriage Crisis in Hashimite Iraq," *History of the Present* 3, no. 2 (Fall 2013): 160–97.

102. "1950–51 Annual Report for Year 1370," in *The Bahrain Government Annual Reports, Vol. IV: 1947–1952* (Cambridge Archive Editions, 1986), 322.

103. "1949–50 Annual Report for Year 1369, in *The Bahrain Government Annual Reports, Vol. IV: 1947–1952* (Cambridge Archive Editions, 1986), 224.

104. "1956 Annual Report for Year 1956," in *The Bahrain Government Annual Reports, Vol. V: 1952–1956* (Cambridge Archive Editions, 1986), 438.

105. David Finnie, "Recruitment and Training of Labor: The Middle East Oil Industry," *Middle East Journal* 12, no. 2 (Spring 1958): 127–43, 141; Belgrave, *Personal Column*, 86.

106. ARC 106841, Letter A. W. Schofield to C. A. P. Southwell, August 13, 1950.

107. Cronin, "Popular Politics, the New State and the Birth of the Iranian Working Class"; FO 371/114774, Letter C. Marshall to M. T. Audsley, July 19, 1955.

108. ARC 59729. Memorandum, C. A. P. Southwell, November 7, 1949.

109. E. A. V. de Candole, "Developments in Kuwait," *Journal of The Royal Central Asian Society*, no. 42 (January 1955): 21–29, 24; Finnie, "Recruitment and Training of Labor," 143.

110. FO 371/126971, Letter K. J. Hird to A. Greenhough, May 21, 1957.

111. FO 371/126971, Telegram B. A. B. Burrows to Foreign Office, June 1, 1957.

112. FO 371/126971, Letter G. W. Bell to C. A. Gault, June 6, 1957.

113. ARC 106890, Memorandum, "Recruitment of Arabs Iraq," June 10, 1957.

114. ARC 106890, Note, "Visit of Messrs. K. W. H. Orner and W. F. Western to Baghdad and Beirut, 10th–18th April, 1957."

115. FO 371/126971, Letter R. A. Beaumont to G. W. Bell, June 11, 1957.

116. ARC 106890, Memorandum, "Recruitment of Arabs," June 20, 1957; "Report on Recruitment Visit to Lebanon and Jordan, November–December 1957," December 18, 1957; and Memorandum, "Recruitment of Arab Staff," June 22, 1957.

117. ARC 106428, Inter-Departmental Memorandum, A. H. Knowles, "Organisation of External Recruitment (ARABS)," May 28, 1958.

118. ARC 106428, Letter E. A. V. Candole to C. A. P. Southwell, May 7, 1958; and Note on "Arab Recruitment," January 21, 1958.

119. FO 371/127020, Letter Agency Kuwait to Residency Bahrain, July 14, 1957.

120. FO 371/74942, M. T. Audsley, "Report on visit to Bahrain, January/February, 1949," April 22, 1949.

121. LAB 13/1128, M. T. Audsley, "Report on visit to Bahrain, 2nd to 7th March, 1951," April 23, 1951.

122. FO 371/98466, Note, C. M. Rose, February 4, 1952; FO 371/104337, Memorandum, "Cost of Living in Bahrain," July 20, 1953.

123. LAB 13/1128, M. T. Audsley, "Visit to Bahrain from 1st to 8th April 1953," May 23, 1953.

124. LAB 13/1128, M. T. Audsley, "Visit to Bahrain from 1st to 8th April 1953," May 23, 1953.

125. LAB 13/1128, M. T. Audsley, "Visit to Bahrain from 1st to 8th April 1953," May 23, 1953.

126. "Shayʾ min al-Akhbar," *al-Iman*, Issue 4, April 1953 (Kuwait: CRSK, 2011.), 284.

127. HSTD 1/1/2, Minutes of the 74th Meeting of the Kuwait Development Board, July 6, 1953.

128. IOR/L/PS/12/3823, "Commercial Agreement between the Sheikh of Koweit and the Kuwait Oil Company," December 23, 1934. The history of these "nationality clauses" is summarized in Errichiello, "Foreign Workforce in the Arab Gulf States."

129. HSTD 1/1/2, Minutes of the 75th Meeting of the Kuwait Development Board, July 13, 1953.

130. HSTD 1/1/2, Minutes of an Extraordinary Meeting of the Kuwait Development Board, July 15, 1953.

131. HSTD 1/1/2, Minutes of the 82nd Meeting of the Kuwait Development Board, September 14, 1953.

132. "Naftuna wa baʿd Muʾathiratih," *al-Raʾid*, Issue 2, April 1952 (CRSK: Kuwait, 1999), 137.

133. Crystal, *Oil and Politics in the Gulf*, 139–47.

134. Manu Goswami, *Producing India: From Colonial Economy to National Space* (University of Chicago Press, 2004), 5.

135. "al-Kuwait fi Shahr," *al-Raʾid*, Issue 3, May 1952 (CRSK: Kuwait, 1999), 286.

136. LAB 13/1597, Letter P. C. D. Archer to A. C. Read, February 22, 1964; FO 371/168728, Amiri speech to the National Assembly, Sabah as-Salim Al Sabah, October 29, 1963.

137. The International Bank for Reconstruction and Development, *The Economic Development of Kuwait* (The Johns Hopkins Press, 1965), 103, 104; Pascal Menoret, *Joyriding in Riyadh: Oil, Urbanism, and Road Revolt* (Cambridge University Press, 2014), 92–94; Toby Craig Jones, *Desert Kingdom: How Oil and Water Forged Modern Saudi Arabia* (Harvard University Press, 2010), 110, 127; Al-Nakib, *Kuwait Transformed*, 104 and chapter 5; Crystal, *Oil and Politics in the Gulf*, 76.

138. Al-Najjar, "Decision Making Process," 108.

139. Al-Najjar, "Decision Making Process," 103, 117; HSTD 1/1/1, Minutes of 53rd Meeting of the Kuwait Development Board, February 2, 1953.

140. Alebrahim, *Kuwait's Politics Before Independence*, 107–108.

141. Al-Nakib, *Kuwait Transformed*, 134–38.

142. Townend Sr., *A History of Shaw Wallace & Co.*

143. Notably the Mesopotamia Persia Corporation Ltd., Gray Paul & Co., and Lynch Brothers. A comprehensive breakdown of this system can be found in CLC/B/123/

MS27729H and CLC/B/123/MS27734, Memorandum, "Description of the amalgamation of businesses and their respective spheres of activity."

144. Kanoo, *The House of Kanoo*, 10.

145. Lienhardt, *Disorientations*, 54; CLC/B/207/MS39073, Letter J. A. Court to General Manager London, March 18, 1953; "Ahmad bin Muhammad Al Ghanim," *Majallat al-Kuwait*, Issue 2–3, March/April 1928 (Reprinted Kuwait: Dar Qurtas, 1999), 104.

146. Kanoo, *The House of Kanoo*; Michael Field, *The Merchants: The Big Business Families of Arabia* (John Murray, 1984); Al-Shaya, *Echoes of Memory*.

147. Al-Najjar, "Decision-Making Process in Kuwait," 453.

148. "Annual Report for Year 1958," in *The Bahrain Government Annual Reports, Vol. VI: 1957–1961* (Cambridge Archive Editions, 1987), 151; "Furas Tijariyya" and "Talabat li-l-Wukala'," *Nashrat Ghurfat Tijarat wa Sina'at al-Kuwait*, Issue 1, Kuwait: September 1960.

149. ARC 106789, Letter H. R. P. Dickson to L. T. Jordan, April 1, 1950.

150. For the Bahraini case see IOR/R/15/2/1363 and CLC/B/207/MS39073, "Annual Report of the Bahrain Chamber of Commerce, 10th February 1959." For Dubai, Al-Sayegh, "Merchants' Role in a Changing Society," 99; "Ta'mim Ham," *Nashrat Ghurfat Tijarat wa Sina'at al-Kuwait*, Issue 1, September 1960, 4; Pete W. Moore, *Doing Business in the Middle East: Politics and Economic Crisis in Jordan und Kuwait* (Cambridge University Press, 2009), 46.

151. "Ghurfat al-Tijara," *al-Ra'id*, Issue 4, May 1952 (CRSK: Kuwait, 1999), 316; "Hadith al-Nas," *al-Ra'id*, Issue 10, March 1953 (CRSK: Kuwait, 1999), 1002; "al-Ghurfat al-Tajariyya," *al-Iman*, Issue 5, May 1953 (CRSK: Kuwait, 2011), 334.

152. "Ta'mim," *Nashrat Ghurfat Tijarat wa Sina'at al-Kuwait*, Issue 1, September 1960.

153. "al-A'mal allati Qamat biha Ghurfat Tijarat al-Kuwait," *Nashrat Ghurfat Tijarat wa Sina'at al-Kuwait*, Issue 1, September 1960.

154. FO 371/168749, Letter A. B. Ball to A. E. Ellwood, December 31, 1962; and Letter Christopher Gandy to K. Mackenzie, October 23, 1963; W. M. Ballantyne, *Legal Development in Arabia: A Selection of Articles and Addresses on the Arabian Gulf* (Graham & Troutman Limited, 1980), 32.

155. CLC/B/207/MS39073; Al-Sayegh, "Merchants' Role in a Changing Society," 99; CLC/B/207/MS39010/015, P. F. D. Tennant, "Report on Kuwait–Bahrain Persian Gulf," November 14–18, 1960; "Ta'mim," *Nashrat Ghurfat Tijarat wa Sina'at al-Kuwait*, Issue 1, September 1960.

156. CLC/B/207/MS39122/012, Letter Eastern Bahrain to GM London, December 11, 1957; "1948–9 Annual Report for Year 1368," in *The Bahrain Government Annual Reports, Vol. IV: 1947–1952* (Cambridge Archive Editions, 1986), 175; Kanoo, *The House of Kanoo*, 133. This is discussed in Boodrookas, "The Making of a Migrant Working Class," 135–37.

157. ARC 106992, "Notes on Labour Recruitment," undated; IOR/R/15/5/251, Memorandum 787, "Monthly Progress Report to the Managing Director, September, 1948," October 10, 1948.

158. ARC 106992, Memorandum General Manager to Resident Accountant, July 5, 1948; LAB 13/483, Report, M. T. Audsley, April 2, 1949.

159. LAB 13/483, Report, M. T. Audsley, April 2, 1949.

160. LAB 13/483, Report, M. T. Audsley, April 2, 1949; HSTD 2/2 Part I, "APPRECIATION OF CONTRACT SITUATION IN KUWAIT – 9 JULY 1953."

161. ARC 106831, Inter-Departmental Memorandum W. P. Doyle to General Manager, May 6, 1956.

162. Fuad I. Khuri, *Tribe and State in Bahrain: The Transformation of Social and Political Authority in an Arab State* (University of Chicago Press, 1980), 140.

163. "Administration Report of the Kuwait Political Agency (1951)," in *Persian Gulf Administration Reports, Vol. XI* (Cambridge Archive Editions, 1989), 218.

164. ARC 106863, Memorandum Ibrahim Rizq to E. A. V. de Candole, March 11, 1957.

165. Al-Bakir, *Min al-Bahrain ila al-Manfa Saint Helena*, 13, 17.

166. Al-Bakir, *Min al-Bahrain ila al-Manfa Saint Helena*, 20, 22.

167. Al-Bakir, *Min al-Bahrain ila al-Manfa Saint Helena*, 20.

168. Al-Bakir, *Min al-Bahrain ila al-Manfa Saint Helena*, 22–23, 27.

169. Al-Khatib and al-Najjar, *al-Kuwait, min al-Imara ila al-Dawla*, 24–25.

170. Al-Khatib and al-Najjar, *al-Kuwait, min al-Imara ila al-Dawla*, 33.

171. Al-Khatib and al-Najjar, *al-Kuwait, min al-Imara ila al-Dawla*, 27; Ahmad al-Khatib, personal interview, January 4, 2018.

172. Ali Hussein Al-ʿAwadhi, *Ahmad al-Khatib: Watan wa Dustur* (Homeland and Constitution) (Kuwait: 2013), 22.

173. Abdel Razzaq Takriti, "Political Praxis in the Gulf: Ahmad al-Khatib and the Movement of Arab Nationalists, 1948–1969," in *Arabic Thought Against the Authoritarian Age: Towards an Intellectual History of the Present*, ed. Jens Hanssen and Max Weiss (Cambridge University Press, 2018); Al-Awadhi, *Ahmad al-Khatib.*

174. "Hadith al-Nas," *al-Raʾid*, Issue 4, May 1952 (CRSK: Kuwait, 1999), 340.

175. "Hawl al-Daman al-Ijtimaʿi" *al-Raʾid*, Issue 2, April 1952 (CRSK: Kuwait, 1999), 150; "Barid al-Raʾid," *al-Raʾid*, Issue 4, May 1952 (CRSK: Kuwait, 1999), 362; "Masʾuliyyat al-Shaʿb," *al-Raʾid*, Issue 5, June 1952 (CRSK: Kuwait, 1999), 428–29.

176. Abdullah Yousif al-Ghanim, "Forward" to *al-Raʾid, Vol. I* (Kuwait: CRSK, 1999).

177. "Hadith al-Nas," *al-Raʾid*, Issue 7, November 1952 (CRSK: Kuwait, 1999), 644.

178. On Bahrain see Fuccaro, *Histories of City and State*, chapter 5.

179. "Hadith al-Suq," *al-Iman*, Issue 1, January 1953 (CRSK: Kuwait City, 2011), 29.

180. "Akhbar Mahalliyya," *al-Iman*, Issue 1, January 1953 (CRSK: Kuwait City, 2011), 67.

181. "Akhbar Mahalliyya," *al-Iman*, Issue 1, January 1953 (CRSK: Kuwait City, 2011), 67.

182. "Yudayiqni," *al-Iman*, Issue 2, February 1953 (CRSK: Kuwait City, 2011), 89.

183. "Hadith al-Suq," *al-Iman*, Issue 9, November 1953 (CRSK: Kuwait City, 2011), 614.

184. FO 371/149098, "Arab Gulf Call," *Voice of the Arabs*, May 17, 1960 at 16.50 GMT.

185. Falah Abdullah al-Mdairis, *al-Tawajjuhat al-Marksiyya al-Kuwaitiyya* (The Kuwaiti Marxist Tendencies) (Kuwait: Dar Qurtas li-l-Nashr, 2003), 26; "Kalimat al-Sha'b" and "Jawla fi al-Kuwait," *al-Sha'b*, Issue 42, August 28, 1958; "Adwa' 'ala al-waqi'," *al-Sha'b*, Issue 45, September 18, 1958.

186. "Kalimatuna al-Ula," *al-Iman*, Issue 1, January 1953 (CRSK: Kuwait, 2011), 12; "Majal al-Qurra'," *al-Iman*, Issue 4, April 1953 (CRSK: Kuwait City, 2011), 282.

187. "al-sha'b Taqaddam: 'Abd al-Rahman al-Bakir," *al-Sha'b*, Issue 12, February 20, 1958; "Ayyuha al-Mas'ulun: Hadhihi Sabiqa Khatira," *Sada al-Iman*, Issue 60, May 27, 1955.

188. "Kalimat al-Tahrir" and "Nadi al-Mu'allimin fi al-'am," *al-Ra'id*, Issue 1, March 1952 (CRSK: Kuwait, 1999), 1, 76.

189. "Khawatir Mushtaraka," *al-Ra'id*, Issue 1, March 1952 (CRSK: Kuwait, 1999), 80; "Naduat al-Ra'id," *al-Ra'id*, Issue 1, March 1952 (CRSK: Kuwait, 1999), 43.

190. "al-Ghala'," *al-Ra'id*, Issue 4, May 1952 (CRSK: Kuwait, 1999), 333.

191. "Hadith al-Nas," *al-Ra'id*, Issue 3, May 1952 (CRSK: Kuwait, 1999), 235–36; "Barid al-Ra'id," *al-Ra'id*, Issue 5, June 1952 (CRSK: Kuwait, 1999), 479; "Min Mushkilatina al-Ijtima'iyya," *al-Ra'id*, Issue 3, May 1952 (CRSK: Kuwait, 1999), 275–78.

192. "Fatwa wa Ahkam," *al-Ma'had al-Dini*, Issue 1, April 1954.

193. "Ahadith al-Suq," *al-Iman*, Issue 8, October 1953 (CRSK: Kuwait, 2011), 513.

194. "al-Kuwait fi Shahr," *al-Ra'id*, Issue 6, October 1952 (CRSK: Kuwait, 1999), 581; "Hadith al-Nas," *Al-Ra'id*, Issue 6, October 1952 (CRSK: Kuwait, 1999), 527; "Haqibat al-Ra'id," *al-Ra'id*, Issue 7, November 1952 (CRSK: Kuwait, 1999) 698.

195. "Ahadith al-Suq," *al-Iman*, Issue 1, January 1953 (CRSK: Kuwait, 2011), 30.

196. "Ahadith al-Suq," *al-Iman*, Issue 1, January 1953 (CRSK: Kuwait, 2011), 30.

197. "Akhbar Mahalliyya," *al-Iman*, Issue 7, July 1953 (CRSK: Kuwait, 2011), 479; "Ahadith al-Suq," *al-Iman*, Issue 5, May 1953 (CRSK: Kuwait, 2011), 324.

198. "Min Muta'ab al-Muwatinin," *al-Iman*, Issue 9, November 1953 (CRSK: Kuwait, 2011), 585.

199. "Hawl al-Daman al-Ijtima'i," *al-Ra'id*, Issue 2, April 1952 (CRSK: Kuwait, 1999), 149.

200. "Majal al-Qurra'," *al-Iman*, Issue 4, April 1953 (CRSK: Kuwait, 2011), 282; "Ahadith al-Suq," *al-Iman*, Issue 14, April 1954 (CRSK: Kuwait, 2011), 389; "al-Kadir al-Habs," *Sada al-Iman*, Issue 54, April 22, 1955.

201. "Liman?" *Al-Iman*, Issue 5, May 1953 (CRSK: Kuwait, 2011), 299.

202. "Majal al-Qurra'," *al-Iman*, Issue 4, April 1953 (CRSK: Kuwait, 2011), 282.

203. "Kulliyat al-Sina'a," *al-Ra'id*, Issue 6, October 1952 (CRSK: Kuwait, 1999), 570; "Hajatuna ila al-Ta'lim al-Sina'i," *al-Ra'id*, Issue 8, January 1953 (CRSK: Kuwait, 1999), 753.

204. NARA, RG 469, ID 2990419, Entry P140, Box 1, Despatch 167, U.S. Consulate Kuwait to Department of State, December 10, 1957.

205. "al-Shahada al-Khalidah," *al-Ra'id*, Issue 1, March 1952 (CRSK: Kuwait, 1999), 92.

206. "Hurriyyat al-Mar'a," *al-Iman*, Issue 1, January 1953 (CRSK: Kuwait, 2011), 23.

207. "Hawla al-Daman al-Ijtimaʿi," *al-Raʾid*, Issue 2, April 1952 (CRSK: Kuwait, 1999), 148.

208. "Masʾuliyya al-Shaʿb," *al-Raʾid*, Issue 5, June 1952 (CRSK: Kuwait, 1999), 427.

209. "al-Daman al-Ijtimaʿi," *al-Raʾid*, Issue 6, October 1952 (CRSK: Kuwait, 1999), 595.

210. "al-Daman al-Ijtimaʿi fi al-Kuwait," *al-Raʾid*, Issue 1, March 1952 (CRSK: Kuwait, 1999), 4.

211. "Khawatir Mushtaraka," 82.

212. "al-Daman al-Ijtimaʿi fi al-Kuwait," 7.

213. "al-Daman al-Ijtimaʿi fi al-Kuwait," 9–11.

214. "al-Daman al-Ijtimaʿi fi al-Kuwait," 10.

215. "al-Daman al-Ijtimaʿi fi al-Kuwait," 11.

216. See also Al-Nakib, "Revisiting Hadar and Badu in Kuwait," and *Kuwait Transformed*, chapter 5.

217. Al-Nakib, "Revisiting Hadar and Badu in Kuwait," and *Kuwait Transformed*, chapter 5.

218. "Majal al-Qurraʾ," *al-Iman*, Issue 15, May 1954 (CRSK: Kuwait, 2011), 516.

219. "Hadith al-Nas," *al-Raʾid*, Issue 7, November 1952 (CRSK: Kuwait, 1999), 644; "Ahadith al-Suq," *al-Iman*, Issue 15, May 1954 (CRSK: Kuwait, 2011), 515.

220. "Qanun al-Jinsiyya wa al-Hijra," 378.

221. "al-Ajnabi," *Sada al-Iman*, Issue 51, April 1, 1955.

222. Al-Khatib and al-Najjar, *al-Kuwait, min al-Imara ila al-Dawla*; "al-Intikhabat," *al-Shaʿb*, Issue 17, March 27, 1958.

223. "Jawla fi al-Kuwait," *al-Shaʿb*, Issue 17, March 27, 1958; "al-Shaʿb Yaqul," *al-Shaʿb*, Issue 16, March 20, 1958.

224. "Kalima: Kuwaiti . . . wa Lākin?" *Al-Shaʿb*, Issue 39, August 7, 1958.

225. "Kalima: Kuwaiti . . . wa Lākin?" *Al-Shaʿb*, Issue 39, August 7, 1958.

226. "al-Hal," *al-Shaʿb*, Issue 48, October 9, 1958.

227. "al-Hal," *al-Shaʿb*, Issue 48, October 9, 1958.

228. "Min al-Khamis ila al-Khamis," *al-Shaʿb*, Issue 45, September 18, 1958.

Chapter 3

1. Personal communication with Khawla Abdelhamid and Hazem Kayali, relatives of Ashraf Lutfi, January 19, 2020.

2. Ghabra, *Palestinians in Kuwait*, 42.

3. NARA, RG 469, ID 2990419, Entry P140, Box 1, Despatch 167, U.S. Consulate Kuwait to the Department of State, December 10, 1957.

4. NARA, RG 469, ID 2990419, Entry P140, Box 1, Despatch 167, U.S. Consulate Kuwait to the Department of State, December 10, 1957.

5. Dietrich, *Oil Revolution*, 79; Nico Schrijver, *Sovereignty over Natural Resources: Balancing Rights and Duties* (Cambridge University Press, 1997); Nelida Fuccaro, "Oilmen, Petroleum Arabism and OPEC: New Political and Public Cultures of Oil in the Arab World, 1959–1964," in *Handbook of OPEC and the Global Energy Order: Past*

Present, and Future Challenges, ed. Dag Harald Claes and Giuliano Garavini (Routledge, 2020), 15–30.

6. Ashraf Lutfi, *Arab Oil: A Plan for the Future* (The Middle East Research and Publishing Center, 1960), 48; Fuccaro, "Oilmen, Petroleum Arabism and OPEC," 27.

7. Lutfi, *Arab Oil*, 40.

8. ARC 106428, Inter-Departmental Memorandum, E. A. V. de Candole to General Manager, January 21, 1958.

9. NARA, RG 469, ID 2990419, Entry P140, Box 1, Despatch 167, U.S. Consulate Kuwait to the Department of State, December 10, 1957.

10. Garavini, *The Rise and Fall of OPEC*, 175.

11. Another account can be found in Mdairis, *al-Mujtamaʿ al-Madani wa-al-Haraka al-Wataniyya fi al-Kuwait*; and in the case of Bahrain in Fuccaro, *Histories of City and State*, 176–86. This chapter is based on Boodrookas, "The Making of a Migrant Working Class," chapter 6. It directly contradicts Wright, *Unruly Labor*, chapter 2, which does not cite Arabic-language source material or this author's dissertation and argues that "labor solidarities increasingly fragmented along national lines" (65).

12. Zachary Lockman, "The Social Roots of Nationalism: Workers and the National Movement in Egypt, 1908–19," *Middle Eastern Studies* 24, no. 4 (October 1988): 445–59; Joel Beinin and Zachary Lockman, *Workers on the Nile: Nationalism, Communism, Islam, and the Egyptian Working Class, 1882–1954* (I. B. Tauris & Co., 1988), chapters 1–3; Cooper, "The Dialectics of Decolonization."

13. Fernando Coronil, *The Magical State: Nature, Money and. Modernity in Venezuela* (University of Chicago Press, 1997), 8.

14. Laleh Khalili, "Crude Knowledge: Petro-Periodicals and Resource Sovereignty," *International Journal of Middle East Studies* 56, no. 3 (2025): 446–64, 446.

15. Vitalis, *America's Kingdom*; Ehsani, "The Social History of Labor in the Iranian Oil Industry"; Khalili, *Sinews of War and Trade*; Wright, *Unruly Labor.*

16. For contemporary accounts, see Le Renard, *Western Privilege*, and Appel, *The Licit Life of Capitalism*.

17. Robinson, *Black Marxism*; Satnam Virdee, "Racialized Capitalism: An Account of its Contested Origins and Consolidation," *The Sociological Review* 67, no. 1 (2019), 3–27; Nancy Fraser, "Expropriation and Exploitation in Racialized Capitalism: A Reply to Michael Dawson," *Critical Historical Studies* 3, no. 1 (Spring 2016): 163–78.

18. Garavini, *The Rise and Fall of OPEC*, 31–32.

19. Francisco Parra, *Oil Politics: A Modern History of Petroleum* (I. B. Tauris, 2004), 34.

20. Alissa, "The Oil Town of Ahmadi since 1946."

21. Alissa, "The Oil Town of Ahmadi since 1946"; Al-Nakib, *Kuwait Transformed*; Ian J. Seccombe, and R. I., Lawless, "Work Camps and Company Towns: Settlement Patterns and the Gulf Oil Industry," Working paper (University of Durham, Center for Middle Eastern and Islamic Studies, 1987); Ehsani, "Social Engineering and the Contradictions of Modernization in Khuzestan's Company Towns"; Bet-Shlimon, *City of Black Gold*, chapter 4.

22. Lienhardt, *Disorientations*, 31.

23. ARC 59729, Memorandum entitled "Kuwait Housing," E. H. O. Elkington to J. M. Pattinson, July 15, 1952.

24. ARC 59729, Minutes of a meeting with Dr. Heald, London, on KOC, April 24, 1953.

25. Personal interview, Qabalan ʿAjnan al-ʿAzimi, November 29, 2017.

26. "Madha Turid Sharikat al-Naft?" *al-Shaʿb*, Issue 44, September 11, 1958.

27. FO 371/98467, Note C. M. Rose, "Kuwait Oil Company Labour Relations," February 12, 1952.

28. Personal interview, Daifullah Falah Sultan, December 4, 2017.

29. Personal interview, Daifullah Falah Sultan, December 4, 2017.

30. ARC 59729, Report by Dr. S. D. McClean, December 1952, "KUWAIT OIL COMPANY - MEDICAL SERVICE RECOMMENDATIONS."

31. Personal interview, Daifullah Falah Sultan, December 4, 2017.

32. IOR/R/15/2/419, Letter Agent Bahrain to Rupert Hay, Resident Gulf, January 8, 1949.

33. ARC 106992, Letter C. A. P. Southwell to L. T. Jordan, October 25, 1949.

34. ARC 106992, Letter L. T. Jordan to C. A. P. Southwell, September 17, 1949, and Memorandum L. T. Jordan to Labour Superintendent, March 29, 1949; ARC 106789, Memorandum London Personnel Department to Kuwait Staff Department, April 25, 1950.

35. ARC 106906, W. P. Doyle, "Notes on a Conversation with H.E. Shaikh Jabir al Ahmad held on 5th December 1956."

36. Field, *The Merchants*, 209.

37. Vitalis, *America's Kingdom*, chapter 3; HQ BBME 0663, Letter Jeoffrey Prior to Lord Kennet, June 25, 1950.

38. ARC 106992, Letter L. T. Jordan to C. A. P. Southwell, February 14, 1949.

39. FO 371/98467, Note C. M. Rose, "Kuwait Oil Company Labour Relations," February 12, 1952.

40. LAB 13/483, Report M. T. Audsley, April 2, 1949.

41. NARA, RG 469, ID 2990419, Entry P140, Box 1, "Economic Summary of the Year 1958," U.S. Consulate Kuwait to Department of State, February 1, 1959.

42. FO 371/74942, Letter W. R. Hay to Ernest Bevin, June 15, 1949.

43. Hay, "Impact of the Oil Industry on the Persian Gulf Shaikhdoms," 371.

44. Vitalis, *America's Kingdom*; Seccombe, "'A Disgrace to American Enterprise'"; Wright, *Unruly Labor.*

45. Al-ʿAjmi, *al-Haraka al-ʿUmmaliyya wa al-Naqabiyya fi al-Kuwait*, 59; Saqr, *Rihla Dakhil al-Dhakira maʿ al-Haraka al-ʿUmaliyya al-Kuwaitiyya*, 23.

46. ARC 106831, Letter L. T. Jordan to C. W. Hamilton, November 25, 1953.

47. ARC 106428, Letter E. Boaden to Philip Southwell, September 13, 1958.

48. FO 371/127021, Telegram B. Burrows to Foreign Office, July 25, 1957; NAI, FP: Mid-Asia, 1923, No. 349, Letter A. Trevor to Foreign Secretary to the Government of India in the Foreign and Political Department, March 28, 1922. For examples elsewhere see Atabaki, Bini, and Ehsani, eds., *Working for Oil.*

49. FO 371/140301, Telegrams G. Middleton to Foreign Office, May 4 and 6, 1959; Finnie, "Recruitment and Training of Labor," 142.

50. ARC 106992, Letter L. T. Jordan to C. A. P. Southwell, June 20, 1948.

51. LAB 13/1597, Despatch No. 74, M. W. Errock to the Earl of Home, July 3, 1963.

52. FO 371/127021, Telegram B. Burrows to Foreign Office, July 25, 1957.

53. FO 371/149091, Letter R. A. Beaumont to A. B. Powell, August 8, 1960.

54. FO 371/149091, Letter J. C. B. Richmond to R. A. Beaumont, June 15, 1960.

55. FO 371/149091, "Summary record of discussion between the Managing Director of the Kuwait Oil Company, the Hon. W. Fraser, and the Political Resident," June 26, 1960.

56. NARA, RG 469, ID 2990419, Entry P140, Box 1, Despatch 53, US Consulate Kuwait to Department of State, August 21, 1956.

57. Finnie, "Recruitment and Training of Labor," 141–42.

58. IOR/R/15/2/664, Order by the Political Agent, Bahrain, April 2, 1940.

59. IOR/R/15/2/664, Telegram Air Officer Commanding British in Hinaidi, Iraq to Agent Bahrain, December 21, 1940; Letter Chief Local Representative Bapco to Agent Bahrain, November 27, 1940; Express Letter Agent Bahrain to Secretary to the Government of India in the External Affairs Department, March 18, 1942. See also Jeff Eamon, "Policing the Bahrain Islands: Labor, Race, and the Historical Origins of Foreign Recruitment" (master's thesis, New York University, May 2015).

60. ARC 106831, Letter L. T. Jordan to C. A. P. Southwell, August 25, 1953.

61. NARA, RG 469, ID 2990419, Entry P140, Box 1, Despatch 53, US Consulate Kuwait to Department of State, August 21, 1956.

62. Willard A. Beling, *Pan Arabism and Labor* (Harvard University Press, 1961), 33; FO 371/140084, "Kuwait: Mr. Halford's Valedictory Despatch," August 13, 1959; LAB 13/1597, Despatch No. 74, M. W. Errock to the Earl of Home, July 3, 1963; FO 371/149090, J. C. B. Richmond to R. A. Beaumont, January 12, 1960; FO 371/149090, Note Roger Stevens, June 3, 1960; FO 371/149091, Letter J. C. B. Richmond to R. A. Beaumont, June 15, 1960.

63. Personal interview, Hassan Falah, January 9, 2018.

64. "1943 Annual Report for Year 1362," in *The Bahrain Government Annual Reports, Vol. III: 1942–1947* (Cambridge Archive Editions, 1986), 208.

65. ARC 106841, Letter A. W. Schofield to C. A. P. Southwell, August 13, 1950.

66. ARC 106428, Inter-Departmental Memorandum, J. G. Considine to Ag. General Manager, July 9, 1958.

67. FO 371/140084, "Kuwait: Mr. Halford's Valedictory Despatch," August 13, 1959; ARC 106721, A. Hijazi, "Notes on a Meeting with H.E. the Minister of Finance and Oil on Wednesday, 1st March 1967," March 4, 1967.

68. Lorimer, *Gazetteer*, Volume II, Part A, 246; Fuccaro, *Histories of City and State in the Persian Gulf*, 108, 161; Belgrave, *Personal Column*, 135; "Tasʿir al-Luhum," *al-Shaʿb*, Issue 43, September 4, 1958; IOR/R/15/2/104, "Statement of Haji Hamad Sahach of Manamah," undated, 1923–1925; "Administration Report of the Kuwait Political Agency (1926)," *Persian Gulf Administration Reports, Vol. VIII* (Cambridge Archive Editions,

1989), 426; "Administration Report of the Kuwait Political Agency (1932)," in *Persian Gulf Administration Reports, Vol. IX* (Cambridge Archive Editions, 1989), 138, 148.

69. IOR/R/15/2/848, Letter Agent Bahrain to Resident Gulf, May 30, 1932.

70. S. J. Thoms, "The Hospital at Bahrein," *Neglected Arabia* 54 (October–December 1902): 12–16, 15.

71. "al-Tarikh: al-Abar al-Irtiwaziyya fi al-Kuwait," *Majallat al-Kuwait*, Issue 6, July/August 1928 (Reprinted Kuwait: Dar Qurtas li-l-Nashr, 1999), 213.

72. Personal interview with Hassan Falah, Kuwait, November 29, 2017; personal interview with Hussein al-Youha, Kuwait, November 27, 2017; personal interview with Hussein Saqr, Kuwait, November 28, 2017; Saqr, *Rihla Dakhil al-Dhakira maʿ al-Haraka al-ʿUmaliyya al-Kuwaitiyya*, 26.

73. Al-Khatib and al-Najjar, *al-Kuwait, min al-Imara ila al-Dawla*, 111; al-ʿAdasani, *Nisf ʿam li-l-Hukm al-Niyabi fi al-Kuwait.*

74. ʿAbdullah Khalid Hatim, *Min Huna Bada'at al-Kuwait* (From Here Began Kuwait) (Dar al-Qabas: Kuwait, 1979), 283.

75. ʿAbdullah Khalid Hatim, *Min Huna Bada'at al-Kuwait* (From Here Began Kuwait) (Dar al-Qabas: Kuwait, 1979), 285.

76. The strike is comprehensively covered in IOR/R/15/2/176. See also Hassan Mohammad Abdulla Saleh, "Labor, Nationalism, and Imperialism in Eastern Arabia: Britain, the Shaikhs and the Gulf Oil Workers in Bahrain, Kuwait and Qatar, 1932–1956" (PhD diss., University of Michigan, 1991), 78–79.

77. Al-Bakir, *Min al-Bahrain ila al-Manfa Saint Helena*, 20.

78. See also Khuri, *Tribe and State in Bahrain*, 197.

79. IOR/R/15/2/176; Fuccaro, *Histories of City and State*, 175–76, 189.

80. Saleh, "Labor, Nationalism, and Imperialism," 83.

81. IOR/R/15/2/408, "Notes of a meeting held at the Agency on 24th December 1943" and "The strike situation as on 28th December 1943"; IOR/R/15/2/713, Bahrain Security Office, "Report on Security of Oil Installations for period ending 31 January 1944."

82. FO 371/39891, Telegram Resident Gulf to External Affairs Department, Government of India, December 30, 1943.

83. IOR/R/15/2/713, Bahrain Security Office, "Report on the security of oil installations for the period ending 1 June 1944"; "1945 Annual Report for Year 1364," in *The Bahrain Government Annual Reports, Vol. III: 1942–1947* (Cambridge Archive Editions, 1986), 235; "1945–6 Annual Report for Year 1365," in *The Bahrain Government Annual Reports, Vol. III: 1942–1947* (Cambridge Archive Editions, 1986), 373.

84. NAI, EA, NE, No. 8(5), Letter Bapco Bahrain to Agent CASOC, Bombay, March 2, 1943.

85. NAI, EA, NE, No. 8(5), Letter Bapco Bahrain to Agent CASOC, Bombay, March 2, 1943.

86. "Administration Report of the Trucial Coast Political Agency (1944)," in *Persian Gulf Administration Reports, Vol. X* (Cambridge Archive Editions, 1989), 401–402.

87. Vitalis, *America's Kingdom*, 95–96.

88. Bet-Shlimon, *City of Black Gold*, 104–105.

89. Ervand Abrahamian, *A History of Modern Iran* (Cambridge University Press, 2008), 109–10.

90. Al-Othman, *With their Bare Hands*, 54; al-'Ajmi, *al-Haraka al-'Ummaliyya wa al-Naqabiyya fi al-Kuwait*, 58.

91. Toby Matthiesen has noted the significance of Saudi and Bahraini worker coordination in "Migration, Minorities, and Radical Networks," 501–502.

92. Al-Khatib and al-Najjar, *al-Kuwait, min al-Imara ila al-Dawla*, 107; al-Mdairis, "The Arab Nationalist Movement of Kuwait from its Origins to 1970," 303.

93. Al-Bakir, *Min al-Bahrain ila al-Manfa Saint Helena*, 29.

94. Hassan Falah, Personal interview, November 29, 2017; "al-'amil Tiltaqi biba'd al-Qada al-Mu'assisin lil-Niqabat," *al-'amil*, October 15, 1989, KU 10/z/310.

95. Personal interview, Daifullah Falah Sultan, December 4, 2017; al-Mdairis, *al-Mujtama' al-Madani wa-al-Haraka al-Wataniyya fi al-Kuwait*, 124–26.

96. Al-Rashoud, "Modern Education and Arab Nationalism in Kuwait, 1911–1961"; and Gerasimos Tsourapas, "Nasser's Educators and Agitators across al-Watan al-'Arabi: Tracing the Foreign Policy Importance of Egyptian Regional Migration, 1952–1967," *British Journal of Middle Eastern Studies* 43, no. 3 (2016): 324–41.

97. 'Adil Muhammad al-Mughni, *Majalat al-Tulabiyya al-Kuwaitiyya al-Qadima* (Old Kuwaiti Student Magazines) (Kuwait: CRSK, 2009).

98. Ali Hussein al-'Awadhi, *al-Haraka al-Wataniyya al-Kuwaitiyya wa-l-'udwan al-Thulathi 'ala Misr* (The Kuwaiti National Movement and the Tripartite Aggression against Egypt) (Kuwait: Dar Qurtas li-l-Nashr, 2019).

99. "Administration Report of the Persian Gulf (November 1952)," in *Persian Gulf Administration Reports, Vol. XI* (Cambridge Archive Editions, 1989), 347; NARA, RG 469, ID 2990419, Entry P140, Box 1, Despatch 238, U.S. Consulate Kuwait to Department of State, February 10, 1958.

100. Beling, *Pan Arabism and Labor*, 15, 32–33, 69.

101. Robert Bianchi, "The Corporatization of the Egyptian Labor Movement," *Middle East Journal* 40, no. 3 (Summer, 1986): 429–44, 435.

102. ARC 106932, Inter-Departmental Memorandum Town Office to Atg. General Manager June 7, 1956; and Town Office, "Notes of a Conversation with Political Agent, Saturday, 9th June 1956." For more on Salama, see Bianchi, "The Corporatization of the Egyptian Labor Movement," 439; and Ellis Goldberg, *Tinker, Tailor, and Textile Worker: Class and Politics in Egypt, 1930–1952* (University of California Press, 1986), 131–38.

103. FO 371/120692, Letter British Embassy Brussels to A. Greenhough, May 29, 1956; and FO 371/114771, Letter M. T. Audsley to D. A. Praber, July 9, 1955.

104. FO 371/120692, Letter Embassy Brussels to A. Greenhough, May 29, 1956.

105. Schrijver, *Sovereignty over Natural Resources*; Garavini, *The Rise and Fall of OPEC*, 41–43; Santiago, *The Ecology of Oil*.

106. Garavini, *The Rise and Fall of OPEC*, chapter 1.

107. Abrahamian, *A History of Modern Iran*.

108. Parra, *Oil Politics*, 30.

109. ARC 106872, Memorandum E. H. O. Elkington to J. M. Pattinson, July 15, 1952, entitled "Kuwait Housing"; David H. Finnie, *Desert Enterprise: The Middle East Oil Industry in its Local Environment* (Harvard University Press, 1958), 83; FO 371/91260, Letter H. G. Jakins to Rupert Hay, October 16, 1951.

110. Gregory Brew, *Petroleum and Progress in Iran: Oil, Development, and the Cold War* (Cambridge University Press, 2022), 192.

111. Hay, "Impact of the Oil Industry on the Persian Gulf Shaikhdoms," 372; Administration Report of the Persian Gulf (1951)," in *Persian Gulf Administration Reports, Vol. XI* (Cambridge Archive Editions, 1989), 208.

112. ARC 30707, "New agreements were offered to two Stores Clerks and a Workshop foreman" and "Summary of Week ending 20 March 1942"; ARC 67329, Letter D. R. Hobson, October 17, 1945.

113. Steven G. Galpern, *Money, Oil, and Empire in the Middle East: Sterling and Postwar Imperialism, 1944–1971* (Cambridge University Press, 2009), chapter 4.

114. These are documented in Vitalis, *America's Kingdom*, 146–55; Matthiesen, "Migration, Minorities, and Radical Networks"; and Bsheer, "A Counter-Revolutionary State."

115. ARC 106992, Letter L. T. Jordan to C. A. P. Southwell, February 14, 1949.

116. Personal interviews, Hassan Falah, November 29, 2017, and January 9, 2018; "Hadith al-Nas," *al-Ra'id*, Issue 1, March 1952 (CRSK: Kuwait, 1999), 49; "Sharikat Aramco," *Sada al-Iman*, Issue 58, May 20, 1955; "Ba'i' Aramco fi al-Sa'udiyya," *al-Sha'b*, February 13, 1958.

117. "Idrab 'Ummal Aramco," *Sada al-Iman*, Issue 60, May 27, 1955; "Baqiyyat Aramco," *Sada al-Iman*, Issue 61, June 4, 1955.

118. "Hawla muhdir al-Ijtima' li-Tahqiq Matalib 'ummal Sharikat Aramco," *al-Qafila*, October 16, 1953; "Mihdar al-Ijtima' al-Ma'qud ma'a al-Hay'a al-Malakiyya," *Sawt al-Bahrain*, Issue 5, January–February 1954; and "Hawla Mihdar al-Ijtima' li-Tahqiq Matalib 'ummal Sharikat Aramco," *Sawt al-Bahrain*, Issue 6, February–March 1954; all in *Sawt al-Bahrayn*, Vol. 1 (Republished Beirut: al-Mu'assasa al-'Arabiyya li al-Dirasa wa al-Nashr, 2003).

119. Al-Bakir, *Min al-Bahrain ila al-Manfa Saint Helena*, 29.

120. FO 371/109945, Note J. W. Wall, October 3, 1954; "1953–54 Annual Report for Year 1954," in *The Bahrain Government Annual Reports, Vol. V: 1952–1956* (Cambridge Archive Editions, 1986), 160.

121. For a more detailed account see Fuccaro, *Histories of City and State*, 176–86.

122. Al-Bakir, *Min al-Bahrain ila al-Manfa Saint Helena*, 57–58.

123. A description can be found in FO 371/109815. See also al-Bakir, *Min al-Bahrain ila al-Manfa Saint Helena*, 66; and Saleh, "Labor, Nationalism, and Imperialism," 236–37.

124. This can be seen in FO 371/109815.

125. Al-Bakir, *Min al-Bahrain ila al-Manfa Saint Helena*, 85.

126. For more see Omar AlShehabi, "Political Movements in Bahrain Across the Long Twentieth Century (1900–2015)," in *The Oxford Handbook of Contemporary*

Middle-Eastern and North African History, ed. Amal Ghazal and Jens Hanssen (Oxford University Press, 2015).

127. "Administration Report of the Sharjah Political Agency (1950)," in *Persian Gulf Administration Reports, Vol. XI* (Cambridge Archive Editions, 1989), 162.

128. "Administration Report of the Muscat Political Agency (1950)," in *Persian Gulf Administration Reports, Vol. XI* (Cambridge Archive Editions, 1989), 191.

129. HQ BBME 0851, Confidential Letter Manager Dubai to H. Musker, June 25, 1956.

130. "Administration Report of the Persian Gulf (September 1952)," in *Persian Gulf Administration Reports, Vol. XI* (Cambridge Archive Editions, 1989), 334.

131. For more details see Crystal, *Oil and Politics in the Gulf*, 139–47.

132. FO 371/98465, "Record of a meeting with the Iraq Petroleum Company at the Foreign Office on the 21st March, 1952"; FO 371/127021, Letter D. C. Carden to Bernard Burrows, November 30, 1957; FO 371/140301, "Supplementary comments on Employment Conditions and Industrial Relations with the Qatar Petroleum Company," K. J. Hird, July 6, 1959.

133. FO 371/132917, Telegram B. Burrows to Foreign Office, August 21, 1958.

134. FO 371/132632, Telegrams Duncan to Foreign Office, August 23, 24, and 25, 1958.

135. "Administration Report of the Persian Gulf (February 1952)," in *Persian Gulf Administration Reports, Vol. XI* (Cambridge Archive Editions, 1989), 275; FO 371/98466, Letter W. R. Hay to R. F. G. Sarell, April 29, 1952; FO 371/120690, Letter C. Marshall to K. J. Hird, October 2, 1956; ARC 106950, Inter-Departmental Memorandum, J. G. Considine to General Manager, March 27, 1957.

136. FO 371/104337, Memorandum, "Cost of Living in Bahrain," July 20, 1953.

137. Personal interview with Hassan Falah and Qabalan ʿAjnan al-ʿAzimi, November 29, 2017, Kuwait.

138. FO 371/149090, J. C. B. Richmond, Enclosure to Kuwait Letter No. 1535/60 of March 2, 1960.

139. Al-ʿAjmi, *al-Haraka al-ʿUmmaliyya wa al-Naqabiyya fi al-Kuwait*, 58.

140. IOR/R/15/2/912, Express Letter Resident Gulf to Foreign New Delhi, November 21, 1946.

141. ARC 106992, Report J. G. Considine to General Manager Ahmadi, November 16, 1949.

142. Al-ʿAjmi, *al-Haraka al-ʿUmmaliyya wa al-Naqabiyya fi al-Kuwait*, 58–59.

143. Personal interview, Hussein Saqr, November 28, 2017; Saqr, *Rihla Dakhil al-Dhakira maʿ al-Haraka al-ʿUmaliyya al-Kuwaitiyya*, 25.

144. ARC 106992, Report J. G. Considine to General Manager Ahmadi, November 16, 1949.

145. ARC 106992, Report J. G. Considine to General Manager Ahmadi, November 16, 1949.

146. Saqr, *Rihla Dakhil al-Dhakira maʿ al-Haraka al-ʿUmaliyya al-Kuwaitiyya*, 25.

147. Al-ʿAjmi, *al-Haraka al-ʿUmmaliyya wa al-Naqabiyya fi al-Kuwait*, 60.

148. Saqr, *Rihla Dakhil al-Dhakira ma' al-Haraka al-'Umaliyya al-Kuwaitiyya*, 25.

149. "Takrim al-Ruwad al-'awa'il alladhina Qadu Idrab 'ummal al-KOC fi Shabat 1952," *al- Tali'a*, May 6, 1975, KU 7/kaf/660.

150. Al-Khatib and al-Najjar, *al-Kuwait, min al-Imara ila al-Dawla*, 159–60; al-'Ajmi, *al-Haraka al-'Ummaliyya wa al-Naqabiyya fi al-Kuwait*, 61–62.

151. "Bidayat al-Haraka al-'ummaliya wa al-Niqabiyya 'ala Lisan Ruwwadiha," *al-'Amil*, October 15, 1984, KU 10/zay/100.

152. Al-Khatib and al-Najjar, *al-Kuwait, min al-Imara ila al-Dawla*, 31.

153. Al-Khatib and al-Najjar, *al-Kuwait, min al-Imara ila al-Dawla*, 159; al-'Ajmi, *al-Haraka al-'Ummaliyya wa al-Naqabiyya fi al-Kuwait*, 60.

154. ARC 106889, D. A. Campbell, "Proclamation Signed by Shaikh Jabir al Ahmad," February 9, 1952.

155. "Takrim al-Ruwad al-'awa'il alladhina Qadu Idrab 'ummal al-KOC fi Shabat 1952."

156. Al-Khatib and al-Najjar, *al-Kuwait, min al-Imara ila al-Dawla*, 160.

157. Al-Khatib and al-Najjar, *al-Kuwait, min al-Imara ila al-Dawla*, 160; al-'Ajmi, *al-Haraka al-'Ummaliyya wa al-Naqabiyya fi al-Kuwait*, 62.

158. ARC 106889, Memorandum entitled "Indoctrination and Training," J. G. Considine to Assistant General Manager (Administration), February 12, 1952.

159. LAB 13/483, "Extract from confidential letter from the Residency at Bahrain dated 9th May 1952, addressed to Mr. Ross."

160. "Administration Report for April 1952," in *Persian Gulf Administration Reports, Vol. XI* (Cambridge Archive Editions, 1989), 298.

161. HSTD 1/1/2, "Minutes of an Extraordinary Meeting of the Development Board held in the Advisory Council Building on Saturday June 20th 1953."

162. HQ BBME 0858, Kuwait Confidential Letter, June 5, 1953.

163. LAB 13/1187, Despatch No. 5, G. W. Bell to Sir Bernard Burrows, March 18, 1956.

164. NARA, RG 469, ARC ID 2990419, Entry P 140, Box 2, Telegram John Foster Dulles to Baghdad, Basra, Beirut, Cairo, Damascus, Dhahran, Jidda, London, Tehran, and Kuwait, August 1, 1955.

165. Personal interview, Hussein al-Youha, Kuwait City, November 27, 2017; "Bidayat al-Haraka al-'ummaliya wa al-Niqabiyya 'ala Lisan Ruwwadiha"; al-Mdairis, "The Arab Nationalist Movement of Kuwait," 300, 304, 411.

166. Al-Mdairis, *al-Tawajjuhat al-Marksiyya al-Kuwaitiyya*, 20–21; AB 13/483, Despatch 40, D. A. Logan to B. A. B. Burrows, September 16, 1954.

167. ARC 106835, Letter L. T. Jordan to C. A. P. Southwell, September 29, 1956; ARC 106906, Letter L. T. Jordan to C. A. P. Southwell, October 30, 1956.

168. ARC 106962, Letter L. T. Jordan to C. A. P. Southwell, December 13, 1956; ARC 106962, Town Office, "Situation Report – December 11th to December 22nd, 1956."

169. ARC 106906, W. P. Doyle, "Notes on a Conversation with Shaikh Jabir al Ahmad held on 27th December 1956."

170. ARC 106962, Notes on conversation, E. A. V. de Candole with Bedr Abdulla Mulla, December 12, 1956.

171. NARA, RG 469, ID 2990419, Entry P140, Box 1, Despatch 136, U.S. Consulate Kuwait to Department of State, December 15, 1956.

172. ARC 108062, Memorandum, "Notes on Public Security Costs," and Letter L. T. Jordan, to C. A. P. Southwell, October 10, 1957.

173. ARC 106831, Memorandum M. L. B. Williamson, "Protective Security Arrangements," December 28, 1956.

174. Beling, *Pan Arabism and Labor*, 28–29.

175. Mitchell, *Carbon Democracy*, 145.

176. Al-Mdairis briefly notes press support in *al-Mujtama' al-Madani wa-al-Haraka al-Wataniyya fi al-Kuwait*, 116.

177. Al-Bakir, *Min al-Bahrain ila al-Manfa Saint Helena*, 23, 26.

178. Al-Bakir, *Min al-Bahrain ila al-Manfa Saint Helena*, 23, 26.

179. "Harakat al-'ummal fi Tunis," *al-Iman*, Issue 4, April 1953 (CRSK: Kuwait, 2011), 230.

180. "Akhbar Mahalliyya," *al-Iman*, Issue 11, January 1954 (CRSK: Kuwait, 2011), 165.

181. "Rukn al-'Ummal," *Sada al-Iman*, Issue 56, May 6, 1955.

182. "Rukn al-'Ummal," *Sada al-Iman*, Issue 51, April 1, 1955.

183. "Rukn al-'Ummal," *Sada al-Iman*, Issue 52, April 15, 1955, Issue 55, April 29, 1955; Issue 58, May 20, 1955.

184. "Rukn al-'Ummal," *Sada al-Iman*, Issue 47, March 4, 1955; "La Niqaba bidun Jimlat Ta'sisiyya," *Sada al-Iman*, Issue 48, March 11, 1955.

185. "Niqabat," *Sada al-Iman*, Issue 46, February 25, 1955.

186. "Rukn al-'Ummal," *Sada al-Iman*, Issue 44, February 11, 1955.

187. "Rukn al-'Ummal," *Sada al-Iman*, Issue 62, June 11, 1955.

188. "Farashu al-Madaris," *Sada al-Iman*, Issue 61, June 4, 1955.

189. "Rukn al-'Ummal," *Sada al-Iman*, Issue 53, April 15, 1955; Issue 56, May 6, 1955.

190. "al-'ummal al-'arab," *Sada al-Iman*, Issue 62, June 11, 1955.

191. "Kayfa Ansha'at al-Niqaba," *Sada al-Iman*, Issue 57, May 13, 1955.

192. "Barid al-Qurra'," *al-Fajr*, Issue 14, May 4, 1955; "Ma'a al-Sha'b," *al-Sha'b*, Issue 60, January 22, 1959.

193. "Khitab min Mudir Da'irat Shu'un al-Muwazzafin," *al-Sha'b*, Issue 45, September 18, 1958.

194. "Ma Nurid min Sharikat al-Naft," *al-Ba'tha*, January 15, 1952; "Shay' min al-Akhbar," *al-Iman*, Issue 10, December 1953 (CRSK: Kuwait, 2011), 699.

195. "Brafu," *al-Sha'b*, Issue 50, October 23, 1958; "Barid al-Qurra',"*al-Fajr*, Issue 14, 4 May 1955; "Madha Turid Sharikat al-Naft?" *Al-Sha'b*, Issue 44, 11 September 1958; "Ma'a al-Sha'b," *al-Sha'b*, September 18, 1958.

196. "Mantiq Sharikat al-Naft," *al-Sha'b*, September 18, 1958.

197. FO 371/132600, "Charlatanism of K.O.C.," *al-Fajr*, September 23, 1958. Translation from FO 371/132600.

198. "Ma'a al-Sha'b," *al-Sha'b*, Issue 45, September 18, 1958; "Jawla fi al-Kuwait," *al-Sha'b*, Issue 43, September 4, 1958.

199. "Ilayka ya . . . Sharikat Naft al-Kuwait!" *Al-Sha'b*, Issue 40, August 14, 1958.

200. "Naftuna wa ba'd Mu'athiratih," *al-Ra'id*, Issue 2, April 1952 (CRSK: Kuwait, 1999), 137; "Khawatir Mushtaraka," *al-Ra'id*, Issue 3, May 1952 (CRSK: Kuwait, 1999), 269.

201. "Mufawadat al-Naft," *Sada al-Iman*, Issue 57, May 13, 1955; "al-Muwazzafun al-Kuwaitiyyun Mudtahadun fi Sharikat al-Naft al-Ajnabiyya," *Sada al-Iman*, Issue 58, May 20, 1955.

202. FO 1016/431, Translation of extracts from *Sada al-Iman*, No. 54, April 22, 1955.

203. "Kifaka ya Sharikat al-Naft," *al-Sha'b*, Issue 55, November 27, 1958; "Sharikat al-Naft Hukuma Mustaqilla," *al-Sha'b*, Issue 46, September 25, 1958.

204. "Ummaluna fi Sharikat al-Naft," *Sada al-Iman*, Issue 60, May 27, 1955.

205. "al-Sha'b Yurid Ighla' al-Mu'ahada la Ta'diliha," *al-Sha'b*, Issue 54, November 20, 1958.

206. "La Imtiyaz bal Ta'mim wa Tasni'," *al-Sha'b*, Issue 5, January 2, 1958.

207. "La Imtiyaz bal Ta'mim wa Tasni'," *al-Sha'b*, Issue 5, January 2, 1958.

208. NARA, RG 469, ID 2990419, Entry P140, Box 1, Despatch 261 US Consulate Kuwait to Department of State, February 28, 1958.

209. "al-Isti'mar . . . wa al-Tamayyuz al-'usuri," *al-Sha'b*, Issue 46, September 25, 1958.

210. "Kwame Nkrumah Yudli bi-Hadith ila *al-Sha'b*," *al-Sha'b*, Issue 30, June 26, 1958.

211. Dietrich, *Oil Revolution*, 67.

212. ARC 106987, Letter Shaikh Jabir al-Ahmad to C. A. P. Southwell, January 6, 1958.

213. FO 371/132600, Memorandum D. M. H. Riches, October 16, 1958.

214. FO 371/132600, Letter D. J. McCarthy to H. W. King, December 4, 1958.

215. ARC 107003, "Work Stoppage and Demonstration, 16th April 1963: Report and Recommendations, Part 1."

216. NARA, RG 469, ID 2990419, Entry P140, Box 1, Despatch 167, U.S. Consulate Kuwait to the Department of State, December 10, 1957.

217. NARA, RG 469, ID 2990419, Entry P140, Box 1, Despatch 1, U.S. Consulate Kuwait to Department of State, July 2, 1957; Despatch 179, U.S. Consulate Kuwait to Department of State, January 3, 1959.

218. FO 1016/553, Letter E. F. Given to A. K. Rothnie, December 28, 1957.

219. NARA, RG 469, ID 2990419, Entry P140, Box 1, Despatch 218, U.S. Consulate Kuwait to Department of State, February 16, 1959.

220. For more on the town office, see ARC 108134.

221. See ARC 106863, including Memorandum for File, L. T. Jordan, October 29, 1957; and Letter, L. T. Jordan to C. A. P. Southwell, April 16, 1957; ARC 106863, Inter-Departmental Memorandum, Ibrahim Rizq to E. A. V. de Candole, April 3, 1957.

222. Vitalis, *America's Kingdom*, 125.

223. "The Ian Fleming Collection of 19th–20th Century Source Material Concerning Western Civilization together with the Originals of the James Bond-007 Tales,"

Lilly Library, Indiana University Bloomington, https://liblilly.sitehost.iu.edu/etexts/fleming/index.shtml, visited May 14, 2025.

224. Fuccaro, *Histories of City and State*, 186.

225. For a much more detailed account of these strikes, see Boodrookas, "The Making of a Migrant Working Class," 235–56.

226. ARC 106992; NAI, EA, Emigration, 1948, Nos. 22–11; NAI, EA, Arab World & Turkey, 1948, Nos. 17(11), Letter Embassy of India, Tehran to Minister of External Affairs and Commonwealth Relations, January 18, 1948; Wright, *Unruly Labor*, chapter 2.

227. Andrea Wright, "Shifting Solidarities: Strikes, Indian Labour and the Arabian Sea Oil Industry, 1946–1953," in *Life Worlds of Middle Eastern Oil: Histories and Ethnographies Oil*, ed. Nelida Fuccaro and Mandana Limbert (Edinburgh University Press, 2023), 251–74, 252; Wright, *Unruly Labor*, chapters 2 and 3. See also Sugata Bose, *A Hundred Horizons: The Indian Ocean in the Age of Global Empire* (Harvard University Press, 2006), 165.

228. FO 371/109947, T. N. Smith, "Report on the Strike of Indian and Pakistani Artisans at Jewan Camp, Kuwait."

229. FO 371/109947, T. N. Smith, "Report on the Strike of Indian and Pakistani Artisans at Jewan Camp, Kuwait."

230. This and other accounts contradict Wright's argument that "labor solidarities increasingly fragmented along national lines" (*Unruly Labor*, 65).

231. "Shay' min al-Akhbar," *al-Iman*, Issue 10, December 1953 (CRSK: Kuwait, 2011), 700.

232. NAI, EA, Emigration, 1948, Nos. 22–11, Note S. K. Chowdhry, October 25, 1948.

233. Hassan Falah, personal interview, November 29, 2017.

234. Qabalan ʿAjnan al-ʿAzimi, personal interview, November 29, 2017.

235. FO 371/149101, Letter Agency Kuwait to Residency Bahrain, February 17, 1960.

Chapter 4

1. NAI, EA, AW&T, 1948, Nos.: 17(11), C. S. Jha, "Report on the Goodwill Mission of to the Persian Gulf," February 28, 1949.

2. William Roger Louis, *The British Empire in the Middle East: Arab Nationalism, The United States, and Postwar Imperialism* (Oxford University Press, 1984), 20.

3. Vitalis, *America's Kingdom*, 26; Bsheer, "A Counter-Revolutionary State"; Ehsani, "The Social History of Labor in the Iranian Oil Industry"; Wright, *Unruly Labor.*

4. Michael Mann, "The Autonomous Power of the State: Its Origins, Mechanisms and Results," *European Journal of Sociology* 25, no. 2 (1984): 185–213, 189.

5. Vitalis, *America's Kingdom*; Ehsani, "The Social History of Labor in the Iranian Oil Industry"; Wright, *Unruly Labor.*

6. Wright makes a similar argument in the context of Abu Dhabi and Qatar in the 1960s in "Migratory Pipelines," 139–49, and more broadly in *Unruly Labor*, chapter 5. This chapter is based on Boodrookas, "The Making of a Migrant Working Class," chapter 7, which is the first comprehensive history of Gulf labor law. Its arguments

significantly differ from those in *Unruly Labor*, which discusses the Bahrain labor law but focuses on the role of corporate and imperial officials, stresses the importance of U.S. precedent, and does not cite either Arabic-language source material or this author's dissertation.

7. Cooper, *Decolonization and African Society*, Introduction.

8. This resembles British attempts to "de-politicize" labor in Egypt. See Beinin and Lockman, *Workers on the Nile*, 7, and chapter 9; Bianchi, "The Corporatization of the Egyptian Labor Movement"; and Goldberg, *Tinker, Tailor, and Textile Worker*.

9. This chapter therefore builds on the arguments of Brown, *The Rule of Law in the Arab World*, chapter 5.

10. This argument builds on Frederick Cooper, *Colonialism in Question: Theory, Knowledge, History* (University of California Press, 2005), 230.

11. FO 371/109946, Letter J. C. Moberly to M. S. Buckmaster, December 2, 1954; al-ʿAjmi, *al-Haraka al-ʿUmmaliyya wa al-Naqabiyya fi al-Kuwait*, 68–82; Hijji, *Kuwait and the Sea*, 132.

12. Personal interview, Hussein Saqr, November 28, 2017.

13. FO 371/98467, Note C. M. Rose, "Kuwait Oil Company Labour Relations," February 12, 1952.

14. FO 371/98467, Note C. M. Rose, "Kuwait Oil Company Labour Relations," February 12, 1952.

15. ARC 106985, Memorandum Labour Superintendent Kuwait to Assistant General Manager, March 9, 1949; NARA, RG 469, ID 2990419, Entry P140, Box 1, Despatch 193 US Consulate Kuwait to Department of State, December 31, 1957.

16. ARC 106992, Letter L. T. Jordan to C. A. P. Southwell, October 24, 1949.

17. "1951–52 Annual Report for Year 1371," in *The Bahrain Government Annual Reports, Vol. IV: 1947–1952* (Cambridge Archive Editions, 1986), 437, 445.

18. "al-Muʿahada al-Kuwaitiyya wa al-Majlis al-Tashriʿi wa al-Shaykh Jabir al-Ahmad Al Sabah!" *Al-Shaʿb*, Issue 56, Year 2, December 25, 1958.

19. "Annual Report for Year 1955," in *The Bahrain Government Annual Reports, Vol. V: 1952–1956* (Cambridge Archive Editions, 1986), 326.

20. There are numerous examples in Beinin and Lockman, *Workers on the Nile*.

21. NARA, RG 469, ID 2990419, Entry P140, Box 1, Despatch 101 U.S. Consulate Kuwait to Department of State, September 1, 1959.

22. ARC 106992, Letter L. T. Jordan to C. A. P. Southwell, October 24, 1949.

23. ARC 106992, Report J. G. Considine to General Manager Ahmadi, November 16, 1949.

24. Saleh, "Labor, nationalism, and imperialism in eastern Arabia," 240–43.

25. LAB 13/1129, Letter M. T. Audsley to A. Greenhough, June 7, 1955.

26. Beinin and Lockman, *Workers on the Nile*, 304.

27. FO 371/74942, M. T. Audsley, "Report on visit to Bahrain, January/February, 1949," April 22, 1949.

28. FO 371/74942, M. T. Audsley, "Report on visit to Bahrain, January/February, 1949," April 22, 1949.

29. FO 371/74942, M. T. Audsley, "Report on visit to Bahrain, January/February, 1949," April 22, 1949.

30. "Intisar al-Sha'b al-'Arabi fi al-Bahrain," *Sada al-Iman*, Issue 57, Year 2, May 13, 1955.

31. LAB 13/1129, Letter M. T. Audsley to A. Greenhough, Overseas Department, June 7, 1955.

32. These notes are preserved as an enclosure to FO 371/114771, Letter M. T. Audsley to A. Greenhough, July 2, 1955.

33. LAB 13/1129, Despatch C. A. Gault to B. A. B. Burrows, April 28, 1955.

34. Beinin and Lockman, *Workers on the Nile*, 304.

35. LAB 13/1157, Letter J. K. Hird to C. Wilson, November 9, 1956.

36. LAB 13/1157, Letter C. Marshall to K. J. Hird, June 23, 1956; D. C. Watt, "Labor Relations and Trades Unionism in Aden, 1952–1960," *Middle East Journal* 16, no. 4 (Autumn 1962): 443–56.

37. LAB 13/1157, Letter C. Marshall to K. J. Hird, June 23, 1956; Watt, "Labor Relations and Trades Unionism in Aden, 1952–1960," 443–56.

38. FO 371/120689, Letter D. M. H. Riches to C. A. Gault, June 18, 1956. Andrea Wright views the U.S. role as much more pivotal in *Unruly Labor*, chapter 5; I also discuss this point in "The Making of a Migrant Working Class," 382.

39. FO 371/120689, "Minutes of a meeting with Caltex at the Foreign Office," July 17, 1956.

40. FO 371/120689, "Minutes of a meeting with Caltex at the Foreign Office," July 17, 1956; FO 371/120689, Note A. C. I. Samuel, June 15, 1956.

41. See FO 371/120689, Minutes of the 49th Meeting of the Labour Law Advisory Committee, April 29, 1956.

42. LAB 13/1157, Letter, C. Marshall to K. J. Hird, June 23, 1956; LAB 13/1157, Telegram B. Burrows to Foreign Office, June 1, 1956.

43. FO 371/120688, Minutes of the 46th Meeting of the Labour Law Advisory Committee, April 8, 1956; Minutes of the 48th Meeting of the Labour Law Advisory Committee, April 22, 1956; Minutes of the 49th Meeting of the Labour Law Advisory Committee, April 29, 1956.

44. LAB 13/1129, Letter M. T. Audsley to A. Greenhough, June 7, 1955; FO 371/120689, Note, A. C. I. Samuel, June 15, 1956.

45. FO 371/120689, Minutes of the 56th Meeting of the Labour Law Advisory Committee, July 8, 1956.

46. FO 371/120688, Minutes of the 46th Meeting of the Labour Law Advisory Committee, April 8, 1956.

47. FO 371/120688, Minutes of the 46th Meeting of the Labour Law Advisory Committee, April 8, 1956.

48. FO 371/120688, Minutes of the 48th Meeting of the Labour Law Advisory Committee, April 22, 1956, and Minutes of the 49th Meeting of the Labour Law Advisory Committee, April 29, 1956.

49. FO 371/120687, Minutes of the 42nd Meeting of the Labour Law Advisory Committee, March 4, 1956.

50. FO 371/120688, Minutes of the 48th Meeting of the Labour Law Advisory Committee, April 22, 1956.

51. FO 371/120689, Gault Bahrain to Foreign Office, July 25, 1956.

52. Beling, *Pan Arabism and Labor*, 35.

53. FO 371/120690, Labour Law Advisory Committee, Cover letter accompanying draft Bahrain Labour Law, October 10, 1956.

54. FO 371/120690, Labour Law Advisory Committee, Cover letter accompanying draft Bahrain Labour Law, October 10, 1956.

55. FO 371/120690, Letter B. A. B. Burrows to A. R. Walmsley, September 4, 1956.

56. FO 371/120690, Labour Law Advisory Committee, Cover letter accompanying draft Bahrain Labour Law, October 10, 1956.

57. Saleh, "Labor, Nationalism, and Imperialism in Eastern Arabia," 250–51.

58. FO 371/127018, Note G. F. Blumer, December 6, 1957.

59. FO 371/127018, Letter C. Marshall to J. F. Walker, November 14, 1957.

60. FO 371/127015, R. Brash to E. F. Given, July 12, 1957.

61. FO 371/127015, Minutes of the 62nd meeting of the Labour Law Advisory Committee, April 21, 1957; FO 371/127017, Minutes of the 72nd Meeting of the Labour Law Advisory Committee, September 13, 1957.

62. FO 371/127018, "Arab Gulf and South" program, *Voice of the Arabs*, October 19, 1957, 4:30 p.m.

63. FO 371/127018, Note G. F. Blumer, January 8, 1958.

64. FO 371/132914, Letter B. A. B. Burrows to Selwyn Lloyd, February 18, 1958.

65. FO 371/149179, Report, I. Dennys, "Labour Inspection in the Territory of Bahrain, Arabian Gulf," 1960.

66. FO 371/149179, Report, I. Dennys, "Labour Inspection in the Territory of Bahrain, Arabian Gulf," 1960.

67. FO 371/140300, Letter K. J. Hird to C. Marshall, May 22, 1959.

68. FO 371/140300, Letter E. F. Given to A. R. Walmsley, July 1, 1959.

69. LAB 13/1597, Letter P. C. D. Archer to A. G. Wallis, February 8, 1962; FO 371/149097, Letter G. H. Middleton to Selwyn Lloyd, January 9, 1960.

70. FO 371/98467, Minute dated February 29, 1952.

71. FO 371/109946, Note C. H. Haines, March 1, 1954.

72. FO 371/98467, Minute dated February 29, 1952.

73. "Matalib ʿAdila," *Sada al-Iman*, Issue 56, May 6, 1955.

74. "Shayʾ min al-Akhbar," *al-Iman*, Issue 4, April 1953 (CRSK: Kuwait, 2011), 284.

75. HSTD 1/2/2, Memorandum from Controller of Development to Finance Committee, January 2, 1954.

76. FO 371/109947, Letter C. J. Pelly to B. A. B. Burrows, May 25, 1954.

77. ARC 106831, Confidential Letter J. G. Considine to Ag. General Manager, August 9, 1956.

78. “Intisar al-Sha'b al-'Arabi fi al-Bahrain,” *Sada al-Iman*, Issue 57, May 13, 1955.

79. Al-Bakir, *Min al-Bahrain ila al-Manfa Saint Helena*, 172.

80. NARA, RG 469, ID 2990419, Entry P140, Box 1, Despatch 164, “Economic Review of the Year 1954,” U.S. Consulate Kuwait to Department of State, February 6, 1955.

81. NARA, RG 469, ID 2990419, Entry P 140, Box 2, Despatch 279, U.S. Consulate Kuwait to Department of State, April 19, 1954.

82. Al-Mdairis, “The Arab Nationalist Movement,” 296.

83. Jill Crystal makes a similar point when discussing Qatar in *Oil and Politics in the Gulf*, 139–47.

84. 'Izz al-Din, *'Ummal al-Kuwait min al-Lu'lu' ila al-Batrul*, 13.

85. LAB 13/1157, Letter J. K. Hird to C. Wilson, November 9, 1956.

86. LAB 13/483, Letter C. E. Kilvington to C. T. E. Ewart-Biggs, July 2, 1954, and Letter Embassy Cairo to W. Lawer, June 18, 1954.

87. HSTD 1/1/1, Minutes of an Extraordinary Meeting of the Development Board held in the Advisory Council Building on Saturday June 20, 1953; al-'Ajmi, *al-Haraka al-'Ummaliyya wa al-Naqabiyya fi al-Kuwait*, 64.

88. 'Izz al-Din, *'Ummal al-Kuwait min al-Lu'lu' ila al-Batrul*, 14.

89. 'Izz al-Din, *'Ummal al-Kuwait min al-Lu'lu' ila al-Batrul*, 14.

90. Saqr, *Rihla Dakhil al-Dhakira ma' al-Haraka al-'Umaliyya al-Kuwaitiyya*, 26.

91. LAB 13/1187, Despatch G. W. Bell to Bernard Burrows, March 18, 1956.

92. 'Izz al-Din, *'Ummal al-Kuwait min al-Lu'lu' ila al-Batrul*, 15.

93. NARA, RG 469, ID 2990419, Entry P140, Box 1, Despatch 205, “Economic Summary of the Year 1958,” U.S. Consulate Kuwait to Department of State, February 1, 1959.

94. FO 1016/553, G. W. Bell, “Kuwait Diary No. 5, covering the period April 25 to May 29, 1957,” May 29, 1957.

95. “Hussain Al-Youha,” AUK Oral History, accessed May 24, 2024, https://oralhistory.auk.edu.kw/items/show/4.

96. Al-Shalal, “The Trade Union Movement in the State of Kuwait,” 159.

97. “Administration Report of the Political Residency (1955),” in *Persian Gulf Administration Reports, Vol. XI* (Cambridge Archive Editions, 1989), 486.

98. LAB 13/1187, Despatch G. W. Bell to Bernard Burrows, March 18, 1956.

99. NARA, RG 469, ID 2990419, Entry P140, Box 1, Despatch 167, U.S. Consulate Kuwait to Department of State, January 31, 1957.

100. “Hadith al-Nas,” *al- Ra'id*, Issue 4, May 1952 (CRSK: Kuwait, 1999), 339.

101. “Ahadith al-Suq,” *al-Iman*, Issue 14, April 1954 (CRSK: Kuwait, 2011), 388; “Hal Sami't?” *Al-Sha'b*, Issue 52, November 6, 1958.

102. For instance, “al-Tafkir al-Ihsa'i,” *al-Iman*, Issue 11, January 1954 (CRSK: Kuwait, 2011), 123.

103. “al-Kadir al-Habs,” *Sada al-Iman*, Issue 54, April 22, 1955.

104. “Ahadith al-Suq,” *al-Iman*, Issue 15, May 1954 (CRSK: Kuwait, 2011), 475.

105. Saqr, *Rihla Dakhil al-Dhakira ma' al-Haraka al-'Umaliyya al-Kuwaitiyya*, 27.

106. NARA, RG 469, ID 2990419, Entry P140, Box 1, "Economic Summary of the Year 1957," U.S. Consulate Kuwait to Department of State, February 1, 1958.

107. Saqr, *Rihla Dakhil al-Dhakira ma' al-Haraka al-'Umaliyya al-Kuwaitiyya*, 28.

108. Saqr, *Rihla Dakhil al-Dhakira ma' al-Haraka al-'Umaliyya al-Kuwaitiyya*, 28.

109. "al-Thaqafa al-'ummaliyya: Nash'atuha – Tatawwuruha – Ahdafuha," *al-Risella*, July 15, 1973, KU 10/ba/030; al-Asbahi, *al-Haraka al-Niqabiyya al-Kuwaitiyya*, 17; Kuwait Trade Union Federation, *Insha' Ma'ahid al-Thaqafiyya al-'ummalliyya fi al-Kuwait* (The Founding of the Workers' Culture Center in Kuwait) (Kuwait: Kuwait Trade Union Federation Press, 1998).

110. LAB 13/1187, Despatch G. W. Bell to Bernard Burrows, March 18, 1956.

111. ARC 106784, Chief Accountant KOC, Meeting Agenda and Notes, November 15, 1948.

112. FO 371/98432, Minutes, Kuwait Oil Company Monthly Liaison Meeting No. 1, November 7, 1952.

113. FO 371/98432, Minutes, Kuwait Oil Company Monthly Liaison Meeting No. 1, November 7, 1952.

114. ARC 106831, Letters L. T. Jordan to C. A. P. Southwell, November 16 and 18, 1953.

115. ARC 108062, Note on "Transfer of Security," L. T. Jordan to C. A. P. Southwell, June 29, 1954; ARC 106835, Letter E. Boaden to C. A. P. Southwell, October 4, 1954.

116. Crystal, "Public Order and Authority: Policing Kuwait."

117. NARA, RG 469, ID 2990419, Entry P140, Box 1, Despatch 193 U.S. Consulate Kuwait to Department of State, December 31, 1957; and NARA, RG 469, ID 2990419, Entry P140, Box 1, Despatch 227, "Economic Summary of the Year 1957," U.S. Consulate Kuwait to Department of State, February 1, 1958.

118. NARA, RG 469, ID 2990419, Entry P140, Box 1, Despatch U.S. Consulate Kuwait to Department of State, December 10, 1957.

119. FO 371/132919, Letter S. L. Egerton to W. J. Adams, August 11, 1958; Letter J. F. Walker to S. L. Eagerton, August 29, 1958.

120. FO 371/127020, Letter K. J. Hird to G. W. Bell, July 8, 1957.

121. FO 371/132919, Letter J. F. Walker to S. L. Eagerton, August 29, 1958.

122. FO 371/109810, Letter C. T. E. Ewart-Biggs to R. W. Bailey, December 3, 1954.

123. FO 371/114588, C. J. Pelly to B. A. B. Burrows, June 13, 1955; B. A. B. Burrows to C. J. Pelly, May 31, 1955.

124. FO 1016/553, Letter B. A. B. Burrows to H. Beeley, March 22, 1957.

125. ARC 106831, Letter L. T. Jordan to C. A. P. Southwell, July 16, 1957.

126. FO 371/148911, Letter J. C. B. Richmond to the Earl of Home, August 14, 1960; al-Khatib and al-Najjar, *al-Kuwait, min al-Imara ila al-Dawla*, 97; al-Mdairis, "The Arab Nationalist Movement of Kuwait," 210–12; Simon Smith, *Kuwait 1950–1965: Britain, the al-Sabah, and Oil* (Oxford University Press, 1999), 97; Al-Nakib, *Kuwait Transformed*, 168.

127. Beinin and Lockman, *Workers on the Nile*, 20. The only extant biographiy of 'Izz al-Din is Salah al-Ansari, "Amin 'Izz al-Din: Mu'arrikh al-Haraka al-Niqabiyya

al-Misriyya" (Historian of the Egyptian Trade Union Movement), *Towards Arab Trade Union Unity*, September 19, 2017, https://arabtradeunionsunity.wordpress.com/2017/09/19. Accessed November 15, 2019.

128. FO 371/127020, Letter K. J Hird to G. W. Bell, July 8, 1957.

129. FO 371/114771, Letter M. T. Audsley to A. Greenhough, July 2, 1955.

130. FO 371/114771, Letter M. T. Audsley to A. Greenhough, July 2, 1955.

131. FO 371/114771, Letter M. T. Audsley to C. Marshall, June 25, 1955.

132. FO 371/114771, Letter M. T. Audsley to A. Greenhough, July 2, 1955.

133. ʿIzz al-Din, *ʿUmmal al-Kuwait min al-Luʾluʾ ila al-Batrul*, Preface.

134. ʿIzz al-Din, *ʿUmmal al-Kuwait min al-Luʾluʾ ila al-Batrul*, Introduction, 3.

135. ʿIzz al-Din, *ʿUmmal al-Kuwait min al-Luʾluʾ ila al-Batrul*, Introduction, 3.

136. ʿIzz al-Din, *ʿUmmal al-Kuwait min al-Luʾluʾ ila al-Batrul*, 6, 7.

137. ʿIzz al-Din, *ʿUmmal al-Kuwait min al-Luʾluʾ ila al-Batrul*, 9, 11.

138. ʿIzz al-Din, *ʿUmmal al-Kuwait min al-Luʾluʾ ila al-Batrul*, 11.

139. ʿIzz al-Din, *ʿUmmal al-Kuwait min al-Luʾluʾ ila al-Batrul*, 11, 12.

140. It is affirmed in Amin ʿIzz al-Din, "al-Hurriyyat al-Niqabiyya fi al-Kuwait," *al-Kuwait*, June 1, 1973, KU 10/zay/100.

141. LAB 13/1187, Letter A. K. Rothnie to A. Greenhough, March 24, 1956.

142. FO 371/127020, Letter C. Marshall to A. K. Rothnie, November 27, 1957.

143. FO 371/132919, Letter C. Marshall to A. K. Rothnie, March 28, 1958.

144. FO 371/132919, Letter C. Marshall to A. K. Rothnie, March 28, 1958; LAB 13/1187, Letter K. J. Hind to Wallis, March 31, 1959.

145. ARC 106982, Translation, "Draft Kuwaiti Labour Law, Private Employment, Non-Governmental Labour Relations," April 7, 1958.

146. FO 371/132919, Letter C. Marshall to A. K. Rothnie, March 28, 1958.

147. FO 371/114771, Letter M. T. Audsley to A. Greenhough, July 2, 1955.

148. FO 371/132914, Letter B. A. B. Burrows to Selwyn Lloyd, February 18, 1958.

149. FO 371/132914, Letter B. A. B. Burrows to Selwyn Lloyd, February 18, 1958.

150. FO 371/132914, Letter B. A. B. Burrows to Selwyn Lloyd, February 18, 1958.

151. FO 371/140274, Note, C. H. Haines, June 25, 1959.

152. ARC 106982, Translation, "Draft Kuwaiti Labour Law, Private Employment, Non-Governmental Labour Relations," April 7, 1958.

153. Marsha Pripstein Posusney, *Labor and the State in Egypt: Workers, Unions, and Economic Restructuring* (Columbia University Press, 1997), 47; Beinin and Lockman, *Workers on the Nile*, 432–35.

154. "Decree No. 43/1960 on Labour Law in the Public Sector," *al-Kuwait al-Yawm*, November 13, 1960.

155. FO 371/132919, Telegram 641, Foreign Office to Kuwait, August 28, 1958.

156. LAB 13/1187, Letter British Embassy Beirut to Treganowan, March 28, 1959.

157. LAB 13/1187, Letter British Embassy Beirut to Treganowan, March 28, 1959.

158. LAB 13/1187, "SOME COMMENTS ON THE PROVISIONS OF THE KUWAIT LABOUR LAW," Kuwait Oil Company, Ahmadi, March 30, 1959.

159. ARC 106983, Memorandum J. G. Considine to Ag. General Manager, July 7, 1958.

160. ARC 106983.

161. FO 371/132919, Note, C. H. Haines, August 21, 1958.

162. ARC 106983, Memorandum J. G. Considine to Ag. General Manager, July 7, 1958.

163. FO 371/132919, Letter S. L. Egerton to W. J. Adams, August 11, 1958; ARC 106983, Memorandum J. G. Considine to Ag. General Manager, July 7, 1958.

164. Beling, *Pan Arabism and Labor*, 36.

165. ARC 106982, Memorandum J. G. Considine to General Manager, June 3, 1958.

166. ARC 106982, Memorandum J. G. Considine to General Manager, June 3, 1958.

167. ARC 106983, "Notes of the meeting held at the Department of Social Affairs between Company and Social Affairs Department Representatives to Discuss 'The Labour Law,'" Translation by Ebrahim Eskandar, June 18, 1958.

168. ARC 106983, "Notes of the meeting held at the Department of Social Affairs between Company and Social Affairs Department Representatives to Discuss 'The Labour Law,'" Translation by Ebrahim Eskandar, June 18, 1958.

169. ARC 106982, Memorandum J. G. Considine to General Manager, June 3, 1958.

170. Al-Khatib and al-Najjar, *al-Kuwait, min al-Imara ila al-Dawla*, 148–49.

171. Al-Mdairis, "The Arab Nationalist Movement of Kuwait," 420.

172. This is extensively discussed in Beinin and Lockman, *Workers on the Nile*. See also Cooper, *Colonialism in Question*, chapter 7.

173. FO 371/140303, Letter Agency Kuwait to Arabian Department Foreign Office, April 19, 1959.

174. FO 371/140303, Letter Agency Kuwait to Arabian Department Foreign Office, April 19, 1959.

175. FO 371/140303, Letter Agency Kuwait to Arabian Department Foreign Office, April 19, 1959.

176. FO 371/148912, Letter J. C. B. Richmond to the Earl of Home, October 18, 1960.

177. NARA, RG 0469, Entry P 205, Container 1, Despatch 245, U.S. Consulate Kuwait to Department of State, March 23, 1959.

178. NARA, RG 469, ID 2990419, Entry P140, Box 1, Despatch 162, U.S. Consulate Kuwait to Department of State, November 25, 1959.

179. NARA, RG 469, ID 2990419, Entry P140, Box 1, Despatch 237, "Economic Summary of the Year 1959," U.S. Consulate Kuwait to Department of State, February 1, 1960.

180. FO 371/149115, Letter Agency Kuwait to Residency Bahrain, December, 29 1959.

181. FO 371/149101, Kuwait Nationality Law, Emiri Decree No. 15 of 1959; Beaugrand, *Stateless in the Gulf*, 76; Al-Nakib, *Kuwait Transformed*, 94–95.

182. FO 371/149101, Kuwait Nationality Law, Emiri Decree No. 15 of 1959; Beaugrand, *Stateless in the Gulf*, 76; Al-Nakib, *Kuwait Transformed*, 94–95.

183. Mohammad S. Al Haddad, "The Effect of Detribalization and Sedentarization on the Socio-economic Structure of the Tribes of the Arabian Peninsula: Ajman Tribes as a Case Study" (PhD diss., University of Kansas, 1981), 108.

184. "Iʿlan," *Kuwait al-Yawm*, July 15, 1962, KU 3/zay/400.

185. Beaugrand, *Stateless in the Gulf*, 70.

186. FO 371/148911, Letter J. C. B. Richmond to the Earl of Home, August 14, 1960.

187. NARA, RG 0469, Entry P 205, Container 1, Dispatch 24, US Consulate Kuwait to Department of State, July 15, 1959.

188. Atyab Al-Shatti, "Administrative Deportation," *Kuwait Times*, June 18, 2022.

189. FO 371/149115, "Passport Regulations," Emiri Decree No. 16 of 1959, December 5, 1959.

190. FO 371/140081, Telegram 88, Halford to Foreign Office, February 3, 1959; Telegram 91, Halford to Foreign Office, February 5, 1959.

191. FO 371/140083, Telegram 317, Kuwait to Foreign Office, May 17, 1959.

192. FO 371/140083, Telegram 318, Kuwait to Foreign Office, May 18, 1959.

193. Al-Moosa, "The Arab Nationalist Movement of Kuwait," 200.

194. FO 371/148912, Letter R. A. Beaumont to J. C. B. Richmond, September 28, 1960.

195. Beaugrand, *Stateless in the Gulf.*

196. Al Moosa, *Bedouin and Shanty Settlements*, 992.

197. Cooper, *Citizenship, Inequality, and Difference*, 25.

Chapter 5

1. The debate is traced in "Majlis al-Umma," *al-Tali'a*, Issue 87, June 24, 1964; "Majlis al-Umma," *al-Tali'a*, Issue 89, July 8, 1964; and ARC 108134, "Report for the Period Ending 24th March 1963." The only scholarly mentions are al-'Ajmi, *al-Haraka al-'Ummaliyya wa al-Naqabiyya fi al-Kuwait*, 85; and al-Mdairis, "The Arab Nationalist Movement," 301 and *al-Mujtama' al-Madani wa-al-Haraka al-Wataniyya fi al-Kuwait*, 126.

2. "Majlis al-Umma," *al-Tali'a*, Issue 87, June 24, 1964; "Majlis al-Umma," *al-Tali'a*, Issue 89, July 8, 1964.

3. Al-Asbahi, *al-Haraka al-Niqabiyya al-Kuwaitiyya*, 30; al-'Ajmi, *al-Haraka al-'Ummaliyya wa al-Naqabiyya fi al-Kuwait*, 85.

4. Al-Khatib and al-Najjar, *al-Kuwait, min al-Imara ila al-Dawla*, 158.

5. For a contemporary analysis of a comparable struggle, see Mikdashi, *Sextarianism*, chapter 1.

6. For more on the regional implications of the coup, see Takriti, "Colonial Coups and the War on Popular Sovereignty."

7. "Hal Nahnu Mustaqillun Haqqan?" *Al-Tali'a*, Issue 413, February 24, 1973.

8. Cooper, *Colonialism in Question*, 230.

9. Julian Go, "Reverberations of Empire: How the Colonial Past Shapes the Present," *Social Science History* 48 (2023): 1–18, 6.

10. Al-Khatib and al-Najjar, *al-Kuwait, min al-Imara ila al-Dawla*, 197; a summary of the imperial perspective can be found in Smith, *Kuwait 1950–1965*, chapters 5 and 6.

11. Zahlan, *The Making of the Modern Gulf States*, 47–48; al-Khatib and al-Najjar, *al-Kuwait, min al-Imara ila al-Dawla*,197; Smith, *Kuwait 1950–1965*.

12. Al-Khatib and al-Najjar, *al-Kuwait, min al-Imara ila al-Dawla*, 192, 200–10.

13. For a full account of its proceedings, see National Assembly of Kuwait, *al-Majlis al-Ta'sisi: Mahadir Ijtima'at Lajnat al-Dustur* (The Constituent Assembly: Minutes of the Meetings of the Constitution Committee) (Kuwait: al-Amana, 2013).

14. Al-Khatib and al-Najjar, *al-Kuwait, min al-Imara ila al-Dawla*, 251.

15. Al-Khatib and al-Najjar, al-Kuwait, *min al-Imara ila al-Dawla*, 221. For more on Egyptian specialists in the Gulf see Brown, *The Rule of Law in the Arab World*, chapter 5, especially footnote 25.

16. See KU 10/Ha/400, for instance "al-'Atilun 'an al-'amal," *al-Tali'a*, July 24, 1963, KU 10/Ha/400; "Manba' al-Sharr wa al-Jarima," *Hadha al-Usbu'*, December 19, 1963, KU 10/Ha/400.

17. ARC 108134, "Report for the Period Ending 28th June 1963."

18. "Kathrat al-Mutasaillin," *al-Hadaf*, July 3, 1963; "Khatar al-Mutasaillin," *al-Tali'a*, July 7, 1963, "Kalimat al-Ra'i al-'Am," *al-Ra'i al-'Am*, April 29, 1964, all KU 3/ba/560.

19. "Faltakun al-KuwaitHhiya al-Ra'ida," *Adwa' al-Madina*, April 14, 1964, KU 3/ba/560.

20. "7 Alaf Mutasallilan fi Arba'a Shuhur," *al-Hadaf*, June 5, 1963, KU 3/ba/560.

21. "Sura wa Ta'liq," *al-Tali'a*, December 11, 1963, KU 3/ba/560.

22. See for instance "Wizarat al-Shu'un Tusdir Ihsa'iyya 'ummaliya 'an al-'ummal al-Musajjilin Tashmal al-'ummal al-Mutasaillin," *al-Watan*, December 23, 1963, KU 10/ba/010.

23. "al-Nuhud bi-al-Quwa al-'Amila fi al-Kuwait," *al-Muwathaf*, Issue 7, July 1962.

24. "Ba'd al-Mushkilat al-Insaniyya allati Tuqabil Munazzim al-Adah al-Hukumiyya," *al-Muwathaf*, Issue 2, October 1960.

25. "Hasr al-'ummal al-Ajnabiyyin fi al-Kuwait," *al-Watan*, June 10, 1963, KU 10/ba/010; "Sharh wa Ta'liq," *al-Muwathaf*, Issue 4, May 1961; FO 371/168728, Amiri speech to the National Assembly, Sabah as-Salim Al Sabah, October 29, 1963; "li-Istikmal Takhtit al-Barnamij al-Sina'i al-Qadim," *Akhbar al-Kuwait*, August 17, 1963, KU 10/ba/010; "Wazarat al-Shu'un Tusajjil 80,000 'amil Ghayr Kuwaiti," *al-Watan*, July 24, 1963, KU 10/ba/010.

26. Untitled, *al-Tali'a*, August 28, 1963, KU 10/ba/010; "Wazarat al-Shu'un Tushajjil 125,000 'amil Baynahum 5,000 Kuwaiti," *Akhbar al-Kuwait*, August 27, 1963, KU 10/ba/010.

27. "Tansiq Khutta Jadida bayna al-Dakhiliyya wa al-Shu'un," *Adwa' al-Kuwait*, September 16, 1963, 3/ba/560; "Man' Tajshil al-Mutasallilin fi al-Qita'ayn al-Rasmi wa al-Ahli," *al-Tali'a*, April 15, 1964, KU 3/ba/560.

28. "Wazir al-Dakhiliyya Yu'lin Fard al-Riqaba 'ala al-Hudud li-Man' Dukhul al-Mutasallilin," *Akhbar al-Kuwait*, June 5, 1963, KU 3/ba/560.

29. "Muda'afat Markaz al-Hirasa 'ala al-Sawahil li-Man' al-Tasallul," *al-Ra'i al-'Am*, September 6, 1963, KU 3/ba/560; "Ta'ziz Quwa al-Shurta 'ala Tul al-Hudud al-Barriyya wa al-Bahriyya," *Adwa' al-Kuwait*, March 10, 1964, KU 3/a/560; "Insha' Shabakat Radar fi Jazirat Failaka li-Dabt Lanshat al-Mutasallilin wa Ta'ziz Quwat Haras al-Sawahil," *Adwa' al-Kuwait*, August 4, 1963, KU 3/ba/560.

30. "Kayfa Tajrd ʿamaliyyat Ibʿad al-Mutasallilin," *al-Taliʿa*, January 3, 1964, KU 3/ba/560; Untitled article, *Adwaʾ al-Kuwait*, April 16, 1964, KU 3/ba/560.

31. "Asʾila Haʾira . . . wa al-Jawab," *al-Muwathaf*, Issue 7, July 1962.

32. Untitled article, *al-Watan*, May 2, 1963, KU 10/ba/010.

33. "ʿan Mashakil al-ʿamal wa al-ʿummal," *al-Watan*, November 4, 1963, KU 10/Ha/200.

34. ARC 108134, "Report for the Period Ending 31st January 1964" and "Report for the Period Ending 29th February 1964," CLC/B/207/MS39020, Letter Eastern Bahrain to Goldsmith London, March 17, 1964.

35. "Mudir Idarat al-Jawazat wa al-Jinsiyya Yathaddath ʿan Tatawwurat Idarat al-Jawazat wa Ahammiyyat al-Iqama bi-nisba li-l-Muwatinin," *al-Raʾi al-ʿAm*, January 1, 1964, KU 3/Ha/000; "Jawazat al-Safr Badaʾat ʾIdhan Murur . . . wa Tatawarat li-Wathiqa Rasmiyya," *al-Qabas*, June 25, 1979, KU 3/Ha/040.

36. "Idarat al-Jinsiyya wa al-Jawazat wa al-Iqama," *Adwaʾ al-Kuwait*, February 25, 1966, KU 3/Ha/000.

37. "Saʿiduna ʿala al-Hadd min al-Kafalat," *Sawt al-Khalij*, February 8, 1973, KU 3/Ha/400.

38. "Asʾila Haʾira . . . wa al-Jawab," *al-Muwathaf*, Issue 7, July 1962.

39. "Tanthim Shuʾun al-ʿummal," *al-Watan*, 14 March 1963, KU 10/ba/010; ARC 108134, "Report for the Period Ending 14th June 1963."

40. "Majlis al-Umma Yuqir b-il-Ijmaʿ Tawsiyat al-Lajna bi-Tasnif al-ʿummal al-Kuwaitiyyin," *Akhbar al-Kuwait*, May 29, 1963, KU 10/ba/030; "al-Tahqiq fi al-Ishaʿat al-Mudilla ʿan Tasnif al-ʿummal," *al-Taliʿa*, Issue 26, April 3, 1963.

41. For more see al-Mdairis, "The Arab Nationalist Movement of Kuwait," 371, 392.–93.

42. "al-Radd ʿala Mushawwihi al-Haqiqa," *al-Taliʿa*, March 17, 1963; "Lamasat," *Sawt al-Khalij*, March 28, 1963; "ʿummal Kuwaitiyyun wa ʿummal ʿarab," *Adwaʾ al-Kuwait*, June 4, 1963, all in KU 10/ba/030.

43. "al-Hall al-ʿamali li-Ibʿad al-Mutasallilin," *al-Taliʿa*, May 6, 1964, KU 3/ba/560.

44. "Aghrab ʿamaliyya Taʿahhud Taquwum biha Sharikat Istighlal Tawrid al-ʿummal ila Sharikat ʿan Tariq al-Munaqasa al-Sirriyya," *Akhbar al-Kuwait*, August 1963, KU 10/Ha/200; "Kana Yuhawil Istiqdam al-ʿummal min al-ʿarabiyya al-Muttahida bi-Sura Ghayr Qanuniyya," *Akhbar al-Kuwait*, August 8, 1963, KU 10/ha/000; "Maʿ al-ʿummal," *al-Taliʿa*, Issue 158, December 8, 1965.

45. "Thalath Sharikat Raʾsmaliha Tawrid al-ʿummal Liqaʾ Wusumat min Ujurihim," *Akhbar al-Kuwait*, July 6, 1963, KU 10/Ha/200.

46. "Raʾi al-Taliʿa," *al-Taliʿa*, April 15, 1964, KU 3/ba/560.

47. "Iʿtiqal 223 Mutasallilan Dakhalu al-Bilad Khilsa khilal Usbuʿ," *al-Raʾi al-ʿAm*, June 6, 1968, KU 3/ba/560.

48. See for instance "Kayfa Yaʿish al-ʿummal fi al-Kuwait," *al-Hadaf*, August 28, 1963, KU 10/Ha/000; "al-ʿummal wa al-Sayf," *Hadha al-Usbuʿ*, June 10, 1965, KU 10/Ha/000.

49. "Nahnu al-ʿummal al-muʿadhdhabun fi al-Kuwait," *Sawt al-Khalij*, November 11, 1963, KU 10/Ha/000.

50. "al-Kadhun fi Masnaʿ al-Tabuq," *al-Taliʿa*, Issue 1, June 20, 1962; "Wazir al-Shuʾun al-Ijtimaʿiyya Mustaʿidd li-Muqabala al-ʿummal," *al-Taliʿa*, Issue 5, July 11, 1962.

51. "al-Kadhun fi Masnaʿ al-Tabuq," *al-Taliʿa*, Issue 1, June 20, 1962; "Wazir al-Shuʾun al-Ijtimaʿiyya Mustaʿidd li-Muqabala al-ʿummal," *al-Taliʿa*, Issue 5, July 11, 1962.

52. Al-Khatib and al-Najjar, *al-Kuwait, min al-Imara ila al-Dawla*, 230; see KU 10/ba/030, including "Muʾamarat Shuʿubiyya," *al-Nadal* (Beirut), April 1, 1963.

53. Hamad H. Albloshi, "Arab Nationalism and the Politics of 'Othering' in Kuwait: Evidence From Al-taliʿa," *British Journal of Middle Eastern Studies* (2024): 1–24.

54. "al-Dukhulaʾ ʿala al-Kuwait," *al-Risala*, July 14, 1963; "Man Hum al-Dukhulaʾ?" *Al-Risala*, July 21, 1963; "3,000 Mutasallil Irani fi Shahr Wahid," *al-Risala*, November 7, 1966; and "al-Khalij al-ʿArabi . . . wa Khatar al-Mutasallilin," *Akhbar al-Kuwait*, September 1, 1964, all in KU 3/ba/560.

55. "Risalat al-Usbuʿ," *al-Hadaf*, August 21, 1963, KU 3/ba/560; "ʿurubat al-Kuwait fi Khatar!" *Al-Risala*, November 3, 1963, KU 3/ba/560.

56. "al-Iraniyyun fi kull Makan!" *Al-Risala*, April 20, 1964, KU 3/ba/560.

57. "al-Hall al-ʿamali li-Ibʿad al-Mutasallilin," *al-Taliʿa*, May 6, 1964; "Risala ila Mutasallil," *Adwaʾ al-Kuwait*, April 14, 1964, both in KU 3/baa/560.

58. "Ana . . . Kufaiti," *al-Taliʿa*, April 21, 1964; and "Kufaiti Mal Afshal," *al-Hadaf*, September 2, 1964, both in KU 3/ba/560.

59. Notable examples are Al-Nakib, *Kuwait Transformed* and "Revisiting Hadar and Badu in Kuwait," and Khaldoun al-Naqeeb, *Siraʿ al-Qabila wa al-Dimuqratiyya: Halat al-Kuwait* (Saqi, 1996).

60. National Assembly of Kuwait, *al-Majlis al-Taʾsisi*.

61. "Barid al-Raʾi al-ʿAmm," *al-Raʾi al-ʿAm*, July 31, 1964, KU 3/zay/400.

62. "Jinsiyyat Ahl al-Badiya," *al-Taliʿa*, April 19, 1964, KU 3/zay/400.

63. "Mashakil al-Jinsiyya," *al-Taliʿa*, November 27, 1963, KU 3/zay/400; "Kalam Sarih hawl al-Jinsiyya wa al-Tajannus," *al-Watan*, November 25, 1963, KU 3/zay/400.

64. "al-ʿaʾishun fi Miyah al-Asina," *al-Raʾi al-ʿAm*, August 7, 1961, KU 3/zay/400; "Ila Mata Yastamir Hadha al-Dajij?" *Al-Risala*, December 24, 1961, KU 3/zay/400; "Inna al-ʿarabi Laysa Ajnabiyyan," *al-Hadaf*, December 31, 1962, KU 3/Ha/400; "Hadith al-Ithnayn: maʿ al-Ajanib," *Adwaʾ al-Kuwait*, September 1, 1963, KU 3/Ha/400; "al-Shuʿubiyyun al-Naddasun," *Hadha al-Usbuʿ*, July 1, 1965, KU 3/Ha/400; "al-Ajanib . . . Yaʾkuluna," *al-Taliʿa*, July 7, 1965, KU 3/zay/400; "al-ʿarabi mu Ajnabi wa Ana Muʾaddab," *Hadha al-Usbuʿ*, April 26, 1966, KU 3/Ha/400.

65. "La Yujaz lil-Nazihin al-Takhalli ʿan Jinsiyyat Filasitin," *al-Raʾi al-ʿAm*, November 2, 1961, KU 3/zay/400.

66. "al-Badu fi al-Kuwait," *al-Hadaf*, July 31, 1963, and "al-Badu fi al-Kuwait: al-Tariq Ila Tawtin al-Badu," *al-Hadaf*, July 24, 1963, both KU 18/zay/370.

67. For more see Al-Nakib, *Kuwait Transformed* and "Revisiting Hadar and Badu in Kuwait," and al-Naqeeb, *Sira' al-Qabila wa al-Dimuqratiyya.*

68. Mohammad Homam AlHashimy, "Bedouins and Bedouin Life in Kuwait," Kuwait Planning Board, January 1967, KU 18/zay/370.

69. "Majlis al-Umma Yunaqish fi Jalsa Khassa Jami' ma Yattasilu b-Mustaqbal al-Jinsiyya al-Kuwaitiyya," *Akhbar al-Kuwait*, November 24, 1963, KU 3/zay/000.

70. "Ashab al-Haqq fi al-Jinsiyya wa Mu'tadun 'alayha," *al-Tali'a*, April 21, 1964, KU 3/zay/400.

71. "Ashab al-Haqq fi al-Jinsiyya wa Mu'tadun 'alayha," *al-Tali'a*, April 21, 1964, KU 3/zay/400; and Sunail Shuhaiber, "Political Development in Kuwait: Continuity and Change in an Arab Independent Gulf State" (PhD diss., St. Catherine's College, University of Oxford, 1982), 112–13.

72. "Jinsiyyat Ahl al-Badiya," *al-Tali'a*, April 19, 1964, KU 3/zay/400.

73. "Khawatir," *al-Risala*, December 1, 1963, KU 3/zay/600.

74. "al-Bahithun 'an: Jinsiyyatihim," *al-Hadaf*, February 1, 1966, KU 3/zay/600.

75. Al-Nakib, "Revisiting Hadar and Badu in Kuwait."

76. "Ra'i al-Tali'a: Mashakil al-Jinsiyya," *al-Tali'a*, November 27, 1963, KU 3/zay/400; "Majlis al-Umma Yunaqish Mawdu' al-Jinsiyya fi Jalisa Muthira," *al-Ra'i al-'Am*, November 24, 1963, KU 3/zay/400; "Majlis al-Umma Yunaqish fi Jalsa Khassa Jami' ma Yattasilu b-Mustaqbal al-Jinsiyya al-Kuwaitiyya," *Akhbar al-Kuwait*, November 24, 1963, KU 3/zay/000; "li-Usbu' al-Mahalli," *Dunya al-'uruba*, October 30, 1963, KU 3/zay/000.

77. Sara Rahnama, *The Future Is Feminist: Women and Social Change in Interwar Algeria* (Cornell University Press, 2023), 172.

78. Similar anxieties would resurface in debates surrounding HIV/AIDS in the 1980s and 1990s, creating an interesting parallel. See Laura Frances Goffman, "Waiting for AIDS in Kuwait," *Radical History Review* 140 (May 2021): 21–48.

79. "Hal Atazawwaj 'arabiyya am Ajnabiyya?" *Hadha al-Usbu'*, July 14, 1966, KU 18/ha/358.

80. "Hawl Mushkilat al-Zawaj bi-l-Ajnabiyyat," *al-Risala*, July 15, 1962, KU 18/ha/358; "Inna al-'arabi laysa Ajnabiyyan," *al-Hadaf*, December 31, 1962, KU 3/Ha/400.

81. "al-Athar al-Say' al-Ladhi Yukhallifuhu al-Zawj bi-l-Ajnabiyyat 'ala al-'a'ila," *Akhbar al-Kuwait*, September 4 and 11, 1962, KU 18/ha/358.

82. The Kuwait University Newspaper Archive file 18/ha/358 includes a remarkable array of articles on the "foreigner marriage crisis."

83. "al-Zawaj bi-l-Ajnabiyyat," *al-Kuwait*, August 1, 1964, KU 18/ha/358; "Zawaj al-Kuwaitiyyin min Ghayrihim Bayna al-Rafad wa al-Qubul," *al-Nahda*, March 22, 1975, KU 18/ha/358.

84. "Limadha la Yatizawwaju al-Kuwaiti min Kuwaitiyya?" *Al-Yaqutha*, May 17, 1971, KU 18/ha/358.

85. "Matlub Isti'rad Fatayyat min al-Kharij," *al-Nahda*, May 11, 1968; "al-Zawaj min Ajnabiyyat," *Usrati*, June 22, 1968, KU 18/ha/358.

86. "Ma' Awwal Ra'isa Tahrir Kuwaitiyya," *al-Tali'a*, Issue 155, November 17, 1965.

87. "Qissa bi-Qalam Qari'," *Usrati*, March 22, 1969, KU 18/ha/358.

88. "al-Zawaj fi al-Kuwait," *Usrati*, August 1, 1966, KU 18/ha/358. For an anthropological account of the Arab–Kuwaiti divide, see Longva, *Walls Built on Sand*, 55–56.

89. See *Usrati* pieces in KU 18/ha/358.

90. "al-Zawaj fi al-Kuwait," *Usrati*, August 1, 1966, KU 18/ha/358.

91. "al-Zawaj," *Usrati*, September 1, 1966, KU 18/ha/358.

92. "Man Tatizawwaju al-Kuwaitiyya?" *Usrati*, June 15, 1966, KU 18/ha/358.

93. "Ra'i al-Mar'a al-Kuwaitiyya fi al-Zawaj min Ghayr Kuwaiti," *al-Nahda*, July 15, 1972, KU 18/ha/358.

94. "Hawl Zawaj al-Mar'a al-Kuwaitiyya min Ghayr al-Kuwaiti," *al-Nahda*, July 22, 1972, KU 18/ha/358.

95. "Ghayr Kuwaitiyyin fi al-Kuwait Man Hum wa Ayna Hum?" *Usrati*, June 21, 1969, KU 3/Ha/400.

96. "Ila Sa'adat Wazir al-Dakhiliyya," *Usrati*, November 11, 1969, KU 3/zay/400; "Ila Sa'adat Wazir al-Dakhiliyya," *Usrati*, November 28, 1970, KU 3/zay/600.

97. Haya al-Mughni, *Women in Kuwait: The Politics of Gender* (Saqi Books, 2001.).

98. "Man Tatizawwaju al-Kuwaitiyya?" *Usrati*, June 15, 1966, KU 18/ha/358.

99. "al-Zawaj fi al-Kuwait," *Usrati*, August 1, 1966, KU 18/ha/358.

100. "Hawl al-Zawaj min Ghayr al-Kuwaiti Marra Ukhra," *al-Nahda*, August 15, 1972, KU 18/ha/358.

101. "al-Zawaj fi al-Kuwait," *Usrati*, August 1, 1966, KU 18/ha/358.

102. FO 371/168785, Memorandum, P. C. D. Archer, "Labour Developments in Kuwait," June 6, 1963.

103. "Sharh wa Aa'liq," *al-Muwathaf*, Issue 4, May 1961.

104. National Assembly of Kuwait, *al-Majlis al-Ta'sisi*, 33, 118.

105. National Assembly of Kuwait, *al-Majlis al-Ta'sisi*, 285.

106. "al-'ummal Yutalibun bi-Dirasat Awda'ihim wa Raf' al-Ghubn 'anhum," *al-Risala*, September 20, 1964, KU 10/Ha/200.

107. "Shakawa al-Nas," *al-Ra'i al-'Am*, January 26, 1963, KU 7/mim/390.

108. Sami al-Munais, *al-Tali'a wa al-Ma'raka al-Dimuqratiyya* (The Vanguard and the Democratic Struggle) (Kuwait: Sharikat Kathima li-l-Nashr wa al-Tarjima wa al-Tawzi', 1984), 9.

109. "Niqabat al-'ummal fi al-Kuwait," *al-Tali'a*, Issue 25, March 27, 1963.

110. FCO 8/642, R. L. Morris, "Kuwait and the Neutral Zone Social, Industrial and Labour Developments," November 4, 1967.

111. See the "International Relations" chapter of Kuwait Ministry of Social Affairs and Labor, *Annual Report for Year 1964* (Kuwait Government Press, 1965); "Wa Tawahinakum," *Adwa' al-Madina*, December 24, 1963, KU 10; "al-Fajwa . . . wa al-'ummal . . . fī al-'Alam wa fi al-Kuwait," *al-Hadaf*, October 9, 1963, KU 10/Ha/000; "Majlis al-Umma" *al-Tali'a*, Issue 87, June 24, 1964 and Issue 89, July 8, 1964; "Ma' al-'ummal," *al-Tali'a*, Issue 74, March 25, 1964.

112. FO 371/168785, P. C. D. Archer, "Labour Developments in Kuwait," June 6, 1963.

113. Al-Asbahi, *al-Haraka al-Niqabiyya al-Kuwaitiyya*, 17; Saqr, *Rihla Dakhil al-Dhakira ma' al-Haraka al-'Umaliyya al-Kuwaitiyya*, 27–30.

114. Saqr, *Rihla Dakhil al-Dhakira ma' al-Haraka al-'Umaliyya al-Kuwaitiyya*, 31–32; personal interview, Daifullah Falah Sultan, December 4, 2017.

115. Saqr, *Rihla Dakhil al-Dhakira ma' al-Haraka al-'Umaliyya al-Kuwaitiyya*, 33.

116. Saqr, *Rihla Dakhil al-Dhakira ma' al-Haraka al-'Umaliyya al-Kuwaitiyya*, 33; al-Khatib and al-Najjar, *al-Kuwait, min al-Imara ila al-Dawla*, 164; personal interview, Hussein Saqr, November 28, 2017.

117. Al-Mdairis, "The Arab Nationalist Movement," 301, 305.

118. Saqr, *Rihla Dakhil al-Dhakira ma' al-Haraka al-'Umaliyya al-Kuwaitiyya*, 35; al-Asbahi, *al-Haraka al-Niqabiyya al-Kuwaitiyya*, 20.

119. "Bayan Hawl Idrab Sa'iqi al-Sayyarat fi al-Jamarik wa al-Mawani," *al-Risala*, April 30, 1963, KU 3/h/040; "Jabir al-Ahmad Yaqul: Babi Maftuh lil-Mutadhallimin," *Sawt al-Khalij*, April 4, 1963, KU 3/h/041; ARC 107003, "Work Stoppage and Demonstration, April 16th, 1963, Report," April 22, 1963; "Idrab 'ummal wa Muwadhafin Mina al-Shuwaikh," *al-Tali'a*, Issue 26, April 3, 1963; "Bayan min Da'irat al-Jamarik wa al-Mawani," *al-Tali'a*, Issue 30, May 1, 1963.

120. Personal interview, Daifullah Falah Sultan, December 4, 2017.

121. FO 371/168785, P. C. D. Archer, "Labour Developments in Kuwait," June 6, 1963.

122. Goffman, *Disorder and Diagnosis*, 145; "Intaha Idrab Mumarridi Mustashfa al-'izam," *al-Ra'i al-'Am*, July 8, 1963, KU 3/h/040.

123. FO 371/174625, Letter Christopher Gandy to J. A. Snellgrove, March 31, 1964.

124. "'ummal al-Ashghal Yadribun Yawm Ams 'an al-'amal,"*Akhbar al-Kuwait*, March 10, 1964, KU 3/h/040.

125. ARC 108134, "Report for the Period Ending 30th April 1964"; "Idrab fi Wizarat al-Kahraba'," *al-Risala*, April 12, 1964, and "Niqabat," *al-Risala*, May 31, 1964, both KU 3/h/040.

126. "al-'ummal Yutalibun bi-Dirasat Awda'ihim wa Raf' al-Ghubn 'anhum," *al-Risala*, September 20, 1964, KU 10/Ha/200.

127. Personal interview, Qabalan 'Ajnan al-'Azimi, November 29, 2017.

128. FO 371/149091, "Summary record of discussion between the Managing Director of the Kuwait Oil Company, the Hon. W. Fraser, and the Political Resident," June 26, 1960.

129. FO 371/149091, Letter J. C. B. Richmond, to R. A. Beaumont, June 15, 1960.

130. FO 371/168785, P. C. D. Archer, "Labour Developments in Kuwait," June 6, 1963.

131. FO 371/149090, Letter J. C. B. Richmond to R. A. Beaumont, January 12, 1960; ILO IC 6-7-173-1, Memorandum, Kuwait Oil Company, 1966.

132. "Majlis al-Umma Jalsa al-Thulatha'," *al-Tali'a*, May 20, 1964, KU 7/mim/390.

133. See for instance "Sharikat al-Naft Tuqabil Talab Ta'yin al-Kuwaitiyyin al-'atilin 'an al-'amal bi-l-Tajahul wa al-Barud," *Akhbar al-Kuwait*, July 23, 1963, KU 7./mim/390.

134. "Khutuwat 'ala al-Tariq," *al-Nahda*, November 8, 1969, KU 7/kaf/620.

135. BP 106434, Letter HLS/DECS/115, H. L. Scott to D. E. C. Steel, November 13, 1962.

136. BP 106434, Letter HLS/DECS/115, H. L. Scott to D. E. C. Steel, November 13, 1962.

137. LAB 13/1597, Despatch No. 74, M. W. Errock to the Earl of Home, Foreign Office, July 3, 1963.

138. ARC 107003, "Work Stoppage and Demonstration, April 16th, 1963, Report," April 22, 1963.

139. "Sharikat al-Naft Mas'uliyya 'an Idrab 'ummaluha," *Akhbar al-Kuwait*, April 17, 1963, KU 7/mim/390; "Idrab 3,000 'amil fi al-Ahmadi," *al-Hadaf*, April 17, 1963, KU 7/miim/390; "al-Idrab alladhi Shall al-Ahmadi," *al-Hadaf*, April 24, 1963, KU 7/mim/390; "Idrab 'ummal Sharikat al-Bitrul al-Wataniyya" *al-Tali'a*, Issue 28, April 17, 1963.

140. ARC 107003, "Work Stoppage and Demonstration, April 16th, 1963, Report," April 22, 1963.

141. ARC 107003, "Meeting at Ministry of Finance and Industry, Kuwait. Monday, 22nd April 1963"; and "Minutes of the Meeting held at the Governate, Ahmadi, on Sunday, 28th April, 1963"; FO 371/168728, Letter J. C. B. Richmond to R. S. Crawford, April 28, 1963; "Matalib 'ummal Sharikat Naft al-Kuwait al-Mahduda," *al-Tali'a*, Issue 29, April 24, 1963.

142. ARC 107003, "Minutes of the Meeting held at the Governate, Ahmadi, on Sunday, 28th April, 1963."

143. ARC 107003, "Minutes of the Meeting held at the Governate, Ahmadi, on Sunday, 28th April, 1963."

144. ARC 107003, "Meeting at Ministry of Finance and Industry, Kuwait. Monday, 22nd April 1963."

145. "al-Muwafaqa 'ala Insha' Niqaba li-'ummal Sharikat al-Naft," *al-Ra'i al-'Am*, April 29, 1963, KU 7/mim/390.

146. "Assarat Sharikat Naft al-Kuwait al-Mustaqilla 'ala Rafad Talab al-'ummal al-'adila," *al-Tali'a*, December 4, 1963, KU 3/mim/390.

147. "al-Tasnif al-Tabqi . . . wa al-Nawadi . . . wa Matalib al-'ummal," *al-Tali'a*, November 27, 1963, KU 7/mim/390; "Hatta Mata Yabqa Diya' al-'ummal Masdaran lil-Bu'sihim?" *Al-Tali'a*, December 18, 1963, KU 10/Ha/200.

148. "Ijtima' bi-l-Ahmadi li-Bahth Matalib 'ummal al-Naft," *al-Ra'i al-'Am*, April 28, 1963, KU 7/mim/390; "al-Miyah al-Maliha wa al-Sakan fi al-'ishash wa al-Tasrih al-Kayfi wa al-Tamiyyaz al-'usuri," *Dunya al-'uruba*, May 4, 1963, KU 7/mim/390.

149. See for instance "Matalib 'ummal Sharikat al-Bitrul al-Mudribin," *Sabah al-Khayr* (Lebanon), April 18, 1963, KU 7/mim/390.

150. "Sharikat al-Naft 'atiba 'ala al-'ummal li'Annahum lam Yu'limuha Musbaqan li-l-Idrab," *Akhbar al-Kuwait*, April 18, 1963, KU 7/mim/390; ARC 108134, "Report for the Period Ending 2nd October 1963," and Aide Memoire, "Notes on Calls Made on Saturday, 28th September 1963."

151. “Sharikat Naft al-Kuwait Tatahayal ʿala al-Qanun bi-Sarf al-ʿummal qabl Ishiqaqihim Taʿwid al-Khidma,” *Akhbar al-Kuwait*, July 4, 1963, KU 7/mim/390; “Mumathilun ʿummal Sharikat al-Naft Yashkun Hadr Huquqihim li-Saʿadat Wazir al-Shuʾun,” *Akhbar al-Kuwait*, July 15, 1963, KU 7/mim/390.

152. “Majlis al-Umma Jalsa al-Thulathaʾ,” *al-Taliʿa*, May 20, 1964, KU 7/mim/390; ARC 108134, “Report for the Period Ending 2nd October 1963.”

153. FO 371/174625, Letter M. W. Errock to J. A. Snellgrove, February 5, 1964.

154. FO 371/168785, P. C. D. Archer, “Labour Developments in Kuwait,” June 6, 1963.

155. ARC 107003, “Work Stoppage and Demonstration, April 16th, 1963, Report,” April 22, 1963.

156. FO 371/185444, R. L. Morris, “Note of a discussion on 17 February on industrial relations at the Kuwait Oil Company,” February 18, 1966.

157. FO 371/185396, “Extract from Annual Report: Social & Industrial Policies & Labour Developments in Arab States of the Middle East during 1965.” This idea has been debunked by more careful studies such as Al Haddad, “The Effect of Detribalization and Sedentarization.”

158. FCO 8/70, R. L. Morris, Report on Labour, Social and Industrial Developments in Abu Dhabi, December 5, 1967.

159. LAB 13/1597, Despatch No. 74, M. W. Errock to the Earl of Home, July 3, 1963; FO 371/149090, Note, Roger Stevens, June 3, 1960.

160. ARC 107003, “Work Stoppage and Demonstration, April 16th, 1963, Report,” April 22, 1963.

161. FO 371/168728, Letter J. C. B. Richmond to R. S. Crawford, April 28, 1963.

162. FO 371/168785, P. C. D. Archer, “Labour Developments in Kuwait,” June 6, 1963.

163. ARC 108129, Memorandum, “Employee Relations Meeting – Bahrain,” J. G. Considine to Managing Director, August 14, 1963.

164. See for instance “Idrab al-ʿummal al-ʿarab fi ʿAden,” *al-Taliʿa*, Issue 59, November 27, 1963; “Akhbar min al-Khalij al-ʿArabi,” *al-Taliʿa*, Issue 35, June 12, 1963.

165. “Wazir al-ʿamal wa Muhafdh al-Ahmadi Yuʿalajan Dhulamat ʿummal Sharikat Naft al-Kuwait,” *Akhbar al-Kuwait*, KU 7/kaf/660, July 25, 1963; “ʿummal Sharikat Naft al-Kuwait Yujaddidun Shakawahum ila Wazir al-Shuʾun wa al-ʿamal,” *Akhbar al-Kuwait*, September 21, 1963, KU 7/mim/390.

166. FO 371/168785, P. C. D. Archer, “Labour Developments in Kuwait,” June 6, 1963, and October 1963; “Muhafdh al-Ahmadi Yahul dun Idrab ʿamali Shamil fi Sharikat al-Naft,” *Akhbar al-Kuwait*, September 14, 1963, KU 7/mim/390; “al-Qurraʾ Yaktubun,” *Akhbar al-Kuwait*, September 19, 1963, KU 7/mim/390; FO 371/168785.

167. “Yajibu an la Yastamir Sallab Huquq al-ʿummal al-ʿadila,” *al-Taliʿa*, November 7, 1963, KU 7/mim/390; FO 371/174625, Letter M. W. Errock to J. A. Snellgrove, February 5, 1964.

168. “Maʿ al-ʿummal,” *al-Taliʿa*, Issue 136, June 23, 1965; Issue 138, July 7, 1965; Issue 139, July 14, 1965; and Issue 154, November 10, 1965.

169. “Raʾi al-Taliʿa: al-Niqabat fi al-Kuwait,” *al-Taliʿa*, Issue 39, July 10, 1963. See also “Maʿ al-ʿummal,” *al-Taliʿa*, Issue 70, February 19, 1964; and Issue 76, April 8, 1964.

170. LAB 13/1597, Letter M. C. S. Weston to T. A. H. Tyler, May 8, 1963.

171. "al-Muwafaqa ʿala Inshaʾ Niqaba li-ʿummal Sharikat al-Naft," *al-Raʾi al-ʿAm*, April 29, 1963, KU 10/zay/100.

172. "Niqabat," *al-Risala*, May 31, 1964, KU 3/h/040.

173. "al-Haraka al-ʿummaliyya fi al-Kuwait," *al-Risala*, April 24, 1963, KU 10/zay/100.

174. ARC 107003, "Minutes of the Resumed Meeting Held at the Governate, Ahmadi, on Wednesday, 1st May 1963," and "Minutes Prepared by the State, State of Kuwait Ministry of the Interior Ahmadi Governate."

175. "Majlis al-Umma Jalsa al-Thulathaʾ," *al-Taliʿa*, May 20, 1964, KU 7/mim/390.

176. "al-Banud allati Uqirra Majlis al-Umma Tahqiqaha Safaan li-ʿummal Sharikat al-Naft," *Akhbar al-Kuwait*, May 20, 1964, KU 7/mim/390.

177. ARC 106520, "Review of Kuwait Oil Company's Position Against the Specific Provisions of Articles in the Labour Law," November 14, 1970.

178. "Law No 38 of the Year 1964," *Kuwait al-Youm*, August 9, 1964.

179. LAB 13/1597, Letter P. C. D. Archer, December 24, 1964.

180. "Majlis al-Umma Jalsa al-Thulathaʾ," *al-Taliʿa*, May 20, 1964, KU 7/mim/390.

181. "Hadith al-Dawawin," *al-Taliʿa*, March 20, 1963, KU 10/ba/030; "Yajibu al-Iʿtiraf bi-Jamiʿ Huquq al-ʿummal wa Laysa Baʿdaha," *al-Taliʿa*, November 20, 1963, KU 10/zay/100.

182. "al-Miyah al-Maliha wa al-Sakan fi al-ʿishash wa al-Tasrih al-Kayfi wa al-Tamiyyaz al-ʿusuri," *Dunya al-ʿuruba*, May 4, 1963, KU 7/mim/390.

183. "Jabir al-Ahmad Yaqul: babi Maftuh lil-Mudhlamin," *Sawt al-Khalij*, April 4, 1963, KU 3/h/041.

184. Al-Mdairis, "The Arab Nationalist Movement," 301.

185. Al-Asbahi, *al-Haraka al-Niqabiyya al-Kuwaitiyya*, 30.

186. "Law No 38 of the Year 1964," *Kuwait al-Yawm*, August 9, 1964.

187. ARC 108134, "Report for the Period Ending 30th June, 1964," July 1, 1964.

188. "Akthariyyat al-Nuwwab Tuʿarid Daman Huquq wa Karamat al-ʿummal," *al-Taliʿa*, Issue 86, June 17, 1964; "Majlis al-Umma," *al-Taliʿa*, Issue 89, July 8, 1964; "Raʾi al-Taliʿa," *al-Taliʿa*, Issue 86, June 17, 1964.

189. "al-Mada 55," *al-Taliʿa*, Issue 87, June 24, 1964; "Ma Hiya al-Marahil allati Marra biha Qanun al-ʿamal Qabl an Yantahi Majlis al-Umma min al-Nadhar fih," *al-Taliʿa*, Issue 90, July 15, 1964; ILO FO 164-A-20-271 S. K. Burgan, Mission Report, Kuwait, January 26–31, 1970.

190. "Raʾi al-Taliʿa," *al-Taliʿa*, Issue 90, July 15, 1964.

191. "Maʿ al-ʿummal," *al-Taliʿa*, Issue 153, November 3, 1965; Issue 161, January 5, 1966; and Issue 167, February 16, 1966.

192. "ʿummal Sharikat al-Naft Yubashirun bi-Taʾsis Awwal Niqaba ʿummaliyya iihum fi al-Ahmadi," *Akhbar al-Kuwait*, August 12, 1964, KU 7/mim/350; "al-ʿummal Yataqaddamun bi-Talabat li-Tashkīl Niqabatihim al-ʿummaliyya," *al-Taliʿa*, August 26, 1964, KU 10/zay/100; "Niqabat fi al-Kuwait . . . Badaʾat Tadhhar ila al-Wujud," *al-Taliʿa*, October 28, 1964, KU 10/z/100.

193. Saqr, *Rihla Dakhil al-Dhakira maʿ al-Haraka al-ʿUmaliyya al-Kuwaitiyya*, 38.

194. Personal interview, Hassan Falah, January 9, 2018.

195. Saqr, *Rihla Dakhil al-Dhakira maʿ al-Haraka al-ʿUmaliyya al-Kuwaitiyya*, 39.

196. "Niqabat fi al-Kuwait . . . Badaʾat Tadhhar ila al-Wujud," *al-Taliʿa*, Issue 104, October 28, 1964.

197. LAB 13/1597, Letter P. C. D. Archer, December 24, 1964.

198. Saqr, *Rihla Dakhil al-Dhakira maʿ al-Haraka al-ʿUmaliyya al-Kuwaitiyya*, 51.

199. For a discussion of corporatism in the Egyptian labor movement see Beinin and Lockman, *Workers on the Nile*, 7–8, 455, and Bianchi, "The Corporatization of the Egyptian Labor Movement."

200. Saqr, *Rihla Dakhil al-Dhakira maʿ al-Haraka al-ʿUmaliyya al-Kuwaitiyya*, 46; Personal interview, Hussein Saqr, November 28, 2017.

201. Al-Khatib and al-Najjar, *al-Kuwait, min al-Imara ila al-Dawla*, 166; Saqr, *Rihla Dakhil al-Dhakira maʿ al-Haraka al-ʿUmaliyya al-Kuwaitiyya*, 42–45.

Chapter 6

1. "Maʿ al-ʿummal," *al-Taliʿa*, Issue 150, September 29, 1965.

2. "Maʿ al-ʿummal," *al-Taliʿa*, Issue 145, August 25, 1965.

3. "Maʿ al-ʿummal," *al-Taliʿa*, Issue 147, September 8, 1965.

4. "Maʿ al-ʿummal," *al-Taliʿa*, Issue 148, September 15, 1965.

5. "Maʿ al-ʿummal," *al-Taliʿa*, Issue 177, May 4, 1966; "Maʿ al-ʿummal," *al-Taliʿa*, Issue 237, July 10, 1968; "al-Duktur ʿAbd al-ʿAziz al-Sultan: ʿindana Tamyiz ʿusuri Qabili," *al-Yaqutha*, November 22, 1971, KU 3/zay/000.

6. Takriti, *Monsoon Revolution*, chapter 5; al-Mdairis, "The Arab Nationalist Movement," 377–79.

7. Omar Hesham AlShehabi, "Divide and Rule in Bahrain and the Elusive Pursuit for a United Front: The Experience of the Constitutive Committee and the 1972 Uprising," *Historical Materialism* 21, no. 1 (2013): 94–127.

8. Toby Matthiesen, "Red Arabia: Anti-Colonialism, the Cold War, and the Long Sixties in the Gulf States," in *The Routledge Handbook of the Global Sixties: Between Protest and Nation-Building*, ed. Chen Jian et al. (Taylor and Francis, 2018); Bsheer, "A Counter-Revolutionary State," 273–74.

9. Glen Balfour-Paul, *The End of Empire in the Middle East: Britain's Relinquishment of Power in Her Last Three Arab Dependencies* (Cambridge University Press, 1991).

10. For more on the role of elite families see Sunail Shuhaiber, "Political Development in Kuwait: Continuity and Change in an Arab Independent Gulf State" (PhD diss., St. Catherine's College, University of Oxford, 1982), 110–13.

11. Al-Mdairis, *al-Tawajjuhat al-Marksiyya al-Kuwaitiyya*, 43–46, 49; al-Mdairis, "The Arab Nationalist Movement," 411; al-Khatib and al-Najjar, *al-Kuwait, min al-Imara ila al-Dawla*, 27–28.

12. Posousney, *Labor and the State in Egypt*; Beinin and Lockman, *Workers on the Nile*.

13. This differs from strikes in Qatar, which, as Jill Crystal argues, often excluded noncitizens. See *Oil and Politics in the Gulf*, chapter 5.

14. It thus builds on work in other postcolonial contexts, such as Aminzade, *Race, Nation, and Citizenship in Postcolonial Africa*.

15. Julian Go, "Three Tensions in the Theory of Racial Capitalism," *Sociological Theory* 39, no. 1 (2021): 38–47, 41.

16. Jaakko Heiskanen, *Ethnos of the Earth: International Order and the Emergence of Ethnicity* (Cambridge University Press, 2024), 3, 155.

17. David R. Roediger, *The Wages of Whiteness: Race and the Making of the American Working Class* (Verso, 2007), 13.

18. Ahmad al-Khatib and Ghanim al-Najjar, *al-Kuwait, min al-Dawla ila al-Imara: Dhikrayyat al-ʿamal al-Watani wa-al-Qawmi* (Kuwait, from State to Emirate: Memoirs of National and Patriotic Work) (Beirut: al-Markaz al-Thaqafi al-ʿArabi, 2009).

19. Zahlan, *The Making of the Modern Gulf States*, 50.

20. Al-Mdairis, "The Arab Nationalist Movement," 276.

21. FO 371/185397, Letter Embassy Kuwait to Michael Stewart, August 7, 1966.

22. FO 371/185396, Telegram Jackson Kuwait to Foreign Office, May 12, 1966.

23. FO 371/185397, Letter C. C. R. Battiscombe to A. E. Chamier, June 25, 1966; Letter J. A. N. Graham to A. E. D. Chamier, September 26, 1966; Letter J. A. N. Graham to M. S. Weir, May 24, 1966; al-Munais, *al-Taliʿa wa al-Maʿraka al-Dimuqratiyya*, 198.

24. FO 371/185397, Letter J. A. N. Graham to A. E. D. Chamier, October 3, 1966, and Letter D. J. Makinson to J. A. N. Graham, October 17, 1966.

25. FO 371/179741, Letter W. H. Luce to R. S. Crawford, March 15, 1965.

26. FO 371/179741, Telegram Kuwait to Foreign Office, March 29, 1965, and Letter G. N. Jackson to R. S. Crawford, March 29, 1965.

27. FO 371/179741, Minutes, J. S. H. Shattock, August 18, 1965, "Counter Subversion Committee Working Group on the Persian Gulf (Including Kuwait) held 12 August 1965."

28. FO 371/185397, Letter Embassy Kuwait to Michael Stewart, August 7, 1966.

29. FO 371/185396, Letter J. A. N. Graham to M. S. Weir, May 11, 1966; FO 371/185397, Letter J. A. N. Graham to A. E. D. Chamier, September 26, 1966.

30. FO 371/185431, Letter C. C. R. Battiscombe to A. E. D. Chamier, July 4, 1966.

31. "Mashakil al-Jinsiyya wa al-Tajannus," *al-Watan*, February 28, 1975, KU 3/zay/400.

32. "al-Mashʿan: al-Jinsiyya li-Ghayr al-Kuwaitiyya al-Mutazawwija min Kuwaiti Tunna Baʿda Khams Sanawat," *al-Siyasa*, November 3, 1970, KU 3/zay/400; "Kayfa Yahsul al-Muwaiin ʿala al-Jinsiyya wa mata Yahiqq lahu al-Tajannus," *Majallat al-Kuwait*, July 1, 1970, KU 3/zay/400.

33. "Hiwar maʿ Sulayman al-Mashʿan Hawl al-Jinasi wa al-Mutajannisin," *Sawt al-Khalij*, November 5, 1970, KU 3/zay/400; "Hatta Musaʿadat al-Zawaj," *al-Raʾi al-ʿAm*, February 5, 1974, KU 3/zay/400.

34. "al-Jinsiyya al-Kuwaitiyya," *al-Watan*, January 15, 1968, KU 3/zay/400; "Tawqiʿ Thamanuhu Milyuni Dular . . . wa Muqawala bi-Milyuni Dinar," *al-Watan*, January 15,

1968, KU 3/zay/400; "Madha 'an Kiyan al-Kuwaitiyyin ya Hukumatuna?" *al-Watan*, June 23, 1969, KU 3/zay/400; "La Tawtin al-Wafidin," *al-Watan*, January 23, 1967, KU 3/Ha/400.

35. Beaugrand, *Stateless in the Gulf*, 40, 78, 94.

36. "Isha'at al-Janasi al-Mabi'a," *Sawt al-Khalij*, June 4, 1970, KU 3/zay/000; "Mashakil al-Jinsiyya wa al-Tajannus," *al-Watan*, February 28, 1975, KU 3/zay/400.

37. FO 371/185396, Kuwait Home Service, Kuwaiti Premier's National Assembly Statement of May 3, 1966; "Qadiya al-Sahafa wa al-Ittihadat wa al-Niqabat wa al-Muwadhafin fi Bayan al-Hukuma," *al-Tali'a*, Issue 177, May 4, 1966.

38. FO 371/185444, "Note of a discussion on 17 February on industrial relations at the Kuwait Oil Company," R. L. Morris, February 18, 1966.

39. FCO 8/642, "Kuwait and the Neutral Zone Social, Industrial and Labour Developments," R. L. Morris, November 4, 1967.

40. FCO 8/642, "Notes of a discussion on arab labour affairs at the US Embassy, Beirut, on Monday, 5 February, 1968," R. L. Morris and J. P. Gordon.

41. "Muhawala Jadida li-'irqalat Insha' al-Niqabat al-'ummaliyya," *al-Tali'a*, Issue 109, December 2, 1964.

42. "Samah al-Qanun wa Samah Wizarat al-Shu'un," *al-Tali'a*, Issue 113, January 6, 1965.

43. "al-Niqabat Tatahaddath ila al-Tali'a," *al-Tali'a*, Issue 128, April 28, 1965; "Ma' al-'ummal," *al-Tali'a*, Issue 124, March 24, 1965; "al-Shu'un al-Ijtima'iyya Tarakat al-'ummal Wahdahum bi-Qawimun Ta'assuf Sharikat al-Naft," *al-Tali'a*, Issue 127, April 21, 1965.

44. Al-Asbahi, *al-Haraka al-Niqabiyya al-Kuwaitiyya*, 39, 134; Saqr, *Rihla Dakhil al-Dhakira ma' al-Haraka al-'Umaliyya al-Kuwaitiyya*, 64.

45. FCO 8/642, Letter J. C. Radcliffe to A. Ibbott, October 7, 1968.

46. "Ma' al-'ummal," *al-Tali'a*, Issue 150, September 29, 1965.

47. "Tahdid Qaww'id Sarf Ujur al-hukumiyyin Ghayr al-Kuwaitiyyin al-'amilin fi al-Wizarat al-Mukhtalifa," *al-Ra'i al-'Am*, August 4, 1973, KU 10/alif/210; "Ujur wa 'alawat al-'ummal Ghayr al-Kuwaitiyyin," *al-Risala*, August 12, 1973, KU 10/alif/215.

48. Frederick Cooper, "French Africa, 1947–48: Reform, Violence, and Uncertainty in a Colonial Situation," *Critical Inquiry* 40, no. 4 (Summer 2014).

49. "Ma' al-'ummal," *al-Tali'a*, Issue 214, January 24, 1968.

50. FCO 8/70, Letter R. D. Gordon to R. L. Morris, February 29, 1968.

51. Andrea Wright discusses the rise of contracting in the Gulf from the corporate and imperial perspective in "Migratory Pipelines," chapter 3; "Imperial Labour," 78; and *Unruly Labor*, chapters 6–7, but reaches different conclusions regarding its origins and focuses exclusively on corporate and imperial actors. See also Boodrookas, "The Making of a Migrant Working Class," chapter 8.

52. ARC 108129, Memorandum, "Employee Relations Meeting – Bahrain," J. G. Considine to Managing Director, August 14, 1963.

53. There are numerous examples in Atabaki, Bini, and Ehsani, eds., *Working for Oil*, in the Introduction (3) and chapters by Tyler Priest (231), Andrew Lawrence (149),

Helge Ryggvik (108), and Stefano Tijerina (53). See also Santiago, *The Ecology of Oil*, 149; Appel, *The Licit Life of Capitalism*, chapters 3–4; Zachary Davis Cuyler, "Building Shared Power: The Trans-Arabian Pipeline and the Technopolitics of Anti-sectarian Labor Mobilization in Lebanon, 1950–1964," *Labor History* 60, no. 1 (2019): 57–77, 66.

54. ARC 108129, Memorandum, "Employee Relations Meeting – Bahrain," J. G. Considine to Managing Director, August 14, 1963.

55. ARC 108129, Memorandum, "Employee Relations Meeting – Bahrain," J. G. Considine to Managing Director, August 14, 1963.

56. FCO 8/70, Foreign and Commonwealth Office, Overseas Labour Consultative Committee, Second Meeting Minutes, February 2, 1968.

57. "al-Mas'uliyya al-Ula lil-Niqabat" *al-Tali'a*, Issue 128, April 28, 1965.

58. "Ahdat al-Haraka al-'ummaliyya," *al-Tali'a*, Issue 131, May 20, 1965.

59. "al-Haqiqa allati Yuqakkiduha Idrab al-'ummal al-Iraniyyin fi al-Mina'," *al-Tali'a*, Issue 158, December 8, 1965.

60. "Ma' al-'ummal," *al-Tali'a*, Issue 170, March 9, 1966.

61. FCO 8/70, Letter R. D. Gordon to R. L. Morris, February 29, 1968.

62. ILO RL 271-3-1 Letter Hussein Saqer Abdul Latif to H. A. Dunning, September 8, 1968; ILO RL 271-3-01, Minute Sheet, D. S. Raj, September 5, 1968.

63. "Nahnu 'Arab Sharikat Naft al-Kuwait," *al-Tali'a*, July 17, 1968, KU 7/mim/390; FCO 8/642, "Kuwait and the Neutral Zone Social, Industrial and Labour Developments," R. L. Morris, November 4, 1967.

64. "Ma' al-'ummal," *al-Tali'a*, Issue 235, June 26, 1968.

65. "al-Tamiyiz al-'usuri Siyasa 'alaniyya fi al-Kuwait," *al-Tali'a*, Issue 253, November 6, 1968; "'afwan ya Sa'ada al-Wazir," *al-Tali'a*, Issue 251, October 23, 1968; "Ma' al-Fadila al-Thalitha ya Sa'ada al-Wazir," *al-Tali'a*, Issue 254, November 13, 1968.

66. LAB 13/2141, "Note of a discussion on Arab labour affairs at the U.S. Embassy on 5th February, 1969."

67. Al-'Ajmi, *al-Haraka al-'Ummaliyya wa al-Naqabiyya fi al-Kuwait*, 85.

68. "Ma' al-'ummal," *al-Tali'a*, Issue 178, May 10, 1967.

69. "Nash'at al-Haraka al-'ummaliyya fi al-Kuwait," *al-Risala*, December 1, 1968, KU 10/H/220; "al-Haraka al-'ummaliyya fi al-Kuwait," *al-Tali'a*, November 20, 1968, KU 10/H/220.

70. Al-Khatib and al-Najjar, al-Kuwait, *min al-Dawla ila al-Imara*, 23; al-Mdairis, "The Arab Nationalist Movement," 279; al-Najjar, "Decision-Making Process in Kuwait," 59–63.

71. "Ma' al-'ummal," *al-Tali'a*, Issue 199, October 4, 1967; "Kalla: Hadhihi laysa Bawadir Khatira," *al-Tali'a*, March 6, 1968, KU 10/zay/100.

72. ILO WED 3-271, Memorandum Director Beirut Office to Director General, Geneva, December 22, 1966; ILO FO 164-20-271 O. Ribeiro, Mission Report, Kuwait, December 9–13, 1966.

73. ILO WED 3-271, Letter Mohamed Sedki Behairy to Paul B. J. Chu, January 6, 1966; ILO WED 3-271, ILO Regular Program of Technical Assistance, Report on Workers' Education in Kuwait, 1967.

74. FO 371/185444, Letter J. A. N. Graham to R. L. Morris, June 21, 1966.

75. LAB 13/2141, Letter from Labour Attaché, British Embassy, Lebanon, February 23, 1967.

76. FCO 8/642, R. L. Morris, "Kuwait and the Neutral Zone Social, Industrial and Labour Developments," November 4, 1967.

77. ILO RL 271-3-01 Memorandum Director, Beirut Office to Director-General, Geneva, February 6, 1967.

78. "Tafah al-Kayl ya Wizarat al-iʿanat," *al-Taliʿa*, Issue 244, August 28, 1968.

79. FCO 8/642, Letter R. D. Gordon to R. L. Morris, April 19, 1967.

80. "Hawl Niqabat ʿummal wa Mustakhdimi Sharikat al-Bitrul al-Wataniyya," *al-Taliʿa*, February 4, 1968, KU 7/kaf/660.

81. "Liqaʾ maʿ Hussein Saqr wa Hassan Falah," *al-Taliʿa*, April 28, 1973, KU 10/zay/310.

82. Dietrich, *Oil Revolution*, 110–16; Garavini, *The Rise and Fall of OPEC*, chapter 3.

83. Dietrich, *Oil Revolution*, 161.

84. "ʿAbdullah al-Tariqi Yarudd ʿala *al-Raʾi al-ʿAm*," *al-Taliʿa*, Issue 165, February 2, 1966.

85. "Naqma Shaʿbiyya Kabira," *al-Taliʿa*, Issue 119, February 17, 1965.

86. Garavini, *The Rise and Fall of OPEC*, 156; Dietrich, *Oil Revolution*, 113.

87. Khalili, "Crude Knowledge."

88. "al-Umma al-ʿarabiyya wa al-Bitrul," *al-Taliʿa*, Issue 63, December 25, 1963; "al-Bitrul fi Oman," *al-Taliʿa*, Issue 93, August 12, 1964; "al-Naft al-ʿarabi," *al-Taliʿa*, Issue 100, September 30, 1964; "Bitruliyat," *al-Taliʿa*, Issue 102, October 14, 1964.

89. "Kayfa Yumkin Istikhdam al-Bitrul li-Khidmat al-Qadaya al-Qawmiyya," *al-Taliʿa*, Issue 161, December 29, 1965.

90. "Jamiʿat al-Bitrul al-ʿarabiyya," *al-Taliʿa*, Issue 86, June 17, 1964.

91. Christopher R. W. Dietrich, "'Arab Oil Belongs to the Arabs': Raw Material Sovereignty, Cold War Boundaries, and the Nationalisation of the Iraq Petroleum Company, 1967–1973," *Diplomacy and Statecraft* 22, no. 3 (2011): 450–79.

92. ARC 106721, "Notes on a Meeting with H.E. the Minister of Finance and Oil on Wednesday, 1st March 1967," by A. Hijazi, March 4, 1967.

93. FCO 8/641, Letter R. D. Gordon to A. E. D. Chamier, March 27, 1967.

94. FCO 8/610, Letter D. E. S. Blatherwick to A. Ibbott, April 1, 1968.

95. "Tabaqa Fadalat al-Mawaʾid Tujahid baʿd aʾiha li-lʿummal," *al-Taliʿa*, Issue 251, October 23, 1968; see series starting with "Maʿ al-ʿummal," *al-Taliʿa*, Issue 260, January 1, 1969.

96. "Maʿ al-ʿummal," *al-Taliʿa*, Issue 164, January 19, 1966; "Maʿ al-ʿummal," *al-Taliʿa*, Issue 218, February 21, 1968.

97. "Maʿ al-ʿummal," *al-Taliʿa*, Issue 236, July 3, 1968.

98. "Hiwar maʿ Wizarat al-Maliyya wa al-Naft," *al-Taliʿa*, Issue 225, April 17, 1968; "al-Takwit wa al-Tatfish," *al-Taliʿa*, Issue 227, May 1, 1968; "ʿajib! Rubʿ Qarn min al-Tadrib?," *al-Taliʿa*, Issue 171, March 16, 1966.

99. "Hawl al-Tadrib al-Mihni wa Sina'at al-Bitrul," *al-Tali'a*, Issue 206, November 22, 1967; "Ma' al-'ummal: Hawl al-Tadrib al-Mihni," *al-Tali'a*, Issue 207 and Issue 208, November 29, 1967, and December 6, 1967.

100. ILO FO 164-A-20-271 P. Akrawee, Mission Report, Kuwait, November 25–28, 1967; FCO 8/642, "Kuwait and the Neutral Zone Social, Industrial and Labour Developments," R. L. Morris, November 4, 1967; "Dirasa 'an al-Quwa al-'amila fi al-Kuwait," *al-Siyasa*, February 23, 1971, KU 10/Ha/000.

101. "Tadrib al-'ummal Yahtaj ila Takhtit," *Sawt al-Khalij*, May 17, 1973, KU 10/Ha/600; "Qalu fi Nadwat Ittihad al-'ummal," *al-Qabas*, May 22, 1973, KU 10/zaay/310; "al-'Amila al-Kuwaitiyya Tushakkil 7% fi al-Qita' al-Mushtarak," *al-Siyasa*, April 26, 1976, KU 10/zay/300; "Insha' Hay'a 'amma min al-Hukuma wa Ashab al-'amal wa al-'ummal," *al-Watan*, October 31, 1975, KU 10/Ha/600.

102. FCO 8/642, Letter R. D. Gordon to R. L. Morris, February 11, 1968; al-Asbahi, *al-Haraka al-Niqabiyya al-Kuwaitiyya*, 41.

103. "Ma hi Mushkil al-Kulliyya al-Sina'iyya," *al-Tali'a*, Issue 229, May 8, 1968.

104. ILO FO 164-20-271, S. K. Jain, Mission Report, Kuwait, May 14–16, 1961.

105. "Muhandis Kuwaiti Yaktub min Britanya hawl Mawdu' al-Quwa al-'amila al-Kuwaitiyya," *al-Tali'a*, Issue 399, November 4, 1972. This is also an argument made by Iskander, *Does Skill Make Us Human?*

106. "Sami al-Munays Yatahaddath 'an: Waqi' al-Tadrib al-Mihni fi al-Kuwait," *al-Tali'a*, Issue 421, April 21, 1973.

107. For more on the discourse of skill see Iskander, *Does Skill Make Us Human?*

108. "Sharikat al-Zayt al-'arabiyya . . . al-Yabaniyya . . . wa 'ummaluha . . . wa A'malha," *al-Tali'a*, Issue 33, May 29, 1963.

109. "Ma' al-'ummal," *al-Tali'a*, Issue 129, May 5, 1965.

110. "Ma' al-'ummal," *al-Tali'a*, Issue 140, July 21, 1965; "Kalima li-l-'ummal," *al-Tali'a*, July 4, 1966, KU 7/mim/390.

111. "Ma' al-'ummal," *al-Tali'a*, Issue 141, July 28, 1965.

112. Saqr, *Rihla Dakhil al-Dhakira ma' al-Haraka al-'Umaliyya al-Kuwaitiyya*, 57, 60.

113. For more on the labor movement and foreign policy, see al-Mdairis, *al-Mujtama' al-Madani wa-al-Haraka al-Wataniyya fi al-Kuwait*, 158–67.

114. Dietrich, *Oil Revolution*, 124.

115. "Silah al-Bitrul fi al-Ma'raka," *al-Tali'a*, Issue 180, May 24, 1967; "al-Harb wa al-Bitrul," *al-Tali'a*, Issue 181, May 31, 1967; "Ra'i al-Tali'a," *al-Tali'a*, Issue 182, June 7, 1967.

116. FCO 8/642, "Kuwait and the Neutral Zone Social, Industrial and Labour Developments," R. L. Morris, November 4, 1967.

117. Dietrich, *Oil Revolution*, chapter 4; Garavini, *The Rise and Fall of OPEC*, 171; Dietrich, "'Arab Oil Belongs to the Arabs,'" 460.

118. FCO 8/642, Letter J. C. Radcliffe to A. Ibbott, October 7, 1968.

119. LAB 13/2141, Letter Labour Attaché, February 23, 1967.

120. LAB 13/2141, Letter Labour Attaché, February 23, 1967.

121. Saqr, *Rihla Dakhil al-Dhakira ma' al-Haraka al-'Umaliyya al-Kuwaitiyya*, 53.

122. Al-Asbahi, *al-Haraka al-Niqabiyya al-Kuwaitiyya*, 72–73.

123. Personal interview, Hassan Falah, January 9, 2018.

124. "Wazir al-Shu'un: Limadha al-Takhawuf min Mashru' Qanun al-'ammal fi Qita' al-Naft?" *Al-Ra'i al-'Am*, April 28, 1969, KU 7/kaf/660.

125. "Mazaya al-Qanun Raqam 43 li-Sanat 1968 bi-Ta'dil Qanun al-'ammal fi Qita' al-'Ahli," *al-Tali'a*, Issue 239, July 24, 1968.

126. ARC 106520, Memorandum I. A. Huneidi to H.G.R., "The Applicability of Kuwaiti Labour Law to Casual, Temporary and Part-Time Employees," February 2, 1969.

127. LAB 13/2141, "Note of a discussion on Arab labour affairs at the U.S. Embassy on Monday, 9th December 1968."

128. Parliamentary Question, Rashid Saif, October 28, 1968, KU 7/kaf/660.

129. "Man Hum Ashab al-Maslaha fi al-Qanun al-Jadid li-'ummal al-Naft?" *Al-Tali'a*, Issue 242, August 14, 1968.

130. "al-Qanun Huwa al-Qanun ya Sharikat al-Naft," *al-Tali'a*, Issue 244, August 28, 1968.

131. Parliamentary Question, Rashid Saif, October 28, 1968, KU 7/kaf/660.

132. "Sharikat al-Naft la Takhsha Hasiban wa la Hisaban," *al-Tali'a*, July 7, 1968, KU 7/kaf/000; "al-Khata' . . . wa al-Natija," *al-Risala*, March 9, 1969, KU 7/kaf/660; "Sharikat al-Naft al-Mutasattila Tatamada fi al-Tahaddi," *al-Risala*, November 3, 1968, KU 7/kaf/660.

133. "al-Hukuma al-Khafiyya fi al-Kuwait," *al-Tali'a*, October 30, 1968, KU 7/mim/390.

134. "'an su' Niyya wa su' Qisd Ahmalat al-Sharikat Tadarib al-'ummal al-Kuwaitiyyin," *al-Risala*, October 27, 1968, KU 7/mim/390.

135. "Ma' al-'ummal," *al-Tali'a*, October 30, 1968, KU 7/kaf/660.

136. "Biyan Sadir 'an Ittihad 'ummal al-Bitrul Yu'lin al-Idrab," *al-Tali'a*, Issue 246, September 18, 1968; "Wazir al-Shu'un al-Ijtima'iyya wa al-'amal Yastankir Mawaqif Sharikat al-Naft," *Akbar al-Kuwait*, September 21, 1968, KU 7/kaf/660.

137. "Ihtimam al-Hukuma bi-Matalib 'ummal al-Naft qad Yuddi ila Ilga' Idrabihim al-Muqarrar Yawm al-Ithnayn al-Qadim," *al-Siyasa*, September 18, 1968, KU 7/kaf/660; "al-Hiwar bayna al-'ummal wa al-Shu'un Yantahi ila al-Qiti'a," *al-Tali'a*, Issue 250, October 16, 1968.

138. "Haqqaq Idrab 'ummal al-Bitrul Hadafahu qabl Mawa'idihi," *al-Tali'a*, Issue 247, September 25, 1968.

139. "al-Hiwar bayna al-'ummal wa al-Shu'un Yantahi ila al-Qiti'a," *al-Tali'a*, Issue 250, October 16, 1968; "'afwan ya Sa'adat al-Wazir," *al-Tali'a*, Issue 251, October 23, 1968.

140. "Shahida Majlis al-Umma Jalsa Hada," *al-Ra'i al-'Am*, January 22, 1969, KU 7/kaf/660.

141. ARC 106490, Cable, Lee to Henshaw, January 19, 1969.

142. ARC 106490, Cable, Lee to Henshaw, January 20, 1969.

143. "al-Idrab bimathabat Indhar," *al-Tali'a*, January 22, 1969, KU 7/kaf/660.

144. "Idrab 'ummal al-Naft 48 Sa'a," *al-Risala*, January 26, 1969, KU 7/kaf/660.

145. ARC 106490, Cable Henshaw to Lee, January 20, 1969.

146. "al-Idrab bimathabat Indhar," *al-Tali'a*, January 22, 1969, KU 7/kaf/660.

147. "al-Hukuma al-Khafifa Marratan Thaniya," *al-Tali'a*, January 22, 1969, KU 7/kaf/660.

148. ARC 106490, Cable Lee to Henshaw, January 21, 1969.

149. FCO 8/1045, Telegram Kuwait to Foreign and Commonwealth Office, January 21, 1969; ARC 106490, Cable Lee to Henshaw, January 22, 1969.

150. FCO 8/1045, Telegram Falle Kuwait to Foreign and Commonwealth Office, January 19, 1969.

151. "al-Tanaqud al-Iqlimi fi al-Kuwait," *al-Siyasa*, December 23, 1971, KU 3/Ha/400.

152. ARC 106490, Cable Lee to Henshaw, January 22, 1969.

153. ARC 106490, Cable Lee to Henshaw, January 19, 1969.

154. ARC 106490, Cable Lee to Henshaw, January 22, 1969.

155. ARC 106490, Letter James E. Lee to Shaikh Abdullah al Jaber, January 26, 1969.

156. Personal interview, Hassan Falah, January 9, 2018.

157. See for instance "Inkhidad Intaj al-Naft min Milyuni Baramil ila 600 alf fi 'aqab i'lan al-Idrab allati A'lanahu 'ummal al-Naft," *al-Ra'i al-'Am*, January 23, 1969, KU 7/lam/390.

158. ARC 106490, A. Hijazi, Memorandum, "Call on His Highness the Amir," Kuwait, January 25, 1969.

159. ARC 106490, A. Hijazi, Memorandum, "Call on His Highness the Amir," Kuwait, January 25, 1969.

160. ARC 106490, Letter James E. Lee to K. R. Henshaw, KOC London, January 29, 1969.

161. FCO 8/1045, Letter J. C. Radcliffe to A. Ibbott, February 4, 1969.

162. FCO 8/1045, Letter J. C. Radcliffe to A. Ibbott, February 4, 1969.

163. Saqr, *Rihla Dakhil al-Dhakira ma' al-Haraka al-'Umaliyya al-Kuwaitiyya*, 55.

164. ARC 106490, Letter K. R. Henshaw to J. E. Lee, January 24, 1969.

165. Al-Mdairis, *al-Mujtama' al-Madani wa-al-Haraka al-Wataniyya fi al-Kuwait*, 127.

166. Al-Mdairis, "The Arab Nationalist Movement," 411, 415; al-Mdairis, *al-Tawajjuhat al-Marksiyya al-Kuwaitiyya*, 46, 46–57.

167. Al-Mdairis, "The Arab Nationalist Movement," 411, 415; al-Mdairis, *al-Tawajjuhat al-Marksiyya al-Kuwaitiyya*, 46, 46–57.

168. "al-Khata' . . . wa al-Natija," *al-Risala*, March 9, 1969, KU 7/kaf/660.

169. FCO 8/1045, Letter R. F. Sharp to A. Ibbott, October 28, 1969.

170. FCO 8/1045, Letters J. C. Radcliffe to A. Ibbott, June 19 and July 2, 1969. I never felt it was appropriate to ask Hassan Falah if the reports of torture were accurate, but both the British embassy and KOC believed that they were.

171. ARC 106520, Memorandum A. J. Horan, "Labour Law 43 – 1968," February 9, 1969.

172. ARC 106490, Translation of "Explanatory Memorandum of Law No. 28 of the Year 1969 Concerning Labour in the Oil-Business Sector," *Kuwait al-Yawm* No. 732, June 22, 1969.

173. ARC 106950, "Law No. 28 of the Year 1969 Concerning Labour in the Oil Business Sector, al-Kuwait al-Yaum, No. 732, 22 June 1969."

174. "Ra'i al-Tali'a" and "al-Hukuma . . . Muhami Sharikat al-Naft," *al-Tali'a*, Issue 302, November 4, 1970.

175. FCO 8/1045, Letter J. C. Radcliffe to A. Ibbott, May 14, 1969.

176. FCO 8/1045, Letter A. Ibbott to J. C. B. Weiatt, October 15, 1968; "Istithna' al-Sharikat al-Wataniyya min Ahkam al-Qanun wa Qasr Huquq al-Taqa'ud 'ala al-Kuwaitiyyin," *al-Ra'i al-'Am*, May 12, 1969, KU 7/kaf/660; "Wazir al-Shu'un: Limadha al-Takhawwuf min Mashru' Qanun al-'amal fe Qita' al-Naft?" *al-Ra'i al-'Am*, April 28, 1969, KU 7/kaf/660.

177. ARC 106520, Memorandum I. A. Huneidi to H. G. R., February 2, 1969, "The Applicability of Kuwaiti Labour Law to Casual, Temporary and Part-Time Employees."

178. FCO 8/1045, Letter J. C. Radcliffe to A. Ibbott, July 2, 1969.

179. ARC 106541, Ministry of Social Affairs and Labour, Department of Labour Relations, "Memorandum on the Outcome of the Meetings of the Committee Set up to Review the Complaint of the Federation of Petroleum Workers and the Kuwaiti Confederation of Workers"; "Muthakkarat Ittihad 'ummal al-Bitrul al-Marfu'a ila Majlis al-Wuzara'," *al-Tali'a*, February 18, 1970, KU 7/kaf/660; "Ma'sat al-'ummal fi Sharikat al-Naft," *al-Tali'a*, Issue 308, December 23, 1970; "Nadhra Thaniya 'ala Sharikat al-Naft al-Ajnabiyya fi al-Haqlayn al-Istithmari wa al-'amali," *al-Tali'a*, Issue 291, August 5, 1970; "Liqa' ma': Muhammad 'Abd al-Muhsin al-'Usaymi," *al-Risala*, August 29, 1971, KU 10/zay/310; "Ra'is Niqabat 'ummal Naft al-Kuwait," *al-Risala*, August 15, 1971, KU 10/zay/120.

180. Quote from "Khutuwat 'ala al-Tariq," *al-Nahda*, November 8, 1969, KU 7/kaf/620; see also "'ummal Sharikat Naft al-Kuwait Uu'anun min Mushkila Kathira Ahammuha: al-Ihtiyal 'ala al-Qanun wa Ta'hid," *al-Risala*, June 27, 1971, KU 10/zay/100; "Aqul," *al-Tali'a*, January 13, 1971, KU 7/kaf/620; "al-Tali'a Turudd 'ala Wizarat al-Maliyya," *al-Tali'a*, Issue 295, September 2, 1970.

181. "Fasl Jadid fi Sira' al-'ummal fi Sharikat al-Naft," *al-Tali'a*, April 3, 1971, KU 7/kaf/660.

182. "Nadhra Thaniya 'ala Sharikat al-Naft al-Ajnabiyya fi al-Haqlayn al-Istithmari wa al-'amali," *al-Tali'a*, Issue 291, August 5, 1970.

183. "al-Hudud Maftuha li-Kull Akh 'arabi," *al-Ra'i al-'Am*, September 18, 1967, KU 3/Ha/400; "Kayfa Tahsul 'ala al-Tashira . . . wa Ma Hiya Shurut al-Iqama?" *al-Kuwait*, November 16, 1965, KU 10/Ha/000.

184. "Mawjah Istinkar 'arabiyya lil-Quyud al-Kuwaitiyya al-Jadida," al-*Jumhuriyya* (Egypt), March 12, 1969, KU 3/Ha/410.

185. Parliamentary Question, Ali al-Mouash, December 30, 1969, KU 3/Ha/410.

186. "Hal Yuhiq lil-Zawj an Yalhaq bi-Zawjatih al-'amila fi al-Kuwait," *al-Yaqutha*, March 9, 1970, KU 3/Ha/410; "Muda'afat 'adad al-'uzzab," *al-Nahda*, February 17, 1973, KU 3/Ha/410.

187. "al-Maslaha min Talab al-Nuwab il-Gha' al-Tashira," *al-Yaqutha*, March 2, 1971, KU 3/Ha/410; "Hawl Maqalat al-Yaqutha," *al-Ra'id*, March 25, 1971, KU 3/Ha/410.

188. Hasan, *al-Filastiniyyun fi al-Kuwait*, 37, 162.

189. Hasan, *al-Filastiniyyun fi al-Kuwait*, 83–100, 114, 121.

190. Ghabra, *Palestinians in Kuwait*, 43.

191. FCO 8/1388, Letter S. Falle to A. A. Acland, April 29, 1970.

192. FCO 8/1388, Memo S. Falle to Michael Stewart, "Revolution in Kuwait: Why, How, When and Its Effect on our Interests," April 22, 1970.

193. Al-Khatib and al-Najjar, *al-Kuwait, min al-Dawla ila al-Imara*, 33–34, 42; Saqr, *Rihla Dakhil al-Dhakira ma' al-Haraka al-'Umaliyya al-Kuwaitiyya*, 71.

194. Al-Mdairis, "The Arab Nationalist Movement," 417.

195. "Program of Patriotic and Democratic Work (Barnamaj al-'amal al-Watani al-Dimuqrati)" from the Progressive Democrats (al-Taqaddamiyyun al-Dimuqratiyyun), republished in *al-Munais, al-Tali'a wa al-Ma'raka al-Dimuqratiyya*, 61.

196. "'ummal al-Kuwait Yadkhulun al-Intikhabat bi-Thalath Murashhin," *al-Tali'a*, Issue 307, December 16, 1970.

197. "Liqa' ma' Murashhi al-'ummal," *al-Tali'a*, Issue 308, December 23, 1970.

198. Ashraf Lutfi, *OPEC Oil* (Beirut: The Middle East Research and Publishing Center, 1968), 4.

199. Lutfi, *OPEC Oil*, 36–37.

200. Lutfi, *OPEC Oil*, 36.

201. Lutfi, *OPEC Oil*, 83.

Chapter 7

1. ILO TF 271-2-A-1-1, K. Inoue, Report on Kuwait, "Manpower Assessment and Planning Project," March 21, 1974.

2. ILO TF 271-2-A-1-1, Letter M. Yasin to The Chief, Sectoral Employment Branch, ILO, January 31, 1974.

3. ILO TF 271-2-A-1-1, Letter Mohammad Yasin to K. Inoue, November 13, 1974.

4. ILO TF 271-2-A-1-1, Letter M. Yasin to The Chief, Sectoral Employment Policies Branch, May 22, 1974.

5. ILO TF 271-2-A-1-1, Letter Mohammad Yasin to K. Inoue, June 29, 1974.

6. ILO TF 271-2-A-1-1, Letter Abdelmohsin Ahmad Al-Doweisan to Resident Representative ILO, August 9, 1976.

7. ILO TF 271-2-A-1-1, Letter Khalid Yassir to A. Abughanem, September 15, 1976.

8. The best economic account of this shift is Omar AlShehabi's chapter in *Transit States*, ed. Khalaf, AlShehabi, and Hanieh.

9. Parra, *Oil Politics*, 159, 194. The only scholarly reference to the role of Kuwaiti workers' oil nationalization is a brief mention in al-Mdairis, *al-Mujtama' al-Madani wa-al-Haraka al-Wataniyya fi al-Kuwait*, 154–55.

10. Al-Mdairis, *al-Tawajjuhat al-Marksiyya al-Kuwaitiyya*, 71–78; personal interview, Ahmad al-Diyyan, March 2, 2018.

11. Marral Shamshiri, "Revolutionary Transnationalism in the Persian Gulf Iranian-Arab Solidarity in Dhufar in the 1970s," *Comparative Studies of South Asia, Africa*

and the Middle East 43, no. 3 (2023): 343–57; Al-Mdairis, *al-Tawajjuhat al-Marksiyya al-Kuwaitiyya*, 62–63.

12. "al-Mas'ala al-Wataniyya wa-l-'alaqa bayna al-Qawmiyyatayn al-'arabiyya wa-l-'iraniyya," *al-Tali'a*, March 25, 1970, KU 18/zay/510; "Hawla al-Mas'ala al-Wataniyya . . . wa-Qadiyyat al-Muhajirin al-'iraniyyin wa-l-Mutasililin," *al-Tali'a*, July 15, 1970, KU 18/zay/510; "Ittihad al-'ummal wa-l-Dawr al-Tarikhi li-l-Nidal al-'ummali," *al-Tali'a*, Issue 404, December 16, 1972; "Lana Kalima Ayna al-Niqabat fi Hadhihi al-Naqalat?" *Al-Tali'a*, Issue 397, October 21, 1972.

13. Hasan, *al-Filastiniyyun fi al-Kuwait*, 124–26.

14. "Satawajih al-Kuwait al-Munafasa al-Shadida 'ala al-Quwa al-'amila al-Fanniya fi al-Mustaqbal al-Qarib," *al-Watan*, December 17, 1972, KU 10/Ha/620.

15. Department of Planning and Statistics, State of Kuwait, *Statistics Abstract in 25 Years* (Kuwait: Central Statistics Office, 1990), 40.

16. "al-Khubara' Yuqaddirun Hajat al-Kuwait ila Ziyada fi al-Aydi al-'amila Hatta '75," *al-Siyasa*, August 30, 1971, KU 10.

17. "'ayna Tatawajjahu al-Quwa al-Kuwaytiyya al-'amila?" *Al-Tali'a*, Issue 395, October 7, 1972; "al-Quwa al-'amila wa al-Hijra al-Mu'akasa fi al-Kuwait," *al-Nahda*, January 6, 1975, KU 18/zay/820; "Mundhu 'am 1965, Qita' al-Bina' Yuwajih Nazifan wa Naqsan fi al-Aydi al-'amila," *Ajiyal*, December 21, 1975, KU 10/Ha/200; "Taqrir Majlis al-Takhtit bi-Ihtiyajat al-Yad al-'amila Yahtaj ila Taqyim 'amali," *al-Siyasa*, May 24, 1975, KU 10/Ha/010; "Mushkilat al-'amila," *al-Nahda*, August 9, 1975, KU 10/Ha/210; "Tanzim al-Quwa al-'amila fi al-Kuwait," *al-Kuwaiti*, July 27, 1975, KU 10/Ha/000.

18. Department of Manpower Planning, Planning Council, State of Kuwait, "Economic and Social Indexes for the Development of Human Resources in the Area of Use and Manpower," July 1974; "Majlis al-Takhtit: al-Kuwait bihaja ila Akthar min Rub' Milyun Wafid," *al-Siyasa*, April 30, 1975, KU 10/Ha/210.

19. Mohammad Yasin, "Responsibilities, Functions and Staffing Requirements of the Department of Manpower Planning," Kuwait, October 1974.

20. "La Yujad 'azmat fi al-'aydi al-'amila fi al-Kuwait bal Suw' Tawzi' laha," *Ajiyal*, March 21, 1976, KU 10/Ha/200.

21. Mohammad Yasin, "Need of Adjusting Population Census Data of Kuwait," Planning Board, Manpower Planning Department, Kuwait, October 1974.

22. "Kharitat Idariya Mufassalah li-l-Quwa al-'amila fi al-Kuwait wa Mada Hajat al-Bilad fi al-Sanawat al-Qadima," *al-Siyasa*, May 3, 1975, KU 10/Ha/010.

23. "'i'dad al-Mar'a al-Kuwaitiyya lil-Musahama fi al-Tanmiya al-Qawmiyya," *al-Siyasa*, December 12, 1972, KU 10/waw. For more on this effort in nursing, see Goffman, *Disorder and Diagnosis*, chapter 5.

24. "Risalat al-'adada Muhawalat Intihar Ahmad Muhammad Ahmad," *al-Tali'a*, Issue 292, August 12, 1970; "Ma'sat 'a'ila wa Mi'at al-'a'ilat," *al-Tali'a*, Issue 293, August 19, 1970.

25. "Mahrumun min Kull Shay' Li'annahum bila Jinsiyya," *al-Tali'a*, Issue 343, October 2, 1971.

26. "Istifta' al-Watan Hawla Fath Bab al-Tajnis," *al-Watan*, March 21, 1972, KU 3/zay/400; "Madha Ya'ni Fath Bab al-Ziyarat lil-Kuwait wa Manh al-Jinsiyya 'an Mustahiqiha?" *Al-Nahda*, April 1, 1972, KU 3/zay/400; "Ara' fi al-Jinsiyya wa al-Iqama al-da'ima," *al-Qabas*, April 13, 1972, KU 3/zay/400; "'ila al-Sada 'uda' Lajnat Tahqiq al-Jinsiyya al-Kuwaitiyya," *al-Siyasa*, May 20, 1973, KU 3/zay/600; "Mas'alat al-Jinsiyya," *al-Tali'a*, Issue 289, July 23, 1970.

27. "al-Siyasa Tusajjil Aghrab al-Qisas Hawl Qanun al-Jinsiyya," *al-Siyasa*, March 30, 1975, KU 3/zay/000; "Sinn al-Dhahab . . . wa Marbat al-Hamir," *al-Yaqutha*, April 7, 1975, KU 3/zay/000.

28. "al-Tarikh Yal'an al-Qada alladhin Sabbabu al-Hazima li-Shu'ubihim," *al-Siyasa*, December 4, 1972, KU 3/zay/600.

29. "Jinsiyya bi-al-Ta'sis Yajibu Shatbuha," *al-Tali'a*, Issue 382, July 8, 1972; "Mashakil al-Jinsiyya wa-al-Tajannus," *al-Watan*, February 28, 1975, KU 3/zay/400; "Matlub Ta'dil Qanun al-Jinsiyya," *al-Siyasa*, March 22, 1975, KU 3/zay/000; "Istifta' al-Nahda," *al-Nahda*, June 26, 1976, KU 3/zay/400.

30. "al-Bayan wa al-Jinsiya," *al-Tali'a*, Issue 287, July 8, 1970.

31. "Sulaiman al-Mish'an: Qanun al-Jinsiya bihaja ila Ta'dil," *Sawt al-Khalij*, April 18, 1968, KU 3/zay/000; "Kayfa Yahsul al-Muwaiin 'ala al-Jinsiyya wa Mata Yahiqqu lahu al-Tajannus," *Majallat al-Kuwait*, July 1, 1970, KU 3/zay/400.

32. "al-Jinsiyya . . . Tawzi' Faqr am Tawzi' Ghani?" *Al-Qabas*, July 31, 1972, KU 3/zay/400.

33. Untitled article, *Mir'at al-Umma*, January 5, 1972, KU 3/zay/400.

34. "Kalimat al-Yaqutha," *al-Yaqutha*, June 8, 1970, KU 3/zay/000; "Anwar al-Nuri: Ma' Manh al-Jinsiyya lakin Dimn Dawabit wa Hudud," *al-Qabas*, April 7, 1974, KU 3/zay/400; "al-Jinsiyya al-Kuwaitiyya: Man hum aladhina Yastahiqunaha?" *al-Nahda*, August 31, 1974, KU 3/zay/400; "al-Tajnis Matlub . . . wa Lakin," *al-Yaqutha*, March 11, 1974, KU 3/zay/400; "al-Siyasa Mahalliyya," *al-Siyasa*, August 21, 1973, KU 3/zay/400; "Naduwat al-Watan 3," *al-Watan*, February 28, 1975, KU 3/zay/400; "al-Kuwait fi Usbu'," *al-Tali'a*, Issue 345, October 16, 1971.

35. "al-Jinsiyya," *al-Tali'a*, Issue 282, June 3, 1970; "Mas'alat al-Jinsiyya," *al-Tali'a*, Issue 289, July 23, 1970; "Story of a Kuwaiti," *Sawt al-Khalij*, May 6, 1971, KU 3/zay/400; "Mahrumun min Kull Shay' li'annahum Bila Jinsiyya," *al-Tali'a*, Issue 343, October 2, 1971, and Issue 346, October 23, 1971.

36. "Kuwaitiyuun ma' Waqf al-Tanfidh!" *al-Ra'i al-'Am*, February 28, 1975, KU 3/zay/600.

37. "al-Liwa' al-Thuwayni: al-Dakhiliya la Tamani' fi Manh Tadhakir al-Murur li-Afrad al-Jaysh wa-l-Shurta," *al-Ra'i al-'Am*, May 29, 1976, KU 3/Ha/020; "Hal Nutbiq at-Tajnis bi-l-Quwwa wa-Fawran?" *Ajiyal*, April 8, 1973, KU 3/zay/600; "Iqtihah bi-Manh al-'arab al-Muqimin al-Jinsiyya al-Kuwaitiyya," *al-Ra'i al-'Am*, June 17, 1973, KU 3/zay/400; "Kuwaitiyyun bila Jinsiyya," *Sawt al-Khalij*, April 9, 1970, KU 3/zay/1970.

38. "Iqtirah Qanun bi-Manah al-Jinsiyya li-Buna' al-Badiyya al-'amilin bil-Dawla," *al-Ra'i al-'Am*, June 4, 1973, KU 3/zay/000.

39. "Kuwaitiyyin Manfiyyun fi al-Kuwait," al-Tali'a, Issue 347, October 30, 1971; "al-Kanadira wa al-Jinsiyya," al-Qabas, January 18, 1973, KU 3/zay/400; "al-Jinsiyya . . . Mushkila Ula min ayy Mushkila Ukhra fi al-Kuwait," al-Siyasa, May 25, 1972, KU 3/zay/600; "Arju i'adat al-Nadhar fi Mawdi' al-Jinsiyya," al-Ra'i al-'Am, January 19, 1973, KU 3/zay/600; "Sannah fi al-Kuwait . . . dun Jinsiyya" al-Siyasa, June 6, 1975, KU 3/zay/600; "Mata Tuhall Mushkilat al-Jinsiyya lil-Talaba?" al-Siyasa, December 31, 1975, KU 3/ zay/400.

40. "Kitab ila Wazir al-Dakhiliyya min Fatah Kuwaitiyya," *al-Siyasa*, April 13, 1973, KU 3/zay/600.

41. "al-Ibn Yahmil al-Jinsiyya . . . wa al-Umm la Tahmiluha," *al-Siyasa*, April 6, 1975, KU 3/zay/600.

42. "La Yumkin lil-Insan an Ya'ish Bila Huwiyya," *al-Siyasa*, July 27, 1974, KU 3/zay/600.

43. "Ara' fi al-Jinsiyya wa al-Iqama al-Da'ima," *al-Qabas*, April 13, 1972, KU 3/zay/400; "Ara' fi al-Jinsiyya wa al-Iqama al-Da'ima," *al-Qabas*, February 9, 1974, KU 3/zay/400; "Nadwa 'an al-Jinsiyya Yashtarikuha al-Duwayj wa al-Mas'ud," *al-Ra'i al-'Am*, April 7, 1975, KU 3/zay/400.

44. "Ara' fi al-Jinsiyya wa al-Iqama al-Da'ima," *al-Qabas*, March 23, 1974, KU 3/zay/400.

45. "al-Dakhiliyya Tushakkil Lajna li-Darasa Muqarahat Majlis al-Takhtit Manh al-Iqama al-Da'ima li-Ba'd al-Muqimin al-'arab," *al-Siyasa*, December 28, 1972, KU 3/zay/000.

46. "Jinsiyya bi-l-Ta'sis Yajibu Shatbuha," *al-Tali'a*, Issue 382, July 8, 1972; "Mashakil al-Jinsiyya wa al-Tajnis," *al-Watan*, February 28, 1975, KU 3/zay/400; "Matlub Ta'dil Qanun al-Jinsiyya," *al-Siyasa*, March 22, 1975, KU 3/zay/000.

47. "Mashakil al-Jinsiyya wa al-Tajnis," *al-Watan*, March 2, 1975, KU 3/zay/400.

48. "Ara' fi al-Jinsiyya wa al-Iqama al-Da'ima," *al-Qabas*, March 23, 1974, KU 3/zay/400.

49. "al-Ittihad al-'amm li-'ummal al-Kuwait . . . Tarikh wa Nidal," *al-'Amil*, November 1, 1975, KU 10/zay/310.

50. For more see KU 10/zay/310 and al-Mdairis, *al-Mujtama' al-Madani wa-al-Haraka al-Wataniyya fi al-Kuwait*, 158–67.

51. "al-Hukuma Tahrimuhum min al-Jinsiyya wa al-KOC Tafsiluhum min al-'amal," *al-Tali'a*, Issue 354, December 18, 1971.

52. "al-KOC: Watha'iq Sirriyya Hawla al-Tawdhif," *al-Tali'a*, Issue 289, July 23, 1970.

53. "'ummal Sharikat Naft al-Kuwait Yu'anan min Hushkila Kathira Ahammuha: al-Ihtiyal 'ala al-Qanun wa Ta'hid," *al-Risala*, June 27, 1971, KU 10/zay/100.

54. "al-Tamayyuz al-'ansuri fi Sharikat al-Naft," *al-Tali'a*, Issue 205, November 15, 1967; "Ma' al-'ummal," *al-Tali'a*, Issue 224, April 10, 1968.

55. "Ma' al-'ummal," *al-Tali'a*, Issue 224, April 10, 1968.

56. "al-Bayan wa al-Jinsiyya," *al-Tali'a*, Issue 287, July 8, 1970.

57. "Ba'da an Tabayyana lil-'ummal anna al-Kalam Shay' . . . wa al-Tatbiq Shay' Akhar," *al-Tali'a*, Issue 351, November 27, 1971.

58. "Mushkila Tabhath 'an Hall fi Sharikat al-Zayt al-Yabaniyya," *al-Tali'a*, Issue 418, March 24, 1973.

59. "al-Hukuma Tahrimuhum min al-Jinsiyya wa al-KOC Tafsiluhum min al-'amal," *al-Tali'a*, Issue 354, December 18, 1971.

60. "al-Ittihad al-'amm li-'Ummal al-Kuwait fi al-'awwal min 'Iyar," *al-Watan*, May 2, 1976, KU 10/zay/310; "al-Duktur 'Abd al-'Aziz al-Sultan: 'induna Tamyiz 'unsuri Qabuli," *al-Yaqutha*, November 22, 1971, KU 3/zay/000.

61. "Fi Mahrajan al-Ittihad al-'almi li-'Ummal al-Kuwait," *al-Tali'a*, Issue 406, December 30, 1972; "Ma' Hussein Saqr wa Hassan Falah," *al-Tali'a*, Issue 422, April 28, 1973; "al-'awda' al-Nafsiyya allati Yuwajihuha al-Wafidun Takammil dawr al-'awda' al-Ijtima'iyya wa al-Ma'ishiyya," *al-Tali'a*, March 29, 1975, KU 3/Ha/400; Untitled article, *al-Risala*, January 18, 1973, KU 10/zay/310.

62. See KU 10/jim/030, including "al-Mu'adhabun fi al-Kuwait," *Majallat al- Ra'id*, January 14, 1971; "La Budda min Ta'dil Qanun al-'amal fi al-Qitaiyn al-Hukumi wa al-Ahli li-T'amin al-'ummal min al-Hawadith," *al-Tali'a*, February 20, 1971, KU 10/mim/000; "Ma Hiya 'awda' al-'amila fi al-Qita' al-'ahli?" *Al-Tali'a*, March 11, 1971, KU 10/Ha/020; "Surat 'an al-Waqi' al-Mu'lim li'ummal al-Qita' al-'ahli," *al-Ra'i al-'Am*, July 3, 1973, KU 10/miim/018; "Hikayat 'ummal al-Bina' fi al-Kuwait," *al-'Amil*, September 1, 1975, KU 10/ha/310.

63. "Wathiqat 'ummaliyya," *al-Tali'a*, Issue 292, August 12, 1970.

64. "at-Tanaqud al-Iqlimi fi al-Kuwait," *al-Siyasa*, December 23, 1971, KU 3/Ha/400.

65. "Qawanin al-'amal al-Ja'ira fi al-Kuwait," *al-Tali'a*, Issue 420, April 14, 1973; "al-Ittihad al-'am li-'ummal al-Kuwait Yutrih Wajhat Nadharihi bi-sha'n al-Takhtit wa-al-Tanmiyya al-Iqtisadiyya fi al-Kuwait," *al-Siyasa*, May 15, 1973, KU 10/zay/310; "Liqa' ma' Hussein Saqr wa Hassan Falah," *al-Tali'a*, April 28, 1973, KU 10/zay/310; "'ilaj al-Awda' bi-'ayn Wahida!" *Al-Tali'a*, April 20, 1974, KU 10/Ha/230; "al-Hijra al-Mu'aksa wa Atharha 'ala al-Kuwait," *al-'Amil*, Issue 6, December 15, 1975, KU 10/Ha/220; "Hal Kanat al-Mihma Himayat al-Malikin am al-'amilin?" *Al-Tali'a*, June 8, 1974, KU 10/alif/200; "Azmat al-Hijra al-M'aksa," *al-Watan*, March 1, 1975, KU 7/lam/350.

66. "Barnamaj al-'amal al-Watani, wa Qadaya al-'amal wa al-'ummal," *al-Tali'a*, January 11, 1975, KU 10/Ha/010.

67. "Matlub I'ada al-Nadhar bi-Qanun al-'amal," *al-Yaqutha*, June 4, 1973, KU 10/mim/010; "Qanun al-'amal fi al-Qita' al-Ahli li-Maslahat al-'amil am Rabb al-'amal?" *al-Siyasa*, July 25, 1973, KU 10/mim/010.

68. "al-Qadaya al-Khams allati Tamus 75% min Muwatini al-Kuwait," *al-Tali'a*, Issue 427, June 2, 1973.

69. "Qawanin al-'amal al-Ja'ira fi al-Kuwait," *al-Tali'a*, Issue 420, April 14, 1973; "Sami al-Munais Yatakallam 'an: Waqi' al-Tadrib al-Mihni fi al-Kuwait," *al-Tali'a*, Issue 421, April 21, 1973.

70. "Tawhid Qawan'in al-'amal fi al-Kuwait," *al-Tali'a*, May 13, 1975, KU 10/alif/010; "al-Makassib wa al-Maham al-Matruha," *al-Tali'a*, February 27, 1974, KU 10/zay/100;

"'ard wa Naqd li-Tashri'at al-'amal fi al-Qita' al-Khas fi al-Kuwait," *al-'Amil*, July 1, 1976, KU 10/mim/010.

71. "Tumuhat al-Haraka al-'amaliyya fi al-Kuwait," *al-Risala*, April 27, 1975, KU 10/zay/210; "Nasir al-Faraj fi Hiwar ma' al-Risala," *al-Risala*, May 30, 1976, KU 10/zay/310; "al-Ittiadd al-'amm li-'Ummal al-Kuwait fi al-'Awwal min 'Ayar," *al-Watan*, May 2, 1976, KU 10/zay/310.

72. "Bi-Munasabat 'id al-'ummal al-'alami, Tawhid Qawanin al-'amal fi al-Kuwait," *al-Tali'a*, May 6, 1975, KU 10/mim/000.

73. "70 Nunashikum al-Daght 'ala Sharikat al-Naft li-Tatbiq al-Qanun Raqam 28 'ala Jami' al-'ummal al-Kuwaitiyyin wa Ghayr Kuwaitiyyin," *al-Tali'a*, Issue 346, October 23, 1971; ILO ACD 8-1-271, Letter Ian Lagergran, Deputy Chief of the International Labour Standards Department, ILO, to the Dierctor-General, Ministry of Social Affairs and Labor, Government of Kuwait, November 23, 1973.

74. ILO ACD 8-1-271, Letter Undersecretary Kuwait Ministry of Social Affairs and Labor to Director-General, ILO November 5, 1973.

75. "Barnamij al-'amal al-Niqabi fi al-Kuwait," *al-Tali'a*, November 16, 1974, KU 10/zay/322.

76. ILO WED 1-271, Kuwait Trade Union Federation Institute for Workers' Culture, "Program for Trade Union Work in Kuwait," November 1974; "Hadith Bariz fi Masirat al-Haraka al-'ummaliyya," *al-Tali'a*, April 27, 1974; and "Al-Mu'tamar al-Awwal li-Ittihad Niqabat al-Qita' al-Hukumi Yakhtitim A'malahu al-Yawm," *Akhbar al-Kuwait*, April 27, 1974, KU 10/zay/322.

77. "Sarah Akbar," AUK Oral History Project, accessed May 25, 2024, https://oralhistory.auk.edu.kw/items/show/7.

78. Goffman, *Disorder and Diagnosis*, 148–59.

79. "Indimam al-Mar'a al-Kuwaitiyya ila al-Haraka al-Niqabiyya," *al-Tali'a*, Issue 468, March 30, 1974.

80. "Laila Ahmad," AUK Oral History Project, accessed May 25, 2024, https://oralhistory.auk.edu.kw/items/show/27.

81. "al-Ittihad al-'amm li-'ummal al-Kuwait fi al-Awwal min Ayyar," *al-Watan*, May 2, 1976, KU 10/zay/310.

82. "al-Tajnis, Qadiyya Sayulahiquha Majlis al-Umma Hatta Yahull Mashakil al-Alif min al-Muwatinin," *al-Siyasa*, March 29, 1975, KU 3/zay/600; "Majlis al-Umma Yulahiq Mawdu' al-Tajnis," *al-Siyasa*, March 30, 1975, KU 3/zay/000; "Fima Yutabi' Majlis al-Umma al-Yawm Munaqashat Mawdu' al-Jinsiyya," *al-Siyasa*, February 1, 1975, KU 3/zay/410.

83. "Ta'dil Qanun al-Jinsiyya Faraghat min Ta'dilihi al-Lajna al-Mukallafa wa-Sayunaqash Qariban," *al-Siyasa*, November 27, 1975, KU 3/zay/200.

84. "Qanun al-Qita' al-Ahli fihi Thagharat wa-Yahtaj ila Ta'dil," *al-Siyasa*, January 7, 1974, KU 10/mim/010.

85. "To Improve Workers' Conditions Government Considering Labour Law Amendment," *The Daily Mail*, May 8, 1975, KU 10/mim/000.

86. CLC/B/207/MS39128/003, National Bank of Kuwait, Balance Sheet and Profit and Loss Account, 1965.

87. "Ittihad al-Muqawilin Ghadib liannahu Didd Tashghil al-Kuwaitiyyin," *al-Tali'a*, Issue 252, October 30, 1968.

88. "Ijtima' Muhim li-l-Lajna al-Da'ima li-Wad' Usus wa Qawa'id Tasarih al-'amal li-Hall Mushkilat al-'amala fi al-Bilad wa Tabsit 'ijra'at al-'Iqama," *al-Ra'i al-'Am*, January 21, 1975, KU 10/Ha/200; "Ittihamat Mutabadila," *al-Hadaf*, September 21, 1967, KU 10/Ha/230; "Ittihad al-Muqawilin Yuthir Mushkilat al-Aydi al-'amila," *al-Ra'i al-'Am*, June 30, 1975, KU 10/Ha/210.

89. "al-Hulul al-Muwaqqatah wa al-Jadhriyyah li-Azmat al-'amila fi Sina'at al-Bina' wa al-Tashiyd," *al-Muqaawal*, Issue 2, August 1975, KU 10/Ha/230; "Waqf Hijrat al-Yad al-'amila min al-Kuwait," *al-Watan*, September 17, 1975, KU 10/Ha/230.

90. "Takhtit al-Quwwa al-'amila," *al-Muqawil*, February 1978, KU 10/Ha/000.

91. "Takhtit al-Quwwa al-'amila," *al-Muqawil*, February 1978, KU 10/Ha/000.

92. "Bila Ritush," *al-Ra'i al-'Am*, January 5, 1966, KU 10/jim/000.

93. "Ittihad al-Muqawilin Ghadib li'annahu Didd Tashghil al-Kuwaitiyyin," *al-Tali'a*, Issue 252, October 30, 1968.

94. Sami Awadh, "Islamic Political Groups in Kuwait: Roots and Influences" (PhD diss., University of Portsmouth, 1999), 88; Ali A. Alkandari, "The Muslim Brotherhood in Kuwait, 1941–2000: A Social Movement within the Social Domain" (PhD diss., University of Exeter, 2014), chapter 3.

95. Beinin and Lockman, *Workers on the Nile*, 371, 384.

96. "al-'ummal," *al-Mujtama'*, Issue 1, March 17, 1970.

97. "al-'ummal," *al-Mujtama'*, Issue 8, 1970.

98. "Mu'askarat li-l-'amal," *al-Mujtama'*, Issue 12, 1970.

99. See for instance "Kayfa Tusaytiru al-Haraka al-Yahudiyya 'ala al-Siyasah wa al-Tijara fi al-Wilayat al-Muttahida" in Issue 16 and "al-Ahzab al-Shuyu'iyya fi al-Duwal al-'Arabiyya" in Issue 30.

100. "al-'ummal wa al-Istighlal al-Siyasi fi al-Kuwait," *al-Mujtama'*, October 1, 1974, KU 10/alif/210.

101. Al-Khatib and al-Najjar, *al-Kuwait, min al-Dawla ila al-Imara*, 29–81.

102. Al-Mdairis, "The Arab Nationalist Movement," 420; al-Khatib and al-Najjar, *al-Kuwait, min al-Dawla ila al-Imara*, 28–29.

103. "al-Naqabiyyun lam Ya'rifu Haqdqat al-Iqtirah," *Sawt al-Khalij*, November 29, 1973, KU 10/zay/510.

104. "Program of Patriotic Work for the Deputies of the People," October 1974, republished in al-Munais, *al-Tali'a wa al-Ma'raka al-Dimuqratiyya*.

105. Jill Crystal also briefly makes this point in *Oil and Politics in the Gulf*, 86.

106. "Ra'i al-Tali'a," *al-Tali'a*, Issue 349, November 13, 1971; "Majlis al-Umma," *al-Tali'a*, Issue 354, December 18, 1971; "Ziyadat Ghayr al-Kuwaitiyyin fi al-Dawla," *al-Tali'a*, Issue 355, December 25, 1971; "li-Ziyadat Ghayr al-Kuwaytiyyin wa al-'amilin fi al-Qita' al-Ahli wa al-Sharikat," *al-Tali'a*, Issue 351, November 27, 1971.

107. Personal interviews, Hassan Falah.

108. "Mundhu Khams Sanawat wa al-ʿummal Ghayr al-Kuwaitiyyin Yantazirun al-Indimam ila al-Niqabat . . . wa Lakinnahum lam Yahaulu baʿd ʿala Shahadat Husn al-Suluk," *al-Taliʿa*, Issue 267, February 18, 1970.

109. ILO WED 1-271, Summary of Discussion of meeting between Hussein al-Youha, Mr. Chu, and Mr. Sarraf, June 12, 1973.

110. ILO RL 271-3-1 Letter Hussein Saqer to H. A. Dunning, ILO, September 8, 1968; ILO RL 271-3-01, Minute Sheet, D. S. Raj, September 5, 1968.

111. See *al-Taliʿa* series "Liqaʾat fi al-Niqabat," specifically Issues 383–85 and 388–90.

112. Personal interview, Hussein Saqr, November 28, 2017; ARC 108129, Telex Kuwait to London, September 19, 1970; "Idrab ʿummal al-Minaʾ Taht Madhillat al-Sharʿiyya . . . wa Lakin," *al-Taliʿa*, Issue 426, May 26, 1973; "al-ʿUmmal fi al-Qitaʿ al- ʾahli," *al-Taliʿa*, Issue 428, June 9, 1973; "Idrab al-ʿummal fi Minaʾ al-Shuwaikh," September 7, 1971, *al-Mujtamaʿ*, KU 10/zay/510.

113. "Idrab ʿumal al-Minaʾ Taht Midhallat al-Sharʿiyya . . . wa Lakin," *al-Taliʿa*, Issue 426, May 26, 1973; "al-ʿamal fi al-Qitaʿ al-ʾahli," *al-Taliʿa*, Issue 428, June 9, 1973.

114. "Bayan min Niqabat al-Asmidaa," *al-Taliʿa*, Issue 386, August 5, 1972; "ʾIla Mata Tastamirr al-ʾAwsaʿ ʿala Halatiha fi Sharikat al-ʾAsmida al-Kimawiyya?," *al-Taliʿa*, Issue 405, December 23, 1972; "ʾIstighlal Bishʿ fi Sharikat al-ʾAsmida al-Kimawiyya," *al-Taliʿa*, Issue 394, September 30, 1972; "ʿUmmal Niqabat al-ʾAsmidah: ʾImma Tahqiq al-Matalib ʾaw al-ʾIdrab," *al-Taliʿa*, Issue 415, March 10, 1973.

115. "Baʿd Ma Jara fi al-ʾAsmida al-Kimawiyyaa: Hal ʾasbahat al-Tafriqah Bayn al-Kuwaitiyyin wa Ghayr al-Kuwaitiyyin (ʿurfan)?" *Al-Taliʿa*, Issue 408, January 13, 1973.

116. "Naqabat ʿUmmal al-ʾAsmida Tutawuj Juhudha al-Muthmira bi-Tahqiq Makasib Jadidah lil-ʿummal," *al-Taliʿa*, Issue 418, March 31, 1973; "Sharikat al-ʾAsmida al-Kimawiyya Tatarajiʿ ʿan Wuʿudhiha lil-ʿummal wa Tarfad Jadwal al-Usbuʿ al-Madi," *al-Taliʿa*, Issue 419, April 7, 1973; "ʿUmmal al-Kimawiyya Yatasaʾalun," *al-Taliʿa*, Issue 420, April 14, 1973; "Ittifaq ʾawwali li-Taswiyat Mushkil ʿummal al-ʾasmida al-Kimawiyya," *al-Taliʿa*, Issue 425, May 19, 1973.

117. "Tasrih ʿAshwaʾi li-ʿummal wa-Saʾiqi al-Sayyarat fi Wizarat al-ʾAshghal," *al-Taliʿa*, Issue 428, June 9, 1973.

118. "ʾAkhbar ʿUmmaliyya," *al-Taliʿa*, March 11, 1972, KU 10/zay/300; "Wa ʾAkhiran Dhaharat Niqabat Muwadhafi al-Bunuk ʾila al-Wujud," *al-Hadaf*, January 25, 1973, KU 10/zay/100.

119. "Raʾis Niqabat al-Bunuk: Nurid al-Ziyadat bi-ʾAthar Rajʿi Iʿtibaran min ʿAm 71," *al-Qabas*, December 19, 1973, KU 10/zay/100; "Rafʿ Idrab al-ʿAmilin fi al-Bunuk baʿda Istimrarihi 8 Ayyam," *al-Taliʿa*, June 22, 1974, KU 10/zay/600.

120. "Barnamaj al-ʿAmal al-Niqabi fi al-Kuwait," *al-Taliʿa*, November 16, 1974, KU 10/zay/322.

121. Al-Mdairis, *al-Mujtamaʿ al-Madani wa-al-Haraka al-Wataniyya fi al-Kuwait*, 110.

122. "Wajhat Nadhar al-Mudir al-Tijari li-Bank al-Khalij Yaʿqub al-Juʿan fi al-Idrab," *al-Risala*, June 16, 1974, KU 10/zay/600; "ʿAwdat al-Muwajaha fi Qitaʿ al-ʿAmal

al-Masrafi," *al-Siyasa*, December 31, 1975, KU 10/zay/400; "Lajnat al-Bunuk Tarfud Mashru' al-Shu'un li-Ziyadat Rawatib al-Muwadhafin," *al-Siyasa*, May 2, 1976, KU 10/zay/510; "Wazir al-Shu'un Yatadakhkhal li-Hall Niza' al-Bunuk," *al-Watan*, May 23, 1976, KU 10/zay/510; "Wuqi'at al-Ittifaqiyya bayn al-Bunuk wa Naqabat al-Muwadhafin," *al-Ra'i al-'Am*, May 28, 1976, KU 10/zay/510.

123. "Muhammad Fahd al-'Uwayda," *al-Risala*, December 23, 1973, KU 10/zay/310; "Bayan min al-Ittihad al-'āmm li-'ummal al-Kuwait bisha'n Matalib 'ummal Masna' al-Asbist," *al-Siyasa*, December 10, 1974, KU 10/zay/310; "Tahiyya wa-Ba'd," *al-Tali'a*, Issue 295, September 2, 1970.

124. "Hatta al-Yawm Nunaqish Faqat al-Tajnis," *Ajiyal*, January 27, 1974, KU 3/zay/400.

125. "Ara' fi al-Jinsiyya wa-al-Iqama al-Da'ima," *al-Qabas*, December 23, 1974, KU 3/zay/400.

126. "al-Qabliyya Ta'ud ila al-Kuwait," *al-Watan*, October 16, 1974, KU 18/zay/350.

127. "Kuwaitiyyun ma' Naqs al-Muwatana," *al-Yaqutha*, July 4, 1972, KU 3/zay/400.

128. "Ara' fi al-Jinsiyya wa-l-Iqama al-Da'ima," *al-Qabas*, December 23, 1974, KU 3/zay/400; "Fima Yutabi' Majlis al-'umma al-Yawm Munaqashat Mawdu' al-Jinsiyya," *al-Siyasa*, February 1, 1975, KU 3/zay/410.

129. ILO UNDP/TA 271-3-A-1, Letter C. H. Sanadiki to S. Burgan, April 25, 1971.

130. "Nashatat al-Ittihad al-'amm li-'ummal al-Kuwait," *al-Siyasa*, November 4, 1973, KU 10/zay/310.

131. "Iqtiharat Hawla al-Daman al-Ijtima'i," *al-Tali'a*, Issue 347, October 30, 1971.

132. ILO UNDP/TA 271-3-A-1, Letter, Arthur Patterson to C. H. Sanadiki, September 23, 1971; ILO UNDP/TA 271-3-A-1, Memorandum C. H. Sanadiki to S. K. Burgan, September 15, 1971.

133. "Akhbar 'Ummaliyya," *al-Tali'a*, Issue 405, December 23, 1972.

134. "al-Wafd Yabhat ma' al-Mas'ulin Sighah li-Tatbiq al-Qanun al-'iraqi dun Ta'ariduh ma' al-Andhima al-Ma'mul biha fi al-Kuwait," *al-Siyasa*, November 12, 1974, KU 10/alif/600.

135. "al-Ittihad al-'amm li-'ummal al-Kuwait Ya'idd Mashru' Qanun li-l-Ta'minat al-Ijtima'iyya Hadafuh Tashji' al-Kuwaitiyyin 'ala al-'amal fi al-Qita' al-Ahli," *al-Siyasa*, January 6, 1974, KU 10/Ha/610; "al-Ittihad al-'amm li-l-'ummal Yashra' li-l-Nuwab," *al-Siyasa*, April 26, 1974, KU 10/zay/310; al-Khatib and al-Najjar, *al-Kuwait, min al-Dawla ila al-Imara*, 44; "al-Ittihad al-'amm li-'ummal wa-Mustakhdimi al-Kuwait A'adda al-Mashru' wa-Rafa'ahu ila Majlis al-Umma wa-Majlis al-Wuzara'," *Akhbar al-Kuwait*, February 2, 1974, KU 10/alif/610.

136. "Ittihad 'ummal al-Kuwait Yutalib al-Hukuma bi-l-Isdar fi Iqar Qanun al-Ta'minat" *al-Siyasa*, August 8, 1976, KU 10/del/610; "Tasjil 'ashr Mulahadhat Hawla Qanun al-Ta'minat al-Ijtima'iyya," *al-Siyasa*, August 20, 1976, KU 10/del/600; al-Asbahi, *al-Haraka al-Niqabiyya al-Kuwaitiyya*, 99–100; "Qanun al-Ta'minat al-Ijtima'iyya min Ahamm al-Makasib Allati Haqqaqaha Itthad al-'ummal," *al-Tali'a*, October 28, 1989, KU 10/zay/310.

137. "al-Jinsiyya wa al-Tajannus," *Mir'at al-Umma*, July 5, 1972, KU 3/zay/600; "Mashakil al-Jinsiyya wa al-Iqama," *al-Nahda*, July 15, 1972, KU 3/zay/200; "al-Jinsiyya liman Atamma al-Dirasa al-Thanawiyya wa Ghayr Muntami ila Ayy Jinsiyya 'ukhra," *Akhbar al-Kuwait*, March 10, 1973, KU 3/zay/000; "al-Lajna al-Khassa bi-Ri'asat al-Lawa' al-Shwayni Tandhur fi 'adad Mahdud min al-Talabat Yawm al-Sabt," *al-Siyasa*, October 5, 1972, KU 3/zay/400;

"al-Masha'an Yuwaddih Shurut Talab al-Jinsiyya," *al-Ra'i al-'Am*, October 13, 1972, KU 3/zay/400.

138. "al-Jinsiyya al-Kuwaytiyya: Man Mum Alladhina Yastahiqunaha?" *Al-Nahda*, August 31, 1974, KU 3/zay/400.

139. "al-Jinsiyya al-Kuwaytiyya li-Rijal al-Shurta alladhina Amdawa fi al-Khidma Akthar min 20 'Aman," *al-Siyasa*, September 21, 1976, KU 3/zay/400; "Hawl Tajnis al-Daf'a al-'awla min Rijal al-Jaysh wa al-Shurta," *al-Ra'i al-'Am*, October 4, 1976, KU 3/zay/400.

140. "Hunaak 3 Lajan lil-Nadhar wa Tahaqqaq fi Talabat al-Jinsiyya al-Kuwaytiyya," *al-Siyasa*, December 12, 1974, KU 3/zay/400.

141. "al-Hukuma Mutamassika bi-Mabadi'iha fi al-Jinsiyya," *al-Hadaf*, June 22, 1972, KU 3/zay/400; "Wazir al-Dakhiliyya: al-Jinsiyya Tu'ta li-Mustahiqiha Faqat," *al-Nahda*, September 16, 1972, KU 3/zay/400.

142. "Lajnat al-Jinsiyya al-Khassa bil-Tullab Tadrus 15 Talaban Tawafaq 'ala Ba'diha wa Tu'ajil al-Akhar," *al-Siyasa*, October 1, 1974, KU 3/zay/410.

143. "Wafaqna 'ala Tajnis 150 Taliban min Khiriji al-Thanawiyya," *al-Siyasa*, May 19, 1975, KU 3/zay/400; "150 Taliban wa Taliba Yahsulun 'ala al-Jinsiyya," *al-Watan*, June 3, 1975, 3/zay/400; "Manh al-Jinsiyya al-Kuwaytiyya ila 'adad min Ri'aya ad-Duwal al-'arabiyya," *al-Watan*, January 21, 1975, KU 3/zay/400; "'Akthar Talibi al-Jinsiyya Tanqusuhum al-Bayanat wa al-Awraq al-Thubutiyya," *al-Ra'i al-'Am*, May 13, 1978, KU 3/zay/200.

144. "Marsum Amiri bi-Sahb al-Jinsiyya al-Kuwaitiyya min Ba'a al-Muwatinin li-'adam Shar'īya wa Dusturiyya al-Husul 'alayha," *al-Siyasa*, December 31, 1973, KU 3/zay/700.

145. "Isqat al-Jinsiyya 'an Arba'a Hasalu 'alayha bi-Tariqat al-Ghish," *al-Siyasa*, April 30, 1975, KU 3/zay/700.

146. "Wazir al-Dakhiliyyaa wa al-Difa' Ya'qidu Nadwa Suhufiyya," *al-Siyasa*, February 16, 1975, KU 3/Ha/400.

147. "Mushakil al-Jinsiyya wa al-Tajannus," *al-Watan*, February 28, 1975, KU 3/zay/400.

148. "'uqfal Milaf al-Jinsiyya bi-Bayan Tawil 'alqah Wazir al-Dakhiliyya wa al-Difaa' fi Majlis al-Umma," *al-Siyasa*, April 2, 1975, KU 3/zay/000; "La Tahmilu Sa'ad, al-'abdullah Mushkilat al-Jinsiyya," *Sawt al-Khalij*, April 17, 1975, KU 3/zay/400.

149. "al-Ra'as al-'unaym: Intahayna min al-Jinsiyyaa wa Sanabhath Mashru'at al-Qawanin al-Mudrajat 'ala al-Jadwal," *al-Ra'i al-'Am*, April 6, 1975, KU 3/zay/000.

150. "Tawsiyyat bi-Tajnis al-Kafa'at al-'arabiyya wa al-Iqama al-Da'ima wa Haqq al-Milkiyya al-Khassa," *al-Ra'i al-'Am*, April 10, 1975, KU 3/zay/400.

151. "al-Majlis Yutabi' Munaqashat Qanun al-Jinsiyyaa wa al-Tajnis," *al-Watan*, April 2, 1975, KU 3/zay/000.

152. "Khalid al-Mas'ud Yuhajim al-Hukuma wa Yad'u li-Tajnis al-'arab," *al-Watan*, April 7, 1975, KU 3/zay/400; "Nadwa 'an al-Jinsiyya Yashtarikuha al-Duwaij wa al-Mas'ud," *al-Ra'i al-'Am*, April 7, 1975, KU 3/zay/400.

153. "Iqtirah bi-'an Yakun Manh al-Jinsiyya lit-Taliba aladhin Atammu Dirasatihim fi al-Kuwait 'ilzamiyya," *al-Siyasa*, June 6, 1975, KU 3/zay/400; "Istifta' al-Nahda," *al-Nahda*, June 26, 1976, KU 3/zay/400; "Ta'dil Qanun al-Jinsiyya Faraghat min Ta'dilihi al-Lajnah al-Mukalafa wa Sayunaqash Qariban," *al-Siyasa*, November 27, 1975, KU 3/zay/200.

154. "'Azmat al-Hijra al-Mu'akisa," *al-Watan*, March 1, 1975, KU 7/laam/350; "Hal Tabqa al-Hukuma al-Taraf al-Wahid al-Mas'ul 'an al-Tadrib al-Tanmuway dun Musahamah Kafiyya min al-Qita' al-Khas?" *Al-Siyasa*, August 19, 1975, KU 10/Ha/600.

155. "Wazir al-Shu'un al-Ijtima'iyya wa al-'amal Yusdir Thalath Qararat," *al-Risala*, January 25, 1973, KU 10/ba/000.

156. "'awwal Dirasa Midaniyya Tastahdif Ru'ya Wadiha li-Haya 22 Alaf 'amil," *Mir'at al-Umma*, August 7, 1974.

157. "Waqf Hijrat al-Yad al-'amila min al-Kuwait," *al-Watan*, September 17, 1975, KU 10/Ha/230.

158. "Wazarat al-Shu'un al-Ijtima'iyya wa al-'amal Tara ann laha al-Huqiyya fi al-Muwafaqa 'ala Manh al-Iqamat li-Hasr al-Quwa al-'amila wa I'ta' al-Fursa li-l-Aydi al-'amila al-Wataniyya" *al-Siyasa*, August 30, 1974, KU 10/ba/000.

159. "Awwal Idrab min Naw'ihi fi al-'alam!" *Al-Siyasa*, September 9, 1975, KU 10/ba/010.

160. "Mishan Explains New Rules for Residence and Work Permits," *The Daily News*, March 6, 1975, KU 3/Ha/410.

161. "Tashilat Kabira lil-Iqama wa al-Ziyara," *al-Siyasa*, March 9, 1975, KU 3/Ha/400.

162. "Mu'amalat al-Iqama 'aw al-Ziyara Batat Mayssara," *al-Watan*, April 21, 1975, KU 3/Ha/400.

163. "Mushkilat al-Jinsiyya wa al-Ziyara wa al-Iqama wa Dukhul al-Filastiniyyin 'ila al-Bilad," *al-Risala*, April 2, 1978, KU 3/zay/200.

164. "Husn al-Suluk Laysa Daruriyyan lil-Iqama," *al-Siyasa*, March 6, 1975, KU 3/Ha/410.

165. "'ad Wazir al-Shu'un min Misr," *al-Ra'i al-'Am*, December 28, 1974, KU 10/Ha/210.

166. "al-Kuwait Tu'ayyid al-Ittifaqat al-Thuna'iyya li-T'amin al-Quwa al-'amila," *al-Ra'i al-'Am*, July 8, 1975, KU 10/Ha/230; "Yudarris Istirad Mullhiqin lil-'ummal fi al-Sifarat al-Kuwaitiyya," *al-Siyasa*, April 3, 1975, KU 10/Ha/210.

167. "Dirasat 'arabiyya Mushtaraka Tushim fiha al-Kuwait Hawla al-Aydi al-'amila," *al-Watan*, December 8, 1975, KU 10/Ha/200; ILO TF 271-2-A-4-1, Sabry H. Tawfik, "Tentative plan of work," March 20, 1976, and Progress report No. 2, July 1, 1976.

168. "al-Kuwait Ya'ani min Nuqs al-Aydi al-'amila wa Lakin," *Ajiyal*, November 16, 1975, KU 20/Ha/230.

169. "Mushkilat Nadrat al-'amila," *al-Watan*, October 16, 1974, KU 10/Ha/230.

170. AlShehabi, "Histories of Migration to the Gulf"; Longva, *Walls Built on Sand*, 30.

171. Nasra Shah et al., "Foreign Domestic Workers in Kuwait: Who employs How Many," *Asian and Pacific Migration Journal* 11, no. 2 (2002): 247–69.

172. "Rackets within rackets?" *Kuwait Times*, January 25, 1978, KU 10/ha/321.

173. "Strict laws of Egyptian government," *Kuwait Times*, January 21, 1978, KU 10/ha/321.

174. "Wad' Nidhamayn li-Khidam al-Manazil wa-Tahdid Amakin Sakan al-Muqimin," *al-Ra'i al-'Am*, April 1, 1975, KU 10/h/321.

175. "al-Shu'un Tutabi' Awda' Khidam al-Manazil li-Khalq 'alaqa Sahiha ma'a Makhdmihim," *al-Siyasa*, April 29, 1975, KU 10/ha/321.

176. "Wizarat al-Shu'un Tulahiq Samasirat al-Takhdim," *al-Ra'i al-'Am*, February 28, 1975, KU 10/ha/321.

177. "al-Kuwait bu'ani min Naqs al-'aydi al-'amila wa Lakin," *Ajiyal*, November 16, 1975, KU 20/Ha/230.

178. "Tandhim Shurut wa-'awda' Iqamat al-Khadam al-Khususiyyin," *al-Ra'i al-'Am*, September 22, 1977, KU 10/ha/321.

179. Garavini, *The Rise and Fall of OPEC*, 191.

180. Dietrich, *Oil Revolution*, chapter 6; Garavini, *The Rise and Fall of OPEC*, 174.–206.

181. Dietrich, *Oil Revolution*, 238.

182. See for instance Garavini, *The Rise and Fall of OPEC*, 182–83, 203–209.

183. LAB 13/2141, R. L. Morris, First Secretary Labour, Embassy Beirut, "Memorandum on Industrial Relations in the American Independent Oil Company (Aminoil)," July 4, 1970.

184. Personal interview, Daifullah Falah Sultan, December 4, 2017.

185. "'ummal Sharikat Aminoil Yuhaddidun Matalibhum fi 'arida Qaddamuha ila Mudir 'am al-Sharika," *al-Tali'a*, December 14, 1964, KU 7/mim/390; "'aghrab 'amaliyya Ta'sifiyya fi Sharikat 'amn 'awil: al-Sharika Tazuru Taqarir Tibbiyya li-Takhallus min al-'ummal," *al-Tali'a*, July 4, 1965, KU 7/sin; "Hal Sijarat al-'amil al-'arabi Wahdaha Tahriq wa Tadammir?" *al-Risala*, March 29, 1966, KU 7/sin.

186. LAB 13/2141, R. L. Morris, "Memorandum on Industrial Relations in the American Independent Oil Company (Aminoil)," July 4, 1970.

187. "Aminoil Employees Go on Strike Next Sunday," *The Daily News*, March 6, 1972.

188. "al-Dars al-Thamin min Najah 'umal al-Aminoil," *al-Tali'a*, March 18, 1972, KU 7/kaf/660.

189. "al-Ittihad al-'am li-'umal al-Kuwait Yad'u al-Niqabat lil-Idrab al-'am," *Akhbar al-Kuwait*, March 11, 1972, KU 10/zay/310.

190. "Akhbar 'umaliyya," *al-Tali'a*, March 11, 1972, KU 10/zay/300.

191. FCO 8/1840, Letter J. J. Beale to G. Lockton, March 16, 1972.

192. “al-Dars al-Thamin min Najah ʿumal al-Aminoil,” *al-Taliʿa*, March 18, 1972, KU 7/kaf/660.

193. “ʾawwal Abril al-Qadim Yashhad ʾAdham Idrab fi al-Bilad ila ʾidha Tarajaʿat al-KOC,” *al-Taliʿa*, March 25, 1972, KU 7/mim/390.

194. “al-Niqaba Tusir ʿala Ziyadat ʾujur al-ʿamilin Ghayr al-Kuwaitiyyin bi-ʾathar Rajʿai,” *al-Risala*, May 28, 1972, KU 7/mim/350.

195. FCO 8/1840, Diplomatic Report No. 266/72, “Trade Unions in Kuwait,” Ambassador Kuwait to the Secretary of State for Foreign and Commonwealth Affairs, April 18, 1972.

196. FCO 8/1840, Diplomatic Report No. 266/72, “Trade Unions in Kuwait,” Ambassador Kuwait to the Secretary of State for Foreign and Commonwealth Affairs, April 18, 1972.

197. FCO 8/1840, Diplomatic Report No. 266/72, “Trade Unions in Kuwait,” Ambassador Kuwait to the Secretary of State for Foreign and Commonwealth Affairs, April 18, 1972.

198. FCO 8/1840, Letter J. J. Beale to G. Lockton, March 16, 1972.

199. FCO 8/1840, Diplomatic Report No. 266/72, “Trade Unions in Kuwait,” Ambassador Kuwait to the Secretary of State for Foreign and Commonwealth Affairs, April 18, 1972.

200. FCO 8/1840, Diplomatic Report No. 266/72, “Trade Unions in Kuwait,” Ambassador Kuwait to the Secretary of State for Foreign and Commonwealth Affairs, April 18, 1972.

201. “Mata Yahsul ʿummal Sharikat al-Naft ʿala Huquqihim?” *Mirʾat al-Umma*, July 26, 1972, KU 7/kaf/660.

202. “Niqabat ʿummal Sharikat Naft al-Kuwait Tuʿlin al-Idrab Yawm as-Sabt al-Qadim,” *al-Siyasa*, June 4, 1972, KU 7/mim/350.

203. “Kitab min ʿummal Sharikat az-Zayt al-Amrikiyya ila Sumu Wali al-ʿahd Yuhaddid fih Matalibahum al-Khassa bi-Ziyadat al-Ujur,” *al-Siyasa*, October 14, 1972, KU 7/sin.

204. “Bayan Ham min an-Niqaba Yadaʿ an-Nuqat Fawqa al-Huruf” *Akhbar al-Kuwait*, August 23, 1972, KU 7/sin; “Munaqashat al-Qanun 28 bi-Shaʾn al-ʿamal fi Qitaʿ an-Naft wa Dawr al-Hukuma wa ash-Sharikat Izaʾ Huquq al-ʿummal,” *al-Siyasa*, November 17, 1972, KU 7/lam/350.

205. “Taʿliq Idrab al-ʿamal li-Usbuʿain,” *al-Raʾi al-ʿAm*, December 1, 1972, KU 7/mim/390.

206. “ʾanna la Nunkir al-Juhud allati Badhaluha Wazir al-Shuʾun wa fi al-Waqt Nafsih lam Nalqi Minhu al-Taʾyid al-Kafi,” *al-Siyasa*, December 12, 1972, KU 7/sin.

207. “Ittihad ʿummal al-Naft Yutalib Majlis al-Umma biʿada al-Nadhar fi al-Taʿdilat al-Akhira li-Qanun Qitaʿ al-Naft,” *al-Raʾi al-ʿAm*, November 1, 1972, KU 7/kaf/660.

208. “al-Mawqif al-Mabdaʾi al-Niqabi Tijah Kaffat al-Qadaiya al-ʿUmaliyya,” *al-Siyasa*, December 18, 1972, KU 10/zay/100; “Niqabat ʿumal al-Aminoil Turid ʿala Wazir al-Shuʾun,” *al-Ittihad*, January 1, 1973, KU 7/sin.

209. "al-Hukuma Sahabat Qanun al-ʿamal wa ʿaddalat fih li-Yanasib Maslahat al-Kuwait wa al-ʿummal wa Laysa Sharikat al-Naft," *al-Raʾi al-ʿAm*, November 23, 1972, KU 10/mim/000.

210. "Sanasaʿa li-Hall al-Khilaf bayn al-ʿummal wa Sharikat "Aminoil" Wazir al-Shuʾun al-Ijtimaʿiyya ila al-Raʾi al-ʿAm," *al-Raʾi al-ʿAm*, December 17, 1972, KU 7/sin.

211. "Sharikat al-Bitrul al-Wataniyya al-Kuwaytiyya wa Mustaqbal al-Kuwait al-Sinaʿī," *al-Taliʿa*, Issue 238, July 17, 1968.

212. "Istithnaʾ al-Sharikat al-Wataniyya min Ahkam al-Qanun wa Qasr Huquq al-Taqaʿud ʿala al-Kuwaitiyyin," *al-Raʾi al-ʿAm*, May 12, 1969, KU 7/kaf/660; "Li-Hisab man Zadat Asʿar al-Binzin," *al-Hadaf*, August 10, 1972, KU 7/lam/390; "KNPC – Labour Union Seek Solution To Problems," *The Kuwait Daily News*, March 17, 1972, KU 7/lam/350.

213. "Hawla Niqabat ʿummal wa Mustakhdimi Sharikat al-Bitrul al-Wataniyya," *al-Taliʿa*, February 4, 1968, KU 7/kaf/660; "Mulid Niqaba Jadida Sharikat al-Bitrul al-Wataniyya al-Kuwaitiyya," *al-Taliʿa*, Issue 255, November 20, 1968; "Wizarat al-Shuʾun al-Ijtimaʿiyya wa al-ʿamal Tukhriq Itifaqiyya al-Hurriyat al-Niqabiyya," *al-Taliʿa*, Issue 262, January 15, 1969.

214. "Limadha la Tasri Majaniyyat al-ʿilaj ʿala al-Jamiʿ," and "Ila Mata Hadhihi al-Asalib fi Sharikat al-Bitrul?" *al-Risala*, December 26, 1971, KU 7/lam/350; "Badal al-Intiqal wa Ujr al-Saʿa fi Sharikat al-Bitrul al-Wataniyya," *al-Taliʿa*, Issue 348, November 6, 1971.

215. "Niqabat al-Bitrul al-Wataniyya Tarfud Mashruʿ al-Sharika li-Ziyadat al-Ujur," *al-Taliʿa*, Issue 389, August 26, 1972; "Istiyaʾ Shamil fi Jamiʿ al-Niqabat li-Qarar Rafaʿ Asʿar al-Mahruqat," *al-Taliʿa*, Issue 387, August 12, 1972.

216. "al-Bahth ʿan "Wataniyya" al-Sharikat al-Wataniyya," *al-Taliʿa*, Issue 388, August 19, 1972; "Asbab Shakwa ʿummal Sharikat al-Bitrul al-Wataniyya," *Sawt al-Khalij*, October 12, 1972, 7/lam/390; "Niqabat al-Bitrul al-Wataniyya Tataʿahhad bi-Tahqiq Ziada lil-ʿummal al-ʿarab," *al-Taliʿa*, Issue 397, October 21, 1972.

217. Quote from "Asbab Shakwa ʿummal Sharikat al-Bitrul al-Wataniyya," *Sawt al-Khalij*, October 12, 1972, 7/lam/390. See also "Istajabat Sharikat al-Bitrul al-Wataniyya li-Matalib al-ʿummal wa-Zadat Rawatib al-Kuwaitiyyin," *al-Raʾi al-ʿAm*, October 14, 1972, KU 7/lam/350; "Ikhwanuna min Ghayr al-Kuwaitiyyin Awwalan," *al-Siyasa*, October 16, 1972, KU 7/lam/390.

218. "Niqabat ʿummal al-Bitrul al-Wataniyya Tataʿahhad bi-Tahqiq al-Ziyada li-Ghayr al-Kuwaitiyyin," *al-Raʾi al-ʿAm*, October 16, 1972, KU 7/lam/350.

219. "Ziyada Rawatib Muwadhafi wa ʿummal Sharikat al-Bitrul al-Wataniyya bi-Hayth Tashmal al-Jamiʿ wa al-Kuwaitiyyin bi-Athar Rajʿi," *al-Raʾi al-ʿAm*, November 23, 1972, KU 7/lam/390; "KNPC, Labour Union Reach Agreement," *The Daily News*, July 15, 1973, KU 7/lam/350.

220. "Sharikat al-Bitrul al-Wataniyya Mutalaba bi-Taʾmin al-ʿilaj wa al-Dawaʾ li-ʿummalha," *al-Risala*, February 18, 1973, KU 7/lam/380; "Majlis Idarat Niqabat ʿummal Sharikat al-Bitrul al-Wataniyya Yuwaddih wa Yuhadhdhir al-Sharika fi Uslub Mufawadatiha," *al-Risala*, June 17, 1973, KU 7/lam/350.

221. "al-KOC Ta'tabir Tahdid Niqabat 'ummal Sharikat Naft al-Kuwait bi-l-Idrab bi-annah la Mubarrir Lah," *al-Siyasa*, June 5, 1973, KU 7/mim/390; "Niqabat 'Ummal Sharikat Naft al-Kuwait Tuhaddid: al-Idrab al-Shamil Khilal Usbu'," *al-Qabas*, May 29, 1973, KU 7/mim/390; "'Ummal Naft al-Kuwait . . . Nahnu Natalib bi-Absat al-Huquq!" *Sawt al-Khalij*, June 21, 1973, KU 7/mim/390; "al-'amilun fi Sharikat Naft al-Kuwait Yusirun 'ala al-Idrab," *al-Tali'a*, Issue 427, June 2, 1973.

222. "Ilgha' al-Idrab al-KOC ba'd Ittifaq al-Niqaba wa al-Sharika," *al-Qabas*, July 12, 1973, KU 7/mim/390.

223. "Madha Hahduthu fi al-Sharika al-'amrikiyya?" *Al-Tali'a*, Issue 344, October 9, 1971; "Shu'un 'ummaliyya," *al-Tali'a*, Issue 346, October 23, 1971; "Niqabat 'ummal Sharikat al-Zayt al-'amrikiyya Tuhadid bi-l-Idrab wa Tatakaddam bi-Jadwal Shamil Mu'ad al-Mashru' al-Sharika li-Ziyadat al-Rawatib," *al-Siyasa*, March 21, 1973, KU 7/sin.

224. "'Ummal al-Zayt al-'amrikiyya Yu'ayyidun Qarar Niqabatihim Radd al-Ziyada al-Muftarahah," *al-Ra'i al-'Am*, February 23, 1973, KU 7/sin; "Ittasa' al-Khilaf bayn al-Aminoil wa 'ummaliha ba'd Qarar bi Ziyadat al-Ruwatib Radfadathu al-Niqaba," *al-Ra'i al-'Am*, March 20, 1973, KU 7/sin.

225. "al-Sharika Lam Tu'tina Siwa 39% min Huquqina wa Barqat bayn al-Kuwaitiyyin wa Ghayr al-Kuwaitiyyin bil-'athar al-Rij'iyyah lil-Ziyadat," *al-Siyasa*, April 6, 1973, KU 7/sin; "'Umal al-Aminoil hal Yu'linun al-Idrab?" *Al-Hadaf*, July 26, 1973, KU 7/sin; "al-Siyasa Mahaliyya," *al-Siyasa*, July 27, 1973, KU 7/kaf/660.

226. "'ala Nahw ma Infaradati bih Akhbar al-Kuwait 'umal al-Aminoil Yanfidhun al-Idrab," *Akhbar al-Kuwait*, August 19, 1973, KU 7/sin; "Wazir al-Shu'un Yu'lin al-Ittihad bayna 'umal wa Sharikat al-Aminoil," *al-Qabas*, September 2, 1973, KU 7/sin; "Tandid bi-l-Mawqif al-Mutaqallib wa Nashr Jadwal bi-l-Ziyadat," *al-Ra'i al-'Am*, September 5, 1973, KU 7/sin.

227. "Idrab 'umal al-Aminoil," *al-Tali'a*, September 15, 1973, KU 7/sin; "Bayyan min Majlis Idarat Niqabat 'ummal Aminoil," *al-Ra'i al-'Am*, September 8, 1973, KU 7/sin.

228. "Idrab 'ummal al-Aminoil al-Yawm wa al-Sharika Tawwaqif al-Intaj," *al-Ra'i al-'Am*, September 9, 1973, KU 7/sin.

229. Al-Asbahi, *al-Haraka al-Niqabiyya al-Kuwaitiyya*, 80–81.

230. "Idrab 'umal al-Aminoil," *al-Tali'a*, September 15, 1973, KU 7/sin.

231. "Idrab 'umal al-Aminoil," *al-Ra'i al-'Am*, September 10, 1973, KU 7/sin; "Ittfaq Inha' al-Munaza'a al-Tawila," *al-Tali'a*, November 24, 1973, KU 7/sin.

232. Al-Asbahi, *al-Haraka al-Niqabiyya al-Kuwaitiyya*, 82.

233. "Akhiran . . . Intahat Khilafat al-Aminoil ma' 'ummalha," *al-Qabas*, November 19, 1973, KU 7/sin; "Sharikat al-Zayt al-'amrikiyya Tusri' fi Tanfidh Tahwil al-'ummal al-Yawmayn 'ila Shahriyyin wa Ziyadat Rawatibhim," *Akhbar al-Kuwait*, November 24, 1973, KU 7/sin; "al-Assas al-Jadid li-'alaqat al-'ujur bayna al-Aminoil wa Niqabat 'ummalha," *al-Qabas*, November 25, 1973, KU 7/sin.

234. Al-Asbahi, *al-Haraka al-Niqabiyya al-Kuwaitiyya*, 80.

235. "al-Asas al-Jadid li-'alaqat al-'ujur bayna al-Aminoil wa Niqabat 'ummalha," *al-Qabas*, September 12, 1973, KU 7/sin; "Wazir al-Shu'un Yuraddid 'ala 'al-Hadaf'," *al-Hadaf*, August 2, 1973, KU 10/zay/524.

236. "al-Bitrul al-'arabi," *al-Tali'a*, Issue 279, May 13, 1970; "al-Bitruliyat," *al-Tali'a*, Issue 301, October 28, 1970; "Nadwat al-Bitrul wa-al-Inma' al-Iqtisadi al-'arabi," *al-Tali'a*, Issue 304, November 18, 1970; "Ittifaqiyyat al-Musharaka Naksa Khatira li-al-'arab," *al-Tali'a*, Issue 406, December 30, 1972.

237. "Malayin 'ummal al-'arab wa-al-'alam Yadu'mun Nidal 'ummal wa-Sha'b al-'Iraq Yuhayyun Qarar al-Ta'mim," *al-Tali'a*, Issue 385, July 29, 1972; "Niqabi Misri Yatahaddath 'an Ta'mim al-Naft al-'Iraqi wa-Dawr Mas'uliyat al-Tabaqa al-'amila al-Misriya," *al-Tali'a*, Issue 387, August 12, 1972; "Liqa' ma' al-Wafd al-'amili al-Kubi fi Baghdad . . . wa Hadith 'an al-Ta'mim wa al-Tadamun wa al-Thawrat al-Taharruriyya," *al-Tali'a*, Issue 392, September 16, 1972; "al-Naft k-Silah," *al-Tali'a*, Issue 400, November 18, 1972.

238. "Tabaqat Fudlat al-Mu'a'id Tajahid ba'd I'aha lil-'ummal," *al-Tali'a*, Issue 251, October 23, 1968; "Muqabala Muhammad 'Ayish Ra'is al-Ittihad al-'amm li-'ummal al-'Iraq," *al-Tali'a*, Issue 384, July 22, 1972.

239. Parra, *Oil Politics*, 156–59, 194; Garavini, *The Rise and Fall of OPEC*, 209.

240. "Mawqifuna min al-Musharaka," *al-Tali'a*, Issue 409, January 27, 1973; "Silah al-Bitrul wa ma Yajibu an Tafhamahu Amrika," *al-Tali'a*, Issue 429, June 16, 1973.

241. "al-Musharika bayn al-Shakl wa al-Madmun," *al-Tali'a*, Issue 460, February 2, 1974.

242. "Hamla Qawiyyah 'ala Ittifaqiyyat al-Musharika fi Majlis al-Umma," *al-Tali'a*, Issue 410, February 3, 1973; "Majlis al-Umma," *al-Tali'a*, Issue 412, February 17, 1973.

243. "Nadwat al-Ittihad al-'am li-'ummal al-Kuwait 'an al-Musharika al-Naftiyya," *al-Ra'i al-'Am*, February 15, 1973, KU 10/zay/310; "al-Ittihad al-'am li-Niqabat al-'ummal al-Kuwait," *al-Tali'a*, Issue 411, February 10, 1973.

244. "Ma' Hussein Saqr wa Hassan Falah," *al-Tali'a*, Issue 422, April 28, 1973.

245. Parra, *Oil Politics*, 156–59, 194; Garavini, *The Rise and Fall of OPEC*, 209. For a detailed account of parliamentary debates see Shuhaiber, "Political Development in Kuwait," chapter 5.

246. Dietrich, *Oil Revolution*, 263.

247. "'ummal Libya wa al-Kuwait Yad'un al-Istimrar Silah al-Naft," *al-Tali'a*, Issue 464, March 2, 1974.

248. "Niqabat al-KOC Tahuth al-'amilin 'ala al-'isra' fi al-Tabar' fi al-M'arika," *al-Qabas*, November 12, 1972, KU 7/mim/350; "Ittihad al-'ummal Yuhi Yawm al-Tadamun ma' al-Tabaqa al-'amila wa al-Thawra fi al-Khalij," *al-Siyasa*, June 9, 1973, KU 10/zay/310; "Yawm al-Tadamun ma'a 'ummal Mantaqat al-Khalij al-'Arabi wa 'Uman," *al-Tali'a*, June 16, 1973, KU 10/zay/310; "Bayan min al-Ittihad al-'am li-'ummal al-Kuwait," *al-Siyasa*, October 11, 1973, KU 10/zay/310.

249. "Labour Unions Call For Nationalisation Of U.S. Interests," *The Daily News*, October 14, 1973, KU 10/zay/310.

250. "'ummal al-Naft Yuqifun al-Dakh li-Muddat Thalathah Ayyam," *al-Tali'a*, October 25, 1973, KU 7/lam/390.

251. Al-Asbahi, *al-Haraka al-Niqabiyya al-Kuwaitiyya*, 84.

252. "al-ʿusaymi Yashrah Asalib al-ʿummal wa Mawaqifihim al-Batuliyya Khilal al-Harb," *Akhbar al-Kuwait*, November 27, 1973, KU 10/zay/310.

253. "ʿummal al-Naft al-Mudribun Yaqulun: Yajib Muajahat Amrika bi-Silah al-Naft wa Muqataʿat al-Bidaʾiʿ al-Amerikiyya," *al-Taliʿa*, October 25, 1973, KU 7./lam/350.

254. "al-Aminoil . . . Dawla um Sharika?" *Al-Ittihaad*, June 1, 1973, KU 7/sin.

255. Al-Asbahi, *al-Haraka al-Niqabiyya al-Kuwaitiyya*, 84; personal interview, Hassan Falah, January 9, 2018.

256. Quoted in Garavini, *The Rise and Fall of OPEC*, 221. From "Minutes of the Secretary of State's Staff Meeting," October 26, 1973, in *Foreign Relations of the United States, 1969–1976*, Volume XXXVI, Energy Crisis, 1969–1974, https://history.state.gov/historicaldocuments/frus1969-76v36/d229.

257. "ʿummal Sharikat al-Bitrul al-Wataniyya Yuʾayyidun Taʾmim al-Hukuma li-l-Sharika wa Yarfadun Rudud al-Fiʿl al-Salbiyya," *al-Siyasa*, April 9, 1975, KU 7/lam/350.

258. "Hal Taʿtina al-Mushtaraka Haqq al-Saytara ʿala Tharwatina al-Wataniyya?" *Al-Taliʿa*, Issue 465, March 9, 1974.

259. "al-Hayʾat al-Shaʿbiyya Tarfud Ittifaqiyya al-Mushtarakaa wa Tatalib bi-Taʾmim Shamil wa Fawri," *al-Taliʿa*, Issue 470, April 13, 1974.

260. "Dhakaʾ al-Hukuma fi Khidmat al-Sharikat," *al-Taliʿa*, Issue 472, April 27, 1974.

261. Parra, *Oil Politics*, 193–94.

262. Parra, *Oil Politics*, 193–94.

263. Garavini's *Rise and Fall of OPEC in the Twentieth Century* is exemplary here.

264. Al-Khatib and al-Najjar, *al-Kuwait, min al-Dawla ila al-Imara*, 49–51, 59–61. The only academic reference is al-Mdairis, *al-Mujtamaʿ al-Madani wa-al-Haraka al-Wataniyya fi al-Kuwait*, 154–55.

265. Al-Asbahi, *al-Haraka al-Niqabiyya al-Kuwaitiyya*, 85.

266. Garavini, *The Rise and Fall of OPEC in the Twentieth Century*, 254.

267. Personal interview, Daifullah Falah Sultan, December 4, 2017.

268. "Mushkilat al-Bitrul al-Wataniyya wa ʿummaluha," *al-Qabas*, March 8, 1974, KU 7/lam/350.

269. "Idrab Shamil liʿummal al-Qitaʿ al-Nafti idha lam Tastajib al-Sharikat," *al-Taliʿa*, August 3, 1974, KU 7/kaf/660.

270. "Fi al-Imkan Hall Nizaʿ al-Bitrul al-Wataniyya wa ʿummalaha bidun al-Lujuʾ ila al-Idrab," *al-Siyasa*, August 2, 1974, KU 7/lam/350.

271. "Idrab ʿummal al-Bitrul . . . ila Waqt Akhar," *al-Yaqutha*, August 26, 1974, KU 7/kaf/660.

272. "al-Lajna al-Tashriʿiyya Tunaqish Qanun al-ʿamal fi al-Qitaʿ al-ʾahli," *al-Raʾi al-ʿAm*, March 31, 1975, KU 10/mim/000.

273. "Kayf Yandhur ʿummal al-Naft ila Tahqiq Matalibihim?" *Al-Taliʿa*, August 31, 1974, KU 7/mim/350; "Sumud ʿummal al-Conoco fi Wajh al-Qamaʿ wa al-Irhab," *al-Taliʿa*, September 28, 1974, KU 7/kaf/660.

274. "al-Wazir al-ʿayyar lil-Hadaf: ʿummal al-Bitrul Rafadu al-Daʿwa allati Wajjahatuha Ilayhim lil-Mufawada," *al-Hadaf*, August 22, 1974, KU 7/kaf/660.

275. "al-ʿummal Yusiʾun Fahm al-ʿamal al-Niqabi," *Sawt al-Khalij*, September 12, 1974, KU 10/zay/500.

276. ILO UNDP/TA 271-3-A-1, Letter M. E. El-Defrawi, Country Representative Kuwait to K. Tidmirsh, Director ILO Activities Middle East/Europe, September 3, 1974.

277. "Matlub Khisma Qimat al-Ishtirak fi al-Niqabat min Rawatib al-ʿummal," *al-Risala*, September 22, 1974, KU 10/zay/100.

278. "al-ʿummal wa Huququhum al-Daʾiʿa bayna al-Hukuma wa Majlis al-Umma wa al-Sharikat!" *Sawt al-Khalij*, December 21, 1974, KU 10/Ha/200.

279. "Sharikat al-Conoco Tufsil 29 ʿamilan li-Idrabihim ʿan al-ʿamal," *al-Siyasa*, August 11, 1975, KU 10/zay/500.

Conclusion

1. For more on this period see al-Khatib, *al-Kuwait, min al-Dawla ila al-Imara*, and Tétreault, *Stories of Democracy*.

2. "Qanun al-Jinsiyya lam Yuhrim al-Marʾa al-Kuwaitiyya min Huquqiha bal Haris aydan ʿala Huquq Awladiha," *al-Siyasa*, April 23, 1979, KU 3/zay/000; "al-Wakil Sulayman al-Mushaʿan Yuʾakkid: Manh al-Jinsiyya al-Kuwaytiyya ʿala Darajatayn la Yaʿni ay Tafriqa aw Tamyyiz," *al-Anbaʾ*, May 4, 1979, KU 3/zay/400; "al-Kuwaitiyyun bi-al-Taʾsis wa bi-al-Tajannus Mutasawun fi al-Huquq wa al-Wajibat," *al-Qabas*, June 4, 1980, KU 3/zay/400.

3. "Hawl Zawaj al-Wafidin bi-al-Aramil wa al-Mutallaqat al-Kuwaitiyyat bighyat al-Husul ʿala al-Jinsiyya," *al-Anbaʾ*, June 15, 1978, KU 3/zay/200.

4. For more detail see Beaugrand, *Stateless in the Gulf.*

5. See Lori, *Offshore Citizens*, 1.

6. Claire Beaugrand has argued that the *bidun* and "migrant workers" must be discussed in the same analytical frame in "Framing Nationality in the Migratory Context," *Middle East Law and Governance* 6, no. 3 (2014): 173–203.

7. Saud Alsanousi, *Saaq al-Bamboo* (The Bamboo Stalk) (Beirut: Arab Scientific Publishers, 2013); "Musalsal Saq al-Bambu Yatajawwaz al-Khutut al-Humr fi al-Mujtamaʿat al-Khalijiyya," *BBC Arabic*, June 18, 2016, https://www.bbc.com/arabic/multimedia/2016/06/160618_gulf_bamboo_leg.

8. Beaugrand, *Stateless in the Gulf*, 131.

9. Babar, "The 'Enemy Within'"; Human Rights Watch, "Kuwait: Government Critics Stripped of Citizenship," October 19, 2014; Beaugrand, *Stateless in the Gulf*, 127.

10. Onn Winckler, *Arab Political Demography: Population Growth, Labor Migration and Natalist Policies* (Sussex Academic Press, 2017), 134.

11. "Prevent Exploitation, Kuwaiti Urges ILO," *Arab Times*, December 8, 1985.

12. "al-Kuwait Tahtaj ila ʾurubba ʿala Suʾ Muʿamalat al-ʿummal al-ʿarab," *al-Watan*, March 21, 1980, KU 10/ba/000; "Idrab 1200 ʿamil Hindi fi al-Qurayn," *al-Anbaʾ*, March 4, 1989, KU 10/zay/500.

13. ILO MIG 1-271, "Statement of Don Stillman, Director of Governmental & International Affairs, International Union, UAW, on Workers' Rights in Kuwait to the Overseas Private Investment Corporation," November 12, 1991; ILO MIG 1-271, Memorandum SLB 1/93, "Rules tightened on domestic service agencies."

14. "80 Alf Muqim ʿIraqi!" *Al-Siyasa*, December 1, 1993, KU 10/zay/520.

15. Mai Al-Nakib, "'The People are Missing'—Palestinians in Kuwait," *Deleuze Studies* 8, no. 1 (2014): 23–44.

16. "MP Safaa al-Hashim—'Expats Are Opportunistic Bacteria," *Arab Times*, February 16, 2018.

17. Nasra M. Shah, Lubna Alkazi, and Batul K. Sadliwala, "Threats, Victims or Allies? Migrant Communities in Kuwait's COVID19 Response," *Middle East Institute*, January 12, 2021, https://www.mei.edu/publications/threats-victims-or-allies-migrant-communities-kuwaits-covid19-response; Abdullah al-Khonaini, "How Covid-19 Stress-Tested Relations between Residents & Citizens in Kuwait," *Gulf International Forum*, https://gulfif.org/how-covid-19-stress-tested-relations-between-residents-citizens-in-kuwait/.

18. "The COVID-19 Crisis Is Fueling More Racist Discourse towards Migrant Workers in the Gulf," *Migrant-Rights.org*, April 5, 2020, https://www.migrant-rights.org/2020/04/the-covid-19-crisis-is-fueling-more-racist-discourse-towards-migrant-workers-in-the-gulf/.

19. Vora and Le Renard, "Who Is 'Indian' in the Gulf?"

20. Emma Day, "Why Kuwait's Only Female MP Needs to Be on Your Radar," *Emirates Woman*, May 15, 2017, https://emirateswoman.com/why-kuwaits-only-female-mp-needs-to-be-on-your-radar/.

21. "In Kuwait, the Discourse on Migrant Workers Is Lively and Divided," *Migrant-Rights.org*, August 7, 2018, https://www.migrant-rights.org/2018/08/in-kuwait-the-discourse-on-migrant-workers-is-lively-and-divided/.

22. Rhacel Salazar Parreñas, *Unfree: Migrant Domestic Work in Arab States* (Stanford University Press, 2022), 48 and chapter 1, footnote 34; "Philippines Takes Extreme Measures, as Kuwait Continues to Mismanage Workers' Rights," *Migrant-rights.org*, February 15, 2018, https://www.migrant-rights.org/2018/02/philippines-takes-extreme-measures-as-kuwait-continues-to-mismanage-workers-rights/.

23. "Kuwait Expels Philippine Envoy amid Tensions over Domestic Workers," *Arab News*, April 25, 2018, https://www.arabnews.com/node/1291346/middle-east.

24. Adam Taylor, "Kuwait Plans to Create a Huge DNA Database of Residents and Visitors. Scientists Are Appalled," *The Washington Post*, September 14, 2016, https://www.washingtonpost.com/news/worldviews/wp/2016/09/14/kuwait-plans-to-create-a-huge-dna-database-of-resident-and-visitors-scientists-are-appalled/; "Slave Markets Found on Instagram and Other Apps," *BBC Arabic*, October 31, 2019, https://www.bbc.co.uk/news/technology-50228549.

25. "4 More Held in Fingerprint Surgery Case," *Times of India*, September 22, 2022, http://timesofindia.indiatimes.com/articleshow/94362841.cms?utm_source=contentofinterest&utm_medium=text&utm_campaign=cppst.

26. Zahra Babar and Neha Vora, "The 2022 World Cup and Migrants' Rights in Qatar: Racialised Labour Hierarchies and the Influence of Racial Capitalism," *The Political Quarterly* 93, no. 3 (July/September 2022): 498–507.

27. Faisal Hamadah, "Kafala and Social Reproduction: Migration Governance Regimes and Labour Relations in the Gulf," in *The South Asia to Gulf Migration Governance Process*, ed. Crystal Ennis and Nicolas Blarel (Bristol University Press, 2022), 173–89.

28. "Sandigan Kuwait: From Survivors to Defenders," *Migrant-Rights.org*, Web, July 23, 2018, accessed May 15, 2020.

29. "Kuwait union opens doors to all migrant workers," Twitter account of the Kuwait Trade Union Federation, November 8, 2019; AFL-CIO Solidarity Center, March 26, 2019.

30. "Eight Unionists Arrested," *Kuwait Times*, September 30, 1976, and "Trade Unionists Freed on Bail," *Kuwait Times*, October 2, 1976.

31. "Niqabat ʿUmal al-Bitrul al-Wataniyya Tatlub min ʾidarat al-Sharika Muraʿat al-Huquq al-Niqabiyya," *al-ʿamil*, May 1, 1977, 7/lam/350.

32. Al-Najjar, "Decision-Making Process in Kuwait," 73.

33. Personal interview, Ahmad al-Diyyan, March 2, 2018; al-Mdairis, *al-Mujtamaʿ al-Madani wa-al-Haraka al-Wataniyya fi al-Kuwait*, 139–46.

34. "Kuwait Tahtaj ila ʾurba ʿala Suʾ Muʿamalat al-ʿummal al-ʿarab," *al-Watan*, March 21, 1980, KU 10/ba/000.

35. Falah al-Mdairis discusses this in *al-Mujtamaʿ al-Madani wa-al-Haraka al-Wataniyya fi al-Kuwait*, 147.

36. Al-Shalal, "The Trade Union Movement in the State of Kuwait," 126.

37. ILO MIG 1-271, "Report on Mission to Kuwait," October 10–14, 1986.

38. Al-Munais, *al-Taliʿa wa al-Maʿraka al-Dimuqratiyya*, 183.

39. "al-Ittihad al-ʿamm li-ʿummal al-Kuwait Yastankir ʿadam Manh Haqq al-Intikhab lil-Mutajannas," *al-Watan*, July 1, 1986, KU 10/zay/310; "Ittihad al-ʿummal Yarfud al-Taʿdilat al-Akhira ʿala Qanun al-Jinsiyya," *al-Watan*, March 13, 1982, KU 10/zay/310; "al-Taqrir al-Idari: Ittihad ʿummal al-Bitrul: Tahqiq al-Mazid min al-Makasib Yatlub Mudaʿafa al-Juhd," *al-ʿAmil*, April 10, 1978, KU 10/zay/300.

40. "al-Haraka al-Niqabiyya al-Kuwaitiyya," *al-ʿAmil*, December 15, 1984, KU 10./zay/100.

41. Personal interview, Hussein al-Youha, November 27, 2017.

42. Saqr, *Rihla Dakhil al-Dhakira maʿ al-Haraka al-ʿUmaliyya al-Kuwaitiyya*.

43. There are numerous retrospective pieces in KU 10/zay/100.

44. "Niqabat ʿummal al-Bitrul al-Wataniyya Tatlub min Idarat al-Sharika Muraʿat al-Huquq al-Niqabiyya," *al-ʿAmil*, May 1, 1977, 7/lam/350.

45. This is documented in KU 10/zay/500.

46. See for instance "Idrab ʿummal al-Naft bi-l-Kuwait bisabab Khutat al-Hukuma li-Khafid," *BBC Arabic*, April 17, 2016, https://www.bbc.com/arabic/middleeast/2016/04/160417_kuwait_oil_strike.

47. https://www.youtube.com/watch?v=IoUnpVsMA6Y, posted March 22, 2016, accessed June 12, 2020.

48. "al-Kuwait: Idrab Shamil Yatal Mu'assasat al-Naft," *al-Arabiyya*, April 17, 2016..

49. Khalili, "Crude Knowledge," 464.

50. Fahad Ahmad Bishara, "The Many Voyages of Fateh Al-Khayr: Unfurling the Gulf in the Age of Oceanic History," *International Journal of Middle East Studies* (2020): 1–16, 14.

51. "al-ʿummal Yatalibun bi-Tandhim al-ʿamala al-Wafida wa Yadʿun al-Hukuma ila Musanada al-Ittihad," *al-Watan*, April 1, 1981, KU 10/zay/310.

52. "al-ʿamala al-Asiyawiyya Tahrim al-Shabab al-Kuwaiti min Furas al-ʿamal," *al-ʿAmil*, July 1, 1987, KU 10/zay/100.

53. "Sanʿlin al-Idrab Yawm Tataʾ al-ʿamala al-Ajnabiyya ʾard al-Waan," *al-Qabas*, October 1, 1992, KU 10/zay/500.

54. Untitled, *al-Qabas*, January 12, 1973, KU 10/waw/500; al-Asbahi, *al-Haraka al-Niqabiyya al-Kuwaitiyya*, 139.

55. Hamadah, "Kafala and Social Reproduction," 177.

56. "al-Matlub Qanun lil-Daman al-Ijtimaʿi bi-Hadaf al-Had min Hijrat al-Aydi al-ʿamila al-ʿarabiyya," *al-Siyasa*, April 28, 1979, KU 10/Ha/230; "Ittihad al-ʿummal Yatalib bi-ʾilghaʾ Qarar Qatʿ 'Rubuʿ al-Ratib' mimman Yaʿmalun bi-l-Qitaʿ al-Ahli," *al-Watan*, December 18, 1981, KU 10/zay/310; *al-ʿAmil*, "Bidayat al-Haraka al-amaliyya wa al-Niqabiyya ʿala Lisan Ruadiha," October 15, 1984. KU 10/zay/100.

57. "Sanʿarid ay Tawajjuh li-Taqlis Hajm al-ʿamala al-ʿarabiyya," *al-Anbaʾ*, November 1, 1982, KU 10/zay/310.

58. Al-Asbahi, *al-Haraka al-Niqabiyya al-Kuwaitiyya*, 144.

59. "Kuwait and Bahrain Unions Become First in the Gulf to Forge an Official Trade Union Relationship with Nepal," *ITUC Press Department*, Web, January 16, 2012, accessed May 15, 2020.

60. "'The Kafala Is a System of Slavery': An Interview with the Kuwait Trade Union Federation," *Migrant Rights*, August 2, 2014, Web, accessed June 10, 2020.

61. "Samu ʾAmir al-Bilad Yalqi al-Nutq al-Sami bʿad ʾIdaʾ Sumuih al-Yamin al-Dusturiyya ʾImam Majlis al-Umma," *Kuwait News Agency*, December 20, 2023, https://www.kuna.net.kw/ArticleDetails.aspx?id=3127446; Kristin Diwan, "Kuwait's New Emir: A Frank Speech Signals a Sharp Change in Direction," *The Arab Gulf States Institute*, January 3, 2024, https://agsiw.org/kuwaits-new-emir-a-frank-speech-signals-a-sharp-change-in-direction/.

62. "Kuwait Hotline to Report Citizenship Fraud Stirs Up Election Debate," *The National*, March 28, 2024. https://www.thenationalnews.com/news/gulf/2024/03/18/kuwait-citizenship-fraud-hotline-elections/.

63. "'Stateless Overnight,'" *France24*.

64. "Everyone 'Under Review' as Kuwait Revokes Citizenship of Nearly 50,000 People," *The National*, August 11, 2025, https://www.thenationalnews.com/news/mena/2025/08/11/everyone-under-review-as-kuwait-revokes-citizenship-of-nearly-50000-people/.

Bibliography

Interviews

Conducted by the author

Qablan ʿAjnan al-ʿAzimi | November 29, 2017—Kuwait City
Ahmad al-Diyyan | March 2, 2018—Kuwait City
Hassan Falah | November 29, 2017, and May 25, 2018—Kuwait City
Dr. Sultan Mohammad al-Hashmi | October 26, 2017—Muscat, Oman
Dr. Ahmad al-Khatib | January 4, 2018—Kuwait City
Ahmad al-Sadoun | February 7, 2018—Kuwait City
Hussein Saqr | November 28, 2017—Kuwait City
Daifullah Falah Sultan | December 4, 2017—Kuwait City
Hussein al-Youha | November 27, 2017—Kuwait City and Fintas, Kuwait
Omani interviews (Names elided to protect confidentiality)
September 14, 2017—Nakhal, Oman
September 14, 2017—Nakhal, Oman
September 21, 2017—Nakhal, Oman
September 22, 2017—Nakhal, Oman

From the American University of Kuwait Oral History and Documentation Project

"Laila Ahmad," accessed May 25, 2024, https://oralhistory.auk.edu.kw/items/show/27.
"Sarah Akbar," accessed May 25, 2024, https://oralhistory.auk.edu.kw/items/show/7.
"Hussein al-Youha," accessed May 25, 2024, https://oralhistory.auk.edu.kw/items/show/4.

Private Archives

American University of Beirut, Archives and Special Collections Department [AUB]

Linda Sadaka Archival Collection [LSAC]
BP (British Petroleum) Archive, University of Warwick, Coventry, United Kingdom [ARC]
Caird Library, National Maritime Museum Greenwich, United Kingdom [NMM]
British India Steam Navigation Company Records [BIS]
Churchill College, Cambridge, United Kingdom; Churchill Archives Centre, Papers of Major-General William Hasted [HSTD]
Georgetown University Library, Booth Family Center for Special Collections, Washington, D.C. [GU]
Mulligan, William E., Papers [WEMP]
Rentz, George S., Jr., Papers [GSRP]
Guildhall Library, London Metropolitan Archives, London [GL]
Eastern Bank Records [EB]
Inchcape Group Records [ICG]
Hong Kong and Shanghai Banking Corporation Archive, London [HSBC]
British Bank of the Middle East/Imperial Bank of Persia Records [BBME]
Kuwait University, Center for Gulf & Arabian Peninsula Studies Newspaper Archive, Kuwait City [KU]

State and International Organization Archives

India Office Records, British Library, London [IOR]
Bahrain Agency Records [R/15/2]
Kuwait Agency Records [R/15/5]
Muscat Agency Records [R/15/6]
Persian Gulf Residency Records [R/15/1]
Political and Judicial Files [L/P&J]
Political and Secret Files [L/P&S]
International Labor Organization, Geneva, Switzerland [ILO]
Maharashtra State Archives, Mumbai, India [MSA]
Political Department Records [P]
Revenue Department Records [R]
National Archives of India, New Delhi, India [NAI]
Department of Commerce and Industry Records [DCI]
External Affairs [EA]
Foreign and Political Department Records [FP]
Foreign Department Records [F]
Near East [NE]
Secret [S]
National Archives of the United Kingdom, Kew [NAUK]
Foreign Office Records [FO]
Foreign and Commonwealth Office Records [FCO]
Labour Office Records [LAB]
National Archives and Records Administration, United States, College Park, MD [NARA]

Records of the Department of State [DS]
Agency for International Development [AID]
Bureau of Economic Affairs [BEA]
International Cooperation Administration [ICA]
Bureau of Near Eastern and South Asian Affairs [NESAA]
Records of the U.S. Information Agency [USIA]

Private and Research Libraries

Center for Research and Study of Kuwait, Kuwait [CRSK]
Kuwait Trade Union Federation Library, Kuwait [KTUF]
Sultan Qaboos University Library, Muscat, Oman [SQU]
National Library of Kuwait, Kuwait [NLK]
Kuwait Chamber of Commerce and Industry Library, Kuwait [KCCI]
American University of Kuwait Library, Kuwait [AUK]

Newspapers

The Arab World | Dunya al-ʿuruba
The Caravan | al-Qafila (Bahrain)
City Lights | Adwaʾ al-Madina
The Contractor | al-Muqawil
The Dawn | al-Fajr
The Delegation | al-Baʿtha
Echo of the Faith | Sada al-Iman
The Employee | al-Muwathaf
The Faith | al-Iman
The Firebrand | al-Qabas
Generations | Ajiyal
The Goal | al-Hadaf
Good Morning | Sabah al-Khayr
The Kuwait Chamber of Commerce Newsletter | Nashrat Ghurfat Tijarat wa Sinaʿat al-Kuwait
Kuwait Magazine | Majallat al-Kuwait
Kuwait News | Akhbar al-Kuwait
Kuwait Today | Kuwait al-Yawm
The Kuwaiti | al-Kuwaiti
Lights of Kuwait | Adwaʾ al-Kuwait
My Family | Usrati
Mirror of the Nation | Mirʾat al-Umma
The Mission | al-Risala
The Nation | al-Watan
The News | al-Anbaʾ
The People | al-Shaʿb
The Pioneer | al-Raʾid
Politics | al-Siyasa

Public Opinion | al-Ra'i al-'Am
The Pyramids | al-Ahram (Egypt)
The Religious Institute | al-Ma'had al-Dini
The Renaissance | al-Nahda
The Republic | al-Jumhuriyya (Egypt)
The Society | al-Mujtama'
The Union | al-Ittihad
The Vanguard | al-Tali'a
The Vigilant | al-Yaqutha
The Voice of Bahrain | Sawt al-Bahrain (Bahrain)
The Voice of the Gulf | Sawt al-Khalij
This Week | Hadha al-Usbu'
The Worker | al-'Amil

In English

The Kuwait Daily News
Kuwait Times
Neglected Arabia

Published Sources

Abdallah, Mohammad Hassan. *al-Haraka al-Adabiyya wa al-Fikriyya fi al-Kuwait* (The Literary and Intellectual Movement in Kuwait). Rabitat al-Adaba' al-Kuwaitiyyn, 1973.

Abrahamian, Ervand. *Iran Between Two Revolutions*. Princeton University Press, 1983.

Abrahamian, Ervand. *A History of Modern Iran*. Cambridge University Press, 2008.

Abu-Hakima, Ahmad Mustafa. *The Modern History of Kuwait*. Luzac, 1983.

Al-'Adasani, Khalid Sulayman. *Nisf 'am li-l-Hukm al-Niyabi fi al-Kuwait* (Half a Year of Parliamentary Rule in Kuwait). Beirut, 1947.

Ahmad, Attiya. "Beyond Labor: Foreign Residents in the Persian Gulf States." In *Migrant Labor in the Persian Gulf*, edited by Mehran Kamrava and Zahra Babar. Columbia University Press, 2012.

Ahmad, Attiya. *Everyday Conversions: Islam, Domestic Work, and South Asian Migrant Women in Kuwait*. Duke University Press, 2017.

Aidi, Hisham. "Exporting Race: Norms, Categories, & 'The All-American Skin Game.'" *Daedalus* 154, no. 2 (2025): 204–28.

Al-'Ajmi, Muhammad Mas'ud. *al-Haraka al-'Ummaliyya wa al-Naqabiyya fi al-Kuwait: al-Nash'a wa Bidayat al-Takwayn* (The Labor and Trade Union Movement in Kuwait: Its Establishment and Early Formation). Sharikat al-Rabi'an li-l-Nashr, 1982.

Al-'Akari, 'Abd al-Nabi. *al-Tandhimat al-Yasariyya fi al-Jazira wa-al-Khalij al-'Arabi* (Leftist Movements in the Arabian Peninsula and Arab Gulf). Dar al-Kunuz al-Adabiyya, 2003.

Alebrahim, Abdulrahman. "The Balancing Powers in Kuwait and the 1938 Majlis Movement." *AlMuntaqa* 4, no. 2 (December 2021/January 2022): 8–26.

Alebrahim, Abdulrahman. *Kuwait's Politics Before Independence: The Role of the Balancing Powers*. Gerlach Press, 2019.

Alessa, Shamlan Y. *The Manpower Problem in Kuwait*. Kegan Paul International, 1981.

Alhajeri, Abdullah. "Citizenship and Political Participation in the State of Kuwait: The Case of National Assembly (1963–1996)." PhD diss., Durham University, 2004.

Alissa, Reem. "Building for Oil: Corporate Colonialism, Nationalism and Urban Modernity in Ahmadi, 1946–1992." PhD diss., U.C. Berkeley, 2012.

Alissa, Reem. "The Oil Town of Ahmadi since 1946: From Colonial Town to Nostalgic City." *Comparative Studies of South Asia, Africa and the Middle East* 33, no. 1 (2013): 41–58.

Alkandari, Ali A. "The Muslim Brotherhood in Kuwait, 1941–2000: A Social Movement within the Social Domain." PhD diss., University of Exeter, 2014.

Alnuaimi, Hessa. "The Role of Colonial Knowledge in Building the Arab Gulf's Migration Regime." *Asian Journal of Middle Eastern and Islamic Studies* 16, no. 4 (2022): 382–401.

Alsanousi, Saud. *Saq al-Bambu* (The Bamboo Stalk). Arab Scientific Publishers, 2013.

Alsayed, Wafa. "Beyond Instrumentalism: Arab Nationalism and the Foreign Policy of Kuwait in the 1960s and 1970s." *The Middle East Journal* 76, no. 2 (Summer 2022): 199–221.

Aminzade, Ronald. *Race, Nation, and Citizenship in Postcolonial Africa: The Case of Tanzania*. Cambridge University Press, 2013.

Amrith, Sunil. *Crossing the Bay of Bengal: The Furies of Nature and the Fortunes of Migrants*. Harvard University Press, 2013.

Anderson, Benedict. *Imagined Communities: Reflections on the Origin and Spread of Nationalism*. Verso, 1983.

Anderson, Bridget, Matthew J. Gibney, and Emanuela Paoletti, eds. *The Social, Political and Historical Contours of Deportation*. Springer, 2013.

Anderson, Kyle J. *The Egyptian Labor Corps: Race, Space, and Place in the First World War*. University of Texas Press, 2021.

Al-Ansari, Salah. "Amin ʿIzz al-Din: Muʾarrikh al-Haraka al-Niqabiyya al-Misriyya" (Amin ʿIzz al-Din: Historian of the Egyptian Trade Union Movement). *Towards Arab Trade Union Unity*, September 19, 2017, https://arabtradeunionsunity.wordpress.com/2017/09/19. Accessed November 15, 2019.

Anscombe, Frederick F. "An Anational Society: Eastern Arabia in the Ottoman Period." In *Transnational Connections in the Arab Gulf*, edited by Madawi al-Rasheed. Routledge, 2005.

Al-ʿAnzi, Rashid Ḥamad. *al-Bidun fi al-Kuwait* (The Bidun in Kuwait). Dar Qurtas li-l-Nashr wa-l-Tawziʿ, 1994.

Appel, Hannah. *The Licit Life of Capitalism: US Oil in Equatorial Guinea*. Duke University Press, 2019.

Appel, Hannah, Arthur Mason, and Michael Watts, eds. *Subterranean Estates: Life Worlds of Oil and Gas*. Cornell University Press, 2015.

Arendt, Hannah. *The Origins of Totalitarianism*. Penguin, 2017.

Arrighi, Giovanni, and Fortunata Piselli. "Capitalist Development in Hostile Environments: Feuds, Class Struggles, and Migrations in a Peripheral Region of Southern Italy." *Review* (Fernand Braudel Center) 10, no. 4 (Spring 1987): 649–751.

Al-Asbahi, Ahmad Sa'id. *al-Haraka al-Niqabiyya al-Kuwaitiyya: Lamha Tarikhiyya* (The Kuwait Trade Union Movement: A Historical Overview). The Kuwait Trade Union Federation Press, 2009.

Atabaki, Touraj. "Far from Home, But at Home: Indian Migrant Workers in the Iranian Oil Industry." *Studies in History* 31, no. 1 (2015): 85–114.

Atabaki, Touraj, Elisabetta Bini, and Kaveh Ehsani, eds. *Working for Oil: Comparative Social Histories of Labor in Petroleum*. Palgrave Macmillan, 2018.

Al-Atiqi, Suliman. "The Origins of Kuwaiti Nationalism: Rashid Rida's Influence on Kuwaiti National Identity." *The Arab Studies Journal* 23, no. 1 (2015): 78–122.

Awadh, Sami. "Islamic Political Groups in Kuwait: Roots and Influences." PhD diss., University of Portsmouth, 1999.

Al-'Awadhi, Ali Hussein. *al-Haraka al-Wataniyya al-Kuwaitiyya wa-l-'udwan al-Thulathi 'ala Misr* (The Kuwaiti National Movement and the Tripartite Aggression against Egypt). Dar Qurtas li-l-Nashr, 2019.

Al-'Awadhi, Ali Hussein. *Ahmad al-Khatib: Watan wa Dustur* (Homeland and Constitution). Kuwait, 2013.

Babar, Zahra. "The "Enemy Within"—Citizenship-Stripping in the Post–Arab Spring GCC." *Middle East Journal* 71, no. 4 (2017): 525–43.

Babar, Zahra, and Neha Vora. "The 2022 World Cup and Migrants' Rights in Qatar: Racialised Labour Hierarchies and the Influence of Racial Capitalism." *The Political Quarterly* 93, no. 3 (July/September 2022): 498–507.

Baghoolizadeh, Beeta. *The Color Black: Enslavement and Erasure in Iran*. Duke University Press, 2024.

Al-Bakir, Abd al-Rahman. *Min al-Bahrain ila al-Manfa Saint Helena* (From Bahrain to Exile in St. Helena). Dar Maktabat al-Haya, 1965.

Bal, Charanpal Singh. "Dealing with Deportability: Deportation Laws and the Political Personhood of Temporary Migrant Workers in Singapore." *Asian Journal of Law and Society*, no. 2 (2015): 267–84.

Baldwin, M. Page. "Subject to Empire: Married Women and the British Nationality and Status of Aliens Act." *Journal of British Studies* 40, no. 4 (2001): 522–56.

Balfour-Paul, Glen. *The End of Empire in the Middle East: Britain's Relinquishment of Power in her Last Three Arab Dependencies*. Cambridge University Press, 1991.

Balibar, Étienne. "What Is a Border?" In *Politics and the Other Scene*. Verso, 2002.

Ballantyne, W. M. *Legal Development in Arabia: A Selection of Articles and Addresses on the Arabian Gulf*. Graham & Troutman Limited, 1980.

Bamberg, James H. *British Petroleum and Global Oil 1950–1975: The Challenge of Nationalism*. Cambridge University Press, 2000.

Banko, Lauren. *The Invention of Palestinian Citizenship, 1918–1947.* Edinburgh University Press, 2016.

Banko, Lauren. "Keeping Out the 'Undesirable Elements': The Treatment of Communists, Transients, Criminals, and the Ill in Mandate Palestine." *The Journal of Imperial and Commonwealth History* 47, no. 6 (2019): 1153–80.

Banko, Lauren. "Claiming Identities in Palestine: Migration and Nationality under the Mandate." *Journal of Palestine Studies* 46 (2017): 26–43.

Barak, On. "Outsourcing: Energy and Empire in the Age of Coal, 1820–1911." *International Journal of Middle East Studies* 47, no. 3 (2015): 425–45.

Bardawil, Fadi A. *Revolution and Disenchantment: Arab Marxism and the Binds of Emancipation.* Duke University Press, 2020.

Barnwell, Kristi N. "Overthrowing the Shaykhs: The Trucial States at the Intersection of Anti-Imperialism, Arab Nationalism, and Politics, 1952–1966." *Arab Studies Journal* 24, no. 2 (2016): 72–95.

Barry, Andrew. "The Oil Archives." In *Subterranean Estates: Life Worlds of Oil and Gas,* edited by Hannah Appel, Arthur Mason, and Michael Watts. Cornell University Press, 2015.

Bawalsa, Nadim. *Transnational Palestine: Migration and the Right of Return Before 1948.* Stanford University Press, 2022.

Beattie, J. M. *Policing and Punishment in London, 1660–1750.* Oxford University Press, 2001.

Beaugrand, Claire. "Framing Nationality in the Migratory Context." *Middle East Law and Governance* 6, no. 3 (2014): 173–203.

Beaugrand, Claire. *Stateless in the Gulf: Migration, Nationality and Society in Kuwait.* I. B. Tauris, 2017.

Beblawi, Hazim. "The Rentier State in the Arab World." In *The Rentier State,* edited by Hazim Beblawi and Giacomo Luciani. Croom Helm, 1987.

Beinin, Joel, and Zachary Lockman. *Workers on the Nile: Nationalism, Communism, Islam, and the Egyptian Working Class, 1882–1954.* I. B. Tauris & Co., 1988.

Beinin, Joel, Bassam Haddad, and Sherene Seikaly, eds. *A Critical Political Economy of the Middle East and North Africa.* Stanford University Press, 2021.

Belgrave, Charles Dalrymple. *Personal Column.* Hutchinson & Co. Ltd., 1960.

Beling, Willard A. *Pan Arabism and Labor.* Harvard University Press, 1961.

Beling, Willard A. "Recent Developments in Labor Relations in Bahrayn." *Middle East Journal* 13, no. 2 (Spring 1959): 156–69.

Berda, Yael. *Colonial Bureaucracy and Contemporary Citizenship: Legacies of Race and Emergency in the Former British Empire.* Cambridge University Press, 2023..

Berda, Yael. "Managing Dangerous Populations: Colonial Legacies of Security and Surveillance." *Sociological Forum* 28, no. 3 (Sept. 2013): 627–30.

Bet-Shlimon, Arbella. *City of Black Gold: Oil, Ethnicity, and the Making of Modern Kirkuk.* Stanford University Press, 2019.

Bhabha, Homi K. *Nation and Narration.* Routledge, 1991.

Bhattacharya, Tithi. *Social Reproduction Theory: Remapping Class, Recentering Oppression*. Pluto Press, 2017.

Bhattacharyya, Gargi. *Rethinking Racial Capitalism: Questions of Reproduction and Survival*. Rowman & Littlefield International, 2018.

Bianchi, Robert. "The Corporatization of the Egyptian Labor Movement." *Middle East Journal* 40, no. 3 (Summer 1986): 429–44.

Bini, Elisabetta. "Oil Workers, Trade Unions and the Emergence of Oil Nationalism in Libya, 1956–1969." *EUI MWP*, no. 27 (2012).

Bishara, Fahad Ahmad. "The Many Voyages of Fateh Al-Khayr: Unfurling the Gulf in the Age of Oceanic History." *International Journal of Middle East Studies* (2020): 1–16.

Bishara, Fahad Ahmad. "Narrative and the Historian's Craft in the Arab Historiography of the Persian Gulf." In The *Persian Gulf in Modern Times: People, Ports, and History*, edited by Lawrence G. Potter. Palgrave Macmillan, 2014.

Bishara, Fahad Ahmad. *A Sea of Debt: Law and Economic Life in the Western Indian Ocean, 1780–1950*. Cambridge University Press, 2017.

Boodrookas, Alex. "Crackdowns and Coalitions in Kuwait." *Middle East Report Online*, June 18, 2018.

Boodrookas, Alex. "The Making of a Migrant Working Class: Contesting Citizenship in the Persian Gulf, 1925–1975." PhD diss., NYU, 2020.

Boodrookas, Alex, and Arang Keshavarzian. "The Forever Frontier of Urbanism: Historicizing Gulf Cities." *International Journal of Urban and Regional Research* 43, no. 1 (2019): 14–29.

Bose, Sugata. *A Hundred Horizons: The Indian Ocean in the Age of Global Empire*. Harvard University Press, 2006.

Bosniak, Linda. *The Citizen and the Alien: Dilemmas of Contemporary Membership*. Princeton University Press, 2006.

Bredbenner, Candice Lewis. *A Nationality of Her Own: Women, Marriage, and the Law of Citizenship*. University of California Press, 1998.

Brew, Gregory. *Petroleum and Progress in Iran: Oil, Development, and the Cold War*. Cambridge University Press, 2022.

Brubaker, Rogers. *Citizenship and Nationhood in France and Germany*. Harvard University Press, 1992.

Bsheer, Rosie. "A Counter-Revolutionary State: Popular Movements and the Making of Saudi Arabia." *Past and Present* 238, no. 1 (February 2018): 233–77.

Buckley, Michelle. "Locating Neoliberalism in Dubai: Migrant Workers and Class Struggle in the Autocratic City." *Antipode* 45, no. 2 (2012): 256–74.

Al-Bulushi, Yousuf. "Thinking Racial Capitalism and Black Radicalism from Africa: An Intellectual Geography of Cedric Robinson's World-System." *Geoforum* 132 (June 2022): 252–62.

Burawoy, Michael. "The Functions and Reproduction of Migrant Labor: Comparative Material from Southern Africa and the United States." *American Journal of Sociology* 81, no. 5 (1976): 1050–87.

Can, Lâle. *Spiritual Subjects: Central Asian Pilgrims and the Ottoman Hajj at the End of* Empire. Stanford University Press, 2020.

de Candole, E. A. V. "Developments in Kuwait." *Journal of The Royal Central Asian Society*, no. 42 (January 1955): 21–29.

Canning, Kathleen. *Languages of Labor and Gender: Female Factory Work in Germany, 1850–1914*. Cornell University Press, 1996.

Caplan, Jane, and John Torpey, eds. *Documenting Individual Identity: The Development of State Practices in the Modern World*. Princeton University Press, 2001.

Castells, Manual. "Immigrant Workers and the Class Struggles in Advanced Capitalism: The West European Experience." *Politics and Society* 5, no. 1 (1975): 33–67.

Chalcraft, John. *The Invisible Cage: Syrian Migrant Workers in Lebanon*. Stanford University Press, 2008.

Chalcraft, John. "Labour Protest and Hegemony in Egypt and the Arabian Peninsula." In. *Social Movements in the Global South: Dispossession, Development and Resistance*, edited by Sara C. Motta and Alf Gunvald Nilsen. Palgrave Macmillan, 2011.

Chalcraft, John. "Migration and Popular Protest in the Arabian Peninsula and the Gulf in the 1950s and 1960s." *International Labor and Working-Class History*, no. 79 (2011): 28–47.

Chalcraft, John. "Migration Politics in the Arabian Peninsula." In *The Transformation of the Gulf: Politics, Economics and the Global Order*, edited by David Held and Kristian Ulrichsen. Routledge, 2012.

Chatty, Dawn. "The Bedouin of Central Oman." *The Journal of Oman Studies* 6, no. 1 (1983): 149–62.

Citino, Nathan J. *From Arab Nationalism to OPEC: Eisenhower, King Sa'ud, and the Making of U.S.-Saudi Relations*. Indiana University Press, 2002.

Cohen, Elizabeth F. "The Political Economy of Immigrant Time: Rights, Citizenship, and Temporariness in the Post-1965 Era." *Polity*, no. 47 (2015): 337–51.

Cole, Camille. "Empire on Edge: Land, Law, and Capital in Gilded Age Basra." PhD diss., Yale University, 2020.

Cook-Martín, David. "Temp Nations? A Research Agenda on Migration, Temporariness, and Membership." *American Behavioral Scientist* 63, no. 9 (2019): 1389–403.

Cooper, Frederick. *Colonialism in Question: Theory, Knowledge, History*. University of California Press, 2005.

Cooper, Frederick. *Citizenship between Empire and Nation: Remaking France and French Africa, 1945–1960*. Princeton University Press, 2014.

Cooper, Frederick. *Citizenship, Inequality, and Difference*. Princeton University Press, 2018.

Cooper, Frederick. *Decolonization and African Society: The Labor Question in French and British Africa*. Cambridge University Press, 1996.

Cooper, Frederick. "The Dialectics of Decolonization: Nationalism and Labor Movements in Postwar French Africa." In *Tensions of Empire: Colonial Cultures in a Bourgeois World*, edited by Frederick Cooper and Ann Laura Stoler, University of California Press, 1997.

Cooper, Frederick. "French Africa, 1947–48: Reform, Violence, and Uncertainty in a Colonial Situation." *Critical Inquiry* 40, no. 4 (Summer 2014).

Cooper, Frederick. "Postcolonial Studies and the Study of History." In *Postcolonial Studies and Beyond*, edited by Ania Loomba, Suvir Kaul, Matti Bunzl, Antoinette Burton, and Jed Esty. Duke University Press, 2005.

Coronil, Fernando. *The Magical State: Nature, Money and Modernity in Venezuela.* University of Chicago Press, 1997.

Crinson, Mark. "Abadan: Planning and Architecture under the Anglo-Iranian Oil Company." *Planning Perspectives* 12, no. 3 (1997): 341–59.

Cronin, Stephanie. "Popular Politics, the New State and the Birth of the Iranian Working Class: The 1929 Abadan Oil Refinery Strike." *Middle Eastern Studies* 46, no. 5 (2010): 699–732.

Cross, G. S. *Immigrant Workers in Industrial France: The Making of a New Labouring Class.* Temple University Press, 1983.

Crystal, Jill. *Kuwait: The Transformation of an Oil State.* Westview Press, 1992.

Crystal, Jill. *Oil and Politics in the Gulf: Rulers and Merchants in Kuwait and Qatar.* Cambridge University Press, 1990.

Crystal, Jill. "Public Order and Authority: Policing Kuwait." In *Monarchies and Nations: Globalisation and Identity in the Arab States of the Gulf*, edited by Paul Dresch and James Piscatori. I. B. Taurus, 2005.

Cuyler, Zachary Davis. "Building Shared Power: The Trans-Arabian Pipeline and the Technopolitics of Anti-Sectarian Labor Mobilization in Lebanon, 1950–1964." *Labor History* 60, no. 1 (2019): 57–77.

Cuyler, Zachary Davis. "Tapline, Welfare Capitalism, and Mass Mobilization in Lebanon, 1950–1964." In *Working for Oil: Comparative Social Histories of Labor in the Global Oil Industry*, edited by Touraj Atabaki, Elisabetta Bini, and Kaveh Ehsani. Palgrave Macmillan, 2018.

al-Dailami, Ahmad. "'Purity and Confusion': The Hawala between Persians and Arabs in the Contemporary Gulf." In *The Persian Gulf in Modern Times: People, Ports, and History*, edited by Lawrence Potter. Palgrave Macmillan, 2014.

Davidson, Christopher. "Arab Nationalism and British Opposition in Dubai, 1920–66." *Middle Eastern Studies* 43, no. 6 (November 2007): 879–92.

Davis, Muriam Haleh. *Markets of Civilization: Islam and Racial Capitalism in Algeria.* Duke University Press, 2022.

De Genova, Nicholas P. "Denizenship." In *Precarity and Belonging: Labor, Migration, and Noncitizenship*, edited by Catherine S. Ramírez, Sylvanna M. Falcón, Juan Poblete, Steven C. McKay and Felicity Amaya Schaeffer. Rutgers University Press, 2021.

De Genova, Nicholas P. "The Legal Production of Mexican/Migrant 'Illegality.'" *Latino Studies* 2 (2004): 160–85.

De Genova, Nicholas P. "Migrant 'Illegality' and Deportability in Everyday Life." *Annual Review of Anthropology* 31 (2002): 419–47.

De Genova, Nicholas, and Ananya Roy. "Practices of Illegalisation." *Antipode* 52, no. 2 (March 2020): 352–64.

Department of Manpower Planning, Planning Council, State of Kuwait. "Economic and Social Indexes for the Development of Human Resources in the Area of Use and Manpower." July 1974.

Department of Planning and Statistics, State of Kuwait. *Statistics Abstract in 25 Years*. Central Statistics Office, 1990.

Dickson, H. R. P. *The Arab of the Desert: A Glimpse into Badawin Life in Kuwait and Sau'di Arabia*. George Allen & Unwin Ltd., 1967.

Dickson, Violet. *Forty Years in Kuwait*. George Allen & Unwin Ltd., 1971.

Dietrich, Christopher R. W. *Oil Revolution: Anticolonial Elites, Sovereign Rights, and the Economic Culture of Decolonization*. Cambridge University Press, 2017.

Dietrich, Christopher R. W. "'Arab Oil Belongs to the Arabs': Raw Material Sovereignty, Cold War Boundaries, and the Nationalisation of the Iraq Petroleum Company, 1967–1973." *Diplomacy and Statecraft* 22, no. 3 (2011): 450–79.

Al-Diyyin, Ahmad ʿAli. *al-Dimuqratiyya fi al-Kuwait* (Democracy in Kuwait). Dar Qurtas li-l-Nashr wa-l-Tawziʿ, 2005.

Al-Diyyin, Ahmad ʿAli. *Ahhdaath wa-Wujuh min al-Dhakira* (Events and Faces from Memory). Dar Qurtas li-l-Nashr wa-l-Tawziʿ, 2021.

Dobe, Michael Edward. "A Long Slow Tutelage in Western Ways of Work: Industrial Education and the Containment of Nationalism in Anglo-Iranian and ARAMCO, 1923–1963." PhD diss., Rutgers University, 2008.

Dresch, Paul. "Foreign Matter: The Place of Strangers in Gulf Society." In *Globalization and the Gulf*, edited by John W. Fox, Nada Mourtada-Sabbah, and Mohammed al-Mutawa. Routledge, 2006.

Dresch, Paul, and James Piscatori, eds. *Monarchies and Nations: Globalisation and Identity in the Arab States of the Gulf*. I. B. Tauris, 2013.

Dubois, Laurent. *A Colony of Citizens: Revolution and Slave Emancipation in the French Caribbean, 1787–1804*. University of North Carolina Press, 2004.

Du Bois, W. E. B. *Black Reconstruction in America: An Essay toward a History of the Part Which Black Folk Played in the Attempt to Reconstruct Democracy in America, 1860–1880*. Oxford University Press, 2007.

Eamon, Jeff. "Policing the Bahrain Islands: Labor, Race, and the Historical Origins of Foreign Recruitment." Master's thesis, New York University, May 2015.

Ehsani, Kaveh. "Social Engineering and the Contradictions of Modernization in Khuzestan's Company Towns: A Look at Abadan and Masjed-Soleyman." *International Review of Social History* 48, no. 3 (2003): 361–99.

Ehsani, Kaveh. "The Social History of Labor in the Iranian Oil Industry: The Built Environment and the Making of the Industrial Working Class (1908–1941)." PhD diss., Leiden University, 2014.

Ennis, Crystal A. *Millennial Dreams in Oil Economies: Job Seeking and the Global Political Economy of Labour in Oman*. Cambridge University Press, 2024.

Ennis, Crystal A., and Nicolas Blarel, eds. *The South Asia to Gulf Migration Governance Process*. Bristol University Press, 2022.

Errichiello, Gennaro. "Foreign Workforce in the Arab Gulf States (1930–1950): Migration Patterns and Nationality Clause." *International Migration Review* 46, no. 2 (Summer 2012): 389–413.

Esch, Elizabeth, and David Roediger. "One Symptom of Originality: Race and the Management of Labour in the History of the United States." *Historical Materialism* 17, no. 4 (2009): 3–43.

Ferguson, James. *Global Shadows: Africa in the Neoliberal World Order*. Duke University Press, 2006.

Ferguson, James. "Mobile Workers, Modernist Narratives: A Critique of the Historiography of Transition on the Zambian Copperbelt." *Journal of Southern African Studies* 16, no. 4 (December 1990): 603–21.

Ferguson, James. "Seeing Like an Oil Company: Space, Security, and Global Capital in Neoliberal Africa." *American Anthropologist* 107, no. 3 (September 2005): 377–82.

Field, Michael. *The Merchants: The Big Business Families of Arabia*. John Murray, 1984.

Finnie, David H. *Desert Enterprise: The Middle East Oil Industry in Its Local Environment*. Harvard University Press, 1958.

Finnie, David. "Recruitment and Training of Labor: The Middle East Oil Industry." *Middle East Journal* 12, no. 2 (Spring 1958): 127–43.

Fitzpatrick, Matthew P. *Purging the Empire. Mass Expulsions in Germany, 1871–1914*. Oxford University Press, 2015.

Foucault, Michel. "Nietzche, Geneology, History." In *Language, Counter-Memory, Practice: Selected Essays and Interviews*, edited by D. F. Bouchard. Cornell University Press, 1977.

Foucault, Michel. *Security, Territory, Population: Lectures at the Collège de France, 1977–78*. Palgrave Macmillan, 2007.

Franklin, Robert Lee. "The Indian Community in Bahrain: Labour Immigration in a Plural Society." PhD diss., Harvard University, 1985.

Fraser, Nancy. "Expropriation and Exploitation in Racialized Capitalism: A Reply to Michael Dawson." *Critical Historical Studies* 3, no. 1 (Spring 2016): 163–78.

Fraser, Nancy. "Roepke Lecture in Economic Geography—From Exploitation to Expropriation: Historic Geographies of Racial Capitalism." *Economic Geography* 94, no. 1 (2018): 1–17.

Fraser, Nancy, and Linda Gordon. "A Genealogy of Dependency: Tracing a Keyword of the U.S. Welfare State." *Signs: Journal of Women in Culture and Society* 19, no. 2 (Winter 1994): 309–36.

Fuccaro, Nelida. *Histories of City and State in the Persian Gulf: Manama since 1800*. Cambridge University Press, 2009.

Fuccaro, Nelida. "Oilmen, Petroleum Arabism and OPEC: New Political and Public Cultures of Oil in the Arab World, 1959–1964." In *Handbook of OPEC and the Global Energy Order: Past Present, and Future Challenges*, edited by Dag Harald Claes and Giuliano Garavini. Routledge, 2020.

Fuccaro, Nelida. "Pearl Towns and Early Oil Cities: Migration and Integration in the Arab Coast of the Persian Gulf." In *The City in the Ottoman Empire: Migration and the making of urban modernity*, edited by Ulrike Freitag. Routledge, 2011.

Fuccaro, Nelida, and Mandana E. Limbert, eds. *Life Worlds of Middle Eastern Oil: Histories and Ethnographies of Black Gold*. Edinburgh University Press, 2023.

Gabaccia, Donna, Franca Iacovetta, and Fraser Ottanelli. "Laboring across National Borders—Class, Gender, and Militancy in the Proletarian Mass Migrations." *International Labor and Working-Class History* 66, no. 1 (2004): 57–77.

Galpern, Steven G. *Money, Oil, and Empire in the Middle East: Sterling and Postwar Imperialism, 1944–1971*. Cambridge University Press, 2009.

Garavini, Giuliano. *The Rise and Fall of OPEC in the Twentieth Century*. Oxford University Press, 2019.

Gardner, Andrew. *City of Strangers: Gulf Migration and the Indian Community in Bahrain*. Cornell University Press 2010.

Gardner, Andrew M. "Why Do They Keep Coming? Labor Migrants in the Persian Gulf States." In *Migrant Labor in the Persian Gulf*, edited by Mehran Kamrava and Zahra Babar. Columbia University Press, 2012.

Gargash, Anwar M. "Political Participation in Kuwait and the United Arab Emirates: 1938–1979." PhD diss., University of Cambridge, 1989.

Getachew, Adom. *Worldmaking after Empire: The Rise and Fall of Self-Determination*. Princeton University Press, 2019.

Ghabra, Shafeeq. *Palestinians in Kuwait: The Family and the Politics of Survival*. Westview Press, 1987.

Ghabra, Shafeeq. *al-Kuwait: Dirasa fi Aliyat al-Dawla wa-l-Sulta wa-l-Mujtama*ʿ (A Study of the State Apparatus, Power, and Society). Dar Qurtas li-l-Nashr wa-l-Tawziʿ, 1995.

Go, Julian. "Reverberations of Empire: How the Colonial Past Shapes the Present." *Social Science History* 48 (2023): 1–18.

Go, Julian. "Three Tensions in the Theory of Racial Capitalism." *Sociological Theory* 39, no. 1 (2021): 38–47.

Goffman, Laura Frances. *Disorder and Diagnosis: Health and the Politics of Everyday Life in Modern Arabia*. Stanford University Press, 2024.

Goffman, Laura Frances. "Medical Frontiers: Health, Empire, and Society in the Gulf and Arabian Peninsula, 1862–1959." PhD diss., Georgetown University, 2019.

Goffman, Laura Frances. "Popular Politics and Epidemics in Eastern Arabia." *Labor: Studies in Working-Class History* 20, no. 2 (2023): 74–94.

Goffman, Laura Frances. "Waiting for AIDS in Kuwait," *Radical History Review* 140 (May 2021): 21–48.

Goldberg, Ellis. *Tinker, Tailor, and Textile Worker: Class and Politics in Egypt, 1930–1952*. University of California Press, 1986.

Gordon, Linda, and Nancy Fraser. "A Genealogy of Dependency: Tracing a Keyword of the U.S. Welfare State." *Signs* 19, no. 2 (Winter 1994): 309–36.

Goswami, Manu. *Producing India: From Colonial Economy to National Space.* University of Chicago Press, 2004.

Graeber, David. *Debt: The First 5,000 Years.* Melville House Publishing, 2011.

Gramsci, Antonio. "Some Aspects of the Southern Question." In *Selections from Political Writings (1921–1926)*, edited and translated by Quintin Hoare. Lawrence and Wishart, 1978.

Greene, Julie. "Rethinking the Boundaries of Class: Labor History and Theories of Class and Capitalism." *Labor* 18, no. 2 (2021): 92–112.

Gulf Labour Markets and Migration [Hereafter GLMM]. "GCC: Total Population and Percentage of Nationals and Non-nationals in GCC Countries." https://gulfmigration.grc.net/gcc-total-population-and-percentage-of-nationals-and-non-nationals-in-gcc-countries-national-statistics-mid-2020-2/.

Al-Gurg, Easa Saleh. *The Wells of Memory: An Autobiography.* John Murray, 1998.

H-Diplo Roundtable Review of Oil Revolution. XX, no. 10 (October 29, 2018).

Al Haddad, Mohammad S. "The Effect of Detribalization and Sedentarization on the Socio-Economic Structure of the Tribes of the Arabian Peninsula: Ajman Tribes as a Case Study." PhD diss., University of Kansas, 1981.

Hahamovitch, Cindy. "Creating Perfect Immigrants: Guestworkers of the World in Historical Perspective." *Labor History* 44, no. 1 (February 2003): 69–94.

Hall, Stuart. "When Was 'the Postcolonial'? Thinking at the Limit." In *The Post-Colonial Question: Common Skies, Divided Horizons*, edited by Iain Chambers and Lidia Curti. Routledge, 1996.

Halliday, Fred. *Arabia without Sultans.* Penguin, 1974.

Halliday, Fred. "Labour Migration in the Arab World: The Ugly Face of the New Economic Order." *Labour, Capital and Society* 15, no. 1 (April 1982): 8–22.

Halliday, Fred. "Migration and the Labor Force in the Oil Producing States of the Middle East." *Development and Change* 8, no. 3 (1977): 263–91.

Hamadah, Faisal. "Kafala and Social Reproduction: Migration Governance Regimes and Labour Relations in the Gulf." In *The South Asia to Gulf Migration Governance Process*, edited by Crystal Ennis and Nicolas Blarel. Bristol University Press, 2022.

Hammad, Hanan. *Industrial Sexuality: Gender, Urbanization, and Social Transformation in Egypt.* University of Texas Press, 2016.

Hammar, Tomas. *Democracy and the Nation-State: Aliens, Denizens, and Citizens in a World of International Migration.* Gower Pub. Co., 1990.

Hanieh, Adam. *Capitalism and Class in the Gulf Arab States.* Palgrave Macmillan, 2011.

Hanieh, Adam. "Overcoming Methodological Nationalism: Spatial Perspectives on Migration to the Gulf Arab States." In *Transit States: Labour, Migration & Citizenship in the Gulf*, edited by Abdulhadi Khalaf, Omar AlShehabi, and Adam Hanieh. Pluto Press, 2015.

Hanieh, Adam. "Rethinking Class and State in the Gulf Cooperation Council." In *A Critical Political Economy of the Middle East and North Africa*, edited by Joel Beinin, Bassam Haddad, and Sherene Seikaly. Stanford University Press, 2021.

Hanley, Will. *Identifying with Nationality: Europeans, Ottomans, and Egyptians in Alexandria*. Columbia University Press, 2017.

Hanley, Will. "Papers for Going, Papers for Staying: Identification and Subject Formation in the Eastern Mediterranean." In *A Global Middle East: Mobility, Materiality and Culture in the Modern Age, 1880–1950*, edited by Liat Kozma, Cyrus Schayegh, and Avner Wishnitzer. I. B. Tauris, 2014.

Harms, Robert. "Introduction." In *The Indian Ocean Slavery in the Age of Abolition*, edited by Robert W. Harms, Bernard K. Freamon, and David W. Blight. Yale University Press, 2013.

Harris, Kevan. *A Social Revolution: Politics and the Welfare State in Iran*. University of California Press, 2007.

Hasan, Bilal. *al-Filastiniyyun fi al-Kuwait: Bahth Ihsa'i* (The Palestinians in Kuwait: A Statistical Study). The Palestinian Liberation Organization, 1974.

Hashim, Saeed Khalil. "The Influence of Iraq on the Nationalist Movements of Kuwait and Bahrain 1920–1961." PhD diss., University of Exeter, 1984.

Hatim, ʿAbdullah Khalid. *Min Huna Badaʾat al-Kuwait* (From Here Began Kuwait). 2nd ed. Dar al-Qabas, 1979.

Hay, Rupert. "Impact of the Oil Industry on the Persian Gulf Shaikhdoms." *Middle East Journal* 9, no. 4 (1955): 361–72.

Heiskanen, Jaakko. *Ethnos of the Earth: International Order and the Emergence of Ethnicity*. Cambridge University Press, 2024.

Herb, Michael. *The Wages of Oil: Parliaments and Economic Development in Kuwait and the UAE*. Cornell University Press, 2014.

Al-Hijji, Yacoub Yusuf. *Kuwait and the Sea: A Brief Social and Economic History*. Translated by Fahad Ahmad ʿIsa Bishara. Arabian Publishing, 2010.

Holston, James. *Insurgent Citizenship: Disjunctions of Democracy and Modernity in Brazil*. Princeton University Press, 2008.

Hopper, Matthew S. *Slaves of One Master: Globalization and Slavery in Arabia in the Age of Empire*. Yale University Press, 2015.

Human Rights Watch. "Building Towers, Cheating Workers: Exploitation of Migrant Construction Workers in the United Arab Emirates." November 11, 2006.

Human Rights Watch. "Kuwait: Government Critics Stripped of Citizenship." October 19, 2014.

The International Bank for Reconstruction and Development. *The Economic Development of Kuwait*. The Johns Hopkins Press, 1965.

Iskander, Natasha. *Does Skill Make Us Human? Migrant Workers in 21st-Century Qatar and Beyond*. Princeton University Press, 2021.

Ismael, Jacqueline S. *Kuwait: Dependency and Class in a Rentier State*. University Press of Florida, 1993.

ʿIzz al-Din, Amin. *ʿUmmal al-Kuwait min al-Luʾluʾ ila al-Batrul* (Workers of Kuwait from Pearls to Oil). Kuwait Government Press, 1958.

ʿIzz al-Din, Amin. "al-Haraka al-Niqabiyya fi al-Kuwait" (The Trade Union Movement in Kuwait). Unpublished paper, Ministry of Information Library, Kuwait, 1972.

Jafari, Peyman. "Linkages of Oil and Politics: Oil Strikes and Dual Power in the Iranian Revolution." *Labor History* 60, no. 1 (2019): 24–43.

Jamal, Muhammad ʿAbd al-Hadi. *Aswaq al-Kuwait al-Qadima* (The Old Markets of Kuwait). Center for Research and Study of Kuwait, 2001.

Jones, Martha S. *Birthright Citizens: A History of Race and Rights in Antebellum America*. Cambridge University Press, 2018.

Jones, Toby Craig. *Desert Kingdom: How Oil and Water Forged Modern Saudi Arabia*. Harvard University Press, 2010.

Joseph, Suad, ed. *Gender and Citizenship in the Middle East*. Syracuse University Press, 2000.

Joseph-Gabriel, Annette K. *Reimagining Liberation: How Black Women Transformed Citizenship in the French Empire*. Illinois University Press, 2019.

Joyce, Miriam. "The Bahraini Three on St. Helena, 1956–1961." *Middle East Journal* 54, no. 4 (Autumn 2000): 613–23.

Kamrava, Mehran, and Zahra Babar. *Migrant Labor in the Persian Gulf*. Columbia University Press, 2012.

Kanna, Ahmed. *Dubai: The City as Corporation*. Minnesota University Press, 2011.

Kanna, Ahmed. "A Politics of Non-Recognition? Biopolitics of Arab Gulf Worker Protests in the Year of Uprisings." *Interface* 4, no. 1 (2012): 146–64.

Kanna, Ahmed, Amélie Le Renard, and Neha Vora. *Beyond Exception: New Interpretations of the Arabian Peninsula*. Cornell University Press, 2020.

Kanoo, Khaled M. *The House of Kanoo: A Century of an Arabian Family Business*. The London Centre of Arabian Studies, 1997.

Kassamali, Sumayya. "Understanding Race and Migrant Domestic Labor in Lebanon." *Middle East Report Online*, July 13, 2021.

Kathiravelu, Laavanya. *Migrant Dubai: Low Wage Workers and the Construction of a Global City*. Palgrave Macmillan, 2016.

Keshavarzian, Arang. "From Port Cities to Cities with Ports: Toward a Multiscalar History of Persian Gulf Urbanism in the Twentieth Century." In *Gateways to the World: Port Cities in the Persian Gulf*, edited by Mehran Kamrava. Oxford University Press, 2018.

Keshavarzian, Arang. *Making Space for the Gulf: Histories of Regionalism and the Middle East*. Stanford University Press, 2024.

Khalaf, ʿAbd al-Hadi. "Labor Movements in Bahrain." *Middle East Report Online*, May 4, 1985.

Khalaf, Abdulhadi, Omar AlShehabi, and Adam Hanieh, eds. *Transit States: Labour, Migration and Citizenship in the Gulf*. Pluto Press, 2015.

Khalili, Laleh. "Crude Knowledge: Petro-Periodicals and Resource Sovereignty." *International Journal of Middle East Studies* 56, no. 3 (2025): 446–64.

Khalili, Laleh. *Sinews of War and Trade: Shipping and Capitalism in the Arabian Peninsula*. Verso, 2020.

Al-Khatib, Ahmad, and Ghanim al-Najjar. *al-Kuwait, min al-Imara ila al-Dawla: Dhikrayyat al-ʿamal al-Watani wa al-Qawmi* (Kuwait, from Emirate to State: Memoirs of National and Patriotic Work). al-Markaz al-Thaqafi al-ʿArabi, 2007.

Al-Khatib, Ahmad, and Ghanim al-Najjar. *al-Kuwait, min al-Dawla ila al-Imara: Dhikrayyat al-ʿamal al-Watani wa-al-Qawmi* (Kuwait, from State to Emirate: Memoirs of National and Patriotic Work). al-Markaz al-Thaqafi al-ʿArabi, 2009.

Khazʿal, Ḥusayn Khalaf al-Shaykh. *Tarikh al-Kuwait al-Siyasi* (The Political History of Kuwait). Dar al-Kutub, 1962.

Kholoussy, Hanan. *For Better, For Worse: The Marriage Crisis That Made Modern Egypt*. Stanford University Press, 2010.

Khuri, Fuad I. *Tribe and State in Bahrain: The Transformation of Social and Political Authority in an Arab State*. University of Chicago Press, 1980.

Koch, Natalie. "Is Nationalism Just for Nationals? Civic Nationalism for Noncitizens and Celebrating National Day in Qatar and the UAE." *Political Geography* 54 (2016): 43–53.

Kraut, Julia Rose. *Dissent: A History of Ideological Exclusion and Deportation in the United States*. Harvard University Press, 2020.

Kuwait Ministry of Social Affairs and Labor. *Annual Report for Year 1964*. Kuwait Government Press, 1965.

Kuwait Trade Union Federation. *Insha' Maʿahid al-Thaqafiyya al-ʿummalliyya fi al-Kuwait* (The Founding of the Workers' Culture Center in Kuwait). Kuwait Trade Union Federation Press, 1998.

Labor Office, National Democratic Action Society. *al-Haraka al-ʿummaliyya al-Niqabiyya al-Bahrainiyya wa-ʿalaqatuha bi-l-Haraka al-Wataniyya al-Siyasiyya* (The Bahraini Labor and Trade Union Movement and Its Relations with the Political National Movement). Bahrain, 2014.

Lackner, Helen. *A House Built on Sand: A Political Economy of Saudi Arabia*. Ithaca Press, 1978.

Lake, Marilyn, and Henry Reynolds. *Drawing the Global Colour Line: White Men's Countries and the International Challenge of Racial Equality*. Cambridge University Press, 2008.

Lawson, Fred. "Class and State in Kuwait." *MERIP Reports*, no. 132 (1985): 16–32.

Lesch, Ann M. "Palestinians in Kuwait." *Journal of Palestine Studies* 20, no. 4 (Summer 1991): 42–54.

Lewis, Mary Dewhurst. *The Boundaries of the Republic: Migrant Rights and the Limits of Universalism in France, 1918–1940*. Stanford University Press, 2007.

Lienhardt, Peter. *Disorientations, A Society in Flux: Kuwait in the 1950s*. Edited by Ahmed Al-Shahi. Ithica Press, 1993.

Lienhardt, Peter. "Town Politics in Eastern Arabia in the 1950s." *Journal of Arabian Studies* 5, no. 1 (2015): 1–14.

Lim, Julian. "Immigration, Plenary Powers, and Sovereignty Talk: Then and Now." *The Journal of the Gilded Age and Progressive Era* (2020): 1–13.

Limbert, Mandana E. "Caste, Ethnicity, and the Politics of Arabness in Southern Arabia." *Comparative Studies of South Asia, Africa, & the Middle East* 34, no. 3 (2014): 590–98.

Limbert, Mandana E. *In the Time of Oil: Piety, Memory, & Social Life in an Omani Town*. Stanford University Press, 2010.

Lockman, Zachary. *Comrades and Enemies: Arab and Jewish Workers in Palestine, 1906–1948*. University of California Press, 1996.

Lockman, Zachary. "The Social Roots of Nationalism: Workers and the National Movement in Egypt, 1908–19." *Middle Eastern Studies* 24, no. 4 (October 1988): 445–59.

Longhurst, Henry. *Adventures in Oil: The Story of British Petroleum*. Sidgwick and Jackson, 1959.

Longva, Anh Nga. *Walls Built on Sand: Migration, Exclusion, and Society in Kuwait*. Westview Press, 1997.

Lori, Noora. "National Security and the Management of Migrant Labor: A Case Study of the United Arab Emirates." *Asian and Pacific Migration Journal* 20, nos. 3–4 (2011): 315–37.

Lori, Noora. *Offshore Citizens: Permanent Temporary Status in the Gulf*. Cambridge University Press, 2019.

Lorimer, John Gordon. *Gazetteer of the Persian Gulf 'Omān, and Central Arabia*. Government of India Press, 1908.

Louër, Laurence. *Transnational Shia Politics: Religious and Political Networks in the Gulf*. Columbia University Press, 2008.

Louis, William Roger. *The British Empire in the Middle East: Arab Nationalism, The United States, and Postwar Imperialism*. Oxford University Press, 1984.

Low, Michael Christopher. *Imperial Mecca: Ottoman Arabia and the Indian Ocean Hajj*. Columbia University Press, 2020.

Lutfi, Ashraf. *Arab Oil: A Plan for the Future*. The Middle East Research and Publishing Center, 1960.

Lutfi, Ashraf. *OPEC Oil*. The Middle East Research and Publishing Center, 1968.

MacLean, Matthew. "Spatial Transformations and the Emergence of the 'National': Infrastructures and the Formation of the United Arab Emirates, 1950–1980." PhD diss., New York University, 2017.

Mahdavi, Pardis. *Crossing the Gulf: Love and Family in Migrant Lives*. Stanford University Press, 2016.

Mann, Michael. "The Autonomous Power of the State: Its Origins, Mechanisms and Results." *European Journal of Sociology* 25, no. 2 (1984): 185–213.

Marshall, T. H., and Tom Bottomore. *Citizenship and Social Class*. Pluto Press, 1992.

Masoudi, Abbas. *Idari az Shaikh Nishinha-yi Khalij-i Fars* (Observations of the Shaikh on the Persian Gulf). Iran-i-Chap, 1966.

Massey, Doreen. *Space, Place and Gender*. Polity Press, 1994.

Massey, Doreen. *Spatial Divisions of Labour: Social Structures and the Geography of Production*. Macmillan, 1995.

Massey, Douglass S. "Towards a Theory of International Migration." *Eastern Journal of European Studies* 3, no. 2 (December 2012): 9–35.

Massey, Douglass S., Joaquin Arango, Graeme Hugo, Ali Kouaouci, Adela Pellegrino, and J. Edward Taylor. "Theories of International Migration: A Review and Appraisal." *Population and Development Review* 19, no. 3 (September 1993): 431–66.

Mathew, Johan. *Margins of the Market: Trafficking and Capitalism across the Arabian Sea*. University of California Press, 2016.

Mathew, Johan. "Trafficking Labor: Abolition and the Exchange of Labor across the Arabian Sea, 1861–1947." *Slavery & Abolition* 33, no. 1 (March 2012): 139–56.

Matthiesen, Toby. "Migration, Minorities, and Radical Networks: Labour Movements and Opposition Groups in Saudi Arabia, 1950–1975." *International Review of Social History* 59, no. 3 (2014): 473–504.

Matthiesen, Toby. "Red Arabia: Anti-Colonialism, the Cold War, and the Long Sixties in the Gulf States." In *The Routledge Handbook of the Global Sixties: Between Protest and Nation-Building*, edited by Chen Jian, Martin Klimke, Masha Kirasova, Mary Nolan, Marilyn Young, and Joanna Waley-Cohen. Taylor and Francis, 2018.

Mbembe, Achille. "Provisional Notes on the Postcolony." *Africa: Journal of the International African Institute* 62, no. 1 (1992): 3–37.

McDow, Thomas F. *Buying Time: Debt and Mobility in the Western Indian Ocean*. Ohio University Press, 2018.

Al-Mdairis, Falah Abdullah. "The Arab Nationalist Movement of Kuwait from its Origins to 1970." PhD diss., University of Oxford, 1987.

Al-Mdairis, Falah Abdullah. *al-Mujtamaʿ al-Madani wa-al-Haraka al-Wataniyya fi al-Kuwait* (Civil Society and the Kuwaiti National Movement). Dar Qurtas li-l-Nashr, 2000.

Al-Mdairis, Falah Abdullah. *al-Haraka al-Dusturiyya fi al-Kuwait* (The Constitutional Movement in Kuwait). Dar Qurtas li-l-Nashr, 2002.

Al-Mdairis, Falah Abdullah. *al-Tawajjuhat al-Marksiyya al-Kuwaitiyya* (The Kuwaiti Marxist Tendencies). Dar Qurtas li-l-Nashr, 2003.

Al-Mdairis, Falah Abdullah. "al-Dawr al-Siyasi li-l-Ḥaraka al-Niqabiyya al-ʿumaliyya fi al-Kuwait (The Political Role of the Trade Union Movement in Kuwait, 1964–1994)." *Shuʾun al-Ijtimaʿiyya*, no. 44 (Winter 1994).

Al-Mdairis, Falah Abdullah. *Malamih Awliyya Hawl Nashʾat al-Tajammuʿat wa al-Tandhimat al-Siyasiyya fi al-Kuwait, 1938–1975* (The Primary Ambitions of Political Groups and Organizations in Kuwait). Dar Qurtas li-l-Nashr, 1994.

Melamed, Jodi. "Racial Capitalism." *Critical Ethnic Studies* 1, no. 1 (2015): 76–85.

Menoret, Pascal. *Joyriding in Riyadh: Oil, Urbanism, and Road Revolt*. Cambridge University Press, 2014.

Mezzadra, Sandro, and Brett Neilson. *Border as Method, or, The Multiplication of Labor*. Duke University Press, 2013.

Miers, Suzanne. "Slavery and the Slave Trade in Saudi Arabia and the Arab States on the Persian Gulf, 1921–63." In *Abolition and Its Aftermath in Indian Ocean Africa and Asia*, edited by Gwen Campbell. Routledge, 2005.

Mies, Maria. *Patriarchy and Accumulation on a World Scale: Women in the International Division of Labor*. Zed Books, 1986.

Mikdashi, Maya. "Sex and Sectarianism: The Legal Architecture of Lebanese Citizenship." *Comparative Studies of South Asia, Africa, & the Middle East* 34, no. 2 (2014): 279–93.

Mikdashi, Maya. *Sextarianism: Sovereignty, Secularism, and the State in Lebanon.* Stanford University Press, 2022.

Mitchell, Timothy. *Carbon Democracy: Political Power in the Age of Oil.* Verso, 2011.

Mitchell, Timothy. "Ten Propositions on Oil." In *A Critical Political Economy of the Middle East and North Africa*, edited by Joel Beinin, Bassam Haddad, and Sherene Seikaly. Stanford University Press, 2021.

Molotch, Harvey, and Davide Ponzini, eds. *The New Arab Urban: Gulf Cities of Wealth, Ambition, and Distress.* NYU Press, 2019.

Mongia, Radhika. *Indian Migration and Empire: A Colonial Genealogy.* Duke University Press, 2018.

Mongia, Radhika. "Race, Nationality, Mobility: A History of the Passport." *Public Culture* 11, no. 3 (Fall 1999): 527–56.

Moore, Pete W. *Doing Business in the Middle East: Politics and Economic Crisis in Jordan und Kuwait.* Cambridge University Press, 2009.

Al-Moosa, Abdulrasoul A. "Bedouin and Shanty Settlements in Kuwait." PhD diss., University of London, 1976.

Al-Moosa, Abdulrasool, and Keith McLachlan. *Immigrant Labour in Kuwait.* Croom Helm, 1985.

Motomura, Hiroshi. *Americans in Waiting: The Lost Story of Immigration and Citizenship in the United States.* Oxford University Press, 2006.

Mueller, Chelsi. *The Origins of the Arab-Iranian Conflict: Nationalism and Sovereignty in the Gulf between the World Wars.* Cambridge University Press, 2020.

Al-Mughni, Haya. *Women in Kuwait: The Politics of Gender.* Saqi, 2001.

al-Munais, Sami. *al-Tali'a wa al-Ma'raka al-Dimuqratiyya* (The Vanguard and the Democratic Struggle). Sharikat Kathima li-l-Nashr wa al-Tarjima wa al-Tawzi', 1984.

Mutiwi', 'Abdullah. *Safhat min Tarikh al-Haraka al-'ummaliyya al-Bahrainiyya* (Pages from the History of the Bahraini Workers' Movement). Dar al-Kunuz al-Adabiyya, 2006.

Nadjmabadi, Shahnaz R. "Cross-Border Networks: Labour Migration from Iran to the Arab Countries of the Persian Gulf." *Anthropology of the Middle East* 5, no. 1 (Spring 2010): 18–33.

Al-Nafisi, Abdullah F. *al-Kuwait: al-Ra'i al-Akhar* (Kuwait: Another Opinion). Dar Taha, 1978.

Naguib, Rim. "The Ideological Deportation of Foreigners and 'Local Subjects of Foreign Extraction' in Interwar Egypt." *Arab Studies Journal* 28, no. 2 (Fall 2020.).

Al-Najjar, Ghanim Hamad. "Decision-Making Process in Kuwait: The Land Acquisition Policy as a Case Study." PhD diss., University of Exeter, 1984.

Al-Najjar, Ghanim Hamad. *Madkhal li-l-Tatawwur al-Siyasi fi al-Kuwait* (An Introduction to Political Development in Kuwait). Dar Qurtas li-l-Nashr, 1994.

Nakhleh, Emile. "Labor Markets and Citizenship in Bahrayn and Qatar." *Middle East Journal* 31, no. 2 (Spring, 1977): 143–56.

Al-Nakib, Farah. *Kuwait Transformed: A History of Oil and Urban Life*. Stanford University Press, 2016.

Al-Nakib, Farah. "Public Space and Public Protest in Kuwait, 1938–2012." *City* 18, no. 6 (2014): 723–34.

Al-Nakib, Farah. "Revisiting Hadar and Badu in Kuwait: Citizenship, Housing, and the Construction of a Dichotomy." *International Journal of Middle Eastern Studies* 46, no. 1 (2014): 5–30.

Al-Nakib, Mai. "'The People are Missing'—Palestinians in Kuwait." *Deleuze Studies* 8, no. 1 (2014): 23–44.

Al-Naqeeb, Khaldoun. *Sira' al-Qabila wa al-Dimuqratiyya: Halat al-Kuwait* (The Struggle of Tribalism and Democracy: The Situation of Kuwait). Saqi, 1996.

National Assembly of Kuwait, *al-Majlis al-Ta'sisi: Mahadir Ijtima'at Lajnat al-Dustur* (The Constituent Assembly: Minutes of the Meetings of the Constitution Committee). al-Amana, 2013.

Ngai, Mae. *Impossible Subjects: Illegal Aliens and the Making of Modern America*. Princeton University Press, 2004.

Okruhlik, Gwenn. "Rentier Wealth, Unruly Law, and the Rise of Opposition: The Political Economy of Oil States." *Comparative Politics* 31, no. 3 (1999): 295–315.

Olin Wright, Erik. "Rethinking, Once Again, the Concept of Class Structure." In *The Debate on Classes*, edited by Erik Olin Wright. Verso, 1989.

Onley, James. *The Arabian Frontier of the British Raj: Merchants, Rulers, and the British in the Nineteenth Century Gulf*. Oxford University Press, 2007.

Onley, James. "Transnational Merchants in the Nineteenth-Century Gulf: The Case of the Safar Family." In *Transnational Connections and the Arab Gulf*, edited by Madawi al-Rasheed. Routledge, 2005.

al-Othman, Nasser. *With their Bare Hands: The Story of the Oil Industry in Qatar*. Translated by Ken Whittingham. Longman, 1984.

Owen, Roger. *Migrant Workers in the Gulf*. Minority Rights Group, 1992.

Parolin, Gianluca Paolo. *Citizenship in the Arab World: Kin, Religion and Nation-State*. Amsterdam University Press, 2009.

Parra, Francisco. *Oil Politics: A Modern History of Petroleum*. I. B. Tauris, 2004.

Parreñas, Rhacel Salazar. *Unfree: Migrant Domestic Work in Arab States*. Stanford University Press, 2022.

Peck, Jamie. *Work-Place: The Social Regulation of Labor Markets*. The Guilford Press, 1996.

Peirce, Leslie. *Morality Tales: Law and Gender in the Ottoman Court of Aintab*. University of California Press, 2003.

Piore, Michael J. *Birds of Passage: Migrant Labor and Industrial Societies*. Cambridge University Press, 1979.

Polanyi, Karl. *The Great Transformation: The Political and Economic Origins of Our Time*. Beacon Press, 2007.

Posusney, Marsha Pripstein. *Labor and the State in Egypt: Workers, Unions, and Economic Restructuring*. Columbia University Press, 1997.

Potter, Lawrence G., ed. *The Persian Gulf in Modern Times: People, Ports, and History.* Palgrave Macmillan, 2014.

Priest, Tyler. "Crude History." *Reviews in American History* 43, no. 2 (2015): 333–39.

Project on Middle East Political Science. "The Politics of Rentier States in the Gulf." POMEPS 33 (January 2019). https://pomeps.org/wp-content/uploads/2019/02/POMEPS_Studies_33.pdf.

Pursley, Sara. *Familiar Futures: Time, Selfhood, and Sovereignty in Iraq.* Stanford University Press, 2019.

Pursley, Sara. "The Stage of Adolescence: Anticolonial Time, Youth Insurgency, and the Marriage Crisis in Hashimite Iraq." *History of the Present* 3, no. 2 (Fall 2013): 160–97.

Al-Qina'i, Yusuf bin 'Isa. *Safhat min Tarikh al-Kuwait* (Pages from the History of Kuwait). Dhat al-Salasil, 1988.

Quintana, Maria L. *Contracting Freedom: Race, Empire, and U.S. Guestworker Programs.* University of Pennsylvania Press, 2022.

Al-Ragam, Asseel. "Towards a Critique of an Architectural Nahda: A Kuwaiti Example." PhD diss., University of Pennsylvania, 2008.

Al-Ragam, Asseel. "Negotiating the Politics of Exclusion: Georges Candilis, Housing and the Kuwaiti Welfare State." *International Journal of Urban and Regional Research* 41, no. 2 (2017): 235–50.

Rahnama, Sara. *The Future Is Feminist: Women and Social Change in Interwar Algeria.* Cornell University Press, 2023.

Ramnath, Kalyani. *Boats in a Storm: Law, Migration, and Decolonization in South and Southeast Asia, 1942–1962.* Stanford University Press, 2023.

Al-Rasheed, Madawi, and Robert Vitalis. *Counter-Narratives: History, Contemporary Society, and Politics in Saudi Arabia and Yemen.* Palgrave Macmillan, 2004

Al-Rashoud, Talal. "Modern Education and Arab Nationalism in Kuwait, 1911–1961." PhD diss., SOAS University of London, 2017.

Razavian, Mohammad Taghi. "Iranian Communities in the Persian Gulf: A Geographical Analysis." PhD diss., University of London, 1975.

Le Renard, Amélie. *Western Privilege: Work, Intimacy, and Postcolonial Hierarchies in Dubai.* Stanford University Press, 2021.

Le Renard, Amélie, and Neha Vora. "Interrogating Race in Gulf Studies." *POMEPS Studies,* no. 44 (September 2021): 96–101.

Robinson, Cedric J. *Black Marxism: The Making of the Black Radical Tradition.* University of North Carolina Press, 2000.

Robinson, Shira N. *Citizen Strangers: Palestinians and the Birth of Israel's Liberal Settler State.* Stanford University Press, 2013.

Roediger, David R. *The Wages of Whiteness: Race and the Making of the American Working Class.* Verso, 2007.

Ross, Michael L. *The Oil Curse: How Petroleum Wealth Shapes the Development of Nations.* Princeton University Press, 2012.

Rumaihi, Muhammad. *Beyond Oil: Unity and Development in the Gulf.* Translated by James Dickins. Al Saqi Books, 1986.

Al-Rushaid, Abd al-ʿAziz. *Tarikh al-Kuwait* (History of Kuwait). Dar Maktabat al-Haya, 1978.

Russell, Sharon Stanton. "Politics and Ideology in Migration Policy Formation: The Case of Kuwait." *International Migration Review* 23, no. 1 (Spring 1989): 24–47.

Al-Sabah, Amal Yusuf al-ʿAdhbi. *al-Hijrah ila al-Kuwait min ʿam 1957 ila 1975: Dirasah fi Jugharafiyat al-Sukkan* (Migration to Kuwait from 1957 to 1975: A Study in Population Geography). Kuwait University Press, 1978.

Saleh, Hassan Mohammad Abdulla. "Labor, Nationalism, and Imperialism in Eastern Arabia: Britain, the Shaikhs and the Gulf Oil Workers in Bahrain, Kuwait and Qatar, 1932–1956." PhD diss., University of Michigan, 1991.

Salih, Kamal Osman. "The 1938 Kuwait Legislative Council." *Middle Eastern Studies* 28, no. 1 (1992): 66–100.

Saleh, Zainab. "On Iraqi Nationality: Law, Citizenship, and Exclusion," *The Arab Studies Journal* 21, no. 1 (2013): 48–78.

Samin, Nadal. *Of Sand or Soil: Genealogy and Tribal Belonging in Saudi Arabia.* Princeton University Press, 2015.

Santiago, Myrna I. *The Ecology of Oil: Environment, Labor and the Mexican Revolution, 1900–1938.* Cambridge University Press, 2006.

Saqr, Hussein. *Rihla Dakhil al-Dhakira maʿ al-Haraka al-ʿUmaliyya al-Kuwaitiyya* (A Trip Down Memory Lane with the Kuwaiti Workers' Movement). The Kuwait Trade Union Federation Press, Undated.

Sassen, Saskia. *Guests and Aliens.* New Press, 1999.

Sassen, Saskia. *The Mobility of Labor and Capital: A Study in International Investment and Labor Flow.* Cambridge University Press, 1988.

Al-Sayegh, Fatma. "Merchants' Role in a Changing Society: The Case of Dubai, 1900–90." *Middle Eastern Studies* 34, no. 1 (January 1998): 87–102.

Schrijver, Nico. *Sovereignty over Natural Resources: Balancing Rights and Duties.* Cambridge University Press, 1997.

Scott, Joan. *Gender and the Politics of History.* Columbia University Press, 1988.

Seccombe, Ian J. "'A Disgrace to American Enterprise': Italian Labour and the Arabian American Oil Company in Saudi Arabia, 1944–54." *Immigrants & Minorities: Historical Studies in Ethnicity, Migration and Diaspora* 5, no. 3 (1986): 233–57.

Seccombe, Ian J. "Labour Migration to the Arabian Gulf: Evolution and Characteristics 1920–1950." *British Society for Middle Eastern Studies Bulletin* 10, no. 1 (1983): 3–20.

Seccombe, Ian J., and R. I. Lawless. "Foreign Worker Dependence in the Gulf, and the International Oil Companies: 1910–50." *International Migration Review,* 20, no. 3 (Autumn 1986): 548–74.

Seccombe, Ian J., and R. I. Lawless. "Work Camps and Company Towns: Settlement Patterns and the Gulf Oil Industry." Working paper, University of Durham, Center for Middle Eastern and Islamic Studies, 1987.

Segal, Eran. "Merchants' Networks in Kuwait: The Story of Yusuf Al-Marzuk." *Middle Eastern Studies* 45, no. 5 (2009): 709–17.

Shafiee, Katayoun. *Machineries of Oil: An Infrastructural History of BP in Iran*. The MIT Press, 2018.

Shafir, Gershon, ed. *The Citizenship Debates: A Reader*. University of Minnesota Press, 1998.

Shah, Nasra. "Asian Women Workers in Kuwait." *International Migration Review* 25, no. 3 (1991): 464–86.

Shah, Nasra, Makhdoom A. Shah, Rafiqul Islam Chowdhury, and Indu Menon. "Foreign Domestic Workers in Kuwait: Who Employs How Many." *Asian and Pacific Migration Journal* 11, no. 2 (2002): 247–69.

El Shakry, Omnia. "'History without Documents': The Vexed Archives of Decolonization in the Middle East." *American Historical Review* 120, no. 3 (2015): 920–34.

Al-Shalal, Khalid Ahmed. "The Trade Union Movement in the State of Kuwait: A Socio-Historical and Analytical Study." PhD diss., Michigan State University, 1983.

Shamshiri, Marral. "Revolutionary Transnationalism in the Persian Gulf Iranian-Arab Solidarity in Dhufar in the 1970s." *Comparative Studies of South Asia, Africa and the Middle East* 43, no. 3 (2023): 343–57.

Al-Shaya, Abdul-Azeez Mohammad. *Echoes of Memory*. Translated by Ali Tahir. The National Council for Culture, Arts & Letters, 2015.

AlShehabi, Omar Hesham. *Contested Modernity: Sectarianism, Nationalism, and Colonialism in Bahrain*. Oneworld Academic, 2019.

AlShehabi, Omar Hesham. "Divide and Rule in Bahrain and the Elusive Pursuit for a United Front: The Experience of the Constitutive Committee and the 1972 Uprising." *Historical Materialism* 21, no. 1 (2013): 94–127.

AlShehabi, Omar Hesham. "Policing Labour in Empire: The Modern Origins of the Kafala Sponsorship System in the Gulf Arab States." *British Journal of Middle Eastern Studies* (2019): 1–20.

AlShehabi, Omar. "Political Movements in Bahrain across the Long Twentieth Century (1900–2015)." In *The Oxford Handbook of Contemporary Middle-Eastern and North African History*, edited by Amal Ghazal and Jens Hanssen. Oxford University Press, 2015.

Shuhaiber, Sunail. "Political Development in Kuwait: Continuity and Change in an Arab Independent Gulf State." PhD diss., St. Catherine's College, University of Oxford, 1982.

Silver, Beverly J. *Forces of Labor: Workers' Movements and Globalization Since 1870*. Cambridge University Press, 2003.

Singh, Nikhil Pal. "On Race, Violence, and 'so-called Primitive Accumulation.'" *Social Text* 34, no. 3 (September 2016): 27–50.

Singha, Radhika. "Finding Labor from India for the War in Iraq: The Jail Porter and Labor Corps, 1916–1920." *Comparative Studies in Society and History* 49, no. 2 (April 2007): 412–45.

Singha, Radhika. "Punished by Surveillance: Policing 'Dangerousness' in Colonial India, 1872–1918." *Modern Asian Studies* 49, no. 2 (2015): 241–69.

Smith, Benjamin. *Hard Times in the Land of Plenty: Oil Politics in Iran and Indonesia.* Cornell University Press, 2007.

Smith, Simon. *Kuwait 1950–1965: Britain, the al-Sabah, and Oil.* Oxford University Press, 1999.

Somers, Margaret. *Genealogies of Citizenship: Markets, Statelessness, and the Right to Have Rights.* Cambridge University Press, 2008.

Soysal, Yasemin Nuhoğlu. *Limits of Citizenship: Migrants and Postnational Membership in Europe.* University of Chicago Press, 1994.

State of Kuwait, Department of Planning and Statistics. *Statistics Abstract in 25 Years.* Central Statistics Office, 1990.

Stephenson, Lindsey R. "Between Modern and National Education: The 'Ajam Schools of Bahrain and Kuwait." *Arabian Humanities* (2020).

Stephenson, Lindsey R. "Rerouting the Persian Gulf: The Transnationalization of Iranian Migrant Networks, c. 1900–1940." PhD diss., Princeton University, 2018.

Stoler, Laura Ann. *Along the Archival Grain: Epistemic Anxieties and Colonial Common Sense.* Princeton University Press, 2008.

Suzuki, Hideaki. "Baluchi Experiences Under Slavery and the Slave Trade of the Gulf of Oman and the Persian Gulf, 1921–1950." *Journal of the Middle East and Africa* 4 (2013): 205–23.

Al-Tajir, Mahdi Abdalla. *Bahrain 1920–1945: Britain, the Shaikh and the Administration.* Croon Helm, 1987.

Takriti, Abdel Razzaq. "Colonial Coups and the War on Popular Sovereignty." *American Historical Review* 124, no. 3 (June 2019): 878–909.

Takriti, Abdel Razzaq. *Monsoon Revolution: Republicans, Sultans, and Empires in Oman 1965–1976.* Oxford University Press, 2013.

Takriti, Abdel Razzaq. "Political Praxis in the Gulf: Ahmad al-Khatib and the Movement of Arab Nationalists, 1948–1969." In *Arabic Thought Beyond the Liberal Age: New Directions in Middle East Intellectual History*, edited by Jens Hanssen and Max Weiss. Princeton University Press, 2018.

Tatour, Lana. "Citizenship as Domination: Settler Colonialism and the Making of Palestinian Citizenship in Israel." *Arab Studies Journal* 27, no. 2 (Fall 2019): 8–39.

Tejel, Jordi, and Ramazan Hakkı Öztan, eds. *Regimes of Mobility: Borders and State Formation in the Middle East, 1918–1946.* Edinburgh University Press, 2022.

Tétreault, Mary Ann. *Stories of Democracy: Politics and Society in Contemporary Kuwait.* Columbia University Press, 2000.

Tétreault, Mary Ann, and Haya al-Mughni. "Gender, Citizenship and Nationalism in Kuwait." *British Journal of Middle Eastern Studies* 22, no. 1/2 (1995): 64–80.

Tétreault, Mary Ann, and Haya al-Mughni. "Modernization and Its Discontents: State and Gender in Kuwait." *Middle East Journal* 49, no. 3 (Summer 1995): 403.–17.

Tetzlaff, Stefan. "The Turn of the Gulf Tide: Empire, Nationalism, and South Asian Labor Migration to Iraq, c. 1900–1935." *International Labor and Working-Class History*, no. 79 (Spring 2011): 7–27.

Thiollet, Hélène. "Immigration Rentier States." *Journal of Ethnic and Migration Studies* V50, no. 3 (2024): 657–79.

Thompson, Edward P. *The Making of the English Working Class.* Vintage Books, 1980.

Tilly, Charles. *Citizenship, Identity, and Social History.* Cambridge University Press, 1996.

Tinker, Hugh. *A New System of Slavery: The Export of Indian Labour Overseas 1830–1920.* Hansib Publishing Limited, 1993.

Torpey, John C. "Coming and Going: On the State Monopolization of the Legitimate Means of Movement." *Sociological Theory* 16, no. 3 (November 1998): 239–59.

Torpey, John. "The Great War and the Birth of the Modern Passport System." In *Documenting Individual Identity: The Development of State Practices in the Modern World*, edited by Jane Caplan and John Torpey. Princeton University Press, 2001.

Torpey, John C. *The Invention of the Passport: Surveillance, Citizenship and the State.* Cambridge University Press, 2000.

Toth, Anthony B. "Tribes and Tribulations: Bedouin Losses in the Saudi and Iraqi Struggles over Kuwait's Frontiers, 1921–1943." *British Journal of Middle Eastern Studies* 32, no. 2 (2005): 145–67.

Townend Sr., Harry. *A History of Shaw Wallace & Co. and Shaw Wallace & Co. Ltd.* Sree Saraswaty Press, 1965.

Traboulsi, Fawwaz. *Dhufar: Shahada min Zaman al-Thawra* (Dhofar: Witness from the Time of Revolution). Riyad al-Rays lil-Kutub wa al-Nashr, 2004.

Troutt Powell, Eve M. *Tell This in My Memory: Stories of Enslavement in Egypt, Sudan and the Late Ottoman Empire.* Stanford University Press, 2012.

Tsourapas, Gerasimos. "Nasser's Educators and Agitators across al-Watan al-'Arabi: Tracing the Foreign Policy Importance of Egyptian Regional Migration, 1952–1967." *British Journal of Middle Eastern Studies* 43, no. 3 (2016): 324–41.

'Umri, Muhammad 'Amir Sa'id. *al-Hijrat al-Sukkaniyya wa Atharuha fi al-Tarikh al-'Omani, 1913–1970* (The Population Migrations and their Influence in Omani History). Oman, 2011.

United Nations, Department of Economic and Social Affairs, Population Division. International Migration Report 2015: Highlights (ST/ESA/SER.A/375). 2016.

van der Linden, Marcel. "The 'Globalization' of Labor and Working-Class History and its Consequences." *International Labor and Working-Class History* 65 (2004): 136–56.

Verdery, Katherine. "Transnationalism, Nationalism, Citizenship, and Property: Eastern Europe Since 1989." *American Ethnologist* 25, no. 2 (May 1998): 291–306.

Virdee, Satnam. "Racialized Capitalism: An Account of Its Contested Origins and Consolidation." *The Sociological Review* 67, no. 1 (2019): 3–27.

Vitalis, Robert. *America's Kingdom: Mythmaking on the Saudi Oil Frontier.* Stanford University Press, 2009.

Vitalis, Robert. "Black Gold, White Crude: An Essay on American Exceptionalism, Hierarchy, and Hegemony in the Gulf." *Diplomatic History* 26, no. 2 (2002), 185.–213.

Vora, Neha. *Impossible Citizens: Dubai's Indian Diaspora*. Duke University Press, 2013..

Vora, Neha. "Producing Diasporas and Globalization: Indian Middle-Class Migrants in Dubai." *Anthropological Quarterly* 31, no. 2 (2008): 377–406.

Vora, Neha, and Ahmed Kanna. "De-Exceptionalizing the Field: Anthropological Reflections on Migration, Labor, and Identity in Dubai." *Arab Studies Journal* 26, no. 2 (2018): 74–100.

Vora, Neha, and Natalie Koch. "Everyday Inclusions: Rethinking Ethnocracy, Kafala, and Belonging in the Arabian Peninsula." *Studies in Ethnicity and Nationalism* 15, no. 3 (December 2015): 540–52.

Watt, D. C. "Labor Relations and Trades Unionism in Aden, 1952–1960." *Middle East Journal* 16, no. 4 (Autumn 1962): 443–56.

Watts, Michael. "Oil Talk." *Development and Change* 44, no. 4 (2013): 1013–26.

Watts, Michael. "Resource Curse? Governmentality, Oil and Power in the Niger Delta, Nigeria." *Geopolitics* 9, no. 1 (2004): 50–80.

Wells, Madeleine, and Rivka Azoulay. "Contesting Welfare State Politics in Kuwait." *Middle East Report*, no. 272 (2014): 43–47.

Willis, John M. "Making Yemen Indian: Rewriting the Boundaries of Imperial Arabia." *International Journal of Middle Eastern Studies* 41, no. 1 (2009): 23–38.

Winckler, Onn. *Arab Political Demography: Population Growth, Labor Migration and Natalist Policies*. Sussex Academic Press, 2017.

Wolfe-Hunnicutt, Brandon. *The Paranoid Style in American Diplomacy: Oil and Arab Nationalism in Iraq*. Stanford University Press, 2021.

Wright, Andrea. *Between Dreams and Ghosts: Indian Migration and Middle Eastern Oil*. Stanford University Press, 2021.

Wright, Andrea. "From Slaves to Contract Workers: Genealogies of Consent and Security in Indian Labor Migration." *Journal of World History* 32, no. 1 (March 2021): 29–43.

Wright, Andrea. "Imperial Labour: Labour, Security and the Depoliticization of Oil Production in the Arabian Peninsula." In *South Asian Migrations in Global History: Labor, Law, and Wayward Lives*, edited by Neilesh Bose. Bloomsbury, 2021.

Wright, Andrea. "Migratory Pipelines: Labor and Oil in the Arabian Sea." PhD diss., University of Michigan, 2015.

Wright, Andrea. *Unruly Labor: A History of Oil in the Arabian Sea*. Stanford University Press, 2024.

Yamada, Makio, and Steffen Hertog. "Introduction: Revisiting Rentierism—With a Short Note by Giacomo Luciani." *British Journal of Middle Eastern Studies* 47, no. 1 (2020): 1–5.

Yergin, Daniel. *The Prize: The Epic Quest for Oil, Money, and Power*. Touchstone, 1992..

Yılmaz, İlkay. *Ottoman Passports: Security and Geographic Mobility, 1876–1908*. Syracuse University Press, 2023.

Zahlan, Rosemarie Said. *The Making of the Modern Gulf States: Kuwait, Bahrain, Qatar, the United Arab Emirates, and Oman*. Ithaca Press, 1989.

Al-Zayadi, Mufid. *al-Tayyarat al-Fikriyya fi al-Khalij al-ʿArabi, 1938–1971* (The Intellectual Trends in the Arab Gulf). Center for Studies of Arab Unity, 2000.

Zolberg, Aristide R. "The Dawn of Cosmopolitan Denizenship." *Indiana Journal of Global Legal Studies* 7, no. 2 (Spring 2000): 511–18.

Index

al-ʿAbd al-Razzaq, Saʿud, 125–26
al-Abdullah, Saʿad, 130, 136, 144, 170–71, 200
Abdullah al-Salem Al Sabah: ascension to throne, 49; death, 157; hiring practices, 63; independence, 129; as moderate reformist, 67, 130; and press freedom, 115, 160; transportation workers strike (1952), 90–91
Abu Dhabi: coups, 128; labor strikes (1950), 88; labor strikes (1963), 150, 163; oil production, 186; passport and sponsorship system, 47
Abu Dhabi Petroleum Company, 163
Abunda, Mary Ann, 219
Aden, 106
ADMA Das Island, 163
al-ʿAdsani, Suleiman, 43
al-ʿAdtham Hospital, 145
agency agreements, 65–66, 70
agricultural workers, 108
Ahmad, Ahmad Mohammad, 187
Ahmad, Attiya, 11
al-Ahmad, Jabir, 79, 91, 96, 104, 179
Ahmadi, Kuwait, 78–79, 146
Ahmed, Jelaluddin, 33
ʿAisi, ʿAshur, 90, 91
al-ʿAjmi, Mohammad Massud, 89
Akbar, Sarah, 193
Al Sabah family: crackdown on dissent, 159–67; origins, 41, 42; struggle against, 157. *See also individual names*
Alebrahim, Abdulrahman, 65
Alewat, Abdu Ali, 24–25
Algeria, 20, 167, 204
Alghanim, 66
AlHashimy, Mohammad, 138
Ali bin Ahmad, 104
Ali Al Khalifa, 83
Alsanousi, Saud, 217
AlShehabi, Omar, 30, 37
al-ʿAmil (The Worker), 192
Aminoil (American Arabian Oil Company): labor strikes (1963), 145; labor strikes (1969), 175; labor strikes (1972), 204–5, 206; labor strikes (1973), 208–10; workers at, 156, 169
Anderson, Benedict, 15
Anglo-Iranian Oil Company, 87
Anglo-Persian Oil Company, 33–34, 39, 56
anticolonial activists, 16, 74, 83, 87–88, 110. *See also* Arab nationalism/nationalists
apartheid, 15, 159, 165, 190
Arab League, 130, 144

Arab nationalism/nationalists: citizenship and nationality access, 16; on communism, 123; divide with Kuwaiti nationalists, 69–70; in Kuwait National Assembly, 125; and Majlis Movement, 43, 83; noncitizen rights, 165, 196; noncitizen rights and labor legislation, 134–35; Shuwaikh School incident (1959), 115, 122; Suez Crisis, 92. *See also* Arab Nationalist Movement (ANM); al-Khatib, Ahmad; labor movement, and Arab nationalism (1945–1959)
Arab Nationalist Movement (ANM): anti-Iranian xenophobia, 135, 164; expulsion of Kuwaiti branch, 157; and socialism, 133–34; splinter within, 156. *See also* Arab nationalism/ nationalists
Arab Nationalist Movement, Kuwait: disbanding of, 179–80; expulsion from ANM, 157; founding, 68, 85; al-Qatami in, 120; unionization efforts, 3, 92, 153–54; working-class base, 145
Arab nationalist press: attacks on KOC, 114; calls for unionization, 144; on inflation fears, 70; Iranians scapegoated, 69; labor legislation, 112–13, 172–74; noncitizen rights and labor legislation, 134–35; Shuwaikh Port strike (1965), 164
Arab Oil (Lutfi), 76–77
Arab Petroleum Congress (1959), 77, 96
Arabian Oil Company: labor strikes (1965, 1967), 170–71; labor strikes (1969), 175; stateless workers, 191
Arab–Israeli war (1967), 171–72
Arab–Israeli war (1973), 211–12
Aramco: deportation in labor conflicts, 39; domestic workers for, 50; labor stoppages (1945), 84; labor strikes (1953), 87; labor strikes (1963), 163; press criticism of, 93; public relations efforts, 97; racial segregation, 79; wages, 58, 89
Archer, P. C. D., 143
Arco, 207
Arendt, Hannah, 12
al-ʿArfi, Nasser, 155
al-Asbahi, Ahmad Said, 156, 172, 209
al-ʿAsimi, Mohammad Abdul Mohsin, 180
Audsley, M. T., 62–63, 80, 105–6, 116
autocratic governance and deportation (1935–1955), 35–39
Awazim tribe, 149
al-ʿAyyar, Hamad Mubarak, 210

Bahrain: British power entrenchment, 30; deportations from, 24–26, 29, 32, 35–39; employment census, 61; girls' education, 61; independence, 156–57; Iranian claims on, 32–33, 39–40; labor legislation (1954–1957), 103–9; labor sponsorship, 37–39; labor strikes (1930s–1940s), 83–84; labor strikes (1954), 80–81, 87–88; labor strikes (1963), 163; nationality legislation, 33–35; noncitizen populations in, 5; uprising (1972), 156. *See also* Bahrain Petroleum Company (Bapco); labor legislation, and fear complex; oil industry
Bahrain Labor Federation, 107
Bahrain Petroleum Company (Bapco): contract workers, 56; deportations, 39; domestic workers, 108–9; Indian workers, 38, 100; labor law drafting, 107, 109; labor strikes (1930s–1940s), 83–84; labor strikes (1963), 163; ownership of, 106; press criticism of, 93; racism, 80; wages, 58–59, 63. *See also* Bahrain; oil industry
Bahraini press, 67–68, 87, 92–93
Bahraini trade union federation, 223

al-Bakir, Abdul Rahman: campaign for abolition, 54; exile from Bahrain, 24–25, 108; Higher Executive Committee, 85, 87–88; labor law drafting, 105; labor strikes, 83; passport application, 47–48; publishing, 67–68, 93
Balibar, Étienne, 13
The Bamboo Stalk (Alsanousi), 217
Bandung Conference, 96
banking industry, labor organizing in, 198
al-Barrack, Mohammad, 83
Basra, Iraq, 80–81
Beaugrand, Claire, 122, 124, 217
Bedouin: economic collapse, 54; and labor movement, 149–50; naturalization as first-tier citizens, 160; naturalization debates, 72, 122, 124, 137–39, 188–89; in oil industry, 55, 191; stereotypes, 44, 128, 198
Beinin, Joel, 105
Belgrave, Charles: deportations by, 36, 80; general labor strikes (1954), 88; girls' education, 61; industrial relations, 104; labor sponsorship, 37–39; nationality laws in Bahrain, 33, 35; opposition to al-Bakir, 47; on sex work, 37; on training and promotion, 82; wage suppression, 58–59; on workers' living conditions, 63
Bhattacharyya, Gargi, 15
Bishara, Fahad, 22–23, 222
Bosniak, Linda, 11
Boumédiène, Houari, 4, 204
British empire: and citizenship in Gulf, 12–15; divide-and-rule policies, 14, 162–64; and exile (1900–1929), 24–27; labor control strategies, 4–5; and labor legislation, 100–101; movement control in Kuwait, 44–45; in Persian Gulf, 27–31; post–World War I, 31–35; withdrawal from Persian Gulf, 156–57. *See also* labor legislation, and fear complex (1952–1961)
British government: fear of citizen–noncitizen alliances, 161–64; suppression of Kuwaiti nationalism, 159–60
British Petroleum: and Kuwait Oil Company (KOC), 2–3, 87; on labor strike (1969), 174
business elites: limitations on ILO study, 182–83; and Majlis Movement, 40, 42–44, 49, 83; as middlemen in labor recruitment industry, 66–67; monopolization of trade, 65–66, 70; in National Assembly, 127–28; nationality as generator of wealth, 13, 51, 64; opposition to reforms, 194–96; pushback against in press, 67–74

Caltex (California Texas Oil Company), 106
Can, Lâle, 28
Center for Workers' Culture, 113, 144–45, 153, 193
Chambers of Commerce, 66, 153, 214
citizenship: debated in Kuwaiti press, 68–74; and empire, 12–15; forms and accessibility, 11; and labor movement (1960s), 167–76; as mechanism of exclusion, 6; versus nationality, 11–12; and naturalization, 5–6, 121–22; stripping of, 25–26, 200, 217, 223; tabiʿiyya conception of, 42; tiered, 6, 121, 160, 216. *See also* labor movement; nationality; noncitizens
class: and Arab nationalism, 145, 153, 186; consciousness, 93–94; and deportation (1920–1950), 39–47; and inflation, 70–71; and marriage, 142; and nationality, 13, 35, 41–42, 44, 51, 71–72, 74, 190–92, 198; in the press, 93–94; and rentier theory, 8; solidarity across the boundaries of nationality, 2, 16–17, 20, 77, 135, 153, 156, 165, 186, 208–10, 222–23; as understood by Islamic activists, 195–96

communism: and immigration, 114–15; and labor camps, 59, 60
Communist Parties, 84
communists, purges of, 123
Comoro Islands, 216–17
Conoco, 214
constitutional period: beginning of first (1962), 126–28, 129–30; end of first (1976), 216–18, 220–22; return of electoral politics (1992), 218; suspension of parliament (2024), 223–24
continuities of independence (1960–1963), 129–35. *See also* decolonization
Cooper, Frederick, 128–29
Coronil, Fernando, 77
corporatism and Kuwaiti trade unions, 157–58
coups, 128
COVID-19 pandemic, 218
crackdowns on dissent: (1959), 115; (1965), 159–67; (1976–1992), 216–18; (2024), 223–24
Crystal, Jill, 64, 88
Curzon, Lord, 30

al-Daʿij, Ahmad, 188, 189–90
Das Island, labor strikes (1963), 150, 163
De Genova, Nicholas, 10–11
debt bondage, 53, 54
decolonization: incompleteness of, 13, 20, 103, 129, 158; and labor movements, 19–20, 144, 157–58; and oil nationalization, 19, 77–78, 167–68. *See also* continuities of independence (1960–1963)
Demafelis, Joanna, 218
denizenship. *See* noncitizens
deportation: and empire, 12–15; and gender, 37; Kuwait recession and, 111; and labor conflicts, 39, 97; noncitizen labor deportability, 57. *See also* deportation states (1900–1950); labor legislation, and fear complex (1952–1961); *specific countries*
deportation states (1900–1950): overview, 24–27, 47–48; deportation and autocratic governance (1935–1955), 35–39; deportation and class (1920–1950), 39–47; empire and exile (1900–1929), 24–27; nationality invention (1920–1940), 25, 31–35. *See also* deportation; labor legislation, and fear complex (1952–1961); nationality; oil boom (1940–1955)
Dhahran, Saudi Arabia: labor strikes (1953), 80–81
Dhofar Liberation Front (Oman), 156
Dickson, H. R. P., 55, 66
Dietrich, Christopher, 167, 204
al-Diyyan, Ahmad, 186, 192
domestic workers: exemptions for, 50, 118, 152; exemptions for, Bahrain, 108–9; gendering, 202–3; immigration regulation reforms, 201; international attention on, 218–19. *See also* labor legislation; labor movement; noncitizens, as workers
al-Dueiri, Fahad, 71–72
Dulles, John Foster, 92

economic collapse in Gulf, 53–54
economic inevitability, 7–8
education: and Arab nationalism, 85; of Palestinians, 179; of women or girls, 61, 71
Egypt: economic conditions, 186; elite mediation in labor disputes, 104; Free Officers coup, 84–85; and Kuwait in ILO, 144. *See also* Suez Crisis
Egyptian media, 67, 69, 109
Egyptian orientalism in Kuwait (1952–1959), 102, 109–15
Egyptians: as legal advisors, 130; as teachers in Kuwait, 69, 85
Ehsani, Kaveh, 17

empire and imperialism: and deportation, 12–15, 24–27. *See also* British empire
enslavement, 15, 27, 53–54
exclusion: and citizenship, 6, 50; and migration studies, 10–11; of noncitizens from labor movement, 97–98, 197–98; of noncitizens from social services, 194–203. *See also* citizenship; labor movement
Exclusive Agreements, 28–29

al-Fajr (The Dawn), 94, 96, 114
Falah, Hassan: detention, 177; on government inaction, 178; Khafji labor strike (1967), 170–71; labor law of 1968, 172, 172–74; National Assembly elections, 165–66; on privatization of oil, 221; as worker representative, 147–48
al-Faraj, Nasser, 193, 220
Federation of Kuwaiti Contractors, 194–95
Federation of Petroleum Workers: fracture in labor movement, 185, 208–9; labor strikes (1967), 171; labor strikes (1969), 174–75; labor strikes (1972), 205–8; labor strikes (1974), 213–14
feminist challenge (1964–1975), 16, 127, 136–37, 139–43
Fleming, Ian, 97
Fuccaro, Nelida, 25, 39–40, 76, 97

Gaddafi, Muammar, 204
GEFONT Support Group-Kuwait, 223
gender: and deportations, 37; imbalance, 56; labor restrictions on women, 118; and the "marriage crisis," 139–43; movement controls, 122; women as domestic workers, 202–3; women in Kuwaiti workforce, 187, 193, 198; women's labor erased, 61. *See also* gender and nationality
gender and nationality: in Bahrain, 33, 34; in Gulf states, 15, 16; in Kuwait, 46, 121, 136–37, 160, 188. *See also* gender
General Federation of Arab Workers, 193
Ghabra, Shafeeq, 55
Ghana, 95–96
al-Ghanim, Khalid, 126
Go, Julian, 129, 158
Goffman, Laura, 31, 193
Goswami, Manu, 64
Government Sector Union Federation, 3
Government Workers' Cadre, 112, 118
Graeber, David, 28
Gulf Oil, 2–3. *See also* Kuwait Oil Company (KOC)
Gulf states: nationalization of oil, 204; noncitizen populations in, 5; participation agreement with oil majors, 210–11; stateless people (the *bidun*), 216–17
Gulf studies: central tropes, 7–8; and naturalization, 5–6

Habash, George, 68
al-Hadaf, 137–38
Hall, Stuart, 13
Hamadah, Faisal, 219
Hanieh, Adam, 8
Hanley, Will, 51
al-Hashem, Safa, 218
Hasted, William, 57, 59, 60
Hay, Rupert, 80
al-Ha'ya (mass movement). *See* Higher Executive Committee (HEC)
Heiskanen, Jaakko, 158
Henjam Island, 32
Higher Executive Committee (HEC) (Bahrain), 87–88, 104–5, 108, 110–11, 116
History of Kuwait (Tarikh al-Kuwait) (al-Rushaid), 40
Hopper, Matthew, 53–54
al-Humaidi, Ya'qub, 123

ICATU (International Confederation of Arab Trade Unions), 85–86, 92, 171–72, 220
ICFTU (International Confederation of Free Trade Unions), 85–86
ILO (International Labor Organization). *See* International Labor Organization (ILO)
al-Iman, 69, 70, 72–73, 93, 98, 112–13. *See also* National Culture Club (Kuwait)
independence of Kuwait: overview, 125–29, 154; continuities of independence (1960–1963), 129–35; feminist challenge (1964–1975), 139–43; Kuwaitis without nationality, 136–39; labor movement and rights, 143–51; unionization (1964–1965), 151–54. *See also* Kuwait; labor legislation; labor movement; oil boom (1940–1955); oil industry and immigration (1971–1976); political radicalism (1965–1970)
India, 100
Indian workers: as contract workers, 56–57, 78; as domestic workers, 50; labor strikes (1940s), 84; labor strikes (1953), 97–98; labor strikes (1963), 147; NOCs (No Objection Certificates), 38; in oil sector, Bahrain, 38, 83, 100. *See also* racism, in oil industry
inflation, 10, 52, 57–58, 60, 70–71, 83–84
International Confederation of Arab Trade Unions (ICATU), 85–86, 92, 171–72, 220
International Confederation of Free Trade Unions (ICFTU), 85–86
International Labor Organization (ILO): abuses of noncitizen workers, 217; KOC report, 146; Kuwaiti labor law, 153, 193; Kuwaiti membership, 114, 144; Kuwaiti trade unions, 165, 166, 220; labor opposition meetings with, 214; labor sponsorship, 223; manpower assessment and planning, 182–83, 187; social security system discussions, 199; on technical training in Kuwait, 169
Iran: claims on Bahrain, 32–33; consolidation of nation-state, 32; land ownership by foreigners, 32–33; left-wing movements, 186; nationalization of oil, 86–87; oil discovery, 30; strike (1946), 84; visit of Shah to Kuwait, 176
Iranians: deportations from Bahrain, 37; deportations from Kuwait, 44; increasing Arab nationalist acceptance of, 186; labor sponsorship in Bahrain, 37; migrations by, 55–56; oil boom, 50; popular feeling against in Bahrain, 39–40; popular feeling against in Kuwait, 69, 72, 134, 135, 139, 164
Iraq: consolidation of nation-state, 32; economic conditions, 186; KOC recruitment, 62, 66; loss of Kuwaiti labor movement records, 22; nationalist coup, 123; Nationality Law (1924), 33; nationalization of oil, 20, 204; occupation of Kuwait, 22, 217–18; and Organization of Petroleum Exporting Countries (OPEC), 167; threats to Kuwait, 129–30
Iraq Petroleum Company: labor strikes (1946), 84; nationalization of oil, 204; wages, 88
Iraqi Communist Party: labor strikes (1946), 84
Isa Al Khalifa, 32
Iskander, Natasha, 60
Islamic activists, 195–96, 220
Islamic Guidance Society, 91
ʿIzz al-Din, Amin, 115–19

al-Jabir, Abdullah, 166, 175–76
Jahra, battle of, 41, 121
Japanese oil firms: Arabian Oil Company, 170–71, 175, 191; bid for oil concession, 95
Jassim bin Muhammad al-Shirawi, 32

al-Jaua'n, Yacoub, 214
Jewan Camp, 59–60, 97, 110
Jordan, L. T., 115

kafala (sponsorship) system. *See* labor sponsorship
Kamil, Fathi, 145
Kanna, Ahmed, 11
Keshavarzian, Arang, 18, 21
Khafji labor strikes (1965, 1967), 170–71
Khalaf, Khalid, 96
Khalili, Laleh, 77, 221
al-Kharafi, Khalid, 120
al-Khashti, Fahad 'Atia, 90
al-Khatib, Ahmad: Arab Nationalist Movement (ANM) in Kuwait, disbanding, 179–80; Arab Nationalist Movement (ANM) in Kuwait, founding, 85; career, 68; constitution drafting, 130; on crackdown of 1965, 159; on crackdown of 1976, 216; on deportations from Kuwait, 44; as editor of *Sada al-Iman*, 93–94; Kuwaiti Progressive Democratic Movement, 180; on labor movement and oil nationalization, 213; labor movement organization, 145; memoirs as source, 23; National Assembly elections alliance with candidates, 166; on noncitizens in organized labor, 126; on statebuilding, 221; unionization efforts, 3, 92, 153; on worker rights, 133. *See also* Arab nationalism/nationalists
al-Khoajih, Ahmad, 172
Kissinger, Henry, 212
KNPC (Kuwait National Petroleum Company), 174, 207–8, 213–14
KOC (Kuwait Oil Company). *See* Kuwait Oil Company (KOC)
KOC Union, 165, 222
Kuwait: census, 112; deportation and class, 40–47; deportations from, 29–30, 111, 159–60, 218; divides in politics, 167–68; economic recession, 111; elections (1967), 3, 165–66; elections (1971), 180; elections, local, 73; gender imbalance, 56; movement control, 44–45; nationalization of oil, 18–21, 185, 204, 210–13, 221–22; noncitizen populations, 5, 9; OAPEC, 204; participation agreement with oil majors, 210–11; trade monopolization, 65–66, 70. *See also* deportation states (1900–1950); independence of Kuwait; Kuwait Oil Company (KOC); labor legislation; labor movement; labor strikes; nationality; oil boom (1940–1955); oil industry and immigration (1971–1976); political radicalism (1965–1970)
Kuwait Development Board: firing practices, 63–64; industrial relations, 110; infrastructure construction, 57; labor camps, 59; labor sponsorship, 46–47; wage suppression, 59
Kuwait Graduates' Club, 94, 220
Kuwait Magazine (Majallat al-Kuwait), 40–41
Kuwait National Petroleum Company (KNPC), 174, 207–8, 213–14
Kuwait Oil Company (KOC): contract workers, 56–57; criticisms and responses, 76; and deportation, 45; divide-and-rule policies, 162–64; domestic workers for, 50; hiring practices, 178; industrial relations, 104; and labor contractors, 66–67; labor law, 109–10, 114; labor law (1968), 172–74; labor law drafting, 105–6, 117, 118–19, 120–21; and nationality question, 46–47; noncitizen workers fired (1971), 191–92; ownership of, 2, 77, 87; public relations efforts, 96–97; racism, 2–3, 61–62, 76–77, 82, 146, 149–50; sabotage, 92–93; security force, 113–14; strike plan, 81; training and promotion, 81–82, 146, 168–70; unionization attempts, 84, 86; wages, 58, 89; water wells, 55. *See also* Kuwait; oil boom (1940–1955)

Kuwait Oil Company, labor strikes: (1940s–1950s), 89–91; (1957), 114; (1960s), 146–50; (1963), 126, 163; (1969), 174–75; (1972), 205–7; (1973), 208, 211–12; (1993), 222
Kuwait Oil Company (KOC) Union, 165, 222
Kuwait Radio, 120
Kuwait Trade Union Federation (KTUF): call for restitution of democracy, 220; founding, 158, 171; labor law unification, 1, 2, 192–93; labor legislation (1968), 177; labor strikes (1972), 205; Migrant Workers Office, 223; naturalization of oil, 211; noncitizen membership, 197; noncitizen rights, 222–23; repression (post-1976), 220; role in politics, 190–91; and Sandigan (Filipino trade union), 219; social security system discussions, 199; support for Nepali workers, 223; transformation of Kuwaiti politics, 167; women's committee, 193
Kuwaiti government employees: contract workers, 57; labor strikes (1964), 145; labor strikes within (1950s), 91–92; noncitizen workers removed, 132; retroactive overtime payments, 155
Kuwaiti Land Acquisition Program, 65
Kuwaiti *Nahda*, 40–42
Kuwaiti press: Aramco labor struggles coverage, 87; attacks on KOC, 114; Bahraini labor law coverage, 110–11; calls for desegregation, 94–95; censorship of, 162, 177–78, 217; debates on citizenship, 68–74; on deportations from Kuwait, 159–60; discourse of political economy, 70–72; on foreigner marriage debate, 139–43; on labor legislation, 112–13, 125; on noncitizen workers, 131–32; opposition to reforms, 194–95; pushback against elites, 68–74; support for trade unions, 148–49. *See also specific publications*
Kuwaiti Progressive Democratic Movement, 180
Kuwaiti Teachers' Club, 68–69, 71, 110–11. See also *al-Ra'id*

labor, sovereignty, and citizenship (1960s), 167–76
labor camps, segregation in, 57, 59–60, 78–80. *See also* racism, in oil industry
labor control in oil industry (1930–1955), 53–63
labor legislation. *See also* deportation states (1900–1950); labor movement; oil boom (1940–1955); oil industry and immigration (1971–1976)
labor legislation, and fear complex (1952–1961): overview, 100–103, 123–24; Bahrain labor law (1954–1957), 103–9; Egyptian orientalism in Kuwait (1952–1959), 102, 109–15; Kuwaiti legislation (1959), 115–23
labor legislation, Bahrain (1954–1957), 103–9
labor legislation, Kuwait: citizen and noncitizen differences, 1–2; domestic workers, 50, 118, 152, 201–3; law of 1940 (Pearling Law), 103; law of 1959, 115–23; law of 1959, drafting, 102, 109–15; law of 1964, 151–54; law of 1968, 172–74, 177–78; reform movement (1970s), 192–94
labor movement: citizen and noncitizen rights (overview), 1–5, 16–17, 19–20; and nationalization of oil (overview), 17–21. *See also* Arab nationalism/nationalists; labor legislation; labor strikes; nationality; noncitizens, as workers; oil boom (1940–1955); oil industry and immigration (1971–1976); political radicalism (1965–1970)

labor movement, and Arab nationalism (1945–1959): overview, 5, 74, 75–78, 98–99; exclusions of non-Arabs, 97–98; labor and nationalism in Kuwait, 89–97; the radical fifties, 82–89; segregation and its discontents, 78–82
labor movement, Bahrain: Higher Executive Committee (HEC), 87–88, 104–5, 108, 110–11, 116; labor strikes (1930s–1940s), 83–84; labor strikes (1954), 80–81, 87–88
labor movement, Kuwait: citizen and noncitizen rights, 16–17, 128, 143–51; in electoral politics, 165–67, 180; exclusion of noncitizens, 97–98, 197–98; fragmentation (1970–1975), 203–14; and immigration restrictions, 222; loss of early records, 22; and nationalism (1960s), 167–76; and nationalization of oil, 185, 203–14, 221–22; oil politics reconfiguration, 180–81; repression of (post-1976), 217, 220; and rights of citizens and noncitizen, 155–59; and statebuilding, 221–23; unionization (1964–1965), 151–54; unionization, early efforts, 3–4; unions, crackdown on, 160–67, 166–67; unions, noncitizen membership, 97–98, 125–27, 134–35, 152–53, 197–98, 222
labor recruitment: bulk labor contractors, 66–67; contractors under scrutiny, 134; reforms targeting recruitment agencies, 217–18; regime as broker, 201–3; Safat Square as labor market, 49–50
labor sponsorship: in Bahrain, 37–39; calls for end to, 223; in Gulf, 26–27, 30, 47; in Kuwait, 45, 46–47, 133
labor strikes: Bahrain (1930s–1940s), 83–84; Bahrain (1954), 87–88; Gulf region (1940s), 84; Gulf region (1963), 150, 163; Gulf region (1967), 171–72; racism and strike plan, 80–82. *See also* Kuwait Oil Company (KOC), labor strikes; labor movement
labor strikes, Kuwait: against Conoco (1975), 214; by Federation of Petroleum Workers (1969), 174–75; against Kuwait National Petroleum Company (KNPC) (1974), 213–14; multiple (1965–1967), 170–72; multiple (1970s), 204–8; multiple (1995), 221; by noncitizen and citizen workers (1963–1964), 145–46; by noncitizen workers (1956), 112; by noncitizen workers (1970s), 197–98; by noncitizen workers (1989), 217; by Oil and Petrochemical Workers Federation (1973), 211–12; outside oil industry (1937), 83; outside oil industry (1956), 112; against privatization (2016), 221; in public sector (1975), 201; work stoppages (1920s), 83
Labour Law Advisory Committee (Bahrain), 105–7, 108
land ownership: and monopolies, 70; and nationality, 34–35, 51, 64–65; and sovereignty, 28–29, 32–33
Le Renard, Amélie, 218
Libya, 20, 204
Lienhardt, Peter, 7–8, 65
Lockman, Zachary, 9, 105
Longhurst, Henry, 54
Lutfi, Ashraf, 75–77, 78, 98–99, 168, 180–81

al-Madaf, Khalid, 166
al-Maʿhad al-Dini, 70
Majlis Movement, 40, 42–44, 49, 83
marriage, mixed citizenship, 139–43, 160, 188, 216, 223
Marshall, Cyril, 106–8, 116
Marxism, 156
al-Marzouq, Ghnaima, 141, 142–43
al-Mashaʿn, Suleiman, 132–33, 160, 187, 201

Massey, Doreen, 10
al-Mdairis, Falah, 22
media: Bahraini press, 67–68, 87, 92–93; Egyptian, 67, 69, 109; Kuwait Radio, 120; and labor activism, 82–89, 92–93. *See also* Arab nationalist press; Kuwaiti press
method and sources of study, 20–23
Mexico, nationalization of oil, 20
"migrant worker" as term, 11
migration: historical, 53–54; reverse, 183, 186–87; as strategy of resistance, 88–89; and xenophobia in Kuwait, 68–69, 72–73, 131–35, 164, 218. *See also* noncitizens
migration models, 7–8, 9–11, 52
Mikdashi, Maya, 15
Mitchell, Timothy, 17–18
Mohammad, Abdul Ghafar, 47
Mohammad, Abdullah Suleiman, 189
Mongia, Radhika, 15
al-Moosa, Abdulrasoul, 124
Mosaddegh, Mohammad, 86
movement controls: in Bahrain, 33; inequalities, 36–37; in Kuwait, 44–45, 122; and oil boom, 55–56
Movement for Democratic Work in Kuwait, 186
Mubarak, Abdullah (Al Sabah), 45, 46, 90, 113–14, 122
Mubarak Al Sabah, 29, 42
al-Mughni, Haya, 143
al-Mujtama', 195–96
Mulla Hafiz, 32
Mulla Saleh, Abdullah, 46–47, 75, 90
Mulligan, Bill, 79
al-Munais, Sami, 3, 145, 151, 170, 180, 190
Municipal Workers Union, 3, 92
Muscat, 84, 88
Muslim Brotherhood, 195–96

al-Nafisi, Ahmad, 180
al-Nahda, 142
al-Najjar, Ghanim, 65
Al-Nakib, Farah, 40, 65, 139
Nasir bin Mubarak Al Sabah, 40
Nasser, Gamal Abdel: and Arab nationalism, 84–85; defeat by Israel, 156; and ICATU, 85–86; nationalization of Suez Canal, 95; rivalry with Qassim, 130; and al-Youha, 4
National Assembly of Kuwait: dissolution (1976), 216; return of electoral politics (1992), 218; suspension of (2024), 223–24. *See also* independence of Kuwait
National Bank of Kuwait, 91
National Bloc (al-Qatami), 196
National Committee of Clubs (Kuwait), 92
National Culture Club (Kuwait), 69, 110. See also *al-Iman*
National Oil Company (Kuwait), 177
National Youth Block, 43
nationality: ambiguity of, 28–29; Bahrain legislation, 33–35; as basis of divide-and-rule, 14, 158–59, 162–64; versus citizenship, 11–12; and gender, 15, 16, 33, 34, 46, 121, 136–37; as generator of wealth, 13, 51, 64; invention of (1920–1940), 25, 31–35; and land ownership, 34–35; in Qatar, 88; and racism, 2–3, 13–15, 51–52. *See also* citizenship; deportation states (1900–1950); noncitizens; oil boom (1940–1955); oil industry and immigration (1971–1976); stateless people (the *bidun*)
nationality, Kuwait: ambiguity, 63–64, 111; and gender, 46, 121, 136–37, 160; as generator of wealth, 51, 64; and land ownership, 51; legislation of 1948, 45–46; legislation of 1959, 121–23; on patrilineal descent, 26–27; and patronage, 72–74; and stateless Kuwaitis, 136–39; tiered, 121, 160, 190, 216; and wages (1948–1959), 63–74

nationality regime: challenges to (1970–1975), 185–94; opposition to reforms, 200–201; patronage, 72–74
nationalization of oil: divisions within Organization of Petroleum Exporting Countries (OPEC), 167–68; and labor movement, 17–21, 86–87; and labor movement fragmentation, Kuwait, 208–14; and labor movement, Kuwait, 185, 203–8, 221–22
Nepali workers, 223
Ngai, Mae, 10–11
al-Nibari, Abdullah, 180
Nkrumah, Kwame, 95–96
No Objection Certificates (NOCs), 38, 45. *See also* labor sponsorship
noncitizen populations: in Gulf states, 5, 9; in Kuwait mid-century, 49–50
noncitizens: marriage to citizens, 139–43, 160, 188, 216, 223; minimal rights of, 12; and naturalization, 5–6; rights of and statebuilding, 222; as scapegoats, 68–69, 72–73, 131–35, 164, 218; and socialism, 132–34. *See also* citizenship; deportation states (1900–1950); deportations; migration; nationality; stateless people (the *bidun*)
noncitizens, as workers: activists, 219; Arab noncitizens and residency, 178; in Bahrain trade union legislation, 108–9; contract workers, 163–64, 178; excluded from social security system (Kuwait), 198–99; exploitation of in global North, 11; hiring limits sought by citizens, 107; international attention on, 218–19; labor strikes (1960s), 145–47; labor strikes (1965), 164; labor strikes (1967), 171–72; labor strikes (1970s), 197–98; labor strikes (1975), 214; reverse migration, 183, 186–87; undocumented, 120; vulnerabilities under autocratic rule, 217–18. *See also* domestic workers; labor legislation; labor legislation, and fear complex (1952–1961); labor movement; noncitizens; stateless people (the *bidun*)

Occidental Petroleum, 204
Oil and Petrochemical Workers Federation, 211–12
oil boom (1940–1955): overview, 49–52, 74; labor control (1930–1955), 53–63; wages and nationality (1948–1959), 63–74. *See also* Kuwait; Kuwait Oil Company (KOC); labor legislation; labor movement; nationality; oil industry
oil boycott (oil crisis of 1970s), 211–12
oil industry: Bahrain, 58–59, 63, 79, 82, 104; and deportation, 13–14, 39; divide-and-rule policies, 14, 158–59, 162–64; hiring, training, and promotion, 60–63, 81–82, 146, 168–70; post-independence influence of companies, 128; reconfiguration of power (1960s), 180–81; recruitment methods, 57–59; sabotage, 92–93; wages, 58–59, 62, 63–74, 87–89. *See also* Bahrain Petroleum Company (Bapco); Kuwait Oil Company (KOC); labor legislation; labor movement; labor strikes; oil boom (1940–1955); oil industry and immigration (1971–1976); racism, in oil industry; *specific companies*
oil industry and immigration (1971–1976): overview, 182–85, 214–15; challenging the nationality regime (1970–1975), 185–94; exclusions of noncitizens (1973–1976), 194–203; nationalization and labor movement fragmentation (1970–1975), 203–14. *See also* Kuwait; labor legislation; labor movement; nationality; oil industry

Oman, 5, 50, 128, 156
OPEC Oil (Lutfi), 180–81
Organization of Arab Petroleum Exporting Countries (OAPEC), 186, 204, 211–12
Organization of Petroleum Exporting Countries (OPEC): appointment of Lutfi, 77; attack on Vienna headquarters, 213; divisions within, 167–68; "fifty-fifty" principle, 86; nationalization of oil, 204, 212–13; oil revenues, 186; participation agreement with oil majors, 210–11; threat of embargo, 171
al-Othman, Laila, 141–42, 143
Othman, Othman Khalil, 130, 136, 144
Ottoman empire, 29, 33, 37

Pahlavi regime, 32–33
Pakistani workers, 39, 78, 79, 91, 97–98, 147. *See also* racism, in oil industry
Palestine and oil, 211–12
Palestinians: deportations from Kuwait, 218; discrimination in hiring, 57; eligibility to join trade unions, 161; fired and replaced from public sector jobs, 197; and Kuwaiti nationality, 137; and labor movement, 149–50; and oil boom, 55; refugees in Kuwait, 179; as teachers, 69, 85
Parra, Francisco, 86, 212, 213
patronage networks, 65, 66, 72–74
pearl divers, 37, 53, 54, 82, 103
Pérez Alfonzo, Juan Pablo, 86
PFLOAG (Popular Front for the Liberation of the Occupied Arab Gulf), 156, 186
Philippines, 218–19
PLO (Palestine Liberation Organization), 179, 218
Polanyi, Karl, 13
political economy, 51–52, 62–63, 70–72
political radicalism (1950s), 82–89
political radicalism (1965–1970): overview, 155–59, 179–81; crackdown (1965), 159–67; labor, sovereignty, and citizenship (1960s), 167–76; revolution fears (1969–1970), 176–79. *See also* labor legislation; labor movement, and Arab nationalism; oil industry and immigration (1971–1976)
Popular Front for the Liberation of the Occupied Arab Gulf (PFLOAG), 156, 186
Popular Revolutionary Movement (PRM), 2, 157, 176–77
Pursley, Sara, 22

al-Qaddumi, Hani, 45
al-Qafila (The Caravan), 67
al-Qaradawi, Yusuf, 195
Qasim bin Muhammad al-Ibrahim, 40
Qassim, Abdul Karim, 129–30, 159
al-Qatami, Jassim, 115, 119–20, 126, 196
Qatar: abolition campaign, 54; independence, 156–57; labor disputes, 39; labor sponsorship, 47; labor strikes (1940s), 84; labor strikes (1950s), 88; labor strikes (1959), 80–81; labor strikes (1963), 150, 163; nationality, 64; nationalization of oil, 204; noncitizen populations, 5, 9; noncitizen workers, 219; oil boom, 50; oil production, 186; wages, 87
Qatar Petroleum Company, 67, 88, 163

racism: at American University of Beirut, 68; in labor legislation, 102–3, 105–6. *See also* labor legislation; nationality; oil industry
racism, in oil industry: calls for desegregation, 94–95; fear of political backlash, 80; in Gulf, 13–15; hiring, training, and promotion, 60–63, 81–82, 146, 168–70; in labor camps, 57, 59–60, 78–80; as means

of control, 76–82; and nationality, 2–3, 13–15, 51–52; post-independence continuities, 129
Rahnama, Sara, 140
al-Ra'i al-'Am, 178, 194
al-Ra'id, 68–69, 70, 71–72, 94, 112. *See also* Kuwaiti Teachers' Club
Ramírez Sánchez, Ilich (Carlos the Jackal), 213
al-Rashid, Mohammad, 126
Rashid Rida, Muhammad, 40
al-Rashoud, Talal, 85
rentier theory, 7–8
resource nationalism. *See* nationalization of oil
revolution fears (1969–1970), 176–79
Reza Shah Pahlavi, 32–33
Robinson, Cedric, 14, 15
al-Ruba'i, Ahmad, 177, 186
al-Rujaib, Hamad, 116
al-Rumi, Khalid, 90
al-Rushaid, Abdul Aziz, 40–42

Sabah al-Salem (Al Sabah), 157
Sada al-Iman, 87, 93–95, 96, 110, 113
Safat Square, Kuwait, 49–50
Saif, Rashid, 165, 165–66, 169, 172, 174
al-Salim, Salim Sabah, 202
Sandigan (Filipino trade union), 219
Saqr, Hussein: and Center for Workers' Culture, 113, 145; committee to Ministry of Social Affairs and Labor, 156; elections (1971), 180; Khafji labor strike (1967), 170–71; Kuwait Trade Union Federation (KTUF), 171; on labor in politics, 190–91; on labor organizing, 89; on labor strikes (1969), 176; noncitizen rights, 155, 156; statebuilding, 221; on stateless workers in oil industry, 191, 192
Sarawi, Abdul Aziz, 166
Sassen, Saskia, 9
Saudi Arabia: battle of Jahra, 41; consolidation of nation-state, 32; deportation in labor conflicts, 39; inflation fears, 58; Khafji labor strike (1965), 170; labor strikes (1953), 87; labor strikes and stoppages (1940s), 84; land confiscations of Bahrainis, 32; Marxist-Leninist factions, 156; nationalization of oil, 204; noncitizen populations in, 5; OAPEC, 204; oil boom, 50
Sawt al-Bahrain (The Voice of Bahrain), 68
Sawt al-Khalij, 152
segregation, labor movements, and Arab nationalism, 76–82. *See also* racism, in oil industry
sex industry and deportations, 37
al-Sha'b (The People), 23, 73–74, 94, 95–96, 113, 114
Shah of Iran (Mohammad Reza Shah), 176
Shah of Iran (Reza Shah), 32–33
Shamlan, Abdul Aziz, 24–25
Shamlan, Sa'ad, 83
Sharjah, 88, 128
Al-Shaya, Abdul-Azeez, 29
Shell Qatar, 163
al-Shirawi, Ahmad, 83
al-Shirawi, Muhammad Qasim, 107
Shuwaikh Camp, 59
Shuwaikh Port strikes: (1963), 145; (1965), 164; (1973), 197
Shuwaikh School incident (1959), 115, 122
skilled labor: calls for more training, 71; shortage and training, 60–61; shortages and racism, 116–17
Social Affairs and Labor Ministry (Kuwait): labor complaints to, 156; labor disputes, 147–48, 170–71, 174, 205, 207–10; labor law (1964), 150–54; labor law drafting (1975), 194; migration management and

Social Affairs and Labor Ministry (Kuwait) (*Cont.*)
work permits, 131–33, 187, 201–3; nationality and residency, 189–90; noncitizen complaints to, 134; on union demands, 214; unionization restrictions, 166–67; vocational training, 169
Social Affairs Department (Kuwait): and Center for Workers' Culture, 113; labor disputes, 120–21; labor law (1959), 117–20, 143; migration management and work permits, 111–13, 120; prioritized by ʿIzz al-Din, 116
Social Reform Society (Kuwait), 195–96
social security system (Kuwait), 198–99
socialism and noncitizens, 133–34
South Asians, xenophobia of, 218
South Yemen, independence, 156
sponsorship of labor. *See* labor sponsorship
statebuilding: and labor legislation, 101–3; and labor movement, 221–23
stateless people (the *bidun*): in Gulf states, 6; and Kuwaiti independence, 136–39; movements for rights, 216–17; in oil industry, 191–92; and patriarchal legislation, 16; reforms by government, 199–200; social consequences, 183–84, 188–89. *See also* citizenship; marriage, mixed citizenship; nationality; noncitizens; noncitizens, as workers
Stegner, Wallace, 97
Stephenson, Lindsey, 32
Strover Report, 111–13
Suez Crisis: British in Bahrain, 24; protests in Bahrain, 61, 108; protests in Gulf, 85; protests in Kuwait, 92, 120; public awareness of nationalization, 95; strike plan at KOC, 81. *See also* Egypt
sukhra (forced labor), 53
Sultan, Daifullah Falah, 85, 205

Takriti, Abdel Razzaq, 12
*al-Tali*ʿa (The Vanguard): on contractors, 153; on elections (1971), 180; internationalist orientation, 186; Iranians caricatured, 135; on KOC hiring practices, 178; on Kuwait National Petroleum Company (KNPC), 207–8; on labor legislation (1968), 177; local and global news, 130; on nationalization of oil, 210–11; on noncitizen workers' rights, 1, 134; on noncitizens and labor movement, 155, 164, 165; on noncitizens in public sector, 196–97; on stateless people, 191; strike coverage (1963), 148; strike coverage (1969), 174; strike coverage (1972), 205; suspension of, 159–60, 177; Tariki writing in, 168, 210; on unionization, 144, 151, 152; on unionization crackdown, 162, 166
Tariki, Abdullah, 75, 95, 167, 168, 204, 210
Tétreault, Mary Ann, 42
trade monopolization, 65–66, 70
trade unions. *See* labor movement
training and promotion in oil industry, 60–63, 81–82, 146, 168–70
Troutt Powell, Eve, 14
Trucial States, 47. *See also* United Arab Emirates (UAE)
Tudeh (Iranian Communist Party), 84

unemployment, Kuwait, 131, 183, 194–95
unionization. *See* labor movement
United Arab Emirates (UAE): independence, 156–57; nationalization of oil, 204; noncitizen populations in, 5; oil boom, 50; stateless people (the *bidun*), 216–17
United States: citizens of excluded from oil industry, 34; commercial

competition, 32; immigration controls and nationality legislation, 15
UNRWA, 57
Usrati (My Family), 141–43

Venezuela, 167
Voice of Bahrain, 93
Voice of the Arabs (radio), 67, 69, 109
Voice of the Gulf, 214
"The Voice of the Worker," 162
Vora, Neha, 218

wage rates in oil industry, 58–59, 62, 87–89
wages and nationality (1948–1959), 63–74
women, 3, 61, 71, 118. *See also* gender
Workers of Kuwait ('Izz al-Din), 116–17
World War I, 30–31, 56
World War II, 58, 83–84

xenophobia, 68–69, 72–73, 131–35, 164, 218

Yamani, Ahmed Zaki, 21, 204, 210–13
Yasin, Mohammad, 182–83, 187
Yergin, Daniel, 18
al-Youha, Hussein: arrest, 220; career, 1–4, 145; committee to Ministry of Social Affairs and Labor, 156; conviction of, 177; dissention within labor movement, 209; in imperial files, 22; Kuwait Trade Union Federation (KTUF), 171; labor law unification, 193; noncitizen rights, 165; on statebuilding, 221; unionization efforts, 92
Yusuf bin 'Isa al-Qina'i, 40, 68

Zayani, Abdul Wahab, 32
Zureiq, Constantine, 68

Kolibri 360 GmbH
Ferdinand-Jühlke-Straße 7
99095 Erfurt, Deutschland
produktsicherheit@kolibri360.de